To El...
yo...
Kind Thoughts of Happy days.
1961

THE PAGEANT OF
ENGLISH POETRY

THE PAGEANT OF
ENGLISH POETRY

BEING 1150 POEMS AND EXTRACTS
BY 300 AUTHORS

'Poets by death are conquered, but the wit
Of poets triumphs over it.'—COWLEY.

HUMPHREY MILFORD
OXFORD UNIVERSITY PRESS
LONDON, NEW YORK, TORONTO AND MELBOURNE
1914

NOTE

THE 1150 poems and extracts, by more than 300 authors, contained in this volume cover a period of upwards of 600 years. The poets appear in alphabetical order, and their poems are also printed in the alphabetical order of first lines. This plan has been adopted for convenience in reference, and it has been departed from only in the case of Shakespeare, the extracts from whose works follow the commonly accepted order of the plays, the selected sonnets, however, being given in the alphabetical order of their first lines.

At the beginning of the book there is a list of authors, giving their full names and the dates of birth and death where known ; and at the end are two indexes, one of first lines of the poems, in which the authors are indicated, and the other a subject index, in which an attempt has been made at classification.

It would have been impossible to print so many poems in one volume if all had been given in full, and very long ballads are necessarily omitted. Only such headings as have been adopted by the poets themselves have been given as a rule. While some pieces have been included because they are familiar or enshrine some time-honoured phrase or thought, or for their author's sake, the volume, large as it is, contains comparatively little verse of poor quality, and not a little that is unfamiliar to the general reader.

Many anthologies have been collated, and the compiler gladly acknowledges his indebtedness to earlier gleaners in the field, but he has exercised his own judgement, and he has not been content without consulting the earliest or most authentic sources for the words. As regards accuracy of text, it is claimed that this volume is superior to any collection made on a similar scale.

The work of living poets has been excluded, but the volume includes a number of copyright poems which are given by the kind permission of the following : Messrs. George Bell & Sons (Coventry Patmore) ; Messrs. Chatto & Windus (George MacDonald, A. W. E. O'Shaughnessy, and R. L. Stevenson) ; Mr. Bertram Dobell (James Thomson and T. Traherne) ; The Houghton Mifflin Company (O. W. Holmes, H. W. Longfellow, and J. G. Whittier); Messrs. Longmans & Company (W. E. H. Lecky) ; Messrs. Macmillan & Company (T. E. Brown) ; and Mr. Nutt (W. E. Henley).

R. M. LEONARD.

March, 1909.

LIST OF AUTHORS

THE PAGEANT

OF

ENGLISH POETRY

1. IT MUST BE SO—PLATO, THOU REASON'ST WELL

IT must be so—Plato, thou reason'st well,
Else whence this pleasing hope, this fond desire,
This longing after immortality ?
Or whence this secret dread and inward horror
Of falling into nought ? Why shrinks the soul
Back on herself and startles at destruction ?
—'Tis the Divinity that stirs within us,
'Tis Heaven itself that points out an hereafter,
And intimates Eternity to man.
Eternity !—thou pleasing-dreadful thought !
Through what variety of untried being—
Through what new scenes and changes must we pass !
The wide, the unbounded prospect lies before me ;
But shadows, clouds, and darkness rest upon it.
Here will I hold :—If there 's a Power above us
(And that there is, all nature cries aloud
Through all her works), he must delight in Virtue ;
And that which he delights in must be happy :
But—when ?—or where ?—*This* world was made for Caesar.
I'm weary of conjectures :—This must end them.
                       [*Laying his hand on his sword.*
Thus I am doubly armed ; my death and life,
My bane and antidote are both before me.
This in a moment brings me to an end,
But this informs me I shall never die.
The soul, secured in her existence, smiles
At the drawn dagger and defies its point.
The stars shall fade away, the sun himself
Grow dim with age, and nature sink in years ;
But thou shalt flourish in immortal youth,
Unhurt amidst the war of elements,
The wrecks of matter, and the crush of worlds.
                     J. ADDISON (*Cato*).

2. THE SPACIOUS FIRMAMENT ON HIGH

THE spacious firmament on high,
With all the blue ethereal sky,
And spangled heavens, a shining
   frame,
Their great Original proclaim.
The unwearied sun, from day to
   day,
Does his Creator's power display ;
And publishes to every land
The work of an Almighty hand.

Soon as the evening shades prevail,
The moon takes up the wondrous
   tale ;
And nightly to the listening earth,
Repeats the story of her birth ;

Whilst all the stars that round
   her burn,
And all the planets in their turn,
Confirm the tidings as they roll,
And spread the truth from pole
   to pole.

What though in solemn silence all
Move round the dark terrestrial
   ball ;
What though nor real voice nor
   sound
Amid their radiant orbs be found?
In reason's ear they all rejoice,
And utter forth a glorious voice ;
For ever singing, as they shine,
' The hand that made us is divine.'
            J. ADDISON.

3. HE MANY A CREATURE DID ANATOMIZE

HE many a creature did anatomize,
   Almost unpeopling water, air, and land ;
Beasts, fishes, birds, snails, caterpillars, flies,
   Were laid full low by his relentless hand,
That oft with gory crimson was distained :
   He many a dog destroyed, and many a cat
Of fleas his bed, of frogs the marshes drained,
   Could tellen if a mite were lean or fat,
And read a lecture o'er the entrails of a gnat.
           M. AKENSIDE (*The Virtuoso*).

4. THE HAND OF NATURE

THE hand of Nature on peculiar minds
Imprints a different bias, and to each
Decrees its province in the common toil.
. . . Some within a finer mould
She wrought and tempered with a purer flame.
To these the Sire Omnipotent unfolds
The world's harmonious volume, there to read
The transcript of Himself. On every part
They trace the bright impressions of His hand ;
In earth, or air, the meadow's purple stores,
The moon's mild radiance, or the virgin's form
Blooming with rosy smiles, they see portrayed
That uncreated Beauty which delights
The Mind supreme. They also feel her charms,
Enamoured : they partake the eternal joy.
        M. AKENSIDE (*The Pleasures of the Imagination*).

5. FROM 'LINES WRITTEN BY A DEATH-BED'

But ah, though peace indeed is
    here,
And ease from shame, and rest
    from fear ;
Though nothing can dismarble now
The smoothness of that limpid
    brow ;
Yet is a calm like this, in truth,
The crowning end of life and youth?
And when this boon rewards the
    dead,
Are all debts paid, has all been
    said ?
And is the heart of youth so light,
Its step so firm, its eye so bright,
Because on its hot brow there blows
A wind of promise and repose
From the far grave, to which it goes?

Because it has the hope to come,
One day, to harbour in the tomb ?
Ah no, the bliss youth dreams is
    one
For daylight, for the cheerful sun,
For feeling nerves and living
    breath—
Youth dreams a bliss on this side
    death.
It dreams a rest, if not more deep,
More grateful than this marble
    sleep.
It hears a voice within it tell—
' Calm 's not life's crown, though
    calm is well.'
'Tis all perhaps which man ac-
    quires :
But 'tis not what our youth desires.
                        M. Arnold.

6. WORDSWORTH AND GOETHE

But Wordsworth's eyes avert their
    ken
From half of human fate ;
And Goethe's course few sons of
    men
May think to emulate.

For he pursued a lonely road,
His eyes on Nature's plan ;
Neither made man too much a
    God,
Nor God too much a man.

Strong was he, with a spirit free
From mists, and sane, and clear ;
Clearer, how much ! than ours :
    yet we
Have a worse course to steer.

For though his manhood bore the
    blast
Of a tremendous time,
Yet in a tranquil world was passed
His tenderer youthful prime.

But we, brought forth and reared
    in hours
Of change, alarm, surprise—
What shelter to grow ripe is ours ?
What leisure to grow wise ?

    .   .   .   .   .   .

Too fast we live, too much are tried,
Too harassed, to attain
Wordsworth's sweet calm, or
    Goethe's wide
And luminous view to gain.

M. Arnold (*Stanzas in memory of the Author of ' Obermann '*).

7. CALM SOUL OF ALL THINGS

Calm Soul of all things ! make it
    mine
To feel, amid the city's jar,
That there abides a peace of thine,
Man did not make, and cannot mar.

The will to neither strive nor cry,
The power to feel with others give.
Calm, calm me more ; nor let me
    die
Before I have begun to live.

M. Arnold (*Lines written in Kensington Gardens*).

8. THE FORSAKEN MERMAN

COME, dear children, let us away;
Down and away below.
Now my brothers call from the bay;
Now the great winds shorewards
    blow ;
Now the salt tides seawards flow ;
Now the wild white horses play,
Champ and chafe and toss in the
    spray.
Children dear, let us away.
This way, this way.

Call her once before you go.
Call once yet.
In a voice that she will know :
' Margaret ! Margaret ! '
Children's voices should be dear
(Call once more) to a mother's ear :
Children's voices, wild with pain.
Surely she will come again.
Call her once and come away.
This way, this way.
' Mother dear, we cannot stay.'
The wild white horses foam and
    fret.
Margaret ! Margaret !

Come, dear children, come away
    down.
Call no more.
One last look at the white-walled
    town,
And the little grey church on the
    windy shore.
Then come down.
She will not come though you call
    all day.
Come away, come away.

Children dear, was it yesterday
We heard the sweet bells over the
    bay ?
In the caverns where we lay,
Through the surf and through the
    swell,
The far-off sound of a silver bell ?
Sand-strewn caverns, cool and
    deep,

Where the winds are all asleep ;
Where the spent lights quiver and
    gleam ;
Where the salt weed sways in the
    stream ;
Where the sea-beasts ranged all
    round
Feed in the ooze of their pasture-
    ground ;
Where the sea-snakes coil and
    twine,
Dry their mail and bask in the
    brine ;
Where great whales come sailing
    by,
Sail and sail, with unshut eye,
Round the world for ever and ay ?
When did music come this way ?
Children dear, was it yesterday ?

Children dear, was it yesterday
(Call yet once) that she went
    away ?
Once she sate with you and me,
On a red gold throne in the heart
    of the sea,
And the youngest sate on her knee.
She combed its bright hair, and she
    tended it well,
When down swung the sound of
    the far-off bell.
She sighed, she looked up through
    the clear green sea.
She said : ' I must go, for my kins-
    folk pray
In the little grey church on the
    shore to-day.
'Twill be Easter-time in the
    world—ah me !
And I lose my poor soul, Merman,
    here with thee.'
I said : ' Go up, dear heart,
    through the waves.
Say thy prayer, and come back to
    the kind sea-caves.'
She smiled, she went up through
    the surf in the bay.
Children dear, was it yesterday ?

Children dear, were we long
    alone ?
' The sea grows stormy, the little
    ones moan.
Long prayers,' I said, 'in the world
    they say.
Come,' I said, and we rose through
    the surf in the bay.
We went up the beach, by the
    sandy down
Where the sea-stocks bloom, to the
    white-walled town.
Through the narrow paved streets,
    where all was still,
To the little grey church on the
    windy hill.
From the church came a murmur
    of folk at their prayers,
But we stood without in the cold
    blowing airs.
We climbed on the graves, on the
    stones, worn with rains,
And we gazed up the aisle through
    the small leaded panes.
She sate by the pillar ; we saw
    her clear :
' Margaret, hist ! come quick, we
    are here
Dear heart,' I said, ' we are long
    alone.
The sea grows stormy, the little
    ones moan.'
But, ah, she gave me never a look,
For her eyes were sealed to the
    holy book.
Loud prays the priest ; shut stands
    the door.
Come away, children, call no
    more.
Come away, come down, call no
    more.

Down, down, down,
Down to the depths of the sea.
She sits at her wheel in the hum-
    ming town,
Singing most joyfully.
Hark, what she sings : ' O joy,
    O joy,

For the humming street, and the
    child with its toy.
For the priest, and the bell, and
    the holy well.
For the wheel where I spun,
And the blessed light of the sun.'
And so she sings her fill,
Singing most joyfully,
Till the shuttle falls from her hand,
And the whizzing wheel stands
    still.
She steals to the window, and looks
    at the sand ;
And over the sand at the sea ;
And her eyes are set in a stare ;
And anon there breaks a sigh,
And anon there drops a tear,
From a sorrow-clouded eye,
And a heart sorrow-laden,
A long, long sigh,
For the cold strange eyes of a little
    Mermaiden,
And the gleam of her golden hair.

Come away, away, children.
Come, children, come down.
The hoarse wind blows colder ;
Lights shine in the town.
She will start from her slumber
When gusts shake the door ;
She will hear the winds howling,
Will hear the waves roar.
We shall see, while above us
The waves roar and whirl,
A ceiling of amber,
A pavement of pearl.
Singing, ' Here came a mortal,
But faithless was she.
And alone dwell for ever
The kings of the sea.'

But, children, at midnight,
When soft the winds blow ;
When clear falls the moonlight ;
When spring-tides are low :
When sweet airs come seaward
From heaths starred with broom ;
And high rocks throw mildly
On the blanched sands a gloom :
Up the still, glistening beaches,

Up the creeks we will hie ;
Over banks of bright seaweed
The ebb-tide leaves dry.
We will gaze, from the sand-hills,
At the white, sleeping town ;
At the church on the hill-side—

And then come back down.
Singing, ' There dwells a loved one,
But cruel is she.
She left lonely for ever
The kings of the sea.'

                                M. ARNOLD.

9. PHILOMELA

HARK ! ah, the Nightingale !
The tawny-throated !
Hark ! from that moonlit cedar
    what a burst !
What triumph ! hark—what pain !

O Wanderer from a Grecian shore,
Still, after many years, in distant
    lands,
Still nourishing in thy bewildered
    brain
That wild, unquenched, deep-
    sunken, old-world pain—
Say, will it never heal ?
And can this fragrant lawn
With its cool trees, and night,
And the sweet tranquil Thames,
And moonshine and the dew,
To thy racked heart and brain
Afford no balm ?
Dost thou to-night behold
Here, through the moonlight on
    this English grass,

The unfriendly palace in the Thra-
    cian wild ?
Dost thou again peruse
With hot cheeks and seared eyes
The too clear web, and thy dumb
    Sister's shame ?
Dost thou once more assay
Thy flight, and feel come over
    thee,
Poor Fugitive, the feathery change
Once more, and once more seem to
    make resound
With love and hate, triumph and
    agony,
Lone Daulis, and the high Cephis-
    sian vale ?
Listen, Eugenia—
How thick the bursts come
    crowding through the leaves !
Again—thou hearest !
Eternal Passion !
Eternal Pain !

                                M. ARNOLD.

10. FROM ' EMPEDOCLES ON ETNA '

LIKE us the lightning fires
Love to have scope and play.
The stream, like us, desires
An unimpeded way.
Like us, the Libyan wind delights
    to roam at large.

Streams will not curb their
    pride
The just man not to entomb,
Nor lightnings go aside
To leave his virtues room,
Nor is the wind less rough that
blows a good man's barge.

Nature, with equal mind,
Sees all her sons at play,
Sees man control the wind,
The wind sweep man away ;
Allows the proudly-riding and the
    foundering bark.

. . . . .

Is it so small a thing
To have enjoyed the sun,
To have lived light in the spring,
To have loved, to have thought,
    to have done ;
To have advanced true friends, and
    beat down baffling foes ;

That we must feign a bliss
Of doubtful future date,
And while we dream on this
Lose all our present state,
And relegate to worlds yet distant
    our repose ?

Not much, I know, you prize
What pleasures may be had,
Who look on life with eyes
Estranged, like mine, and
    sad :
And yet the village churl feels the
    truth more than you,

Who 's loath to leave this life
Which to him little yields :
His hard-tasked sunburnt wife,
His often-laboured fields ;
The boors with whom he talked,
    the country spots he knew.

.   .   .   .   .

I say, Fear not ! life still
Leaves human effort scope !
But, since life teems with ill,
Nurse no extravagant hope.
Because thou must not dream, thou
    need'st not then despair !
                    M. ARNOLD.

11. SHAKESPEARE

OTHERS abide our question. Thou art free.
We ask and ask : Thou smilest and art still,
Out-topping knowledge. For the loftiest hill
That to the stars uncrowns his majesty,
Planting his steadfast footsteps in the sea,
Making the Heaven of Heavens his dwelling-place,
Spares but the cloudy border of his base
To the foiled searching of mortality :
And thou, who didst the stars and sunbeams know,
Self-schooled, self-scanned, self-honoured, self-secure,
Didst walk on Earth unguessed at. Better so !
All pains the immortal spirit must endure,
All weakness that impairs, all griefs that bow,
Find their sole voice in that victorious brow.
                                    M. ARNOLD.

12. REQUIESCAT

STREW on her roses, roses,
    And never a spray of yew.
In quiet she reposes :
    Ah ! would that I did too.

Her mirth the world required :
    She bathed it in smiles of
        glee.
But her heart was tired, tired,
    And now they let her be.

Her life was turning, turning,
    In mazes of heat and sound.
But for peace her soul was yearn-
        ing,
    And now peace laps her round.

Her cabined, ample Spirit,
    It fluttered and failed for breath.
To-night it doth inherit
    The vasty Hall of Death.
                    M. ARNOLD.

13. FROM 'THE SCHOLAR GIPSY'

Thou waitest for the spark from heaven! and we,
  Light half-believers of our casual creeds,
    Who never deeply felt, nor clearly willed,
  Whose insight never has borne fruit in deeds,
    Whose vague resolves never have been fulfilled;
      For whom each year we see
  Breeds new beginnings, disappointments new;
    Who hesitate and falter life away,
    And lose to-morrow the ground won to-day—
  Ah! do not we, wanderer! await it too?

.   .   .   .

Still nursing the unconquerable hope,
  Still clutching the inviolable shade,
    With a free onward impulse brushing through,
  By night, the silvered branches of the glade—
    Far on the forest skirts, where none pursue,
      On some mild pastoral slope
  Emerge, and resting on the moonlit pales,
    Freshen thy flowers as in former years
    With dew, or listen with enchanted ears,
  From the dark dingles, to the nightingales!

But fly our paths, our feverish contact fly!
  For strong the infection of our mental strife,
    Which, though it gives no bliss, yet spoils for rest;
  And we should win thee from thy own fair life,
    Like us distracted, and like us unblest.
      Soon, soon thy cheer would die,
  Thy hopes grow timorous, and unfixed thy powers,
    And thy clear aims be cross and shifting made;
    And then thy glad perennial youth would fade,
  Fade, and grow old at last, and die like ours.

Then fly our greetings, fly our speech and smiles!
  —As some grave Tyrian trader, from the sea,
    Descried at sunrise an emerging prow
  Lifting the cool-haired creepers stealthily,
    The fringes of a southward-facing brow
      Among the Aegean isles;
  And saw the merry Grecian coaster come,
    Freighted with amber grapes, and Chian wine,
    Green, bursting figs, and tunnies steeped in brine;
  And knew the intruders on his ancient home,

The young light-hearted masters of the waves;
  And snatched his rudder, and shook out more sail;
    And day and night held on indignantly
O'er the blue Midland waters with the gale,
  Betwixt the Syrtes and soft Sicily,
    To where the Atlantic raves
Outside the western straits; and unbent sails
  There, where down cloudy cliffs, through sheets of foam,
  Shy traffickers, the dark Iberians come;
And on the beach undid his corded bales.

M. ARNOLD.

14. ON THE RHINE

VAIN is the effort to forget.
Some day I shall be cold, I know,
As is the eternal moon-lit snow
Of the high Alps, to which I go:
But ah, not yet! not yet!

Vain is the agony of grief.
'Tis true, indeed, an iron knot
Ties straitly up from mine thy lot,
And were it snapt—thou lov'st me not!
But is despair relief?

Awhile let me with thought have done;
And as this brimmed unwrinkled Rhine

And that far purple mountain line
Lie sweetly in the look divine
Of the slow-sinking sun;

So let me lie, and calm as they
Let beam upon my inward view
Those eyes of deep, soft, lucent hue—
Eyes too expressive to be blue,
Too lovely to be grey.

Ah Quiet, all things feel thy balm!
Those blue hills too, this river's flow,
Were restless once, but long ago.
Tamed is their turbulent youthful glow:
Their joy is in their calm.

M. ARNOLD.

15. MORALITY

WE cannot kindle when we will
The fire that in the heart resides,
The spirit bloweth and is still,
In mystery our soul abides:
  But tasks in hours of insight willed
  Can be through hours of gloom fulfilled.

With aching hands and bleeding feet
We dig and heap, lay stone on stone;
We bear the burden and the heat
Of the long day, and wish 'twere done.
  Not till the hours of light return
  All we have built do we discern.

M. ARNOLD.

16. THE SONG OF CALLICLES

—WHAT Forms are these coming
So white through the gloom?
What garments out-glistening
The gold-flowered broom?

What sweet-breathing Presence
Out-perfumes the thyme?
What voices enrapture
The night's balmy prime?—

B 3

'Tis Apollo comes leading
His choir, the Nine.
—The Leader is fairest,
But all are divine.

They are lost in the hollows,
They stream up again.
What seeks on this mountain
The glorified train ?—

They bathe on this mountain
In the spring by their road.
Then on to Olympus,
Their endless abode.

—Whose praise do they mention,
Of what is it told ?—
What will be for ever,
What was from of old.

First hymn they the Father
Of all things : and then
The rest of Immortals,
The action of men.

The Day in its hotness,
The strife with the palm ;
The Night in its silence,
The Stars in their calm.

M. ARNOLD (*Empedocles on Etna*).

17. I'LL LOVE NO MORE

I LOVED thee once, I'll love no more,
    Thine be the grief as is the blame ;
Thou art not what thou wast before,
    What reason I should be the same ?
        He that can love unloved again,
        Hath better store of love than brain :
    God send me love my debts to pay,
    While unthrifts fool their love away !

Nothing could have my love o'erthrown,
    If thou hadst still continued mine ;
Yea, if thou hadst remained thy own,
    I might perchance have yet been thine.
        But thou thy freedom didst recall,
        That, if thou might, elsewhere inthrall :
    And then how could I but disdain
    A captive's captive to remain ?   SIR R. AYTON.

18. FROM 'THE WIDOW OF GLENCOE'

Do not lift him from the bracken,
    Leave him lying where he
        fell—
Better bier ye cannot fashion :
    None beseems him half so well
As the bare and broken heather,
    And the hard and trampled sod,
Whence his angry soul ascended
    To the judgement-seat of God !
Winding-sheet we cannot give
        him—
    Seek no mantle for the dead,
Save the cold and spotless covering
    Showered from heaven upon his
        head.

Leave his broadsword as we found
        it,
    Bent and broken with the blow,
That, before he died, avenged him
    On the foremost of the foe.
Leave the blood upon his bosom—
    Wash not off that sacred stain ;
Let it stiffen on the tartan,
    Let his wounds unclosed remain,
Till the day when he shall show
        them
    At the throne of God on high,
When the murderer and the mur-
        dered
    Meet before their Judge's eye.
W. E. AYTOUN.

19. DEAD DUNDEE

SOUND the fife, and cry the
    slogan—
Let the pibroch shake the air
With its wild triumphal music,
    Worthy of the freight we bear.
Let the ancient hills of Scotland
    Hear once more the battle song
Swell within their glens and
    valleys
    As the clansmen march along !
Never from the field of combat,
    Never from the deadly fray,
Was a nobler trophy carried
    Than we bring with us to-day ;
Never, since the valiant Douglas
    On his dauntless bosom bore
Good King Robert's heart—the
    priceless—
    To our dear Redeemer's shore !

Lo ! we bring with us the hero—
    Lo ! we bring the conquering
        Graeme,
Crowned as but becomes a victor
    From the altar of his fame ;
Fresh and bleeding from the battle
    Whence his spirit took its flight,
Midst the crashing charge of
    squadrons,
    And the thunder of the fight !
Strike, I say, the notes of triumph,
    As we march o'er moor and lea !
Is there any here will venture
    To bewail our dead Dundee ?
Let the widows of the traitors
    Weep until their eyes are dim !
Wail ye may full well for
    Scotland—
    Let none dare to mourn for him !

W. E. AYTOUN (*The Burial March of Dundee*).

20. THE REFUSAL OF CHARON

WHY look the distant mountains
    So gloomy and so drear ?
Are rain-clouds passing o'er them,
    Or is the tempest near ?
No shadow of the tempest
    Is there, nor wind nor rain—
'Tis Charon that is passing by,
    With all his gloomy train.

The young men march before him,
    In all their strength and
        pride ;
The tender little infants,
    They totter by his side ;
The old men walk behind him,
    And earnestly they pray—
Both old and young imploring
    him
    To grant some brief delay.

' O Charon ! halt, we pray thee,
    Beside some little town,
Or near some sparkling fountain,
    Where the waters wimple down !
The old will drink and be refreshed,
    The young the disc will fling,
And the tender little children
    Pluck flowers beside the spring.'

' I will not stay my journey,
    Nor halt by any town,
Near any sparkling fountain,
    Where the waters wimple down :
The mothers coming to the well
    Would know the babes they
        bore,
The wives would clasp their hus-
    bands,
    Nor could I part them more.'
                        W. E. AYTOUN.

21. THE WORLD'S A BUBBLE

THE World's a bubble, and the Life of Man
          Less than a span :
In his conception wretched, from the womb
          So to the tomb ;
Curst from his cradle, and brought up to years
          With cares and fears.
Who then to frail mortality shall trust,
But limns on water, or but writes in dust.

FRANCIS BACON, LORD VERULAM.

22. LUCIFER'S SONG

THOU hast more music in thy
          voice
    Than to the spheres is given,
And more temptations on thy lips
    Than lost the angels Heaven.
Thou hast more brightness in thine
          eyes
    Than all the stars which burn,
More dazzling art thou than the
          throne
    We fallen dared to spurn.

Go, search through Heaven—the
          sweetest smile
    That lightens there is thine ;
And through hell's burning dark-
          ness breaks
    No frown so fell as mine.
One smile—'twill light, one tear—
          'twill cool ;
    These will be more to me
Than all the wealth of all the worlds,
    Or boundless power could be.

P. J. BAILEY (*Festus*).

23. WE LIVE IN DEEDS

WE live in deeds, not years ; in thoughts, not breaths ;
In feelings, not in figures on a dial.
We should count time by heart-throbs. He most lives
Who thinks most, feels the noblest, acts the best.
Where imperfection ceaseth, heaven begins.

P. J. BAILEY (*Festus*).

24. FISHERMAN'S SONG

No fish stir in our heaving net,
And the sky is dark and the night is wet ;
And we must ply the lusty oar,
For the tide is ebbing from the shore ;
And sad are they whose faggots burn,
So kindly stored for our return.

Our boat is small, and the tempest raves,
And nought is heard but the lashing waves
And the sullen roar of the angry sea
And the wild winds piping drearily ;
Yet sea and tempest rise in vain,
We'll bless our blazing hearths again.

Push bravely, mates ! Our guiding star
Now from its towerlet streameth far,
And now along the nearing strand,
See, swiftly moves yon flaming brand.
Before the midnight watch be past
We'll quaff our bowl and mock the blast.

JOANNA BAILLIE.

25. LIFE ! I KNOW NOT WHAT THOU ART

LIFE ! I know not what thou art,
But know that thou and I must part ;
And when, or how, or where we met
I own to me 's a secret yet.

Life ! we've been long together
Through pleasant and through cloudy weather ;
'Tis hard to part when friends are dear—
Perhaps 'twill cost a sigh, a tear ;
—Then steal away, give little warning,
   Choose thine own time ;
Say not Good Night,—but in some brighter clime
   Bid me Good Morning.

A. L. BARBAULD.

26. SPRING

SWEET daughter of a rough and
      stormy sire,
Hoar Winter's blooming child,
   delightful Spring !
   Whose unshorn locks with leaves
   And   swelling   buds   are
      crowned ;

From the green islands of eternal
      youth
(Crowned with fresh blooms, and
   ever-springing shade)
Turn, hither turn thy step,
   O thou, whose powerful voice,

More sweet than softest touch of
      Doric reed,
Or Lydian flute, can soothe the
      madding winds,
And through the stormy deep
Breathe thy own tender calm.
. . . .

Sweet is thy reign, but short : the
      red dogstar
Shall scorch thy tresses ; and the
      mower's scythe
   Thy greens, thy flowerets all,
   Remorseless shall destroy.

Reluctant shall I bid thee then
      farewell ;
For O ! not all that Autumn's lap
      contains,
   Nor Summer's ruddiest fruits,
   Can aught for thee atone,

Fair Spring ! whose simplest pro-
      mise more delights,
Than all their largest wealth, and
      through the heart
   Each joy and new-born hope
   With softest influence breathes.

A. L. BARBAULD (*Ode to Spring*).

27. AS I LAYE A-THYNKYNGE

The last lines of ' Thomas Ingoldsby '

As I laye a-thynkynge, a-thynkynge, a-thynkynge,
Merrie sang the Birde as she sat upon the spraye ;
    There came a noble Knyghte,
    With his hauberke shynynge brighte,
    And his gallant heart was lyghte,
        Free and gaye ;
As I laye a-thynkynge, he rode upon his waye.

As I laye a-thynkynge, a-thynkynge, a-thynkynge,
Sadly sang the Birde as she sat upon the tree !
    There seemed a crimson plain,
    Where a gallant Knyghte lay slayne,
    And a steed with broken rein
        Ran free,
As I laye a-thynkynge, most pitiful to see !

As I laye a-thynkynge, a-thynkynge, a-thynkynge,
Merrie sang the Birde as she sat upon the boughe ;
    A lovely Mayde came bye,
    And a gentil youthe was nyghe,
    And he breathed many a syghe
        And a vowe ;
As I laye a-thynkynge, her hearte was gladsome now.

As I laye a-thynkynge, a-thynkynge, a-thynkynge,
Sadly sang the Birde as she sat upon the thorne ;
    No more a youth was there,
    But a Maiden rent her haire,
    And cried in sad despaire
        ' That I was borne ! '
As I laye a-thynkynge, she perished forlorne.

As I laye a-thynkynge, a-thynkynge, a-thynkynge,
Sweetly sang the Birde as she sat upon the briar ;
    There came a lovely Childe,
    And his face was meek and mild,
    Yet joyously he smiled
        On his sire ;
As I laye a-thynkynge, a Cherub mote admire.

But I laye a-thynkynge, a-thynkynge, a-thynkynge,
And sadly sang the Birde as it perched upon a bier ;
    That joyous smile was gone,
    And the face was white and wan,
    As the downe upon the Swan
        Doth appear,
As I laye a-thynkynge—oh ! bitter flowed the tear !

As I laye a-thynkynge, the golden sun was sinking,
O merrie sang that Birde as it glittered on her breast
    With a thousand glorious dyes,
    While, soaring to the skies,
    'Mid the stars she seemed to rise,
      As to her nest ;
As I laye a-thynkynge, her meaning was exprest :—
    'Follow, follow me away,
    It boots not to delay ',—
    'Twas so she seemed to saye,
      ' HERE IS REST ! '

                    R. H. BARHAM.

28. AULD ROBIN GRAY

WHEN the sheep are in the fauld, when the cows come hame,
And a' the weary warld to quiet rest are gane,
The woes of my heart fa' in showers frae my ee
Unkenned by my gudeman, who soundly sleeps by me.

Young Jamie loo'd me weel, and sought me for his bride ;
But saving ae crown-piece he'd naething else beside.
To make the crown a pound, my Jamie gaed to sea ;
And the crown and the pound, oh ! they were baith for me !

Before he had been gane a twelvemonth and a day,
My father brak his arm, our cow was stown away ;
My mother she fell sick—my Jamie was at sea—
And Auld Robin Gray, oh ! he came a-courting me.

My father cou'dna work—my mother cou'dna spin ;
I toiled day and night, but their bread I cou'dna win,
Auld Rob maintained them baith, and wi' tears in his ee
Said, 'Jenny, oh ! for their sakes, will you marry me ?'

My heart it said na, and I looked for Jamie back ;
But hard blew the winds, and his ship was a wrack ;
His ship it was a wrack ! Why didna Jenny dee ?
Or, wherefore am I spared to cry out, Woe is me ?

My father argued sair—my mother didna speak,
But she looked in my face till my heart was like to break ;
They gied him my hand, but my heart was in the sea ;
And so Auld Robin Gray, he was gudeman to me.

I hadna been his wife a week but only four,
When mournfu' as I sat on the stane at my door,
I saw my Jamie's ghaist—I cou'dna think it he,
Till he said : ' I'm come hame, my love, to marry thee ! '

Oh sair, sair did we greet, and mickle say of a'.
Ae kiss we took, nae mair—I bad him gang awa.
I wish that I were dead, but I'm no like to dee ;
For O, I am but young to cry out, Woe is me !

I gang like a ghaist, and I carena much to spin ;
I darena think o' Jamie, for that wad be a sin.
But I will do my best a gude wife ay to be,
For auld Robin Gray, oh ! he is sae kind to me.

                                        ANNE, LADY BARNARD.

29. THE PLAINT OF THE NIGHTINGALE

As it fell upon a day
In the merry month of May,
Sitting in a pleasant shade
Which a grove of myrtles
    made,
Beasts did leap and birds did sing,
Trees did grow and plants did
    spring,
Every thing did banish moan
Save the Nightingale alone.
She, poor bird, as all forlorn,
Leaned her breast up-till a thorn,
And there sung the dolefull'st ditty
That to hear it was great pity.
Fie, fie, fie, now would she cry ;
Tereu, tereu, by and by :
That to hear her so complain
Scarce I could from tears refrain ;
For her griefs so lively shown
Made me think upon my own.
—Ah, thought I, thou mourn'st
    in vain,

None takes pity on thy pain :
Senseless trees, they cannot hear
    thee,
Ruthless bears, they will not
    cheer thee ;
King Pandion, he is dead,
All thy friends are lapped in
    lead :
All thy fellow birds do sing
Careless of thy sorrowing :
Whilst as fickle fortune smiled,
Thou and I were both beguiled.
Every one that flatters thee,
Is no friend in misery.
Words are easy, like the wind :
Faithful friends are hard to
    find.
Every man will be thy friend,
Whilst thou hast wherewith to
    spend ;
But if store of crowns be scant,
No man will supply thy want.

                                        R. BARNEFIELD.

30. BLACKMWORE MAIDENS

THE primrwose in the sheäde do
    blow,
The cowslip in the zun,
The thyme upon the down do grow,
The clote where streams do run ;
An' where do pretty maïdens grow
An' blow, but where the tow'r
Do rise among the bricken tuns,
In Blackmwore by the Stour.

If you could zee their comely gaït,
An' pretty feäces' smiles,
A-trippèn on so light o' waïght,
An' steppèn off the stiles ;
A-gwaïn to church, as bells do swing
An' ring within the tow'r,
You'd own the pretty maïdens'
    pleäce
Is Blackmwore by the Stour.

If you vrom Wimborne took your
        road,
To Stower or Paladore,
An' all the farmers' housen show'd
Their daughters at the door ;
You'd cry to bachelors at
        hwome—
' Here, come : 'ithin an hour
You'll vind ten maïdens to your
        mind,
In Blackmwore by the Stour.'

An' if you look'd 'ithin their door,
To zee em in their pleäce,
A-doèn housework up avore
Their smilèn mother's feäce ;
You'd cry—' Why, if a man
        would wive
An' thrive, 'ithout a dow'r,
Then let en look en out a wife
In Blackmwore by the Stour.'

As I upon my road did pass
A school-house back in Maÿ,
There out upon the beäten grass
Wer maïdens at their plaÿ ;
An' as the pretty souls did tweil
An' smile, I cried, ' The flow'r
O' beauty, then, is still in bud
In Blackmwore by the Stour.'

W. BARNES.

31. THE MOTHERLESS CHILD

THE zun'd a-zet back t'other night,
        But in the zettèn pleäce
The clouds, a-redden'd by his
        light,
        Still glow'd avore my feäce.
An' I've a-lost my Meäry's smile,
I thought ; but still I have her chile
Zoo like her, that my eyes can
        treäce
The mother's in her daughter's
        feäce.
O little feäce so near to me,
An' like thy mother's gone ; why
        need I zay,
Sweet night cloud, wi' the glow o'
        my lost day,
Thy looks be always dear to me !

The zun'd a-zet another night ;
        But, by the moon on high,
He still did zend us back his light
        Below a cwolder sky.
My Meäry 's in a better land
I thought, but still her chile 's at
        hand,
An' in her chile she'll zend me on
Her love, though she herself 's
        a-gone.
O little chile so near to me,
An' like thy mother gone ; why
        need I zay,
Sweet moon, the messenger vrom
        my lost day,
Thy looks be always dear to
        me.

W. BARNES.

32. AN EPITAPH

RENOWNÈD Spenser, lie a thought more nigh
To learnèd Chaucer ; and rare Beaumont, lie
A little nearer Spenser ; to make room
For Shakespeare in your three-fold four-fold tomb.
To lodge all four in one bed make a shift
Until Doomsday ; for hardly will a fifth,
Betwixt this day and that, by fates be slain,
For whom your curtains may be drawn again.

If your precedency in death do bar
A fourth place in your sacred sepulchre,
Under this sacred marble of thine own,
Sleep, rare tragedian, Shakespeare, sleep alone :
Thy unmolested peace, in an unshared cave,
Possess as lord, not tenant, of thy grave ;
That unto us and others it may be
Honour hereafter to be laid by thee.　　W. BASSE.

33.　THE PREACHER

STILL thinking I had little time to live,
My fervent heart to win men's souls did strive ;
I preached as never sure to preach again,
And as a dying man to dying men.

.　　.　　.　　.　　.　　.　　.　　.

Though God be free, He works by instruments,
And wisely fitteth them to His intents.
A proud unhumbled preacher is unmeet
To lay proud sinners humbled at Christ's feet ;
So are the blind to tell men what God saith,
And faithless men to propagate the faith :
The dead are unfit means to raise the dead,
And enemies to give the children bread ;
And utter strangers to the life to come
Are not the best conductors to our home.
They that yet never learned to live and die,
Will scarcely teach it others feelingly.　　R. BAXTER.

34.　AT THE CLOSE OF THE DAY

AT the close of the day, when the hamlet is still,
And mortals the sweets of forgetfulness prove,
When nought but the torrent is heard on the hill,
And nought but the nightingale's song in the grove :
'Twas thus, by the cave of the mountain afar,
While his harp rung symphonious, a hermit began ;
No more with himself or with nature at war,
He thought as a sage, though he felt as a man.

.　　.　　.　　.　　.　　.　　.　　.

' 'Tis night, and the landscape is lovely no more :
I mourn, but, ye woodlands, I mourn not for you ;
For morn is approaching, your charms to restore,
Perfumed with fresh fragrance, and glittering with dew ;
Nor yet for the ravage of winter I mourn ;
Kind Nature the embryo blossoms will save :
But when shall spring visit the mouldering urn—
Or when shall it dawn on the night of the grave ? '
　　　　　　　　　　J. BEATTIE (*The Hermit*).

35. BUT WHO THE MELODIES OF MORN CAN TELL?

BUT who the melodies of morn can tell—
The wild brook babbling down the mountain side;
The lowing herd, the sheepfold's simple bell;
The pipe of early shepherd dim descried
In the lone valley; echoing far and wide
The clamorous horn along the cliffs above;
The hollow murmur of the ocean-tide;
The hum of bees, the linnet's lay of love,
And the full choir that wakes the universal grove?

The cottage curs at early pilgrim bark;
Crowned with her pail the tripping milkmaid sings;
The whistling ploughman stalks afield; and, hark!
Down the rough slope the ponderous wagon rings;
Thro' rustling corn the hare astonished springs;
Slow tolls the village clock the drowsy hour;
The partridge bursts away on whirring wings;
Deep mourns the turtle in sequestered bower,
And shrill lark carols from her aerial tour.

J. BEATTIE (*The Minstrel*).

36. THE TOMBS IN WESTMINSTER ABBEY

MORTALITY, behold, and fear,
What a change of flesh is here!
Think how many royal bones
Sleep within this heap of stones;
Here they lie, had realms and lands,
Who now want strength to stir their hands;
Where from their pulpits sealed with dust,
They preach, 'In greatness is no trust!'
Here's an acre sown indeed
With the richest, royal'st seed,
That the earth did e'er suck in
Since the first man died for sin;
Here the bones of earth have cried,
'Though gods they were, as men they died;'
Here are sands, ignoble things,
Dropt from the ruined sides of kings.
Here's a world of pomp and state
Buried in dust, once dead by fate.

F. BEAUMONT.

37. AT THE MERMAID

WHAT things have we seen
Done at the Mermaid! heard words that have been
So nimble, and so full of subtle flame,
As if that every one from whence they came
Had meant to put his whole wit in a jest,

And had resolved to live a fool the rest
Of his dull life ; then when there hath been thrown
Wit able enough to justify the town
For three days past ; wit that might warrant be
For the whole city to talk foolishly
Till that were cancelled ; and when we were gone,
We left an air behind us, which alone
Was able to make the two next companies
Right witty ; though but downright fools, more wise !
> F. BEAUMONT (*Letter to Ben Jonson*).

38. DRINK AND DROWN SORROW

DRINK to-day, and drown all sorrow,
You shall perhaps not do it to-morrow :
But, while you have it, use your breath ;
There is no drinking after death.

Wine works the heart up, wakes the wit,
There is no cure 'gainst age but it :
It helps the headache, cough, and ptisick,
And is for all diseases physic.

Then let us swill, boys, for our health ;
Who drinks well, loves the commonwealth.
And he that will to bed go sober
Falls with the leaf, still in October.
> F. BEAUMONT AND J. FLETCHER (*The Bloody Brother*).

39. LAY A GARLAND ON MY HEARSE

LAY a garland on my hearse
  Of the dismal yew ;
Maidens, willow branches bear ;
  Say, I dièd true.

My love was false, but I was firm
  From my hour of birth.
Upon my buried body lie
  Lightly, gentle earth !
> F. BEAUMONT AND J. FLETCHER
> (*The Maid's Tragedy*).

40. TAKE, OH ! TAKE THOSE LIPS AWAY

TAKE, oh ! take those lips away,
  That so sweetly were forsworn,
And those eyes like break of day,
  Lights that do mislead the morn !
But my kisses bring again,
Seals of love, though sealed in vain.

Hide, oh ! hide those hills of snow,
  Which thy frozen bosom bears,
On whose tops the pinks that grow
  Are of those that April wears !
But first set my poor heart free,
Bound in those icy chains by thee.
> F. BEAUMONT AND J. FLETCHER
> (*The Bloody Brother*).

41. ON MY DEAR SON

CAN I, who have for others oft compiled
The songs of death, forget my sweetest child,
Which, like a flower crushed, with a blast is dead,
And ere full time hangs down his smiling head,
Expecting with clear hope to live anew,
Among the angels fed with heavenly dew ?
We have this sign of joy, that many days,
While on the earth his struggling spirit stays,
The name of Jesus in his mouth contains,
His only food, his sleep, his ease from pains.
O may that sound be rooted in my mind,
Of which in him such strong effect I find.
Dear Lord, receive my son, whose winning love
To me was like a friendship, far above
The course of nature, or his tender age ;
Whose looks could all my bitter griefs assuage ;
Let his pure soul—ordained seven years to be
In that frail body, which was part of me—
Remain my pledge in heaven, as sent to show
How to this port at every step I go.   SIR J. BEAUMONT.

42. BAD TIMES

WHY slander we the times ?
    What crimes
Have days and years, that we
Thus charge them with iniquity ?
If we would rightly scan,
It's not the times are bad, but man.

If thy desire it be
    To see
The times prove good, be thou
But such thyself, and surely know
That all thy days to thee
Shall spite of mischief happy be.
                    JOSEPH BEAUMONT.

43. IF THOU WILT EASE THINE HEART

IF thou wilt ease thine heart
Of love and all its smart,
    Then sleep, dear, sleep ;
And not a sorrow
    Hang any tear on your eye-
        lashes ;
        Lie still and deep,
    Sad soul, until the sea-wave
        washes
The rim o' the sun to-morrow,
    In eastern sky.

But wilt thou cure thine heart
Of love and all its smart,
    Then die, dear, die ;
'Tis deeper, sweeter,
    Than on a rose-bank to lie
        dreaming
        With folded eye ;
    And there alone, amid the
        beaming
Of love's stars, thou'lt meet her
    In eastern sky.

T. L. BEDDOES (*Death's Jest-Book*)

44. LOVE IN FANTASTIC TRIUMPH SAT

Love in fantastic triumph sat,
    Whilst bleeding hearts around him flowed:
For whom fresh pains he did create,
    And strange tyrannic power he showed.
From thy bright eyes he took his fires,
    Which round about in sport he hurled;
But 'twas from mine he took desires
    Enough to undo the amorous world.

From me he took his sighs and tears,
    From thee his pride and cruelty;
From me his languishments and fears,
    And every killing dart from thee.
Thus thou and I the God have armed,
    And set him up a deity,
But my poor heart alone is harmed,
    Whilst thine the victor is, and free.   A. Behn.

45. THE PROSPECT IN AMERICA

The Muse, disgusted at an age and clime
    Barren of every glorious theme,
In distant lands now waits a better time,
    Producing subjects worthy fame.

In happy climes, where from the genial sun
    And virgin earth such scenes ensue,
The force of art by nature seems outdone,
    And fancied beauties by the true:

In happy climes, the seat of innocence,
    Where nature guides and virtue rules,
Where men shall not impose for truth and sense
    The pedantry of courts and schools:

There shall be sung another golden age,
    The rise of empire and of arts,
The good and great inspiring epic rage,
    The wisest heads and noblest hearts.

Not such as Europe breeds in her decay;
    Such as she bred when fresh and young,
When heavenly flame did animate her clay,
    By future poets shall be sung.

Westward the course of empire takes its way;
    The four first acts already past,
A fifth shall close the drama with the day;
    Time's noblest offspring is the last.
                G. Berkeley (On the Prospect of planting
                        Arts and Learning in America).

46. I CARE FOR NOBODY, NOT I

THERE was a jolly miller once
Lived on the river Dee ;
He worked and sang from morn
till night,
No lark more blithe than he.

And this the burden of his
song
For ever used to be :—
I care for nobody, not I,
If no one cares for me.

I. BICKERSTAFFE (*Love in a Village*).

47. THE END OF LIFE

SURE the last end
Of the good man is peace ! How calm his exit !
Night-dews fall not more gently to the ground,
Nor weary worn-out winds expire so soft.
Behold him ! in the evening tide of life,
A life well spent, whose early care it was
His riper years should not upbraid his green :
By unperceived degrees he wears away ;
Yet, like the sun, seems larger at his setting !
High in his faith and hopes, look how he reaches
After the prize in view ! and, like a bird
That 's hampered, struggles hard to get away !
Whilst the glad gates of sight are wide expanded
To let new glories in, the first fair fruits
Of the fast-coming harvest.

R. BLAIR (*The Grave*).

48. FROM 'AUGURIES OF INNOCENCE'

A ROBIN redbreast in a cage
Puts all Heaven in a rage.
A dove-house filled with doves
and pigeons
Shudders Hell through all its
regions.
A dog starved at his master's gate
Predicts the ruin of the state.
A horse misused upon the road
Calls to Heaven for human blood.
Each outcry of the hunted hare
A fibre from the brain does tear.
A skylark wounded in the wing,
A cherubim does cease to sing.
The game-cock clipped and armed
for fight
Does the rising sun affright.
Every wolf's and lion's howl
Raises from Hell a human soul.

The wild deer, wandering here and
there,
Keeps the human soul from care.
The lamb misused breeds public
strife,
And yet forgives the butcher's
knife.
He who shall hurt the little wren
Shall never be beloved by men.
He who the ox to wrath has
moved
Shall never be by woman loved.
The wanton boy that kills the fly
Shall feel the spider's enmity.
He who torments the chafer's
sprite
Weaves a bower in endless night.
The caterpillar on the leaf
Repeats to thee thy mother's grief.

Kill not the moth nor butter-
fly,
For the last judgement draweth
nigh.

He who shall train the horse to war
Shall never pass the polar bar.
The beggar's dog and widow's cat,
Feed them and thou wilt grow fat.

W. BLAKE.

49. THE BUILDING OF JERUSALEM

AND did those feet in ancient time
  Walk upon England's moun-
    tains green ?
And was the holy Lamb of God
  On England's pleasant pastures
    seen ?
And did the Countenance Divine
  Shine forth upon our clouded
    hills ?
And was Jerusalem builded here
  Among these dark Satanic Mills?

Bring me my bow of burning gold !
  Bring me my arrows of desire !
Bring me my spear ! O clouds,
  unfold !
  Bring me my chariot of fire !
I will not cease from mental fight,
  Nor shall my sword sleep in my
    hand,
Till we have built Jerusalem
  In England's green and pleasant
    land.

W. BLAKE (*Milton*).

50. A TEAR IS AN INTELLECTUAL THING

BUT vain the sword and vain the bow,
They never can work War's overthrow.
The hermit's prayer and the widow's tear
Alone can free the world from fear.

For a tear is an intellectual thing,
And a sigh is the sword of an angel king,
And the bitter groan of the martyr's woe,
Is an arrow from the Almighty's bow.

W. BLAKE (*The Grey Monk*).

51. I TOLD MY LOVE

I TOLD my love, I told my love,
  I told her all my heart ;
Trembling, cold, in ghastly fears,
  Ah ! she doth depart.

Soon as she was gone from me,
  A traveller came by,
Silently, invisibly—
  O! was no deny.

W. BLAKE.

52. THE NEW DISPENSATION

JESUS was sitting in Moses' chair.
They brought the trembling woman there.
Moses commands she be stoned to death.
What was the sound of Jesus' breath ?
He laid His hand on Moses' law ;
The ancient Heavens, in silent awe,
Writ with curses from pole to pole,
All away began to roll.

W. BLAKE (*The Everlasting Gospel*).

53. THE LAMB

LITTLE Lamb, who made thee ?
  Dost thou know who made thee?
Gave thee life, and bid thee feed,
By the stream and o'er the mead ;
Gave thee clothing of delight,
Softest clothing, woolly, bright ;
Gave thee such a tender voice,
Making all the vales rejoice ?
  Little Lamb, who made thee ?
  Dost thou know who made thee?

Little Lamb, I'll tell thee,
  Little Lamb, I'll tell thee :
He is callèd by thy name,
For He calls Himself a Lamb.
He is meek, and He is mild ;
He became a little child.
I a child, and thou a lamb,
We are callèd by His name.
  Little Lamb, God bless thee !
  Little Lamb, God bless thee !
                    W. BLAKE.

54. MOCK ON, MOCK ON, VOLTAIRE, ROUSSEAU

Mock on, mock on, Voltaire, Rousseau ;
  Mock on, mock on ; 'tis all in vain !
You throw the sand against the wind,
  And the wind blows it back again.

And every sand becomes a gem
  Reflected in the beams divine ;
Blown back they blind the mocking eye,
  But still in Israel's paths they shine.

                                    W. BLAKE.

55. THE LITTLE BLACK BOY

MY mother bore me in the southern wild,
  And I am black, but O my soul is white ;
White as an angel is the English child,
  But I am black, as if bereaved of light.

My mother taught me underneath a tree,
  And, sitting down before the heat of day,
She took me on her lap and kissèd me,
  And, pointing to the east, began to say :

' Look on the rising sun,—there God does live,
  And gives His light, and gives His heat away ;
And flowers and trees and beasts and men receive
  Comfort in morning, joy in the noonday.

' And we are put on earth a little space,
  That we may learn to bear the beams of love ;
And these black bodies and this sunburnt face
  Is but a cloud, and like a shady grove.

' For when our souls have learned the heat to bear,
  The cloud will vanish, we shall hear His voice,
Saying : "Come out from the grove, My love and care,
  And round My golden tent like lambs rejoice." '

Thus did my mother say, and kissèd me ;
  And thus I say to little English boy.
When I from black, and he from white cloud free,
  And round the tent of God like lambs we joy,

I'll shade him from the heat, till he can bear
  To lean in joy upon our father's knee ;
And then I'll stand and stroke his silver hair,
  And be like him, and he will then love me.

W. BLAKE.

56. TO SPRING

O THOU with dewy locks, who lookest down
Through the clear windows of the morning, turn
Thine angel eyes upon our western isle,
Which in full choir hails thy approach, O Spring !

The hills tell each other, and the list'ning
Valleys hear ; all our longing eyes are turned
Up to thy bright pavilions : issue forth,
And let thy holy feet visit our clime.

Come o'er the eastern hills, and let our winds
Kiss thy perfumèd garments ; let us taste
Thy morn and evening breath ; scatter thy pearls
Upon our love-sick land that mourns for thee.

O deck her forth with thy fair fingers ; pour
Thy soft kisses on her bosom ; and put
Thy golden crown upon her languished head,
Whose modest tresses were bound up for thee.

W. BLAKE.

57. 'SONGS OF INNOCENCE'

PIPING down the valleys wild,
  Piping songs of pleasant glee,
On a cloud I saw a child,
  And he laughing said to me :

'Pipe a song about a Lamb ! '
  So I piped with merry cheer.
'Piper, pipe that song again ; '
  So I piped : he wept to hear.

'Drop thy pipe, thy happy pipe ;
  Sing thy songs of happy cheer:'
So I sang the same again,
  While he wept with joy to hear.

'Piper, sit thee down and write
  In a book, that all may read.'
So he vanished from my sight,
  And I plucked a hollow reed,

And I made a rural pen,
  And I stained the water clear,
And I wrote my happy songs
  Every child may joy to hear.

W. BLAKE.

58. TIGER! TIGER! BURNING BRIGHT

Tiger! Tiger! burning bright
In the forests of the night,
What immortal hand or eye
Could frame thy fearful sym-
    metry?

In what distant deeps or skies
Burnt the fire of thine eyes?
On what wings dare he aspire?
What the hand dare seize the
    fire?

And what shoulder, and what
    art,
Could twist the sinews of thy
    heart?
And when thy heart began to beat,
What dread hand? and what
    dread feet?

What the hammer? what the
    chain?
In what furnace was thy brain?
What the anvil? what dread
    grasp
Dare its deadly terrors clasp?

When the stars threw down their
    spears,
And watered heaven with their
    tears,
Did he smile his work to see?
Did he who made the Lamb make
    thee?

Tiger! Tiger! burning bright
In the forests of the night,
What immortal hand or eye
Dare frame thy fearful symmetry?
                              W. Blake.

59. TO THE MUSES

Whether on Ida's shady brow,
    Or in the chambers of the East,
The chambers of the sun, that now
    From ancient melody have
    ceased;

Whether in Heav'n ye wander
    fair,
    Or the green corners of the earth,
Or the blue regions of the air
    Where the melodious winds
    have birth;

Whether on crystal rocks ye rove,
    Beneath the bosom of the sea
Wandering in many a coral grove,
    Fair Nine, forsaking Poetry!

How have you left the ancient love
    That bards of old enjoyed in
    you!
The languid strings do scarcely
    move!
    The sound is forced, the notes
    are few!
                              W. Blake.

60. THE VOICE OF THE ANCIENT BARD

Youth of delight, come hither,
And see the opening morn,
Image of truth new-born.
Doubt is fled, and clouds of reason,
Dark disputes and artful teasing.
Folly is an endless maze,
Tangled roots perplex her ways.

How many have fallen there!
They stumble all night over bones
    of the dead,
And feel they know not what but
    care,
And wish to lead others, when
    they should be led.
                              W. Blake.

61. DOVER CLIFFS

On these white cliffs, that calm above the flood
Uplift their shadowy heads, and at their feet
Scarce hear the surge that has for ages beat,
Sure many a lonely wanderer has stood ;
And while the distant murmur met his ear,
And o'er the distant billows the still eve
Sailed slow, has thought of all his heart must leave
To-morrow ; of the friends he loved most dear ;
Of social scenes from which he wept to part.
But if, like me, he knew how fruitless all
The thoughts that would full fain the past recall ;
Soon would he quell the risings of his heart,
And brave the wild winds and unhearing tide,
The world his country, and his God his guide.

W. L. Bowles.

62. IN THE MERRY MONTH OF MAY

In the merry month of May,
In a morn by break of day,
Forth I walked by the wood-side,
Whenas May was in his pride :
There I spièd all alone
Phillida and Corydon.
Much ado there was, God wot !
He would love and she would not.
She said, Never man was true ;
He said, None was false to you.
He said, He had loved her long ;
She said, Love should have no wrong.
Corydon would kiss her then ;

She said, Maids must kiss no men
Till they did for good and all ;
Then she made the shepherd call
All the heavens to witness truth
Never loved a truer youth.
Thus with many a pretty oath,
Yea and nay, faith and troth,
Such as silly shepherds use
When they will not love abuse,
Love, which had been long de-
    luded,
Was with kisses sweet concluded ;
And Phillida with garlands gay
Was made the Lady of the May.

N. Breton.

63. FROM ' FAREWELL TO TOWN '

Now next, my gallant youths, farewell ;
    My lads that oft have cheered my heart !
My grief of mind no tongue can tell,
    To think that I must from you part.
I now must leave you all, alas,
And live with some old lobcock ass !

And now, farewell, thou gallant lute,
    With instruments of music's sounds :
Recorder, cittern, harp and flute,
    And heavenly descants on sweet grounds ;
I now must leave you all, indeed,
And make some music on a reed !

.   .   .   .   .

And now, farewell, both spear and shield,
    Caliver, pistol, arquebus ;
See, see, what sighs my heart doth yield,
    To think that I must leave you thus ;
And lay aside my rapier blade,
And take in hand a ditching spade.

.   .   .   .

And now, farewell, each dainty dish,
    With sundry sorts of sugared wine!
Farewell, I say, fine flesh and fish,
    To please this dainty mouth of mine !
I now, alas, must leave all these,
And make good cheer with bread and cheese.
N. BRETON.

64. LOVE, DRINK, AND DEBT

I HAVE been in love, and in debt, and in drink,
    This many and many a year,
And those are three plagues enough, any should think,
    For one poor mortal to bear.
'Twas love made me fall into drink,
    And drink made me run into debt,
And though I have struggled, and struggled, and strove,
    I cannot get out of them yet.

There 's nothing but money can cure me,
    And rid me of all my pain !
      'Twill pay all my debts,
      And remove all my lets,
And my mistress, that cannot endure me,
    Will love me, and love me again :
Then I'll fall to my loving and drinking amain !
A. BROME.

65. LOVE UNACCOUNTABLE

'TIS not her birth, her friends, nor yet her treasure,
Nor do I covet her for sensual pleasure,
Nor for that old morality
Do I love her, 'cause she loves me.
Sure he that loves his lady 'cause she 's fair,
Delights his eye, so loves himself, not her.
Something there is moves me to love, and I
Do know I love, but know not how, nor why.
A. BROME.

66. NO COWARD SOUL IS MINE

No coward soul is mine,
No trembler in the world's storm-troubled sphere:
    I see Heaven's glories shine,
And faith shines equal, arming me from fear.

    O God within my breast,
Almighty, ever-present Deity!
    Life—that in me has rest,
As I—undying life—have power in Thee!

    Vain are the thousand creeds
That move men's hearts: unutterably vain;
    Worthless as withered weeds,
Or idlest froth amid the boundless main,

    To waken doubt in one
Holding so fast by thine infinity;
    So surely anchored on
The steadfast rock of immortality.

    With wide-embracing love
Thy spirit animates eternal years,
    Pervades and broods above,
Changes, sustains, dissolves, creates, and rears.

    Though earth and man were gone,
And suns and universes ceased to be,
    And Thou wert left alone,
Every existence would exist in thee.

    There is not room for Death
Nor atom that his might could render void:
    Thou—Thou art Being and Breath,
And what Thou art may never be destroyed.

                E. Brontë.

67. THE OLD STOIC

Riches I hold in light esteem,
    And Love I laugh to scorn;
And lust of fame was but a dream,
    That vanished with the morn:

And if I pray, the only prayer
    That moves my lips for me
Is, 'Leave the heart that now I bear,
    And give me liberty!'

Yes, as my swift days near their goal,
    'Tis all that I implore;
In life and death a chainless soul,
    With courage to endure.

                E. Brontë.

68. MY GARDEN

A GARDEN is a lovesome thing, God wot !
  Rose plot,
 Fringed pool,
Ferned grot—
  The veriest school
  Of peace ; and yet the fool
Contends that God is not—
Not God ! in gardens ! when the eve is cool ?
  Nay, but I have a sign :
  'Tis very sure God walks in mine.

T. E. BROWN.

69. HE THAT LOOKS STILL ON YOUR EYES

HE that looks still on your eyes,
  Though the winter have begun
To benumb our arteries,
  Shall not want the summer's sun.

He that still may see your cheeks,
  Where all rareness still reposes,
Is a fool, if e'er he seeks
  Other lilies, other roses.

He to whom your soft lip yields,
  And perceives your breath in kissing,
All the odours of the fields,
  Never, never, shall be missing.
    Welcome, welcome ! do I sing,
    Far more welcome than the Spring;
    He that parteth from you never
    Shall enjoy a Spring for ever.

W. BROWNE.

70. THE SUBJECT OF ALL VERSE

UNDERNEATH this sable hearse
Lies the subject of all verse,
Sidney's sister, Pembroke's
    mother,
Death, ere thou hast slain another,
Fair and learned and good as she,
Time shall throw a dart at thee.
Marble piles let no man raise
To her name ; for after days,
Some kind woman, born as
    she,
Reading this, like Niobe,
Shall turn marble, and become
Both her mourner and her tomb.

W. BROWNE.

71. VENUS, BY ADONIS' SIDE

VENUS, by Adonis' side,
Crying kissed, and kissing cried,
Wrung her hands and tore her hair,
For Adonis dying there.
' Stay,' quoth she, ' Oh, stay and
   live !
Nature, surely, doth not give
To the earth her sweetest flowers,
To be seen but some few hours.'

On his face, still as he bled,
For each drop a tear she shed,
Which she kissed or wiped away,
Else had drowned him where he
   lay.
' Fair Proserpina,' quoth she,
' Shall not have thee yet from me ;
Nor thy soul, to fly begin ;
While my lips can keep it in !'

    Here she ceased again. And some
    Say, Apollo would have come
    To have cured his wounded limb,
    But that she had smothered him.   W. BROWNE.

72. BUT THEN THE THRUSHES SANG

            BUT then the thrushes sang
And shook my pulses and the elms' new leaves ;
At which I turned, and held my finger up,
And bade him mark that, howsoe'er the world
Went ill, as he related, certainly
The thrushes still sang in it. At the word
His brow would soften,—and he bore with me
In melancholy patience, not unkind,
While breaking into voluble ecstasy
I flattered all the beauteous country round,
As poets use, the skies, the clouds, the fields,
The happy violets hiding from the roads
The primroses run down to, carrying gold ;
The tangled hedgerows, where the cows push out
Impatient horns and tolerant churning-mouths
'Twixt dripping ash-boughs,—hedge-rows all alive
With birds, and gnats, and large white butterflies
Which look as if the May-flower had caught life
And palpitated forth upon the wind ;
Hills, vales, woods, netted in a silver mist,
Farms, granges, doubled up among the hills ;
And cattle grazing in the watered vales,
And cottage-chimneys smoking from the woods,
And cottage-gardens smelling everywhere,
Confused with smell of orchards. ' See,' I said,
' And see ! is God not with us on the earth ?
And shall we put Him down by aught we do ?
Who says there 's nothing for the poor and vile
Save poverty and wickedness ? behold !'
And ankle-deep in English grass I leaped
And clapped my hands, and called all very fair.
             E. B. BROWNING (*Aurora Leigh*).

73. THE CRY OF THE CHILDREN

Do ye hear the children weeping, O my brothers,
  Ere the sorrow comes with years ?
They are leaning their young heads against their mothers,
  And *that* cannot stop their tears.
The young lambs are bleating in the meadows,
  The young birds are chirping in the nest,
The young fawns are playing with the shadows,
  The young flowers are blowing toward the west—
But the young, young children, O my brothers,
  They are weeping bitterly !
They are weeping in the playtime of the others,
  In the country of the free.

Do you question the young children in the sorrow,
  Why their tears are falling so ?
The old man may weep for his to-morrow
  Which is lost in Long Ago ;
The old tree is leafless in the forest,
  The old year is ending in the frost,
The old wound, if stricken, is the sorest,
  The old hope is hardest to be lost.
But the young, young children, O my brothers,
  Do you ask them why they stand
Weeping sore before the bosoms of their mothers,
  In our happy Fatherland ?

They look up with their pale and sunken faces,
  And their looks are sad to see,
For the man's hoary anguish draws and presses
  Down the cheeks of infancy.
' Your old earth,' they say, ' is very dreary ;
  Our young feet,' they say, ' are very weak ;
Few paces have we taken, yet are weary—
  Our grave-rest is very far to seek.
Ask the aged why they weep, and not the children ;
  For the outside earth is cold ;
And we young ones stand without, in our bewildering.
  And the graves are for the old.'

   .   .   .   .

Alas, alas, the children ! they are seeking
  Death in life, as best to have ;
They are binding up their hearts away from breaking,
  With a cerement from the grave.
Go out, children, from the mine and from the city,
  Sing out, children, as the little thrushes do ;

C

Pluck you handfuls of the meadow cowslips pretty,
　　Laugh aloud to feel your fingers let them through !
But they answer, ' Are your cowslips of the meadows
　　Like our weeds anear the mine ?
Leave us quiet in the dark of the coal-shadows,
　　From your pleasures fair and fine !

' For oh,' say the children, ' we are weary,
　　And we cannot run or leap ;
If we cared for any meadows, it were merely
　　To drop down in them and sleep.
Our knees tremble sorely in the stooping,
　　We fall upon our faces, trying to go ;
And, underneath our heavy eyelids drooping,
　　The reddest flower would look as pale as snow ;
For, all day, we drag our burden tiring
　　Through the coal-dark, underground—
Or, all day, we drive the wheels of iron
　　In the factories, round and round.'

　　.　　.　　.　　.　　.　　.　　.　　.

And well may the children weep before you !
　　They are weary ere they run ;
They have never seen the sunshine, nor the glory
　　Which is brighter than the sun.
They know the grief of man, without its wisdom ;
　　They sink in man's despair, without its calm ;
Are slaves, without the liberty in Christdom,
　　Are martyrs, by the pang without the palm,—
Are worn, as if with age, yet unretrievingly
　　The harvest of its memories cannot reap,—
Are orphans of the earthly love and heavenly.
　　Let them weep ! let them weep !

They look up, with their pale and sunken faces,
　　And their look is dread to see,
For they mind you of their angels in high places,
　　With eyes turned on Deity !—
' How long,' they say, ' how long, O cruel nation,
　　Will you stand, to move the world, on a child's heart,—
Stifle down with a mailed heel its palpitation,
　　And tread onward to your throne amid the mart ?
Our blood splashes upward, O gold-heaper,
　　And your purple shows your path !
But the child's sob in the silence curses deeper
　　Than the strong man in his wrath.'

E. B. BROWNING.

74. A PORTRAIT

FACE and figure of a child,—
  Though too calm, you think,
    and tender,
  For the childhood you would
    lend her.

Yet child-simple, undefiled,
  Frank, obedient,—waiting still
  On the turnings of your will.

. . . .

And if any poet knew her,
  He would sing of her with
    falls
  Used in lovely madrigals.

And if any painter drew her,
  He would paint her unaware
  With a halo round the hair.
            E. B. BROWNING.

75. HOW DO I LOVE THEE ?

How do I love thee ? Let me count the ways.
I love thee to the depth and breadth and height
My soul can reach, when feeling out of sight
For the ends of Being and ideal Grace.
I love thee to the level of every day's
Most quiet need, by sun and candlelight.
I love thee freely, as men strive for Right ;
I love thee purely, as they turn from Praise.
I love thee with the passion put to use
In my old griefs, and with my childhood's faith.
I love thee with a love I seemed to lose
With my lost saints,—I love thee with the breath,
Smiles, tears, of all my life !—and, if God choose,
I shall but love thee better after death.
        E. B. BROWNING (*Sonnets from the Portuguese*).

76. THE SEA-MEW

How joyously the young sea-mew
Lay dreaming on the waters blue,
Whereon our little bark had thrown
A little shade, the only one,—
But shadows ever man pursue.

Familiar with the waves and free
As if their own white foam were he,
His heart upon the heart of ocean
Lay learning all its mystic motion,
And throbbing to tne throbbing sea.

And such a brightness in his eye,
As if the ocean and the sky
Within him had lit up and nurst
A soul God gave him not at first
To comprehend their majesty.

We were not cruel, yet did sunder
His white wing from the blue waves under,
And bound it, while his fearless eyes
Shone up to ours in calm surprise,
As deeming us some ocean wonder !

We bore our ocean bird unto
A grassy place, where he might view
The flowers that curtsy to the bees,
The waving of the tall green trees,
The falling of the silver dew.

But flowers of earth were pale to him
Who had seen the rainbow fishes swim ;
And when earth's dew around him lay
He thought of ocean's wingèd spray,
And his eye waxèd sad and dim.

The green trees round him only made
A prison with their darksome shade ;
And drooped his wing, and mournèd he
For his own boundless glittering sea—
Albeit he knew not they could fade.

Then One her gladsome face did bring,
Her gentle voice's murmuring,
In ocean's stead his heart to move
And teach him what was human love—
He thought it a strange, mournful thing.

He lay down in his grief to die
(First looking to the sea-like sky
That hath no waves !), because, alas !
Our human touch did on him pass,
And with our touch, our agony.   E. B. Browning.

77. I THOUGHT ONCE HOW THEOCRITUS HAD SUNG

I thought once how Theocritus had sung
Of the sweet years, the dear and wished-for years,
Who each one in a gracious hand appears
To bear a gift for mortals, old or young :
And, as I mused it in his antique tongue,
I saw, in gradual vision through my tears,
The sweet, sad years, the melancholy years,
Those of my own life, who by turns had flung
A shadow across me.   Straightway I was 'ware,
So weeping, how a mystic Shape did move
Behind me, and drew me backward by the hair,
And a voice said in mastery while I strove, . .
' Guess now who holds thee ? '—' Death,' I said.   But, there,
The silver answer rang, . . ' Not Death, but Love.'
        E. B. Browning (*Sonnets from the Portuguese*).

78. A THOUGHT FOR A LONELY DEATH-BED

IF God compel thee to this destiny,
To die alone,—with none beside thy bed
To ruffle round with sobs thy last word said,
And mark with tears the pulses ebb from thee,—
Pray then alone—'O Christ, come tenderly!
By thy forsaken Sonship in the red
Drear wine-press,—by the wilderness outspread,—
And the lone garden where Thine agony
Fell bloody from Thy brow,—by all of those
Permitted desolations, comfort mine!
No earthly friend being near me, interpose
No deathly angel 'twixt my face and Thine,
But stoop Thyself to gather my life's rose,
And smile away my mortal to Divine.'

E. B. BROWNING (*To E. C.*).

79. IF THOU MUST LOVE ME

IF thou must love me, let it be for nought
Except for love's sake only. Do not say
'I love her for her smile . . . her look . . . her way
Of speaking gently, . . for a trick of thought
That falls in well with mine, and certes brought
A sense of pleasant ease on such a day'—
For these things in themselves, Belovèd, may
Be changed, or change for thee,—and love, so wrought,
May be unwrought so. Neither love me for
Thine own dear pity's wiping my cheeks dry,—
A creature might forget to weep, who bore
Thy comfort long, and lose thy love thereby!
But love me for love's sake, that evermore
Thou mayst love on, through love's eternity.

E. B. BROWNING (*Sonnets from the Portuguese*).

80. THE SLEEP

He giveth his beloved sleep.—*Ps.* cxxvii. 2.

OF all the thoughts of God that are
Borne inward unto souls afar,
Along the Psalmist's music deep,
Now tell me if that any is,
For gift or grace, surpassing this—
'He giveth His belovèd, sleep'?

What would we give to our beloved?
The hero's heart, to be unmoved,
The poet's star-tuned harp, to sweep,

The patriot's voice, to teach and rouse,
The monarch's crown, to light the brows ?—
He giveth His belovèd, sleep.

What do we give to our beloved ?
A little faith all undisproved,
A little dust to overweep,
And bitter memories to make
The whole earth blasted for our sake.
He giveth His belovèd, sleep.

' Sleep soft, beloved ! ' we sometimes say,
But have no tune to charm away
Sad dreams that through the eye-lids creep.
But never doleful dream again
Shall break the happy slumber when
He giveth His belovèd, sleep.

O earth, so full of dreary noises !
O men, with wailing in your voices !
O delvèd gold, the wailers heap !
O strife, O curse, that o'er it fall !
God strikes a silence through you all,
And giveth His belovèd, sleep.

His dews drop mutely on the hill ;
His cloud above it saileth still,
Though on its slope men sow and reap.
More softly than the dew is shed,
Or cloud is floated overhead,
He giveth His belovèd, sleep.

Aye, men may wonder while they scan
A living, thinking, feeling man
Confirmed in such a rest to keep ;
But angels say, and through the word
I think their happy smile is *heard*—
' He giveth His belovèd, sleep.'

For me, my heart that erst did go
Most like a tired child at a show,
That sees through tears the mummers leap,
Would now its wearied vision close,
Would child-like on His love repose,
Who giveth His belovèd, sleep.

And, friends, dear friends,—when it shall be
That this low breath is gone from me,
And round my bier ye come to weep,
Let One, most loving of you all,
Say, ' Not a tear must o'er her fall ;
He giveth His belovèd, sleep.'

                              E. B. BROWNING.

81. COMFORT

SPEAK low to me, my Saviour, low and sweet
From out the hallelujahs, sweet and low,
Lest I should fear and fall, and miss Thee so,
Who art not missed by any that entreat.
Speak to me as to Mary at Thy feet!
And if no precious gums my hands bestow,
Let my tears drop like amber, while I go
In reach of Thy divinest voice complete
In humanest affection—thus, in sooth,
To lose the sense of losing. As a child,
Whose song-bird seeks the wood for evermore,
Is sung to in its stead by mother's mouth,
Till, sinking on her breast, love-reconciled,
He sleeps the faster that he wept before.

E. B. BROWNING.

82. THE CYGNET FINDS THE WATER

THE cygnet finds the water, but the man
Is born in ignorance of his element
And feels out blind at first, disorganized
By sin i' the blood,—his spirit-insight dulled
And crossed by his sensations. Presently
He feels it quicken in the dark sometimes,
When, mark, be revere ., be obedient,
For such dumb motions of imperfect life
Are oracles of vital Deity
Attesting the Hereafter. Let who says
' The soul's a clean white paper ', rather say,
A palimpsest, a prophet's holograph
Defiled, erased and covered by a monk's,—
The apocalypse, by a Longus! poring on
Which obscene text, we may discern perhaps
Some fair, fine trace of what was written once,
Some upstroke of an alpha and omega
Expressing the old scripture.

E. B. BROWNING (Aurora Leigh).

83. THE FACE OF ALL THE WORLD IS CHANGED

THE face of all the world is changed, I think,
Since first I heard the footsteps of thy soul
Move still, oh, still, beside me, as they stole
Betwixt me and the dreadful outer brink
Of obvious death, where I, who thought to sink,
Was caught up into love, and taught the whole
Of life in a new rhythm. The cup of dole
God gave for baptism, I am fain to drink,

And praise its sweetness, Sweet, with thee anear.
The names of country, heaven, are changed away
For where thou art or shalt be, there or here ;
And this . . . this lute and song . . . loved yesterday
(The singing angels know) are only dear,
Because thy name moves right in what they say.

> E. B. BROWNING (*Sonnets from the Portuguese*).

84. THE POETS

THERE, obedient to her praying, did I read aloud the poems
Made to Tuscan flutes, or instruments more various of our own ;
Read the pastoral parts of Spenser—or the subtle interflowings
Found in Petrarch's sonnets—here 's the book—the leaf is folded
    down !

Or at times a modern volume—Wordsworth's solemn-thoughted idyl,
Howitt's ballad-verse, or Tennyson's enchanted reverie,—
Or from Browning some 'Pomegranate', which, if cut deep down the
    middle,
Shows a heart within blood-tinctured, of a veined humanity.

> E. B. BROWNING (*Lady Geraldine's Courtship*).

85. HIRAM POWERS'S GREEK SLAVE

THEY say Ideal beauty cannot enter
The house of anguish. On the threshold stands
An alien Image with enshackled hands,
Called the Greek Slave ! as if the artist meant her
(That passionless perfection which he lent her,
Shadowed not darkened where the sill expands)
To, so, confront man's crimes in different lands
With man's ideal sense. Pierce to the centre,
Art's fiery finger !—and break up ere long
The serfdom of this world ! appeal, fair stone,
From God's pure heights of beauty against man's wrong !
Catch up in thy divine face, not alone
East griefs but west,—and strike and shame the strong,
By thunders of white silence, overthrown.

> E. B. BROWNING.

86. TO GEORGE SAND

A DESIRE

THOU large-brained woman and large-hearted man,
Self-called George Sand ! whose soul, amid the lions
Of thy tumultuous senses, moans defiance,
And answers roar for roar, as spirits can !
I would some mild miraculous thunder ran
Above the applauded circus, in appliance

Of thine own nobler nature's strength and science,
Drawing two pinions, white as wings of swan,
From thy strong shoulders, to amaze the place
With holier light ! that thou to woman's claim
And man's, mightst join beside the angel's grace
Of a pure genius sanctified from blame,—
Till child and maiden pressed to thine embrace,
To kiss upon thy lips a stainless fame.

A RECOGNITION

True genius, but true woman ! dost deny
Thy woman's nature with a manly scorn,
And break away the gauds and armlets worn
By weaker women in captivity ?
Ah, vain denial ! that revolted cry
Is sobbed in by a woman's voice forlorn !—
Thy woman's hair, my sister, all unshorn,
Floats back dishevelled strength in agony,
Disproving thy man's name ! and while before
The world thou burnest in a poet-fire,
We see thy woman-heart beat evermore
Through the large flame. Beat purer, heart, and higher,
Till God unsex thee on the heavenly shore,
Where unincarnate spirits purely aspire.

E. B. BROWNING.

87. THE LADY'S YES

'Yes,' I answered you last night ;
'No,' this morning, sir, I say.
Colours seen by candle-light
Will not look the same by day.

When the viols played their best,
Lamps above, and laughs below,
Love me sounded like a jest,
Fit for *yes* or fit for *no*.

Call me false or call me free—
Vow, whatever light may shine,
No man on your face shall see
Any grief, for change on mine.

Yet the sin is on us both ;
Time to dance is not to woo ;
Wooing light makes fickle troth,
Scorn of *me* recoils on *you*.

Learn to win a lady's faith
Nobly, as the thing is high,
Bravely, as for life and death—
With a loyal gravity.

Lead her from the festive boards,
Point her to the starry skies,
Guard her, by your truthful words,
Pure from courtship's flatteries.

By your truth she shall be true,
Ever true, as wives of yore ;
And her *yes*, once said to you,
SHALL be Yes for evermore.

E. B. BROWNING.

88. YET LOVE, MERE LOVE

YET, love, mere love, is beautiful indeed
And worthy of acceptation. Fire is bright,
Let temple burn, or flax. An equal light
Leaps in the flame from cedar-plank or weed.
And love is fire ; and when I say at need
I love thee . . mark ! . . *I love thee !* . . in thy sight
I stand transfigured, glorified aright,
With conscience of the new rays that proceed
Out of my face toward thine. There 's nothing low
In love, when love the lowest : meanest creatures
Who love God, God accepts while loving so.
And what I *feel*, across the inferior features
Of what I *am*, doth flash itself, and show
How that great work of Love enhances Nature's.

> E. B. BROWNING (*Sonnets from the Portuguese*).

89. FLUSH OR FAUNUS

YOU see this dog. It was but yesterday
I mused forgetful of his presence here
Till thought on thought drew downward tear on tear,
When from the pillow, where wet-cheeked I lay,
A head as hairy as Faunus, thrust its way
Right sudden against my face,—two golden-clear
Great eyes astonished mine,—a drooping ear
Did flap me on either cheek to dry the spray !
I started first, as some Arcadian,
Amazed by goatly god in twilight grove ;
But, as the bearded vision closelier ran
My tears off, I knew Flush, and rose above
Surprise and sadness,—thanking the true PAN,
Who, by low creatures, leads to heights of love.

> E. B. BROWNING.

90. MY STAR

ALL that I know
   Of a certain star,
Is, it can throw
   (Like the angled spar)
Now a dart of red,
   Now a dart of blue,
Till my friends have said
   They would fain see, too,
My star that dartles the red and the blue !
Then it stops like a bird ; like a flower, hangs furled :
   They must solace themselves with the Saturn above it.
What matter to me if their star is a world ?
   Mine has opened its soul to me ; therefore I love it.

> R. BROWNING.

91. LIFE IN A LOVE

ESCAPE me ?
Never—
Beloved !
While I am I, and you are you,
  So long as the world contains us both,
  Me the loving and you the loath,
While the one eludes, must the other pursue.
My life is a fault at last, I fear :
  It seems too much like a fate, indeed !
  Though I do my best I shall scarce succeed.
But what if I fail of my purpose here ?
It is but to keep the nerves at strain,
  To dry one's eyes and laugh at a fall,
And, baffled, get up and begin again,—
  So the chace takes up one's life, that 's all.
While, look but once from your farthest bound
  At me so deep in the dust and dark,
No sooner the old hope drops to ground
  Than a new one, straight to the self-same mark,
        I shape me—
        Ever
        Removed !

R. BROWNING.

92. PROSPICE

FEAR death ?—to feel the fog in my throat,
    The mist in my face,
When the snows begin, and the blasts denote
    I am nearing the place,
The power of the night, the press of the storm,
    The post of the foe ;
Where he stands, the Arch Fear in a visible form,
    Yet the strong man must go :
For the journey is done and the summit attained,
    And the barriers fall,
Though a battle 's to fight ere the guerdon be gained,
    The reward of it all.
I was ever a fighter, so—one fight more,
    The best and the last !
I would hate that death bandaged my eyes, and forbore,
    And bade me creep past.
No ! let me taste the whole of it, fare like my peers
    The heroes of old, ·
Bear the brunt, in a minute pay glad life's arrears
    Of pain, darkness and cold.

For sudden the worst turns the best to the brave,
  The black minute's at end,
And the elements' rage, the fiend-voices that rave,
  Shall dwindle, shall blend,
Shall change, shall become first a peace, then a joy,
  Then a light, then thy breast,
O thou soul of my soul! I shall clasp thee again,
  And with God be the rest! R. BROWNING.

93. GROW OLD ALONG WITH ME

GROW old along with me!
The best is yet to be,
The last of life, for which the first was made:
Our times are in His hand
Who saith 'A whole I planned,
Youth shows but half; trust God: see all, nor be afraid!'

Then, welcome each rebuff
That turns earth's smoothness rough,
Each sting that bids nor sit nor stand but go!
Be our joys three-parts pain!
Strive, and hold cheap the strain;
Learn, nor account the pang; dare, never grudge the throe!

Not on the vulgar mass
Called 'work', must sentence pass,
Things done, that took the eye and had the price;
O'er which, from level stand,
The low world laid its hand,
Found straightway to its mind, could value in a trice:

But all, the world's coarse thumb
And finger failed to plumb,
So passed in making up the main account;
All instincts immature,
All purposes unsure,
That weighed not as his work, yet swelled the man's amount:

Thoughts hardly to be packed
Into a narrow act,
Fancies that broke through language and escaped;
All I could never be,
All, men ignored in me,
This, I was worth to God, whose wheel the pitcher shaped.

So, take and use Thy work!
Amend what flaws may lurk,
What strain o' the stuff, what warpings past the aim!
My times be in Thy hand!
Perfect the cup as planned!
Let age approve of youth, and death complete the same!
    R. BROWNING (*Rabbi Ben Ezra*).

94. THE NELSON TOUCH

Here 's to Nelson's memory !
'Tis the second time that I, at sea,
Right off Cape Trafalgar here,
Have drunk it deep in British Beer.
Nelson for ever—any time
Am I his to command in prose or rhyme !
Give me of Nelson only a touch,
And I save it, be it little or much.

R. Browning (Nationality in Drinks).

95. RUDEL TO THE LADY OF TRIPOLI

I know a Mount, the gracious Sun perceives
First when he visits, last, too, when he leaves
The world ; and, vainly favoured, it repays
The day-long glory of his steadfast gaze
By no change of its large calm front of snow.
And underneath the Mount, a Flower I know,
He cannot have perceived, that changes ever
At his approach ; and, in the lost endeavour
To live his life, has parted, one by one,
With all a flower's true graces, for the grace
Of being but a foolish mimic sun,
With ray-like florets round a disk-like face.
Men nobly call by many a name the Mount
As over many a land of theirs its large
Calm front of snow like a triumphal targe
Is reared, and still with old names, fresh ones vie,
Each to its proper praise and own account :
Men call the Flower, the Sunflower, sportively.

Oh, Angel of the East, one, one gold look
Across the waters to this twilight nook,
—The far sad waters, Angel, to this nook !

Dear Pilgrim, art thou for the East indeed ?
Go ! Saying ever as thou dost proceed,
That I, French Rudel, choose for my device
A sunflower outspread like a sacrifice
Before its idol. See ! These inexpert
And hurried fingers could not fail to hurt
The woven picture ; 'tis a woman's skill
Indeed ; but nothing baffled me, so, ill
Or well, the work is finished. Say, men feed
On songs I sing, and therefore bask the bees
On my flower's breast as on a platform broad :
But, as the flower's concern is not for these
But solely for the sun, so men applaud
In vain this Rudel, he not looking here
But to the East—the East ! Go, say this, Pilgrim dear !

R. Browning.

96. 'HOW THEY BROUGHT THE GOOD NEWS FROM GHENT TO AIX' [16—]

I SPRANG to the stirrup, and Joris, and he;
I galloped, Dirck galloped, we galloped all three;
' Good speed ! ' cried the watch, as the gate-bolts undrew;
' Speed ! ' echoed the wall to us galloping through;
Behind shut the postern, the lights sank to rest,
And into the midnight we galloped abreast.

Not a word to each other ; we kept the great pace
Neck by neck, stride by stride, never changing our place ;
I turned in my saddle and made its girths tight,
Then shortened each stirrup, and set the pique right,
Rebuckled the cheek-strap, chained slacker the bit,
Nor galloped less steadily Roland a whit.

'Twas moonset at starting ; but while we drew near
Lokeren, the cocks crew and twilight dawned clear ;
At Boom, a great yellow star came out to see ;
At Düffeld, 'twas morning as plain as could be ;
And from Mecheln church-steeple we heard the half-chime,
So Joris broke silence with ' Yet there is time ! '

At Aerschot, up leaped of a sudden the sun,
And against him the cattle stood black every one,
To stare through the mist at us galloping past,
And I saw my stout galloper Roland at last,
With resolute shoulders, each butting away
The haze, as some bluff river headland its spray.

And his low head and crest, just one sharp ear bent back
For my voice, and the other pricked out on his track ;
And one eye's black intelligence,—ever that glance
O'er its white edge at me, his own master, askance !
And the thick heavy spume-flakes which aye and anon
His fierce lips shook upwards in galloping on.

By Hasselt, Dirck groaned ; and cried Joris, ' Stay spur !
Your Roos galloped bravely, the fault 's not in her,
We'll remember at Aix '—for one heard the quick wheeze
Of her chest, saw the stretched neck and staggering knees,
And sunk tail, and horrible heave of the flank,
As down on her haunches she shuddered and sank.

So we were left galloping, Joris and I,
Past Looz and past Tongres, no cloud in the sky ;
The broad sun above laughed a pitiless laugh,
'Neath our feet broke the brittle bright stubble like chaff ;
Till over by Dalhem a dome-spire sprang white,
And ' Gallop ', gasped Joris, ' for Aix is in sight ! '

' How they'll greet us ! '—and all in a moment his roan
Rolled neck and croup over, lay dead as a stone ;
And there was my Roland to bear the whole weight
Of the news which alone could save Aix from her fate,
With his nostrils like pits full of blood to the brim,
And with circles of red for his eye-sockets' rim.

Then I cast loose my buffcoat, each holster let fall,
Shook off both my jack-boots, let go belt and all,
Stood up in the stirrup, leaned, patted his ear,
Called my Roland his pet-name, my horse without peer ;
Clapped my hands, laughed and sang, any noise, bad or good,
Till at length into Aix Roland galloped and stood.

And all I remember is, friends flocking round
As I sat with his head 'twixt my knees on the ground ;
And no voice but was praising this Roland of mine,
As I poured down his throat our last measure of wine,
Which (the burgesses voted by common consent)
Was no more than his due who brought good news from Ghent.

R. BROWNING.

97. IT 'S WISER BEING GOOD THAN BAD

IT 's wiser being good than bad ;
    It 's safer being meek than fierce :
It 's fitter being sane than mad.
    My own hope is, a sun will pierce
The thickest cloud earth ever stretched
    That, after Last, returns the First,
Though a wide compass round be fetched ;
    That what began best, can't end worst,
Nor what God blessed once, prove accurst.

R. BROWNING (*Apparent Failure*).

98. THE PATRIOT

AN OLD STORY

IT was roses, roses, all the way,
    With myrtle mixed in my path like mad :
The house-roofs seemed to heave and sway,
    The church-spires flamed, such flags they had,
A year ago on this very day !

The air broke into a mist with bells,
    The old walls rocked with the crowd and cries.
Had I said, ' Good folk, mere noise repels—
    But give me your sun from yonder skies ! '
They had answered, ' And afterward, what else ? '

Alack, it was I who leaped at the sun
  To give it my loving friends to keep!
Naught man could do, have I left undone:
  And you see my harvest, what I reap
This very day, now a year is run.

There's nobody on the house-tops now—
  Just a palsied few at the windows set;
For the best of the sight is, all allow,
  At the Shambles' Gate—or, better yet,
By the very scaffold's foot, I trow.

I go in the rain, and, more than needs,
  A rope cuts both my wrists behind;
And I think, by the feel, my forehead bleeds,
  For they fling, whoever has a mind,
Stones at me for my year's misdeeds.

Thus I entered, and thus I go!
  In triumphs, people have dropped down dead.
'Paid by the World,—what dost thou owe
  Me?' God might question: now instead,
'Tis God shall repay! I am safer so.

                                    R. BROWNING.

99.   ITALY

  ITALY, my Italy!
Queen Mary's saying serves for me—
      (When fortune's malice
      Lost her, Calais)
Open my heart and you will see
Graved inside of it, 'Italy.'
Such lovers old are I and she;
So it always was, so shall ever be!

              R. BROWNING (*De Gustibus—*).

100.   THE LOST LEADER

JUST for a handful of silver he left us,
  Just for a riband to stick in his coat—
Found the one gift of which fortune bereft us,
  Lost all the others she lets us devote;
They, with the gold to give, doled him out silver,
  So much was theirs who so little allowed:
How all our copper had gone for his service!
  Rags—were they purple, his heart had been proud!
We that had loved him so, followed him, honoured him,
  Lived in his mild and magnificent eye,
Learned his great language, caught his clear accents,
  Made him our pattern to live and to die!

Shakespeare was of us, Milton was for us,
  Burns, Shelley, were with us,—they watch from their graves !
He alone breaks from the van and the freemen,
  He alone sinks to the rear and the slaves !

We shall march prospering,—not through his presence ;
  Songs may inspirit us,—not from his lyre ;
Deeds will be done,—while he boasts his quiescence,
  Still bidding crouch whom the rest bade aspire :
Blot out his name, then, record one lost soul more,
  One task more declined, one more footpath untrod,
One more triumph for devils and sorrow for angels,
  One wrong more to man, one more insult to God !
Life's night begins : let him never come back to us !
  There would be doubt, hesitation and pain,
Forced praise on our part—the glimmer of twilight,
  Never glad confident morning again !
Best fight on well, for we taught him,—strike gallantly,
  Menace our heart ere we master his own ;
Then let him receive the new knowledge and wait us,
  Pardoned in Heaven, the first by the throne !

R. BROWNING.

101. A WOMAN'S LAST WORD

LET's contend no more, Love,
  Strive nor weep :
All be as before, Love,
  —Only sleep !

What so wild as words are ?
  I and thou
In debate, as birds are,
  Hawk on bough !

See the creature stalking
  While we speak !
Hush and hide the talking,
  Cheek on cheek !

What so false as truth is,
  False to thee ?
Where the serpent's tooth is,
  Shun the tree—

Where the apple reddens
  Never pry—
Lest we lose our Edens,
  Eve and I !

Be a god and hold me
  With a charm !
Be a man and fold me
  With thine arm !

Teach me, only teach, Love !
  As I ought
I will speak thy speech, Love,
  Think thy thought—

Meet, if thou require it,
  Both demands,
Laying flesh and spirit
  In thy hands.

That shall be to-morrow
  Not to-night :
I must bury sorrow
  Out of sight :

—Must a little weep, Love.
  (Foolish me !)
And so fall asleep, Love,
  Loved by thee.

R. BROWNING.

102. NAY BUT YOU, WHO DO NOT LOVE HER

NAY but you, who do not love her,
  Is she not pure gold, my mistress ?
Holds earth aught—speak truth—above her ?
  Aught like this tress, see, and this tress,
And this last fairest tress of all,
So fair, see, ere I let it fall ?

Because, you spend your lives in praising ;
  To praise, you search the wide world over :
So, why not witness, calmly gazing,
  If earth holds aught—speak truth—above her ?
Above this tress, and this I touch
But cannot praise, I love so much !

                                        R. BROWNING.

103. HOME-THOUGHTS FROM THE SEA

NOBLY, nobly Cape Saint Vincent to the North-West died away ;
Sunset ran, one glorious blood-red, reeking into Cadiz Bay ;
Bluish mid the burning water, full in face Trafalgar lay ;
In the dimmest North-East distance, dawned Gibraltar grand and grey ;
' Here and here did England help me : how can I help England ? '—
    say,
Whoso turns as I, this evening, turn to God to praise and pray,
While Jove's planet rises yonder, silent over Africa.

                                        R. BROWNING.

104. OH, GOOD GIGANTIC SMILE O' THE BROWN OLD EARTH

OH, good gigantic smile o' the brown old earth,
  This autumn morning ! How he sets his bones
To bask i' the sun, and thrusts out knees and feet
For the ripple to run over in its mirth ;
  Listening the while, where on the heap of stones
The white breast of the sea-lark twitters sweet.

                        R. BROWNING (*James Lee's Wife*).

105. HOME-THOUGHTS, FROM ABROAD

OH, to be in England
Now that April's there,
And whoever wakes in England
Sees, some morning, unaware,
That the lowest boughs and the brushwood sheaf
Round the elm-tree bole are in tiny leaf,
While the chaffinch sings on the orchard bough
In England—now !

And after April, when May follows,
And the whitethroat builds, and all the swallows !
Hark, where my blossomed pear-tree in the hedge
Leans to the field and scatters on the clover
Blossoms and dewdrops—at the bent spray's edge—
That 's the wise thrush ; he sings each song twice over,
Lest you should think he never could recapture
The first fine careless rapture !
And though the fields look rough with hoary dew,
All will be gay when noontide wakes anew
The buttercups, the little children's dower
—Far brighter than this gaudy melon-flower !

R. BROWNING.

106. FROM ' ONE WORD MORE '

RAFAEL made a century of sonnets,
Made and wrote them in a certain volume
Dinted with the silver-pointed pencil
Else he only used to draw Madonnas :
These the world might view—but One, the volume.
Who that one, you ask ? Your heart instructs you.
Did she live and love it all her life-time ?
Did she drop, his lady of the sonnets,
Die, and let it drop beside her pillow
Where it lay in place of Rafael's glory,
Rafael's cheek so duteous and so loving—
Cheek, the world was wont to hail a painter's,
Rafael's cheek, her love had turned a poet's ?

You and I would rather read that volume
(Taken to his beating bosom by it),
Lean and list the bosom-beats of Rafael,
Would we not ? than wonder at Madonnas.

. . . .

Dante once prepared to paint an angel :
Whom to please ? You whisper ' Beatrice '.
While he mused and traced it and retraced it
(Peradventure with a pen corroded
Still by drops of that hot ink he dipped for,
When, his left-hand i' the hair o' the wicked,
Back he held the brow and pricked its stigma,
Bit into the live man's flesh for parchment,
Loosed him, laughed to see the writing rankle,
Let the wretch go festering through Florence)—
Dante, who loved well because he hated,
Hated wickedness that hinders loving,
Dante standing, studying his angel,—
In there broke the folk of his Inferno.

. . . .

You and I would rather see that angel,
Painted by the tenderness of Dante,
Would we not ?—than read a fresh Inferno.

.   .   .   .   .   .

God be thanked, the meanest of His creatures
Boasts two soul-sides, one to face the world with,
One to show a woman when he loves her.

.   .   .   .   .   .

Oh, their Rafael of the dear Madonnas,
Oh, their Dante of the dread Inferno.
Wrote one song—and in my brain I sing it,
Drew one angel—borne, see, on my bosom !

R. BROWNING.

107. AFTER

TAKE the cloak from his face, and
        at first
    Let the corpse do its worst.

How he lies in his rights of a
        man !
    Death has done all death
        can.
And, absorbed in the new life he
        leads,
    He recks not, he heeds
Nor his wrong nor my vengeance
        —both strike
    On his senses alike,

And are lost in the solemn and
        strange
    Surprise of the change.

Ha, what avails death to erase
    His offence, my disgrace ?
I would we were boys as of old
    In the field, by the fold :
His outrage, God's patience, man's
        scorn
    Were so easily borne.

I stand here now, he lies in his
        place :
    Cover the face.

R. BROWNING.

108. FROM ' A GRAMMARIAN'S FUNERAL '

THAT low man seeks a little thing to do,
    Sees it and does it :
This high man, with a great thing to pursue,
    Dies ere he knows it.
That low man goes on adding one to one,
    His hundred 's soon hit :
This high man, aiming at a million,
    Misses an unit.
That, has the world here—should he need the next,
    Let the world mind him !
This, throws himself on God, and unperplext
    Seeking shall find Him.
So, with the throttling hands of Death at strife,
    Ground he at grammar ;
Still, thro' the rattle, parts of speech were rife :
    While he could stammer

He settled *Hoti's* business—let it be !—
    Properly based *Oun*—
Gave us the doctrine of the enclitic *De*,
    Dead from the waist down.
Well, here 's the platform, here 's the proper place.
    Hail to your purlieus,
All ye highfliers of the feathered race,
    Swallows and curlews !
Here 's the top-peak ! the multitude below
    Live, for they can, there.
This man decided not to Live but Know—
    Bury this man there ?
Here—here 's his place, where meteors shoot, clouds form,
    Lightnings are loosened,
Stars come and go ! let joy break with the storm,
    Peace let the dew send !
Lofty designs must close in like effects :
    Loftily lying,
Leave him—still loftier than the world suspects,
    Living and dying.

R. BROWNING.

109. THE YEAR'S AT THE SPRING

THE year 's at the spring,
And day 's at the morn ;
Morning 's at seven ;
The hill-side 's dew-pearled ;

The lark 's on the wing ;
The snail 's on the thorn ;
God 's in His heaven—
All 's right with the world !

R. BROWNING (*Pippa Passes*).

110. MISCONCEPTIONS

THIS is a spray the Bird clung to,
    Making it blossom with pleasure,
Ere the high tree-top she sprung to,
    Fit for her nest and her treasure.
    Oh, what a hope beyond measure
Was the poor spray's, which the flying feet hung to,—
So to be singled out, built in, and sung to !

This is a heart the Queen leant on,
    Thrilled in a minute erratic,
Ere the true bosom she bent on,
    Meet for love's regal dalmatic.
    Oh, what a fancy ecstatic
Was the poor heart's, ere the wanderer went on—
Love to be saved for it, proffered to, spent on !

R. BROWNING.

111. WARING

I

WHAT'S become of Waring
Since he gave us all the slip,
Chose land-travel or seafaring,
Boots and chest or staff and
  scrip,
Rather than pace up and down
Any longer London-town ?

Who'd have guessed it from his
  lip
Or his brow's accustomed bearing,
On the night he thus took ship
Or started landward ?—little car-
  ing
For us, it seems, who supped
  together
(Friends of his too, I remember)
And walked home through the
  merry weather,
The snowiest in all December.
I left his arm that night myself
For what 's-his-name's, the new
  prose-poet
That wrote the book there, on
  the shelf—
How, forsooth, was I to know it
If Waring meant to glide away
Like a ghost at break of day ?
Never looked he half so gay !

He was prouder than the Devil :
How he must have cursed our
  revel !
Aye, and many other meetings,
Indoor visits, outdoor greetings,
As up and down he paced this
  London,
With no work done, but great
  works undone,
Where scarce twenty knew his
  name.
Why not, then, have earlier
  spoken,
Written, bustled ?   Who's to
  blame
If your silence kept unbroken ?

' True, but there were sundry
  jottings,
Stray-leaves, fragments, blurrs
  and blottings,
Certain first steps were achieved
Already which '—(is that your
  meaning ?)
' Had well borne out whoe'er
  believed
In more to come ! ' But who
  goes gleaning
Hedge-side chance-blades, while
  full-sheaved
Stand cornfields by him ? Pride,
  o'erweening
Pride alone, puts forth such
  claims
O'er the day's distinguished
  names.

Meantime, how much I loved him,
I find out now I've lost him :
I, who cared not if I moved him,
Who could so carelessly accost
  him,
Henceforth never shall get free
Of his ghostly company.

.   .   .   .   .   .

II

' When I last saw Waring . . .'
(How all turned to him who
  spoke—
You saw Waring ?   Truth or
  joke ?
In land-travel, or sea-faring ?)
' We were sailing by Triest,
Where a day or two we harboured :
A sunset was in the West,
When, looking over the vessel's
  side,
One of our company espied
A sudden speck to larboard.
And, as a sea-duck flies and
  swims
At once, so came the light craft
  up,

With its sole lateen sail that trims
And turns (the water round its
    rims
Dancing, as round a sinking cup)
And by us like a fish it curled,
And drew itself up close beside,
Its great sail on the instant furled,
And o'er its planks, a shrill voice
    cried
(A neck as bronzed as a Lascar's),
"Buy wine of us, you English
    Brig ?
Or fruit, tobacco and cigars ?
A pilot for you up to Triest ?
Without one, look you ne'er so
    big,
They 'll never let you up the
    bay !
We natives should know best."
I turned, and "Just those fellows'
    way",
Our captain said, "The 'long-
    shore thieves
Are laughing at us in their sleeves."

' In truth, the boy leaned laughing
    back ;
And one, half-hidden by his side
Under the furled sail, soon I
    spied,
With great grass hat and kerchief
    black,

Who looked up with his kingly
    throat,
Said somewhat, while the other
    shook
His hair back from his eyes to
    look
Their longest at us ; then the boat,
I know not how, turned sharply
    round,
Laying her whole side on the sea
As a leaping fish does ; from the
    lee,
Into the weather, cut somehow
Her sparkling path beneath our
    bow ;
And so went off, as with a bound,
Into the rosy and golden half
Of the sky, to overtake the sun
And reach the shore, like the sea-
    calf
Its singing cave ; yet I caught one
Glance ere away the boat quite
    passed,
And neither time nor toil could
    mar
Those features : so I saw the last
Of Waring ! '—You ? Oh, never
    star
Was lost here, but it rose afar !
Look East, where whole new
    thousands are !
In Vishnu-land what Avatar ?
                    R. BROWNING.

112. YOU'LL LOVE ME YET

You'll love me yet !—and I can tarry
    Your love's protracted growing:
June reared this bunch of flowers you carry,
    From seeds of April's sowing.

I plant a heartful now : some seed
    At least is sure to strike,
And yield—what you'll not pluck indeed,
    Not love, but, may be, like !

You'll look at least on love 's remains,
    A grave 's one violet:
Your look ?—that pays a thousand pains,
    What 's death ?—you'll love me yet !
                    R. BROWNING (*Pippa Passes*).

113. FROM 'JUNE'

AND what if cheerful shouts, at noon,
　　Come, from the village sent,
Or songs of maids, beneath the moon,
　　With fairy laughter blent ?
And what if, in the evening light,
Betrothèd lovers walk in sight
　　Of my low monument ?
I would the lovely scene around
Might know no sadder sight nor sound.

I know, I know I should not see
　　The season's glorious show,
Nor would its brightness shine for me,
　　Nor its wild music flow ;
But if around my place of sleep,
The friends I love should come to weep,
　　They might not haste to go.
Soft airs, and song, and light, and bloom
Should keep them lingering by my tomb.

These to their softened hearts should bear
　　The thought of what has been,
And speak of one who cannot share
　　The gladness of the scene ;
Whose part in all the pomp that fills
The circuit of the summer hills,
　　Is—that his grave is green ;
And deeply would their hearts rejoice
To hear, again, his living voice.

W. C. BRYANT.

114. SO LIVE, THAT WHEN THY SUMMONS COMES

So live, that when thy summons comes to join
The innumerable caravan, which moves
To that mysterious realm, where each shall take
His chamber in the silent halls of death,
Thou go not, like the quarry-slave at night,
Scourged to his dungeon ; but, sustained and soothed
By an unfaltering trust, approach thy grave,
Like one who wraps the drapery of his couch
About him, and lies down to pleasant dreams.

W. C. BRYANT (*Thanatopsis*).

115. TO THE FRINGED GENTIAN

THOU blossom bright with autumn dew,
And colourèd with heaven's own blue,
That openest when the quiet light
Succeeds the keen and frosty night.

Thou comest not when violets lean
O'er wandering brooks and springs unseen,
Or columbines, in purple dressed,
Nod o'er the ground-bird's hidden nest.

Thou waitest late and com'st alone,
When woods are bare and birds are flown,
And frosts and shortening days portend
The aged year is near his end.

Then doth thy sweet and quiet eye
Look through its fringes to the sky,
Blue—blue—as if that sky let fall
A flower from its cerulean wall.

I would that thus, when I shall see
The hour of death draw near to me,
Hope, blossoming within my heart,
May look to heaven as I depart.

W. C. BRYANT.

116. TO A WATERFOWL

WHITHER, midst falling dew,
While glow the heavens with the last steps of day,
Far, through their rosy depths, dost thou pursue
    Thy solitary way?

Vainly the fowler's eye
Might mark thy distant flight to do thee wrong,
As, darkly painted on the crimson sky,
    Thy figure floats along.

Seek'st thou the plashy brink
Of weedy lake, or marge of river wide,
Or where the rocking billows rise and sink
    On the chafed ocean-side?

There is a Power whose care
Teaches thy way along that pathless coast—
The desert and illimitable air—
    Lone wandering, but not lost.

.   .   .   .

He who, from zone to zone,
Guides through the boundless sky thy certain flight,
In the long way that I must tread alone,
    Will lead my steps aright.

W. C. BRYANT.

117. FROM 'ARTIST AND MODEL'

Is it not pleasant to wander
  In town on Saturday night,
While people go hither or thither,
  And shops shed cheerful light ?
And, arm in arm, while our shadows
  Chase us along the panes,
Are we not quite as cosy
  As down among country lanes ?

Nobody knows us, heeds us,
  Nobody hears or sees,
And the shop-lights gleam more gladly
  Than the moon on hedges and trees ;
And people coming and going,
  All upon ends of their own,
Though they work a spell on the spirit,
  Move it more finely alone.

The sound seems harmless and pleasant
  As the murmur of brook and wind ;
The shops with the fruit and the pictures
  Have sweetness to suit my mind ;

And nobody knows us, heeds us,
  And our loving none reproves,—
I, the poor figure-painter !
  You, the lady he loves !

And what if the world should scorn you,
  For now and again, as you do,
Assuming a country kirtle,
  And bonnet of straw thereto,
Or the robe of a vestal virgin,
  Or a nun's grey gabardine,
And keeping a brother and sister
  By standing and looking divine ?

And what if the world, moreover,
  Should silently pass me by,
Because, at the dawn of the struggle,
  I labour some stories high !
Why, there's comfort in waiting, working,
  And feeling one's heart beat right,—
And rambling alone, love-making,
  In London on Saturday night.
        R. BUCHANAN.

118. LIZ

THE crimson light of sunset falls
  Through the grey glamour of the murmuring rain,
And creeping o'er the housetops crawls
  Through the black smoke upon the broken pane,
Steals to the straw on which she lies,
  And tints her thin black hair and hollow cheeks,
Her sun-tanned neck, her glistening eyes,—
  While faintly, sadly, fitfully she speaks.
But when it is no longer light,
  The pale girl smiles, with only One to mark,
And dies upon the breast of Night,
  Like trodden snowdrift melting in the dark.
        R. BUCHANAN.

119. SONG IN THE VALLEY OF HUMILIATION

He that is down, needs fear no
  fall,
He that is low, no pride :
He that is humble, ever shall
Have God to be his guide.

I am content with what I have,
Little be it, or much :
And, Lord, contentment still I
  crave,
Because Thou savest such.

Fullness to such a burden is
That go on pilgrimage :
Here little, and hereafter bliss,
Is best from age to age.
      J. BUNYAN (*The Pilgrim's Progress*).

120. TO BE A PILGRIM

Who would true valour see,
Let him come hither ;
One here will constant be,
Come wind, come weather.
There 's no discouragement,
Shall make him once relent
His first avowed intent
To be a pilgrim.

Who so beset him round
With dismal stories,
Do but themselves confound,
His strength the more is.

No lion can him fright,
He'll with a giant fight,
But he will have a right
To be a pilgrim.

  Hobgoblin, nor foul fiend,
Can daunt his spirit ;
He knows he at the end
Shall life inherit.
Then fancies fly away,
He'll fear not what men say,
He'll labour night and day
To be a pilgrim.

      J. BUNYAN (*The Pilgrim's Progress*).

121. OLD SCOTIA'S GRANDEUR

From scenes like these old Scotia's grandeur springs,
  That makes her loved at home, revered abroad :
Princes and lords are but the breath of kings,
  ' An honest man 's the noblest work of God ; '
And certes, in fair virtue's heavenly road,
  The cottage leaves the palace far behind ;
What is a lordling's pomp ? a cumbrous load,
  Disguising oft the wretch of human kind,
Studied in arts of hell, in wickedness refined !
      R. BURNS (*The Cotter's Saturday Night*).

122. FOR A' THAT AND A' THAT

Is there, for honest poverty,
  That hangs his head, and a' that ?
The coward-slave, we pass him by,
  We dare be poor for a' that !
    For a' that, and a' that,
      Our toils obscure, and a' that ;
    The rank is but the guinea's stamp ;
      The man 's the gowd for a' that.

What tho' on hamely fare we dine,
  Wear hodden-grey, and a' that;
Gie fools their silks, and knaves their wine,
  A man's a man for a' that.
      For a' that, and a' that,
        Their tinsel show, and a' that;
      The honest man, tho' e'er sae poor
        Is King o' men for a' that.

Ye see yon birkie, ca'd a lord,
  Wha struts and stares, and a' that;
Tho' hundreds worship at his word,
  He's but a coof for a' that:
      For a' that, and a' that,
        His riband, star, and a' that,
      The man of independent mind,
        He looks and laughs at a' that.

A prince can mak a belted knight,
  A marquis, duke, and a' that;
But an honest man's aboon his might,
  Guid faith he mauna fa' that!
      For a' that, and a' that,
        Their dignities, and a' that,
      The pith o' sense, and pride o' worth,
        Are higher rank than a' that.

Then let us pray that come it may,
  As come it will for a' that;
That sense and worth, o'er a' the earth,
  May bear the gree, and a' that.
      For a' that, and a' that,
        It's coming yet, for a' that,
      That man to man the warld o'er,
        Shall brothers be for a' that.

                                              R. Burns.

123. A' FOR OUR RIGHTFU' KING

It was a' for our rightfu' King,
  We left fair Scotland's strand;
It was a' for our rightfu' King,
  We e'er saw Irish land,
        My dear,
  We e'er saw Irish land.

Now a' is done that men can do,
  And a' is done in vain;
My love and native land farewell,
  For I maun cross the main,
        My dear,
  For I maun cross the main.

He turned him right and round about
  Upon the Irish shore;
And gae his bridle-reins a shake,
  With adieu for evermore,
        My dear,
  Adieu for evermore.

The sodger from the wars returns,
  The sailor frae the main;
But I hae parted frae my love,
  Never to meet again,
        My dear,
  Never to meet again.

When day is gane, and night is come,
And a' folk boune to sleep,
I think on him that 's far awa',
The lee-lang night, and weep,
My dear,
The lee-lang night, and weep.

R. BURNS.

124. JOHN ANDERSON MY JO

JOHN ANDERSON my jo, John,
When we were first acquent,
Your locks were like the raven,
Your bonnie brow was brent;
But now your brow is beld, John,
Your locks are like the snow;
But blessings on your frosty pow,
John Anderson, my jo.

John Anderson my jo, John,
We clamb the hill thegither;
And mony a canty day, John,
We've had wi' ane anither:
Now we maun totter down, John,
And hand in hand we'll go,
And sleep thegither at the foot,
John Anderson, my jo.

R. BURNS.

125. FROM THE 'ADDRESS TO THE TOOTHACHE'

My curse upon your venomed stang,
That shoots my tortured gums alang,
And thro' my lugs gies monie a twang,
Wi' gnawing vengeance;
Tearing my nerves wi' bitter pang,
Like racking engines!

When fevers burn, or ague freezes,
Rheumatics gnaw, or cholic squeezes;
Our neighbour's sympathy may ease us,
Wi' pitying moan;
But thee—thou hell o' a' diseases!
Ay mocks our groan.

R. BURNS.

126. MY HEART'S IN THE HIGHLANDS

My heart's in the Highlands, my heart is not here;
My heart's in the Highlands a-chasing the deer;
Chasing the wild deer, and following the roe,
My heart's in the Highlands, wherever I go.
Farewell to the Highlands, farewell to the North,
The birth-place of valour, the country of worth;
Wherever I wander, wherever I rove,
The hills of the Highlands for ever I love.

Farewell to the mountains, high cover'd with snow ;
Farewell to the straths and green valleys below ;
Farewell to the forests and wild-hanging woods ;
Farewell to the torrents and loud-pouring floods.
My heart 's in the Highlands, my heart is not here ;
My heart 's in the Highlands a-chasing the deer ;
Chasing the wild deer, and following the roe,
My heart 's in the Highlands, wherever I go.

R. BURNS.

127.   MY LOVE IS LIKE A RED RED ROSE

MY love is like a red red rose
 That 's newly sprung in June :
My love is like the melodie
 That 's sweetly played in tune.

As fair art thou, my bonnie lass,
 So deep in love am I :
And I will love thee still, my dear,
 Till a' the seas gang dry.

Till a' the seas gang dry, my dear,
 And the rocks melt wi' the sun :
And I will love thee still, my dear,
 While the sands o' life shall run.

And fare thee weel, my only love,
 And fare thee weel awhile !
And I will come again, my love,
 Tho' it were ten thousand mile.

R. BURNS.

128.   MARY MORISON

O MARY, at thy window be,
It is the wished, the trysted hour !
Those smiles and glances let me
     see,
That make the miser's treasure
     poor :
How blythely wad I bide the
     stoure,
A weary slave frae sun to sun,
Could I the rich reward secure,
The lovely Mary Morison.

Yestreen, when to the trembling
     string
The dance gaed thro' the lighted
     ha',
To thee my fancy took its wing,
I sat, but neither heard nor saw :

Tho' this was fair, and that was
     braw,
And yon the toast of a' the
     town,
I sighed, and said among them a',
' Ye are na Mary Morison.'

O Mary, canst thou wreck his
     peace,
Wha for thy sake wad gladly
     die ?
Or canst thou break that heart of
     his,
Whase only faut is loving thee ?
If love for love thou wilt na gie,
At least be pity to me shown !
A thought ungentle canna be
The thought o' Mary Morison.

R. BURNS.

129.   BONNIE LESLEY

O SAW ye bonnie Lesley
 As she gaed o'er the border ?
She 's gane, like Alexander,
 To spread her conquests farther.

To see her is to love her,
 And love but her for ever ;
For Nature made her what she is,
 And never made anither !

Thou art a queen, fair Lesley,
  Thy subjects we, before thee :
Thou art divine, fair Lesley,
  The hearts o' men adore thee.

The Deil he could na scaith
    thee,
  Or aught that wad belang thee ;
He'd look into thy bonnie face,
  And say, ' I canna wrang thee.'

The Powers aboon will tent thee ;
  Misfortune sha'na steer thee ;
Thou'rt like themselves sae lovely,
  That ill they'll ne'er let near
    thee.

Return again, fair Lesley,
  Return to Caledonie !
That we may brag we hae a lass
  There 's nane again sae bonnie.
            R. BURNS.

130. A PRAYER IN THE PROSPECT OF DEATH

O THOU unknown Almighty Cause
  Of all my hope and fear !
In whose dread presence, ere an hour,
  Perhaps I must appear !

If I have wandered in those paths
  Of life I ought to shun ;
As something, loudly in my breast,
  Remonstrates I have done ;

Thou know'st that Thou hast formèd me
  With passions wild and strong ;
And listening to their witching voice
  Has often led me wrong.

Where human weakness has come short,
  Or frailty stept aside,
Do Thou, All-Good ! for such Thou art,
  In shades of darkness hide.

Where with intention I have erred,
  No other plea I have,
But, Thou art good ; and Goodness still
  Delighteth to forgive.
            R. BURNS.

131. OF A' THE AIRTS THE WIND CAN BLAW

OF a' the airts the wind can blaw,
  I dearly like the west,
For there the bonnie lassie lives,
  The lassie I lo'e best :
There wild woods grow, and rivers
    row,
  And mony a hill between ;
But day and night my fancy's
    flight
  Is ever wi' my Jean.

I see her in the dewy flowers,
  I see her sweet and fair :
I hear her in the tunefu' birds,
  I hear her charm the air :
There 's not a bonnie flower that
    springs
  By fountain, shaw, or green ;
There 's not a bonnie bird that
    sings,
  But minds me o' my Jean.
            R. BURNS.

132. AULD LANG SYNE

SHOULD auld acquaintance be forgot,
    And never brought to min' ?
Should auld acquaintance be forgot,
    And auld lang syne ?
      For auld lang syne, my dear,
        For auld lang syne,
      We'll tak a cup o' kindness yet,
        For auld lang syne.

We twa hae run about the braes,
    And pu'd the gowans fine ;
But we've wander'd mony a weary foot
    Sin' auld lang syne.

We twa hae paidled i' the burn,
    From morning sun till dine ;
But seas between us braid hae roar'd
    Sin' auld lang syne.

And here 's a hand, my trusty fiere,
    And gie 's a hand o' thine ;
And we'll tak a right guid-willie waught,
    For auld lang syne.

And surely ye'll be your pint-stowp,
    And surely I'll be mine ;
And we'll tak a cup o' kindness yet
    For auld lang syne.
      For auld lang syne, my dear,
        For auld lang syne,
      We'll tak a cup o' kindness yet,
        For auld lang syne.   R. BURNS.

133. THE SELKIRK GRACE

SOME hae meat, and canna eat,
And some wad eat that want it;
But we hae meat and we can eat,
And sae the Lord be thankit.   R. BURNS.

134. THEN GENTLY SCAN YOUR BROTHER MAN

THEN gently scan your brother
    man,
    Still gentler sister woman ;
Tho' they may gang a kennin
    wrang,
    To step aside is human.
One point must still be greatly dark,
    The moving why they do it ;
And just as lamely can ye mark,
    How far perhaps they rue it.

Who made the heart, 'tis He alone
    Decidedly can try us ;
He knows each chord, its various
    tone,
    Each spring, its various bias.
Then at the balance let 's be mute,
    We never can adjust it ;
What 's done we partly may
    compute,
    But know not what 's resisted.

R. BURNS (*Address to the Unco Guid.*)

135. THE TRUE PATHOS

To make a happy fire-side clime
    To weans and wife,
That 's the true pathos and sublime
    Of human life.

R. BURNS (*To Dr. Blacklock*).

136. BONNIE DOON

YE banks and braes o' bonnie Doon,
    How can ye bloom sae fresh and fair ?
How can ye chant, ye little birds,
    And I sae weary fu' o' care ?
Thou'lt break my heart, thou warbling bird,
    That wantons thro' the flowering thorn :
Thou minds me o' departed joys,
    Departed never to return.

Aft hae I roved by bonnie Doon,
    To see the rose and woodbine twine ;
And ilka bird sang o' its love,
    And fondly sae did I o' mine.
Wi' lightsome heart I pu'd a rose.
    Fu' sweet upon its thorny tree ,
And my fause lover stole my rose,
    But ah ! he left the thorn wi' me.

R. BURNS.

137. THE RELIGION OF HUDIBRAS

FOR his Religion, it was fit
To match his learning and his
    wit ;
'Twas Presbyterian true blue ;
For he was of that stubborn crew
Of errant saints, whom all men
    grant
To be the true Church Militant ;
Such as do build their faith upon
The holy text of pike and gun ;
Decide all controversies by
Infallible artillery ;
And prove their doctrine orthodox
By apostolic blows and knocks ;
Call fire and sword and desola-
    tion,
A godly thorough Reformation ;

.   .   .   .   .   .

Compound for sins they are in-
    clined to,
By damning those they have no
    mind to :
Still so perverse and opposite,
As if they worshipped God for
    spite.

.   .   .   .   .   .

Rather than fail they will defy
That which they love most ten-
    derly,
Quarrel with minced pies, and
    disparage
Their best and dearest friend—
    plum-porridge ;
Fat pig or goose itself oppose
And blaspheme custard through
    the nose.

S. BUTLER (*Hudibras*).

D

138. MEN AND WOMEN

FOR women first were made for men,
Not men for them : It follows, then,
That men have right to every one,
And they no freedom of their own;
And therefore men have power to choose,
But they no charter to refuse.

S. BUTLER (*Hudibras*).

139. THE MORN

THE sun had long since, in the lap
Of Thetis, taken out his nap,
And, like a lobster boiled, the morn
From black to red began to turn.

S. BUTLER (*Hudibras*).

140. MODERN PROWESS IN WAR

'TIS true, our modern way of war
Is grown more politic by far,
But not so resolute and bold,
Nor tied to honour as the old.
For now they laugh at giving battle,
Unless it be to herds of cattle,
Or fighting convoys of provision,
The whole design o' the expedition.

. . . . . .

For 'tis not now, who 's stout and bold ?
But who bears hunger best and cold ?
And he 's approved the most deserving
Who longest can hold out at starving :
And he that routs most pigs and cows
The formidablest man of prowess.

So th' emperor Caligula,
That triumphed o'er the British sea
Took crabs and oysters prisoners,
And lobsters, 'stead of cuirassiers ;
Engaged his legions in fierce bustles,
With periwinkles, prawns and mussels,
And led his troops with furious gallops,
To charge whole regiments of scallops ;
Not like their ancient way of war,
To wait on his triumphal car ;
But when he went to dine or sup,
More bravely ate his captives up,
And left all war, by his example,
Reduced to victualling of a camp well.

S. BUTLER (*Hudibras*).

141. A JACOBITE TOAST

God bless the King!—I mean the Faith's Defender ;
God bless (no harm in blessing) the Pretender !
But who Pretender is, or who is King,
God bless us all !—that 's quite another thing.

J. Byrom.

142. ALAS! THE LOVE OF WOMEN.

Alas! the love of women ! it is known
  To be a lovely and a fearful thing ;
For all of theirs upon that die is thrown,
  And if 'tis lost, life hath no more to bring
To them but mockeries of the past alone,
  And their revenge is as the tiger's spring,
Deadly, and quick, and crushing ; yet, as real
Torture is theirs, what they inflict they feel.

George Gordon, Lord Byron (Don Juan).

143. AVE MARIA

Ave Maria ! blessèd be the hour !
  The time, the clime, the spot, where I so oft
Have felt that moment in its fullest power
  Sink o'er the earth so beautiful and soft,
While swung the deep bell in the distant tower,
  Or the faint dying day-hymn stole aloft,
And not a breath crept through the rosy air,
And yet the forest leaves seemed stirred with prayer.

Ave Maria ! 'tis the hour of prayer !
  Ave Maria ! 'tis the hour of love !
Ave Maria ! may our spirits dare
  Look up to thine and to thy Son's above !
Ave Maria ! oh that face so fair !
  Those downcast eyes beneath the Almighty dove—
What though 'tis but a pictured image strike,
That painting is no idol,—'tis too like.

Lord Byron (Don Juan).

144. MAN'S LOVE A THING APART

Man's love is of man's life a thing apart,
  'Tis woman's whole existence ; man may range
The court, camp, church, the vessel, and the mart ;
  Sword, gown, gain, glory, offer in exchange
Pride, fame, ambition, to fill up his heart,
  And few there are whom these cannot estrange ;
Men have all these resources, we but one,
To love again, and be again undone.

Lord Byron (Don Juan).

145. OH, TALK NOT TO ME OF A NAME GREAT IN STORY

Oh, talk not to me of a name great in story;
The days of our youth are the days of our glory;
And the myrtle and ivy of sweet two-and-twenty
Are worth all your laurels, though ever so plenty.

What are garlands and crowns to the brow that is wrinkled?
'Tis but as a dead-flower with May-dew besprinkled.
Then away with all such from the head that is hoary!
What care I for the wreaths that can *only* give glory?

Oh Fame!—if I e'er took delight in thy praises,
'Twas less for the sake of thy high-sounding phrases,
Than to see the bright eyes of the dear one discover,
She thought that I was not unworthy to love her.

There chiefly I sought thee, *there* only I found thee;
Her glance was the best of the rays that surround thee;
When it sparkled o'er aught that was bright in my story,
I knew it was love, and I felt it was glory.

LORD BYRON.

146. ROLL ON, THOU DEEP AND DARK BLUE OCEAN

Roll on, thou deep and dark blue Ocean—roll!
Ten thousand fleets sweep over thee in vain;
Man marks the earth with ruin—his control
Stops with the shore; upon the watery plain
The wrecks are all thy deed, nor doth remain
A shadow of man's ravage, save his own,
When, for a moment, like a drop of rain,
He sinks into thy depths with bubbling groan,
Without a grave, unknelled, uncoffined, and unknown.

His steps are not upon thy paths,—thy fields
Are not a spoil for him,—thou dost arise
And shake him from thee; the vile strength he wields
For earth's destruction thou dost all despise,
Spurning him from thy bosom to the skies,
And send'st him, shivering in thy playful spray
And howling, to his Gods, where haply lies
His petty hope in some near port or bay,
And dashest him again to earth:—there let him lay.

.   .   .   .

Thy shores are empires, changed in all save thee—
Assyria, Greece, Rome, Carthage, what are they?
Thy waters washed them power while they were free,
And many a tyrant since; their shores obey
The stranger, slave, or savage; their decay
Has dried up realms to deserts:—not so thou;—
Unchangeable, save to thy wild waves' play,
Time writes no wrinkle on thine azure brow:
Such as creation's dawn beheld, thou rollest now.

Thou glorious mirror, where the Almighty's form
Glasses itself in tempests ; in all time,—
Calm or convulsed, in breeze, or gale, or storm,
Icing the pole, or in the torrid clime
Dark-heaving—boundless, endless, and sublime—
The image of eternity, the throne
Of the Invisible ; even from out thy slime
The monsters of the deep are made ; each zone
Obeys thee ; thou goest forth, dread, fathomless, alone.

And I have loved thee, Ocean ! and my joy
Of youthful sports was on thy breast to be
Borne, like thy bubbles, onward : from a boy
I wantoned with thy breakers—they to me
Were a delight ; and if the freshening sea
Made them a terror—'twas a pleasing fear,
For I was as it were a child of thee,
And trusted to thy billows far and near,
And laid my hand upon thy mane—as I do here.

LORD BYRON (*Childe Harold's Pilgrimage*).

147. SHE WALKS IN BEAUTY, LIKE THE NIGHT

SHE walks in beauty, like the night
Of cloudless climes and starry skies ;
And all that's best of dark and bright
Meet in her aspect and her eyes :
Thus mellowed to that tender light
Which heaven to gaudy day denies.

One shade the more, one ray the less,
Had half impaired the nameless grace
Which waves in every raven tress,
Or softly lightens o'er her face ;
Where thoughts serenely sweet express
How pure, how dear their dwelling-place.

And on that cheek, and o'er that brow,
So soft, so calm, yet eloquent,
The smiles that win, the tints that glow,
But tell of days in goodness spent,
A mind at peace with all below,
A heart whose love is innocent !

LORD BYRON.

148. SO WE'LL GO NO MORE A-ROVING

So we'll go no more a-roving
So late into the night,
Though the heart be still as loving,
And the moon be still as bright.

For the sword outwears its sheath,
  And the soul wears out the breast,
And the heart must pause to breathe,
  And love itself have rest.

Though the night was made for loving,
  And the day returns too soon,
Yet we'll go no more a-roving
  By the light of the moon.   Lord Byron.

149. THE DESTRUCTION OF SENNACHERIB

The Assyrian came down like the wolf on the fold,
And his cohorts were gleaming in purple and gold;
And the sheen of their spears was like stars on the sea,
When the blue wave rolls nightly on deep Galilee.

Like the leaves of the forest when Summer is green,
That host with their banners at sunset were seen:
Like the leaves of the forest when Autumn hath blown,
That host on the morrow lay withered and strown.

For the Angel of Death spread his wings on the blast,
And breathed in the face of the foe as he passed;
And the eyes of the sleepers waxed deadly and chill,
And their hearts but once heaved, and for ever grew still!

And there lay the steed with his nostril all wide,
But through it there rolled not the breath of his pride;
And the foam of his gasping lay white on the turf,
And cold as the spray of the rock-beating surf.

And there lay the rider distorted and pale,
With the dew on his brow, and the rust on his mail:
And the tents were all silent, the banners alone,
The lances unlifted, the trumpet unblown.

And the widows of Ashur are loud in their wail,
And the idols are broke in the temple of Baal;
And the might of the Gentile, unsmote by the sword,
Hath melted like snow in the glance of the Lord!
    Lord Byron.

150. THE CASTLED CRAG OF DRACHENFELS

The castled crag of Drachenfels
Frowns o'er the wide and winding Rhine,
Whose breast of waters broadly swells
Between the banks which bear the vine,
And hills all rich with blossomed trees,
And fields which promise corn and wine,
And scattered cities crowning these,
Whose far white walls along them shine,
Have strewed a scene, which I should see
With double joy wert *thou* with me.

And peasant girls, with deep blue eyes,
And hands which offer early flowers,
Walk smiling o'er this paradise ;
Above, the frequent feudal towers
Through green leaves lift their walls of grey ;
And many a rock which steeply lowers,
And noble arch in proud decay,
Look o'er this vale of vintage-bowers ;
But one thing want these banks of Rhine,—
Thy gentle hand to clasp in mine !

LORD BYRON (*Childe Harold's Pilgrimage*).

151. THE ISLES OF GREECE

THE isles of Greece, the isles of Greece !
  Where burning Sappho loved and sung,
Where grew the arts of war and peace,
  Where Delos rose, and Phoebus sprung !
Eternal summer gilds them yet,
But all, except their sun, is set.

The mountains look on Marathon—
  And Marathon looks on the sea ;
And musing there an hour alone,
  I dreamed that Greece might still be free ;
For standing on the Persians' grave,
I could not deem myself a slave.

You have the Pyrrhic dance as yet ;
  Where is the Pyrrhic phalanx gone ?
Of two such lessons, why forget
  The nobler and the manlier one ?
You have the letters Cadmus gave—
Think ye he meant them for a slave ?

Fill high the bowl with Samian wine !
  Our virgins dance beneath the shade—
I see their glorious black eyes shine ;
  But gazing on each glowing maid,
My own the burning tear-drop laves,
To think such breasts must suckle slaves.

Place me on Sunium's marbled steep,
  Where nothing, save the waves and I,
May hear our mutual murmurs sweep ;
  There, swan-like, let me sing and die :
A land of slaves shall ne'er be mine—
Dash down yon cup of Samian wine !

LORD BYRON (*Don Juan*).

152. THERE BE NONE OF BEAUTY'S DAUGHTERS

THERE be none of Beauty's
daughters
  With a magic like thee;
And like sweet music on the waters
  Is thy sweet voice to me:
When, as if its sound were causing
The charmèd ocean's pausing,
The waves lie still and gleaming,
And the lulled winds seem dream-
  ing:
And the midnight moon is weav-
  ing
  Her bright chain o'er the deep;
Whose breast is gently heaving,
  As an infant's asleep:
So the spirit bows before thee,
To listen and adore thee;
With a full but soft emotion,
Like the swell of Summer's ocean.

LORD BYRON.

153. THERE'S NOT A JOY THE WORLD CAN GIVE

THERE's not a joy the world can give like that it takes away,
When the glow of early thought declines in feeling's dull decay;
'Tis not on youth's smooth cheek the blush alone, which fades so fast,
But the tender bloom of heart is gone, ere youth itself be past.

Then the few whose spirits float above the wreck of happiness
Are driven o'er the shoals of guilt or ocean of excess:
The magnet of their course is gone, or only points in vain
The shore to which their shivered sail shall never stretch again.

Then the mortal coldness of the soul like death itself comes down;
It cannot feel for others' woes, it dare not dream its own;
That heavy chill has frozen o'er the fountain of our tears,
And though the eye may sparkle still, 'tis where the ice appears.

Though wit may flash from fluent lips, and mirth distract the breast,
Through midnight hours that yield no more their former hope of rest;
'Tis but as ivy-leaves around the ruined turret wreathe,
All green and wildly fresh without, but worn and grey beneath.

O could I feel as I have felt,—or be what I have been,
Or weep as I could once have wept o'er many a vanished scene;
As springs in deserts found seem sweet, all brackish though they be,
So midst the withered waste of life, those tears would flow to me.

LORD BYRON.

154. THE EVE OF WATERLOO

THERE was a sound of revelry by night,
And Belgium's capital had gathered then
Her Beauty and her Chivalry, and bright
The lamps shone o'er fair women and brave men;
A thousand hearts beat happily; and when
Music arose with its voluptuous swell,
Soft eyes looked love to eyes which spake again,
And all went merry as a marriage bell;
But hush! hark! a deep sound strikes like a rising knell!

Did ye not hear it ?—No ; 'twas but the wind,
Or the car rattling o'er the stony street ;
On with the dance ! let joy be unconfined ;
No sleep till morn, when Youth and Pleasure meet
To chase the glowing Hours with flying feet—
But hark !—that heavy sound breaks in once more,
As if the clouds its echo would repeat ;
And nearer, clearer, deadlier than before !
Arm ! Arm ! it is—it is—the cannon's opening roar !

Within a windowed niche of that high hall
Sate Brunswick's fated chieftain ; he did hear
That sound the first amidst the festival,
And caught its tone with Death's prophetic ear ;
And when they smiled because he deemed it near,
His heart more truly knew that peal too well
Which stretched his father on a bloody bier,
And roused the vengeance blood alone could quell ;
He rushed into the field, and, foremost fighting, fell.

Ah ! then and there was hurrying to and fro,
And gathering tears, and tremblings of distress,
And cheeks all pale, which but an hour ago
Blushed at the praise of their own loveliness ;
And there were sudden partings, such as press
The life from out young hearts, and choking sighs
Which ne'er might be repeated ; who could guess
If ever more should meet those mutual eyes,
Since upon night so sweet such awful morn could rise ?

And there was mounting ·in hot haste : the steed,
The mustering squadron, and the clattering car,
Went pouring forward with impetuous speed,
And swiftly forming in the ranks of war ;
And the deep thunder peal on peal afar ;
And near, the beat of the alarming drum
Roused up the soldier ere the morning star ;
While thronged the citizens with terror dumb,
Or whispering, with white lips—' The foe ! they come ! they come ! '

And wild and high the ' Cameron's gathering ' rose !
The war-note of Lochiel, which Albyn's hills
Have heard, and heard, too, have her Saxon foes :—
How in the noon of night that pibroch thrills,
Savage and shrill ! But with the breath which fills
Their mountain-pipe, so fill the mountaineers
With the fierce native daring which instils
The stirring memory of a thousand years,
And Evan's, Donald's fame rings in each clansman's ears !

And Ardennes waves above them her green leaves,
  Dewy with nature's tear-drops as they pass,
Grieving, if aught inanimate e'er grieves,
  Over the unreturning brave,—alas !
Ere evening to be trodden like the grass
Which now beneath them, but above shall grow
In its next verdure, when this fiery mass
Of living valour, rolling on the foe
And burning with high hope shall moulder cold and low.

Last noon beheld them full of lusty life,
  Last eve in Beauty's circle proudly gay,
The midnight brought the signal-sound of strife,
  The morn the marshalling in arms,—the day
Battle's magnificently stern array !
The thunder-clouds close o'er it, which when rent
The earth is covered thick with other clay,
Which her own clay shall cover, heaped and pent,
Rider and horse,—friend, foe,—in one red burial blent !
                    LORD BYRON (*Childe Harold's Pilgrimage*).

155. FROM 'STANZAS TO AUGUSTA'

THOUGH the day of my destiny's over,
  And the star of my fate hath declined,
Thy soft heart refused to discover
  The faults which so many could find ;
Though thy soul with my grief was acquainted,
  It shrunk not to share it with me,
And the love which my spirit hath painted
  It never hath found but in *thee*.

    .   .   .   .

Yet I blame not the world, nor despise it,
  Nor the war of the many with one ;
If my soul was not fitted to prize it,
  'Twas folly not sooner to shun :
And if dearly that error hath cost me,
  And more than I once could foresee,
I have found that, whatever it lost me,
  It could not deprive me of *thee*.

From the wreck of the past, which hath perished,
  Thus much I at least may recall,
It hath taught me that what I most cherished,
  Deserved to be dearest of all :
In the desert a fountain is springing,
  In the wide waste there still is a tree,
And a bird in the solitude singing,
  Which speaks to my spirit of *thee*.   LORD BYRON.

156. TO THE MEMORY OF KIRKE WHITE

UNHAPPY White ! while life was in its spring,
And thy young muse just waved her joyous wing,
The spoiler swept that soaring lyre away,
Which else had sounded an immortal lay.
Oh ! what a noble heart was here undone,
When Science' self destroyed her favourite son !
Yes, she too much indulged thy fond pursuit,
She sowed the seeds, but death has reaped the fruit.
'Twas thine own genius gave the final blow,
And helped to plant the wound that laid thee low :
So the struck eagle, stretched upon the plain,
No more through rolling clouds to soar again,
Viewed his own feather on the fatal dart,
And winged the shaft that quivered in his heart ;
Keen were his pangs, but keener far to feel
He nursed the pinion which impelled the steel ;
While the same plumage that had warmed his nest
Drank the last life-drop of his bleeding breast.

LORD BYRON
(English Bards and Scotch Reviewers).

157.   WHEN WE TWO PARTED

WHEN we two parted
  In silence and tears,
Half broken-hearted
  To sever for years,
Pale grew thy cheek and cold,
  Colder thy kiss ;
Truly that hour foretold
  Sorrow to this.

The dew of the morning
  Sunk chill on my brow—
It felt like the warning
  Of what I feel now.
Thy vows are all broken,
  And light is thy fame :
I hear thy name spoken,
  And share in its shame.

They name thee before me,
  A knell to mine ear ;
A shudder comes o'er me—
  Why wert thou so dear ?
They know not I knew thee,
  Who knew thee too well :—
Long, long shall I rue thee,
  Too deeply to tell.

In secret we met—
  In silence I grieve,
That thy heart could forget,
  Thy spirit deceive.
If I should meet thee
  After long years,
How should I greet thee ?—
  With silence and tears.

LORD BYRON.

158. LORD ULLIN'S DAUGHTER

A chieftain to the Highlands
   bound
  Cries ' Boatman, do not tarry !
And I'll give thee a silver pound
  To row us o'er the ferry.'

' Now be ye would cross
   Lochgyle,
  This dark and stormy water ? '
' O, I'm the chief of Ulva's isle,
  And this Lord Ullin's daughter.

' And fast before her father's
   men
  Three days we've fled together,
For, should he find us in the
   glen,
  My blood would stain the
   heather.

' His horseman hard behind us
   ride ;
  Should they our steps discover,
Then who will cheer my bonny
   bride
  When they have slain her
   lover ? '

Outspoke the hardy Highland
   wight,
  ' I'll go, my chief ! I'm ready ;
It is not for your silver bright,
  But for your winsome lady.

' And, by my word ! the bonny
   bird
  In danger shall not tarry ;
So, though the waves are raging
   white
  I'll row you o'er the ferry.'

By this the storm grew loud
   apace,
  The water-wraith was shrieking ;
And in the scowl of heaven each
   face
  Grew dark as they were
   speaking.

But still, as wilder blew the wind,
  And as the night grew drearer,
Adown the glen rode armèd men—
  Their trampling sounded nearer.

' O haste thee, haste ! ' the lady
   cries,
  ' Though tempests round us
   gather ;
I'll meet the raging of the skies,
  But not an angry father.'

The boat has left a stormy land,
  A stormy sea before her,—
When, oh ! too strong for human
   hand,
  The tempest gathered o'er her.

And still they rode amidst the
   roar
  Of waters fast prevailing :
Lord Ullin reached that fatal
   shore,—
  His wrath was changed to
   wailing.

For sore dismayed, through storm
   and shade,
  His child he did discover :
One lovely hand she stretched for
   aid,
  And one was round her lover.

' Come back ! come back ! ' he
   cried in grief
  Across the stormy water :
' And I'll forgive your Highland
   chief,
  My daughter ! oh my daughter ! '

'Twas vain : the loud waves lashed
   the shore,
  Return or aid preventing ;
The waters wild went o'er his
   child,
  And he was left lamenting.

            T. CAMPBELL.

159. FROM 'THE LAST MAN'

ALL worldly shapes shall melt in
    gloom,
  The Sun himself must die,
Before this mortal shall assume
  Its Immortality !
I saw a vision in my sleep,
That gave my spirit strength to
    sweep
  Adown the gulf of Time !
I saw the last of human mould
That shall Creation's death behold
  As Adam saw her prime !

. . . . . .

' The spirit shall return to Him
  That gave its heavenly spark ;
Yet think not, Sun, it shall be dim
  When thou thyself art dark !
No ! it shall live again and shine
In bliss unknown to beams of
    thine,

By Him recalled to breath
Who captive led captivity,
Who robbed the grave of Victory,
  And took the sting from Death !

' Go, Sun, while Mercy holds me
    up
  On Nature's awful waste
To drink this last and bitter
    cup
  Of grief that man shall taste—
Go, tell the night that hides thy
    face
Thou saw'st the last of Adam's
    race
  On Earth's sepulchral clod
The darkening universe defy
To quench his immortality,
  Or shake his trust in God ! '
                    T. CAMPBELL.

160. FLORINE

COULD I bring back lost youth again
  And be what I have been,
I'd court you in a gallant strain,
  My young and fair Florine.

But mine's the chilling age that chides
  Devoted rapture's glow,
And Love—that conquers all besides—
  Finds Time a conquering foe.

Farewell ! we're severed by our fate
  As far as night from noon ;
You came into the world too late,
  And I depart so soon.   T. CAMPBELL.

161. FROM 'MEN OF ENGLAND'

MEN of England ! who inherit
  Rights that cost your sires their blood !
Men whose undegenerate spirit
  Has been proved on land and flood

By the foes ye've fought, uncounted,
  By the glorious deeds ye've done.
Trophies captured—breaches mounted,
  Navies conquered—kingdoms won !

Yet, remember, England gathers
   Hence but fruitless wreaths of fame,
If the freedom of your fathers
   Glow not in your hearts the same.

What are monuments of bravery,
   Where no public virtues bloom ?
What avail in lands of slavery
   Trophied temples, arch, and tomb ?

T. CAMPBELL.

162. SONG OF HYBRIAS THE CRETAN

My wealth's a burly spear and brand,
And a right good shield of hides untanned
   Which on my arm I buckle :
With these I plough, I reap, I sow,
With these I make the sweet vintage flow,
   And all around me truckle.

But your wights that take no pride to wield
A massy spear and well-made shield,
   Nor joy to draw the sword—
Oh, I bring those heartless, hapless drones,
Down in a trice on their marrow-bones
   To call me King and Lord.

T. CAMPBELL.

163. THE BATTLE OF THE BALTIC

Of Nelson and the North
Sing the glorious day's renown,
When to battle fierce came forth
All the might of Denmark's crown,
And her arms along the deep
   proudly shone,—
By each gun the lighted brand
In a bold determined hand ;
And the Prince of all the land
Led them on.

Like leviathans afloat
Lay their bulwarks on the brine,
While the sign of battle flew
On the lofty British line :
It was ten of April morn by the
   chime :
As they drifted on their path
There was silence deep as death,
And the boldest held his breath
For a time.

But the might of England flushed
To anticipate the scene ;
And her van the fleeter rushed
O'er the deadly space between.
'Hearts of oak !' our captain
   cried ; when each gun
From its adamantine lips
Spread a death-shade round the
   ships,
Like the hurricane eclipse
Of the sun.

Again ! again ! again !
And the havoc did not slack,
Till a feeble cheer the Dane
To our cheering sent us back :
Their shots along the deep slowly
   boom ;
Then ceased—and all is wail
As they strike the shattered sail,
Or in conflagration pale
Light the gloom.

Out spoke the victor then
As he hailed them o'er the wave,
'Ye are brothers! ye are men!
And we conquer but to save;
So peace instead of death let us
      bring:
But yield, proud foe, thy fleet
With the crews at England's feet,
And make submission meet
To our King.'

Then Denmark blessed our chief
That he gave her wounds repose;
And the sounds of joy and grief
From her people wildly rose,
As death withdrew his shades from
      the day;
While the sun looked smiling
      bright
O'er a wide and woful sight,
Where the fires of funeral light
Died away.

Now joy, Old England, raise
For the tidings of thy might
By the festal cities' blaze,
While the wine-cup shines in
      light;
And yet, amidst that joy and
      uproar,
Let us think of them that sleep,
Full many a fathom deep,
By thy wild and stormy steep,
Elsinore!

Brave hearts! to Britain's pride
Once so faithful and so true,
On the deck of fame that died
With the gallant good Riou—
Soft sigh the winds of heaven o'er
      their grave!
While the billow mournful rolls
And the mermaid's song condoles,
Singing glory to the souls
Of the brave!

                              T. CAMPBELL.

164. HOHENLINDEN

On Linden, when the sun was low,
All bloodless lay the untrodden snow,
And dark as winter was the flow
      Of Iser, rolling rapidly.

But Linden saw another sight
When the drum beat at dead of night,
Commanding fires of death to light
      The darkness of her scenery.

By torch and trumpet fast arrayed,
Each horseman drew his battle-blade,
And furious every charger neighed
      To join the dreadful revelry.

Then shook the hills with thunder riven,
Then rushed the steed to battle driven,
And louder than the bolts of heaven
      Far flashed the red artillery.

But redder yet that light shall glow
On Linden's hills of stainèd snow,
And bloodier yet the torrent flow
      Of Iser, rolling rapidly.

'Tis morn, but scarce yon level sun
Can pierce the war-clouds, rolling dun,
Where furious Frank and fiery Hun
    Shout in their sulphurous canopy.

The combat deepens. On, ye brave,
Who rush to glory, or the grave !
Wave, Munich ! all thy banners wave,
    And charge with all thy chivalry !

Few, few shall part, where many meet !
The snow shall be their winding-sheet,
And every turf beneath their feet
    Shall be a soldier's sepulchre.

T. CAMPBELL.

165. DRINKING-SONG OF MUNICH

SWEET Iser ! were thy sunny realm
    And flowery gardens mine,
Thy waters I would shade with
    elm
    To prop the tender vine ;
My golden flagons I would fill
With rosy draughts from every
    hill ;
    And under every myrtle bower
My gay companions should pro-
    long
The laugh, the revel, and the
    song,
    To many an idle hour.

Like rivers crimsoned with the
    beam
    Of yonder planet bright
Our balmy cups should ever
    stream
    Profusion of delight ;
No care should touch the mellow
    heart,
And sad or sober none depart ;
    For wine can triumph over woe,
And Love and Bacchus, brother
    powers,
Could build in Iser's sunny bowers
    A paradise below.

T. CAMPBELL.

166. YE MARINERS OF ENGLAND

YE Mariners of England
That guard our native seas,
Whose flag has braved, a thousand
    years,
The battle and the breeze—
Your glorious standard launch
    again
To match another foe !
And sweep through the deep,
While the stormy winds do
    blow,—
While the battle rages loud and
    long,
And the stormy winds do blow.

The spirits of your fathers
Shall start from every wave !
For the deck it was their field of
    fame,
And Ocean was their grave.
Where Blake and mighty Nelson
    fell
Your manly hearts shall glow,
As ye sweep through the deep,
While the stormy winds do
    blow,—
While the battle rages loud and
    long,
And the stormy winds do blow.

Britannia needs no bulwarks,
No towers along the steep ;
Her march is o'er the mountain waves,
Her home is on the deep.
With thunders from her native oak
She quells the floods below,
As they roar on the shore,
When the stormy winds do blow,—
When the battle rages loud and long
And the stormy winds do blow.

The meteor flag of England
Shall yet terrific burn,
Till danger's troubled night depart
And the star of peace return.
Then, then, ye ocean warriors !
Our song and feast shall flow
To the fame of your name,
When the storm has ceased to blow,—
When the fiery fight is heard no more,
And the storm has ceased to blow.
T. CAMPBELL.

167. FOLLOW THY FAIR SUN

FOLLOW thy fair sun, unhappy shadow,
Though thou be black as night,
And she made all of light ;
Yet follow thy fair sun, unhappy shadow !

Follow her, whose light thy light depriveth !
Though here thou livest disgraced,
And she in heaven is placed ;
Yet follow her whose light the world reviveth !

Follow those pure beams, whose beauty burneth !
That so have scorchèd thee ;
As thou still black must be,
Till her kind beams thy black to brightness turneth !

Follow her, while yet her glory shineth !
There comes a luckless night
That will dim all her light ;
And this the black unhappy shade divineth.

Follow still, since so thy Fates ordainèd !
The sun must have his shade,
Till both at once do fade ;
The sun still proved, the shadow still disdainèd !
T. CAMPION.

168. FOLLOW YOUR SAINT

FOLLOW your saint. Follow, with accents sweet !
Haste you, sad notes, fall at her flying feet !
There, wrapped in cloud of sorrow, pity move,
And tell the ravisher of my soul I perish for her love.
But if she scorns my never-ceasing pain,
Then burst with sighing in her sight, and ne'er return again !

All that I sang, still to her praise did tend.
Still she was first, still she my songs did end ;
Yet she my love and music both doth fly,
The music that her echo is, and beauty's sympathy :
Then let my notes pursue her scornful flight !
It shall suffice that they were breathed and died for her delight.
T. CAMPION.

169. MY SWEETEST LESBIA

My sweetest Lesbia, let us live and love,
And though the sager sort our deeds reprove,
Let us not weigh them.   Heaven's great lamps do dive
Into their west, and straight again revive ;
But, soon as once set is our little light,
Then must we sleep one ever-during night.

If all would lead their lives in love like me,
Then bloody swords and armour should not be ;
No drum nor trumpet peaceful sleeps should move,
Unless alarm came from the Camp of Love.
But fools do live and waste their little light,
And seek with pain their ever-during night.

When timely death my life and fortune ends,
Let not my hearse be vext with mourning friends ;
But let all lovers, rich in triumph, come
And with sweet pastimes grace my happy tomb :
And, Lesbia, close up thou my little light,
And crown with love my ever-during night.

T. CAMPION.

170. LAURA

Rose-cheeked Laura, come ;
Sing thou smoothly with thy
    beauty's
Silent music, either other
    Sweetly gracing.

Lovely forms do flow
From concent divinely framèd ;
Heaven is music, and thy beauty's
    Birth is heavenly.

These dull notes we sing
Discords need for helps to grace
    them ;
Only beauty purely loving
    Knows no discord,

But still moves delight,
Like clear springs renewed by
    flowing,
Ever perfect, ever in them-
    Selves eternal.

T. CAMPION.

171. THE MAN UPRIGHT OF LIFE

The man upright of life, whose guiltless heart is free
From all dishonest deeds, or thought of vanity ;

The man whose silent days in harmless joys are spent,
Whom hopes cannot delude, nor sorrow discontent ;

That man needs neither towers nor armour for defence,
Nor secret vaults, to fly from thunder's violence :

He, only, can behold with unaffrighted eyes
The horrors of the deep, and terrors of the skies.

Thus, scorning all the cares that fate or fortune brings,
He makes the heaven his book ; his wisdom, heavenly things ;

Good thoughts, his only friends ; his wealth, a well-spent age ;
The earth his sober inn, and quiet pilgrimage.

T. CAMPION.

172. THINK'ST THOU TO SEDUCE ME

THINK'ST thou to seduce me then with words that have no meaning ?
Parrots so can learn to prate, our speech by pieces gleaning :
Nurses teach their children so about the time of weaning.

Learn to speak first, then to woo : to wooing much pertaineth :
He that courts us, wanting art, soon falters when he feigneth,
Looks asquint on his discourse and smiles when he complaineth.

Skilful anglers hide their hooks, fit baits for every season,
But with crooked pins fish'st thou, as babes do that want reason.
Gudgeons only can be caught with such poor tricks of treason.

T. CAMPION.

173. THOU ART NOT FAIR

THOU art not fair, for all thy red and white,
   For all those rosy ornaments in thee ;
Thou art not sweet, though made of mere delight,
   Nor fair, nor sweet—unless thou pity me.
I will not soothe thy fancies : thou shalt prove
That beauty is no beauty without love.

Yet love not me, nor seek thou to allure
   My thoughts with beauty, were it more divine ;
Thy smiles and kisses I cannot endure,
   I'll not be wrapped up in those arms of thine :
Now show it, if thou be a woman right,—
Embrace and kiss and love me in despite !

T. CAMPION.

174. TURN ALL THY THOUGHTS TO EYES

TURN all thy thoughts to eyes,
Turn all thy hairs to ears,
Change all thy friends to spies
And all thy joys to fears :
   True love will yet be free
   In spite of jealousy.

Turn darkness into day,
Conjectures into truth,
Believe what th' envious say,
Let age interpret youth :
   True love will yet be free
   In spite of jealousy.

Wrest every word and look,
Rack every hidden thought,
Or fish with golden hook ;
True love cannot be caught :
   For that will still be free
   In spite of jealousy.

T. CAMPION.

175. WERE MY HEART AS SOME MEN'S ARE

WERE my heart as some men's are, thy errors would not move me;
But thy faults I curious find, and speak because I love thee :
Patience is a thing divine, and far, I grant, above me.

Foes sometimes befriend us more, our blacker deeds objecting,
Than the obsequious bosom-guest with false respect affecting :
Friendship is the Glass of Truth, our hidden stains detecting.

When I use of eyes enjoy, and inward light of reason,
Thy observer will I be and censor, but in season :
Hidden mischief to conceal in state and love is treason.

T. CAMPION.

176. WHEN TO HER LUTE CORINNA SINGS

WHEN to her lute Corinna sings,
Her voice revives the leaden strings,
And doth in highest notes appear,
As any challenged echo clear :
But when she doth of mourning speak,
E'en with her sighs, the strings do break.

And as her lute doth live or die,
Led by her passion, so must I ;
For when of pleasure she doth sing,
My thoughts enjoy a sudden spring,
But if she doth of sorrow speak,
E'en from my heart the strings do break.

T. CAMPION.

177. THE PILOT THAT WEATHERED THE STORM

IF hushed the loud whirlwind that ruffled the deep,
  The sky if no longer loud tempests deform ;
When our perils are past, shall our gratitude sleep ?
  No ! Here 's to the Pilot that weathered the storm !

. . . .

And shall not his memory to Britain be dear,
  Whose example, with envy, all nations behold ;
A statesman unbiased by interest or fear,
  By power uncorrupted, untainted by gold ?

Who, when terror and doubt through the universe reigned,
  While rapine and treason their standards unfurled,
The heart and the hopes of his country maintained,
  And one kingdom preserved 'midst the wreck of the world.

. . . .

Lo ! Pitt, when the course of thy greatness is o'er,
  Thy talents, thy virtues, we fondly recall !
Now justly we prize thee, when lost we deplore ;
  Admired in thy zenith, but loved in thy fall.

G. CANNING.

178. A POLITICAL DISPATCH

In matters of commerce the fault of the Dutch
Is offering too little and asking too much.
The French are with equal advantage content,
So we clap on Dutch bottoms just 20 per cent.
    20 per cent, 20 per cent,
We clap on Dutch bottoms just 20 per cent.
Vous frapperez Falck avec 20 per cent.

G. CANNING.

179. SAPPHICS

THE FRIEND OF HUMANITY AND THE KNIFE-GRINDER

Friend of Humanity.

NEEDY Knife-grinder ! whither are you going ?
Rough is the road, your wheel is out of order—
Bleak blows the blast ;—your hat has got a hole in't,
        So have your breeches.

Weary Knife-grinder ! little think the proud ones
Who in their coaches roll along the turnpike-
Road, what hard work 'tis crying all day, ' Knives and
        Scissors to grind O ! '

Tell me, Knife-grinder, how you came to grind knives :
Did some rich man tyrannically use you ?
Was it the 'Squire ? or Parson of the Parish ?
        Or the Attorney ?

Was it the 'Squire, for killing of his game ? or
Covetous Parson, for his tithes distraining ?
Or roguish Lawyer, made you lose your little
        All in a lawsuit ?

(Have you not read the Rights of Man, by Tom Paine ?)
Drops of compassion tremble on my eyelids,
Ready to fall, as soon as you have told your
        Pitiful story.

Knife-grinder.

Story ! God bless you ! I have none to tell, Sir,
Only last night a-drinking at the ' Chequers ',
This poor old hat and breeches, as you see, were
        Torn in a scuffle.

Constables came up for to take me into
Custody ; they took me before the justice ;
Justice Oldmixon put me in the parish-
        Stocks for a vagrant.

I should be glad to drink your Honour's health in
A Pot of Beer, if you will give me Sixpence ;
But for my part, I never love to meddle
                      With politics, Sir.

Friend of Humanity.

I give thee Sixpence ! I will see thee damned first—
Wretch ! whom no sense of wrongs can rouse to vengeance—
Sordid, unfeeling, reprobate, degraded,
                      Spiritless outcast !
(*Kicks the Knife-grinder, overturns his wheel, and exit in a transport of
Republican Enthusiasm and Universal Philanthropy.*)
                                              G. CANNING.

180.   ASK ME NO MORE WHERE JOVE BESTOWS

Ask me no more where Jove
   bestows,
When June is past, the fading rose ;
For in your beauty's orient deep
These flowers, as in their causes,
   sleep.

Ask me no more whither do stray
The golden atoms of the day ;
For in pure love heaven did
   prepare
Those powders to enrich your
   hair.

Ask me no more whither doth
   haste
The nightingale when May is past ;
For in your sweet dividing throat
She winters, and keeps warm her
   note.

Ask me no more where those stars
   'light
That downwards fall in dead of
   night ;
For in your eyes they sit, and there
Fixèd become as in their sphere.

Ask me no more if east or west
The Phoenix builds her spicy nest ;
For unto you at last she flies,
And in your fragrant bosom dies.   T. CAREW.

181.   MEDIOCRITY IN LOVE REJECTED

Give me more love, or more disdain ;
   The torrid or the frozen zone
Bring equal ease unto my pain ;
   The temperate affords me none :
Either extreme, of love or hate,
Is sweeter than a calm estate.

Give me a storm ; if it be love—
   Like Danaë in that golden shower,
I'll swim in pleasure ; if it prove
   Disdain, that torrent will devour
My vulture hopes ; and he 's possessed
Of heaven, that 's from hell released.
Then crown my joys, or cure my pain ;
Give me more love, or more disdain.   T. CAREW.

182. DISDAIN RETURNED

He that loves a rosy cheek,
  Or a coral lip admires ;
Or from star-like eyes doth
    seek
  Fuel to maintain his fires :
As old Time makes these decay,
So his flames must waste away.

But a smooth and steadfast mind,
  Gentle thoughts, and calm
    desires,
Hearts with equal love combined,
  Kindle never-dying fires :—
Where these are not, I despise
Lovely cheeks or lips or eyes.

T. CAREW.

183. UNGRATEFUL BEAUTY THREATENED

Know, Celia, since thou art so proud,
  'Twas I that gave thee thy renown;
Thou hadst in the forgotten crowd
  Of common beauties lived unknown,
Had not my verse exhaled thy name,
And with it imped the wings of Fame.

That killing power is none of thine:
  I gave it to thy voice and eyes;
Thy sweets, thy graces, all are mine;
  Thou art my star, shin'st in my skies;
Then dart not from thy borrowed sphere
Lightning on him that fixed thee there.

Tempt me with such affrights no more,
  Lest what I made I uncreate;
Let fools thy mystic forms adore,
  I know thee in thy mortal state:
Wise poets, that wrapt Truth in tales,
Knew her themselves through all her veils.　　T. CAREW.

184. MARK HOW THE BASHFUL MORN

Mark how the bashful morn in vain
  Courts the amorous marigold
With sighing blasts and weeping rain,
  Yet she refuses to unfold;
But when the planet of the day
Approacheth with his powerful ray
Then she spreads, then she receives
His warmer beams into her virgin leaves.

So shalt thou thrive in love, fond boy ;
  If thy tears and sighs discover
Thy grief, thou never shalt enjoy
  The just reward of a bold lover.
But when with moving accents thou
Shalt constant faith and service vow,
Thy Celia shalt receive those charms
With open ears, and with unfolded arms.　　T. CAREW.

185. TO HIS INCONSTANT MISTRESS

WHEN thou, poor Excommunicate
  From all the joys of Love, shalt see
The full reward and glorious fate
  Which my strong faith shall purchase me,
  Then curse thine own inconstancy!

A fairer hand than thine shall cure
  That heart which thy false oaths did wound;
And to my soul a soul more pure
  Than thine shall by Love's hand be bound,
  And both with equal glory crowned.

Then shalt thou weep, entreat, complain
  To Love, as I did once to thee;
When all thy tears shall be in vain
  As mine were then: for thou shalt be
  Damned for thy false apostasy.   T. CAREW.

186. A LOYAL SONG

[SUNG AT THE THEATRES ROYAL.   FOR TWO VOICES *Published* 1742].

GOD save great George our King,
Long live our noble King,
  God save the King!
Send him victorious,
Happy and glorious,
Long to reign over us,
  God save the King!

O Lord, our God, arise,
Scatter our enemies,
  And make them fall;
Confound their politics,
Frustrate their knavish tricks!
On Thee our hopes we fix—
  God save us all!

Thy choicest gifts in store,
On George be pleased to pour,
  Long may he reign!
May he defend our laws;
And ever give us cause
With heart and voice to sing
  God save the King!   H. CAREY.

187. SALLY IN OUR ALLEY.

OF all the girls that are so smart
  There's none like pretty Sally;
She is the darling of my heart,
  And she lives in our alley.
There is no lady in the land
  Is half so sweet as Sally;
She is the darling of my heart,
  And she lives in our alley.

Her father he makes cabbage-nets
  And through the streets does cry them;
Her mother she sells laces long
  To such as please to buy them:
But sure such folks could ne'er beget
  So sweet a girl as Sally!
She is the darling of my heart,
  And she lives in our alley.

When she is by, I leave my
    work,
  I love her so sincerely ;
My master comes like any Turk,
    And bangs me most severely—
But let him bang his bellyful,
  I'll bear it all for Sally ;
She is the darling of my heart,
  And she lives in our alley.

Of all the days that's in the
    week
  I dearly love but one day—
And that's the day that comes
    betwixt
  A Saturday and Monday ;
For then I'm drest all in my
    best
  To walk abroad with Sally ;
She is the darling of my heart,
  And she lives in our alley.

My master carries me to church,
  And often am I blamed
Because I leave him in the lurch
  As soon as text is named ;

I leave the church in sermon-time
  And slink away to Sally ;
She is the darling of my heart,
  And she lives in our alley.

When Christmas comes about
    again
  O then I shall have money ;
I'll hoard it up, and box and all
  I'll give it to my honey :
And would it were ten thousand
    pounds,
  I'd give it all to Sally ;
She is the darling of my heart,
  And she lives in our alley.

My master and the neighbours all
  Make game of me and Sally,
And, but for her, I'd better be
  A slave and row a galley ;
But when my seven long years are
    out
  O then I'll marry Sally,—
O then we'll wed, and then we'll
    bed,
  But not in our alley !

                H. CAREY.

188. FROM THE MOUNTAINS TO THE CHAMPAIGN

FROM the mountains to the Champaign,
  By the glens and hills along,
Comes a rustling and a tramping,
  Comes a motion as of song :
And this undetermined roving
  Brings delight, and brings good heed ;
Life's no resting, but a moving,
  Let thy life be Deed on Deed !

Keep not standing fixed and rooted,
  Briskly venture, briskly roam ;
Head and hand, where'er thou foot it,
  And stout heart, are still at home.
In each land the sun does visit
  We are gay, whate'er betide :
To give room for wandering is it
  That the world was made so wide.

                T. CARLYLE.

189. TO-DAY

So here hath been dawning
  Another blue Day:
Think wilt thou let it
  Slip useless away?

Out of Eternity
  This new Day is born;
Into Eternity,
  At night, will return.

Behold it aforetime
  No eye ever did:
So soon it for ever
  From all eyes is hid.

Here hath been dawning
  Another blue Day:
Think, wilt thou let it
  Slip useless away?

          T. CARLYLE.

190. CUI BONO

WHAT is Hope? A smiling rainbow
  Children follow through the wet;
'Tis not here, still yonder, yonder:
  Never urchin found it yet.

What is Life? A thawing iceboard
  On a sea with sunny shore;
Gay we sail; it melts beneath us;
  We are sunk, and seen no more.

What is Man? A foolish baby,
  Vainly strives, and fights, and frets;
Demanding all, deserving nothing;
  One small grave is what he gets.

          T. CARLYLE.

191. CORIDON'S SONG

OH, the sweet contentment
The countryman doth find.
  High trolollie lollie loe,
  High trolollie lee,
That quiet contemplation
Possesseth all my mind:
  Then care away,
  And wend along with me.

For courts are full of flattery,
As hath too oft been tried;
  High trolollie lollie loe,
  High trolollie lee,
The city full of wantonness,
And both are full of pride.
  Then care away,
  And wend along with me.

But oh, the honest countryman
Speaks truly from his heart,
  High trolollie lollie loe,
  High trolollie lee,
His pride is in his tillage,
His horses and his cart:
  Then care away,
  And wend along with me.

Our clothing is good sheepskins,
Grey russet for our wives,
  High trolollie lollie loe,
  High trolollie lee,
'Tis warmth and not gay clothing
That doth prolong our lives;
  Then care away,
  And wend along with me.

The ploughman, though he labour
   hard,
Yet on the holiday,
   High trolollie lollie loe,
   High trolollie lee,
No emperor so merrily
Does pass his time away ;
   Then care away,
   And wend along with me.

To recompense our tillage
The heavens afford us showers ;
   High trolollie lollie loe,
   High trolollie lee,
And for our sweet refreshments
The earth affords us bowers :
   Then care away,
   And wend along with me.

The cuckoo and the nightingale
Full merrily do sing,
   High trolollie lollie loe,
   High trolollie lee,
And with their pleasant rounde-
   lays
Bid welcome to the spring :
   Then care away,
   And wend along with me.

This is not half the happiness
The countryman enjoys ;
   High trolollie lollie loe,
   High trolollie lee,
Though others think they have
   as much
Yet he that says so lies :
   Then come away, turn
   Countryman with me.

         J. CHALKHILL.

192. THE MINSTREL'S SONG

OH sing unto my roundelay ;
   Oh drop the briny tear with
   me ;
Dance no more on holiday ;
   Like a running river be !
     My love is dead,
     Gone to his death-bed,
     All under the willow tree !

Black his hair as the winter night,
   White his throat as the summer
   snow,
Red his cheek as the morning
   light,
   Cold he lies in the grave below.

Sweet his tongue as the throstle's
   note ;
   Quick in dance as thought can
   be ;
Deft his tabor, cudgel stout,
   Oh, he lies by the willow tree.

Hark ! the raven flaps his wing
   In the briery dell below ;
Hark ! the death-owl loud doth
   sing,
   To the night-mares as they go.

See ! the white moon shines on
   high ;
   Whiter is my true love's shroud ;
Whiter than the morning sky,
   Whiter than the evening cloud.

Here, upon my true love's grave,
   Shall the barren flowers be laid ;
Not one holy saint to save
   All the coldness of a maid.

With my hands I'll twist the
   briers
   Round his holy corpse to gre ;
Elfin fairy, light your fires,
   Here my body still shall be.

Come, with acorn-cup and thorn,
   Drain my heartis blood away ;
Life and all its good I scorn,
   Dance by night, or feast by day.

Water-witches, crowned with
   reeds,
   Bear me to your deadly tide.
I die ! I come ! my true love
   waits !—
   Thus the damsel spoke, and
   died.

         T. CHATTERTON.

193. THE PARSON

A GOOD man was ther of religioun,
And was a povre PERSOUN of a toun ;
But riche he was of holy thoght and werk.
He was also a lerned man, a clerk,
That Cristes gospel trewely wolde preche ;
His parisshens devoutly wolde he teche.
Benigne he was, and wonder diligent,
And in adversitee ful pacient ;
And swich he was y-preved ofte sythes.
Ful looth were him to cursen for his tythes.

. . . .

He sette nat his benefice to hyre,
And leet his sheep encombred in the myre,
And ran to London, un-to sëynt Poules,
To seken him a chaunterie for soules,
Or with a bretherhed to been withholde ;
But dwelte at hoom, and kepte wel his folde.

. . . .

A bettre preest I trowe that nowher noon is
He wayted after no pompe and reverence,
Ne maked him a spyced conscience,
But Cristes lore, and his apostles twelve,
He taught, and first he folwed it himselve.

G. CHAUCER (*The Canterbury Tales*).

194. THE PERFECT KNIGHT

A KNIGHT ther was, and that a worthy man,
That fro the tyme that he first bigan
To ryden out, he loved chivalrye,
Trouthe and honour, fredom and curteisye,
Ful worthy was he in his lordes werre,
And therto hadde he riden (no man ferre)
As wel in Cristendom as hethenesse,
And ever honoured for his worthinesse.

. . . .

And evermore he hadde a sovereign prys.
And though that he were worthy, he was wys,
And of his port as meke as is a mayde.
He never yet no vileinye ne sayde
In al his lyf, un-to no maner wight.
He was a verray parfit gentil knight.

G. CHAUCER (*The Canterbury Tales*).

195. BALADE OF GOOD COUNCIL

FLEE fro the prees, and dwelle with sothfastnesse,
Suffyce unto thy good, though hit be smal ;
For hord hath hate, and climbing tikelnesse,
Prees hath envye, and wele blent overal ;
Savour no more than thee bihove shal ;
Werk wel thy-self, that other folk canst rede ;
And trouthe shal delivere, hit is no drede.

Tempest thee noght al croked to redresse,
In trust of hir that turneth as a bal :
Gret reste stant in litel besinesse ;
And eek be war to sporne ageyn an al ;
Stryve noght, as doth the crokke with the wal.
Daunte thy-self, that dauntest otheres dede ;
And trouthe shal delivere, hit is no drede.

That thee is sent, receyve in buxumnesse,
The wrastling for this worlde axeth a fal.
Her nis non hoom, her nis but wildernesse :
Forth, pilgrim, forth ! Forth, beste, out of thy stal !
Know thy contree, look up, thank God of al ;
Hold the hye wey, and lat thy gost thee lede :
And trouthe shal delivere, hit is no drede.

ENVOY

Therfore, thou vache, leve thyn old wrecchednesse
Unto the worlde ; leve now to be thral ;
Crye him mercy, that of his hy goodnesse
Made thee of noght, and in especial
Draw unto him, and pray in general
For thee, and eek for other, hevenlich mede ;
And trouthe shal delivere, hit is no drede.

G. CHAUCER (*The Canterbury Tales*).

196. THE PRIORESS EGLANTINE

THER was also a Nonne, a PRIORESSE,
That of hir smyling was ful simple and coy ;
Hir gretteste ooth was but by sëynt Loy ;
And she was cleped madame Eglentyne.
Ful wel she song the service divyne,
Entuned in hir nose ful semely ;
And Frensh she spak ful faire and fetisly,
After the scole of Stratford atte Bowe,
For Frensh of Paris was to hir unknowe.

.   .   .   .

She was so charitable and so pitous,
She wolde wepe, if that she sawe a mous
Caught in a trappe, if it were deed or bledde.
Of smale houndes had she, that she fedde
With rosted flesh, or milk and wastel-breed.
But sore weep she if oon of hem were deed,
Or if men smoot it with a yerde smerte :
And al was conscience and tendre herte.
Ful semely hir wimpel pinched was ;
Hir nose tretys ; hir eyen greye as glas ;
Hir mouth ful smal, and ther-to softe and reed ;
But sikerly she hadde a fair forheed ;
It was almost a spanne brood, I trowe ;
For, hardily, she was nat undergrowe.
Ful fetis was hir cloke, as I was war.
Of smal coral aboute hir arm she bar
A peire of bedes, gauded al with grene ;
And ther-on heng a broche of gold ful shene,
On which ther was first write a crowned A,
And after, *Amor vincit omnia.*

> G. CHAUCER (*The Canterbury Tales*).

197. WHEN THAT APRIL WITH HIS SHOWERS SWEET

WHAN that Aprille with his shoures sote
The droghte of Marche hath perced to the rote,
And bathed every veyne in swich licour,
Of which vertu engendred is the flour ;
Whan Zephirus eek with his swete breeth
Inspired hath in every holt and heeth
The tendre croppes, and the yonge sonne
Hath in the Ram his halfe cours y-ronne,
And smale fowles maken melodye,
That slepen al the night with open yë,
(So priketh hem nature in hir corages) :
Than longen folk to goon on pilgrimages
(And palmers for to seken straunge strondes)
To ferne halwes, couthe in sondry londes ;
And specially, from every shires ende
Of Engelond, to Caunterbury they wende,
The holy blisful martir for to seke,
That hem hath holpen, whan that they were seke.

> G. CHAUCER (*The Canterbury Tales*).

198. THE DOCTOR OF PHYSIC

WITH us ther was a DOCTOUR OF
   PHISYK,
In al this world ne was ther noon
   him lyk
To speke of phisik and of sur-
   gerye;
For he was grounded in astrono-
   mye.
He kepte his pacient a ful greet del
In houres, by his magik naturel.

Wel coude he fortunen the ascen-
   dent
Of his images for his pacient.
He knew the cause of everich
   maladye,
Were it of hoot or cold, or moiste,
   or drye,
And where engendred, and of
   what humour;
He was a verrey parfit practisour.

G. CHAUCER (*The Canterbury Tales*).

199. THE BLIND BOY

OH, say what is that thing called
   light
   Which I can ne'er enjoy?
What is the blessing of the sight?
   Oh, tell your poor blind boy.

You talk of wondrous things you
   see,
   You say ' The sun shines bright.'
I feel him warm; but how can he
   Then make it day or night?

My day or night myself I make,
   Whene'er I wake or play;
And could I ever keep awake
   It would be always day.

With heavy sighs I often hear
   You mourn my hopeless woe:
But, sure, with patience I may
   bear
   A loss I ne'er can know.

Then let not what I cannot have
   My cheer of mind destroy.
While thus I sing, I am a king,
   Although a poor blind boy!   C. CIBBER.

200. THE DYING CHILD

HE could not die when trees were
   green,
   For he loved the time too well.
His little hands, when flowers were
   seen,
   Were held for the bluebell,
   As he was carried o'er the
      green.

His eye glanced at the white-
   nosed bee;
He knew those children of the
   Spring:
When he was well and on the lea
   He held one in his hands to
      sing,
   Which filled his heart with
      glee.

Infants, the children of the Spring!
   How can an infant die
When butterflies are on the wing,
   Green grass, and such a sky?
   How can they die at Spring?
He held his hands for daisies
      white,
   And then for violets blue,
And took them all to bed at night
   That in the green fields grew,
   As childhood's sweet delight.

And then he shut his little eyes,
   And flowers would notice not;
Birds' nests and eggs caused no
   surprise,
   He now no blossoms got:
   They met with plaintive sighs.

> When Winter came and blasts did sigh,
>   And bare were plain and tree,
> As he for ease in bed did lie
>   His soul seemed with the free,
>   He died so quietly.

J. CLARE.

201. MY EARLY HOME

HERE sparrows build upon the trees,
  And stockdove hides her nest ;
The leaves are winnowed by the breeze
  Into a calmer rest :
The black-cap's song was very sweet,
  That used the rose to kiss ;
It made the Paradise complete :
  My early home was this.

The red-breast from the sweetbrier bush
  Dropt down to pick the worm ;
On the horse-chestnut sang the thrush,
  O'er the house where I was born ;
The moonlight, like a shower of pearls,
  Fell o'er this ' bower of bliss ',
And on the bench sat boys and girls :
  My early home was this.

The old house stooped just like a cave,
  Thatched o'er with mosses green ;
Winter around the walls would rave,
  But all was calm within ;
The trees are here all green agen,
  Here bees the flowers still kiss,
But flowers and trees seemed sweeter then :
  My early home was this.

J. CLARE.

202. FROM 'THE FATE OF AMY'

THE flowers the sultry summer kills,
  Spring's milder suns restore ;
But innocence, that fickle charm,
  Blooms once, and blooms no more.

The swains who loved no more admire,
  Their hearts no beauty warms ;
And maidens triumph in her fall
  That envied once her charms.

Lost was that sweet simplicity ;
  Her eye's bright lustre fled ;
And o'er her cheeks, where roses bloomed,
  A sickly paleness spread.

So fades the flower before its time,
  Where canker-worms assail ;
So droops the bud upon its stem
  Beneath the sickly gale.

J. CLARE.

203. EVENING PRIMROSE

WHEN once the sun sinks in the west,
And dew-drops pearl the Evening's breast;
Almost as pale as moonbeams are,
Or its companionable star,
The Evening Primrose opes anew
Its delicate blossoms to the dew;
And hermit-like, shunning the light,
Wastes its fair bloom upon the Night;
Who, blindfold to its fond caresses,
Knows not the beauty he possesses.
Thus it blooms on while Night is by;
When Day looks out with open eye,
'Bashed at the gaze it cannot shun,
It faints, and withers, and is gone.   J. CLARE.

204. QUA CURSUM VENTUS

As ships, becalmed at eve, that lay
  With canvas drooping, side by side,
Two towers of sail at dawn of day
  Are scarce long leagues apart descried;

When fell the night, upsprung the breeze,
  And all the darkling hours they plied,
Nor dreamt but each the self-same seas
  By each was cleaving, side by side:

E'en so—but why the tale reveal
  Of those, whom year by year unchanged,
Brief absence joined anew to feel,
  Astounded, soul from soul estranged?

At dead of night their sails were filled,
  And onward each rejoicing steered—
Ah, neither blame, for neither willed,
  Or wist, what first with dawn appeared!

To veer, how vain! On, onward strain,
  Brave barks! In light, in darkness too,
Through winds and tides one compass guides:
  To that, and your own selves, be true.

But O blithe breeze; and O great seas,
  Though ne'er, that earliest parting past,
On your wide plain they join again,
  Together lead them home at last.

One port, methought, alike they sought,
  One purpose hold where'er they fare,—
O bounding breeze, O rushing seas!
  At last, at last, unite them there!

                        A. H. CLOUGH.

E

205. THE BATHING-PLACE

BUT in the interval here the boiling, pent-up water
Frees itself by a final descent, attaining a basin,
Ten feet wide and eighteen long, with whiteness and fury
Occupied partly, but mostly pellucid, pure, a mirror ;
Beautiful there for the colour derived from the green rocks under ;
Beautiful, most of all, where beads of foam uprising
Mingle their clouds of white with the delicate hue of the stillness,
Cliff over cliff for its sides, with rowan and pendent birch boughs,
Here it lies, unthought of above at the bridge and pathway,
Still more enclosed from below by wood and rocky projection.
You are shut in, left alone with yourself and perfection of water,
Hid on all sides, left alone with yourself and the goddess of bathing.
Here, the pride of the plunger, you stride the fall and clear it ;
Here, the delight of the bather, you roll in beaded sparklings,
Here into pure green depth drop down from lofty ledges.
A. H. CLOUGH (*The Bothie of Tober-na-Vuolich*).

206. COME BACK, COME BACK

COME back, come back, across the flying foam,
We hear faint far-off voices call us home.
. . . .
Come back, come back ; and whither back or why ?
To fan quenched hopes, forsaken schemes to try ;
Walk the old fields ; pace the familiar street ;
Dream with the idlers, with the bards compete.
Come back, come back.

Come back, come back ; and whither and for what ?
To finger idly some old Gordian knot,
Unskilled to sunder, and too weak to cleave,
And with much toil attain to half-believe.
Come back, come back.
. . . .
Come back, come back !
Back flies the foam ; the hoisted flag streams back ;
The long smoke wavers on the homeward track,
Back fly with winds things which the winds obey,
The strong ship follows its appointed way.
A. H. CLOUGH.

207. GREEN FIELDS OF ENGLAND

GREEN fields of England ! wheresoe'er
Across this watery waste we fare,
Your image at our hearts we bear,
Green fields of England, everywhere.

Sweet eyes in England, I must flee
Past where the waves' last confines be,
Ere your loved smile I cease to see,
Sweet eyes in England, dear to me.

Dear home in England, safe and fast
If but in thee my lot lie cast,
The past shall seem a nothing past
To thee, dear home, if won at last;
Dear home in England, won at last.

                              A. H. CLOUGH.

208. THE STREAM OF LIFE

O STREAM descending to the sea,
  Thy mossy banks between,
The flowerets blow, the grasses
    grow,
  The leafy trees are green.

In garden plots the children play,
  The fields the labourers till,
And houses stand on either hand,
  And thou descendest still.

O life descending into death,
  Our waking eyes behold,
Parent and friend thy lapse attend,
  Companions young and old.

Strong purposes our mind possess,
  Our hearts affections fill,
We toil and earn, we seek and
    learn,
  And thou descendest still.

O end to which our currents tend,
  Inevitable sea,
To which we flow, what do we
    know,
  What shall we guess of thee ?

A roar we hear upon thy shore,
  As we our course fulfil ;
Scarce we divine a sun will shine
  And be above us still.

                              A. H. CLOUGH.

209. IN A LONDON SQUARE

PUT forth thy leaf, thou lofty plane,
  East wind and frost are safely gone ;
With zephyr mild and balmy rain
  The summer comes serenely on ;
Earth, air, and sun and skies combine
  To promise all that's kind and fair ;—
But thou, O human heart of mine,
  Be still, contain thyself, and bear.

December days were brief and chill,
  The winds of March were wild and drear,
And, nearing and receding still,
  Spring never would, we thought, be here.
The leaves that burst, the suns that shine,
  Had, not the less, their certain date ;—
And thou, O human heart of mine,
  Be still, refrain thyself, and wait.

                              A. H. CLOUGH.

210.   SAY NOT THE STRUGGLE NAUGHT AVAILETH

SAY not the struggle naught availeth,
  The labour and the wounds are vain,
The enemy faints not, nor faileth,
  And as things have been they remain.

If hopes were dupes, fears may be liars ;
  It may be, in yon smoke concealed,
Your comrades chase e'en now the fliers,
  And, but for you, possess the field.

For while the tired waves, vainly breaking,
  Seem here no painful inch to gain,
Far back, through creeks and inlets making,
  Comes silent, flooding in, the main.

And not by eastern windows only,
  When daylight comes, comes in the light,
In front, the sun climbs slow, how slowly,
  But westward, look, the land is bright !

A. H. CLOUGH.

211.   HOME, ROSE, AND HOME, PROVENCE AND LA PALIE

ITE DOMUM SATURAE, VENIT HESPERUS

THE skies have sunk, and hid the upper snow
(Home, Rose, and home, Provence and La Palie),
The rainy clouds are filing fast below,
And wet will be the path, and wet shall we.
Home, Rose, and home, Provence and La Palie.

Ah dear, and where is he, a year agone
Who stepped beside and cheered us on and on ?
My sweetheart wanders far away from me,
In foreign land or on a foreign sea.
Home, Rose, and home, Provence and La Palie.

The lightning zigzags shoot across the sky
(Home, Rose, and home, Provence and La Palie),
And through the vale the rains go sweeping by ;
Ah me, and when in shelter shall we be ?
Home, Rose, and home, Provence and La Palie.

Cold, dreary cold, the stormy winds feel they
O'er foreign lands and foreign seas that stray
(Home, Rose, and home, Provence and La Palie).
And doth he e'er, I wonder, bring to mind
The pleasant huts and herds he left behind ?
And doth he sometimes in his slumbering see
The feeding kine and doth he think of me,
My sweetheart wandering wheresoe'er it be ?
Home, Rose, and home, Provence and La Palie.

The thunder bellows far from snow to snow
(Home, Rose, and home, Provence and La Palie),
And loud and louder roars the flood below.
Heigh-ho ! but soon in shelter shall we be :
Home, Rose, and home, Provence and La Palie.

Or shall he find before his term be sped,
Some comelier maid that he shall wish to wed ?
(Home, Rose, and home, Provence and La Palie.)
For weary is work, and weary day by day
To have your comfort miles on miles away.
Home, Rose, and home, Provence and La Palie.

Or may it be that I shall find my mate,
And he returning see himself too late ?
For work we must, and what we see, we see,
And God he knows, and what must be, must be,
When sweethearts wander far away from me.
Home, Rose, and home, Provence and La Palie.

The sky behind is brightening up anew
(Home, Rose, and home, Provence and La Palie),
The rain is ending, and our journey too :
Heigh-ho ! aha ! for here at home are we :—
In, Rose, and in, Provence and La Palie.

A. H. CLOUGH.

212. WHERE LIES THE LAND TO WHICH THE SHIP
WOULD GO ?

WHERE lies the land to which the ship would go ?
Far, far ahead, is all her seamen know.
And where the land she travels from ? Away,
Far, far behind, is all that they can say.

On sunny noons upon the deck's smooth face,
Linked arm in arm, how pleasant here to pace ;
Or, o'er the stern reclining, watch below
The foaming wake far widening as we go.

On stormy nights when wild north-westers rave,
How proud a thing to fight with wind and wave !
The dripping sailor on the reeling mast
Exults to bear, and scorns to wish it past.

Where lies the land to which the ship would go ?
Far, far ahead, is all her seamen know.
And where the land she travels from ? Away,
Far, far behind, is all that they can say.

A. H. CLOUGH.

213. WHERE UPON APENNINE SLOPE

WHERE, upon Apennine slope, with the chestnut the oak-trees im-
    mingle,
  Where amid odorous copse bridle-paths wander and wind,
Where under mulberry-branches the diligent rivulet sparkles,
  Or amid cotton and maize peasants their water-works ply,
Where, over fig-tree and orange in tier upon tier still repeated,
  Garden on garden upreared, balconies step to the sky,—
Ah, that I were far away from the crowd and the streets of the city,
  Under the vine-trellis laid, O my beloved, with thee !

A. H. CLOUGH (Amours de Voyage).

214. SHE IS NOT FAIR TO OUTWARD VIEW

SHE is not fair to outward view
  As many maidens be,
Her loveliness I never knew
  Until she smiled on me.
O then I saw her eye was
    bright,
A well of love, a spring of light.

But now her looks are coy and
    cold,
  To mine they ne'er reply,
And yet I cease not to behold
  The love-light in her eye :
Her very frowns are fairer far
Than smiles of other maidens are.

HARTLEY COLERIDGE.

215. WHITHER IS GONE THE WISDOM AND THE POWER

WHITHER is gone the wisdom and the power
That ancient sages scattered with the notes
Of thought-suggesting lyres ? The music floats
In the void air ; e'en at this breathing hour,
In every cell and every blooming bower
The sweetness of old lays is hovering still :
But the strong soul, the self-constraining will,
The rugged root which bare the winsome flower
Is weak and withered. Were we like the fays
That sweetly nestle in the fox-glove bells,
Or lurk and murmur in the rose-lipped shells
Which Neptune to the earth for quit-rent pays,
Then might our pretty modern Philomels
Sustain our spirits with their roundelays.

HARTLEY COLERIDGE.

216. A LITTLE CHILD

A LITTLE child, a limber elf,
Singing, dancing to itself,
A fairy thing with red round
    cheeks
That always finds, and never seeks,
Makes such a vision to the sight
As fills a father's eyes with light ;

And pleasures flow in so thick and
    fast
Upon his heart, that he at last
Must needs express his love's
    excess
With words of unmeant bitterness.

S. T. COLERIDGE (Christabel).

217. THEY HAD BEEN FRIENDS IN YOUTH

ALAS ! they had been friends in youth;
But whispering tongues can poison truth;
And constancy lives in realms above;
And life is thorny; and youth is vain:
And to be wroth with one we love,
Doth work like madness in the brain.
And thus it chanced, as I divine,
With Roland and Sir Leoline.
Each spake words of high disdain
And insult to his heart's best brother:
They parted—ne'er to meet again !
But never either found another
To free the hollow heart from paining—
They stood aloof, the scars remaining,
Like cliffs which had been rent asunder;
A dreary sea now flows between.
But neither heat, nor frost, nor thunder,
Shall wholly do away, I ween,
The marks of that which once hath been.

S. T. COLERIDGE (*Christabel*).

218. LOVE

ALL thoughts, all passions, all delights,
   Whatever stirs this mortal frame,
All are but ministers of Love,
   And feed his sacred flame.

. . . . . .

She wept with pity and delight,
   She blushed with love and virgin-shame;
And like the murmur of a dream,
   I heard her breathe my name.

Her bosom heaved—she stepped aside,
   As conscious of my look she stepped—
Then suddenly, with timorous eye,
   She fled to me and wept.

She half enclosed me with her arms,
   She pressed me with a meek embrace;
And bending back her head, looked up,
   And gazed upon my face.

'Twas partly love and partly fear,
   And partly 'twas a bashful art,
That I might rather feel, than see,
   The swelling of her heart.

S. T. COLERIDGE.

219. NAMES

I ASKED my fair one happy day,
What I should call her in my lay;
  By what sweet name from
    Rome or Greece ;
Lalage, Neaera, Chloris,
Sappho, Lesbia, or Doris,
  Arethusa or Lucrece.

'Ah !' replied my gentle fair,
'Belovèd, what are names but air ?
  Choose thou whatever suits the
    line ;
Call me Sappho, call me Chloris,
Call me Lalage or Doris,
  Only, only call me Thine.'
            S. T. COLERIDGE.

220. KUBLA KHAN

IN Xanadu did Kubla Khan
A stately pleasure-dome decree :
Where Alph, the sacred river, ran
Through caverns measureless to man
    Down to a sunless sea.
So twice five miles of fertile ground
With walls and towers were girdled round :
And here were gardens bright with sinuous rills,
Where blossomed many an incense-bearing tree ;
And here were forests ancient as the hills,
Enfolding sunny spots of greenery.
But oh ! that deep romantic chasm which slanted
Down the green hill athwart a cedarn cover !
A savage place ! as holy and enchanted
As e'er beneath a waning moon was haunted
By woman wailing for her demon-lover !
And from this chasm with ceaseless turmoil seething,
As if this earth in fast thick pants were breathing,
A mighty fountain momently was forced :
Amid whose swift half-intermitted burst
Huge fragments vaulted like rebounding hail,
Or chaffy grain beneath the thresher's flail :
And 'mid these dancing rocks at once and ever
It flung up momently the sacred river.
Five miles meandering with a mazy motion
Through wood and dale the sacred river ran,
Then reached the caverns measureless to man
And sank in tumult to a lifeless ocean :
And 'mid this tumult Kubla heard from far
Ancestral voices prophesying war !

  The shadow of the dome of pleasure
  Floated midway on the waves ;
  Where was heard the mingled measure
  From the fountain and the caves.
It was a miracle of rare device,
A sunny pleasure-dome with caves of ice !

A damsel with a dulcimer
In a vision once I saw:
It was an Abyssinian maid,
And on her dulcimer she played,
Singing of Mount Abora.
Could I revive within me
Her symphony and song,
To such a deep delight 'twould win me,
That with music loud and long,
I would build that dome in air,
That sunny dome! those caves of ice!
And all who heard should see them there,
And all should cry, Beware! Beware!
His flashing eyes, his floating hair!
Weave a circle round him thrice,
And close your eyes with holy dread,
For he on honey-dew hath fed,
And drank the milk of Paradise.   S. T. COLERIDGE.

221. THE RIME OF THE ANCIENT MARINER

IT is an ancient mariner,
And he stoppeth one of three.
' By thy long grey beard and
    glittering eye,
Now wherefore stopp'st thou me ?
' The Bridegroom's doors are
    opened wide
And I am next of kin ;
The guests are met, the feast is
    set :
May'st hear the merry din.'

He holds him with his skinny hand,
' There was a ship,' quoth he.
' Hold off ! unhand me, grey-
    beard loon ! '
Eftsoons his hand dropt he.

He holds him with his glittering
    eye—
The Wedding-Guest stood still,
And listens like a three years'
    child :
The Mariner hath his will.

The Wedding-Guest sat on a stone :
He cannot choose but hear ;
And thus spake on that ancient
    man,
The bright-eyed Mariner.

The ship was cheered, the harbour
    cleared,
Merrily did we drop
Below the kirk, below the hill,
Below the lighthouse top.

The sun came up upon the left,
Out of the sea came he !
And he shone bright, and on the
    right
Went down into the sea.

Higher and higher every day,
Till over the mast at noon—
The Wedding-Guest here beat his
    breast,
For he heard the loud bassoon.

The bride hath paced into the hall,
Red as a rose is she ;
Nodding their heads before her
    goes
The merry minstrelsy.

The Wedding-Guest he beat his
    breast,
Yet he cannot choose but hear ;
And thus spake on that ancient
    man,
The bright-eyed Mariner.

And now the Storm-blast came,
    and he
Was tyrannous and strong :
He struck with his o'ertaking
    wings,
And chased us south along.

With sloping masts and dipping
    prow,
As who pursued with yell and
    blow
Still treads the shadow of his foe
And forward bends his head,
The ship drove fast, loud roared
    the blast,
And southward ay we fled.

And now there came both mist
    and snow
And it grew wondrous cold :
And ice, mast-high, came floating
    by,
As green as emerald.

And through the drifts the snowy
    clifts
Did send a dismal sheen :
Nor shapes of men nor beasts we
    ken—
The ice was all between.

The ice was here, the ice was
    there,
The ice was all around :
It cracked and growled, and
    roared and howled,
Like noises in a swound !

At length did cross an Albatross :
Thorough the fog it came ;
As if it had been a Christian soul,
We hailed it in God's name.

It ate the food it ne'er had eat,
And round and round it flew.
The ice did split with a thunder-
    fit ;
The helmsman steered us through !

And a good south wind sprung
    up behind;
The Albatross did follow,
And every day, for food or play,
Came to the mariner's hollo !

In mist or cloud, on mast or
    shroud,
It perched for vespers nine ;
Whiles all the night, through fog-
    smoke white,
Glimmered the white moonshine.

' God save thee, ancient Mariner !
From the fiends, that plague thee
    thus !—
Why look'st thou so ? '—With my
    cross-bow
I shot the Albatross.

The Sun now rose upon the
    right :
Out of the sea came he,
Still hid in mist, and on the left
Went down into the sea.

And the good south wind still
    blew behind,
But no sweet bird did follow,
Nor any day for food or play
Come to the mariner's hollo !

And I had done a hellish thing,
And it would work 'em woe :
For all averred, I had killed the
    bird
That made the breeze to blow.
Ah wretch ! said they, the bird
    to slay,
That made the breeze to blow !

Nor dim nor red, like God's own
    head,
The glorious Sun uprist :
Then all averred, I had killed the
    bird
That brought the fog and mist.
'Twas right, said they, such birds
    to slay,
That bring the fog and mist.

The fair breeze blew, the white
    foam flew,
The furrow followed free ;
We were the first that ever burst
Into that silent sea.

Down dropt the breeze, the sails
    dropt down,
'Twas sad as sad could be ;
And we did speak only to break
The silence of the sea !

All in a hot and copper sky,
The bloody Sun, at noon,
Right up above the mast did
    stand,
No bigger than the Moon.

Day after day, day after day,
We stuck, nor breath nor motion ;
As idle as a painted ship
Upon a painted ocean.

Water, water, everywhere,
And all the boards did shrink ;
Water, water, everywhere,
Nor any drop to drink.

The very deep did rot : O Christ !
That ever this should be !
Yea, slimy things did crawl with
    legs
Upon the slimy sea.

About, about, in reel and rout
The death-fires danced at night ;
The water, like a witch's oils,
Burnt green and blue and white.

And some in dreams assured were
Of the spirit that plagued us so ;
Nine fathom deep he had followed
    us
From the land of mist and snow.

And every tongue, through utter
    drought,
Was withered at the root ;
We could not speak, no more
    than if
We had been choked with soot.

Ah ! well-a-day ! what evil looks
Had I from old and young !
Instead of the cross, the Albatross
About my neck was hung.

    .   .   .   .   .

Alone, alone, all, all alone,
Alone on a wide wide sea !
And never a saint took pity on
My soul in agony.

The many men, so beautiful !
And they all dead did lie :
And a thousand thousand slimy
    things
Lived on ; and so did I.

I looked upon the rotting sea,
And drew my eyes away ;
I looked upon the rotting deck
And there the dead men lay.

    .   .   .   .   .

Oh sleep ! it is a gentle thing,
Beloved from pole to pole !
To Mary Queen the praise be
    given !
She sent the gentle sleep from
    Heaven,
That slid into my soul.

The silly buckets on the deck,
That had so long remained,
I dreamt that they were filled
    with dew ;
And when I awoke, it rained.

My lips were wet, my throat was
    cold,
My garments were all dank ;
Sure I had drunken in my dreams,
And still my body drank.

I moved, and could not feel my
    limbs :
I was so light—almost
I thought that I had died in sleep,
And was a blessed ghost.

    .   .   .   .   .

The Sun, right up above the mast,
Had fixed her to the ocean :
But in a minute she 'gan stir,
With a short uneasy motion—
Backwards and forwards half her
    length
With a short uneasy motion.

Then, like a pawing horse let go,
She made a sudden bound :
It flung the blood into my head,
And I fell down in a swound.

How long in that same fit I lay,
I have not to declare ;
But ere my living life returned,
I heard and in my soul discerned
Two voices in the air.

' Is it he ? ' quoth one, ' Is this
    the man ?
By Him who died on cross,
With his cruel bow he laid full
    low
The harmless Albatross.

' The spirit who bideth by himself
In the land of mist and snow,
He loved the bird that loved the
    man
Who shot him with his bow.'

The other was a softer voice,
As soft as honeydew :
Quoth he, ' The man hath pen-
    ance done,
And penance more will do.'

. . . . . .

O Wedding-Guest ! this soul hath
    been
Alone on a wide wide sea :
So lonely 'twas, that God Him-
    self
Scarce seemèd there to be.

O sweeter than the marriage-feast,
'Tis sweeter far to me,
To walk together to the kirk
With a goodly company !—

To walk together to the kirk,
And all together pray,
While each to his great Father
    bends,
Old men, and babes, and loving
    friends,
And youths and maidens gay !

Farewell, farewell ! but this I tell
To thee, thou Wedding-Guest !
He prayeth well, who loveth well
Both man and bird and beast.

He prayeth best, who loveth best
All things both great and small ;
For the dear God who loveth us,
He made and loveth all.

The Mariner, whose eye is bright,
Whose beard with age is hoar,
Is gone : and now the Wedding-
    Guest
Turned from the bridegroom's
    door.

He went like one that hath been
    stunned,
And is of sense forlorn :
A sadder and a wiser man,
He rose the morrow morn.
                                S. T. COLERIDGE.

222. AN EPITAPH FOR HIMSELF

STOP, Christian passer-by !—Stop, child of God,
And read with gentle breast. Beneath this sod
A poet lies, or that which once seemed he.—
Oh, lift one thought in prayer for S. T. C. !
That he who many a year with toil of breath
Found death in life, may here find life in death !
Mercy for praise—to be forgiven for fame
He asked, and hoped, through Christ. Do thou the same !
                                S. T. COLERIDGE.

223. THE KNIGHT'S TOMB

WHERE is the grave of Sir Arthur O'Kellyn ?
Where may the grave of that good man be ?—
By the side of a spring, on the breast of Helvellyn,
Under the twigs of a young birch tree !
The oak that in summer was sweet to hear,
And rustled its leaves in the fall of the year,
And whistled and roared in the winter alone,
Is gone,—and the birch in its stead is grown.—
The Knight's bones are dust,
And his good sword rust ;—
His soul is with the saints, I trust.   S. T. COLERIDGE.

224. CURST BE THE GOLD AND SILVER

CURST be the gold and silver which persuade
Weak men to follow far-fatiguing trade.
The lily-peace outshines the silver store,
And life is dearer than the golden ore.
Yet money tempts us o'er the desert brown,
To every distant mart, and wealthy town :
Full oft we tempt the land, and oft the sea,
And are we only yet repaid by thee ?
Ah ! why was ruin so attractive made,
Or why fond man so easily betrayed ?
Why heed we not, whilst mad we haste along,
The gentle voice of peace, or pleasure's song ?
Or wherefore think the flowery mountain's side,
The fountain's murmurs, and the valley's pride,
Why think we these less pleasing to behold,
Than dreary deserts, if they lead to gold ?
            Sad was the hour, and luckless was the day,
            When first from Schiraz' walls I bent my way.
                    W. COLLINS (Persian Eclogues).

225. ODE WRITTEN IN 1746

How sleep the Brave who sink to rest,
By all their Country's wishes blest !
When Spring, with dewy fingers cold,
Returns to deck their hallowed mould,
She there shall dress a sweeter sod,
Than Fancy's feet have ever trod.

By fairy hands their knell is rung,
By forms unseen their dirge is sung ;
There Honour comes, a pilgrim grey,
To bless the turf that wraps their clay,
And Freedom shall awhile repair,
To dwell a weeping hermit there !   W. COLLINS.

226. TO EVENING

If aught of oaten stop or pastoral song
May hope, O pensive Eve, to soothe thine ear,
    Like thy own brawling springs,
    Thy springs, and dying gales,

O Nymph reserved, while now the bright-haired sun
Sits in yon western tent, whose cloudy skirts,
    With brede ethereal wove,
    O'erhang his wavy bed:

Now air is hushed, save where the weak-eyed bat,
With short shrill shriek flits by on leathern wing,
    Or when the beetle winds
    His small but sullen horn,

As oft he rises 'midst the twilight path,
Against the pilgrim borne in heedless hum:
    Now teach me, maid composed,
    To breathe some softened strain,

Whose numbers stealing through thy darkening vale,
May not unseemly with its stillness suit,
    As musing slow I hail
    Thy genial loved return.

For when thy folding-star arising shows
His paly circlet, at his warning lamp
    The fragrant Hours, and Elves
    Who slept in buds the day,

And many a Nymph who wreathes her brows with sedge,
And sheds the freshening dew, and, lovelier still,
    The pensive Pleasures sweet,
    Prepare thy shadowy car.

Then let me rove some wild and heathy scene,
Or find some ruin midst its dreary dells,
    Whose walls more awful nod
    By thy religious gleams.

Or if chill blustering winds or driving rain
Prevent my willing feet, be mine the hut
    That, from the mountain's side,
    Views wilds and swelling floods,

And hamlets brown, and dim-discovered spires,
And hears their simple bell, and marks o'er all
    Thy dewy fingers draw
    The gradual dusky veil.

While Spring shall pour his showers, as oft he wont,
And bathe thy breathing tresses, meekest Eve!
    While Summer loves to sport
    Beneath thy lingering light;

While sallow Autumn fills thy lap with leaves,
Or Winter, yelling through the troublous air,
    Affrights thy shrinking train,
    And rudely rends thy robes;

So long, regardful of thy quiet rule,
Shall Fancy, Friendship, Science, smiling Peace,
    Thy gentlest influence own,
    And love thy favourite name!

W. COLLINS.

227. DIRGE FOR FIDELE

To fair Fidele's grassy tomb
  Soft maids and village hinds shall bring
Each opening sweet of earliest bloom,
  And rifle all the breathing Spring.

No wailing ghost shall dare appear
  To vex with shrieks this quiet grove:
But shepherd lads assemble here,
  And melting virgins own their love.

No withered witch shall here be seen;
  No goblins lead their nightly crew:
The female fays shall haunt the green,
  And dress thy grave with pearly dew!

The redbreast oft at evening hours
  Shall kindly lend his little aid;
With hoary moss, and gathered flowers,
  To deck the ground where thou art laid.

When howling winds, and beating rain,
  In tempests shake the sylvan cell;
Or 'midst the chase on every plain,
  The tender thought on thee shall dwell.

Each lonely scene shall thee restore,
  For thee the tear be duly shed;
Beloved till life can charm no more,
  And mourned till Pity's self be dead.

W. COLLINS.

228. TO MUSIC

WHEN Music, heavenly maid, was young,
While yet in early Greece she sung,
The Passions oft to hear her shell,
Thronged around her magic cell,
Exulting, trembling, raging, fainting,
Possessed beyond the Muse's painting;
By turns they felt the glowing mind,
Disturbed, delighted, raised, refined,

Till once, 'tis said, when all were fired,
Filled with fury, rapt, inspired,
From the supporting myrtles round,
They snatched her instruments of sound,
And as they oft had heard apart
Sweet lessons of her forceful art,
Each, for madness ruled the hour,
Would prove his own expressive power.
                    W. COLLINS (*The Passions*).

229. A HUE AND CRY AFTER FAIR AMORET

FAIR Amoret is gone astray !
    Pursue and seek her, every lover !
I'll tell the signs by which you may
    The wandering shepherdess discover.

Coquet and coy at once her air,
    Both studied, though both seem neglected:
Careless she is, with artful care ;
    Affecting to seem unaffected.

With skill, her eyes dart every glance ;
    Yet change so soon, you'd ne'er suspect them:
For she'd persuade, they wound by chance ;
    Though certain aim and art direct them.

She likes herself, yet others hates
    For that which in herself she prizes,
And, while she laughs at them, forgets
    She is the thing that she despises.   W. CONGREVE.

230. FALSE THOUGH SHE BE TO ME

FALSE though she be to me and
        love,
    I'll ne'er pursue revenge ;
For still the charmer I approve,
    Though I deplore her change.

In hours of bliss we oft have met :
    They could not always last,
And though the present I regret,
    I'm grateful for the past.
                    W. CONGREVE.

231. MUSIC HAS CHARMS

MUSIC has charms to soothe a savage breast,
To soften rocks, or bend a knotted oak.
I've read that things inanimate have moved,
And, as with living souls, have been informed
By magic numbers and persuasive sound.
What then am I ? Am I more senseless grown
Than trees or flint ? O force of constant woe !
'Tis not in harmony to calm my griefs.
                    W. CONGREVE (*The Mourning Bride*).

232. SABINA WAKES

SEE! see, she wakes! Sabina wakes!
  And now the sun begins to rise!
Less glorious is the morn that breaks
  From his bright beams than her fair eyes.

With light united, day they give;
  But different fates ere night fulfil;
How many by his warmth will live!
  How many will her coldness kill!

W. CONGREVE.

233. DIAPHENIA

DIAPHENIA, like the daffadowndilly,
  White as the sun, fair as the lily,
Heigh-ho, how I do love thee!
  I do love thee as my lambs
  Are belovèd of their dams;
How blest were I if thou wouldst prove me.

Diaphenia, like the spreading roses,
  That in thy sweets all sweets encloses,
Fair sweet, how I do love thee!
  I do love thee as each flower
  Loves the sun's life-giving power;
For, dead, thy breath to life might move me.

Diaphenia, like to all things blessèd
  When all thy praises are expressèd,
Dear joy, how I do love thee!
  As the birds do love the spring,
  Or the bees their careful king:
Then in requite, sweet virgin, love me!

H. CONSTABLE.

234. FAREWELL, REWARDS AND FAIRIES

FAREWELL, rewards and fairies,
  Good housewives now may say,
For now foul sluts in dairies
  Do fare as well as they.
And though they sweep their hearths no less
  Than maids were wont to do,
Yet who of late for cleanliness
  Finds sixpence in her shoe?

Lament, lament, old Abbeys,
  The Fairies' lost command!
They did but change Priests' babies,
  But some have changed your land.
And all your children, sprung from thence,
  Are now grown Puritans,
Who live as Changelings ever since
  For love of your demains.

At morning and at evening both
  You merry were and glad,
So little care of sleep or sloth
  These pretty ladies had ;
When Tom came home from
    labour,
  Or Cis to milking rose,
Then merrily went their tabor,
  And nimbly went their toes.

Witness those rings and rounde-
    lays
  Of theirs, which yet remain,
Were footed in Queen Mary's days
  On many a grassy plain ;
But since of late, Elizabeth,
  And later, James came in,
They never danced on any heath
  As when the time hath been.

By which we note the Fairies
  Were of the old Profession.
Their songs were 'Ave Mary's',
  Their dances were Procession.
But now, alas, they all are dead ;
  Or gone beyond the seas ;
Or farther for Religion fled ;
  Or else they take their ease.

A tell-tale in their company
  They never could endure !
And whoso kept not secretly
  Their mirth, was punished, sure;
It was a just and Christian
    deed
  To pinch such black and blue.
Oh how the commonwealth doth
    want
  Such Justices as you !
                    R. CORBET.

235. TO VINCENT CORBET, HIS SON

WHAT I shall leave thee, none can
    tell,
But all shall say I wish thee
    well :
I wish thee, Vin, before all wealth,
Both bodily and ghostly health;
Nor too much wealth nor wit
    come to thee,
So much of either may undo thee.
I wish thee learning not for show,
Enough for to instruct and know ;
Not such as gentlemen require
To prate at table or at fire.

I wish thee all thy mother's graces,
Thy father's fortunes and his
    places.
I wish thee friends, and one at
    court,
Not to build on, but support ;
To keep thee not in doing many
Oppressions, but from suffering
    any.
I wish thee peace in all thy ways,
Nor lazy nor contentious days ;
And, when thy soul and body part,
As innocent as now thou art.
                    R. CORBET.

236. OH, EARLIER SHALL THE ROSEBUDS BLOW

OH, earlier shall the rosebuds blow,
  In after years, those happier years,
And children weep, when we lie low,
  Far fewer tears, far softer tears.

Oh, true shall boyish laughter ring,
  Like tinkling chimes, in kinder times !
And merrier shall the maiden sing :
  And I not there, and I not there.

Like lightning in the summer night
　Their mirth shall be, so quick and free;
And oh! the flash of their delight
　I shall not see, I may not see.

In deeper dream, with wider range,
　Those eyes shall shine, but not on mine:
Unmoved, unblest, by worldly change,
　The dead must rest, the dead shall rest.

W. J. CORY.

237. HERACLITUS

THEY told me, Heraclitus, they told me you were dead;
They brought me bitter news to hear and bitter tears to shed.
I wept as I remembered, how often you and I
Had tired the sun with talking and sent him down the sky.

And now that thou art lying, my dear old Carian guest,
A handful of grey ashes, long, long ago at rest,
Still are thy pleasant voices, thy nightingales, awake;
For Death, he taketh all away, but them he cannot take.

W. J. CORY.

238. MIMNERMUS IN CHURCH

YOU promise heavens free from strife,
　Pure truth, and perfect change of will;
But sweet, sweet is this human life,
　So sweet, I fain would breathe it still:
Your chilly stars I can forgo,
This warm kind world is all I know.

You say there is no substance here,
　One great reality above:
Back from that void I shrink in fear,
　And child-like hide myself in love:
Show me what angels feel. Till then,
I cling, a mere weak man, to men.

You bid me lift my mean desires
　From faltering lips and fitful veins
To sexless souls, ideal quires,
　Unwearied voices, wordless strains:
My mind with fonder welcome owns
One dear dead friend's remembered tones.

Forsooth the present we must give
　To that which cannot pass away;
All beauteous things for which we live
　By laws of time and space decay.
But oh, the very reason why
I clasp them, is because they die.

W. J. CORY.

239. TO CHLORIS

FAREWELL, my sweet, until I come,
  Improved in merit, for thy sake,
With characters of honour, home,
  Such as thou canst not then but take.

To loyalty my love must bow,
  My honour, too, calls to the field,
Where for a lady's busk I now
  Must keen and sturdy iron wield.

Yet, when I rush into those arms,
  Where death and danger do combine,
I shall less subject be to harms
  Than to those killing eyes of thine.

                                    C. COTTON.

240. FROM 'THE RETIREMENT'

GOOD God, how sweet are all things here,
How beautiful the fields appear,
How cleanly do we feed and lie,
Lord ! what good hours do we keep.
    How quietly we sleep.
    What peace, what unanimity !
How innocent from the lewd fashion
Is all our business, all our recreation !

          .   .   .   .   .

How calm and quiet a delight
    Is it, alone,
To read, and meditate, and write ;
By none offended, and offending none.
To walk, ride, sit, or sleep, at one's own ease,
And, pleasing a man's self, none other to displease !

                                    C. COTTON.

241. CONTENTATION

WHO from the busy world retires,
  To be more useful to it still,
And to no greater good aspires
  But only the eschewing ill.
Who with his angle and his books,
  Can think the longest day well spent,
And praises God when back he looks,
  And finds that all was innocent.
This man is happier far than he
  Whom public business oft betrays
Through labyrinths of policy
  To crooked and forbidden ways.

                                    C. COTTON.

242. A PARADISE BELOW

DEAR Chloe, while the busy crowd,
The vain, the wealthy and the
    proud,
  In folly's maze advance ;
Though singularity and pride
Be called our choice, we'll step
    aside,
  Nor join the giddy dance.

Though fools spurn Hymen's
    gentle powers,
We, who improve his golden hours,
  By sweet experience know,
That marriage, rightly understood,
Gives to the tender and the
    good
  A paradise below !
      N. COTTON (*The Fireside*).

243. CHEER UP, MY MATES

CHEER up, my mates, the wind does fairly blow ;
  Clap on more sail, and never spare ;
  Farewell, all lands, for now we are
  In the wide sea of drink, and merrily we go.
Bless me, 'tis hot ! another bowl of wine,
  And we shall cut the burning Line :
Hey, boys ! she scuds away, and by my head I know
  We round the world are sailing now.
What dull men are those who tarry at home,
When abroad they might wantonly roam,
  And gain such experience, and spy, too,
  Such countries and wonders, as I do !
But pr'ythee, good pilot, take heed what you do,
  And fail not to touch at Peru !
  With gold there the vessel we'll store,
  And never, and never be poor,
  No, never be poor any more.

A. COWLEY
*(Sitting and drinking in the chair made out of the
    relics of Sir Francis Drake's ship).*

244. FILL THE BOWL WITH ROSY WINE

FILL the bowl with rosy wine,
Around our temples roses twine,
And let us cheerfully awhile,
Like the wine and roses, smile.
Crowned with roses, we contemn
Gyges' wealthy diadem.

To-day is ours ; what do we fear ?
To-day is ours ; we have it here !
Let 's treat it kindly, that it may
Wish, at least, with us to stay.
Let 's banish business, banish sorrow,
To the gods belongs to-morrow.   A. COWLEY.

245. THE SWALLOW

Foolish prater, what dost thou
So early at my window do?

Cruel bird, thou'st ta'en away
A dream out of my arms to-day;
A dream that ne'er must equalled be

By all that waking eyes may see.
Thou this damage to repair
Nothing half so sweet or fair,
Nothing half so good, canst bring,
Though men say thou bring'st the
　　Spring.　　　　　A. Cowley.

246. LARGE WAS HIS SOUL

Large was his soul; as large a soul as e'er
Submitted to inform a body here;
High as the place 'twas shortly in Heaven to have,
　　But low and humble as his grave.
So high that all the virtues there did come,
　　　　As to their chiefest seat
　　　　Conspicuous and great;
So low, that for me too it made a room.

Knowledge he only sought, and so soon caught
As if for him Knowledge had rather sought;
Nor did more learning ever crowded lie
　　In such a short mortality.
Whene'er the skilful youth discoursed or writ,
　　　　Still did the notions throng
　　　　About his eloquent tongue;
Nor could his ink flow faster than his wit.

His mirth was the pure spirits of various wit,
Yet never did his God or friends forget;
And when deep talk and wisdom came in view,
　　Retired, and gave to them their due.
For the rich help of books he always took,
　　　　Though his own searching mind before
　　　　Was so with notions written o'er,
As if wise Nature had made that her book.
　　　　A. Cowley (*On the death of Mr. William Harvey*).

247. LIFE

Life's a name
　　That nothing here can truly claim;
This wretched inn, where we scarce stay to bait,
　　We call our dwelling-place!

　　And mighty voyages we take,
　　And mighty journeys seem to make,
O'er sea and land, the little point that has no space.
　　Because we fight and battles gain,
Some captives call, and say, ' The rest are slain;'
Because we heap up yellow earth, and so
Rich, valiant, wise, and virtuous seem to grow;

Because we draw a long nobility
From hieroglyphic proofs of heraldry,
And impudently talk of a posterity—
. . . . . .
We grow at last by custom to believe,
  That really we live ;
Whilst all these shadows, that for things we take,
Are but the empty dreams which in Death's sleep we make.
                                        A. COWLEY.

248. WITHOUT AND WITHIN

LOVE in her sunny eyes doth basking play ;
  Love walks the pleasant mazes of her hair ;
Love does on both her lips for ever stray,
  And sows and reaps a thousand kisses there :
In all her outward parts Love's always seen ;
But oh ! he never went within.   A. COWLEY.

249. THE CHRONICLE

MARGARITA first possessed,
If I remember well, my breast ;
    Margarita, first of all !
        But when a while the wanton maid
        With my restless heart had played,
    Martha took the flying ball.

Martha soon did it resign
To the beauteous Catharine.
    Beauteous Catharine gave place
        (Though loath and angry she to part
        With the possession of my heart)
    To Eliza's conquering face.

Eliza till this hour might reign,
Had not she ill counsels ta'en.
    Fundamental laws she broke ;
        And still new favourites she chose,
        Till up in arms my passions rose,
    And cast away her yoke.

Mary then and gentle Anne
Both to reign at once began.
    Alternately they swayed ;
        And sometimes Mary was the fair,
        And sometimes Anne the crown did wear ;
    And sometimes both I obeyed.

Another Mary then arose
And did rigorous laws impose ;
    A mighty tyrant she !
        Long, alas, should I have been
        Under that iron-sceptred Queen,
    Had not Rebecca set me free.

When fair Rebecca set me free,
Twas then a golden time with me.
  But soon those pleasures fled,
    For the gracious Princess died
    In her youth and beauty's pride,
  And Judith reigned in her stead.

One month, three days, and half an hour,
Judith held the sovereign power.
  Wondrous beautiful her face ;
    But so weak and small her wit
    That she to govern was unfit,
  And so Susanna took her place.

But when Isabella came,
Armed with a resistless flame
  And th' artillery of her eye,
    Whilst she proudly marched about
    Greater conquests to find out,
  She beat out Susan by the by.

      .   .   .   .   .   .

But I will briefer with them be,
Since few of them were long with me.
  A higher and a nobler strain
    My present Empress does claim:
    Heleonora, first o' th' name,
  Whom God grant long to reign !

                                    A. COWLEY.

250. POET AND SAINT

POET and Saint ! to thee alone are given
The two most sacred names of earth and heaven,
The hard and rarest union which can be,
Next that of Godhead with humanity.
Long did the Muses banished slaves abide,
And built vain pyramids to mortal pride :
Like Moses, thou (though spells and charms withstand)
Hast brought them nobly home back to their Holy Land.
  Ah, wretched we, poets of earth ! but thou
Wert living the same poet which thou'rt now.
Whilst angels sing to thee their airs divine,
And joy in an applause so great as thine.
Equal society with them to hold,
Thou need'st not make new songs, but say the old.
And they (kind spirits !) shall all rejoice to see
How little less than they exalted man may be.
            A. COWLEY (*On the death of Mr. Crashaw*).

251. SPORT

THE merry waves dance up and down and play,
    Sport is granted to the sea ;
Birds are the quiristers of the empty air,
    Sport is never wanting there ;
The ground doth smile at the spring's flowery birth,
    Sport is granted to the earth ;
The fire its cheering flame on high doth rear,
    Sport is never wanting there.
If all the elements, the earth, the sea,
    Air, and fire, so merry be,
Why is man's mirth so seldom and so small,
    Who is compounded of them all ?

A. COWLEY.

252. DRINKING

THE thirsty earth soaks up the rain,
And drinks, and gapes for drink again.
The plants suck in the earth, and are
With constant drinking fresh and fair ;
The sea itself—which one would think
Should have but little need of drink—
Drinks ten thousand rivers up,
So filled that they o'erflow the cup.
The busy sun—and one would guess
By 's drunken fiery face no less—
Drinks up the sea, and when he 's done,
The moon and stars drink up the sun :
They drink and dance by their own light ;
They drink and revel all the night.
Nothing in nature's sober found,
But an eternal health goes round.
Fill up the bowl then, fill it high,
Fill up the glasses there ; for why
Should every creature drink but Ĭ ;
Why, man of morals, tell me why ?

A. COWLEY.

253. TO HIS MISTRESS

TYRIAN dye why do you wear,
You whose cheeks best scarlet are ?
    Why do you fondly pin
    Pure linens o'er your skin,
    Your skin that 's whiter far ?—
Casting a dusky cloud before a star

Why bears your neck a golden chain ?
Did Nature make your hair in vain,
  Of gold most pure and fine ?
  With gems why do you shine ?
  They, neighbours to your eyes,
Show but like Phosphor when the Sun doth rise.

I would have all my mistress' parts
Owe more to Nature than the arts ;
  I would not woo the dress,
  Or one whose nights give less
  Contentment than the day ;
She's fair whose beauty only makes her gay.

A. COWLEY.

254. WELCOME, GREAT STAGIRITE

WELCOME, great Stagirite ! and teach me now
  All I was born to know.
Thy scholar's victories thou dost far outdo ;
  He conquered th' earth ; the whole world you !
Welcome, learned Cicero ! whose blessed tongue and wit
  Preserves Rome's greatness yet.
Thou art the first of orators ; only he
  Who best can praise thee, next must be.
Welcome, the Mantuan swan, Virgil the wise ;
  Whose verse walks highest, but not flies ;
Who brought green Poesy to her perfect age,
  And mad'st that art which was a rage.
Tell me, ye mighty Three, what shall I do
  To be like one of you ?
But you have climbed the mountain's top ! there sit
  On the calm flourishing head of it ;
And whilst, with wearied steps, we upward go,
  See us, and clouds, below.

A. COWLEY.

255. THE WISH

WELL then, I now do plainly see
This busy world and I shall ne'er agree.
The very honey of all earthly joy
Does, of all meats, the soonest cloy ;
  And they, methinks, deserve my pity
Who for it can endure the stings,
The crowd and buzz and murmurings
  Of this great hive, the city !

Ah yet, ere I descend to the grave,
May I a small house and large garden have ;
And a few friends, and many books, both true,
Both wise, and both delightful too !
   And since Love ne'er will from me flee,—
A Mistress moderately fair,
And good as guardian angels are,
   Only beloved, and loving me !

O founts ! Oh, when in you shall I
Myself eased of unpeaceful thoughts espy ?
O fields ! O woods ! when, when shall I be made
The happy tenant of your shade ?
   Here 's the spring-head of Pleasure's flood !
Here 's wealthy Nature's treasury,
Where all the riches lie that she
   Has coined and stamped for good.

Pride and ambition here
Only in far-fetched metaphors appear ;
Here naught but winds can hurtful murmurs scatter,
And naught but echo flatter.
   The gods, when they descended, hither
From heaven did always choose their way ;
And therefore we may boldly say
   That 'tis the way too thither.

How happy here should I
And one dear She live, and embracing die !
She who is all the world, and can exclude
In deserts solitude.
   I should have then this only fear :
Lest men, when they my pleasures see,
Should all come imitate me,
   And so make a city here.   A. COWLEY.

256. MILTON

AGES elapsed ere Homer's lamp appeared,
And ages ere the Mantuan swan was heard :
To carry nature lengths unknown before,
To give a Milton birth, asked ages more.
Thus genius rose and set at ordered times,
And shot a dayspring into distant climes,
Ennobling every region that he chose ;
He sunk in Greece, in Italy he rose ;
And, tedious years of Gothic darkness passed,
Emerged all splendour in our isle at last.
Thus lovely halcyons dive into the main,
Then show far off their shining plumes again.
     W. COWPER (*Table Talk*).

257. BOOKS

Books are not seldom talismans and spells,
By which the magic art of shrewder wits
Holds an unthinking multitude enthralled.
Some to the fascination of a name
Surrender judgement, hoodwinked.   Some the style
Infatuates, and through labyrinths and wilds
Of error leads them by a tune entranced.
While sloth seduces more, too weak to bear
The insupportable fatigue of thought,
And swallowing, therefore, without pause or choice,
The total grist unsifted, husks and all.

W. Cowper (*The Task*, Bk. vi).

258. EVENING

Come, Evening, once again, season of peace ;
Return, sweet Evening, and continue long !
Methinks I see thee in the streaky west,
With matron-step slow-moving, while the night
Treads on thy sweeping train ; one hand employed
In letting fall the curtain of repose
On bird and beast, the other charged for man
With sweet oblivion of the cares of day :
Not sumptuously adorned, nor needing aid,
Like homely-featured night, of clustering gems :
A star or two, just twinkling on thy brow,
Suffices thee ; save that the moon is thine
No less than hers, not worn indeed on high
With ostentatious pageantry, but set
With modest grandeur in thy purple zone,
Resplendent less, but of an ampler round.

W. Cowper (*The Task*, Bk. iv).

259. ENGLAND

England, with all thy faults, I love thee still—
My country ! and, while yet a nook is left
Where English minds and manners may be found,
Shall be constrained to love thee.   Though thy clime
Be fickle, and thy year most part deformed
With dripping rains, or withered by a frost,
I would not yet exchange thy sullen skies,
And fields without a flower, for warmer France
With all her vines ; nor for Ausonia's groves
Of golden fruitage, and her myrtle bowers.

W. Cowper (*The Task*, Bk. ii).

260. EPITAPH ON A HARE

HERE lies, whom hound did ne'er pursue,
  Nor swifter greyhound follow,
Whose foot ne'er tainted morning dew,
  Nor ear heard huntsman's hallo,

Old Tiney, surliest of his kind,
  Who, nursed with tender care,
And to domestic bounds confined,
  Was still a wild Jack-hare.

Though duly from my hand he took
  His pittance every night,
He did it with a jealous look,
  And, when he could, would bite.

His diet was of wheaten bread,
  And milk, and oats, and straw,
Thistles, or lettuces instead,
  With sand to scour his maw.

On twigs of hawthorn he regaled,
  On pippins' russet peel ;
And, when his juicy salads failed,
  Sliced carrot pleased him well.

A Turkey carpet was his lawn,
  Whereon he loved to bound,
To skip and gambol like a fawn,
  And swing his rump around.

His frisking was at evening hours,
  For then he lost his fear ;
But most before approaching showers,
  Or when a storm drew near.

Eight years and five round-rolling moons
  He thus saw steal away,
Dozing out all his idle noons,
  And every night at play.

I kept him for his humour' sake,
  For he would oft beguile
My heart of thoughts that made it ache,
  And force me to a smile.

But now, beneath this walnut-shade
  He finds his long, last home,
And waits in snug concealment laid,
  Till gentler Puss shall come.

He, still more aged, feels the shocks
  From which no care can save,
And, partner once of Tiney's box,
  Must soon partake his grave.

                    W. COWPER.

261.   THE SOLITUDE OF ALEXANDER SELKIRK

I AM monarch of all I survey,
  My right there is none to dispute;
From the centre all round to the sea
  I am lord of the fowl and the brute.
O solitude! where are the charms
  That sages have seen in thy face?
Better dwell in the midst of alarms
  Than reign in this horrible place.

I am out of humanity's reach,
  I must finish my journey alone,
Never hear the sweet music of speech;
  I start at the sound of my own.
The beasts, that roam over the plain,
  My form with indifference see;
They are so unacquainted with man,
  Their tameness is shocking to me.

Society, friendship, and love,
  Divinely bestowed upon man,
Oh, had I the wings of a dove,
  How soon would I taste you again!
My sorrows I then might assuage
  In the ways of religion and truth,
Might learn from the wisdom of age,
  And be cheered by the sallies of youth.

Religion! what treasure untold
  Resides in that heavenly word!
More precious than silver and gold,
  Or all that this earth can afford.
But the sound of the church-going bell
  These valleys and rocks never heard,
Ne'er sighed at the sound of a knell,
  Or smiled when a sabbath appeared.

Ye winds, that have made me your sport,
  Convey to this desolate shore
Some cordial endearing report
  Of a land I shall visit no more.
My friends, do they now and then send
  A wish or a thought after me?
O tell me I yet have a friend,
  Though a friend I am never to see.

How fleet is a glance of the mind!
  Compared with the speed of its flight,
The tempest itself lags behind,
  And the swift-winged arrows of light.

When I think of my own native land,
  In a moment I seem to be there;
But alas! recollection at hand
  Soon hurries me back to despair.

But the seafowl is gone to her nest,
  The beast is laid down in his lair;
Even here is a season of rest,
  And I to my cabin repair.
There is mercy in every place;
  And mercy, encouraging thought!
Gives even affliction a grace,
  And reconciles man to his lot.   W. COWPER.

262.   I WOULD NOT ENTER ON MY LIST OF FRIENDS

I WOULD not enter on my list of friends
(Though graced with polished manners and fine sense,
Yet wanting sensibility) the man
Who needlessly sets foot upon a worm.
An inadvertent step may crush the snail
That crawls at evening in the public path;
But he that has humanity, forewarned,
Will tread aside and let the reptile live.
The creeping vermin, loathsome to the sight,
And charged perhaps with venom, that intrudes,
A visitor unwelcome, into scenes
Sacred to neatness and repose—th' alcove,
The chamber, or refectory—may die:
A necessary act incurs no blame.

  .   .   .   .

The sum is this.—If man's convenience, health,
Or safety, interfere, his rights and claims
Are paramount, and must extinguish theirs.
                 W. COWPER (*The Task*, Bk. vi).

263.   TO MARY UNWIN

MARY! I want a lyre with other strings;
Such aid from Heaven as some have feigned they drew!
An eloquence scarce given to mortals, new,
And undebased by praise of meaner things!
That, ere through age or woe I shed my wings,
I may record thy worth, with honour due,
In verse as musical as thou art true,—
Verse, that immortalizes whom it sings!

But thou hast little need : there is a book,
By seraphs writ with beams of heavenly light,
On which the eyes of God not rarely look ;
A chronicle of actions just and bright !
　　There all thy deeds, my faithful Mary, shine,
　　And since thou own'st that praise, I spare thee mine.
　　　　　　　　　　　　　　　W. COWPER.

264. THE WINTER EVENING

Now stir the fire, and close the shutters fast,
Let fall the curtains, wheel the sofa round,
And, while the bubbling and loud-hissing urn
Throws up a steamy column, and the cups,
That cheer but not inebriate, wait on each,
So let us welcome peaceful evening in.
Not such his evening who, with shining face,
Sweats in the crowded theatre, and, squeezed
And bored with elbow-points through both his sides,
Outscolds the ranting actor on the stage :
Nor his, who patient stands till his feet throb,
And his head thumps, to feed upon the breath
Of patriots, bursting with heroic rage,
Or placemen, all tranquillity and smiles.
　　　　　　　　　　W. COWPER (*The Task*, Bk. iv).

265. OH THAT THOSE LIPS HAD LANGUAGE

OH that those lips had language ! Life has passed
With me but roughly since I heard thee last.
Those lips are thine—thy own sweet smiles I see,
The same that oft in childhood solaced me ;
Voice only fails, else, how distinct they say,
' Grieve not, my child, chase all thy fears away ! '
The meek intelligence of those dear eyes
(Blest be the art that can immortalize,
The art that baffles time's tyrannic claim
To quench it) here shines on me still the same.
Faithful remembrancer of one so dear,
Oh welcome guest, though unexpected, here !
Who bidd'st me honour with an artless song,
Affectionate, a mother lost so long,
I will obey, not willingly alone,
But gladly, as the precept were her own ;
And, while that face renews my filial grief,
Fancy shall weave a charm in my relief—
Shall steep me in Elysian reverie,
A momentary dream, that thou art she.
　　　　　　　　W. COWPER (*On the receipt of my mother's
　　　　　　　　　　　picture out of Norfolk*).

266. TO A YOUNG LADY

SWEET stream that winds through yonder glade,
Apt emblem of a virtuous maid—
Silent and chaste she steals along,
Far from the world's gay busy throng,
With gentle, yet prevailing, force
Intent upon her destined course ;
Graceful and useful all she does,
Blessing and blest where'er she goes,
Pure-bosomed as that watery glass,
And heaven reflected in her face.

W. COWPER.

267. TO MARY

THE twentieth year is wellnigh past,
Since first our sky was overcast ;
Ah would that this might be the last !
    My Mary !

Thy spirits have a fainter flow,
I see thee daily weaker grow—
'Twas my distress that brought thee low,
    My Mary !

Thy needles, once a shining store,
For my sake restless heretofore,
Now rust disused, and shine no more,
    My Mary !

For though thou gladly wouldst fulfil
The same kind office for me still,
Thy sight now seconds not thy will,
    My Mary !

But well thou playedst the housewife's part,
And all thy threads with magic art
Have wound themselves about this heart,
    My Mary !

Thy indistinct expressions seem
Like language uttered in a dream ;
Yet me they charm, whate'er the theme,
    My Mary !

Thy silver locks, once auburn bright,
Are still more lovely in my sight
Than golden beams of orient light,
    My Mary !

F

For could I view nor them nor thee,
What sight worth seeing could I see ?
The sun would rise in vain for me,
        My Mary !

Partakers of thy sad decline,
Thy hands their little force resign ;
Yet, gently pressed, press gently mine,
        My Mary !

And then I feel that still I hold
A richer store ten thousandfold
Than misers fancy in their gold,
        My Mary !

Such feebleness of limbs thou prov'st
That now at every step thou mov'st
Upheld by two ; yet still thou lov'st,
        My Mary !

And still to love, though pressed with ill,
In wintry age to feel no chill,
With me is to be lovely still,
        My Mary !

But oh ! by constant heed I know
How oft the sadness that I show
Transforms thy smiles to looks of woe,
        My Mary !

And should my future lot be cast
With much resemblance of the past,
Thy worn-out heart will break at last,
        My Mary !

                                    W. COWPER.

268.   A SYMPATHY WITH SOUNDS

THERE is in souls a sympathy with sounds ;
And, as the mind is pitched, the ear is pleased
With melting airs, or martial, brisk or grave :
Some chord in unison with what we hear
Is touched within us, and the heart replies.
How soft the music of those village bells,
Falling at intervals upon the ear
In cadence sweet, now dying all away,
Now pealing loud again, and louder still,
Clear and sonorous, as the gale comes on !
                        W. COWPER (*The Task*, Bk. vi).

269. ON THE LOSS OF THE ROYAL GEORGE

TOLL for the brave—
The brave! that are no more:
  All sunk beneath the wave,
Fast by their native shore.
  Eight hundred of the brave,
Whose courage well was tried,
  Had made the vessel heel
And laid her on her side;
  A land-breeze shook the
    shrouds,
And she was overset;
  Down went the Royal George,
With all her crew complete.

Toll for the brave—
Brave Kempenfelt is gone,
  His last sea-fight is fought,
His work of glory done.
  It was not in the battle,
No tempest gave the shock,

She sprang no fatal leak,
She ran upon no rock;
  His sword was in the sheath,
His fingers held the pen,
  When Kempenfelt went down
With twice four hundred men.

  Weigh the vessel up,
Once dreaded by our foes,
  And mingle with your cup
The tears that England owes;
  Her timbers yet are sound,
And she may float again,
  Full charged with England's
    thunder,
And plough the distant main;
  But Kempenfelt is gone,
His victories are o'er;
  And he and his Eight hundred
Must plough the wave no more.

                    W. COWPER.

270. FROM ' CHARITY '

WHEN one, that holds communion with the skies,
Has filled his urn where these pure waters rise,
And once more mingles with us meaner things,
'Tis even as if an angel shook his wings;
Immortal fragrance fills the circuit wide,
That tells us whence his treasures are supplied.
So, when a ship well-freighted with the stores
The sun matures on India's spicy shores,
Has dropped her anchor and her canvas furled
In some safe haven of our western world,
'Twere vain inquiry to what port she went;
The gale informs us, laden with the scent.
Some seek, when queasy conscience has its qualms,
To lull the painful malady with alms;
But charity, not feigned, intends alone
Another's good—theirs centres in their own;
And, too short-lived to reach the realms of peace,
Must cease for ever when the poor shall cease.
Flavia, most tender of her own good name,
Is rather careless of her sister's fame:
Her superfluity the poor supplies,
But, if she touch a character, it dies.

The seeming virtue weighed against the vice,
She deems all safe, for she has paid the price:
No charity but alms aught values she,
Except in porcelain on her mantel-tree.
How many deeds, with which the world has rung,
From pride, in league with ignorance, have sprung!
But God o'errules all human follies still,
And bends the tough materials to His will.
A conflagration or a wintry flood
Has left some hundreds without home or food;
Extravagance and avarice shall subscribe,
While fame and self-complacence are the bribe.
The brief proclaimed, it visits every pew,
But first the squire's—a compliment but due.
With slow deliberation he unties
His glittering purse—that envy of all eyes!
And, while the clerk just puzzles out the psalm,
Slides guinea behind guinea in his palm;
Till, finding (what he might have found before)
A smaller piece amidst the precious store,
Pinched close between his finger and his thumb,
He half exhibits, and then drops the sum.
Gold, to be sure!—Throughout the town 'tis told
How the good squire gives never less than gold.
From motives such as his, though not the best,
Springs in due time supply for the distressed;
Not less effectual than what love bestows—
Except that office clips it as it goes.

W. COWPER.

271. BOADICEA: AN ODE

WHEN the British warrior queen,
　　Bleeding from the Roman rods,
Sought, with an indignant mien,
　　Counsel of her country's gods,

Sage beneath a spreading oak
　　Sat the Druid, hoary chief;
Every burning word he spoke
　　Full of rage, and full of grief.

' Princess! if our aged eyes
　　Weep upon thy matchless wrongs,
'Tis because resentment ties
　　All the terrors of our tongues.

' Rome shall perish—write that word
　　In the blood that she has spilt;
Perish, hopeless and abhorred,
　　Deep in ruin as in guilt.

'Rome, for empire far renowned
   Tramples on a thousand states;
Soon her pride shall kiss the ground—
   Hark! the Gaul is at her gates!

'Other Romans shall arise,
   Heedless of a soldier's name;
Sounds, not arms, shall win the prize—
   Harmony the path to fame.

'Then the progeny that springs
   From the forests of our land,
Armed with thunder, clad with wings,
   Shall a wider world command.

'Regions Caesar never knew
   Thy posterity shall sway,
Where his eagles never flew,
   None invincible as they.'

Such the bard's prophetic words,
   Pregnant with celestial fire,
Bending, as he swept the chords
   Of his sweet but awful lyre.

She, with all a monarch's pride,
   Felt them in her bosom glow;
Rushed to battle, fought, and died;
   Dying, hurled them at the foe.

'Ruffians, pitiless as proud,
   Heaven awards the vengeance due;
Empire is on us bestowed,
   Shame and ruin wait for you.'

                                        W. COWPER.

272. ALDBOROUGH

HERE, wandering long, amid these frowning fields,
I sought the simple life that Nature yields;
Rapine and Wrong and Fear usurped her place,
And a bold, artful, surly, savage race;
Who, only skilled to take the finny tribe,
The yearly dinner, or septennial bribe,
Wait on the shore, and, as the waves run high,
On the tossed vessel bend their eager eye,
Which to their coast directs its venturous way,
Theirs or the ocean's, miserable prey.
As on their neighbouring beach yon swallows stand,
And wait for favouring winds to leave the land;
While still for flight the ready wing is spread:
So waited I the favouring hour, and fled;

Fled from these shores where guilt and famine reign,
And cried, Ah ! hapless they who still remain ;
Who still remain to hear the ocean roar,
Whose greedy waves devour the lessening shore ;
Till some fierce tide, with more imperious sway,
Sweeps the low hut and all it holds away.

G. CRABBE (*The Village*).

273. HIS MOTHER'S WEDDING-RING

THE ring so worn, as you behold,
So thin, so pale, is yet of gold :
The passion such it was to prove ;
Worn with life's cares, love yet was love.

G. CRABBE.

274. BOOKS

THEY give
New views to life, and teach us how to live ;
They soothe the grieved, the stubborn they chastise,
Fools they admonish, and confirm the wise :
Their aid they yield to all : they never shun
The man of sorrow, nor the wretch undone :
Unlike the hard, the selfish, and the proud,
They fly not sullen from the suppliant crowd ;
Nor tell to various people various things,
But show to subjects what they show to kings.

. . . .

Now bid thy soul man's busy scenes exclude,
And view composed this silent multitude :—
Silent they are, but, though deprived of sound,
Here all the living languages abound ;
Here all that live no more ; preserved they lie,
In tombs that open to the curious eye.
Blessed be the gracious Power, who taught mankind
To stamp a lasting image of the mind !

G. CRABBE (*The Library*).

275. LATE WISDOM

WE'VE trod the maze of error round,
    Long wandering in the winding glade ;
And now the torch of truth is found,
    It only shows us where we strayed :
Light for ourselves, what is it worth,
    When we no more our way can choose ?
For others when we hold it forth,
    They, in their pride, the boon refuse.

By long experience taught, we now
    Can rightly judge of friends and foes,
Can all the worth of these allow,
    And all their faults discern in those.
Relentless hatred, erring love,
    We can for sacred truth forgo ;
We can the warmest friend reprove,
    And bear to praise the fiercest foe :
To what effect ? Our friends are gone
    Beyond reproof, regard or care ;
And of our foes remains there one
    The mild relenting thoughts to share ?

Now 'tis our boast that we can quell
    The wildest passions in their rage ;
Can their destructive force repel,
    And their impetuous wrath assuage :
Ah ! Virtue, dost thou arm, when now
    This bold rebellious race are fled ;
When all these tyrants rest, and thou
    Art warring with the mighty dead ?
                    G. CRABBE (*Reflections*).

276. PHILOMELA

HER supple breast thrills out
Sharp airs, and staggers in a warbling doubt
Of dallying sweetness, hovers o'er her skill,
And folds in waved notes with a trembling bill
The pliant series of her slippery song ;
Then starts she suddenly into a throng
Of short thick sobs, whose thundering volleys float
And roll themselves over her lubric throat
In panting murmurs stilled out of her breast,
That ever-bubbling spring, the sugared nest
Of her delicious soul, that there does lie
Bathing in streams of liquid melody.
        .   .   .   .   .

And while she thus discharges a shrill peal
Of flashing airs, she qualifies their zeal
With the cool epode of a graver note,
Thus high, thus low, as if her silver throat
Would reach the brazen note of War's hoarse bird.
Her little soul is ravished, and so poured
Into loose ecstasies, that she is placed
Above herself, Music's enthusiast !
                    R. CRASHAW (*Music's Duel*).

277. ON GEORGE HERBERT'S 'THE TEMPLE' SENT TO A GENTLEWOMAN

Know you, fair, on what you look ?
Divinest love lies in this book :
Expecting fire from your fair eyes,
To kindle this his sacrifice.
When your hands untie these strings,
Think, you've an angel by the wings ;
One that gladly would be nigh,
To wait upon each morning sigh ;
To flutter in the balmy air
Of your well-perfumèd prayer ;

These white plumes of his he'll lend you,
Which every day to heaven will send you :
To take acquaintance of each sphere,
And all your smooth-faced kindred there.
And though Herbert's name do owe
These devotions, fairest, know
While I thus lay them on the shrine
Of your white hand, they are mine.   R. CRASHAW.

278. ON A PRAYER BOOK SENT TO MRS. M. R.

Lo, here a little volume, but great book !
A nest of new-born sweets,
Whose native fires disdaining
To be thus folded, and complaining
Of these ignoble sheets,
Affect more comely bands,
Fair one, from thy kind hands,
And confidently look
To find the rest
Of a rich binding in your breast !

It is in one choice handful, heaven ; and all
Heaven's royal host; encamped thus small
To prove that true, schools use to tell,
A thousand angels in one point can dwell.

It is love's great artillery,
Which here contracts itself, and comes to lie
Close couched in your white bosom ; and from thence,
As from a snowy fortress of defence,
Against your ghostly foes to take your part,
And fortify the hold of your chaste heart.

It is an armoury of light ;
Let constant use but keep it bright,
        You'll find it yields
To holy hands and humble hearts
        More swords and shields

Than sin hath snares, or hell hath darts.
      Only be sure
      The hands be pure
That hold these weapons, and the eyes
Those of turtles, chaste and true,
      Wakeful, and wise;
Here is a friend shall fight for you;
Hold but this book before your heart,
Let prayer alone to play his part.   R. CRASHAW.

279. SAINT TERESA

O THOU undaunted daughter of desires!
By all thy dower of lights and fires;
By all the eagle in thee, all the dove;
By all thy lives and deaths of love;
By thy large draughts of intellectual day,
And by thy thirsts of love more large than they;
By all thy brim-filled bowls of fierce desire;
By thy last morning's draught of liquid fire;
By the full kingdom of that final kiss
That seized thy parting soul, and sealed thee His;
By all the heavens thou hast in Him
(Fair sister of the seraphim!);
By all of Him we have in thee;
Leave nothing of myself in me.
Let me so read thy life, that I
Unto all life of mine may die!   R. CRASHAW.

280. AN EPITAPH UPON HUSBAND AND WIFE WHO DIED AND WERE BURIED TOGETHER

To these whom death again did wed
This grave's their second marriage-bed.
For though the hand of Fate could force
'Twixt soul and body a divorce,
It could not sever man and wife,
'Cause they both lived but one life.
Peace, good reader, do not weep;
Peace, the lovers are asleep.
They, sweet turtles, folded lie
In the last knot Love could tie.
Let them sleep, let them sleep on,
Till this stormy night be gone,
And the eternal morrow dawn;
Then the curtains will be drawn,
And they wake into that light
Whose day shall never die in night.   R. CRASHAW.

281.   TWO WENT UP INTO THE TEMPLE TO PRAY

Two went to pray ? oh, rather say
One went to brag, the other to pray.

One stands up close, and treads on high,
Where the other dares not send his eye.

One nearer to God's altar trod ;
The other to the altar's God.

R. CRASHAW.

282.   THE SHEPHERD'S SONG

WE saw thee in thy balmy nest,
  Young dawn of our eternal day ;
We saw thine eyes break from the east,
  And chase the trembling shades away.
We saw thee, and we blessed the sight ;
We saw thee by thine own sweet light.

Poor world, said I, what wilt thou do
  To entertain this starry stranger ?
Is this the best thou canst bestow—
  A cold and not too cleanly manger ?
Contend, the powers of heaven and earth,
To fit a bed for this huge birth.

Proud world, said I, cease your contest,
  And let the mighty babe alone ;
The phoenix builds the phoenix' nest,
  Love's architecture is his own.
The babe, whose birth embraves this morn,
Made his own bed ere He was born.

R. CRASHAW (*A Hymn of the Nativity*).

283.   FROM 'WISHES FOR THE SUPPOSED MISTRESS.'

Whoe'er she be,
That not impossible She
That shall command my heart and me ;

Where'er she lie,
Locked up from mortal eye
In shady leaves of destiny :

Till that ripe birth
Of studied Fate stand forth,
And teach her fair steps to our earth ;

Till that divine
Idea take a shrine
Of crystal flesh, through which to shine :

—Meet you her, my Wishes,
Bespeak her to my blisses,
And be ye-called my absent kisses.

I wish her Beauty
That owes not all his duty
To gaudy tire, or glistering shoe-tie ;

Something more than
Taffeta or tissue can,
Or rampant feather, or rich fan.

More than the spoil
Of shops or silkworm's toil,
Or a bought blush, or a set smile.

A face that 's best
By its own beauty drest,
And can, alone, command the rest.

A face, made up
Out of no other shop
Than what Nature's white hand sets ope.

A cheek where youth
And blood, with pen of truth,
Write what the reader sweetly rueth.

A cheek where grows
More than a morning rose ;
Which to no box his being owes.

Lips where all day
A lover's kiss may play
Yet carry nothing thence away.

Looks that oppress
Their richest tires, but dress
And clothe their simplest nakedness.

Eyes that displace
The neighbour diamond, and outface
That sunshine by their own sweet grace.

Tresses that wear
Jewels but to declare
How much themselves more precious are,

Whose native ray
Can tame the wanton day
Of gems, that in their bright shades play.

R. CRASHAW.

284.   EUTHANASIA

WOULDST see blithe looks, fresh cheeks beguile
Age ? wouldst see December smile ?
Wouldst see nests of new roses grow
In a bed of reverend snow ?
Warm thoughts, free spirits, flattering
Winter's self into a spring ?
In sum wouldst see a man that can
Live to be old, and still a man ?
Whose latest and most leaden hours,
Fall with soft wings stuck with soft flowers ;
And, when life's sweet fable ends,
Soul and body part like friends ;
No quarrels, murmurs, no delay—
A kiss, a sigh, and so away.
This rare one, reader, wouldst thou see ?
Hark hither !—and thyself be he.

R. CRASHAW.

285.   A WET SHEET AND A FLOWING SEA

A WET sheet and a flowing sea,
  A wind that follows fast
And fills the white and rustling sail
  And bends the gallant mast ;
And bends the gallant mast, my boys,
  While like the eagle free
Away the good ship flies and leaves
  Old England on the lee.

O for a soft and gentle wind !
  I heard a fair one cry :
But give to me the snoring breeze
  And white waves heaving high ;
And white waves heaving high, my lads,
  The good ship tight and free—
The world of waters is our home,
  And merry men are we.

There 's tempest in yon hornèd moon,
  And lightning in yon cloud ;
But hark the music, mariners !
  The wind is piping loud ;
The wind is piping loud, my boys,
  The lightning flashes free—
While the hollow oak our palace is,
  Our heritage the sea.

A. CUNNINGHAM.

286. HAME, HAME, HAME

HAME, hame, hame, O hame fain wad I be,
O, hame, hame, hame, to my ain countree!

When the flower is i' the bud and the leaf is on the tree,
The larks shall sing me hame in my ain countree.
Hame, hame, hame, O hame fain wad I be,
O hame, hame, hame, to my ain countree!

The green leaf o' loyaltie's beginning for to fa',
The bonnie white rose it is withering an' a';
But I'll water 't wi' the blude of usurping tyrannie,
An' green it will graw in my ain countree.

O, there's nocht now frae ruin my country can save,
But the keys o' kind heaven, to open the grave:
That a' the noble martyrs wha died for loyaltie,
May rise again an' fight for their ain countree.

The great now are gane, a' wha ventured to save,
The new grass is springing on the tap o' their grave;
But the sun thro' the mirk blinks blythe in my e'e,
'I'll shine on ye yet in your ain countree.'

Hame, hame, hame, O hame fain wad I be,
Hame, hame, hame, to my ain countree!

A. CUNNINGHAM.

287.   THE SUN RISES BRIGHT IN FRANCE

THE sun rises bright in France,
   And fair sets he;
But he has tint the blythe blink he had
   In my ain countree.

Oh, it's nae my ain ruin
   That saddens ay my e'e,
But the dear Marie I left behin',
   Wi' sweet bairnies three.

My lanely hearth burned bonnie,
   And smiled my ain Marie;
I've left a' my heart behin'
   In my ain countree.

The bud comes back to summer,
   And the blossom to the bee;
But I'll win back, oh, never,
   To my ain countree.

Oh, I am leal to high Heaven,
   Where soon I hope to be,
An' there I'll meet ye a' soon
   Frae my ain countree!   A. CUNNINGHAM.

288.   CARE-CHARMER SLEEP

CARE-CHARMER Sleep, son of the sable Night,
Brother to Death, in silent darkness born,
Relieve my languish, and restore the light ;
With dark forgetting of my care return.
And let the day be time enough to mourn
The shipwreck of my ill-adventured youth :
Let waking eyes suffice to wail their scorn,
Without the torment of the night's untruth.
Cease, dreams, the images of day-desires,
To model forth the passions of the morrow ;
Never let rising Sun approve you liars
To add more grief to aggravate my sorrow :
   Still let me sleep, embracing clouds in vain,
   And never wake to feel the day's disdain.

S. DANIEL.

289.   LOVE IS A SICKNESS

LOVE is a sickness full of woes,
   All remedies refusing ;
A plant that with most cutting grows,
   Most barren with best using.
      Why so ?
More we enjoy it, more it dies;
If not enjoyed, it sighing cries
      Heigh-ho !

Love is a torment of the mind,
   A tempest everlasting ;
And Jove hath made it of a kind
   Not well, nor full, nor fasting.
      Why so ?
More we enjoy it, more it dies;
If not enjoyed, it sighing cries
      Heigh-ho !

S. DANIEL (*Hymen's Triumph*).

290.   O BLESSED LETTERS

O BLESSED Letters ! that combine in one
All ages past, and make one live with all.
By you we do confer with who are gone,
And the dead-living unto council call ;
By you the unborn shall have communion
Of what we feel and what doth us befall.

   .   .   .   .   .

      What good is like to this,
To do worthy the writing, and to write
Worthy the reading, and the world's delight ?

S. DANIEL (*Musophilus*).

291. WHEN MEN SHALL FIND THY FLOWER, THY GLORY, PASS

WHEN men shall find thy flower, thy glory, pass,
And thou with careful brow, sitting alone,
Receivèd hast this message from thy glass,
That tells the truth and says that all is gone ;
Fresh shalt thou see in me the wounds thou mad'st,
Though spent thy flame, in me the heat remaining :
I that have loved thee thus before thou fad'st—
My faith shall wax, when thou art in thy waning.
The world shall find this miracle in me,
That fire can burn when all the matter 's spent :
Then what my faith hath been thyself shalt see,
And that thou wast unkind thou mayst repent.
 Thou mayst repent that thou hast scorned my tears,
 When Winter snows upon thy sable hairs.

         S. DANIEL.

292. ROBIN'S CROSS

A LITTLE cross
To tell my loss ;
A little bed
To rest my head ;
A little tear is all I crave
Upon my very little grave.

I strew thy bed,
Who loved thy lays,
The tear I shed,
The cross I raise,
With nothing more upon it than—
Here lies the little friend of man.

         G. DARLEY.

293. IT IS NOT BEAUTY I DEMAND

IT is not Beauty I demand,
A crystal brow, the moon's despair,
Nor the snow's daughter, a white hand,
Nor mermaid's yellow pride of hair :

Tell me not of your starry eyes,
Your lips that seem on roses fed,
Your breasts where Cupid trembling lies,
Nor sleeps for kissing of his bed :—

A bloomy pair of vermeil cheeks
Like Hebe's in her ruddiest hours,
A breath that softer music speaks
Than summer winds a-wooing flowers.

These are but gauds : nay, what are lips ?
Coral beneath the ocean-stream,
Whose brink when your adventurer sips
Full oft he perisheth on them.

And what are cheeks but ensigns oft
That wave hot youth to fields of blood ?
Did Helen's breast, though ne'er so soft,
Do Greece or Ilium any good ?

.   .   .   .   .   .

Give me, instead of Beauty's bust,
A tender heart, a loyal mind,
Which with temptation I could trust,
Yet never linked with error find.   G. Darley.

294.   WHEREFORE, UNLAURELLED BOY

Wherefore, unlaurelled Boy,
  Whom the contemptuous Muse will not inspire,
With a sad kind of joy,
  Still sing'st thou to thy solitary lyre ?

The melancholy winds
  Pour through unnumbered reeds their idle woes,
And every Naiad finds
  A stream to weep her sorrow as it flows.

Her sighs unto the air
  The wood-maid's native oak doth broadly tell,
And Echo's fond despair
  Intelligible rocks re-syllable.

Wherefore then should not I,
  Albeit no haughty Muse my breast inspire,
Fated of grief to die,
  Impart it to a solitary lyre ?   G. Darley.

295.   STEEL

Hail, adamantine Steel ! magnetic Lord !
King of the prow, the ploughshare, and the sword !
True to the pole, by thee the pilot guides
His steady helm amid the struggling tides ;
Braves with broad sail the immeasurable sea,
Cleaves the dark air, and asks no star but thee.—
By thee the ploughshare rends the matted plain,
Inhumes in level rows the living grain ;
Intrusive forests quit the cultured ground,
And Ceres laughs, with golden fillets crowned.—
O'er restless realms, when scowling discord flings
Her snakes, and loud the din of battle rings ;
Expiring strength, and vanquished courage feel
Thy arm resistless, adamantine Steel !
          E. Darwin (*The Botanic Garden*).

296. THE PAPYRUS

PAPYRA, throned upon the banks of Nile,
Spread her smooth leaf, and waved her silver style.
The storied pyramid, the laurelled bust,
The trophied arch had crumbled into dust ;
The sacred symbol, and the epic song
(Unknown the character, forgot the tongue),
With each unconquered chief, or sainted maid,
Sunk undistinguished in Oblivion's shade.
Sad o'er the scattered ruins Genius sighed,
And infant Arts but learned to lisp, and died,
Till to astonished realms Papyra taught
To paint in mystic colours sound and thought.
With Wisdom's voice to print the page sublime,
And mark in adamant the steps of Time.

E. DARWIN (The Botanic Garden).

297. THE SOLDIER GOING TO THE FIELD

PRESERVE thy sighs, unthrifty
    girl,
  To purify the air !
Thy tears to thread, instead of
    pearl,
  On bracelets of thy hair.

The trumpet makes the echo
    hoarse,
  And wakes the louder drum.
Expense of grief gains no remorse,
  When sorrow should be dumb.

For I must go where lazy Peace
  Will hide her drowsy head,
And, for the sport of kings,
    increase
  The number of the dead.

But, first, I'll chide thy cruel
    theft :
  Can I in war delight,
Who (being of my heart bereft)
  Can have no heart to fight ?

Thou knowst, the sacred laws of
    old
  Ordained a thief should pay,
To quit him of his theft, sevenfold
  What he had stolen away.

Thy payment shall but double be,
  Oh then with speed resign
My own seducèd heart to me,
  Accompanied with thine.

SIR W. DAVENANT.

298. SHE NE'ER SAW COURTS, YET COURTS COULD HAVE UNDONE

SHE ne'er saw courts, yet courts could have undone,
  With untaught looks and an unpractised heart ;
Her nets, the most prepared could never shun ;
  For Nature spread them in the scorn of art.

She never had in busy cities been,
  Ne'er warmed with hopes, nor e'er allayed with fears ;
Not seeing punishment, could guess no sin ;
  And sin not seeing, ne'er had use of tears.

And as kind Nature with calm diligence
    Her own free virtue silently employs,
Whilst she, unheard, does ripening growth dispense,
    So were her virtues busy without noise.

Whilst her great mistress, Nature, thus she tends,
    The busy household waits no less on her ;
By secret law, each to her beauty bends ;
    Though all her lowly mind to that prefer.
                    SIR W. DAVENANT (*Gondibert*).

299.   THE LARK NOW LEAVES HIS WATERY NEST

THE lark now leaves his watery nest
    And climbing shakes his dewy wings.
He takes this window for the East,
    And to implore your light he sings—
Awake, awake ! the morn will never rise
Till she can dress her beauty at your eyes.

The merchant bows unto the seaman's star,
    The ploughman from the sun his season takes ;
But still the lover wonders what they are
    Who look for day before his mistress wakes.
Awake, awake ! break through your veils of lawn !
Then draw your curtains, and begin the dawn !
                            SIR W. DAVENANT.

300.   THE FOLLY OF KNOWLEDGE

WHY did my parents send me to the schools,
    That I with knowledge might enrich my mind,
Since the desire to know first made men fools,
    And did corrupt the root of all mankind ?
.   .   .   .

I know my body's of so frail a kind,
    As force without, fevers within, can kill ;
I know the heavenly nature of my mind,
    But 'tis corrupted both in wit and will.

I know my soul hath power to know all things,
    Yet is she blind and ignorant in all ;
I know I'm one of nature's little kings,
    Yet to the least and vilest things am thrall.

I know my life's a pain, and but a span ;
    I know my sense is mocked in everything ;
And, to conclude, I know myself a man,
    Which is a proud, and yet a wretched thing.
        SIR J. DAVIES (*The Immortality of the Soul*).

301. WHEREVER GOD ERECTS A HOUSE OF PRAYER

WHEREVER God erects a house of prayer,
The Devil always builds a chapel there :
And 'twill be found upon examination
The latter has the largest congregation :
For ever since he first debauched the mind,
He made a perfect conquest of mankind.

D. DEFOE (*The True-born Englishman*).

302. ART THOU POOR, YET HAST THOU GOLDEN SLUMBERS ?

ART thou poor, yet hast thou golden slumbers ?
    O sweet content !
Art thou rich, yet is thy mind perplexèd ?
    O punishment !
Dost thou laugh to see how fools are vexèd
To add to golden numbers, golden numbers ?
O sweet content ! O sweet, O sweet content !
  Work apace, apace, apace, apace ;
  Honest labour bears a lovely face ;
Then hey nonny nonny, hey nonny nonny !

Canst drink the waters of the crispèd spring ?
    O sweet content !
Swimm'st thou in wealth, yet sink'st in thine own tears ?
    O punishment !
Then he that patiently want's burden bears,
No burden bears, but is a king, a king !
O sweet content ! O sweet, O sweet content !
  Work apace, apace, apace, apace ;
  Honest labour bears a lovely face ;
Then hey nonny nonny, hey nonny nonny !

T. DEKKER (*Patient Grissel*).

303. COLD'S THE WIND

COLD's the wind, and wet's the rain,
Saint Hugh be our good speed !
Ill is the weather that bringeth no gain,
Nor helps good hearts in need.

Troll the bowl, the jolly nut-brown bowl,
And here, kind mate, to thee !
Let's sing a dirge for Saint Hugh's soul,
And down it merrily.

T. DEKKER (*The Shoemaker's Holiday*).

304. GOLDEN SLUMBERS KISS YOUR EYES

GOLDEN slumbers kiss your eyes,
Smiles awake you when you rise.
Sleep, pretty wantons, do not
    cry,
And I will sing a lullaby.
Rock them, rock them, lullaby.

Care is heavy, therefore sleep you.
You are care, and care must keep
    you.
Sleep, pretty wantons, do not cry,
And I will sing a lullaby.
Rock them, rock them, lullaby.

T. DEKKER (*Patient Grissel*).

305. THE THAMES

THAMES ! the most loved of all the Ocean's sons
By his old sire, to his embraces runs,
Hasting to pay his tribute to the sea,
Like mortal life to meet eternity.
   .   .   .   .
Oh, could I flow like thee, and make thy stream
My great example, as it is my theme !
Though deep, yet clear ; though gentle, yet not dull ;
Strong without rage ; without o'erflowing, full.

SIR J. DENHAM (*Cooper's Hill*).

306. A PASSION OF MY LORD OF ESSEX

HAPPY were he could finish forth his fate
   In some unhaunted desert, most obscure
From all societies, from love and hate
   Of worldly folk ; then might he sleep secure ;
Then wake again, and ever give God praise,
   Content with hips and haws and bramble-berry ;
In contemplation spending all his days,
   And change of holy thoughts to make him merry ;
Where, when he dies, his tomb may be a bush,
Where harmless Robin dwells with gentle thrush.

ROBERT DEVEREUX, EARL OF ESSEX.

307. TOM BOWLING

HERE, a sheer hulk, lies poor Tom Bowling,
   The darling of our crew ;
No more he'll hear the tempest howling,
   For Death has broached him to.
His form was of the manliest beauty,
   His heart was kind and soft ;
Faithful below he did his duty,
   And now he 's gone aloft.

Tom never from his word departed,
   His virtues were so rare ;
His friends were many and true-hearted,
   His Poll was kind and fair :

And then he'd sing so blithe and jolly,
　　Ah, many 's the time and oft !
But mirth is turned to melancholy,
　　For Tom is gone aloft.

Yet shall poor Tom find pleasant weather,
　　When He, who all commands,
Shall give, to call Life's crew together,
　　The word to ' pipe all hands '.
Thus Death, who kings and tars dispatches,
　　In vain Tom's life has doffed ;
For though his body 's under hatches,
　　His soul is gone aloft.

C. DIBDIN.

308.　THE IVY GREEN

OH, a dainty plant is the Ivy green,
That creepeth o'er ruins old !
Of right choice food are his meals I ween,
In his cell so lone and cold.
The wall must be crumbled, the stone decayed,
To pleasure his dainty whim :
And the mouldering dust that years have made
Is a merry meal for him.
　　　　Creeping where no life is seen,
　　　　A rare old plant is the Ivy green.

Fast he stealeth on, though he wears no wings,
And a stanch old heart has he.
How closely he twineth, how tight he clings
To his friend the huge Oak Tree !
And slily he traileth along the ground,
And his leaves he gently waves,
As he joyously hugs and crawleth round
The rich mould of dead men's graves.
　　　　Creeping where grim death has been,
　　　　A rare old plant is the Ivy green.

Whole ages have fled and their works decayed,
And nations have scattered been ;
But the stout old Ivy shall never fade,
From its hale and hearty green.
The brave old plant in its lonely days,
Shall fatten upon the past :
For the stateliest building man can raise,
Is the Ivy's food at last.
　　　　Creeping on, where time has been,
　　　　A rare old plant is the Ivy green.

C. DICKENS.

309.   KEITH OF RAVELSTON

THE murmur of the mourning
    ghost
  That keeps the shadowy kine ;—
'Oh, Keith of Ravelston,
  The sorrows of thy line !'

Ravelston, Ravelston,
  The merry path that leads
Down the golden morning hill
  And through the silver meads ;

Ravelston, Ravelston,
  The stile beneath the tree,
The maid that kept her mother's
    kine,
  The song that sang she !

She sang her song, she kept her
    kine,
  She sat beneath the thorn,
When Andrew Keith of Ravelston
  Rode through the Monday morn.

His henchmen sing, his hawk-bells
    ring,
  His belted jewels shine !—
Oh, Keith of Ravelston,
  The sorrows of thy line !

Year after year, where Andrew
    came,
  Comes evening down the glade ;
And still there sits a moonshine
    ghost
  Where sat the sunshine maid.

Her misty hair is faint and fair,
  She keeps the shadowy kine ;—
Oh, Keith of Ravelston,
  The sorrows of thy line !

I lay my hand upon the stile,
  The stile is lone and cold ;
The burnie that goes babbling by
  Says naught that can be told.

Yet, stranger ! here, from year to
    year,
  She keeps her shadowy kine ;—
Oh, Keith of Ravelston,
  The sorrows of thy line !

Step out three steps, where
    Andrew stood—
  Why blanch thy cheeks for
    fear ?
The ancient stile is not alone,
  'Tis not the burn I hear !

She makes her immemorial moan,
  She keeps her shadowy kine ;—
Oh, Keith of Ravelston,
  The sorrows of thy line !

S. DOBELL.

310.   ODE

That time and absence proves
Rather helps than hurts to loves.

ABSENCE, hear thou my protesta-
    tion
  Against thy strength,
  Distance and length :
Do what thou canst for altera-
    tion,
  For hearts of truest mettle
  Absence doth join and time doth
    settle.

Who loves a mistress of such
    quality,
  He soon hath found
  Affection's ground
Beyond time, place, and all
    mortality.
  To hearts that cannot vary
  Absence is present, time doth
    tarry.

My senses want their outward
    motion,
  Which now within
  Reason doth win,
Redoubled by her secret notion;
  Like rich men that take pleasure
  In hiding more than handling
    treasure.

By absence this good means I gain
  That I can catch her
  Where none can watch her,
In some close corner of my brain;
  There I embrace and kiss her
  And so I both enjoy and miss
  her.

                 J. DONNE.

311. THE BAIT

COME live with me, and be my love,
And we will some new pleasures prove
Of golden sands, and crystal brooks,
With silken lines and silver hooks.

There will the river whispering run
Warmed by thy eyes, more than the sun;
And there the enamoured fish will stay,
Begging themselves they may betray.

When thou wilt swim in that live bath,
Each fish, which every channel hath,
Will amorously to thee swim,
Gladder to catch thee, than thou him.

If thou, to be so seen, beest loath,
By sun or moon, thou darkenest both,
And if myself have leave to see,
I need not their light, having thee.

Let others freeze with angling reeds,
And cut their legs with shells and weeds,
Or treacherously poor fish beset,
With strangling snare, or windowy net.

Let coarse bold hands from slimy nest
The bedded fish in banks out-wrest;
Or curious traitors, sleeve-silk flies,
Bewitch poor fishes' wandering eyes.

For thee, thou need'st no such deceit,
For thou thyself art thine own bait:
That fish, that is not catched thereby,
Alas! is wiser far than I.

                 J. DONNE.

312.   DEATH, BE NOT PROUD

DEATH, be not proud, though some have callèd thee
Mighty and dreadful, for thou art not so:
For those, whom thou think'st thou dost overthrow,
Die not, poor Death; nor yet canst thou kill me.
From rest and sleep, which but thy picture be,
Much pleasure, then from thee much more must flow;
And soonest our best men with thee do go,
Rest of their bones and souls' delivery.
Thou'rt slave to Fate, chance, kings, and desperate men,
And dost with poison, war, and sickness dwell;
And poppy or charms can make us sleep as well
And better than thy stroke; why swell'st thou then?
  One short sleep past, we wake eternally,
  And Death shall be no more: Death, thou shalt die.
                                        J. DONNE.

313.   GO AND CATCH A FALLING STAR

Go and catch a falling star,
  Get with child a mandrake root,
Tell me where all past years are,
  Or who cleft the Devil's foot;
Teach me to hear mermaids singing,
Or to keep off envy's stinging,
        And find
        What wind
Serves to advance an honest mind.

If thou beest born to strange sights,
  Things invisible to see,
Ride ten thousand days and nights
  Till age snow white hairs on thee;
Thou, when thou return'st, wilt tell me
All strange wonders that befell thee,
        And swear,
        No where
Lives a woman true and fair.

If thou find'st one, let me know;
  Such a pilgrimage were sweet.
Yet do not; I would not go,
  Though at next door we might meet.
Though she were true when you met her,
And last till you write your letter,
        Yet she
        Will be
False, ere I come, to two or three.   J. DONNE.

314. LOVE'S DEITY

I LONG to talk with some old lover's ghost,
    Who died before the god of love was born.
I cannot think that he, who then loved most,
    Sunk so low as to love one which did scorn.
But since this god produced a destiny,
And that vice-nature, custom, lets it be,
    I must love her that loves not me.

Sure, they which made him god, meant not so much,
    Nor he in his young godhead practised it.
But when an even flame two hearts did touch,
    His office was indulgently to fit
Actives to passives. Correspondency
Only his subject was ; it cannot be
    Love, till I love her, who loves me.

But every modern god will now extend
    His vast prerogative as far as Jove.
To rage, to lust, to write to, to commend,
    All is the purlieu of the god of love.
Oh ! were we wakened by this tyranny
To ungod this child again, it could not be
    I should love her, who loves not me.

Rebel and atheist too, why murmur I,
    As though I felt the worst that love could do ?
Love may make me leave loving, or might try
    A deeper plague, to make her love me too ;
Which, since she loves before, I'm loath to see.
Falsehood is worse than hate ; and that must be,
    If she whom I love, should love me.

J. DONNE.

315. THE GOOD MORROW

I WONDER, by my troth, what thou and I
Did, till we loved ? were we not weaned till then ?
But sucked on country pleasures, childishly ?
Or snored we in the Seven Sleepers' den ?
'Twas so ; but this, all pleasures fancies be ;
If ever any beauty I did see,
Which I desired, and got, 'twas but a dream of thee.

And now good-morrow to our waking souls,
Which watch not one another out of fear ;
For love all love of other sights controls,
And makes one little room an everywhere.
Let sea-discoverers to new worlds have gone ;
Let maps to other, worlds on worlds have shown,
Let us possess one world ; each hath one, and is one.

My face in thine eye, thine in mine appears,
And true plain hearts do in the faces rest ;
Where can we find two better hemispheres
Without sharp north, without declining west ?
Whatever dies, was not mixed equally ;
If our two loves be one, or thou and I
Love so alike that none can slacken, none can die.

J. DONNE.

316. A HYMN TO CHRIST, AT THE AUTHOR'S LAST GOING INTO GERMANY

In what torn ship soever I embark,
That ship shall be my emblem of Thy ark ;
What sea soever swallow me, that flood
Shall be to me an emblem of Thy blood ;
Though Thou with clouds of anger do disguise
Thy face, yet through that mask I know those eyes,
    Which, though they turn away sometimes,
      They never will despise.

I sacrifice this island unto Thee,
And all whom I love there, and who love me ;
When I have put our seas 'twixt them and me,
Put thou Thy seas betwixt my sins and Thee.
As the tree's sap doth seek the root below
In winter, in my winter now I go,
    Where none but Thee, the eternal root
      Of true love, I may know.

.   .   .   .

Seal then this bill of my divorce to all,
On whom those fainter beams of love did fall ;
Marry those loves, which in youth scattered be
On fame, wit, hopes—false mistresses—to Thee.
Churches are best for prayer, that have least light;
To see God only, I go out of sight ;
    And to escape stormy days, I choose
      An everlasting night.

J. DONNE.

317. A HYMN TO GOD THE FATHER

Wilt Thou forgive that sin where I begun,
  Which was my sin, though it were done before ?
Wilt Thou forgive that sin, through which I run,
  And do run still, though still I do deplore ?
When Thou hast done, Thou hast not done ;
    For I have more.

Wilt Thou forgive that sin which I have won
Others to sin, and made my sin their door ?
Wilt Thou forgive that sin which I did shun
A year or two, but wallowed in a score ?
When Thou hast done, Thou hast not done ;
For I have more.

I have a sin of fear, that when I have spun
My last thread, I shall perish on the shore ;
But swear by Thyself, that at my death Thy Son
Shall shine as He shines now, and heretofore :
And, having done that, Thou hast done ;
I fear no more.   J. DONNE.

318. THE PRIVATE OF THE BUFFS

'Some Sikhs and a private of the Buffs having remained behind with
the grog carts, fell into the hands of the Chinese. On the next morning
they were brought before the authorities, and commanded to perform the
Kotow. The Sikhs obeyed ; but Moyse, the English soldier, declaring that
he would not prostrate himself before any Chinaman alive, was imme-
diately knocked upon the head, and his body thrown on a dunghill.'—
The Times (An incident in the China War, which ended in 1860).

Last night, among his fellow
    roughs,
He jested, quaffed, and swore,
A drunken private of the Buffs,
    Who never looked before.
To-day, beneath the foeman's
    frown,
He stands in Elgin's place,
Ambassador from Britain's crown,
    And type of all her race.

Poor, reckless, rude, low-born,
    untaught,
    Bewildered, and alone,
A heart, with English instinct
    fraught,
    He yet can call his own.
Aye, tear his body limb from limb,
    Bring cord, or axe, or flame :
He only knows, that not through
    him
    Shall England come to shame.

Far Kentish hop-fields round him
    seemed,
    Like dreams, to come and go ;
Bright leagues of cherry-blossom
    gleamed,
    One sheet of living snow ;

The smoke, above his father's door,
    In grey soft eddyings hung :
Must he then watch it rise no more,
    Doomed by himself so young ?
Yes, honour calls !—with strength
    like steel
    He put the vision by.
Let dusky Indians whine and
    kneel ;
    An English lad must die.

And thus, with eyes that would
    not shrink,
    With knee to man unbent,
Unfaltering on its dreadful brink,
    To his red grave he went.

Vain, mightiest fleets of iron
    framed ;
    Vain, those all-shattering guns ;
Unless proud England keep, un-
    tamed,
    The strong heart of her sons.
So, let his name through Europe
    ring—
    A man of mean estate,
Who died, as firm as Sparta's king,
    Because his soul was great.
                          SIR F. H. DOYLE.

319. PIGWIGGEN ARMING

AND quickly arms him for the
field,
A little cockle-shell his shield,
Which he could very bravely
wield:
  Yet could it not be pierced:
His spear a bent both stiff and
strong,
And well near of two inches long ;
The pile was of a horse-fly's
tongue,
  Whose sharpness nought re-
versed.

And puts him on a coat of mail,
Which was of a fish's scale,
That when his foe should him
assail,
  No point should be prevailing :
His rapier was a hornet's sting,
It was a very dangerous thing :
For if he chanced to hurt the king,
  It would be long in healing.

His helmet was a beetle's head,
Most horrible and full of dread,
That able was to strike one dead,
  Yet did it well become him :
And for a plume, a horse's hair,
Which being tossèd with the air,
Had force to strike his foe with
fear,
  And turn his weapon from him.

Himself he on an earwig set,
Yet scarce he on his back could
get,
So oft and high he did curvet,
  Ere he himself could settle :
He made him turn, and stop, and
bound,
To gallop, and to trot the round,
He scarce could stand on any
ground,
  He was so full of mettle.

      M. DRAYTON (*Nymphidia*).

320. THE BALLAD OF AGINCOURT

FAIR stood the wind for France,
When we our sails advance,
Nor now to prove our chance,
  Longer will tarry ;
But putting to the main,
At Kaux, the mouth of Seine,
With all his martial train,
  Landed King Harry.

And taking many a fort,
Furnished in warlike sort
Marcheth tow'rds Agincourt
  In happy hour ;
Skirmishing day by day
With those that stopped his way,
Where the French general lay,
  With all his power.

Which in his height of pride,
King Henry to deride,
His ransom to provide
  To the king sending.

Which he neglects the while,
As from a nation vile,
Yet with an angry smile,
  Their fall portending.

And turning to his men,
Quoth our brave Henry then,
Though they to one be ten,
  Be not amazed.
Yet have we well begun,
Battles so bravely won,
Have ever to the sun
  By fame been raised.

And, for myself (quoth he),
This my full rest shall be,
England ne'er mourn for me,
  Nor more esteem me.
Victor I will remain,
Or on this earth lie slain,
Never shall she sustain
  Loss to redeem me.

Poitiers and Cressy tell,
When most their pride did swell,
Under our swords they fell,
   No less our skill is,
Than when our grandsire great,
Claiming the regal seat,
By many a warlike feat,
   Lopped the French lilies.

The Duke of York so dread,
The eager vaward led ;
With the main, Henry sped,
   Amongst his henchmen.
Excester had the rear,
A braver man not there ;
O Lord, how hot they were
   On the false Frenchmen !

They now to fight are gone,
Armour on armour shone,
Drum now to drum did groan,
   To hear was wonder ;
That with the cries they make,
The very earth did shake,
Trumpet to trumpet spake,
   Thunder to thunder.

Well it thine age became,
O noble Erpingham,
Which didst the signal aim
   To our hid forces ;
When from a meadow by,
Like a storm suddenly
The English archery
   Stuck the French horses.

With Spanish yew so strong,
Arrows a cloth-yard long,
That like to serpents stung,
   Piercing the weather ;
None from his fellow starts,
But playing manly parts,
And like true English hearts
   Stuck close together.

When down their bows they threw,
And forth their bilbows drew.
And on the French they flew,
   Not one was tardy ;
Arms were from shoulders sent,
Scalps to the teeth were rent,
Down the French peasants went,
   Our men were hardy.

This while our noble King,
His broad sword brandishing,
Down the French host did ding,
   As to o'erwhelm it ;
And many a deep wound lent,
His arms with blood besprent,
And many a cruel dent
   Bruisèd his helmet.

Gloucester, that Duke so good,
Next of the royal blood,
For famous England stood,
   With his brave brother ;
Clarence, in steel so bright,
Though but a maiden knight,
Yet in that famous fight,
   Scarce such another.

Warwick in blood did wade,
Oxford the foe invade,
And cruel slaughter made,
   Still as they ran up ;
Suffolk his axe did ply,
Beaumont and Willoughby
Bare them right doughtily,
   Ferrers and Fanhope.

Upon Saint Crispin's day
Fought was this noble fray,
Which fame did not delay
   To England to carry ;
Oh, when shall Englishmen
With such acts fill a pen,
Or England breed again
   Such a King Harry ?
               M. DRAYTON.

321. IMMORTALITY IN SONG

How many paltry, foolish, painted things,
That now in coaches trouble every street,
Shall be forgotten, whom no poet sings,
Ere they be well wrapped in their winding-sheet ?
Where I to thee eternity shall give,
When nothing else remaineth of these days,
And queens hereafter shall be glad to live
Upon the alms of thy superfluous praise ;
Virgins and matrons reading these my rhymes,
Shall be so much delighted with thy story,
That they shall grieve they lived not in these times,
To have seen thee, their sex's only glory :
    So shalt thou fly above the vulgar throng,
    Still to survive in my immortal song.   M. DRAYTON.

322. TO HIS COY LOVE

I PRAY thee leave, love me no more,
  Call home the heart you gave me,
I but in vain that saint adore,
  That can, but will not save me :
These poor half-kisses kill me quite;
  Was ever man thus servèd ?
Amidst an ocean of delight,
  For pleasure to be starvèd.

Show me no more those snowy
    breasts,
With azure riverets branched,
Where whilst my eye with plenty
    feasts,
  Yet is my thirst not stanched.

O Tantalus, thy pains ne'er tell,
  By me thou art prevented ;
'Tis nothing to be plagued in hell,
  But thus in heaven tormented.
Clip me no more in those dear arms,
  Nor thy life's comfort call me ;
Oh, these are but too powerful
    charms,
  And do but more enthral me.
But see, how patient I am grown,
  In all this coil about thee ;
Come, nice thing, let my heart alone,
  I cannot live without thee.
              M. DRAYTON.

323. SINCE THERE'S NO HELP, COME LET US KISS AND PART

SINCE there's no help, come let us kiss and part,
Nay, I have done : you get no more of me,
And I am glad, yea, glad with all my heart,
That thus so cleanly I myself can free.
Shake hands for ever, cancel all our vows,
And when we meet at any time again,
Be it not seen in either of our brows
That we one jot of former love retain ;
Now at the last gasp of Love's latest breath,
When, his pulse failing, Passion speechless lies,
When Faith is kneeling by his bed of death,
And Innocence is closing up his eyes,
Now if thou wouldst, when all have given him over,
From death to life thou mightst him yet recover.
                        M. DRAYTON.

324. SOME ATHEIST IN LOVE

SOME atheist or vile infidel in love,
When I do speak of thy divinity,
May blaspheme thus, and say I flatter thee,
And only write my skill in verse to prove.
See miracles, ye unbelieving! see
A dumb-born Muse made to express the mind,
A cripple hand to write, yet lame by kind,
One by thy name, the other touching thee.
Blind were my eyes, till they were seen of thine,
And mine ears deaf by thy fame healèd be;
My vices cured by virtues sprung from thee,
My hopes revived, which long in grave had lyne:
   All unclean thoughts, foul spirits, cast out in me
   By thy great power, and by strong faith in thee.
                          M. DRAYTON.

325. TO THE VIRGINIAN VOYAGE

YOU brave heroic minds,
Worthy your country's name;
  That honour still pursue,
  Go, and subdue,
Whilst loitering hinds
Lurk here at home, with shame.

Britons, you stay too long,
Quickly aboard bestow you,
  And with a merry gale
  Swell your stretched sail,
With vows as strong,
As the winds that blow you.

Your course securely steer,
West and by south forth keep,
  Rocks, lee-shores, nor shoals,
  When Aeolus scowls,
You need not fear,
So absolute the deep.

And cheerfully at sea
Success you still entice,
  To get the pearl and gold,
  And ours to hold
Virginia,
Earth's only Paradise.

Where Nature hath in store
Fowl, venison, and fish,
  And the fruitfullest soil,
  Without your toil,
Three harvests more,
All greater than your wish.

And the ambitious vine
Crowns with his purple mass
  The cedar reaching high
  To kiss the sky,
The cypress, pine
And useful sassafras.

To whom the Golden Age
Still Nature's laws doth give,
  No other cares that tend,
  But them to defend
From winter's rage,
That long there doth not live.

When as the luscious smell
Of that delicious land,
  Above the seas that flows,
  The clear wind throws,
Your hearts to swell
Approaching the dear strand;

In kenning of the shore
(Thanks to God first given)
  O you the happiest men
  Be frolic then,
Let cannons roar
Frighting the wide heaven.

And in regions far
Such heroes bring ye forth,
  As those from whom we came,
  And plant our name,
Under that star
Not known unto our North.

And as there plenty grows
Of laurel everywhere,
  Apollo's sacred tree,
  You may it see,
A poet's brows
To crown, that may sing there.

Thy voyages attend,
Industrious Hackluyt,
  Whose reading shall inflame
  Men to seek fame,
And much commend
To after-times thy wit.

M. DRAYTON.

326. ALEXIS, HERE SHE STAYED

ALEXIS, here she stayed ; among these pines,
Sweet hermitress, she did alone repair ;
Here did she spread the treasure of her hair,
More rich than that brought from the Colchian mines.
She set her by these muskèd eglantines,
The happy place the print seems yet to bear ;
Her voice did sweeten here thy sugared lines,
To which winds, trees, beasts, birds, did lend their ear.
Me here she first perceived, and here a morn
Of bright carnations did o'erspread her face,
Here did she sigh, here first my hopes were born,
And I first got a pledge of promised grace ·
But, ah ! what served it to be happy so,
Sith passèd pleasure double but new woe ?

W. DRUMMOND.

327. LIKE THE IDALIAN QUEEN

LIKE the Idalian Queen,
Her hair about her eyne
With neck and breast's ripe apples to be seen,
At first glance of the morn,
In Cyprus' gardens gathering those fair flowers
Which of her blood were born,
I saw, but fainting saw, my paramours.
The Graces naked danced about the place,
The winds and trees amazed
With silence on her gazed;
The flowers did smile like those upon her face,
And as their aspen stalks those fingers band,
That she might read my case,
A hyacinth I wished me in her hand.

W. DRUMMOND.

328. MY THOUGHTS HOLD MORTAL STRIFE

My thoughts hold mortal strife ;
I do detest my life,
And with lamenting cries
Peace to my soul to bring
Oft call that prince which here doth monarchize :
—But he, grim-grinning King,
Who caitiffs scorns, and doth the blest surprise,
Late having decked with beauty's rose his tomb,
Disdains to crop a weed, and will not come.

W. DRUMMOND.

329. THE BOOK OF NATURE

Of this fair volume which we World do name,
If we the sheets and leaves could turn with care,
Of Him who it corrects, and did it frame,
We clear might read the art and wisdom rare :
Find out His power which wildest powers doth tame,
His providence extending everywhere,
His justice which proud rebels doth not spare,
In every page, no, period of the same.
But silly we, like foolish children, rest
Well pleased with coloured vellum, leaves of gold,
Fair dangling ribands, leaving what is best,
On the great Writer's sense ne'er taking hold ;
Or if by chance our minds do muse on aught,
It is some picture on the margin wrought.

W. DRUMMOND.

330. PHOEBUS ARISE

Phoebus, arise,
And paint the sable skies
With azure, white, and red ;
Rouse Memnon's mother from her Tithon's bed,
That she thy career may with roses spread ;
The nightingales thy coming each where sing ;
Make an eternal spring,
Give life to this dark world which lieth dead ;
Spread forth thy golden hair
In larger locks than thou wast wont before,
And, emperor-like, decore
With diadem of pearl thy temples fair :
Chase hence the ugly night,
Which serves but to make dear thy glorious light.

W. DRUMMOND.

G

331. TO CHLORIS

SEE, Chloris, how the clouds
Tilt in the azure lists,
And how with Stygian mists
Each hornèd hill his giant forehead shrouds ;
Jove thundereth in the air,
The air, grown great with rain,
Now seems to bring Deucalion's days again.
I see thee quake ; come, let us home repair,
Come hide thee in mine arms,
If not for love, yet to shun greater harms.

W. DRUMMOND.

332. SAINT JOHN BAPTIST

THE last and greatest Herald of Heaven's King,
Girt with rough skins, hies to the deserts wild,
Among that savage brood the woods forth bring,
Which he than man more harmless found and mild.
His food was locusts, and what young doth spring,
With honey that from virgin hives distilled ;
Parched body, hollow eyes, some uncouth thing
Made him appear, long since from earth exiled.
There burst he forth : All ye whose hopes rely
On God, with me amidst these deserts mourn ;
Repent, repent, and from old errors turn !
—Who listened to his voice, obeyed his cry ?
Only the echoes, which he made relent,
Rung from their flinty caves, Repent ! Repent !

W. DRUMMOND.

333. THIS WORLD A HUNTING IS

THIS world a hunting is,
The prey poor man, the Nimrod fierce is Death ;
His speedy greyhounds are
Lust, sickness, envy, care,
Strife that ne'er falls amiss,
With all those ills which haunt us while we breathe.
Now, if by chance we fly
Of these the eager chase,
Old age with stealing pace
Casts up his nets, and there we panting die.

W. DRUMMOND.

334. GEORGE VILLIERS, DUKE OF BUCKINGHAM

A MAN so various, that he seemed to be
Not one, but all mankind's epitome:
Stiff in opinions, always in the wrong;
Was everything by starts, and nothing long;
But, in the course of one revolving moon,
Was chemist, fiddler, statesman, and buffoon;
Then all for women, painting, rhyming, drinking,
Beside ten thousand freaks that died in thinking.
Blest madman, who could every hour employ,
With something new to wish, or to enjoy!
Railing and praising were his usual themes,
And both, to show his judgement, in extremes;
So over violent, or over civil,
That every man with him was God or Devil.
In squandering wealth was his peculiar art;
Nothing went unrewarded but desert.
Beggared by fools, whom still he found too late;
He had his jest, and they had his estate.

J. DRYDEN (*Absalom and Achitophel*).

335. DREAMS

DREAMS are but interludes which Fancy makes;
When monarch Reason sleeps, this mimic wakes:
Compounds a medley of disjointed things,
A mob of cobblers, and a court of kings:
Light fumes are merry, grosser fumes are sad:
Both are the reasonable soul run mad;
And many monstrous forms in sleep we see,
That neither were, nor are, nor e'er can be.
Sometimes forgotten things long cast behind
Rush forward in the brain, and come to mind.
The nurse's legends are for truths received,
And the man dreams but what the boy believed.
Sometimes we but rehearse a former play,
The night restores our actions done by day;
As hounds in sleep will open for their prey.
In short, the farce of dreams is of a piece,
Chimeras all; and more absurd, or less.

J. DRYDEN (*The Cock and the Fox*).

336. FAIR, SWEET, AND YOUNG

FAIR, sweet, and young, receive a prize
Reserved for your victorious eyes.
From crowds whom at your feet you see
Oh pity and distinguish me!
As I from thousand beauties more
Distinguish you; and only you adore

Your face for conquest was designed;
Your every motion charms my mind.
Angels, when you your silence break
Forget their hymns to hear you speak;
But when at once they hear and view
Are loath to mount; and long to stay with you.

No graces can your form improve,
But all are lost unless you love.
While that sweet passion you disdain,
Your veil and beauty are in vain.
In pity then prevent my fate,
For, after dying, all reprieve's too late.

                                                J. DRYDEN.

337. SONG FOR SAINT CECILIA'S DAY, 1687

FROM harmony, from heavenly harmony,
        This universal frame began:
    When Nature underneath a heap
        Of jarring atoms lay,
    And could not heave her head,
The tuneful voice was heard from high,
        Arise, ye more than dead!
Then cold, and hot, and moist, and dry
In order to their stations leap,
        And Music's power obey.
From harmony, from heavenly harmony
        This universal frame began:
        From harmony to harmony
Through all the compass of the notes it ran,
The diapason closing full in Man.

What passion cannot Music raise and quell?
        When Jubal struck the chorded shell
    His listening brethren stood around,
        And, wondering, on their faces fell
    To worship that celestial sound.
Less than a god they thought there could not dwell
        Within the hollow of that shell,
        That spoke so sweetly and so well.
What passion cannot Music raise and quell?

        The trumpet's loud clangor
            Excites us to arms,
        With shrill notes of anger
            And mortal alarms.
        The double double double beat
            Of the thundering drum
    Cries 'Hark! the foes come;
    Charge, charge, 'tis too late to retreat!'

The soft complaining flute
In dying notes discovers
    The woes of hopeless lovers,
Whose dirge is whispered by the warbling lute.

Sharp violins proclaim
Their jealous pangs and desperation,
Fury, frantic indignation,
Depth of pains, and height of passion,
    For the fair disdainful dame.

But oh ! what art can teach,
What human voice can reach
    The sacred organ's praise ?
Notes inspiring holy love,
Notes that wing their heavenly ways
    To mend the choirs above.

Orpheus could lead the savage race,
And trees uprooted left their place
    Sequacious of the lyre :
But bright Cecilia raised the wonder higher :
When to her organ vocal breath was given,
An angel heard, and straight appeared—
    Mistaking earth for heaven !

Grand Chorus

As from the power of sacred lays
    The spheres began to move,
And sung the great Creator's praise
    To all the blest above :
So when the last and dreadful hour
This crumbling pageant shall devour,
The trumpet shall be heard on high,
The dead shall live, the living die,
And Music shall untune the sky.

                            J. DRYDEN.

338.   MANKIND

MEN are but children of a larger growth ;
Our appetites are apt to change as theirs,
And full as craving too, and full as vain ;
And yet the soul, shut up in her dark room,
Viewing so clear abroad, at home sees nothing ;
But, like a mole in earth, busy and blind,
Works all her folly up, and casts it outward
To the world's open view.

                    J. DRYDEN (*All for Love*).

339. THE HEAVENLY GIFT OF POESY

O GRACIOUS God ! how far have we
Profaned thy heavenly gift of Poesy !
Made prostitute and profligate the Muse,
Debased to each obscene and impious use,
Whose harmony was first ordained above
For tongues of angels, and for hymns of love !
Oh wretched we ! why were we hurried down
    This lubric and adulterate age—
Nay, added fat pollutions of our own—
        To increase the steaming ordures of the stage ?
          J. DRYDEN (*To the Memory of*
            Mrs. Anne Killigrew).

340. ANTHONY ASHLEY COOPER, EARL OF SHAFTESBURY

OF these the false Achitophel was first ;
A name to all succeeding ages curst :
For close designs and crooked counsels fit,
Sagacious, bold, and turbulent of wit ;
Restless, unfixed in principles and place ;
In power unpleased, impatient of disgrace ;
A fiery soul, which, working out its way,
Fretted the pigmy body to decay,
And o'er-informed the tenement of clay :
A daring pilot in extremity,
Pleased with the danger, when the waves went high
He sought the storms ; but, for a calm unfit,
Would steer too nigh the sands to boast his wit.
Great wits are sure to madness near allied,
And thin partitions do their bounds divide :
Else why should he, with wealth and honour blest,
Refuse his age the needful hours of rest ?
Punish a body which he could not please ;
Bankrupt of life, yet prodigal of ease ?
        J. DRYDEN (*Absalom and Achitophel*).

341. ON MILTON

THREE poets, in three distant ages born,
Greece, Italy and England did adorn.
The first in loftiness of thought surpassed ;
The next in majesty ; in both the last.
The force of nature could no further go ;
To make a third, she joined the former two.
          J. DRYDEN.

342.   ALEXANDER'S FEAST; OR, THE POWER OF MUSIC

'TWAS at the royal feast for Persia won
    By Philip's warlike son—
    Aloft in awful state
    The godlike hero sate
    On his imperial throne;
His valiant peers were placed around,
Their brows with roses and with myrtles bound
(So should desert in arms be crowned);
    The lovely Thais by his side
    Sate like a blooming eastern bride
    In flower of youth and beauty's pride:—
    Happy, happy, happy pair!
    None but the brave,
    None but the brave,
    None but the brave deserves the fair!

    Timotheus, placed on high
Amid the tuneful quire,
With flying fingers touched the lyre:
The trembling notes ascend the sky
And heavenly joys inspire.
The song began from Jove
Who left his blissful seats above—
Such is the power of mighty love!
A dragon's fiery form belied the god;
Sublime on radiant spheres he rode
When he to fair Olympia pressed,
And while he sought her snowy breast,
Then round her slender waist he curled,
And stamped an image of himself, a sovereign of the world.
—The listening crowd admire the lofty sound!
A present deity! they shout around:
A present deity! the vaulted roofs rebound!
    With ravished ears
    The monarch hears;
    Assumes the god,
    Affects to nod,
And seems to shake the spheres.

    The praise of Bacchus then the sweet musician sung,
Of Bacchus ever fair and ever young:
The jolly god in triumph comes!
Sound the trumpets, beat the drums!
Flushed with a purple grace
He shows his honest face:
Now give the hautboys breath; he comes, he comes!
Bacchus, ever fair and young,
Drinking joys did first ordain;

Bacchus' blessings are a treasure,
Drinking is the soldier's pleasure :
Rich the treasure,
Sweet the pleasure,
Sweet is pleasure after pain.

Soothed with the sound, the king grew vain ;
Fought all his battles o'er again,
And thrice he routed all his foes, and thrice he slew the slain.—
The master saw the madness rise,
His glowing cheeks, his ardent eyes :
And, while he heaven and earth defied,
Changed his hand and checked his pride.
He chose a mournful Muse
Soft pity to infuse :
He sung Darius great and good,
By too severe a fate,
Fallen, fallen, fallen, fallen,
Fallen from his high estate,
And weltering in his blood ;
Deserted, at his utmost need,
By those his former bounty fed ;
On the bare earth exposed he lies,
With not a friend to close his eyes.
With downcast looks the joyless victor sate,
Revolving in his altered soul
The various turns of chance below ;
And now and then a sigh he stole,
And tears began to flow.

The mighty master smiled to see
That love was in the next degree ;
'Twas but a kindred sound to move,
For pity melts the mind to love.
Softly sweet, in Lydian measures
Soon he soothed his soul to pleasures.
War, he sung, is toil and trouble ;
Honour but an empty bubble ;
Never ending, still beginning,
Fighting still, and still destroying ;
If the world be worth thy winning,
Think, O think it worth enjoying :
Lovely Thais sits beside thee,
Take the good the gods provide thee !
—The many rend the skies with loud applause
So Love was crowned, but Music won the cause.
The prince, unable to conceal his pain,
Gazed on the fair
Who caused his care,

And sighed and looked, sighed and looked,
Sighed and looked, and sighed again :
At length, with love and wine at once oppressed
The vanquished victor sunk upon her breast.

Now strike the golden lyre again :
A louder yet, and yet a louder strain !
Break his bands of sleep asunder,
And rouse him like a rattling peal of thunder.
Hark, hark ! the horrid sound
Has raised up his head :
As awaked from the dead
And amazed, he stares around.
Revenge, revenge ! Timotheus cries,
See the Furies arise !
See the snakes that they rear
How they hiss in their hair,
And the sparkles that flash from their eyes !
Behold a ghastly band,
Each a torch in his hand !
Those are Grecian ghosts, that in battle were slain,
And unburied remain
Inglorious on the plain :
Give the vengeance due
To the valiant crew !
Behold how they toss their torches on high,
How they point to the Persian abodes
And glittering temples of their hostile gods.
—The princes applaud with a furious joy :
And the King seized a flambeau with zeal to destroy ;
Thais led the way
To light him to his prey,
And like another Helen, fired another Troy !

—Thus, long ago,
Ere heaving bellows learned to blow,
While organs yet were mute,
Timotheus, to his breathing flute
And sounding lyre,
Could swell the soul to rage, or kindle soft desire.
At last divine Cecilia came,
Inventress of the vocal frame ;
The sweet enthusiast from her sacred store
Enlarged the former narrow bounds,
And added length to solemn sounds,
With Nature's mother-wit, and arts unknown before.
—Let old Timotheus yield the prize
Or both divide the crown ;
He raised a mortal to the skies ;
She drew an angel down !   J. DRYDEN.

G 3

343. LIFE A CHEAT

WHEN I consider life, 'tis all a cheat ;
Yet, fooled with hope, men favour the deceit ;
Trust on, and think to-morrow will repay :
To-morrow's falser than the former day ;
Lies worse ; and while it says, we shall be blessed
With some new joys, cuts off what we possessed.
Strange cozenage ! none would live past years again,
Yet all hope pleasure in what yet remain ;
And, from the dregs of life, think to receive
What the first sprightly running could not give.
I'm tired with waiting for this chemic gold,
Which fools us young, and beggars us when old.
                              J. DRYDEN (*Aureng-Zebe*).

344. LOVE HATH A LANGUAGE

LOVE hath a language for all years—
    Fond hieroglyphs, obscure and old—
Wherein the heart reads, writ in tears,
    The tale which never yet was told.

Love hath his meter too, to trace
    Those bounds which never yet were given,
To measure that which mocks at space,
    Is deep as death, and high as heaven.

Love hath his treasure hoards, to pay
    True faith, or goodly service done,—
Dear priceless nothings, which outweigh
    All riches that the sun shines on.
            HELEN, LADY DUFFERIN (*To my Son*).

345. TIMOR MORTIS CONTURBAT ME

I THAT in heill was and gladness
Am trublit now with great sickness
And feblit with infirmitie :—
    Timor Mortis conturbat me.

Our plesance here is all vain glory,
This fals world is but transitory,
The flesh is bruckle, the Feynd is slee :—
    Timor Mortis conturbat me.

The state of man does change and vary,
Now sound, now sick, now blyth, now sary,
Now dansand mirry, now like to die :—
    Timor Mortis conturbat me.

He takis the knichtis in to the field
Enarmit under helm and scheild ;
Victor he is at all mellie :—
   Timor Mortis conturbat me.

That strong unmerciful tyrand
Takis, on the motheris breast sowkand,
The babe full of benignitie :—
   Timor Mortis conturbat me.

He takis the campion in the stour,
The captain closit in the tour,
The lady in bour full of bewtie :—
   Timor Mortis conturbat me.

He spairis no lord for his piscence,
Na clerk for his intelligence ;
His awful straik may no man flee :—
   Timor Mortis conturbat me.

         W. DUNBAR (*The lament for the Makaris
                quhen he was seik*).

346. LONDON

LONDON, thou art of townès *a per se*,
  Sovereign of cities, seemliest in sight,
Of high renown, riches and royalty,
  Of lords, barons, and many a goodly knight,
  Of most delectable lusty ladies bright,
    Of famous prelates in habits clerical,
    Of merchants full of substance and of might :
    London, thou art the flower of cities all !

   .   .   .   .   .   .

Gem of all joy, jasper of jocundity,
  Most mighty carbuncle of virtue and valour ;
Strong Troy in vigour and in strenuity,
  Of royal cities rose and geraflour ;
  Empress of townès, exalt in honour,
    In beauty bearing the throne imperial,
  Sweet Paradise, precelling in pleasure :
    London, thou art the flower of cities all !

                      W. DUNBAR.

347. MY MIND TO ME A KINGDOM IS

MY mind to me a kingdom is !
  Such present joys therein I find
That it excels all other bliss
  That earth affords, or grows by kind.
    Though much I want which most would have,
    Yet still my mind forbids to crave.

No princely pomp, no wealthy store,
　No force to win a victory,
No wily wit to salve a sore,
　No shape to feed a loving eye,
　　To none of these I yield as thrall.
　　For why?　My mind doth serve for all.

I see how plenty surfeits oft;
　And hasty climbers soon do fall.
I see that those which are aloft
　Mishap doth threaten most of all.
　　They get with toil, they keep with fear;
　　Such cares my mind could never bear.

Content to live, this is my stay:
　I seek no more than may suffice.
I press to bear no haughty sway.
　Look, what I lack my mind supplies.
　　Lo, thus I triumph like a king,
　　Content with that my mind doth bring.

Some have too much, yet still do crave!
　I little have, and seek no more.
They are but poor, though much they have;
　And I am rich, with little store.
　　They poor, I rich; they beg, I give;
　　They lack, I leave; they pine, I live.

I laugh not at another's loss;
　· I grudge not at another's pain,
No worldly waves my mind can toss;
　My state at one doth still remain.
　　I fear no foe, I fawn no friend;
　　I loathe not life, nor dread my end.

Some weigh their pleasure by their lust,
　Their wisdom by their rage of will,
Their treasure is their only trust,
　A cloakèd craft their store of skill;
　　But all the pleasure that I find
　　Is to maintain a quiet mind.

My wealth is health and perfect ease,
　My conscience clear, my choice defence.
I neither seek by bribes to please,
　Nor by deceit to breed offence.
　　Thus do I live: thus will I die.
　　Would all did so, as well as I!

Sir E. Dyer.

348. THE FALLING OUT OF FAITHFUL FRIENDS

IN going to my naked bed, as one that would have slept,
I heard a wife sing to her child, that long before had wept.
She sighèd sore, and sang full sweet to bring the babe to rest,
That would not cease ; but crièd still, in sucking at her breast.
She was full weary of her watch, and grievèd with her child ;
She rockèd it, and rated it, till that on her it smiled.
Then did she say, ' Now have I found this proverb true to prove,
The falling out of faithful friends, renewing is of love.'

Then took I paper, pen, and ink, this proverb for to write,
In register for to remain of such a worthy wight.
As she proceeded thus in song unto her little brat
Much matter uttered she of weight, in place whereas she sat :
And provèd plain there was no beast, ne creature bearing life
Could well be known to live in love, without discord and strife.
Then kissèd she her little babe, and sware, by God above,
The falling out of faithful friends, renewing is of love.

She said that neither king, ne prince, ne lord could live aright,
Until their puissance they did prove, their manhood, and their might,
When manhood shall be matchèd so, that fear can take no place,
Then weary works make warriors each other to embrace,
And leave their force that failèd them ; which did consume the rout
That might before have lived their time, their strength and nature out.
Then did she sing, as one that thought no man could her reprove,
The falling out of faithful friends, renewing is of love.

She said she saw no fish, ne fowl, ne beast within her haunt
That met a stranger in their kind, but could give it a taunt.
Since flesh might not endure, but rest must wrath succeed,
And force the fight to fall to play, in pasture where they feed,
So noble Nature can well end the work she hath begun ;
And bridle well that will not cease her tragedy in some.
Thus in her song she oft rehearsed, as did her well behove,
The falling out of faithful friends, renewing is of love.

'I marvel much, pardy,' quoth she, ' for to behold the rout,
To see man, woman, boy, and beast, to toss the world about ;
Some kneel, some crouch, some beck, some check, and some can
  smoothly smile,
And some embrace others in arms, and there think many a wile.
Some stand aloof at cap and knee, some humble, and some stout,
Yet are they never friends in deed, until they once fall out ! '
Thus ended she her song, and said before she did remove
The falling out of faithful friends, renewing is of love.

R. EDWARDS.

349. O MAY I JOIN THE CHOIR INVISIBLE

O MAY I join the choir invisible
Of those immortal dead who live again
In minds made better by their presence : live
In pulses stirred to generosity,
In deeds of daring rectitude, in scorn
For miserable aims that end with self,
In thoughts sublime that pierce the night like stars,
And with their mild persistence urge man's search
To vaster issues.
                                    So to live is heaven.

.   .   .   .

May I reach
That purest heaven, be to other souls
The cup of strength in some great agony,
Enkindle generous ardour, feed pure love,
Beget the smiles that have no cruelty—
Be the sweet presence of a good diffused,
And in diffusion ever more intense.
So shall I join the choir invisible
Whose music is the gladness of the world.

                                    GEORGE ELIOT.

350. ON THE SACRAMENT

HE was the Word that spake it ;
He took the bread and brake it ;
And what the Word did make it,
I do believe and take it.

                                    QUEEN ELIZABETH.

351. A LAMENT FOR FLODDEN

I'VE heard them lilting at our ewe-milking,
    Lasses a' lilting before dawn o' day ;
But now they are moaning on ilka green loaning—
    The Flowers of the Forest are a' wede away.

At bughts, in the morning, nae blythe lads are scorning,
    Lasses are lonely and dowie and wae ;
Nae daffin', nae gabbin', but sighing and sabbing,
    Ilk ane lifts her leglin and hies her away.

In har'st, at the shearing, nae youths now are jeering,
    Bandsters are lyart, and runkled, and grey :
At fair or at preaching, nae wooing, nae fleeching—
    The Flowers of the Forest are a' wede away.

At e'en in the gloaming, nae swankies are roaming
  'Bout stacks wi' the lasses at bogle to play ;
But ilk ane sits drearie, lamenting her dearie—
  The Flowers of the Forest are a' wede away.

Dool and wae for the order, sent our lads to the Border !
  The English, for ance, by guile wan the day ;
The Flowers of the Forest, that fought ay the foremost,
  The prime of our land, lie cauld in the clay.

We'll hear nae mair lilting at our ewe-milking ;
  Women and bairns are heartless and wae ;
Sighing and moaning on ilka green loaning—
  The Flowers of the Forest are a' wede away.

JANE ELLIOT.

352. A POET'S PRAYER

ALMIGHTY Father ! let thy lowly child,
Strong in his love of truth, be wisely bold—
A patriot bard by sycophants reviled,
Let him live usefully, and not die old !
Let poor men's children, pleased to read his lays,
Love, for his sake, the scenes where he hath been;
And, when he ends his pilgrimage of days,
Let him be buried where the grass is green;
Where daisies, blooming earliest, linger late
To hear the bee his busy note prolong,—
There let him slumber, and in peace await
The dawning morn, far from the sensual throng,
Who scorn the wind-flower's blush, the redbreast's lonely song.

E. ELLIOTT.

353. THE LAND WHICH NO ONE KNOWS

  DARK, deep, and cold the current flows
  Unto the sea where no wind blows,
  Seeking the land which no one knows.

  O'er its sad gloom still comes and goes
  The mingled wail of friends and foes,
  Borne to the land which no one knows.

  Why shrieks for help yon wretch, who goes
  With millions, from a world of woes,
  Unto the land which no one knows ?

  Though myriads go with him who goes,
  Alone he goes where no wind blows,
  Unto the land which no one knows.

  For all must go where no wind blows,
  And none can go for him who goes ;
  None, none return whence no one knows.

Yet why should he who shrieking goes
With millions, from a world of woes,
Reunion seek with it or those ?

Alone with God, where no wind blows,
And Death, his shadow—doomed, he goes :
That God is there the shadow shows.

O shoreless Deep, where no wind blows !
And thou, O Land which no one knows !
That God is all, His shadow shows.

E. Elliott.

354.   AMYNTA

My sheep I neglected, I lost my sheep-hook,
And all the gay haunts of my youth I forsook ;
No more for Amynta fresh garlands I wove ;
For ambition, I said, would soon cure my love.
  Oh, what had my youth with ambition to do ?
  Why left I Amynta ? Why broke I my vow ?
        .   .   .   .   .   .

Oh, give me my sheep, and my sheep-hook restore,
I'll wander from love and Amynta no more.
        .   .   .   .   .   .

Alas ! 'tis too late at my fate to repine ;
Poor shepherd, Amynta no more can be thine :
Thy tears are all fruitless, thy wishes are vain,
The moments neglected return not again.

Sir G. Elliott.

355.   THE MONUMENT OF CONCORD FIGHT

By the rude bridge that arched the flood,
  Their flag to April's breeze unfurled,
Here once the embattled farmers stood,
  And fired the shot heard round the world.

The foe long since in silence slept ;
  Alike the conqueror silent sleeps ;
And Time the ruined bridge has swept
  Down the dark stream which seaward creeps.

On this green bank, by this soft stream,
  We set to-day a votive stone ;
That memory may their deed redeem,
  When, like our sires, our sons are gone.

Spirit, that made those heroes dare
  To die, and leave their children free,
Bid Time and Nature gently spare
  The shaft we raise to them and thee.

R. W. Emerson.

356.   GIVE ALL TO LOVE

Give all to love ;
Obey thy heart ;
Friends, kindred, days,
Estate, good-fame,
Plans, credit, and the Muse,—
Nothing refuse.

.   .   .   .   .   .

Cling with life to the maid ;
But when the surprise,
First vague shadow of surmise,
Flits across her bosom young

Of a joy apart from thee,
Free be she, fancy-free ;
Nor thou detain her vesture's hem,
Nor the palest rose she flung
From her summer diadem.

Though thou loved her as thyself,
As a self of purer clay,
Though her parting dims the day,
Stealing grace from all alive ;
Heartily know,
When half-gods go,
The gods arrive.

R. W. Emerson.

357.   GOOD-BYE, PROUD WORLD !

Good-bye, proud world ! I'm going home ;
  Thou art not my friend and I'm not thine.
Long through thy weary crowds I roam :
  A river-ark on the ocean brine,
Long I've been tossed like the driven foam
But now, proud world ! I'm going home.

.   .   .   .

Oh, when I am safe in my sylvan home,
I tread on the pride of Greece and Rome ;
And when I am stretched beneath the pines,
Where the evening star so holy shines,
I laugh at the lore and the pride of man,
At the sophist schools, and the learned clan ;
For what are they all, in their high conceit,
When man in the bush with God may meet ?

R. W. Emerson.

358.   FROM 'THE WORLD-SOUL'

He serveth the servant,
  The brave he loves amain ;
He kills the cripple and the sick,
  And straight begins again ;
For gods delight in gods,
  And thrust the weak aside ;
To him who scorns their charities,
  Their arms fly open wide.

R. W. Emerson.

359. FROM 'A DIRGE'

HEARKEN to yon pine-warbler
  Singing aloft in the tree !
Hearest thou, O traveller,
  What he singeth to me ?

Not unless God made sharp thine
    ear
  With sorrow such as mine,
Out of that delicate lay couldst
    thou
  Its heavy tale divine.

'Go, lonely man,' it saith ;
  'They loved thee from their
      birth ;
Their hands were pure, and pure
    their faith,—
  There are no such hearts on
      earth.
     .   .   .   .   .
'Ye cannot unlock your heart,
  The key is gone with them ;
The silent organ loudest chants
  The master's requiem.'
                    R. W. EMERSON.

360. BRAHMA

IF the red slayer think he slays,
  Or if the slain think he is slain,
They know not well the subtle
    ways
  I keep, and pass, and turn again.

Far or forgot to me is near ;
  Shadow and sunlight are the
      same ;
The vanished gods to me appear ;
  And one to me are shame and
      fame.

They reckon ill who leave me out ;
  When me they fly, I am the
      wings ;
I am the doubter and the doubt,
  And I the hymn the Brahmin
      sings.

The strong gods pine for my abode,
  And pine in vain the sacred
      Seven ;
But thou, meek lover of the good !
  Find me, and turn thy back on
      heaven.
                    R. W. EMERSON.

361. FROM 'THE PROBLEM'

NOT from a vain or shallow thought
His awful Jove young Phidias brought;
Never from lips of cunning fell
The thrilling Delphic oracle ;
Out from the heart of nature rolled
The burdens of the Bible old ;
The litanies of nations came,
Like the volcano's tongue of flame,
Up from the burning core below,—
The canticles of love and woe ;
The hand that rounded Peter's dome,
And groined the aisles of Christian Rome,
Wrought in a sad sincerity ;
Himself from God he could not free ;
He builded better than he knew ;—
The conscious stone to beauty grew.
                    R. W. EMERSON.

362. TO EVA

O FAIR and stately maid, whose eyes
Were kindled in the upper skies
  At the same torch that lighted mine;
For so I must interpret still
Thy sweet dominion o'er my will,
  A sympathy divine.

Ah! let me blameless gaze upon
Features that seem at heart my own;
  Nor fear those watchful sentinels,
Who charm the more their glance forbids,
Chaste-glowing, underneath their lids,
  With fire that draws while it repels.

R. W. EMERSON.

363. FABLE

THE mountain and the squirrel
Had a quarrel;
And the former called the latter
  'Little Prig'.
Bun replied,
'You are doubtless very big;
But all sorts of things and weather
Must be taken in together,
To make up a year
And a sphere.
And I think it no disgrace
To occupy my place.

If I'm not so large as you,
You are not so small as I,
And not half so spry.
I'll not deny you make
A very pretty squirrel track;
Talents differ: all is well and
  wisely put;
If I cannot carry forests on my
  back,
Neither can you crack a
  nut.'

R. W. EMERSON.

364. YE HAPPY SWAINS, WHOSE HEARTS ARE FREE

YE happy swains, whose hearts are free
  From Love's imperial chain,
Take warning, and be taught by me,
  To avoid the enchanting pain.
Fatal the wolves to trembling flocks—
  Fierce winds to blossoms prove—
To careless seamen, hidden rocks—
  To human quiet, love.

Fly the fair sex, if bliss you prize;
  The snake's beneath the flower:
Who ever gazed on beauteous eyes,
  That tasted quiet more?
How faithless is the lovers' joy!
  How constant is their care!
The kind with falsehood do destroy,
  The cruel with despair.   SIR G. ETHEREGE.

365. WRITTEN IN A LITTLE LADY'S LITTLE ALBUM

HEARTS good and true
Have wishes few
In narrow circles bounded,
And hope that lives
On what God gives
Is Christian hope well founded.

Small things are best;
Grief and unrest
To rank and wealth are given;
But little things
On little wings
Bear little souls to heaven.

F. W. FABER.

366. AGED CITIES

I HAVE known cities with the strong-armed Rhine
Clasping their mouldered quays in lordly sweep;
And lingered where the Maine's low waters shine
Through Tyrian Frankfort; and been fain to weep
'Mid the green cliffs where pale Mosella laves
That Roman sepulchre, imperial Treves.
Ghent boasts her street, and Bruges her moonlight square;
And holy Mechlin, Rome of Flanders, stands,
Like a queen-mother, on her spacious lands;
And Antwerp shoots her glowing spire in air.
Yet have I seen no place, by inland brook,
Hill-top, or plain, or trim arcaded bowers,
That carries age so nobly in its look,
As Oxford with the sun upon her towers.   F. W. FABER.

367. ENIGMA ON THE LETTER H

'TWAS whispered in Heaven, 'twas muttered in Hell,
And echo caught softly the sound as it fell;
In the confines of earth 'twas permitted to rest,
And the depth of the ocean its presence confessed;
'Twas seen in the lightning, 'twas heard in the thunder,
'Twill be found in the spheres when they're riven asunder;
'Twas given to man with his earliest breath,
It assists at his birth and attends him in death,
Presides o'er his happiness, honour, and health,
'Tis the prop of his house and the end of his wealth;
It begins every hope, every wish it must bound,
With the husbandman toils, and with monarchs is crowned;
In the heaps of the miser 'tis hoarded with care,
But is sure to be lost in the prodigal heir;
Without it the soldier and sailor may roam,
But woe to the wretch who expels it from home;
In the whispers of conscience it there will be found,
Nor e'er in the whirlwind of passion be drowned;
It softens the heart, and though deaf to the ear,
It will make it acutely and instantly hear;
But in shades let it rest, like an elegant flower,
Oh! breathe on it softly, it dies in an hour.   C. M. FANSHAWE.

368. IN ANCIENT GREECE

OCCASIONED BY A LADY'S MAKING A COPY OF VERSES

In ancient Greece, when Sappho sung
And touched with matchless art the lyre,
Apollo's hand her music strung
And all Parnassus formed the quire.

But sweeter notes and softer lays
From your diviner numbers spring,
Such as himself Apollo plays,
Such as the Heavenly Sisters sing.

H. FELTON.

369. A HUNTING SONG

THE dusky night rides down the sky,
And ushers in the morn ;
The hounds all join in glorious cry,
The huntsman winds his horn,
And a-hunting we will go.

The wife around her husband throws
Her arms, and begs his stay ;
' My dear, it rains, and hails, and snows,
You will not hunt to-day ? '
But a-hunting we will go.

' A brushing fox in yonder wood
Secure to find we seek :
For why ? I carried, sound and good,
A cartload there last week,
And a-hunting we will go.'

Away he goes, he flies the rout,
Their steeds all spur and switch,
Some are thrown in, and some thrown out,
And some thrown in the ditch;
But a-hunting we will go.

At length his strength to faintness worn,
Poor Reynard ceases flight ;
Then, hungry, homeward we return,
To feast away the night.
Then a-drinking we will go.

H. FIELDING.

370. IN THE MUSES' PATHS I STRAY

In the Muses' paths I stray ;
Among their groves and by their sacred springs
My hand delights to trace unusual things,
And deviates from the known and common way :
Nor will in fading silks compose
Faintly the inimitable rose,
Fill up an ill-drawn bird, or paint on glass
The Sovereign's blurred and undistinguished face,
The threatening angel, and the speaking ass.

ANNE FINCH, COUNTESS OF WINCHELSEA (*The Spleen*).

371. TO DEATH

O KING of Terrors! whose unbounded sway
All that have life must certainly obey;
The king, the priest, the prophet, all are thine,
Nor would even God (in flesh) thy stroke decline.
My name is on thy roll, and sure I must
Increase thy gloomy kingdom in the dust.
My soul at this no apprehension feels,
But trembles at thy swords, thy racks, thy wheels,
Thy scorching fevers, which distract the sense,
And snatch us raving, unprepared from hence;
At thy contagious darts, that wound the heads
Of weeping friends who wait at dying beds.—
Spare these, and let thy time be when it will;
My office is to die, and thine to kill.
Gently thy fatal sceptre on me lay,
And take to thy cold arms, insensibly, thy prey.
                ANNE FINCH, COUNTESS OF WINCHELSEA.

372. TO SILVIA

SILVIA, let us from the crowd retire,
    For what to you and me
(Who but each other do desire)
    Is all that here we see?

Apart we'll live, though not alone;
    For who *alone* can call
Those who in deserts live with one
    If in that one they've all?

The world a vast meander is,
    Where hearts confusedly stray;
Where few do hit, whilst thousands miss,
    The happy mutual way.
            ANNE FINCH, COUNTESS OF WINCHELSEA
                    (*The Cautious Lovers*).

373. FROM THE 'RUBAIYÁT OF OMAR KHAYYÁM'

AWAKE! for Morning in the Bowl of Night
Has flung the Stone that puts the Stars to flight,
    And Lo! the Hunter of the East has caught
The Sultán's Turret in a Noose of Light.

Come, fill the Cup, and in the Fire of Spring
The Winter Garment of Repentance fling:
    The Bird of Time has but a little way
To fly—and Lo! the Bird is on the Wing.

Here with a Loaf of Bread beneath the Bough,
A Flask of Wine, a Book of Verse—and Thou
   Beside me singing in the Wilderness—
And Wilderness is Paradise enow.

   .   .   .   .   . .

Think, in this battered Caravanserai
Whose Doorways are alternate Night and Day,
   How Sultán after Sultán with his Pomp
Abode his Hour or two, and went his way.

They say the Lion and the Lizard keep
The Courts where Jamshýd gloried and drank deep ;
   And Bahrám, that great Hunter—the Wild Ass
Stamps o'er his Head, and he lies fast asleep.

I sometimes think that never blows so red
The Rose as where some buried Caesar bled ;
   That every Hyacinth the Garden wears
Dropt in its Lap from some once lovely Head.

And this delightful Herb whose tender Green
Fledges the River's Lip on which we lean—
   Ah, lean upon it lightly ! for who knows
From what once lovely Lip it springs unseen !

Ah, my Belovèd, fill the Cup that clears
To-DAY of past Regrets and future Fears—
   To-morrow ?—Why, To-morrow I may be
Myself with Yesterday's Seven Thousand Years.

Lo ! some we loved, the loveliest and best
That Time and Fate of all their Vintage prest,
   Have drunk their Cup a Round or two before,
And one by one crept silently to Rest.

   .   .   .   .   .

Oh, come with old Khayyám, and leave the Wise
To talk ; one thing is certain, that Life flies ;
   One thing is certain, and the Rest is Lies ;
The Flower that once has blown for ever dies.

Myself when young did eagerly frequent
Doctor and Saint, and heard great Argument
   About it and about : but evermore
Came out by the same Door as in I went.

With them the Seed of Wisdom did I sow,
And with my own hand laboured it to grow :
   And this was all the Harvest that I reaped—
'I came like Water, and like Wind I go.'

   .   .   .   .   .

There was a Door to which I found no Key:
There was a Veil past which I could not see:
　Some little Talk awhile of ME and THEE
There seemed—and then no more of THEE and ME.

　.　　.　　.　　　.　　　.　　　.　　.

'Tis all a Chequer-board of Nights and Days
Where Destiny with Men for Pieces plays:
　Hither and thither moves, and mates, and slays,
And one by one back in the Closet lays.

The Ball no Question makes of Ayes and Noes,
But Right or Left as strikes the Player goes;
　And He that tossed Thee down into the Field,
He knows about it all—HE knows—HE knows!

The Moving Finger writes; and, having writ,
Moves on: nor all thy Piety nor Wit
　Shall lure it back to cancel half a Line,
Nor all thy Tears wash out a Word of it.

　.　　.　　.　　　.　　　.　　　.　　.

Oh Thou, who didst with Pitfall and with Gin
Beset the Road I was to wander in,
　Thou wilt not with Predestination round
Enmesh me, and impute my Fall to Sin?

Oh, Thou, who Man of baser Earth didst make,
And who with Eden didst devise the Snake;
　For all the Sin wherewith the Face of Man
Is blackened, Man's Forgiveness give—and take!

　.　　.　　.　　　.　　　.　　　.　　.

Ah, with the Grape my fading Life provide,
And wash my Body whence the Life has died,
　And in a Winding-sheet of Vine-leaf wrapt,
So bury me by some sweet Garden-side.

That even my buried Ashes such a Snare
Of Perfume shall fling up into the Air,
　As not a True Believer passing by
But shall be overtaken unaware.

Indeed the Idols I have loved so long
Have done my Credit in Men's Eye much wrong:
　Have drowned my Honour in a shallow Cup,
And sold my Reputation for a Song.

Indeed, indeed, Repentance oft before
I swore—but was I sober when I swore?
　And then and then came Spring, and Rose-in-hand
My thread-bare Penitence apieces tore.

And much as Wine has played the Infidel,
And robbed me of my Robe of Honour—well,
   I often wonder what the Vintners buy
One half so precious as the Goods they sell.

Alas, that Spring should vanish with the Rose !
That Youth's sweet-scented Manuscript should close !
   The Nightingale that in the Branches sang,
Ah, whence, and whither flown again, who knows !

Ah Love ! could thou and I with Fate conspire
To grasp this sorry Scheme of Things entire,
   Would not we shatter it to bits—and then
Re-mould it nearer to the Heart's Desire ! E. FITZGERALD.

374. OH, THE SAD DAY !

OH, the sad day !
When friends shall shake their heads, and say
Of miserable me :—
' Hark, how he groans !
Look how he pants for breath !
See how he struggles with the pangs of death ! '
When they shall say of these dear eyes :—
' How hollow, oh, how dim they be !
Mark how his breast doth rise and swell
Against his potent enemy ! '
When some old friend shall step to my bedside,
Touch my chill face, and thence shall gently slide,
But when his next companions say :—
' How does he do ? What hopes ? ' shall turn away,
Answering only, with a lift-up hand :—
' Who can his fate withstand ? '
Then shall a gasp or two do more
Than e'er my rhetoric could before :
Persuade the world to trouble me no more—
Persuade the world to trouble me no more. T. FLATMAN.

375. SONG TO PAN

ALL ye woods and trees and bowers,
All ye virtues and ye powers
That inhabit in the lakes,
In the pleasant springs or brakes,
   Move your feet
    To our sound
   Whilst we greet
    All this ground
With his honour and his name
That defends our flocks from blame.

He is great, and he is just,
He is ever good, and must
Thus be honoured. Daffadillies,
Roses, pinks, and lovèd lilies,
   Let us fling,
   Whilst we sing
   ' Ever holy,
   Ever holy,
Ever honoured, ever young ! '
Thus great Pan is ever sung.
        J. FLETCHER
    (The Faithful Shepherdess).

376. AWAY, DELIGHTS

Away, delights ! Go, seek some other dwelling,
  For I must die.
Farewell, false love. Thy tongue is ever telling
  Lie after lie.
For ever let me rest now from thy smarts.
    Alas, for pity, go,
    And fire their hearts
That have been hard to thee. Mine was not so.

Never again deluding love shall know me,
  For I will die,
And all those griefs, that think to overgrow me,
  Shall be as I.
For ever will I sleep, while poor maids cry,
    ' Alas, for pity, stay,
    And let us die
With thee. Men cannot mock us in the clay.'

J. FLETCHER (*The Captain*).

377. GOD LYAEUS

God Lyaeus, ever young,
Ever honoured, ever sung ;
Stained with blood of lusty grapes,
In a thousand lusty shapes
Dance upon the mazer's brim,
In the crimson liquor swim ;
From thy plenteous hand divine
Let a river run with wine :
  God of Youth, let this day here
  Enter neither care nor fear.

J. FLETCHER (*Valentinian*).

378. HEAR YE, LADIES, THAT DESPISE

Hear ye, ladies, that despise,
  What the mighty love has done ;
Fear examples, and be wise :
  Fair Callisto was a nun ;
Leda, sailing on the stream
  To deceive the hopes of man,
Love accounting but a dream,
  Doted on a silver swan ;
    Danaë, in a brazen tower,
    Where no love was, loved
    a shower.

Hear, ye ladies that are coy,
  What the mighty love can do ;
Fear the fierceness of the boy :
  The chaste moon he makes to woo ;
Vesta, kindling holy fires,
  Circled round about with spies,
Never dreaming loose desires,
  Doting at the altar dies ;
    Ilion, in a short hour, higher
    He can build, and once more
    fire.

J. FLETCHER (*Valentinian*).

379. HENCE, ALL YOU VAIN DELIGHTS

HENCE, all you vain delights,
As short as are the nights
Wherein you spend your folly:
There's naught in this life sweet,
If man were wise to see't,
But only melancholy,
Oh, sweetest melancholy!
Welcome, folded arms, and fixèd eyes,
A sigh that piercing mortifies,
A look that's fastened to the ground,
A tongue chained up, without a sound!
Fountain-heads and pathless groves,
Places which pale passion loves!
Moonlight walks, when all the fowls
Are warmly housed, save bats and owls!
A midnight bell, a parting groan!
These are the sounds we feed upon;
Then stretch our bones in a still gloomy valley;
Nothing's so dainty sweet as lovely melancholy.

J. FLETCHER (*The Nice Valour*).

380. MAN HIS OWN STAR

MAN is his own star; and the soul that can
Render an honest and a perfect man
Commands all light, all influence, all fate;
Nothing to him falls early, or too late.
Our acts our angels are, or good or ill,
Our fatal shadows that walk by us still.

J. FLETCHER (*The Honest Man's Fortune*).

381. NOW THE LUSTY SPRING IS SEEN

Now the lusty Spring is seen;
  Golden yellow, gaudy blue,
  Daintily invite the view.
Everywhere, on every green,
Roses blushing as they blow,
  And enticing men to pull!
Lilies whiter than the snow,
  Woodbines, of sweet honey full:
    All Love's emblems! and all cry,
    'Ladies, if not plucked, we die!'

Yet the lusty Spring hath stayed;
  Blushing red and purest white
  Daintily to Love invite
Every woman, every maid!
Cherries kissing, as they grow;
  And inviting men to taste!
Apples even ripe below,
  Winding gently to the waist!
    All Love's emblems, and all cry,
    'Ladies, if not plucked, we die!'

J. FLETCHER (*Valentinian*).

382.   WOMEN'S LONGING

TELL me what is that only thing
    For which all women long ;
Yet having what they most desire,
    To have it does them wrong ?

'Tis not to be chaste nor fair,
(Such gifts malice may impair),
Richly trimmed, to walk or ride,
Or to wanton unespied,
To preserve an honest name
And so to give it up to fame—
These are toys.   In good or ill
They desire to have their will :
Yet when they have it, they abuse it,
For they know not how to use it.

J. FLETCHER (Women Pleased).

383.   THE LIBRARY A GLORIOUS COURT

THAT place, that does contain
My books, the best companions, is to me
A glorious court, where hourly I converse
With the old sages and philosophers.
And sometimes, for variety, I confer
With kings and emperors, and weigh their counsels ;
Calling their victories, if unjustly got,
Unto a strict account : and in my fancy,
Deface their ill-planned statues.   Can I then
Part with such constant pleasures, to embrace
Uncertain vanities ?   No : be it your care
To augment your heap of wealth ; it shall be mine
To increase in knowledge.   Lights there for my study !

J. FLETCHER (The Elder Brother).

384.   DROP, DROP, SLOW TEARS

DROP, drop, slow tears,
    And bathe those beauteous feet
Which brought from Heaven
    The news and Prince of Peace.
Cease not, wet eyes,
    His mercy to entreat ;
To cry for vengeance
    Sin doth never cease.
In your deep floods
    Drown all my faults and fears ;
Nor let His eye
    See sin, but through my tears.

P. FLETCHER.

385. IMMORTALITY IN BOOKS

SINCE honour from the honourer proceeds,
How well do they deserve, that memorize
And leave in books for all posterities
The names of worthies and their virtuous deeds ;
When all their glory else, like water-weeds
Without their element, presèntly dies,
And all their greatness quite forgotten lies,
And when and how they flourished no man heeds !
How poor remembrances are statues, tombs
And other monuments that men erect
To princes, which remain in closèd rooms,
Where but a few behold them, in respect
Of books, that to the universal eye
Show how they lived ; the other where they lie !

J. FLORIO.

386. THE BROKEN HEART

OH, no more, no more ; too late
  Sighs are spent ; the burning
      tapers
Of a life as chaste as fate,
  Pure as are unwritten papers,
Are burnt out ; no heat, no light
Now remains ; 'tis ever night.

Love is dead ; let lovers' eyes,
Locked in endless dreams,
Th' extremes of all extremes,
Ope no more, for now Love dies.
Now Love dies—implying
Love's martyrs must be ever, ever
      dying.   J. FORD
                 (*The Broken Heart*).

387. BLACK-EYED SUSAN

ALL in the Downs the fleet was moored,
  The streamers waving in the wind,
When black-eyed Susan came aboard.
  ' Oh ! where shall I my true love find ?
Tell me, ye jovial sailors, tell me true,
If my sweet William sails among the crew.'

William, who high upon the yard
  Rocked with the billow to and fro,
Soon as her well-known voice he heard,
  He sighed, and cast his eyes below :
The cord slides swiftly through his glowing hands,
And (quick as lightning) on the deck he stands.

So the sweet lark, high poised in air,
  Shuts close his pinions to his breast,
If chance his mate's shrill call he hear,
  And drops at once into her nest :—
The noblest captain in the British fleet
Might envy William's lip those kisses sweet.

' O Susan, Susan, lovely dear,
   My vows shall ever true remain,
Let me kiss off that falling tear ;
   We only part to meet again.
Change, as ye list, ye winds ; my heart shall be
The faithful compass that still points to thee.

' Believe not what the landmen say,
   Who tempt with doubts thy constant mind.
They'll tell thee, sailors, when away,
   In every port a mistress find :
Yes, yes, believe them when they tell thee so,
For thou art present wheresoe'er I go.

' If to far India's coast we sail
   Thy eyes are seen in diamonds bright,
Thy breath is Afric's spicy gale,
   Thy skin is ivory so white.
Thus every beauteous object that I view
Wakes in my soul some charm of lovely Sue.

' Though battle call me from thy arms
   Let not my pretty Susan mourn ;
Though cannons roar, yet safe from harms
   William shall to his Dear return.
Love turns aside the balls that round me fly,
Lest precious tears should drop from Susan's eye.'

The boatswain gave the dreadful word,
   The sails their swelling bosom spread ;
No longer must she stay aboard ;
   They kissed, she sighed, he hung his head.
Her lessening boat unwilling rows to land ;
' Adieu ! ' she cries ; and waved her lily hand.

J. GAY.

388.   LOVE IN HER EYES SITS PLAYING

LOVE in her eyes sits playing,
   And sheds delicious death ;
Love in her lips is straying,
   And warbling in her breath ;
Love on her breast sits panting,
   And swells with soft desire :
Nor grace, nor charm, is wanting
To set the heart on fire.

J. GAY (Acis and Galatea).

389.   O RUDDIER THAN THE CHERRY

O RUDDIER than the cherry !
O sweeter than the berry !
   O nymph more bright
   Than moonshine night,
Like kidlings blithe and merry
Ripe as the melting cluster !
No lily has such lustre ;
   Yet hard to tame
   As raging flame,
And fierce as storms that bluster.

J. GAY (Acis and Galatea).

390. TO HEALTH

How shall I woo thee, sweetest, rose-lipped fair ?
  When to my eager bosom press thy charms ?
No fleecy lambkins ask my evening care ;
  No morning toils have nerved my youthful arms.

Yet say, O say, bright daughter of the sky,
  Wilt thou still shun the student's midnight oil ?
And, O too partial ! every grace deny
  To all but yonder sturdy sons of toil ?

Would numbers win thee, thou no lay shouldst need,
  Whether the Muses' sacred bond resides
Among the Dryads on the daisied mead,
  Where Cam's fair stream, or silver Isis glides.
                  R. GIFFORD (*Contemplation*).

391. LITTLE, YE SISTER-NINE

LITTLE, ye Sister-Nine, they need your aid
  Whose artless breasts these living scenes inspire.

Even from the straw-roofed cot the note of joy
  Flows full and frequent as the village fair,
Whose little wants the busy hours employ,
  Chanting some rural ditty soothes her care.

Verse sweetens toil, however rude the sound.
  She feels no biting pang the while she sings ;
Nor, as she turns the giddy wheel around,
  Revolves the sad vicissitude of things.
                  R. GIFFORD (*Contemplation*).

392. THE EXILE'S SONG

OH, why left I my hame ?
  Why did I cross the deep ?
Oh, why left I the land
  Where my forefathers sleep ?
I sigh for Scotia's shore,
  And I gaze across the sea,
But I canna get a blink
  O' my ain countrie !

The palm-tree waveth high,
  And fair the myrtle springs ;
And, to the Indian maid
  The bulbul sweetly sings ;
But I dinna see the broom
  Wi' its tassels on the lea,
Nor hear the lintie's sang
  O' my ain countrie !

Oh, here no Sabbath bell
  Awakes the Sabbath morn,
Nor song of reapers heard
  Amang the yellow corn :
For the tyrant's voice is here,
  And the wail of slaverie ;
But the sun of freedom shines
  In my ain countrie !

There's a hope for every woe,
  And a balm for every pain,
But the first joys o' our heart
  Come never back again.
There's a track upon the deep,
  And a path across the sea ;
But the weary ne'er return
  To their ain countrie !
                  R. GILFILLAN.

393. THE VILLAGE PREACHER

A MAN he was to all the country dear,
And passing rich with forty pounds a year ;
Remote from towns he ran his godly race,
Nor e'er had changed, nor wished to change his place ;
Unpractised he to fawn, or seek for power,
By doctrines fashioned to the varying hour ;
Far other aims his heart had learned to prize,
More skilled to raise the wretched than to rise.
His house was known to all the vagrant train,
He chid their wanderings, but relieved their pain ;
The long-remembered beggar was his guest,
Whose beard descending swept his aged breast ;
The ruined spendthrift, now no longer proud,
Claimed kindred there, and had his claims allowed ;
The broken soldier, kindly bade to stay,
Sat by his fire, and talked the night away ;
Wept o'er his wounds, or tales of sorrow done,
Shouldered his crutch, and showed how fields were won.
Pleased with his guests, the good man learned to glow,
And quite forgot their vices in their woe ;
Careless their merits or their faults to scan,
His pity gave ere charity began.

O. GOLDSMITH (*The Deserted Village*).

394. AN ELEGY

ON THE DEATH OF A MAD DOG

GOOD people all, of every sort,
  Give ear unto my song ;
And if you find it wondrous short
  It cannot hold you long.

In Islington there was a man,
  Of whom the world might say
That still a godly race he ran,
  Whene'er he went to pray.

A kind and gentle heart he had,
  To comfort friends and foes ;
The naked every day he clad,
  When he put on his clothes.

And in that town a dog was found,
  As many dogs there be,
Both mongrel, puppy, whelp, and
    hound,
  And curs of low degree.

This dog and man at first were
    friends ;
  But when a pique began,
The dog, to gain some private ends,
  Went mad and bit the man.

Around from all the neighbouring
    streets
  The wondering neighbours ran,
And swore the dog had lost his
    wits,
  To bite so good a man.

The wound it seemed both sore
    and sad
  To every Christian eye ;
And while they swore the dog was
    mad,
  They swore the man would die.

But soon a wonder came to light,
    That showed the rogues they lied :
The man recovered of the bite,
    The dog it was that died.

O. GOLDSMITH.

395. DAVID GARRICK

HERE lies David Garrick, describe me, who can,
An abridgement of all that was pleasant in man ;
As an actor, confessed without rival to shine :
As a wit, if not first, in the very first line :
Yet, with talents like these, and an excellent heart,
The man had his failings, a dupe to his art.
Like an ill-judging beauty, his colours he spread,
And beplastered with rouge his own natural red.
On the stage he was natural, simple, affecting ;
'Twas only that when he was off he was acting.

O. GOLDSMITH (Retaliation).

396. EDMUND BURKE

HERE lies our good Edmund, whose genius was such,
We scarcely can praise it, or blame it too much ;
Who, born for the Universe, narrowed his mind,
And to party gave up what was meant for mankind.
Though fraught with all learning, yet straining his throat
To persuade Tommy Townshend to lend him a vote ;
Who, too deep for his hearers, still went on refining,
And thought of convincing, while they thought of dining ;
Though equal to all things, for all things unfit,
Too nice for a statesman, too proud for a wit ;
For a patriot, too cool ; for a drudge, disobedient ;
And too fond of the <i>right</i> to pursue the <i>expedient</i>.

O. GOLDSMITH (Retaliation).

397. SIR JOSHUA REYNOLDS

HERE Reynolds is laid, and, to tell you my mind,
He has not left a better or wiser behind :
His pencil was striking, resistless, and grand ;
His manners were gentle, complying, and bland
Still born to improve us in every part,
His pencil our faces, his manners our heart :
To coxcombs averse, yet most civilly steering,
When they judged without skill he was still hard of hearing :
When they talked of their Raphaels, Correggios, and stuff,
He shifted his trumpet, and only took snuff.

O. GOLDSMITH (Retaliation).

H

398. MAN WANTS BUT LITTLE

No flocks that range the valley free
    To slaughter I condemn ;
Taught by that Power that pities me,
    I learn to pity them.

But from the mountain's grassy side,
    A guiltless feast I bring ;
A scrip with herbs and fruits supplied,
    And water from the spring.

Then, pilgrim, turn, thy cares forgo ;
    All earth-born cares are wrong :
Man wants but little here below,
    Nor wants that little long.
               O. GOLDSMITH (*Edwin and Angelina*).

399. FROM 'THE TRAVELLER'

REMOTE, unfriended, melancholy, slow,
Or by the lazy Scheldt, or wandering Po,
Or onward, where the rude Carinthian boor
Against the houseless stranger shuts the door ;
Or where Campania's plain forsaken lies,
A weary waste expanding to the skies :
Where'er I roam, whatever realms to see,
My heart untravelled fondly turns to thee ;
Still to my brother turns with ceaseless pain,
And drags at each remove a lengthening chain.

Eternal blessings crown my earliest friend,
And round his dwelling guardian saints attend :
Blest be that spot, where cheerful guests retire
To pause from toil, and trim their evening fire ;
Blest that abode, where want and pain repair,
And every stranger finds a ready chair ;
Blest be those feasts with simple plenty crowned,
Where all the ruddy family around
Laugh at the jests or pranks that never fail,
Or sigh with pity at some mournful tale,
Or press the bashful stranger to his food,
And learn the luxury of doing good.   O. GOLDSMITH.

400. SWEET AUBURN

SWEET Auburn ! loveliest village of the plain,
Where health and plenty cheered the labouring swain,
Where smiling spring its earliest visit paid,
And parting summer's lingering blooms delayed :
Dear lovely bowers of innocence and ease,
Seats of my youth, when every sport could please.

   .   .   .   .

Ill fares the land, to hastening ills a prey,
Where wealth accumulates, and men decay :
Princes and lords may flourish, or may fade
A breath can make them, as a breath has made ;
But a bold peasantry, their country's pride,
When once destroyed, can never be supplied.

. . . .

In all my wanderings round this world of care,
In all my griefs—and God has given my share—
I still had hopes my latest hours to crown,
Amidst these humble bowers to lay me down ;
To husband out life's taper at the close,
And keep the flame from wasting by repose.
I still had hopes, for pride attends us still,
Amidst the swains to show my book-learned skill,
Around my fire an evening group to draw,
And tell of all I felt, and all I saw ;
And, as a hare, whom hounds and horns pursue,
Pants to the place from whence at first she flew,
I still had hopes, my long vexations passed,
Here to return—and die at home at last.

O. GOLDSMITH (*The Deserted Village*).

401. THE SCHOOLMASTER

THERE, in his noisy mansion, skilled to rule,
The village master taught his little school ;
A man severe he was, and stern to view ;
I knew him well, and every truant knew ;
Well had the boding tremblers learned to trace
The day's disasters in his morning face ;
Full well they laughed, with counterfeited glee,
At all his jokes, for many a joke had he ;
Full well the busy whisper, circling round,
Conveyed the dismal tidings when he frowned ;
Yet he was kind ; or if severe in aught,
The love he bore to learning was in fault ;
The village all declared how much he knew ;
'Twas certain he could write, and cypher too ;
Lands he could measure, terms and tides presage,
And e'en the story ran that he could gauge.
In arguing too, the parson owned his skill,
For e'en though vanquished, he could argue still ;
While words of learnèd length and thundering sound
Amazed the gazing rustics ranged around,
And still they gazed, and still the wonder grew,
That one small head could carry all he knew.

O. GOLDSMITH (*The Deserted Village*).

402. HOPE

To the last moment of his breath
    On hope the wretch relies;
And e'en the pang preceding death
    Bids expectation rise.

Hope, like the gleaming taper's light,
    Adorns and cheers our way;
And still, as darker grows the night,
    Emits a brighter ray.

        O. GOLDSMITH (*The Captivity*).

403. WHEN LOVELY WOMAN STOOPS TO FOLLY

WHEN lovely woman stoops to folly,
    And finds too late that men betray,
What charm can soothe her melancholy,
    What art can wash her guilt away?

The only art her guilt to cover,
    To hide her shame from every eye
To give repentance to her lover,
    And wring his bosom, is—to die.

        O. GOLDSMITH (*The Vicar of Wakefield*).

404. OF MONEY

GIVE money me; take friendship whoso list!
    For friends are gone, come once adversity;
When money yet remaineth safe in chest,
    That quickly can thee bring from misery.
Fair face show friends, when riches do abound;
    Come time of proof, 'Farewell, they must away!'
Believe me well, they are not to be found,
    If God but send thee once a lowering day.
        Gold never starts aside; but, in distress,
        Finds ways enough to ease thy heaviness.

        B. GOOGE.

405. MY DEAR AND ONLY LOVE, I PRAY

My dear and only love, I pray
    This noble world of thee
Be governed by no other sway
    But purest monarchy;
For if confusion have a part,
    (Which virtuous souls abhor),
And hold a Synod in thy heart,
    I'll never love thee more.

Like Alexander I will reign,
    And I will reign alone;
My thoughts did evermore disdain
    A rival on my throne.
He either fears his fate too much,
    Or his deserts are small,
That puts it not unto the touch
    To win, or lose, it all.

But I must rule and govern still
And always give the law,
And have each subject at my wil!
And all to stand in awe.
But 'gainst my battery, if I find
Thou shunn'st the prize so sore
As that thou sett'st me up a
blind,
I'll never love thee more !

Or in the empire of thy heart,
Where I should solely be,
Another do pretend a part
And dares to vie with me,

Or if Committees thou erect,
And go on such a score,
I'll sing and laugh at thy neglect,
And never love thee more.

But if thou wilt be constant then,
And faithful of thy word ;
I'll make thee glorious by my pen
And famous by my sword,
I'll serve thee in such noble ways
Were never heard before !
I'll crown and deck thee all with
bays,
And love thee evermore.

J. GRAHAM, MARQUIS OF MONTROSE.

406. IF DOUGHTY DEEDS MY LADY PLEASE

IF doughty deeds my lady please,
Right soon I'll mount my steed ;
And strong his arm, and fast his
seat,
That bears frae me the meed.
I'll wear thy colours in my cap,
Thy picture in my heart ;
And he that bends not to thine eye
Shall rue it to his smart !
Then tell me how to woo thee,
Love ;
O tell me how to woo thee !
For thy dear sake, nae care
I'll take,
Tho' ne'er another trow me.

If gay attire delight thine eye,
I'll dight me in array ;
I'll tend thy chamber door all
night,
And squire thee all the day.

If sweetest sounds can win thine
ear,
These sounds I'll strive to catch;
Thy voice I'll steal to woo thysell,
That voice that nane can match.

But if fond love thy heart can
gain,
I never broke a vow ;
Nae maiden lays her skaith to me,
I never loved but you.
For you alone I ride the ring,
For you I wear the blue ;
For you alone I strive to sing,
O tell me how to woo !
O tell me how to woo thee,
Love ;
O tell me how to woo thee !
For thy dear sake, nae care
I'll take,
Tho' ne'er another trow me.

R. GRAHAM (afterwards Cunninghame-Graham).

407. FROM THE 'HYMN TO ADVERSITY'

DAUGHTER of Jove, relentless power,
Thou tamer of the human breast,
Whose iron scourge and torturing hour
The bad affright, afflict the best !
Bound in thy adamantine chain,
The proud are taught to taste of pain,
And purple tyrants vainly groan
With pangs unfelt before, unpitied and alone.

When first thy sire to send on earth
    Virtue, his darling child, designed,
To thee he gave the heavenly birth,
    And bade to form her infant mind.
Stern rugged nurse ! thy rigid lore
With patience many a year she bore :
What sorrow was thou bad'st her know,
And from her own she learned to melt at others' woe.

     .   .   .   .   .

Thy form benign, O goddess, wear,
    Thy milder influence impart,
Thy philosophic train be there
    To soften, not to wound, my heart.
The generous spark extinct revive,
Teach me to love and to forgive,
Exact my own defects to scan,
What others are, to feel, and know myself a Man.
                                              T. GRAY.

408.   FROM 'THE PROGRESS OF POESY'

A PINDARIC ODE

FAR from the sun and summer-gale,
In thy green lap was Nature's darling laid,
What time, where lucid Avon strayed,
To Him the mighty mother did unveil
Her awful face : the dauntless Child
Stretched forth his little arms, and smiled.
    This pencil take (she said), whose colours clear
Richly paint the vernal year :
Thine too these golden keys, immortal Boy !
This can unlock the gates of Joy ;
Of Horror that, and thrilling fears,
Or ope the sacred source of sympathetic tears.

Nor second He, that rode sublime
    Upon the seraph-wings of Ecstasy,
    The secrets of the Abyss to spy.
He passed the flaming bounds of Place and Time :
    The living Throne, the sapphire-blaze,
Where Angels tremble, while they gaze,
He saw ; but, blasted with excess of light,
Closed his eyes in endless night.
Behold, where Dryden's less presumptuous car,
Wide o'er the fields of Glory bear
Two coursers of ethereal race,
With necks in thunder clothed, and long-resounding pace.

Hark, his hands the lyre explore !
Bright-eyed Fancy hovering o'er,

Scatters from her pictured urn
Thoughts that breathe and words that burn.
But ah ! 'tis heard no more—
Oh ! lyre divine, what daring Spirit
Wakes thee now ? though he inherit
Nor the pride, nor ample pinion,
   That the Theban Eagle bear
Sailing with supreme dominion
   Through the azure deep of air :
Yet oft before his infant eyes would run
Such forms, as glitter in the Muse's ray
With orient hues, unborrowed of the sun :
Yet shall he mount, and keep his distant way
Beyond the limits of a vulgar fate,
Beneath the Good how far—but far above the Great.

                               T. GRAY.

409. ODE TO THE SPRING

Lo ! where the rosy-bosomed Hours,
   Fair Venus' train appear,
Disclose the long-expecting flowers,
   And wake the purple year !
The Attic warbler pours her throat
Responsive to the cuckoo's note,
   The untaught harmony of spring :
While, whispering pleasure as they fly,
Cool Zephyrs through the clear blue sky
   Their gathered fragrance fling.

Where'er the oak's thick branches stretch
   A broader browner shade ;
Where'er the rude and moss-grown beech
   O'er-canopies the glade,
Beside some water's rushy brink
With me the Muse shall sit, and think
   (At ease reclined in rustic state)
How vain the ardour of the crowd,
How low, how little are the proud,
   How indigent the great !

Still is the toiling hand of Care :
   The panting herds repose :
Yet hark, how through the peopled air
   The busy murmur glows :
The insect youth are on the wing,
Eager to taste the honied spring
   And float amid the liquid noon ;
Some lightly o'er the current skim,
Some show their gaily-gilded trim
   Quick-glancing to the sun.

To Contemplation's sober eye
    Such is the race of man:
And they that creep, and they that fly,
    Shall end where they began.
Alike the busy and the gay
But flutter through life's little day,
    In fortune's varying colours dressed:
Brushed by the hand of rough Mischance,
Or chilled by age, their airy dance
    They leave, in dust to rest.

Methinks I hear in accents low
    The sportive kind reply:
Poor moralist! and what art thou?
    A solitary fly!
Thy joys no glittering female meets,
No hive hast thou of hoarded sweets,
    No painted plumage to display;
On hasty wings thy youth is flown;
Thy sun is set, thy spring is gone—
    We frolic, while 'tis May.   T. GRAY.

410.   OPENING PARADISE

SEE the wretch that long has tossed
    On the thorny bed of pain
At length repair his vigour lost,
    And breathe and walk again:
The meanest floweret of the vale,
The simplest note that swells the gale,
The common sun, the air, the skies,
To him are opening Paradise.

                                T. GRAY (*Vicissitude*).

411.   ELEGY WRITTEN IN A COUNTRY CHURCHYARD

THE Curfew tolls the knell of parting day,
The lowing herd wind slowly o'er the lea,
The ploughman homeward plods his weary way,
And leaves the world to darkness and to me.

Now fades the glimmering landscape on the sight,
And all the air a solemn stillness holds,
Save where the beetle wheels his droning flight,
And drowsy tinklings lull the distant folds:

Save that from yonder ivy-mantled tower
The moping owl does to the moon complain
Of such as, wandering near her secret bower,
Molest her ancient solitary reign.

Beneath those rugged elms, that yew-tree's shade,
Where heaves the turf in many a mouldering heap,
Each in his narrow cell for ever laid,
The rude Forefathers of the hamlet sleep.

The breezy call of incense-breathing morn,
The swallow twittering from the straw-built shed,
The cock's shrill clarion, or the echoing horn,
No more shall rouse them from their lowly bed.

For them no more the blazing hearth shall burn,
Or busy housewife ply her evening care:
No children run to lisp their sire's return,
Or climb his knees the envied kiss to share.

Oft did the harvest to their sickle yield,
Their furrow oft the stubborn glebe has broke;
How jocund did they drive their team afield!
How bowed the woods beneath their sturdy stroke!

Let not Ambition mock their useful toil,
Their homely joys, and destiny obscure;
Nor Grandeur hear with a disdainful smile
The short and simple annals of the poor.

The boast of heraldry, the pomp of power,
And all that beauty, all that wealth e'er gave,
Awaits alike the inevitable hour—
The paths of glory lead but to the grave.

Nor you, ye Proud, impute to these the fault
If Memory o'er their tomb no trophies raise,
Where through the long-drawn aisle and fretted vault
The pealing anthem swells the note of praise.

Can storied urn or animated bust
Back to its mansion call the fleeting breath?
Can Honour's voice provoke the silent dust,
Or Flattery soothe the dull cold ear of Death?

Perhaps in this neglected spot is laid
Some heart once pregnant with celestial fire;
Hands, that the rod of empire might have swayed,
Or waked to ecstasy the living lyre.

But Knowledge to their eyes her ample page
Rich with the spoils of time, did ne'er unroll;
Chill Penury repressed their noble rage,
And froze the genial current of the soul.

Full many a gem of purest ray serene
The dark unfathomed caves of ocean bear:
Full many a flower is born to blush unseen,
And waste its sweetness on the desert air.

Some village-Hampden, that with dauntless breast
The little tyrant of his fields withstood,
Some mute inglorious Milton here may rest,
Some Cromwell guiltless of his country's blood.

The applause of listening senates to command,
The threats of pain and ruin to despise,
To scatter plenty o'er a smiling land,
And read their history in a nation's eyes,

Their lot forbade : nor circumscribed alone
Their growing virtues, but their crimes confined ;
Forbade to wade through slaughter to a throne,
And shut the gates of mercy on mankind,

The struggling pangs of conscious truth to hide,
To quench the blushes of ingenuous shame,
Or heap the shrine of Luxury and Pride
With incense kindled at the Muse's flame.

Far from the madding crowd's ignoble strife
Their sober wishes never learned to stray ;
Along the cool sequestered vale of life
They kept the noiseless tenor of their way.

Yet even these bones from insult to protect
Some frail memorial still erected nigh,
With uncouth rhymes and shapeless sculpture decked,
Implores the passing tribute of a sigh.

Their name, their years, spelt by the unlettered muse,
The place of fame and elegy supply :
And many a holy text around she strews,
That teach the rustic moralist to die.

For who, to dumb forgetfulness a prey,
This pleasing anxious being e'er resigned,
Left the warm precincts of the cheerful day,
Nor cast one longing lingering look behind ?

On some fond breast the parting soul relies,
Some pious drops the closing eye requires ;
E'en from the tomb the voice of Nature cries,
E'en in our ashes live their wonted fires.

For thee, who, mindful of the unhonoured dead,
Dost in these lines their artless tale relate ;
If chance, by lonely contemplation led,
Some kindred spirit shall inquire thy fate,—

Haply some hoary-headed swain may say,
' Oft have we seen him at the peep of dawn
Brushing with hasty steps the dews away
To meet the sun upon the upland lawn ;

'There at the foot of yonder nodding beech
That wreathes its old fantastic roots so high,
His listless length at noon-tide would he stretch,
And pore upon the brook that babbles by.

'Hard by yon wood, now smiling as in scorn,
Muttering his wayward fancies he would rove ;
Now drooping, woeful-wan, like one forlorn,
Or crazed with care, or crossed in hopeless love.

'One morn I missed him on the customed hill,
Along the heath, and near his favourite tree ;
Another came : nor yet beside the rill,
Nor up the lawn, nor at the wood was he ;

'The next, with dirges due in sad array
Slow through the church-way path we saw him borne,—
Approach and read (for thou canst read) the lay
Graved on the stone beneath yon aged thorn.'

THE EPITAPH

HERE rests his head upon the lap of earth
A Youth, to Fortune and to Fame unknown ;
Fair Science frowned not on his humble birth,
And Melancholy marked him for her own.

Large was his bounty, and his soul sincere,
Heaven did a recompense as largely send :
He gave to Misery (all he had) a tear,
He gained from Heaven ('twas all he wished) a friend.

No farther seek his merits to disclose,
Or draw his frailties from their dread abode
(There they alike in trembling hope repose),
The bosom of his Father and his God.   T. GRAY.

412. ODE ON THE DEATH OF A FAVOURITE CAT
DROWNED IN A TUB OF GOLD FISHES

'TWAS on a lofty vase's side
Where China's gayest art had dyed
    The azure flowers, that blow ;
Demurest of the tabby kind,
The pensive Selima reclined,
    Gazed on the lake below.

Her conscious tail her joy declared ;
The fair round face, the snowy beard,
    The velvet of her paws,
Her coat, that with the tortoise vies,
Her ears of jet, and emerald eyes
    She saw ; and purred applause.

Still had she gazed; but midst the tide
Two angel forms were seen to glide,
    The Genii of the stream:
Their scaly armour's Tyrian hue
Through richest purple to the view
    Betrayed a golden gleam.

The hapless Nymph with wonder saw:
A whisker first and then a claw
    With many an ardent wish
She stretched in vain to reach the prize.
What female heart can gold despise?
    What Cat's averse to fish?

Presumptuous Maid! with looks intent
Again she stretched, again she bent,
    Nor knew the gulf between.
(Malignant Fate sat by and smiled)
The slippery verge her feet beguiled,
    She tumbled headlong in.

Eight times emerging from the flood
She mewed to every watery God
    Some speedy aid to send.
No Dolphin came, no Nereid stirred:
Nor cruel Tom nor Susan heard,
    A Favourite has no friend.

From hence, ye Beauties, undeceived,
Know, one false step is ne'er retrieved,
    And be with caution bold.
Not all that tempts your wandering eyes
And heedless hearts is lawful prize ·
    Nor all that glisters gold.   T. GRAY.

413. FROM THE 'ODE ON A DISTANT PROSPECT OF ETON COLLEGE'

YE distant spires, ye antique towers,
  That crown the watery glade,
Where grateful Science still adores
  Her Henry's holy shade;
And ye, that from the stately brow
Of Windsor's heights the expanse below
  Of grove, of lawn, of mead survey,
Whose turf, whose shade, whose flowers among
Wanders the hoary Thames along
  His silver-winding way:

Ah, happy hills, ah, pleasing shade,
  Ah, fields beloved in vain,
Where once my careless childhood strayed,
  A stranger yet to pain!
I feel the gales that from ye blow,
A momentary bliss bestow,
  As waving fresh their gladsome wing,
My weary soul they seem to soothe,
And, redolent of joy and youth,
  To breathe a second spring.

.   .   .   .   .

While some, on earnest business
bent,
   Their murmuring labours ply
'Gainst graver hours that bring
    constraint
   To sweeten liberty:
Some bold adventurers disdain
The limits of their little reign,
   And unknown regions dare
    descry:
Still as they run they look behind,
They hear a voice in every wind,
   And snatch a fearful joy.

Alas, regardless of their doom
   The little victims play!
No sense have they of ills to come,
   Nor care beyond to-day:
Yet see how all around them wait
The ministers of human fate,
   And black Misfortune's baleful
    train!

Ah, show them where in ambush
    stand
To seize their prey the murtherous
    band!
   Ah, tell them, they are men!

To each his sufferings: all are
    men,
   Condemned alike to groan,
The tender for another's pain;
   The unfeeling for his own.
Yet, ah! why should they know
   their fate?
Since sorrow never comes too
   late,
   And happiness too swiftly flies.
Thought would destroy their para-
   dise.
No more; where ignorance is
   bliss,
   'Tis folly to be wise.

T. GRAY.

414. FAWNIA

Ah! were she pitiful as she is fair,
   Or but as mild as she is seeming so,
Then were my hopes greater than my despair;
   Then all the world were heaven, nothing woe.
Ah! were her heart relenting as her hand,
   That seems to melt e'en with the mildest touch,
Then knew I where to seat me in a land
   Under the wide heavens, but yet not such:
Just as she shows, so seems the budding rose,
   Yet sweeter far than is an earthly flower;
Sovereign of Beauty! like the spray she grows,
   Compassed she is with thorns and cankered bower:
Yet were she willing to be plucked and worn,
She would be gathered, though she grew on thorn.

Ah! when she sings, all music else be still,
   For none must be comparèd to her note:
Ne'er breathed such glee from Philomela's bill;
   Nor from the Morning-Singer's swelling throat.
Ah! when she riseth from her blissful bed,
   She comforts all the world, as doth the sun;
And at her sight the night's foul vapour 's fled;
   When she is set, the gladsome day is done:
O glorious Sun! imagine me the west,
Shine in my arms, and set thou in my breast!

R. GREENE (Pandosto).

415. THE SHEPHERD'S WIFE'S SONG

Ah what is love ?   It is a pretty thing,
As sweet unto a shepherd as a king,
  And sweeter too :
For kings have cares that wait upon a crown,
And cares can make the sweetest love to frown :
  Ah then, ah then,
If country loves such sweet desires do gain,
What lady would not love a shepherd swain ?

His flocks are folded, he comes home at night,
As merry as a king in his delight,
  And merrier too :
For kings bethink them what the State require,
Where shepherds careless carol by the fire.
  Ah then, ah then,
If country loves such sweet desires gain,
What lady would not love a shepherd swain ?

He kisseth first, then sits as blithe to eat
His cream and curds, as doth the king his meat,
  And blither too :
For kings have often fears when they do sup,
Where shepherds dread no poison in their cup.
  Ah then, ah then,
If country loves such sweet desires gain
What lady would not love a shepherd swain ?
    R. Greene (*Greene's Mourning Garment*).

416. SAMELA

Like to Diana in her summer weed,
Girt with a crimson robe of brightest dye,
  goes fair Samela.
Whiter than be the flocks that straggling feed,
When washed by Arethusa's Fount they lie,
  is fair Samela.
As fair Aurora in her morning grey,
Decked with the ruddy glister of her love,
  is fair Samela.
Like lovely Thetis on a calmèd day,
When as her brightness Neptune's fancy move,
  shines fair Samela.
Her tresses gold, her eyes like glassy streams,
Her teeth are pearl, the breasts are ivory
  of fair Samela.
Her cheeks like rose and lily yield forth gleams
Her brows bright arches framed of ebony :
  thus fair Samela

Passeth fair Venus in her bravest hue,
And Juno in the show of majesty,
              for she 's Samela ;
Pallas, in wit—all three, if you well view,
For beauty, wit, and matchless dignity
              yield to Samela.

          R. GREENE (*Menaphon*).

417. INFIDA'S SONG

SWEET Adon', dar'st not glance
    thine eye—
  N'oserez-vous, mon bel ami ?
Upon thy Venus that must die,
  Je vous en prie, pity me :
N'oserez-vous, mon bel, mon bel,
  N'oserez-vous, mon bel ami ?

See how sad thy Venus lies,
  N'oserez-vous, mon bel ami ?
Love in heart and tears in eyes,
  Je vous en prie, pity me.

Thy face as fair as Paphos brooks,
  N'oserez-vous, mon bel ami ?
Wherein fancy baits her hooks,
  Je vous en prie, pity me.

Thy cheeks like cherries that do
  grow,
  N'oserez-vous, mon bel ami ?
Amongst the Western mounts of
  snow,
  Je vous en prie, pity me.

Thy lips vermilion, full of love,
  N'oserez-vous, mon bel ami ?
Thy neck as silver-white as dove,
  Je vous en prie, pity me.

Thine eyes like flames of holy fires,
  N'oserez-vous, mon bel ami ?
Burn all my thoughts with sweet
  desires,
  Je vous en prie, pity me.

All thy beauties sting my heart,
  N'oserez-vous, mon bel ami ?
I must die through Cupid's dart,
  Je vous en prie, pity me.

Wilt thou let thy Venus die ?
  N'oserez-vous, mon bel ami ?
Adon' were unkind, say I,
  Je vous en prie, pity me.

To let fair Venus die for woe,
  N'oserez-vous, mon bel ami ?
That doth love sweet Adon' so ;
  Je vous en prie, pity me :
N'oserez-vous, mon bel, mon bel,
  N'oserez-vous, mon bel ami ?

        R. GREENE (*Never too late*).

418. MAESIA'S SONG

SWEET are the thoughts that savour of content,
  the quiet mind is richer than a crown,
Sweet are the nights, in careless slumber spent,
  the poor estate scorns Fortune's angry frown.
    Such sweet content, such minds, such sleep, such bliss,
    beggars enjoy, when Princes oft do miss.

The homely house that harbours quiet rest,
  the cottage that affords no pride, nor care,
The mean that 'grees with country music best,
  the sweet consort of mirth and music's fare ;
    Obscurèd life sets down a type of bliss,
    a mind content both crown and kingdom is.

        R. GREENE (*Farewell to Follie*).

419. SEPHESTIA'S SONG TO HER CHILD

WEEP not, my wanton, smile upon
  my knee,
When thou art old there 's grief
  enough for thee.
  Mother's wag, pretty boy,
  Father's sorrow, father's joy.
  When thy father first did see
  Such a boy by him and me,
  He was glad, I was woe,
  Fortune changèd made him so,
  When he left his pretty boy,
  Last his sorrow, first his joy.

. . . . . .

The wanton smiled, father wept,
Mother cried, baby leapt:
More he crowed, more we cried;
Nature could not sorrow hide.
He must go, he must kiss
Child and mother, baby bliss:
For he left his pretty boy,
  Father's sorrow, father's joy.
Weep not, my wanton, smile upon
  my knee,
When thou art old there 's grief
  enough for thee.
        R. GREENE (*Menaphon*).

420. WHAT THING IS LOVE ?

WHAT thing is love ? It is a power divine
  That reigns in us ; or else a wreakful law
That dooms our minds to beauty to incline:
  It is a star whose influence doth draw
    Our hearts to love, dissembling of his might,
    Till he be master of our hearts and sight.

. . . . . .

'Tis now a peace, and then a sudden war,
  A hope consumed before it is conceived ;
At hand it fears, and menaceth afar ;
  And he that gains is most of all deceived:
    It is a secret hidden and not known
    Which one may better feel than write upon.
        R. GREENE (*Menaphon*).

421. ARBASTO'S SONG

WHEREAT erewhile I wept, I laugh ;
  That which I feared, I now despise ;
My victor once, my vassal is ;
  My foe constrained, my weal supplies :
    Thus do I triumph on my foe,
    I weep at weal, I laugh at woe.

My care is cured, yet hath none end ;
  Not that I want, but that I have ;
My chance was change, yet still I stay,
  I would have less, and yet I crave :
    Ay me, poor wretch ! that thus do live,
    Constrained to take, yet forced to give.

She whose delights are signs of death,
  Who when she smiles, begins to lower,
Constant in this that still she change,
  Her sweetest gifts time proves but sour :
    I live in care, crossed with her guile,
    Through her I weep, at her I smile !

R. GREENE (Arbasto).

422. UPON CASTARA'S DEPARTURE

Vows are vain. No suppliant
    breath
Stays the speed of swift-heeled
    Death.
Life with her is gone, and I
Learn but a new way to die.
See the flowers condole, and all
Wither in my funeral.
The bright lily, as if day
Parted with her, fades away.

Violets hang their heads and lose
All their beauty. That the rose
A sad part in sorrow bears,
Witness all those dewy tears,
Which, as pearl or diamond like,
Swell upon her blushing cheek.
All things mourn, but oh, behold
How the withered marigold
Closeth up, now she is gone,
Judging her the setting sun.

W. HABINGTON.

423. WHEN I SURVEY THE BRIGHT CELESTIAL SPHERE

WHEN I survey the bright
    Celestial sphere ;
So rich with jewels hung, that
    Night
Doth like an Ethiop bride
    appear :
My soul her wings doth spread
    And heavenward flies,
The Almighty's mysteries to read
  In the large volumes of the skies.

For the bright firmament
    Shoots forth no flame
So silent, but is eloquent
    In speaking the Creator's name.

No unregarded star
    Contracts its light
Into so small a character,
    Removed far from our human
    sight,

But if we steadfast look
  We shall discern
In it, as in some holy book,
  How man may heavenly knowledge learn.

W. HABINGTON.

424. TO ROSES, IN THE BOSOM OF CASTARA

YE blushing Virgins happy are
  In the chaste nunnery of her breasts,
For he'd profane so chaste a fair,
  Whoe'er should call them Cupid's nests.

Transplanted thus, how bright ye grow,
  How rich a perfume do ye yield !
In some close garden, cowslips so
  Are sweeter than i' th' open field.

In those white cloisters, live secure
    From the rude blasts of wanton breath,
Each hour more innocent and pure,
    Till you shall wither into death.

Then that which, living, gave you room,
    Your glorious sepulchre shall be.
There wants no marble for a tomb,
    Whose breast hath marble been to me.
                                        W. Habington.

425. TO MY MOTHER

When barren doubt, like a late coming snow,
Made an unkind December of my spring,
That all the pretty flowers did droop for woe,
And the sweet birds their love no more would sing;
Then the remembrance of thy gentle faith,
Mother beloved, would steal upon my heart;
Fond feeling saved me from the utter scathe,
And from the hope I could not live apart.
Now that my mind has passed from wintry gloom,
And on the calmèd waters once again
Ascendant Faith circles with silver plume,
That casts a charmèd shade, not now in pain,
Thou child of Christ,—in joy I think of thee,
And mingle prayers for what we both may be.
                                        A. H. Hallam.

426. AGAINST WRITERS THAT CARP AT OTHER MEN'S BOOKS

The readers and the hearers like my books,
And yet some writers cannot them digest;
But what care I? for when I make a feast,
I would my guests should praise it, not the cooks.
                                        Sir J. Harington.

427. OF TREASON

Treason doth never prosper: what's the reason?
For if it prosper, none dare call it treason.
                                        Sir J. Harington.

428. AND SHALL TRELAWNY DIE?

A GOOD sword and a trusty hand !
  A merry heart and true !
King James's men shall under-
    stand
  What Cornish lads can do.

And have they fixed the where
    and when ?
  And shall Trelawny die ?
Here 's twenty thousand Cornish
    men
  Will know the reason why !

Out spake their captain brave and
    bold,
  A merry wight was he :
' If London Tower were Michael's
    hold,
  We'll set Trelawny free !

' We'll cross the Tamar, land to
    land,
  The Severn is no stay,
With " one and all ", and hand in
    hand,
  And who shall bid us nay ?
' And when we come to London
    Wall,
  A pleasant sight to view,
Come forth ! come forth, ye
    cowards all,
  Here 's men as good as you.

' Trelawny he 's in keep and hold,
  Trelawny he may die ;
But here 's twenty thousand
    Cornish bold
  Will know the reason why ! '
             R. S. HAWKER.

429. A BOW-MEETING SONG

'TWAS merry then in England
  (Our ancient records tell),
With Robin Hood and Little
    John
  Who dwelt by down and dell ;
And yet we love the bold outlaw
Who braved a tyrant foe,
Whose cheer was the deer,
  And his only friend the bow !

'Twas merry then in England
  In autumn's dewy morn,
When echo started from her hill
  To hear the bugle-horn.
And beauty, mirth, and warrior
    worth
  In garb of green did go
The shade to invade
  With the arrow and the bow.
             R. HEBER.

430. TO A WELSH AIR

WHY that neck of marble whiteness,
Why that hair of sunny brightness,
  Form of perfect mould,
Why those fringèd eyelids screening
Lights of love and liquid meaning,
  While the heart is cold ?

Shame on her whose pride or malice
With a lover's anguish dallies !
Scorn our scattered reason rallies,
Thou shalt mourn thy tyrant sallies,
Ere that thou art old—young Alice,
  Ere that thou art old !

             R. HEBER.

431. A DIRGE

CALM on the bosom of thy God,
  Young spirit, rest thee now !
Even while with us thy footstep trod,
  His seal was on thy brow.

Dust, to its narrow house beneath !
  Soul, to its place on high !—
They that have seen thy look in death
  No more may fear to die.

Lone are the paths and sad the bowers
  Whence thy meek smile is gone ;
But oh !—a brighter home than ours
  In heaven is now thine own.

                              F. HEMANS.

432. THE BETTER LAND

'I HEAR thee speak of the better land,
Thou callest its children a happy band :
Mother ! oh, where is that radiant shore ?
Shall we not seek it, and weep no more ?
Is it where the flower of the orange blows,
And the fire-flies glance through the myrtle boughs ? '—
    ' Not there, not there, my child ! '

' Is it where the feathery palm-trees rise,
And the date grows ripe under sunny skies ?
Or midst the green islands of glittering seas,
Where fragrant forests perfume the breeze,
And strange, bright birds, on their starry wings,
Bear the rich hues of all glorious things ? '—
    ' Not there, not there, my child ! '

' Is it far away, in some region old,
Where the rivers wander o'er sands of gold ?—
Where the burning rays of the ruby shine,
And the diamond lights up the secret mine,
And the pearl gleams forth from the coral strand ?—
Is it there, sweet mother, that better land ? '—
    ' Not there, not there, my child !

' Eye hath not seen it, my gentle boy !
Ear hath not heard its deep songs of joy ;
Dreams cannot picture a world so fair,
Sorrow and death may not enter there ;
Time doth not breathe on its fadeless bloom,
For beyond the clouds, and beyond the tomb,—
    It is there, it is there, my child ! '

                              F. HEMANS.

433. ENGLAND'S DEAD

Son of the ocean isle !
Where sleep your mighty dead?
Show me what high and stately pile
Is reared o'er Glory's bed.

Go, stranger ! track the deep,
Free, free, the white sail spread !
Wave may not foam, nor wild wind sweep,
Where rest not England's dead.

On Egypt's burning plains,
By the pyramid o'erswayed,
With fearful power the noonday reigns,
And the palm-trees yield no shade.

But let the angry sun
From heaven look fiercely red,
Unfelt by those whose task is done !—
There slumber England's dead.

The hurricane hath might
Along the Indian shore,
And far by Ganges' banks at night
Is heard the tiger's roar.

But let the sound roll on !
It hath no tone of dread
For those that from their toils are gone ;—
There slumber England's dead !

Loud rush the torrent-floods
The western wilds among,
And free in green Columbia's woods
The hunter's bow is strung.

But let the floods rush on !
Let the arrow's flight be sped !
Why should *they* reck whose task is done ?—
There slumber England's dead !

The mountain-storms rise high
In the snowy Pyrenees,
And toss the pine-boughs through the sky
Like rose-leaves on the breeze.

But let the storm rage on !
Let the forest-wreaths be shed :
For the Roncesvalles' field is won,—
There slumber England's dead.

On the frozen deep's repose,
'Tis a dark and dreadful hour,
When round the ship the ice-fields close,
To chain her with their power.

But let the ice drift on !
Let the cold-blue desert spread !
Their course with mast and flag is done,—
Even there sleep England's dead.

The warlike of the isles,
The men of field and wave !
Are not the rocks their funeral piles,
The seas and shores their grave?

Go, stranger ! track the deep,
Free, free, the white sail spread !
Wave may not foam, nor wild wind sweep,
Where rest not England's dead.

F. HEMANS.

434. CASABIANCA

In the battle of the Nile the *Orient* took fire, and her guns were abandoned, except by the Admiral's son, Casabianca.   This boy, about thirteen
years of age, remained at his post until the flames reached the powder,
and perished in the explosion which resulted.

The boy stood on the burning
  deck
  Whence all but he had fled ;
The flame that lit the battle's
  wreck
  Shone round him o'er the dead.

Yet beautiful and bright he stood,
  As born to rule the storm—
A creature of heroic blood,
  A proud, though childlike form.

The flames rolled on—he would
  not go
Without his father's word ;
That father, faint in death below,
  His voice no longer heard.

He called aloud :—' Say, father,
  say,
  If yet my task is done ! '
He knew not that the chieftain
  lay
  Unconscious of his son.

' Speak, father ! ' once again he
  cried,
  ' If I may yet be gone ! '
And but the booming shots replied,
  And fast the flames rolled on.

Upon his brow he felt their breath,
  And in his waving hair,
And looked from that lone post of
  death,
  In still yet brave despair :

And shouted but once more aloud,
  ' My father ! must I stay ? '
While o'er him fast, through sail
  and shroud,
  The wreathing fires made way.

They wrapt the ship in splendour
  wild,
  They caught the flag on high,
And streamed above the gallant
  child,
  Like banners in the sky.

There came a burst of thunder-
  sound—
  The boy—oh, where was he ?
Ask of the winds that far around
  With fragments strewed the
    sea !—

With mast and helm, and penncn
  fair,
  That well had borne their part—
But the noblest thing that perished
  there
  Was that young faithful heart.
            F. Hemans.

435. FROM 'THE MUFFLED DRUM'

The muffled drum was heard
  In the Pyrenees by night,
With a dull, deep rolling sound,
Which told the hamlets round
  Of a soldier's burial-rite.

But it told them not how dear,
  In a home beyond the main,
Was the warrior-youth laid low
  that hour
  By a mountain-stream of Spain.

The oaks of England waved
  O'er the slumber of his race,
But a pine of the Ronceval made moan
  Above *his* last, lone place.

            F. Hemans.

436. OUT OF THE NIGHT

Out of the night that covers me,
  Black as the Pit from pole to pole,
I thank whatever gods may be
  For my unconquerable soul.

In the fell clutch of circumstance
  I have not winced nor cried aloud.
Under the bludgeonings of chance
  My head is bloody, but unbowed.

Beyond this place of wrath and tears
  Looms but the Horror of the shade,
And yet the menace of the years
  Finds and shall find me unafraid.

It matters not how strait the gate,
  How charged with punishments the scroll,
I am the master of my fate:
  I am the captain of my soul.

W. E. HENLEY (*To R. T. H. B.*).

437. ENGLAND, MY ENGLAND

What have I done for you,
    England, my England?
What is there I would not do,
    England, my own?
With your glorious eyes austere,
As the Lord were walking near,
Whispering terrible things and dear
      As the Song on your bugles blown,
        England—
      Round the world on your bugles blown!

Where shall the watchful sun,
    England, my England,
Match the master-work you've done,
    England, my own?
When shall he rejoice agen
Such a breed of mighty men
As come forward, one to ten,
      To the Song on your bugles blown,
        England—
      Down the years on your bugles blown?

Ever the faith endures,
    England, my England:—
'Take and break us: we are yours,
    England, my own!
Life is good, and joy runs high
Between English earth and sky:
Death is death; but we shall die
      To the Song on your bugles blown,
        England—
      To the stars on your bugles blown!

They call you proud and hard,
    England, my England :
You with worlds to watch and ward,
    England, my own !
You whose mailed hand keeps the keys
Of such teeming destinies,
You could know nor dread nor ease
      Were the Song on your bugles blown,
        England,
      Round the Pit on your bugles blown !

Mother of Ships whose might,
    England, my England,
Is the fierce old Sea's delight,
    England, my own,
Chosen daughter of the Lord,
Spouse-in-Chief of the ancient Sword,
There 's the menace of the Word
      In the Song on your bugles blown,
        England—
      Out of heaven on your bugles blown !
                        W. E. HENLEY.

438. NOW THAT THE APRIL OF YOUR YOUTH

Now that the April of your youth adorns
    The garden of your face,
Now that for you each knowing lover mourns,
    And all seek to your grace,
Do not repay affection with scorns.

What though you may a matchless beauty vaunt,
    And all that hearts can move
By such a power, that seemeth to enchant ;
    Yet, without help of love,
Beauty no pleasure to itself can grant.

Then think each minute that you lose a day ;
    The longest youth is short,
The shortest age is long ; Time flies away
    And makes us but his sport,
And that which is not Youth's, is Age's prey.
              LORD HERBERT OF CHERBURY.

439. EASTER

I GOT me flowers to straw Thy way,
I got me boughs off many a tree ;
But Thou wast up by break of day,
And brought'st Thy sweets along with Thee.

The sun arising in the East,
Though he give light, and the East perfume,
If they should offer to contest
With Thy arising, they presume.

Can there be any day but this,
Though many suns to shine endeavour ?
We count three hundred, but we miss :
There is but one, and that one ever.

G. HERBERT.

440. JUDGE NOT THE PREACHER

JUDGE not the preacher, for He is thy judge ;
If thou mistake him, thou conceiv'st Him not :
God calleth preaching folly : do not grudge
To pick out treasures from an earthen pot :
  The worst speak something good ; if all want sense,
  God takes a text, and preacheth patience.

G. HERBERT (The Church Porch).

441. SIN

LORD, with what care hast Thou begirt us round !
Parents first season us ; then schoolmasters
Deliver us to laws ; they send us, bound
To rules of reason, holy messengers,
Pulpits and Sundays, sorrow dogging sin,
Afflictions sorted, anguish of all sizes,
Fine nets and stratagems to catch us in,
Bibles laid open, millions of surprises ;
Blessings beforehand, ties of gratefulness,
The sound of glory ringing in our ears :
Without, our shame ; within, our consciences ;
Angels and grace, eternal hopes and fears !
Yet all these fences and their whole array
One cunning bosom-sin blows quite away.

G. HERBERT.

442. THE QUIDDITY

MY God, a verse is not a crown,
No point of honour, or gay suit,
No hawk, or banquet, or renown,
Nor a good sword, nor yet a lute.
It cannot vault or dance or play,
It never was in France or Spain,
Nor can it entertain the day
With a great stable or demain.

It is no office, art, or news,
Nor the Exchange, or busy hall :
But it is that which, while I use,
I am with Thee : and ' Most take all '.

G. HERBERT.

443. SUNDAY

O DAY most calm, most bright,
The fruit of this, the next world's bud,
The indorsement of supreme delight,
Writ by a friend, and with His blood ;
The couch of Time, Care's balm and bay :
The week were dark but for thy light—
    Thy Torch doth show the way.

.   .   .   .   .

The Sundays of man's life,
Threaded together on Time's string,
Make bracelets to adorn the wife
Of the eternal glorious King :
On Sunday heaven's gate stands ope ;
Blessings are plentiful and rife,
    More plentiful than hope.   G. HERBERT.

444. VIRTUE

SWEET day, so cool, so calm, so bright,
The bridal of the earth and sky,
The dew shall weep thy fall to-night,
    For thou must die.

Sweet rose, whose hue, angry and brave,
Bids the rash gazer wipe his eye,
Thy root is ever in its grave,
    And thou must die.

Sweet spring, full of sweet days and roses,
A box where sweets compacted lie,
My music shows you have your closes,
    And all must die.

Only a sweet and virtuous soul,
Like seasoned timber, never gives ;
But though the whole world turn to coal,
    Then chiefly lives.   G. HERBERT.

445. THE ELIXIR

TEACH me, my God and King,
  In all things Thee to see,
And what I do in anything
  To do it as for Thee.

.   .   .   .

All may of Thee partake
  Nothing can be so mean
Which with his tincture, ' for Thy sake ',
  Will not grow bright and clean.

A servant with this clause
  Makes drudgery divine ;
Who sweeps a room, as for Thy laws,
  Makes that and the action fine.   G. HERBERT.

446. THE PULLEY

WHEN God at first made man,
Having a glass of blessings standing by,
'Let us,' said He, 'pour on him all we can:
Let the world's riches, which dispersèd lie,
    Contract into a span.'

So strength first made a way,
Then beauty flowed, then wisdom, honour, pleasure;
When almost all was out, God made a stay,
Perceiving that, alone of all His treasure,
    Rest in the bottom lay.

'For if I should,' said He,
'Bestow this jewel also on My creature,
He would adore My gifts instead of Me,
And rest in Nature, not the God of Nature:
    So both should losers be.

'Yet let him keep the rest,
But keep them with repining restlessness;
Let him be rich and weary, that at least,
If goodness lead him not, yet weariness
    May toss him to My breast.'   G. HERBERT.

447. TO LAURELS

    A FUNERAL stone
    Or verse, I covet none:
  But only crave
Of you, that I may have
A sacred laurel springing from my grave,
    Which being seen,
  Blessed with perpetual green,
    May grow to be
  Not so much called a tree,
As the eternal monument of me.   R. HERRICK.

448. DELIGHT IN DISORDER

A SWEET disorder in the dress
Kindles in clothes a wantonness;
A lawn about the shoulders thrown
Into a fine distraction;
An erring lace, which here and there
Enthrals a crimson stomacher;
A cuff neglectful, and thereby
Ribands to flow confusedly;
A winning wave, deserving note,
In the tempestuous petticoat;
A careless shoe-string, in whose tie
I see a wild civility;
Do more bewitch me, than when art
Is too precise in every part.
    R. HERRICK.

449. AN ODE FOR BEN JONSON

Ah Ben!
Say how, or when
Shall we, thy guests,
Meet at those lyric feasts,
Made at the Sun,
The Dog, the Triple Tun;
Where we such clusters had,
As made us nobly wild, not
mad?
And yet each verse of thine
Out-did the meat, out-did the
frolic wine.

My Ben!
Or come agen,
Or send to us
Thy wit's great over-plus;
But teach us yet
Wisely to husband it,
Lest we that talent spend;
And having once brought to an
end
That precious stock, the store
Of such a wit the world should
have no more.

R. HERRICK.

450. TO ANTHEA, WHO MAY COMMAND HIM ANYTHING

Bid me to live, and I will live
Thy Protestant to be;
Or bid me love, and I will give
A loving heart to thee.

A heart as soft, a heart as kind,
A heart as sound and free,
As in the whole world thou canst
find,
That heart I'll give to thee.

Bid that heart stay, and it will
stay,
To honour thy decree;
Or bid it languish quite away,
And 't shall do so for thee.

Bid me to weep, and I will weep,
While I have eyes to see;
And, having none, yet I will keep
A heart to weep for thee.

Bid me despair, and I'll despair,
Under that cypress tree;
Or bid me die, and I will dare
E'en death, to die for thee.

Thou art my life, my love, my
heart,
The very eyes of me;
And hast command of every part,
To live and die for thee.

R. HERRICK.

451. TO MUSIC, TO BECALM HIS FEVER

Charm me asleep, and melt me
so
With thy delicious numbers;
That being ravished, hence I go
Away in easy slumbers.
Ease my sick head,
And make my bed,
Thou power that canst sever
From me this ill,
And quickly still,
Though thou not kill
My fever,

Thou sweetly canst convert the
same
From a consuming fire,
Into a gentle-licking flame,
And make it thus expire.
Then make me weep
My pains asleep,
And give me such reposes,
That I, poor I,
May think, thereby,
I live and die
'Mongst roses.

Fall on me like a silent dew,
 Or like those maiden showers,
Which, by the peep of day, do strew
 A baptism o'er the flowers.
  Melt, melt my pains,
  With thy soft strains ;
 That having ease me given,
  With full delight,
  I leave this light,
  And take my flight
   For heaven.

R. HERRICK.

452. TO DAFFODILS

Fair Daffodils, we weep to see
 You haste away so soon ;
As yet the early-rising sun
 Has not attained his noon.
  Stay, stay,
 Until the hasting day
  Has run
 But to the even-song ;
And, having prayed together, we
 Will go with you along.

We have short time to stay as you,
 We have as short a Spring ;
As quick a growth to meet decay,
 As you, or anything.
  We die
As your hours do, and dry
  Away,
Like to the summer's rain ;
Or as the pearls of morning's dew,
 Ne'er to be found again.

R. HERRICK.

453. TO BLOSSOMS

Fair pledges of a fruitful tree,
 Why do ye fall so fast ?
 Your date is not so past,
But you may stay yet here awhile,
 To blush and gently smile,
  And go at last.

What, were ye born to be
 An hour or half's delight,
 And so to bid good-night ?
'Twas pity Nature brought ye forth
 Merely to show your worth,
  And lose you quite.

But you are lovely leaves, where we
 May read how soon things have
 Their end, though ne'er so brave ;
And after they have shown their pride
 Like you, awhile, they glide
  Into the grave.

R. HERRICK.

454. HIS PRAYER FOR ABSOLUTION

For those my unbaptizèd rhymes,
Writ in my wild unhallowed times ;
For every sentence, clause, and word,
That's not inlaid with Thee, my Lord,
Forgive me, God, and blot each line
Out of my book that is not Thine.
But if, 'mongst all, Thou find'st here one
Worthy Thy benediction ;
That one of all the rest shall be
The glory of my work and me.   R. Herrick.

455. TO THE VIRGINS TO MAKE MUCH OF TIME

Gather ye rose-buds while ye may,
    Old time is still a-flying ;
And this same flower that smiles to-day,
    To-morrow will be dying.

The glorious lamp of heaven, the Sun,
    The higher he's a-getting,
The sooner will his race be run,
    And nearer he's to setting.

That age is best which is the first,
    When youth and blood are warmer ;
But being spent the worse and worst
    Times still succeed the former.

Then be not coy, but use your time,
    And while ye may, go marry ;
For having lost but once your prime,
    You may for ever tarry.   R. Herrick.

456. CORINNA'S GOING A-MAYING

Get up, get up for shame, the blooming morn
Upon her wings presents the god unshorn.
    See how Aurora throws her fair
    Fresh-quilted colours through the air :
    Get up, sweet slug-a-bed, and see
    The dew bespangling herb and tree.
Each flower has wept, and bowed toward the east,
Above an hour since, yet you not dressed,
    Nay ! not so much as out of bed ;
    When all the birds have Matins said,
    And sung their thankful hymns ; 'tis sin,
    Nay, profanation to keep in,
Whenas a thousand virgins on this day,
Spring, sooner than the lark, to fetch in May.

Rise, and put on your foliage, and be seen
To come forth, like the spring-time, fresh and green ;
 And sweet as Flora. Take no care
 For jewels for your gown, or hair ;
 Fear not, the leaves will strew
 Gems in abundance upon you ;
Besides, the childhood of the day has kept,
Against you come, some orient pearls unwept.
 Come, and receive them while the light
 Hangs on the dew-locks of the night :
 And Titan on the eastern hill
 Retires himself, or else stands still
Till you come forth. Wash, dress, be brief in praying ;
Few beads are best, when once we go a-Maying.

Come, my Corinna, come ; and coming, mark
How each field turns a street, each street a park
 Made green, and trimmed with trees : see how
 Devotion gives each house a bough,
 Or branch ; each porch, each door, ere this,
 An ark, a tabernacle is,
Made up of whitethorn neatly interwove ;
As if here were those cooler shades of love.
 Can such delights be in the street,
 And open fields, and we not see 't ?
 Come, we'll abroad, and let 's obey
 The proclamation made for May :
And sin no more, as we have done, by staying :
But, my Corinna, come, let 's go a-Maying.

There 's not a budding boy or girl, this day,
But is got up, and gone to bring in May.
 A deal of youth, ere this, is come
 Back, and with whitethorn laden home.
 Some have dispatched their cakes and cream,
 Before that we have left to dream ;
And some have wept, and wooed, and plighted troth,
And chose their priest, ere we can cast off sloth:
 Many a green-gown has been given ;
 Many a kiss both odd and even ;
 Many a glance too has been sent
 From out the eye, love's firmament ;
Many a jest told of the key's betraying
This night, and locks picked, yet we're not a-Maying.

Come, let us go, while we are in our prime,
And take the harmless folly of the time.
 We shall grow old apace and die
 Before we know our liberty.

Our life is short, and our days run
As fast away as does the sun;
And as a vapour, or a drop of rain
Once lost, can ne'er be found again;
So when or you or I are made
A fable, song, or fleeting shade;
All love, all liking, all delight
Lies drowned with us in endless night.
Then while time serves, and we are but decaying,
Come, my Corinna, come, let's go a-Maying.

R. HERRICK.

457. GRACE FOR A CHILD

HERE a little child I stand,
Heaving up my either hand;
Cold as paddocks though they be
Here I lift them up to Thee,
For a benison to fall
On our meat, and on us all. *Amen.*

R. HERRICK.

458. TO ELECTRA

I DARE not ask a kiss,
I dare not beg a smile;
Lest having that, or this,
I might grow proud the while.

No, no, the utmost share
Of my desire, shall be,
Only to kiss that air
That lately kissèd thee.

R. HERRICK.

459. HIS LITANY TO THE HOLY SPIRIT

IN the hour of my distress,
When temptations me oppress,
And when I my sins confess,
Sweet Spirit, comfort me!

When I lie within my bed,
Sick in heart, and sick in head,
And with doubts discomfortèd,
Sweet Spirit, comfort me!

When the artless doctor sees
No one hope, but of his fees,
And his skill runs on the lees,
Sweet Spirit, comfort me!

When his potion and his pill,
His, or none, or little skill,
Meet for nothing but to kill,
Sweet Spirit, comfort me!

. . . .

When the priest his last hath prayed,
And I nod to what is said,
'Cause my speech is now decayed,
Sweet Spirit, comfort me!

R. HERRICK.

460. A THANKSGIVING

LORD, I confess too, when I dine,
    The pulse is Thine,
And all those other bits that be
    There placed by Thee;
The worts, the purslane, and the mess
    Of water-cress,
Which of Thy kindness Thou hast sent;
    And my content
Makes those, and my belovèd beet,
    To be more sweet.

.   .   .   .   .

Lord, 'tis Thy plenty-dropping hand,
    That soils my land,
And giv'st me, for my bushel sown,
    Twice ten for one;
Thou mak'st my teeming hen to lay
    Her egg each day;
Besides my healthful ewes to bear
    Me twins each year;
The while the conduits of my kine
    Run cream for wine.

R. HERRICK (<i>A Thanksgiving to God,
for his house</i>).</div>

461. TO ANTHEA

Now is the time, when all the lights wax dim;
And thou, Anthea, must withdraw from him
Who was thy servant: Dearest, bury me
Under that holy-oak, or gospel-tree;
Where, though thou see'st not, thou mayst think upon
Me, when thou yearly go'st procession;
Or for mine honour, lay me in that tomb
In which thy sacred reliques shall have room;
For my embalming, Sweetest, there will be
No spices wanting when I'm laid by thee.   R. HERRICK.

462. TO DIANEME

SWEET, be not proud of those two eyes,
Which, starlike, sparkle in their skies;
Nor be you proud, that you can see
All hearts your captives, yours yet free;
Be you not proud of that rich hair,
Which wantons with the lovesick air;
Whenas that ruby which you wear,
Sunk from the tip of your soft ear,
Will last to be a precious stone
When all your world of beauty's gone.   R. HERRICK.

I

463. HIS PRAYER TO BEN JONSON

WHEN I a verse shall make,
Know I have prayed thee,
For old religion's sake,
Saint Ben, to aid me.

Make the way smooth for me,
When I, thy Herrick,
Honouring thee, on my knee
Offer my lyric.

Candles I'll give to thee,
And a new altar ;
And thou, Saint Ben, shalt be
Writ in my psalter.   R. HERRICK.

464. UPON JULIA'S CLOTHES

WHENAS in silks my Julia goes,
Then, then, methinks, how sweetly flows
That liquefaction of her clothes.

Next, when I cast mine eyes and see
That brave vibration each way free ;
O how that glittering taketh me !   R. HERRICK.

465. A PRAISE OF HIS LADY

GIVE place, you ladies, and be
    gone ;
  Boast not yourselves at all,
For here at hand approacheth one
  Whose face will stain you all.

I think Nature hath lost the mould
  Where she her shape did take ;
Or else I doubt if Nature could
  So fair a creature make.

.   .   .   .   .   .

The virtue of her lively looks
  Excels the precious stone ;
I wish to have none other books
  To read or look upon.
.   .   .   .   .

In life she is Diana chaste ;
  In truth Penelope ;
In word and eke in deed stead-
    fast ;
  'What will you more ?' say we.
                          J. HEYWOOD.

466. PACK, CLOUDS, AWAY, AND WELCOME DAY

PACK, clouds, away, and welcome, day !
  With night we banish sorrow ;
Sweet air, blow soft ; mount, larks, aloft,
  To give my Love good-morrow !
Wings from the wind to please her mind,
  Notes from the lark I'll borrow ;
Bird, prune thy wing, nightingale, sing,
  To give my Love good-morrow !
To give my Love good-morrow
  Notes from them all I'll borrow.

Wake from thy nest, Robin-redbreast!
  Sing, birds, in every furrow;
And from each bill let music shrill
  Give my fair Love good-morrow!
Blackbird and thrush in every bush,
  Stare, linnet, and cock-sparrow;
You pretty elves, among yourselves,
  Sing my fair Love good-morrow!
To give my Love good-morrow
  Sing, birds, in every furrow!

        T. Heywood (*The Rape of Lucrece*).

467. YE LITTLE BIRDS THAT SIT AND SING

Ye little birds that sit and sing
  Amidst the shady valleys,
And see how Phyllis sweetly walks
  Within her garden-alleys;
Go, pretty birds, about her bower;
Sing, pretty birds, she may not lower;
Ah, me! methinks I see her frown!
  Ye pretty wantons, warble.

Go tell her through your chirping bills,
  As you by me are bidden,
To her is only known my love,
  Which from the world is hidden.
Go, pretty birds, and tell her so;
See that your notes strain not too low,
For still, methinks, I see her frown;
  Ye pretty wantons, warble.

    .   .   .   .   .   .

O fly! make haste! see, see, she falls
  Into a pretty slumber!
Sing round about her rosy bed
  That waking she may wonder.
Say to her, 'tis her lover true
That sendeth love to you, to you;
And when you hear her kind reply
  Return with pleasant warblings.

        T. Heywood (*The Fair Maid of the
        Exchange*).

468. TENDER-HANDED STROKE A NETTLE

Tender-handed stroke a nettle,
  And it stings you for your pains;
Grasp it like a man of mettle,
  And it soft as silk remains.

'Tis the same with common natures,
  Use them kindly, they rebel;
But be rough as nutmeg-graters,
  And the rogues obey you well.

        Aaron Hill.

469.   THE SKYLARK

BIRD of the wilderness,
Blithesome and cumberless,
Sweet be thy matin o'er moorland and lea !
Emblem of happiness,
Blest is thy dwelling-place—
Oh, to abide in the desert with thee !

Wild is thy lay and loud,
Far in the downy cloud ;
Love gives it energy, love gave it birth.
Where, on thy dewy wing,
Where art thou journeying ?
Thy lay is in heaven, thy love is on earth.

O'er fell and fountain sheen,
O'er moor and mountain green,
O'er the red streamer that heralds the day,
Over the cloudlet dim,
Over the rainbow's rim,
Musical cherub, soar, singing, away !

Then, when the gloaming comes,
Low in the heather blooms,
Sweet will thy welcome and bed of love be !
Emblem of happiness,
Blest is thy dwelling-place—
Oh, to abide in the desert with thee !   J. HOGG.

470.   FROM 'MY LOVE SHE 'S BUT A LASSIE YET'

My love she 's but a lassie yet,
A lichtsome lovely lassie yet ;
It scarce wad do
To sit an' woo
Down by the stream sae glassy yet.
But there 's a braw time coming yet,
When we may gang a-roaming yet,
An' hint wi' glee
O' joys to be,
When fa's the modest gloaming yet.

She 's neither proud nor saucy yet,
She 's neither plump nor gaucy yet,
But just a jinking,
Bonny blinking,
Hilty-skilty lassie yet.
But O her artless smile 's mair sweet
Than hinny or than marmalete,
An' right or wrang,
Ere it be lang,
I'll bring her to a parley yet.   J. HOGG.

471.   FROM 'A BOY'S SONG'

WHERE the pools are bright and deep,
Where the grey trout lies asleep,
Up the river and o'er the lea,
That 's the way for Billy and me.

Where the blackbird sings the latest,
Where the hawthorn blooms the sweetest,
Where the nestlings chirp and flee,
That 's the way for Billy and me.

Where the mowers mow the cleanest,
Where the hay lies thick and greenest:
There to trace the homeward bee,
That 's the way for Billy and me.

Where the hazel bank is steepest,
When the shadow falls the deepest,
When the clustering nuts fall free,
That 's the way for Billy and me.

J. HOGG.

472. THE CROOKED FOOTPATH

AH, here it is ! the sliding rail
    That marks the old remembered spot,—
The gap that struck our schoolboy trail,—
    The crooked path across the lot.

It left the road by school and church,
    A pencilled shadow, nothing more,
That parted from the silver birch
    And ended at the farm-house door.

No line or compass traced its plan ;
    With frequent bends to left or right,
In aimless, wayward curves it ran,
    But always kept the door in sight.

The gabled porch, with woodbine green,—
    The broken millstone at the sill,—
Though many a rood might stretch between,
    The truant child could see them still.

No rocks across the pathway lie,—
    No fallen trunk is o'er it thrown,—
And yet it winds, we know not why,
    And turns as if for tree or stone.

Perhaps some lover trod the way
    With shaking knees and leaping heart,—
And so it often runs astray
    With sinuous sweep or sudden start.

Or one, perchance, with clouded brain
    From some unholy banquet reeled,—
And since, our devious steps maintain
    His track across the trodden field.

Nay, deem not thus,—no earthborn will
   Could ever trace a faultless line ;
Our truest steps are human still,—
   To walk unswerving were divine !

Truants from love, we dream of wrath ;—
   Oh, rather, let us trust the more !
Through all the wanderings of the path,
   We still can see our Father's door !

O. W. HOLMES.

473. OLD IRONSIDES

AYE, tear her tattered ensign down !
   Long has it waved on high,
And many an eye has danced to see
   That banner in the sky :
Beneath it rung the battle-shout
   And burst the cannon's roar ;—
The meteor of the ocean air
   Shall sweep the clouds no more.

Her deck, once red with heroes' blood,
   Where knelt the vanquished foe,
When winds were hurrying o'er the flood,
   And waves were white below,
No more shall feel the victor's tread,
   Or know the conquered knee,—
The harpies of the shore shall pluck
   The eagle of the sea !

O better that her shattered hulk
   Should sink beneath the wave ;
Her thunders shook the mighty deep,
   And there should be her grave ;
Nail to the mast her holy flag,
   Set every threadbare sail,
And give her to the god of storms,
   The lightning and the gale.   O. W. HOLMES.

474. BUILD THEE MORE STATELY MANSIONS

BUILD thee more stately mansions, O my soul,
   As the swift seasons roll !
   Leave thy low-vaulted past !
Let each new temple, nobler than the last,
Shut thee from heaven with a dome more vast,
   Till thou at length art free,
Leaving thine outgrown shell by life's unresting sea.
            O. W. HOLMES (*The Chambered Nautilus*).

475. L' INCONNUE

Is thy name Mary, maiden fair ?
　Such should, methinks, its music be ;
The sweetest name that mortals bear
　Were best befitting thee ;
And she to whom it once was given,
Was half of earth and half of heaven.

I hear thy voice, I see thy smile,
　I look upon thy folded hair ;
Ah ! while we dream not they beguile,
　Our hearts are in the snare ;
And she who chains a wild bird's wing
Must start not if her captive sing.

So, lady, take the leaf that falls,
　To all but thee unseen, unknown ;
When evening shades thy silent walls,
　Then read it all alone ;
In stillness read, in darkness seal,
Forget, despise, but not reveal !　　O. W. HOLMES.

476. THE EARTH-BORN SAINT

O BLISSFUL dream ! Our nursery joys
　We know must have an end,
But love and friendship's broken toys
　May God's good angels mend !

The cheering smile, the voice of mirth
　And laughter's gay surprise
That please the children born of earth,
　Why deem that Heaven denies ?

Methinks in that refulgent sphere
　That knows not sun or moon,
An earth-born saint might long to hear
　One verse of ' Bonnie Doon '.
　　　　O. W. HOLMES (*Our Sweet Singer J. A.*).

477. FAREWELL, LIFE ! MY SENSES SWIM

FAREWELL, Life ! my senses swim ;
And the world is growing dim ;
Thronging shadows cloud the light,
Like the advent of the night,—
Colder, colder, colder still
Upward steals a vapour chill—
Strong the earthy odour grows—
I smell the Mould above the
　Rose !

Welcome, Life ! the Spirit strives !
Strength returns, and hope revives ;
Cloudy fears and shapes forlorn
Fly like shadows at the morn,—
O'er the earth there comes a
　bloom—
Sunny light for sullen gloom,
Warm perfume for vapour cold,
I smell the Rose above the Mould.
　　　　　　T. HOOD.

478. IT WAS NOT IN THE WINTER

It was not in the winter
  Our loving lot was cast !
It was the time of roses,
  We plucked them as we passed !

That churlish season never frowned
  On early lovers yet !—
Oh no—the world was newly
    crowned
With flowers, when first we met.

'Twas twilight, and I bade you go,
  But still you held me fast ;—
It was the time of roses,—
  We plucked them as we passed !

What else could peer my glowing
    cheek
  That tears began to stud ?—
And when I asked the like of Love
  You snatched a damask bud,—

And oped it to the dainty core
  Still glowing till the last :—
It was the time of roses,
  We plucked them as we passed !   T. Hood.

479. MY MOTHER BIDS ME SPEND MY SMILES

My mother bids me spend my smiles
  On all who come and call me fair,
As crumbs are thrown upon the tiles,
  To all the sparrows of the air.
But I've a darling of my own
  For whom I hoard my little stock—
What if I chirp him all alone,
  And leave mamma to feed the flock !

                           T. Hood.

480. TO MINERVA

My temples throb, my pulses boil,
  I'm sick of Song, and Ode, and
    Ballad—
So, Thyrsis, take the Midnight Oil,
  And pour it on a lobster salad.

My brain is dull, my sight is foul,
  I cannot write a verse, or read,—
Then, Pallas, take away thine Owl,
  And let us have a lark instead.
                  T. Hood.

481. NO !

No sun—no moon !
No morn—no noon—
No dawn—no dusk—no proper time of day—
  No sky—no earthly view—
  No distance looking blue—
No road—no street—no ' t'other side the way '—
  No end to any Row—
  No indications where the Crescents go—
  No top to any steeple—
No recognitions of familiar people—

No courtesies for showing 'em—
No knowing 'em !—
No travelling at all—no locomotion,
No inkling of the way—no notion—
'No go'—by land or ocean—
No mail—no post—
No news from any foreign coast—
No Park—no Ring—no afternoon gentility—
No company—no nobility—
No warmth, no cheerfulness, no healthful ease,
No comfortable feel in any member—
No shade, no shine, no butterflies, no bees,
No fruits, no flowers, no leaves, no birds—
November !

T. HOOD.

482. FAIR INES

OH, saw ye not fair Ines ?
  She 's gone into the West,
To dazzle when the sun is down,
  And rob the world of rest :
She took our daylight with her,
  The smiles that we love best,
With morning blushes on her
  cheek,
  And pearls upon her breast.

O, turn again, fair Ines,
  Before the fall of night,
For fear the Moon should shine
  alone,
  And stars unrivalled bright ;
And blessèd will the lover be
  That walks beneath their light,
And breathes the love against thy
  cheek
  I dare not even write !

Would I had been, fair Ines,
  That gallant cavalier,
Who rode so gaily by thy side,
  And whispered thee so near !—
Were there no bonny dames at
  home
  Or no true lovers here,
That he should cross the seas to
  win
  The dearest of the dear ?

I saw thee, lovely Ines,
  Descend along the shore,
With bands of noble gentlemen,
  And banners waved before ;
And gentle youth and maidens
  gay,
  And snowy plumes they wore ;—
It would have been a beauteous
  dream,
  —If it had been no more.

Alas, alas, fair Ines,
  She went away with song,
With music waiting on her steps,
  And shoutings of the throng ;
But some were sad, and felt no
  mirth,
  But only Music's wrong,
In sounds that sang Farewell,
  farewell,
  To her you 've loved so long.

Farewell, farewell, fair Ines !
  That vessel never bore
So fair a lady on its deck,
  Nor danced so light before,—
Alas for pleasure on the sea,
  And sorrow on the shore !
The smile that blessed one lover's
  heart
  Has broken many more !

T. HOOD.

483. THE BRIDGE OF SIGHS

ONE more Unfortunate,
Weary of breath,
Rashly importunate,
Gone to her death!

Take her up tenderly,
Lift her with care;
Fashioned so slenderly,
Young, and so fair!

Look at her garments
Clinging like cerements;
Whilst the wave constantly
Drips from her clothing;
Take her up instantly,
Loving, not loathing.—

Touch her not scornfully;
Think of her mournfully;
Gently and humanly;
Not of the stains of her,
All that remains of her
Now is pure womanly.

Make no deep scrutiny
Into her mutiny
Rash and undutiful:
Past all dishonour
Death has left on her
Only the beautiful.

Still, for all slips of hers,
One of Eve's family—
Wipe those poor lips of hers
Oozing so clammily.

Loop up her tresses,
Escaped from the comb,
Her fair auburn tresses;
Whilst wonderment guesses
Where was her home?
Who was her father?
Who was her mother?
Had she a sister?
Had she a brother?
Or was there a dearer one
Still, and a nearer one
Yet, than all other?

Alas! for the rarity
Of Christian charity
Under the sun!

Oh! it was pitiful!
Near a whole city full,
Home she had none!

Sisterly, brotherly,
Fatherly, motherly
Feelings had changed:
Love, by harsh evidence,
Thrown from its eminence;
Even God's providence
Seeming estranged.

Where the lamps quiver
So far in the river,
With many a light
From window and casement,
From garret to basement,
She stood, with amazement,
Houseless by night.

The bleak wind of March,
Made her tremble and shiver;
But not the dark arch,
Or the black flowing river:
Mad from life's history,
Glad to death's mystery
Swift to be hurled—
Anywhere, anywhere,
Out of the world!

In she plunged boldly,
No matter how coldly
The rough river ran,—
Over the brink of it,
Picture it,—think of it,
Dissolute man!
Lave in it, drink of it,
Then, if you can!

Take her up tenderly,
Lift her with care;
Fashioned so slenderly,
Young, and so fair!

Ere her limbs frigidly
Stiffen too rigidly,
Decently,—kindly,—
Smoothe and compose them:
And her eyes, close them,
Staring so blindly!

Dreadfully staring
Through muddy impurity,
As when with the daring
Last look of despairing,
Fixed on futurity.

Perishing gloomily,
Spurred by contumely,
Cold inhumanity,
Burning insanity,

Into her rest.—
Cross her hands humbly
As if praying dumbly,
Over her breast !

Owning her weakness,
Her evil behaviour,
And leaving, with meekness,
Her sins to her Saviour !
                                        T. HOOD.

484.   RUTH

SHE stood breast-high amid the
        corn,
Clasped by the golden light of
        morn,
Like the sweetheart of the sun,
Who many a glowing kiss had won.

On her cheek an autumn flush,
Deeply ripened;—such a blush
In the midst of brown was born,
Like red poppies grown with corn.

Round her eyes her tresses fell,
Which were blackest none could
        tell,
But long lashes veiled a light,
That had else been all too bright.

And her hat, with shady brim,
Made her tressy forehead dim—
Thus she stood amid the stooks,
Praising God with sweetest looks.

Sure, I said, heaven did not mean
Where I reap thou shouldst but glean,
Lay thy sheaf adown and come,
Share my harvest and my home.
                                        T. HOOD.

485.   FROM AN 'ODE: AUTUMN'

THE squirrel gloats on his accomplished hoard,
The ants have brimmed their garners with ripe grain,
        And honey bees have stored
The sweets of Summer in their luscious cells ;
The swallows all have winged across the main ;
But here the Autumn melancholy dwells,
        And sighs her tearful spells
Amongst the sunless shadows of the plain.
        Alone, alone,
        Upon a mossy stone,
She sits and reckons up the dead and gone
With the last leaves for a love-rosary,
Whilst all the withered world looks drearily,
Like a dim picture of the drownèd past
In the hushed mind's mysterious far away,
Doubtful what ghostly thing will steal the last
Into that distance, grey upon the grey.

O go and sit with her, and be o'ershaded
Under the languid downfall of her hair :
She wears a coronal of flowers faded
Upon her forehead, and a face of care ;—
There is enough of withered every where
To make her bower,—and enough of gloom ;
There is enough of sadness to invite,
If only for the rose that died,—whose doom
Is Beauty's,—she that with the living bloom
Of conscious cheeks most beautifies the light ;—
There is enough of sorrowing, and quite
Enough of bitter fruits the earth doth bear,—
Enough of chilly droppings for her bowl ;
Enough of fear and shadowy despair,
To frame her cloudy prison for the soul !　　　T. HOOD.

486.　THE DEATH-BED

WE watched her breathing through the night,
Her breathing soft and low,
As in her breast the wave of life
Kept heaving to and fro !

So silently we seemed to speak—
So slowly moved about !
As we had lent her half our powers
To eke her living out !

Our very hopes belied our fears,
Our fears our hopes belied—
We thought her dying when she slept,
And sleeping when she died !

For when the morn came dim and sad—
And chill with early showers,
Her quiet eyelids closed—she had
Another morn than ours !

　　　T. HOOD.

487.　THE PLOUGH

ABOVE yon sombre swell of land
　　Thou seest the dawn's grave orange hue,
With one pale streak like yellow sand,
　　And over that a vein of blue.

The air is cold above the woods ;
　　All silent is the earth and sky,
Except with his own lonely moods
　　The blackbird holds a colloquy.

Over the broad hill creeps a beam,
　　Like hope that gilds a good man's brow ;
And now ascends the nostril-steam
　　Of stalwart horses come to plough.

Ye rigid ploughmen, bear in mind—
　　Your labour is for future hours,
Advance—spare not—nor look behind—
　　Plough deep and straight with all your powers.
　　　R. H. HORNE.

488. THE HAPPY LIFE

MARTIAL, the things that do attain
  The happy life be these, I find:—
The riches left, not got with pain;
  The fruitful ground, the quiet mind;

The equal friend; no grudge, no strife;
  No charge of rule, nor governance;
Without disease, the healthful life;
  The household of continuance;

The mean diet, no delicate fare;
  True wisdom joined with simpleness;
The night dischargèd of all care,
  Where wine the wit may not oppress;

The faithful wife, without debate;
  Such sleeps as may beguile the night:
Contented with thine own estate,
  Ne wish for death, ne fear his might.

H. HOWARD, EARL OF SURREY.

489. DESCRIPTION OF SPRING

WHEREIN EACH THING RENEWS, SAVE ONLY THE LOVER

THE soote season, that bud and bloom forth brings,
With green hath clad the hill, and eke the vale.
The nightingale, with feathers new, she sings;
The turtle to her make hath told her tale.
Summer is come, for every spray now springs.
The hart hath hung his old head on the pale;
The buck in brake his winter coat he flings;
The fishes fleet with new repairèd scale.
The adder all her slough away she slings;
The swift swallow pursueth the flies small;
The busy bee her honey now she mings;
Winter is worn that was the flowers' bale.
  And thus I see among these pleasant things
  Each care decays; and yet my sorrow springs.

H. HOWARD, EARL OF SURREY.

490. ABOU BEN ADHEM

ABOU BEN ADHEM (may his tribe increase)
Awoke one night from a deep dream of peace,
And saw—within the moonlight in his room,
Making it rich and like a lily in bloom—
An angel, writing in a book of gold.
Exceeding peace had made Ben Adhem bold,
And to the presence in the room he said,
' What writest thou ? '—The vision raised its head,

And, with a look made of all sweet accord,
Answered, ' The names of those who love the Lord.'
' And is mine one ? ' said Abou. ' Nay, not so,'
Replied the angel. Abou spoke more low,
But cheerly still, and said, ' I pray thee, then,
Write me as one that loves his fellow men.'

The angel wrote and vanished. The next night
It came again with a great wakening light,
And showed the names whom love of God had blessed,
And lo ! Ben Adhem's name led all the rest.

J. H. Leigh Hunt.

491. DIRGE

Blest is the turf, serenely blest,
Where throbbing hearts may sink to rest,
Where life's long journey turns to sleep,
Nor ever pilgrim wakes to weep.
A little sod, a few sad flowers,
A tear for long-departed hours,
Is all that feeling hearts request
To hush their weary thoughts to rest.
There shall no vain ambition come
To lure them from their quiet home ;
Nor sorrow lift, with heart-strings riven,
The meek imploring eye to heaven ;
Nor sad remembrance stoop to shed
His wrinkles on the slumberer's head ;
And never, never love repair
To breathe his idle whispers there !

J. H. Leigh Hunt.

492. THE GRASSHOPPER AND THE CRICKET

Green little vaulter in the sunny grass,
Catching your heart up at the feel of June,
Sole voice that 's heard amidst the lazy noon,
When even the bees lag at the summoning brass ;
And you, warm little housekeeper, who class
With those who think the candles come too soon,
Loving the fire, and with your tricksome tune
Nick the glad silent moments as they pass ;

Oh sweet and tiny cousins, that belong,
One to the fields, the other to the hearth,
Both have your sunshine ; both though small are strong
At your clear hearts ; and both seem given to earth
To ring in thoughtful ears this natural song—
Indoors and out, summer and winter, Mirth.

J. H. Leigh Hunt.

493. JENNY KISSED ME WHEN WE MET

JENNY kissed me when we met,
　Jumping from the chair she sat in ;
Time, you thief ! who love to get
　Sweets into your list, put that in.
Say I'm weary, say I'm sad ;
　Say that health and wealth have missed me ;
Say I'm growing old, but add—
　　Jenny kissed me !

J. H. LEIGH HUNT.

494. THE DEAREST POETS

WERE I to name, out of the times gone by,
The poets dearest to me, I should say,
Pulci for spirits, and a fine, free way ;
Chaucer for manners, and close, silent eye ;
Milton for classic taste, and harp strung high ;
Spenser for luxury, and sweet, sylvan play ;
Horace for chatting with, from day to day ;
Shakespeare for all, but most, society.

But which take with me, could I take but one ?
Shakespeare,—as long as I was unoppressed
With the world's weight, making sad thoughts intenser ;
But did I wish, out of the common sun
To lay a wounded heart in leafy rest,
And dream of things far off and healing,—Spenser.

J. H. LEIGH HUNT.

495. MY MOTHER BIDS ME BIND MY HAIR

MY mother bids me bind my hair
　With bands of rosy hue ;
Tie up my sleeves with ribbons rare,
　And lace my bodice blue !

' For why,' she cries, ' sit still and weep,
　While others dance and play ? '
Alas ! I scarce can go, or creep,
　While Lubin is away !

'Tis sad to think the days are gone
　When those we love were near !
I sit upon this mossy stone,
　And sigh when none can hear :

And while I spin my flaxen thread,
　And sing my simple lay,
The village seems asleep, or dead,
　Now Lubin is away !   ANNE HUNTER.

496. FROM 'THE HIGH TIDE ON THE LINCOLNSHIRE COAST'

I SHALL never hear her more
By the reedy Lindis shore,
' Cusha ! Cusha ! Cusha ! ' calling,
Ere the early dews be falling ;
I shall never hear her song,
' Cusha ! Cusha ! ' all along,
Where the sunny Lindis floweth,
  Goeth, floweth ;
From the meads where melick
  groweth,
When the water winding down,
Onward floweth to the town.

I shall never see her more
Where the reeds and rushes quiver,
  Shiver, quiver ;
Stand beside the sobbing river,
Sobbing, throbbing, in its falling,

To the sandy lonesome shore ;
I shall never hear her calling,
' Leave your meadow grasses mel-
  low,
  Mellow, mellow ;
Quit your cowslips, cowslips yel-
  low ;
Come uppe Whitefoot, come uppe
  Lightfoot ;
Quit your pipes of parsley hollow,
  Hollow, hollow ;
Come uppe Lightfoot, rise and
  follow ;
  Lightfoot, Whitefoot ;
From your clovers lift the head ;
Come uppe Jetty, follow, follow,
Jetty, to the milking shed.'
                    JEAN INGELOW.

497. OH, MY LOST LOVE

OH, my lost love, and my own, own love,
  And my love that loved me so !
Is there never a chink in the world above
  Where they listen for words from below ?
Nay, I spoke once, and I grieved thee sore,
  I remember all that I said,
And now thou wilt hear me no more—no more
  Till the sea gives up her dead.

Thou didst set thy foot on the ship, and sail
  To the ice-fields and the snow ;
Thou wert sad, for thy love did naught avail,
  And the end I could not know ;
How could I tell I should love thee to-day,
  Whom that day I held not dear ?
How could I know I should love thee away
  When I did not love thee anear ?
                    JEAN INGELOW (*Supper at the Mill*).

498. PLAYING ON THE VIRGINALS

PLAYING on the virginals,
  Who but I! Sae glad, sae free,
Smelling for all cordials,
  The green mint and marjorie ;
Set among the budding broom,
  Kingcup and daffodilly ;
By my side I made him room :
  O love my Willie !

' Like me, love me, girl o' gowd,'
  Sang he to my nimble strain ;
Sweet his ruddy lips o'erflowed
  Till my heartstrings rang again :
By the broom, the bonny broom,
  Kingcup and daffodilly,
In my heart I made him room :
  O love my Willie !

' Pipe and play, dear heart,' sang he,
  ' I must go, yet pipe and play ;
Soon I'll come and ask of thee
  For an answer yea or nay ' ;
And I waited till the flocks
  Panted in yon waters stilly,
And the corn stood in the shocks :
  O love my Willie !

I thought first when thou didst come,
  I would wear the ring for thee,
But the year told out its sum
  Ere again thou sat'st by me ;
Thou hadst naught to ask that day
  By kingcup and daffodilly ;
I said neither yea nor nay :
  O love my Willie !

JEAN INGELOW (*Supper at the Mill*).

499. TO BEAR, TO NURSE, TO REAR

To bear, to nurse, to rear,
  To watch, and then to lose :
To see my bright ones disappear,
  Drawn up like morning dews—
To bear, to nurse, to rear,
  To watch, and then to lose :
This have I done when God drew near
  Among His own to choose.

To hear, to heed, to wed,
  And with thy lord depart
In tears that he, as soon as shed,
  Will let no longer smart.—
To hear, to heed, to wed,
  This while thou didst I smiled,
For now it was not God who said,
  ' Mother, give Me thy child.'

O fond, O fool, and blind,
  To God I gave with tears ;
But when a man like grace would find,
  My soul put by her fears—
O fond, O fool, and blind,
  God guards in happier spheres ;
That man will guard where he did bind
  Is hope for unknown years.

To hear, to heed, to wed,
  Fair lot that maidens choose,
Thy mother's tenderest words are said,
  Thy face no more she views
Thy mother's lot, my dear,
  She doth in naught accuse ;
Her lot to bear, to nurse, to rear,
  To love—and then to lose.

JEAN INGELOW (*Songs of Seven*).

500. WHEN THE DIMPLED WATER SLIPPETH

WHEN the dimpled water slippeth,
  Full of laughter on its way,
And her wing the wagtail dippeth,
  Running by the brink at play ;
When the poplar leaves a-tremble
  Turn their edges to the light,
And the far-up clouds resemble
  Veils of gauze most clear and
    white ;
And the sunbeams fall and flatter
  Woodland moss and branches
    brown,
And the glossy finches chatter
  Up and down, up and down :
Though the heart be not attending,
  Having music of her own,
On the grass, through meadows
    wending,
  It is sweet to walk alone.

When the falling waters utter
  Something mournful on their
    way,
And departing swallows flutter,
  Taking leave of bank and brae ;
When the chaffinch idly sitteth
  With her mate upon the sheaves,
And the wistful robin flitteth
  Over beds of yellow leaves ;
When the clouds, like ghosts that
    ponder
  Evil fate, float by and frown,
And the listless wind doth wander
  Up and down, up and down :
Though the heart be not attending,
  Having sorrows of her own,
Through the fields and fallows
    wending,
  It is sad to walk alone.

JEAN INGELOW (*Afternoon at a Parsonage*).

501. WITH LEADEN FOOT TIME CREEPS ALONG

WITH leaden foot time creeps along,
  While Delia is away ;
With her, nor plaintive was the song,
  Nor tedious was the day,
Ah ! envious power, reverse my doom ;
  Now double thy career ;
Strain every nerve, stretch every plume,
  And rest them when she 's here.   R. JAGO.

502. SONNET

PREFIXED TO HIS MAJESTY'S INSTRUCTIONS TO HIS DEAREST
SON, HENRY THE PRINCE

GOD gives not kings the style of gods in vain,
For on His throne His sceptre do they sway ;
And as their subjects ought them to obey,
So kings should fear and serve their God again.
If then ye would enjoy a happy reign,
Observe the statutes of your Heavenly King,
And from His Law make all your laws to spring,
Since His lieutenant here ye should remain :
Reward the just ; be steadfast, true, and plain ;
Repress the proud, maintaining ay the right ;
Walk always so as ever in His sight,
Who guards the godly, plaguing the profane,
And so ye shall in princely virtues shine,
Resembling right your mighty King divine.   KING JAMES I.

503. ON THE DEATH OF MR. ROBERT LEVET,
A PRACTISER IN PHYSIC

In misery's darkest cavern known,
His useful care was ever nigh,
Where hopeless anguish poured his groan,
And lonely want retired to die;

No summons mocked by chill delay,
No petty gain disdained by pride,
The modest wants of every day
The toil of every day supplied.

His virtues walked their narrow round,
Nor made a pause, nor left a void:
And sure the Eternal Master found
The single talent well employed.   S. Johnson.

504. BY POVERTY DEPRESSED

Of all the griefs that harass the distressed,
Sure the most bitter is a scornful jest;
Fate never wounds more deep the generous heart
Than when a blockhead's insult points the dart.
Has Heaven reserved, in pity to the poor,
No pathless waste, or undiscovered shore?
No secret island in the boundless main?
No peaceful desert yet unclaimed by Spain?
Quick let us rise, the happy seats explore,
And bear oppression's insolence no more.
This mournful truth is everywhere confessed,
Slow rises worth by poverty depressed.
                    S. Johnson (*London*).

505. CHARLES XII

On what foundation stands the warrior's pride,
How just his hopes let Swedish Charles decide.
A frame of adamant, a soul of fire,
No dangers fright him, and no labours tire;
O'er love, o'er fear, extends his wide domain,
Unconquered lord of pleasure and of pain;
No joys to him pacific sceptres yield,
War sounds the trump, he rushes to the field.
Behold surrounding kings their powers combine,
And one capitulate, and one resign:
Peace courts his hand, but spreads her charms in vain:
'Think nothing gained,' he cries, 'till naught remain,
On Moscow's walls till Gothic standards fly,
And all be mine beneath the polar sky.'

The march begins, in military state,
And nations on his eye suspended wait;
Stern famine guards the solitary coast,
And Winter barricades the realms of frost;
He comes, nor want nor cold his course delay!—
Hide, blushing glory, hide Pultowa's day:
The vanquished hero leaves his broken bands,
And shows his miseries in distant lands;
Condemned a needy supplicant to wait,
While ladies interpose, and slaves debate.
But did not chance at length her error mend?
Did no subverted empire mark his end?
Did rival monarchs give the fatal wound?
Or hostile millions press him to the ground?
His fall was destined to a barren strand,
A petty fortress, and a dubious hand:
He left the name at which the world grew pale,
To point a moral, or adorn a tale.

S. JOHNSON (*The Vanity of Human Wishes*).

506. TO-MORROW

TO-MORROW!
That fatal mistress of the young, the lazy,
The coward, and the fool, condemned to lose
A useless life in waiting for to-morrow—
To gaze with longing eyes upon to-morrow,
Till interposing death destroys the prospect!
Strange! that this general fraud from day to day
Should fill the world with wretches undetected.
The soldier, labouring through a winter's march,
Still sees to-morrow dressed in robes of triumph;
Still to the lover's long-expecting arms
To-morrow brings the visionary bride.
But thou, too old to bear another cheat,
Learn that the present hour alone is man's.

S. JOHNSON (*Irene*).

507. SHAKESPEARE AND JONSON

WHEN Learning's triumph o'er her barbarous foes
First reared the Stage, immortal Shakespeare rose;
Each change of many-coloured life he drew,
Exhausted worlds, and then imagined new;
Existence saw him spurn her bounded reign,
And panting Time toiled after him in vain.
His powerful strokes presiding Truth impressed,
And unresisted passion stormed the breast.

Then Jonson came, instructed from the school,
To please in method, and invent by rule;

His studious patience and laborious art,
By regular approach assayed the heart.
Cold approbation gave the lingering bays,
For those who durst not censure, scarce could praise ;
A mortal born, he met the general doom,
But left, like Egypt's kings, a lasting tomb.

S. Johnson (Drury Lane Prologue, 1747).

508. ON PARENT KNEES A NAKED NEW-BORN CHILD

On parent knees, a naked new-born child,
Weeping thou sat'st while all around thee smiled :
So live, that sinking to thy life's last sleep,
Calm thou may'st smile, whilst all around thee weep.

Sir W. Jones.

509. VENUS' RUNAWAY

Beauties, have you seen this toy,
Callèd Love, a little boy,
Almost naked, wanton, blind ;
Cruel now, and then as kind ?
If he be amongst ye, say ?
He is Venus' runaway.

B. Jonson (Mask).

510. COME, MY CELIA, LET US PROVE

Come, my Celia, let us prove,
While we can, the sports of love,
Time will not be ours for ever,
He, at length, our good will sever ;
Spend not then his gifts in vain ;
Suns that set may rise again :
But if once we lose this light,
'Tis with us perpetual night.
Why should we defer our joys ?
Fame and rumour are but toys.

Cannot we delude the eyes
Of a few poor household spies ?
Or his easier ears beguile,
Thus removed by our wile ?—
'Tis no sin love's fruits to steal ;
But the sweet thefts to reveal,
To be taken, to be seen,
These have crimes accounted
been.

B. Jonson (Volpone).

511. TO CELIA

Drink to me only with thine
    eyes,
And I will pledge with mine ;
Or leave a kiss but in the cup,
And I'll not look for wine.
The thirst that from the soul doth
    rise,
Doth ask a drink divine :
But might I of Jove's nectar sup,
I would not change for thine.

I sent thee late a rosy wreath,
    Not so much honouring thee,
As giving it a hope that there
    It could not withered be.
But thou thereon didst only
    breathe,
    And sent'st it back to me :
Since when it grows, and smells,
    I swear,
    Not of itself, but thee.

B. Jonson (The Forest).

512. THAT WOMEN ARE BUT MEN'S SHADOWS

FOLLOW a shadow, it still flies you;
  Seem to fly it, it will pursue:
So court a mistress, she denies you;
  Let her alone, she will court you.
Say are not women truly, then,
Styled but the shadows of us men?

B. JONSON (*The Forest*).

513. HAVE YOU SEEN BUT A BRIGHT LILY GROW

HAVE you seen but a bright lily grow,
  Before rude hands have touched it?
Have you marked but the fall o' the snow
  Before the soil hath smutched it?
Have you felt the wool of the beaver?
    Or swan's down ever?
Or have smelt o' the bud o' the brier?
    Or the nard in the fire?
Or have tasted the bag of the bee?
O so white! O so soft! O so sweet is she!

B. JONSON (*A Celebration of Charis*).

514. IF I FREELY MAY DISCOVER

IF I freely may discover
What would please me in my lover,
I would have her fair and witty,
Savouring more of court than city;
A little proud, but full of pity:
Light and humorous in her toying;
Oft building hopes, and soon destroying;
Long, but sweet, in the enjoying;
Neither too easy, nor too hard:
All extremes I would have barred.

She should be allowed her passions,
So they were but used as fashions;
Sometimes froward, and then frowning,
Sometimes sickish and then swooning,
Every fit with change still crowning.
Purely jealous I would have her,
Then only constant when I crave her:
'Tis a virtue should not save her.
Thus, nor her delicates would cloy me,
Neither her peevishness annoy me.

B. JONSON (*The Poetaster*).

515. IT IS NOT GROWING LIKE A TREE

It is not growing like a tree
    In bulk, doth make men better be;
Or standing long an oak, three hundred year,
To fall a log at last, dry, bald, and sere:
            A lily of a day
            Is fairer far in May,
Although it fall and die that night;
It was the plant and flower of light.
In small proportions we just beauties see;
And in short measures life may perfect be.
            B. Jonson (*A Pindaric Ode to the Memory
                of Sir L. Carey and Sir H. Morison*).

516. THE KISS

O that joy so soon should waste!
    Or so sweet a bliss
    As a kiss
Might not for ever last!
So sugared, so melting, so soft, so
    delicious,
The dew that lies on roses,

When the morn herself discloses,
Is not so precious.
Oh, rather than I would it smother,
Were I to taste such another,
    It should be my wishing
    That I might die with kissing.
        B. Jonson (*Cynthia's Revels*)

517. HYMN TO DIANA

Queen and huntress, chaste and fair,
    Now the sun is laid to sleep,
Seated in thy silver chair
    State in wonted manner keep:
        Hesperus entreats thy light,
        Goddess excellently bright.

Earth, let not thy envious shade
    Dare itself to interpose;
Cynthia's shining orb was made
    Heaven to clear when day did close;
        Bless us then with wishèd sight,
        Goddess excellently bright.

Lay thy bow of pearl apart,
    And thy crystal shining quiver;
Give unto the flying hart
    Space to breathe, how short soever,
        Thou that mak'st a day of night,
        Goddess excellently bright.
            B. Jonson (*Cynthia's Revels*).

518. SHAKESPEARE

SOUL of the age !
The applause, delight, the wonder of our stage,
My Shakespeare, rise ! I will not lodge thee by
Chaucer, or Spenser, or bid Beaumont lie
A little further, to make thee a room :
Thou art a monument without a tomb,
And art alive still, while thy book doth live,
And we have wits to read, and praise to give.

That I not mix thee so my brain excuses ;
I mean, with great but disproportioned Muses.
For, if I thought my judgement were of years,
I should commit thee, surely, with thy peers.
And tell how far thou didst our Lyly outshine
Or sporting Kyd, or Marlowe's mighty line.

And though thou hadst small Latin and less Greek,
From thence, to honour thee, I will not seek
For names ; but call forth thundering Aeschylus,
Euripides, and Sophocles to us,
Paccuvius, Accius, him of Cordova dead
To life again, to hear thy buskin tread
And shake a stage ; or when thy sock was on,
Leave thee alone, for the comparison
Of all that insolent Greece or haughty Rome
Sent forth ; or since did from their ashes come.

Triumph, my Britain ! Thou hast one to show
To whom all scenes of Europe homage owe.
He was not of an age, but for all time !
And all the Muses still were in their prime,
When, like Apollo, he came forth to warm
Our ears, or, like a Mercury, to charm.
Nature herself was proud of his designs,
And joyed to wear the dressing of his lines,
Which were so richly spun, and woven so fit
As, since, she will vouchsafe no other wit.
The merry Greek, tart Aristophanes,
Neat Terence, witty Plautus, now not please ;
But antiquated and deserted lie,
As they were not of Nature's family.

Yet must I not give Nature all ! Thy art,
My gentle Shakespeare, must enjoy a part.
For though the Poet's matter Nature be
His art doth give the fashion. And that he
Who casts to write a living line, must sweat
(Such as thine are), and strike the second heat

Upon the Muses' anvil, turn the same
(And himself with it), that he thinks to frame;
Or for the laurel he may gain a scorn!
For a good Poet's made as well as born;
And such wert thou! Look how the father's face
Lives in his issue; even so, the race
Of Shakespeare's mind and manners brightly shines
In his well-turnèd and true-filèd lines;
In each of which he seems to shake a lance
As brandished at the eyes of Ignorance.

Sweet Swan of Avon! what a sight it were
To see thee in our water yet appear,
And make those flights upon the banks of Thames
That so did take Eliza, and our James!

                         B. JONSON.

519.   STILL TO BE NEAT

STILL to be neat, still to be dressed,
As you were going to a feast;
Still to be powdered, still perfumed:
Lady, it is to be presumed,
Though art's hid causes are not found,
All is not sweet, all is not sound.

Give me a look, give me a face,
That makes simplicity a grace;
Robes loosely flowing, hair as free:
Such sweet neglect more taketh me,
Than all the adulteries of art;
They strike mine eyes, but not my heart.

            B. JONSON (*The Silent Woman*).

520.   ON THE PORTRAIT OF SHAKESPEARE

THIS figure that thou here seest put,
It was for gentle Shakespeare cut,
Wherein the graver had a strife
With Nature, to outdo the life.
   Oh, could he but have drawn his wit
As well in brass, as he has hit
His face, the print would then surpass
All that was ever writ in brass.
   But, since he cannot, reader, look
Not on his picture, but his book.

         B. JONSON (*In the First Folio of
Shakespeare's Works*, 1623).

521. TRUTH

TRUTH is the trial of itself,
  And needs no other touch ;
And purer than the purest gold,
  Refine it ne'er so much.

It is the life and light of love,
  The sun that ever shineth,
And spirit of that special grace,
  That faith and love defineth.

It is the warrant of the word,
  That yields a scent so sweet,
As gives a power to faith to tread
  All falsehood under feet.   B. JONSON.

522. AN EPITAPH ON SALATHIEL PAVY
(A CHILD OF QUEEN ELIZABETH'S CHAPEL)

WEEP with me, all you that read
  This little story ;
And know, for whom a tear you shed,
  Death's self is sorry.
'Twas a child, that so did thrive
  In grace and feature,
As Heaven and Nature seemed to strive
  Which owned the creature.

Years he numbered scarce thirteen,
  When Fates turned cruel ;
Yet three filled zodiacs had he been
  The stage's jewel ;
And did act, what now we moan,
  Old men so duly,
As sooth, the Parcæ thought him one,
  He played so truly.

So, by error, to his fate
  They all consented ;
But, viewing him since (alas, too late !),
  They have repented ;
And have sought, to give new birth,
  In baths to steep him :
But, being so much too good for earth ;
  Heaven vows to keep him.   B. JONSON.

523. TO MY WORTHY AND HONOURED FRIEND
MASTER GEORGE CHAPMAN

WHOSE work could this be, Chapman, to refine
Old Hesiod's ore, and give it thus ! but thine,
Who hadst before wrought in rich Homer's mine.

What treasure hast thou brought us ! and what store
Still, still, dost thou arrive with at our shore,
To make thy honour, and our wealth the more !

If all the vulgar tongues that speak this day
Were asked of thy discoveries, they must say,
To the Greek coast thine only knew the way.

Such passage hast thou found, such returns made,
As now of all men, it is called thy trade,
And who make thither else, rob or invade. B. JONSON.

524. EPITAPH ON ELIZABETH L. H.

WOULDST thou hear what man can say
In a little ? Reader, stay.

Underneath this stone doth lie
As much beauty as could die ;
Which in life did harbour give
To more virtue than doth live.
If at all she had a fault,
Leave it buried in this vault.
One name was *Elizabeth*,
The other, let it sleep with death :
Fitter, where it died, to tell
Than that it lived at all. Farewell. B. JONSON.

525. LET US DRINK AND BE MERRY

LET us drink and be merry, dance, joke, and rejoice,
With claret and sherry, theorbo and voice !
The changeable world to our joy is unjust,
    All treasure's uncertain,
    Then down with your dust !
In frolics dispose your pounds, shillings, and pence,
For we shall be nothing a hundred years hence.

Then why should we turmoil in cares and in fears,
Turn all our tranquill'ty to sighs and to tears ?
Let 's eat, drink, and play till the worms do corrupt us,
    'Tis certain, *Post mortem*
    Nulla voluptas.
For health, wealth and beauty, wit, learning and sense,
Must all come to nothing a hundred years hence.

                                   T. JORDAN.

526. A THING OF BEAUTY IS A JOY FOR EVER

A THING of beauty is a joy for ever :
Its loveliness increases ; it will never
Pass into nothingness ; but still will keep
A bower quiet for us, and a sleep
Full of sweet dreams, and health, and quiet breathing
Therefore, on every morrow, are we wreathing
A flowery band to bind us to the earth,
Spite of despondence, of the inhuman dearth

Of noble natures, of the gloomy days,
Of all the unhealthy and o'er-darkened ways
Made for our searching : yes, in spite of all,
Some shape of beauty moves away the pall
From our dark spirits. Such the sun, the moon,
Trees old and young, sprouting a shady boon
For simple sheep ; and such are daffodils
With the green world they live in ; and clear rills
That for themselves a cooling covert make
'Gainst the hot season ; the mid-forest brake,
Rich with a sprinkling of fair musk-rose blooms :
And such too is the grandeur of the dooms
We have imagined for the mighty dead ;
All lovely tales that we have heard or read :
An endless fountain of immortal drink,
Pouring unto us from the heaven's brink.
Nor do we merely feel these essences
For one short hour ; no, even as the trees
That whisper round a temple become soon
Dear as the temple's self, so does the moon,
The passion poesy, glories infinite,
Haunt us till they become a cheering light
Unto our souls, and bound to us so fast,
That, whether there be shine, or gloom o'ercast,
They always must be with us, or we die.

J. Keats (Endymion).

527. LA BELLE DAME SANS MERCI

' Ah, what can ail thee, wretched wight,
    Alone and palely loitering ?
The sedge is withered from the lake,
    And no birds sing.

' Ah, what can ail thee, wretched wight,
    So haggard and so woe-begone ?
The squirrel's granary is full,
    And the harvest 's done.

' I see a lily on thy brow,
    With anguish moist and fever dew;
And on thy cheeks a fading rose
    Fast withereth too.'

' I met a lady in the meads
    Full beautiful, a faery's child;
Her hair was long, her foot was light,
    And her eyes were wild.

' I set her on my pacing steed,
    And nothing else saw all day long ;
For sideways would she lean, and sing
    A faery's song.

'I made a garland for her head,
  And bracelets too, and fragrant zone ;
She looked at me as she did love,
  And made sweet moan.

'She found me roots of relish sweet,
  And honey wild, and manna dew ;
And sure in language strange she said,
  "I love thee true."

'She took me to her elfin grot,
  And there she gazed, and sighèd deep,
And there I shut her wild sad eyes—
  So kissed to sleep.

'And there we slumbered on the moss,
  And there I dreamed, ah woe betide,
The latest dream I ever dreamed
  On the cold hill side.

'I saw pale kings, and princes too,
  Pale warriors, death-pale were they all ;
They cried—"La belle Dame sans merci
  Hath thee in thrall !"

'I saw their starved lips in the gloam
  With horrid warning gapèd wide,
And I awoke and found me here
  On the cold hill side.

'And this is why I sojourn here
  Alone and palely loitering,
Though the sedge is withered from the lake,
  And no birds sing.'

                                    J. KEATS.

528. SONNET

Written on a blank page in Shakespeare's Poems, facing
' A Lover's Complaint '

BRIGHT star, would I were steadfast as thou art—
Not in lone splendour hung aloft the night
And watching, with eternal lids apart,
Like nature's patient, sleepless Eremite,
The moving waters at their priestlike task
Of pure ablution round earth's human shores,
Or gazing on the new soft-fallen mask
Of snow upon the mountains and the moors—
No—yet still steadfast, still unchangeable,
Pillowed upon my fair love's ripening breast,
To feel for ever its soft fall and swell,
Awake for ever in a sweet unrest,
Still, still to hear her tender-taken breath,
And so live ever—or else swoon to death.   J. KEATS.

529. HAPPY IS ENGLAND

Happy is England! I could be content
To see no other verdure than its own;
To feel no other breezes than are blown
Through its tall woods with high romances blent:
Yet do I sometimes feel a languishment
For skies Italian, and an inward groan
To sit upon an Alp as on a throne,
And half forget what world or worldling meant.
Happy is England, sweet her artless daughters;
Enough their simple loveliness for me,
Enough their whitest arms in silence clinging:
Yet do I often warmly burn to see
Beauties of deeper glance, and hear their singing,
And float with them about the summer waters.

J. Keats.

530. IN A DREAR-NIGHTED DECEMBER

In a drear-nighted December,
Too happy, happy tree,
Thy branches ne'er remember
Their green felicity:
The north cannot undo them,
With a sleety whistle through
    them;
Nor frozen thawings glue them
From budding at the prime.

In a drear-nighted December,
Too happy, happy brook,
Thy bubblings ne'er remember
Apollo's summer look;

But with a sweet forgetting,
They stay their crystal fretting,
Never, never petting
About the frozen time.

Ah! would 'twere so with many
A gentle girl and boy!
But were there ever any
Writhed not at passèd joy?
To know the change and feel it,
When there is none to heal it,
Nor numbed sense to steal it,
Was never said in rhyme.

J. Keats.

531. ON FIRST LOOKING INTO CHAPMAN'S HOMER

Much have I travelled in the realms of gold,
And many goodly states and kingdoms seen;
Round many western islands have I been
Which bards in fealty to Apollo hold.
Oft of one wide expanse had I been told
That deep-browed Homer ruled as his demesne:
Yet did I never breathe its pure serene
Till I heard Chapman speak out loud and bold:
Then felt I like some watcher of the skies
When a new planet swims into his ken;
Or like stout Cortez when with eagle eyes
He stared at the Pacific—and all his men
Looked at each other with a wild surmise—
Silent, upon a peak in Darien.

J. Keats.

532. ODE TO A NIGHTINGALE

My heart aches, and a drowsy numbness pains
　My sense, as though of hemlock I had drunk,
Or emptied some dull opiate to the drains
　One minute past, and Lethe-wards had sunk:
'Tis not through envy of thy happy lot,
　But being too happy in thine happiness,—
　　That thou, light-wingèd Dryad of the trees,
　　　In some melodious plot
　Of beechen green, and shadows numberless,
　　Singest of summer in full-throated ease.

O, for a draught of vintage! that hath been
　Cooled a long age in the deep-delvèd earth,
Tasting of Flora and the country green,
　Dance, and Provençal song, and sunburnt mirth!
O for a beaker full of the warm South,
　Full of the true, the blushful Hippocrene,
　　With beaded bubbles winking at the brim
　　　And purple-stainèd mouth;
　That I might drink, and leave the world unseen,
　　And with thee fade away into the forest dim:

Fade far away, dissolve, and quite forget
　What thou among the leaves hast never known,
The weariness, the fever, and the fret
　Here, where men sit and hear each other groan;
Where palsy shakes a few, sad, last grey hairs,
　Where youth grows pale, and spectre-thin, and dies;
　　Where but to think is to be full of sorrow
　　　And leaden-eyed despairs,
　Where Beauty cannot keep her lustrous eyes,
　　Or new Love pine at them beyond to-morrow.

Away! away! for I will fly to thee,
　Not charioted by Bacchus and his pards,
But on the viewless wings of Poesy,
　Though the dull brain perplexes and retards:
Already with thee! tender is the night,
　And haply the Queen-Moon is on her throne,
　　Clustered around by all her starry Fays;
　　　But here there is no light,
　Save what from heaven is with the breezes blown
　　Through verdurous glooms and winding mossy ways.

I cannot see what flowers are at my feet,
　Nor what soft incense hangs upon the boughs,
But, in embalmèd darkness, guess each sweet
　Wherewith the seasonable month endows

The grass, the thicket, and the fruit-tree wild ;
  White hawthorn, and the pastoral eglantine ;
    Fast fading violets covered up in leaves ;
      And mid-May's eldest child,
  The coming musk-rose, full of dewy wine,
    The murmurous haunt of flies on summer eves.

Darkling I listen ; and for many a time
  I have been half in love with easeful Death,
Called him soft names in many a musèd rhyme,
  To take into the air my quiet breath ;
Now more than ever seems it rich to die,
  To cease upon the midnight with no pain,
    While thou art pouring forth thy soul abroad
      In such an ecstasy !
  Still wouldst thou sing, and I have ears in vain—
    To thy high requiem become a sod.

Thou wast not born for death, immortal Bird !
  No hungry generations tread thee down ;
The voice I hear this passing night was heard
  In ancient days by emperor and clown :
Perhaps the self-same song that found a path
  Through the sad heart of Ruth, when, sick for home,
    She stood in tears amid the alien corn ;
      The same that oft-times hath
  Charmed magic casements, opening on the foam
    Of perilous seas, in faery lands forlorn.

Forlorn ! the very word is like a bell
  To toll me back from thee to my sole self !
Adieu ! the fancy cannot cheat so well
  As she is famed to do, deceiving elf.
Adieu ! adieu ! thy plaintive anthem fades
  Past the near meadows, over the still stream,
    Up the hill-side ; and now 'tis buried deep
      In the next valley-glades :
  Was it a vision, or a waking dream ?
    Fled is that music :—Do I wake or sleep ?

J. KEATS.

533. SONNET TO SLEEP

O SOFT embalmer of the still midnight,
Shutting, with careful fingers and benign,
Our gloom-pleased eyes, embowered from the light,
Enshaded in forgetfulness divine :
O soothest Sleep ! if so it please thee, close
In midst of this thine hymn my willing eyes,
Or wait the ' Amen ' ere thy poppy throws
Around my bed its lulling charities.

Then save me, or the passèd day will shine
Upon my pillow, breeding many woes,—
Save me from curious Conscience, that still lords
Its strength for darkness, burrowing like a mole;
Turn the key deftly in the oilèd wards,
And seal the hushèd Casket of my Soul.

J. KEATS.

534. SORROW

O SORROW,
Why dost borrow
The natural hue of health, from vermeil lips ?—
To give maiden blushes
To the white rose bushes ?
Or is 't thy dewy hand the daisy tips ?

O Sorrow,
Why dost borrow
The lustrous passion from a falcon-eye ?—
To give the glow-worm light ?
Or, on a moonless night,
To tinge, on siren shores, the salt sea-spry ?

O Sorrow,
Why dost borrow
The mellow ditties from a mourning tongue ?—
To give at evening pale
Unto the nightingale,
That thou mayst listen the cold dews among ?

O Sorrow,
Why dost borrow
Heart's lightness from the merriment of May ?—
A lover would not tread
A cowslip on the head,
Though he should dance from eve till peep of day—
Nor any drooping flower
Held sacred for thy bower,
Wherever he may sport himself and play.

To Sorrow
I bade good-morrow,
And thought to leave her far away behind;
But cheerly, cheerly,
She loves me dearly;
She is so constant to me, and so kind:
I would deceive her
And so leave her,
But ah ! she is so constant and so kind.

. . . .

Come then, Sorrow !
    Sweetest Sorrow !
Like an own babe I nurse thee on my breast :
    I thought to leave thee
    And deceive thee,
But now of all the world I love thee best.

    There is not one,
    No, no, not one
But thee to comfort a poor lonely maid ;
    Thou art her mother,
    And her brother,
Her playmate, and her wooer in the shade.

J. KEATS (Endymion).

535. ODE TO AUTUMN

SEASON of mists and mellow fruitfulness,
Close bosom-friend of the maturing sun ;
Conspiring with him how to load and bless
With fruit the vines that round the thatch-eaves run ;
To bend with apples the mossed cottage-trees,
And fill all fruit with ripeness to the core ;
To swell the gourd, and plump the hazel shells
With a sweet kernel ; to set budding more,
And still more, later flowers for the bees,
Until they think warm days will never cease,
For Summer has o'erbrimmed their clammy cells.

Who hath not seen thee oft amid thy store ?
Sometimes whoever seeks abroad may find
Thee sitting careless on a granary floor,
Thy hair soft-lifted by the winnowing wind ;
Or on a half-reaped furrow sound asleep,
Drowsed with the fume of poppies, while thy hook
Spares the next swath and all its twinèd flowers ;
And sometimes like a gleaner thou dost keep
Steady thy laden head across a brook ;
Or by a cider press, with patient look,
Thou watchest the last oozings hours by hours.

Where are the songs of Spring ? Aye, where are they ?
Think not of them, thou hast thy music too,—
While barrèd clouds bloom the soft-dying day,
And touch the stubble-plains with rosy hue ;
Then in a wailful choir the small gnats mourn
Among the river sallows, borne aloft
Or sinking as the light wind lives or dies ;
And full-grown lambs loud bleat from hilly bourn
Hedge-crickets sing ; and now with treble soft
The red-breast whistles from a garden-croft ;
And gathering swallows twitter in the skies.   J. KEATS.

536. THE MERMAID TAVERN

Souls of Poets dead and gone,
What Elysium have ye known,
Happy field or mossy cavern,
Choicer than the Mermaid Tavern?
Have ye tippled drink more fine
Than mine host's Canary wine?
Or are fruits of Paradise
Sweeter than those dainty pies
Of venison? O generous food!
Dressed as though bold Robin Hood
Would, with his maid Marian,
Sup and bowse from horn and can.

I have heard that on a day
Mine host's sign-board flew away,
Nobody knew whither, till
An astrologer's old quill
To a sheepskin gave the story,
Said he saw you in your glory,
Underneath a new old sign
Sipping beverage divine,
And pledging with contented smack
The Mermaid in the Zodiac!

Souls of Poets dead and gone,
What Elysium have ye known,
Happy field or mossy cavern,
Choicer than the Mermaid Tavern?

J. KEATS.

537. SONNET TO HOMER

Standing aloof in giant ignorance,
Of thee I hear and of the Cyclades,
As one who sits ashore and longs perchance
To visit dolphin-coral in deep seas.
So thou wast blind;—but then the veil was rent,
For Jove uncurtained Heaven to let thee live,
And Neptune made for thee a spumy tent,
And Pan made sing for thee his forest-hive;
Aye on the shores of darkness there is light,
And precipices show untrodden green,
There is a budding morrow in midnight,
There is a triple sight in blindness keen;
Such seeing hadst thou, as it once befell
To Dian, Queen of Earth and Heaven and Hell.

J. KEATS.

538. ON THE GRASSHOPPER AND CRICKET

The poetry of earth is never dead:
When all the birds are faint with the hot sun,
And hide in cooling trees, a voice will run
From hedge to hedge about the new-mown mead
That is the grasshopper's—he takes the lead
In summer luxury,—he has never done
With his delights, for when tired out with fun
He rests at ease beneath some pleasant weed.
The poetry of earth is ceasing never:
On a lone winter evening, when the frost
Has wrought a silence, from the stove there shrills
The cricket's song, in warmth increasing ever,
And seems to one in drowsiness half lost,
The grasshopper's among some grassy hills.   J. KEATS.

539. ODE ON A GRECIAN URN

THOU still unravished bride of quietness,
  Thou foster-child of silence and slow time,
Sylvan historian, who canst thus express
  A flowery tale more sweetly than our rhyme:
What leaf-fringed legend haunts about thy shape
  Of deities or mortals, or of both,
    In Tempe, or the dales of Arcady?
  What men or gods are these? What maidens loath?
What mad pursuit? What struggle to escape?
    What pipes and timbrels? What wild ecstasy?

Heard melodies are sweet, but those unheard
  Are sweeter; therefore, ye soft pipes, play on;
Not to the sensual ear, but, more endeared,
  Pipe to the spirit ditties of no tone:
Fair youth, beneath the trees, thou canst not leave
  Thy song, nor ever can those trees be bare;
    Bold Lover, never, never canst thou kiss,
Though winning near the goal—yet, do not grieve;
    She cannot fade, though thou hast not thy bliss,
  For ever wilt thou love, and she be fair!

Ah, happy, happy boughs! that cannot shed
  Your leaves, nor ever bid the Spring adieu;
And, happy melodist, unwearièd,
  For ever piping songs for ever new;
More happy love! more happy, happy love!
  For ever warm and still to be enjoyed,
    For ever panting, and for ever young;
All breathing human passion far above,
  That leaves a heart high-sorrowful and cloyed,
    A burning forehead, and a parching tongue.

Who are these coming to the sacrifice?
  To what green altar, O mysterious priest,
Lead'st thou that heifer lowing at the skies,
  And all her silken flanks with garlands drest?
What little town by river or sea-shore,
  Or mountain-built with peaceful citadel,
    Is emptied of this folk, this pious morn?
And, little town, thy streets for evermore
  Will silent be; and not a soul, to tell
    Why thou art desolate, can e'er return.

O Attic shape! Fair attitude! with brede
  Of marble men and maidens overwrought,
With forest branches and the trodden weed;
  Thou silent form! dost tease us out of thought

As doth eternity: cold Pastoral !
When old age shall this generation waste,
Thou shalt remain, in midst of other woe
Than ours, a friend to man, to whom thou say'st,
Beauty is truth, truth beauty,'—that is all
Ye know on earth, and all ye need to know.

J. KEATS.

540. TO ONE WHO HAS BEEN LONG IN CITY PENT

To one who has been long in city pent,
'Tis very sweet to look into the fair
And open face of heaven,—to breathe a prayer
Full in the smile of the blue firmament.
Who is more happy, when, with heart's content,
Fatigued he sinks into some pleasant lair
Of wavy grass, and reads a debonair
And gentle tale of love and languishment ?
Returning home at evening, with one ear
Catching the notes of Philomel,—an eye
Watching the sailing cloudlet's bright career,
He mourns that day so soon has glided by :
E'en like the passage of an angel's tear
That falls through the clear ether silently.

J. KEATS.

541. WHEN I HAVE FEARS THAT I MAY CEASE TO BE

When I have fears that I may cease to be
Before my pen has gleaned my teeming brain,
Before high-pilèd books, in charactery,
Hold like rich garners the full ripened grain ;
When I behold, upon the night's starred face,
Huge cloudy symbols of a high romance,
And think that I may never live to trace
Their shadows, with the magic hand of chance ;
And when I feel, fair creature of an hour,
That I shall never look upon thee more,
Never have relish in the faery power
Of unreflecting love ;—then on the shore
Of the wide world I stand alone, and think
Till love and fame to nothingness do sink.

J. KEATS.

542. MORNING

Hues of the rich unfolding morn,
That, ere the glorious sun be born,
By some soft touch invisible
Around his path are taught to swell ;—

Thou rustling breeze so fresh and gay,
That dancest forth at opening day,
And brushing by with joyous wing,
Wakenest each little leaf to sing ;—

Ye fragrant clouds of dewy steam,
By which deep grove and tangled stream
Pay, for soft rains in season given,
Their tribute to the genial heaven ;—

. . . .

Oh ! timely happy, timely wise,
Hearts that with rising morn arise !
Eyes that the beam celestial view
Which evermore makes all things new !

J. Keble (*The Christian Year*).

543. SWEET NURSLINGS OF THE VERNAL SKIES.

Sweet nurslings of the vernal skies,
    Bathed in soft airs, and fed with dew,
What more than magic in you lies,
    To fill the heart's fond view ?

. . . .

Relics ye are of Eden's bowers,
    As pure, as fragrant, and as fair,
As when ye crowned the sunshine hours
    Of happy wanderers there.

J. Keble (*The Christian Year*).

544. WE NEED NOT BID, FOR CLOISTERED CELL

We need not bid, for cloistered cell,
Our neighbour and our work farewell,
Nor strive to wind ourselves too high
For sinful man beneath the sky :

The trivial round, the common task,
Would furnish all we ought to ask ;
Room to deny ourselves ; a road
To bring us, daily, nearer God.

Seek we no more ; content with these
Let present Rapture, Comfort, Ease,
As Heaven shall bid them, come and go :—
The secret this of Rest below.

J. Keble (*The Christian Year*).

545. WHO EVER SAW THE EARLIEST ROSE

Who ever saw the earliest rose
  First open her sweet breast?
Or, when the summer sun goes down,
The first soft star in evening's crown
  Light up her gleaming crest?

. . . .

But there's a sweeter flower than e'er
  Blushed on the rosy spray—
A brighter star, a richer bloom
Than e'er did western heaven illume
  At close of summer day.

'Tis Love, the last best gift of Heaven;
  Love gentle, holy, pure;
But tenderer than a dove's soft eye,
The searching sun, the open sky,
  She never could endure.

J. Keble (*The Christian Year*).

546. SIC VITA

Like to the falling of a star,
Or as the flights of eagles are,—
Or like the fresh spring's gaudy hue,
Or silver drops of morning dew;
Or like a wind that chafes the flood,
Or bubbles which on water stood:
Even such is man, whose borrowed light
Is straight called in, and paid to night.
The wind blows out, the bubble dies;
The spring entombed in autumn lies;
The dew dries up, the star is shot;
The flight is past—and man forgot.

H. King.

547. A DIRGE

What is the existence of man's life,
But open war, or slumbered strife;
Where sickness to his sense presents
The combat of the elements;
And never feels a perfect peace
Till Death's cold hand signs his release?

. . . .

It is a weary interlude—
Which doth short joys, long woes, include,
The world the stage, the prologue tears,
The acts vain hopes and varied fears;
The scene shuts up with loss of breath,
And leaves no epilogue but death.

H. King.

548. AIRLY BEACON

Airly Beacon, Airly Beacon;
  O the pleasant sight to see
Shires and towns from Airly Beacon,
  While my love climbed up to me!

Airly Beacon, Airly Beacon;
  O the happy hours we lay
Deep in fern on Airly Beacon,
  Courting through the summer's day!

Airly Beacon, Airly Beacon;
  O the weary haunt for me,
All alone on Airly Beacon,
  With his baby on my knee!

C. KINGSLEY.

549. MY LITTLE DOLL

I ONCE had a sweet little doll, dears,
  The prettiest doll in the world;
Her cheeks were so red and so white, dears,
  And her hair was so charmingly curled.
But I lost my poor little doll, dears,
  As I played in the heath one day;
And I cried for more than a week, dears,
  But I never could find where she lay.

I found my poor little doll, dears,
  As I played in the heath one day:
Folks say she is terribly changed, dears,
  For her paint is all washed away,
And her arms trodden off by the cows, dears,
  And her hair not the least bit curled:
Yet for old sakes' sake she is still, dears,
  The prettiest doll in the world.

C. KINGSLEY.

550. A FAREWELL

To C. E. G.

My fairest child, I have no song to give you;
  No lark could pipe in skies so dull and grey;
Yet, if you will, one quiet hint I'll leave you,
  For every day.

I'll tell you how to sing a clearer carol
  Than lark who hails the dawn or breezy down,
To earn yourself a purer poet's laurel
  Than Shakespeare's crown.

Be good, sweet maid, and let who can be clever,
  Do lovely things, not dream them, all day long;
And so make Life and Death, and that For Ever,
  One grand sweet song.

C. KINGSLEY.

551. THE SANDS OF DEE

‘ O MARY, go and call the cattle home,
 And call the cattle home,
 And call the cattle home
 Across the sands of Dee ’ ;
The western wind was wild and dank with foam,
 And all alone went she.

The western tide crept up along the sand,
 And o’er and o’er the sand,
 And round and round the sand,
 As far as eye could see.
The rolling mist came down and hid the land :
 And never home came she.

‘ Oh ! is it weed, or fish, or floating hair,
 A tress of golden hair,
 A drownèd maiden’s hair
 Above the nets at sea ?
Was never salmon yet that shone so fair
 Among the stakes of Dee.’

They rowed her in across the rolling foam,
 The cruel crawling foam,
 The cruel hungry foam,
 To her grave beside the sea :
But still the boatmen hear her call the cattle home
 Across the sands of Dee.

C. KINGSLEY.

552. ON THE DEATH OF A CERTAIN JOURNAL

The *Christian Socialist*, started by the Council of Associates for
promotion of Co-operation.

So die, thou child of stormy dawn,
Thou winter flower, forlorn of nurse ;
Chilled early by the bigot’s curse,
The pedant’s frown, the worldling’s yawn.

Fair death, to fall in teeming June,
When every seed which drops to earth
Takes root, and wins a second birth
From steaming shower and gleaming moon.

Fall warm, fall fast, thou mellow rain ;
Thou rain of God, make fat the land ;
That roots which parch in burning sand
May bud to flower and fruit again,

To grace, perchance, a fairer morn
In mightier lands beyond the sea,
While honour falls to such as we
From hearts of heroes yet unborn,

Who in the light of fuller day,
Of purer science, holier laws,
Bless us, faint heralds of their cause,
Dim beacons of their glorious way.

Failure ?   While tide-floods rise and boil
Round cape and isle, in port and cove,
Resistless, star-led from above :
What though our tiny wave recoil ?   C. KINGSLEY.

553. THE BAD SQUIRE

THE merry brown hares came leaping
    Over the crest of the hill,
Where the clover and corn lay sleeping
    Under the moonlight still.

Leaping late and early,
    Till under their bite and their tread
The swedes and the wheat and the barley
    Lay cankered and trampled and dead.

A poacher's widow sat sighing
    On the side of the white chalk bank,
Where under the gloomy fir-woods
    One spot in the ley throve rank.

She watched a long tuft of clover,
    Where rabbit or hare never ran ;
For its black sour haulm covered over
    The blood of a murdered man.

She thought of the dark plantation,
    And the hares, and her husband's blood,
And the voice of her indignation
    Rose up to the throne of God.

' I am long past wailing and whining—
    I have wept too much in my life :
I've had twenty years of pining
    As an English labourer's wife.

' A labourer in Christian England,
    Where they cant of a Saviour's name,
And yet waste men's lives like the vermin's
    For a few more brace of game.

' There's blood on your new foreign shrubs, squire,
    There's blood on your pointer's feet ;
There's blood on the game you sell, squire,
    And there's blood on the game you eat.

'You have sold the labouring-man, squire,
  Body and soul to shame,
To pay for your seat in the House, squire,
  And to pay for the feed of your game.

'You made him a poacher yourself, squire,
  When you'd give neither work nor meat,
And your barley-fed hares robbed the garden
  At our starving children's feet;

'When, packed in one reeking chamber,
  Man, maid, mother, and little ones lay;
While the rain pattered in on the rotting bride-bed,
  And the walls let in the day.

'When we lay in the burning fever
  On the mud of the cold clay floor,
Till you parted us all for three months, squire,
  At the dreary workhouse door.

'We quarrelled like brutes, and who wonders?
  What self-respect could we keep,
Worse housed than your hacks and your pointers,
  Worse fed than your hogs and your sheep?

'Our daughters with base-born babies
  Have wandered away in their shame,
If your misses had slept, squire, where they did,
  Your misses might do the same.

'Can your lady patch hearts that are breaking
  With handfuls of coals and rice,
Or by dealing out flannel and sheeting
  A little below cost price?

'You may tire of the jail and the workhouse,
  And take to allotments and schools,
But you've run up a debt that will never
  Be paid us by penny-club rules.

'In the season of shame and sadness,
  In the dark and dreary day,
When scrofula, gout, and madness
  Are eating your race away;

'When to kennels and liveried varlets
  You have cast your daughter's bread,
And, worn out with liquor and harlots,
  Your heir at your feet lies dead;

'When your youngest, the mealy-mouthed rector,
  Lets your soul rot asleep to the grave,
You will find in your God the protector
  Of the freeman you fancied your slave.'

She looked at the tuft of clover,
    And wept till her heart grew light ;
And at last, when her passion was over,
    Went wandering into the night.

But the merry brown hares came leaping
    Over the uplands still,
Where the clover and corn lay sleeping
    On the side of the white chalk hill.

C. KINGSLEY.

554. ODE TO THE NORTH-EAST WIND

WELCOME, wild North-easter !
    Shame it is to see
Odes to every zephyr ;
    Ne'er a verse to thee.
Welcome, black North-easter !
    O'er the German foam ;
O'er the Danish moorlands,
    From thy frozen home.
Tired we are of summer,
    Tired of gaudy glare.
Showers soft and steaming,
    Hot and breathless air.
Tired of listless dreaming,
    Through the lazy day :
Jovial wind of winter
    Turn us out to play !
Sweep the golden reed-beds ;
    Crisp the lazy dyke ;
Hunger into madness
    Every plunging pike.
Fill the lake with wild-fowl ;
    Fill the marsh with snipe ;
While on dreary moorlands
    Lonely curlew pipe.
Through the black fir-forest
    Thunder harsh and dry,
Shattering down the snow-flakes
    Off the curdled sky.
Hark ! The brave North-easter !
    Breast-high lies the scent,
On by holt and headland,
    Over heath and bent.
Chime, ye dappled darlings,
    Through the sleet and snow.

Who can over-ride you ?
    Let the horses go !
Chime, ye dappled darlings,
    Down the roaring blast
You shall see a fox die
    Ere an hour be past.
Go ! and rest to-morrow,
    Hunting in your dreams,
While our skates are ringing
    O'er the frozen streams.
Let the luscious South-wind
    Breathe in lovers' sighs,
While the lazy gallants
    Bask in ladies' eyes.
What does he but soften
    Heart alike and pen ?
'Tis the hard grey weather
    Breeds hard English men.
What's the soft South-wester ?
    'Tis the ladies' breeze,
Bringing home their true-loves
    Out of all the seas :
But the black North-easter,
    Through the snowstorm hurled,
Drives our English hearts of oak
    Seaward round the world.
Come, as came our fathers,
    Heralded by thee,
Conquering from the eastward,
    Lords by land and sea.
Come ; and strong within us
    Stir the Vikings' blood ;
Bracing brain and sinew ;
    Blow, thou wind of God !

C. KINGSLEY.

555. YOUNG AND OLD

When all the world is young, lad
　And all the trees are green ;
And every goose a swan, lad,
　And every lass a queen ;
Then hey for boot and horse, lad,
　And round the world away ;
Young blood must have its course,
　lad,
　And every dog his day.

When all the world is old, lad,
　And all the trees are brown ;
And all the sport is stale, lad,
　And all the wheels run down :
Creep home, and take your place
　there,
　The spent and maimed among :
God grant you find one face there
　You loved when all was young.
　　　　　　　　C. Kingsley.

556. A CHILD

A child's a plaything for an
　hour ;
　Its pretty tricks we try
For that or for a longer space ;
　Then tire, and lay it by.

But I knew one, that to itself
　All seasons could control ;
That would have mocked the
　sense of pain
　Out of a grievéd soul.

Thou straggler into loving arms,
　Young climber up of knees,
When I forget thy thousand ways,
　Then life and all shall cease. 　C. Lamb.

557. FROM 'A FAREWELL TO TOBACCO'

For I must (nor let it grieve thee,
Friendliest of plants, that I must)
　leave thee.
For thy sake, Tobacco, I
Would do anything but die,
And but seek to extend my days
Long enough to sing thy praise.
But as she who once hath been
A king's consort, is a queen
Ever after, nor will bate
Any tittle of her state,
Though a widow, or divorced,
So I, from thy converse forced,
The old name and style retain,
A right Katherine of Spain ;

And a seat, too, 'mongst the joys
Of the blest Tobacco boys ;
Where, though I, by sour physi-
　cian,
Am debarred the full fruition
Of thy favours, I may catch
Some collateral sweets, and snatch
Sidelong odours, that give life
Like glances from a neighbour's
　wife ;
And still live in the by-places
And the suburbs of thy graces ;
And in thy borders take delight,
An unconquered Canaanite.
　　　　　　　　C. Lamb.

558. THE OLD FAMILIAR FACES

I have had playmates, I have had companions,
In my days of childhood, in my joyful school-days,
All, all are gone, the old familiar faces.

I have been laughing, I have been carousing,
Drinking late, sitting late, with my bosom cronies,
All, all are gone, the old familiar faces.

I loved a love once, fairest among women ;
Closed are her doors on me, I must not see her—
All, all are gone, the old familiar faces.

I have a friend, a kinder friend has no man ;
Like an ingrate, I left my friend abruptly ;
Left him, to muse on the old familiar faces.

Ghost-like I paced round the haunts of my childhood.
Earth seemed a desert I was bound to traverse,
Seeking to find the old familiar faces.

Friend of my bosom, thou more than a brother,
Why wert not thou born in my father's dwelling ?
So might we talk of the old familiar faces—

How some they have died, and some they have left me,
And some are taken from me ; all are departed ;
All, all are gone, the old familiar faces.   C. LAMB.

559. WRITTEN AT CAMBRIDGE (1819)

I WAS not trained in academic bowers,
And to those learnèd streams I nothing owe
Which copious from those twin fair founts do flow ;
Mine have been anything but studious hours.
Yet can I fancy, wandering 'mid thy towers,
Myself a nursling, Granta, of thy lap ;
My brow seems tightening with the doctor's cap,
And I walk *gownèd* ; feel unusual powers.
Strange forms of logic clothe my admiring speech,
Old Ramus' ghost is busy at my brain ;
And my skull teems with notions infinite.
Be still, ye reeds of Camus, while I teach
Truths, which transcend the searching Schoolmen's vein,
And half had staggered that stout Stagirite !   C. LAMB.

560. A SONNET ON CHRISTIAN NAMES
(*Written in the album of Edith Southey*)

IN Christian world Mary the garland wears !
Rebecca sweetens on a Hebrew's ear ;
Quakers for pure Priscilla are more clear ;
And the light Gaul by amorous Ninon swears.
Among the lesser lights how Lucy shines !
What air of fragrance Rosamond throws around !
How like a hymn doth sweet Cecilia sound !
Of Marthas, and of Abigails, few lines
Have bragged in verse. Of coarsest household stuff
Should homely Joan be fashionèd. But can
You Barbara resist, or Marian ?
And is not Clare for love excuse enough ?
Yet, by my faith in numbers, I profess,
These all, than Saxon Edith, please me less.   C. LAMB.

561. HESTER

WHEN maidens such as Hester die,
Their place ye may not well supply,
Though ye among a thousand try,
        With vain endeavour.

A month or more hath she been dead,
Yet cannot I by force be led
To think upon the wormy bed,
        And her together.

A springy motion in her gait,
A rising step, did indicate
Of pride and joy no common rate,
        That flushed her spirit.

I know not by what name beside
I shall it call :—if 'twas not pride,
It was a joy to that allied,
        She did inherit.

Her parents held the Quaker rule,
Which doth the human feeling cool,
But she was trained in Nature's school,
        Nature had blest her.

A waking eye, a prying mind,
A heart that stirs, is hard to bind,
A hawk's keen sight ye cannot blind,
        Ye could not Hester.

My sprightly neighbour, gone before
To that unknown and silent shore,
Shall we not meet, as heretofore,
        Some summer morning,

When from thy cheerful eyes a ray
Hath struck a bliss upon the day,
A bliss that would not go away,
        A sweet forewarning ?   C. LAMB.

562. AH, WHAT AVAILS THE SCEPTRED RACE

AH, what avails the sceptred race,
    Ah, what the form divine !
What every virtue, every grace !
    Rose Aylmer, all were thine.
Rose Aylmer, whom these wakeful eyes
    May weep, but never see,
A night of memories and of sighs
    I consecrate to thee.   W. S. LANDOR.

563.   AROUND THE CHILD

AROUND the child bend all the three
Sweet Graces—Faith, Hope, Charity.
Around the man bend other faces—
Pride, Envy, Malice, are his Graces.

W. S. LANDOR.

564.   CHILD OF A DAY

CHILD of a day, thou knowest not
    The tears that overflow thine urn,
The gushing eyes that read thy lot,
    Nor, if thou knewest, couldst return !

And why the wish ? the pure and blest
    Watch like thy mother o'er thy sleep
O peaceful night ! O envied rest !
    Thou wilt not ever see her weep.

W. S. LANDOR.

565.   HOW MANY VOICES GAILY SING

How many voices gaily sing,
' O happy morn, O happy spring
Of life ! ' Meanwhile there comes o'er me
A softer voice from Memory,
And says, ' If loves and hopes have flown
With years, think too what griefs are gone ! '

W. S. LANDOR.

566.   THE MAID'S LAMENT

I LOVED him not ; and yet now he is gone
        I feel I am alone.
I checked him while he spoke ; yet, could he speak,
        Alas ! I would not check.
For reasons not to love him once I sought,
        And wearied all my thought
To vex myself and him ; I now would give
        My love, could he but live
Who lately lived for me, and when he found
        'Twas vain, in holy ground
He hid his face amid the shades of death.
        I waste for him my breath
Who wasted his for me ; but mine returns,
        And this lorn bosom burns
With stifling heat, heaving it up in sleep,
        And waking me to weep
Tears that had melted his soft heart : for years
        Wept he as bitter tears.

'Merciful God!' such was his latest prayer,
  'These may she never share!'
Quieter is his breath, his breast more cold
  Than daisies in the mould,
Where children spell, athwart the churchyard gate,
  His name and life's brief date.
Pray for him, gentle souls, whoe'er you be,
  And, oh, pray too for me!   W. S. LANDOR.

567. I STROVE WITH NONE

I STROVE with none; for none was worth my strife.
Nature I loved and, next to Nature, Art;
I warmed both hands before the fire of life;
It sinks, and I am ready to depart.   W. S. LANDOR.

568. IN CLEMENTINA'S ARTLESS MIEN

IN Clementina's artless mien
  Lucilla asks me what I see,
And are the roses of sixteen
      Enough for me?

Lucilla asks, if that be all,
  Have I not culled as sweet before:
Ah yes, Lucilla! and their fall
  I still deplore.

I now behold another scene,
  Where Pleasure beams with heaven's own light,
More pure, more constant, more serene,
      And not less bright:

Faith, on whose breast the Loves repose,
  Whose chain of flowers no force can sever,
And Modesty who, when she goes,
      Is gone for ever.   W. S. LANDOR.

569. IRELAND NEVER WAS CONTENTED

IRELAND never was contented.
Say you so? You are demented.
Ireland was contented when
All could use the sword and pen,
And when Tara rose so high
That her turrets split the sky,
And about her courts were seen
Liveried angels robed in green,
Wearing, by St. Patrick's bounty,
Emeralds big as half the county.   W. S. LANDOR.

570. MY SERIOUS SON

My serious son! I see thee look
First on the picture, then the book.
I catch the wish that thou couldst paint
The yearnings of the ecstatic saint.
Give it not up, my serious son!
Wish it again, and it is done.
Seldom will any fail who tries
With patient hand and steadfast eyes,
And wooes the true with such pure sighs.

W. S. LANDOR.

571. NO DOUBT THY LITTLE BOSOM BEATS

No doubt thy little bosom beats
    When sounds a wedding bell,
No doubt it pants to taste the sweets
    That songs and stories tell.

Awhile in shade content to lie,
    Prolong life's morning dream,
While others rise at the first fly
    That glitters on the stream.   W. S. LANDOR.

572. NO, MY OWN LOVE OF OTHER YEARS

No, my own love of other years!
    No, it must never be.
Much rests with you that yet endears,
    Alas! but what with me?

Could those bright years o'er me revolve
    So gay, o'er you so fair,
The pearl of life we would dissolve,
    And each the cup might share.

You show that truth can ne'er decay,
    Whatever fate befalls;
I, that the myrtle and the bay
    Shoot fresh on ruined walls.   W. S. LANDOR.

573. PROUD WORD YOU NEVER SPOKE

Proud word you never spoke, but you will speak
    Four not exempt from pride some future day.
Resting on one white hand a warm wet cheek,
    Over my open volume you will say,
'This man loved *me!*' then rise and trip away.

W. S. LANDOR.

574. THE MAID I LOVE NE'ER THOUGHT OF ME

THE maid I love ne'er thought of me
Amid the scenes of gaiety;
But when her heart or mine sank low,
Ah, then it was no longer so.
From the slant palm she raised her head,
And kissed the cheek whence youth had fled.
Angels! some future day for this,
Give her as sweet and pure a kiss.

                              W. S. LANDOR.

575. ROBERT BROWNING

THERE is delight in singing, though none hear
Beside the singer; and there is delight
In praising, though the praiser sit alone
And see the praised far off him, far above.
Shakespeare is not our poet, but the world's,
Therefore on him no speech! and brief for thee,
Browning! Since Chaucer was alive and hale,
No man hath walked along our roads with step
So active, so inquiring eye, or tongue
So varied in discourse. But warmer climes
Give brighter plumage, stronger wing: the breeze
Of Alpine heights thou playest with, borne on
Beyond Sorrento and Amalfi, where
The Siren waits thee, singing song for song.

                              W. S. LANDOR.

576. TWENTY YEARS HENCE

TWENTY years hence my eyes may grow
If not quite dim, yet rather so,
Still yours from others they shall know
          Twenty years hence.

Twenty years hence though it may hap
That I be called to take a nap
In a cool cell where thunder-clap
          Was never heard,

There breathe but o'er my arch of grass
A not too sadly sighed *Alas*,
And I shall catch, ere you can pass,
          That wingèd word.

                              W. S. LANDOR.

577.　WELL I REMEMBER HOW YOU SMILED

WELL I remember how you smiled
　　To see me write your name upon
The soft sea-sand—'*O ! what a child !*
　　You think you're writing upon stone !'

I have since written what no tide
　　Shall ever wash away, what men
Unborn shall read o'er ocean wide
　　And find Ianthe's name again.　　W. S. LANDOR.

578.　WHY REPINE ?

WHY, why repine, my pensive friend,
　　At pleasures slipt away ?
Some the stern Fates will never lend,
　　And all refuse to stay.

I see the rainbow in the sky,
　　The dew upon the grass,
I see them, and I ask not why
　　They glimmer or they pass.

With folded arms I linger not
　　To call them back ; 'twere vain ;
In this, or in some other spot,
　　I know they'll shine again.　　W. S. LANDOR.

579.　THE CHILD OF MISERY

COLD on Canadian hills or Minden's plain,
Perhaps that parent mourned her soldier slain ;
Bent o'er her babe, her eye dissolved in dew,
The big drops mingling with the milk he drew
Gave the sad presage of his future years,—
The child of misery, baptized in tears.
　　　　　　　J. LANGHORNE (*The Country Justice*).

580.　UNCONSCIOUS CEREBRATION

SAY not that the past is dead.
Though the Autumn leaves are shed,
Though the day's last flush has flown,
Though the lute has lost its tone—
Still within, unfelt, unseen,
Lives the life that once has been ;
With a silent power still
Guiding heart or brain or will,
Lending bias, force, and hue
To the things we think and do.
Strange ! how aimless looks or words
Sometimes wake forgotten chords,
Bidding dreams and memories leap
From a long unbroken sleep.
　　　　　　　W. E. H. LECKY.

581. THE LIBERTY OF THE IMPRISONED ROYALIST

WHAT though I cannot see my King,
 Either in 's person, or his coin,
Yet contemplation is a thing
 Which renders what I have not, mine.
My King from me no adamant can part,
Whom I do wear engraven in my heart.

My soul 's free as the ambient air
 Although my baser part 's immured;
Whilst loyal thoughts do still repair
 To accompany my solitude.
And though Rebellion do my body bind,
My King can only captivate my mind.

. . . . .

I am that bird, which they combine
 Thus to deprive of liberty;
Who, though they do my corpse confine
 Yet, maugre hate, my soul is free:
And, though immured, yet can I chirp and sing,
' Disgrace to rebels, glory to my King !'

SIR R. L'ESTRANGE.

582. TO CHLOE

SAY, in these latter days of ours,
When love exerts his usual powers,
 What difference lies between us ?
In Chloe's self at once I boast,
What bards of every age might
 toast,
 A Muse, a Grace, a Venus.

In Chloe are a thousand charms,
Though envy call her sex to arms,
 And giggling girls might flout
  her.
The Muse inhabits in her mind,
A Venus in her form we find,
 The Graces all about her.

R. LLOYD.

583. WHEN YOUTHFUL FAITH HATH FLED

WHEN youthful faith hath fled,
 Of loving take thy leave ;
Be constant to the dead—
 The dead cannot deceive.

Sweet modest flowers of spring,
 How fleet your balmy day !
And man's brief year can bring
 No secondary May,

No earthly burst again
 Of gladness out of gloom,
Fond hope and vision vain,
 Ungrateful to the tomb.

But 'tis an old belief
 That on some solemn shore,
Beyond the sphere of grief,
 Dear friends shall meet once
  more.

Beyond the sphere of time,
 And Sin and Fate's control,
Serene in endless prime
 Of body and of soul.

That creed I fain would keep,
 That hope I'll not forgo,
Eternal be the sleep
 Unless to waken so.

J. G. LOCKHART

584. TO LOVE

LOVE guards the roses of thy lips,
    And flies about them like a bee ;
If I approach he forward skips,
    And if I kiss he stingeth me.

Love in thine eyes doth build his bower,
    And sleeps within their pretty shine,
And if I look the boy will lower,
    And from their orbs shoot shafts divine.

.   .   .   .

Love, let me cull her choicest flowers,
    And pity me, and calm her eye,
Make soft her heart, dissolve her lowers,
    Then will I praise thy deity.   T. LODGE.

585. LOVE, IN MY BOSOM, LIKE A BEE

LOVE, in my bosom, like a bee,
    Doth suck his sweet.
Now with his wings he plays with me,
    Now with his feet.
Within mine eyes he makes his nest,
His bed amidst my tender breast,
My kisses are his daily feast ;
And yet he robs me of my rest !
    Ah ! wanton, will ye ?

And if I sleep, then percheth he,
    With pretty flight,
And makes his pillow of my knee
    The livelong night.
Strike I my lute, he tunes the string ;
He music plays if so I sing,
He lends me every lovely thing,
Yet cruel he my heart doth sting :
    Whist, wanton, still ye !

Else I with roses every day
    Will whip you hence,
And bind you, when you long to play,
    For your offence.
I'll shut mine eyes to keep you in ;
I'll make you fast it for your sin ;
I'll count your power not worth a pin.
—Alas ! what hereby shall I win,
    If he gainsay me ?

What if I beat the wanton boy
    With many a rod ?
He will repay me with annoy
    Because a god !
Then sit thou safely on my knee ;
Then let thy bower my bosom be ;
Lurk in mine eyes, I like of thee ;
O Cupid, so thou pity me.
    Spare not, but play thee !
        T. LODGE.

586. TO PHYLLIS

MY Phyllis hath the morning sun,
    At first, to look upon her ;
And Phyllis hath morn-waking birds
    Her risings for to honour.
My Phyllis hath prime-feathered flowers
    That smile when she treads on them ;

And Phyllis hath a gallant flock
    That leap, since she doth own them.
But Phyllis hath so hard a heart,
    (Alas that she should have it !)
As yields no mercy to desert,
    Nor grace to those that crave it.
        T. LODGE.

587. TO THE CUCKOO

HAIL, beauteous stranger of the grove !
  Thou messenger of Spring !
Now Heaven repairs thy rural seat,
  And woods thy welcome ring.

What time the daisy decks the green,
  Thy certain voice we hear :
Hast thou a star to guide thy path,
  Or mark the rolling year ?

Delightful visitant ! with thee
  I hail the time of flowers,
And hear the sound of music sweet
  From birds among the bowers.

The schoolboy, wandering through the wood
  To pull the primrose gay,
Starts, the new voice of Spring to hear,
  And imitates thy lay.

What time the pea puts on the bloom,
  Thou fliest thy vocal vale,
An annual guest in other lands,
  Another Spring to hail.

Sweet bird ! thy bower is ever green,
  Thy sky is ever clear ;
Thou hast no sorrow in thy song,
  No winter in thy year !

Oh, could I fly, I'd fly with thee !
  We'd make, with joyful wing,
Our annual visit o'er the globe,
  Companions of the Spring.   J. LOGAN.

588. THE WARDEN OF THE CINQUE PORTS

A MIST was driving down the British Channel,
  The day was just begun,
And through the window-panes, on floor and panel,
  Streamed the red autumn sun.

It glanced on flowing flag and rippling pennon,
  And the white sails of ships ;
And, from the frowning rampart, the black cannon
  Hailed it with feverish lips.

Sandwich and Romney, Hastings, Hythe, and Dover
  Were all alert that day,
To see the French war-steamers speeding over,
  When the fog cleared away.

Sullen and silent, and like couchant lions,
  Their cannon, through the night,
Holding their breath, had watched, in grim defiance,
  The sea-coast opposite.

And now they roared at drum-beat from their stations
  On every citadel ;
Each answering each, with morning salutations,
  That all was well.

And down the coast, all taking up the burden,
  Replied the distant forts,
As if to summon from his sleep the Warden
  And Lord of the Cinque Ports.

Him shall no sunshine from the fields of azure,
  No drum-beat from the wall,
No morning gun from the black fort's embrasure,
  Awaken with its call !

No more, surveying with an eye impartial
  The long line of the coast,
Shall the gaunt figure of the old Field Marshal
  Be seen upon his post !

For in the night, unseen, a single warrior,
  In sombre harness mailed,
Dreaded of man, and surnamed the Destroyer,
  The rampart wall had scaled.

He passed into the chamber of the sleeper,
  The dark and silent room,
And as he entered, darker grew, and deeper,
  The silence and the gloom.

He did not pause to parley or dissemble,
  But smote the Warden hoar ;
Ah ! what a blow ! that made all England tremble,
  And groan from shore to shore.

Meanwhile, without, the surly cannon waited,
  The sun rose bright o'erhead ;
Nothing in Nature's aspect intimated
  That a great man was dead.

        H. W. LONGFELLOW.

589. THE SLAVE'S DREAM

BESIDE the ungathered rice he lay,
 His sickle in his hand ;
His breast was bare, his matted hair
 Was buried in the sand.
Again, in the mist and shadow of sleep,
 He saw his Native Land.

Wide through the landscape of his dreams
   The lordly Niger flowed ;
Beneath the palm-trees on the plain
   Once more a king he strode ;
And heard the tinkling caravans
   Descend the mountain-road.

He saw once more his dark-eyed queen
   Among his children stand ;
They clasped his neck, they kissed his cheeks,
   They held him by the hand !—
A tear burst from the sleeper's lids
   And fell into the sand.

And then at furious speed he rode
   Along the Niger's bank ;
His bridle-reins were golden chains,
   And, with a martial clank,
At each leap he could feel his scabbard of steel
   Smiting his stallion's flank.

Before him, like a blood-red flag,
   The bright flamingoes flew ;
From morn till night he followed their flight,
   O'er plains where the tamarind grew,
Till he saw the roofs of Caffre huts,
   And the ocean rose to view.

At night he heard the lion roar,
   And the hyena scream,
And the river-horse, as he crushed the reeds
   Beside some hidden stream ;
And it passed, like a glorious roll of drums,
   Through the triumph of his dream.

The forests, with their myriad tongues,
   Shouted of liberty ;
And the Blast of the Desert cried aloud,
   With a voice so wild and free,
That he started in his sleep and smiled
   At their tempestuous glee.

He did not feel the driver's whip,
   Nor the burning heat of day ;
For Death had illumined the Land of Sleep,
   And his lifeless body lay
A worn-out fetter, that the soul
   Had broken and thrown away !

                  H. W. LONGFELLOW.

590. THE DAY IS DONE

Come, read to me some poem,
  Some simple and heartfelt lay,
That shall soothe this restless feeling,
  And banish the thoughts of day.

Not from the grand old masters,
  Not from the bards sublime,
Whose distant footsteps echo
  Through the corridors of time.

For, like strains of martial music,
  Their mighty thoughts suggest
Life's endless toil and endeavour;
  And to-night I long for rest.

. . . . . .

And the night shall be filled with music,
  And the cares that infest the day
Shall fold their tents, like the Arabs,
  And as silently steal away.
                    H. W. Longfellow.

591. CHILDREN

Come to me, O ye children!
  For I hear you at your play,
And the questions that perplexed me
  Have vanished quite away.

Ye open the eastern windows,
  That look towards the sun,
Where thoughts are singing swallows
  And the brooks of morning run.

In your hearts are the birds and the sunshine,
  In your thoughts the brooklet's flow,
But in mine is the wind of Autumn
  And the first fall of the snow.

Ah! what would the world be to us
  If the children were no more?
We should dread the desert behind us
  Worse than the dark before.

What the leaves are to the forest,
  With light and air for food,
Ere their sweet and tender juices
  Have been hardened into wood,

That to the world are children;
  Through them it feels the glow
Of a brighter and sunnier climate
  Than reaches the trunks below.

Come to me, O ye children!
  And whisper in my ear
What the birds and the winds are singing
  In your sunny atmosphere.

For what are all our contrivings,
  And the wisdom of our books,
When compared with your caresses,
  And the gladness of your looks?

Ye are better than all the ballads
  That ever were sung or said;
For ye are living poems,
  And all the rest are dead.
                    H. W. Longfellow.

592. GOD'S ACRE

I like that ancient Saxon phrase, which calls
  The burial-ground God's Acre! It is just;
It consecrates each grave within its walls,
  And breathes a benison o'er the sleeping dust.

God's Acre! Yes, that blessed name imparts
  Comfort to those who in the grave have sown
The seed that they had garnered in their hearts,
  Their bread of life, alas! no more their own.

Into its furrows shall we all be cast,
  In the sure faith that we shall rise again
At the great harvest, when the archangel's blast
  Shall winnow, like a fan, the chaff and grain.

Then shall the good stand in immortal bloom
  In the fair gardens of that second birth,
And each bright blossom mingle its perfume
  With that of flowers which never bloomed on earth.

With thy rude ploughshare, Death, turn up the sod,
  And spread the furrow for the seed we sow;
This is the field and Acre of our God,
  This is the place where human harvests grow!

H. W. LONGFELLOW.

593. THE ARROW AND THE SONG

I shot an arrow into the air,
It fell to earth, I knew not where;
For, so swiftly it flew, the sight
Could not follow it in its flight.

I breathed a song into the air,
It fell to earth, I knew not where;
For who has sight so keen and strong
That it can follow the flight of song?

Long, long afterward, in an oak,
I found the arrow, still unbroke;
And the song, from beginning to end,
I found again in the heart of a friend.

H. W. LONGFELLOW.

594. SONG OF THE SILENT LAND

Into the Silent Land!
Ah! who shall lead us thither?
Clouds in the evening sky more
    darkly gather,
And shattered wrecks lie thicker
    on the strand.
Who leads us with a gentle hand
Thither, O thither,
Into the Silent Land?

Into the Silent Land!
To you, ye boundless regions
Of all perfection! Tender morning-
    visions
Of beauteous souls! The Future's
    pledge and band!

Who in Life's battle firm doth
    stand,
Shall bear Hope's tender blossoms
Into the Silent Land!

O Land! O Land!
For all the broken-hearted
The mildest herald by our fate
    allotted,
Beckons, and with inverted torch
    doth stand
To lead us with a gentle hand
To the land of the great Departed,
Into the Silent Land!

H. W. LONGFELLOW.

595. THE WRECK OF THE HESPERUS

IT was the schooner Hesperus,
    That sailed the wintry sea;
And the skipper had taken his little daughter,
    To bear him company.

Blue were her eyes as the fairy-flax,
    Her cheeks like the dawn of day,
And her bosom white as the hawthorn buds
    That ope in the month of May.

The skipper he stood beside the helm,
    His pipe was in his mouth,
And he watched how the veering flaw did blow
    The smoke now West, now South.

Then up and spake an old Sailor,
    Had sailed the Spanish Main,
' I pray thee, put into yonder port,
    For I fear a hurricane.

' Last night, the moon had a golden ring,
    And to-night no moon we see ! '
The skipper he blew a whiff from his pipe,
    And a scornful laugh laughed he.

Colder and louder blew the wind,
    A gale from the North-east,
The snow fell hissing in the brine,
    And the billows frothed like yeast.

Down came the storm, and smote amain
    The vessel in its strength ;
She shuddered and paused, like a frighted steed,
    Then leaped her cable's length.

' Come hither ! come hither ! my little daughter,
    And do not tremble so ;
For I can weather the roughest gale
    That ever wind did blow.'

He wrapped her warm in his seaman's coat
    Against the stinging blast ;
He cut a rope from a broken spar,
    And bound her to the mast.

' O father ! I hear the church-bells ring,
    O say, what may it be ? '
' 'Tis a fog-bell on a rock-bound coast ! '—
    And he steered for the open sea.

' O father ! I hear the sound of guns,
    O say what may it be ? '
' Some ship in distress, that cannot live
    In such an angry sea ! '

'O father! I see a gleaming light,
 O say what may it be?'
But the father answered never a word,
 A frozen corpse was he.

Lashed to the helm, all stiff and stark,
 With his face turned to the skies,
The lantern gleamed through the gleaming snow
 On his fixed and glassy eyes.

Then the maiden clasped her hands and prayed
 That savèd she might be;
And she thought of Christ, who stilled the wave
 On the Lake of Galilee.

And fast through the midnight dark and drear,
 Through the whistling sleet and snow,
Like a sheeted ghost the vessel swept
 Towards the reef of Norman's Woe.

And ever the fitful gusts between
 A sound came from the land;
It was the sound of the trampling surf,
 On the rocks and the hard sea-sand.

The breakers were right beneath her bows,
 She drifted a dreary wreck,
And a whooping billow swept the crew
 Like icicles from her deck.

She struck where the white and fleecy waves
 Looked soft as carded wool,
But the cruel rocks they gored her side
 Like the horns of an angry bull.

Her rattling shrouds, all sheathed in ice,
 With the masts went by the board;
Like a vessel of glass she stove and sank,—
 Ho! ho! the breakers roared!

At daybreak on the bleak sea-beach
 A fisherman stood aghast,
To see the form of a maiden fair
 Lashed close to a drifting mast.

The salt sea was frozen on her breast,
 The salt tears in her eyes;
And he saw her hair, like the brown sea-weed,
 On the billows fall and rise.

Such was the wreck of the Hesperus,
 In the midnight and the snow!
Christ save us all from a death like this,
 On the reef of Norman's Woe.

       H. W. LONGFELLOW.

596. HAROUN AL RASCHID

ONE day, Haroun Al Raschid read
A book wherein the poet said :—

' Where are the kings, and where the rest
Of those who once the world possessed ?

' They're gone with all their pomp and show,
They're gone the way that thou shalt go.

' O thou who choosest for thy share
The world, and what the world calls fair,

' Take all that it can give or lend,
But know that death is at the end ! '

Haroun Al Raschid bowed his head :
Tears fell upon the page he read.

H. W. LONGFELLOW.

597. A PSALM OF LIFE

What the heart of the young man said to the Psalmist

TELL me not, in mournful numbers,
　Life is but an empty dream !
For the soul is dead that slumbers,
　And things are not what they
　　seem.

Life is real ! Life is earnest !
　And the grave is not its goal ;
Dust thou art, to dust returnest,
　Was not spoken of the soul.

Not enjoyment, and not sorrow,
　Is our destined end or way ;
But to act, that each to-morrow
　Find us farther than to-day.

Art is long, and Time is fleeting,
　And our hearts, though stout
　　and brave,
Still, like muffled drums, are
　　beating
　Funeral marches to the grave.

In the world's broad field of battle,
　In the bivouac of Life,
Be not like dumb, driven cattle !
　Be a hero in the strife !

Trust no Future, howe'er pleasant !
　Let the dead Past bury its
　　dead !
Act,—act in the living Present !
　Heart within, and God o'erhead !

Lives of great men all remind us
　We can make our lives sub-
　　lime,
And, departing, leave behind us
　Footprints on the sands of
　　time ;—

Footprints, that perhaps another,
　Sailing o'er life's solemn main,
A forlorn and shipwrecked brother,
　Seeing, shall take heart again.

Let us, then, be up and doing,
　With a heart for any fate ;
Still achieving, still pursuing,
　Learn to labour and to wait.

H. W. LONGFELLOW.

598. EXCELSIOR

The shades of night were falling fast,
As through an Alpine village passed
A youth, who bore, 'mid snow and ice,
A banner with the strange device,
    Excelsior !

His brow was sad ; his eye beneath
Flashed like a falchion from its sheath,
And like a silver clarion rung
The accents of that unknown tongue,
    Excelsior !

In happy homes he saw the light
Of household fires gleam warm and bright;
Above, the spectral glaciers shone,
And from his lips escaped a groan,
    Excelsior !

'Try not the pass !' the old man said ;
'Dark lowers the tempest overhead,
The roaring torrent is deep and wide !'
And loud that clarion voice replied,
    Excelsior !

' O stay,' the maiden said, ' and rest
Thy weary head upon this breast !'
A tear stood in his bright blue eye,
But still he answered, with a sigh,
    Excelsior !

' Beware the pine-tree's withered branch !
Beware the awful avalanche !'
This was the peasant's last Good-night.
A voice replied, far up the height,
    Excelsior !

At break of day, as heavenward
The pious monks of Saint Bernard
Uttered the oft-repeated prayer,
A voice cried through the startled air,
    Excelsior !

A traveller, by the faithful hound,
Half-buried in the snow was found,
Still grasping in his hand of ice
That banner with the strange device,
    Excelsior !

There in the twilight cold and grey,
Lifeless, but beautiful, he lay,
And from the sky, serene and far,
A voice fell, like a falling star,
    Excelsior !   H. W. Longfellow.

599. FROM 'RESIGNATION'

THERE is no flock, however watched and tended,
    But one dead lamb is there!
There is no fireside, howsoe'er defended,
    But has one vacant chair!

The air is full of farewells to the dying,
    And mournings for the dead;
The heart of Rachel, for her children crying,
    Will not be comforted!

Let us be patient! These severe afflictions
    Not from the ground arise,
But oftentimes celestial benedictions
    Assume this dark disguise.

   .   .   .   .   .   .

She is not dead, the child of our affection,
    But gone unto that school
Where she no longer needs our poor protection,
    And Christ himself doth rule.

In that great cloister's stillness and seclusion,
    By guardian angels led,
Safe from temptation, safe from sin's pollution,
    She lives, whom we call dead.

H. W. LONGFELLOW.

600. THE ARSENAL AT SPRINGFIELD

THIS is the Arsenal. From floor to ceiling,
    Like a huge organ, rise the burnished arms;
But from their silent pipes no anthem pealing
    Startles the villages with strange alarms.

Ah! what a sound will rise, how wild and dreary,
    When the death-angel touches those swift keys!
What loud lament and dismal Miserere
    Will mingle with their awful symphonies!

I hear even now the infinite fierce chorus,
    The cries of agony, the endless groan,
Which, through the ages that have gone before us,
    In long reverberations reach our own.

On helm and harness rings the Saxon hammer,
    Through Cimbric forest roars the Norseman's song,
And loud, amid the universal clamour,
    O'er distant deserts sounds the Tartar gong.

I hear the Florentine, who from his palace
    Wheels out his battle-bell with dreadful din,
And Aztec priests upon their teocallis
    Beat the wild war-drums made of serpent's skin;

The tumult of each sacked and burning village;
  The shout that every prayer for mercy drowns;
The soldiers' revels in the midst of pillage;
  The wail of famine in beleaguered towns;

The bursting shell, the gateway wrenched asunder,
  The rattling musketry, the clashing blade;
And ever and anon, in tones of thunder,
  The diapason of the cannonade.

Is it, O man, with such discordant noises,
  With such accursèd instruments as these,
Thou drownest Nature's sweet and kindly voices,
  And jarrest the celestial harmonies?

Were half the power that fills the world with terror,
  Were half the wealth bestowed on camps and courts,
Given to redeem the human mind from error,
  There were no need of arsenals or forts:

The warrior's name would be a name abhorrèd!
  And every nation that should lift again
Its hand against a brother, on its forehead
  Would wear for evermore the curse of Cain!

Down the dark future, through long generations,
  The echoing sounds grow fainter and then cease;
And like a bell, with solemn, sweet vibrations,
  I hear once more the voice of Christ say, 'Peace!'

Peace! and no longer from its brazen portals
  The blast of War's great organ shakes the skies!
But beautiful as songs of the immortals,
  The holy melodies of love arise.

H. W. LONGFELLOW.

601. FROM 'THE BUILDING OF THE SHIP'

THOU, too, sail on, O Ship of State!
Sail on, O Union, strong and great!
Humanity with all its fears,
With all the hopes of future years,
Is hanging breathless on thy fate!
We know what Master laid thy keel,
What Workmen wrought thy ribs of steel,
Who made each mast, and sail, and rope,
What anvils rang, what hammers beat,
In what a forge and what a heat
Were shaped the anchors of thy hope!
Fear not each sudden sound and shock,
'Tis of the wave and not the rock;

L

'Tis but the flapping of the sail,
And not a rent made by the gale !
In spite of rock and tempest's roar,
In spite of false lights on the shore,
Sail on, nor fear to breast the sea !
Our hearts, our hopes, are all with thee,
Our hearts, our hopes, our prayers, our tears,
Our faith triumphant o'er our fears,
Are all with thee,—are all with thee !

H. W. LONGFELLOW.

602.   THE VILLAGE BLACKSMITH

UNDER a spreading chestnut-tree
  The village smithy stands ;
The smith, a mighty man is he,
  With large and sinewy hands ;
And the muscles of his brawny arms
  Are strong as iron bands.

His hair is crisp, and black, and long ;
  His face is like the tan ;
His brow is wet with honest sweat,
  He earns whate'er he can,
And looks the whole world in the face,
  For he owes not any man.

Week in, week out, from morn till night,
  You can hear his bellows blow ;
You can hear him swing his heavy sledge,
  With measured beat and slow,
Like a sexton ringing the village bell,
  When the evening sun is low.

And children coming home from school
  Look in at the open door ;
They love to see the flaming forge,
  And hear the bellows roar,
And catch the burning sparks that fly
  Like chaff from a threshing-floor.

He goes on Sunday to the church,
  And sits among his boys ;
He hears the parson pray and preach,
  He hears his daughter's voice
Singing in the village choir,
  And it makes his heart rejoice.

It sounds to him like her mother's voice
  Singing in Paradise !
He needs must think of her once more,
  How in the grave she lies ;
And with his hard, rough hand he wipes
  A tear out of his eyes.

Toiling,—rejoicing,—sorrowing,
  Onward through life he goes ;
Each morning sees some task begin,
  Each evening sees it close ;
Something attempted, something done,
  Has earned a night's repose.

Thanks, thanks to thee, my worthy friend,
  For the lesson thou hast taught !
Thus at the flaming forge of life
  Our fortunes must be wrought ;
Thus on its sounding anvil shaped
  Each burning deed and thought.

H. W. LONGFELLOW.

603. VICTOR GALBRAITH

UNDER the walls of Monterey
At daybreak the bugles began to play,
   Victor Galbraith !
In the mist of the morning damp and grey,
These were the words they seemed to say,
   ' Come forth to thy death,
   Victor Galbraith ! '

Forth he came, with a martial tread ;
Firm was his step, erect his head ;
   Victor Galbraith,
He who so well the bugle played,
Could not mistake the words it said :
   ' Come forth to thy death,
   Victor Galbraith ! '

He looked at the earth, he looked at the sky,
He looked at the files of musketry,
   Victor Galbraith !
And he said, with a steady voice and eye,
' Take good aim ; I am ready to die ! '
   Thus challenges death
   Victor Galbraith.

Twelve fiery tongues flashed straight and red,
Six leaden balls on their errand sped ;
   Victor Galbraith
Falls on the ground, but he is not dead ;
His name was not stamped on those balls of lead,
   And they only scathe
   Victor Galbraith.

Three balls are in his breast and brain,
But he rises out of the dust again,
   Victor Galbraith !
The water he drinks has a bloody stain ;
' O kill me, and put me out of my pain ! '
   In his agony prayeth
   Victor Galbraith.

Forth dart once more those tongues of flame,
And the bugler has died a death of shame,
   Victor Galbraith !
His soul has gone back to whence it came,
And no one answers to the name,
   When the Sergeant saith,
   ' Victor Galbraith ! '

Under the walls of Monterey
By night a bugle is heard to play,
          Victor Galbraith !
Through the mist of the valley damp and grey
The sentinels hear the sound, and say,
          ' That is the wraith
          Of Victor Galbraith ! '

H. W. LONGFELLOW.

604. TO AMARANTHA

That she would dishevel her hair.

AMARANTHA, sweet and fair,
Ah, braid no more that shining
          hair !
As my curious hand or eye
Hovering round thee, let it fly.

Let it fly as unconfined
As its calm ravisher the wind,
Who hath left his darling, the east,
To wanton o'er that spicy nest.

Every tress must be confessed ;
But neatly tangled at the best ;
Like a clue of golden thread
Most excellently ravellèd.

Do not, then, wind up that light
In ribands, and o'ercloud in night,
Like the sun in 's early ray ;
But shake your head and scatter
          day.

R. LOVELACE.

605. ON THE DEATH OF MRS. ELIZABETH FILMER

CHASTE as the air whither she 's
          fled,
She, making her celestial bed
In her warm alabaster, lay
As cold as in this house of clay ;
Nor were the rooms unfit to feast,
Or circumscribe this angel-guest ;
The radiant gem was brightly set
In as divine a carcanet ;
For which the clearer was not
          known,
Her mind, or her complexion ;
Such an everlasting grace,
Such a beatific face

Incloisters here this narrow floor
That possessed all hearts before.

Thus, although this marble must,
As all things, crumble into dust,
And though you find this fair-built
          tomb
Ashes, as what lies in its womb :
Yet her saint-like name shall
          shine
A living glory to this shrine,
And her eternal fame be read,
When all but very virtue 's dead.

R. LOVELACE.

606. TO LUCASTA, ON GOING BEYOND THE SEAS

IF to be absent were to be
          Away from thee ;
     Or that when I am gone
     You or I were alone ;
     Then, my Lucasta, might I crave
Pity from blustering wind, or swallowing wave.

But I'll not sigh one blast or gale
   To swell my sail,
    Or pay a tear to 'suage
    The foaming blue god's rage ;
For whether he will let me pass
Or no, I'm still as happy as I was.

Though seas and land betwixt us both,
   Our faith and troth,
    Like separated souls,
    All time and space controls :
Above the highest sphere we meet
Unseen, unknown, and greet as Angels greet.

So then we do anticipate
   Our after-fate,
    And are alive i' the skies,
    If thus our lips and eyes
Can speak like spirits unconfined
In Heaven, their earthy bodies left behind.
R. LOVELACE.

607. GRATIANA DANCING, AND SINGING

SEE, with what constant motion,
Even, and glorious as the sun,
  Gratiana steers that noble frame,
    Soft as her breast, sweet as her voice,
    That gave each winding law and poise,
  And swifter than the wings of Fame.

She beat the happy pavèment—
By such a star made firmament,
  Which now no more the roof envies !
    But swells up high, with Atlas even,
    Bearing the brighter, nobler heaven,
  And, in her, all the deities.

Each step trod out a lover's thought,
And the ambitious hopes he brought
  Chained to her brave feet with such arts,
    Such sweet command and gentle awe,
    As, when she ceased, we sighing saw
  The floor lay paved with broken hearts.

So did she move, so did she sing,
Like the harmonious spheres that bring
  Unto their rounds their music's aid ;
    Which she performèd such a way
    As all the enamoured world will say,
'The Graces danced, and Apollo played !'
R. LOVELACE.

608. TO LUCASTA, ON GOING TO THE WARS

TELL me not, Sweet, I am unkind
  That from the nunnery
Of thy chaste breast and quiet
    mind,
  To war and arms I fly.

True, a new mistress now I
    chase,
  The first foe in the field;
And with a stronger faith embrace
  A sword, a horse, a shield.

    Yet this inconstancy is such
      As you too shall adore;
    I could not love thee, Dear, so much,
      Loved I not Honour more.

R. LOVELACE.

609. TO ALTHEA FROM PRISON

WHEN Love with unconfinèd wings
  Hovers within my gates,
And my divine Althea brings
  To whisper at the grates;
When I lie tangled in her hair
  And fettered to her eye,
The birds that wanton in the air
  Know no such liberty.

When flowing cups run swiftly
    round
  With no allaying Thames,
Our careless heads with roses
    bound,
  Our hearts with loyal flames;
When thirsty grief in wine we
    steep,
  When healths and draughts go
    free—
Fishes that tipple in the deep
  Know no such liberty.

When (like committed linnets) I
  With shriller throat shall sing
The sweetness, mercy, majesty
  And glories of my King;
When I shall voice aloud how
    good
He is, how great should be,
Enlargèd winds, that curl the
    flood
  Know no such liberty.

Stone walls do not a prison
    make,
  Nor iron bars a cage;
Minds innocent and quiet take
  That for an hermitage:
If I have freedom in my love
  And in my soul am free,
Angels alone, that soar above,
  Enjoy such liberty.

R. LOVELACE.

610. A MONUMENT IN ARCADIA

O YOU that dwell where shepherds reign,
  Arcadian youths, Arcadian maids,
To pastoral pipe who danced the plain,
  Why pensive now beneath the shades?

Approach her virgin tomb, they cry,
  Behold the verse inscribed above:
Once too in Arcady was I—
  Behold what dreams are life and love!

E. LOVIBOND.

611. THE COURTIN'

GOD makes sech nights, all white an' still
    Fur 'z you can look or listen,
Moonshine an' snow on field an' hill,
    All silence an' all glisten.

Zekle crep' up quite unbeknown
    An' peeked in thru' the winder,
An' there sot Huldy all alone,
    'Ith no one nigh to hender.

A fireplace filled the room's one side
    With half a cord o' wood in—
There warn't no stoves (tell comfort died)
    To bake ye to a puddin'.

The wa'nut logs shot sparkles out
    Towards the pootiest, bless her,
An' leetle flames danced all about
    The chiny on the dresser.

Agin the chimbley crook-necks hung,
    An' in amongst 'em rusted
The ole queen's-arm that gran'ther Young
    Fetched back f'om Concord busted.

The very room, coz she was in,
    Seemed warm f'om floor to ceilin',
An' she looked full ez rosy agin
    Ez the apples she was peelin'.

'Twas kin' o' kingdom-come to look
    On sech a blessed cretur,
A dogrose blushin' to a brook
    Ain't modester nor sweeter.

He was six foot o' man, A 1,
    Clear grit an' human natur',
None couldn't quicker pitch a ton
    Nor dror a furrer straighter.

He'd sparked it with full twenty gals,
    Hed squired 'em, danced 'em, druv 'em,
Fust this one, an' then thet, by spells—
    All is, he couldn't love 'em.

But long o' her his veins 'ould run
    All crinkly like curled maple,
The side she breshed felt full o' sun
    Ez a south slope in Ap'il.

She thought no v'ice hed sech a swing
    Ez hisn in the choir;
My! when he made Ole Hunderd ring,
    She *knowed* the Lord was nigher.

An' she'd blush scarlit, right in prayer,
    When her new meetin'-bunnet
Felt somehow thru' its crown a pair
    O' blue eyes sot upun it.

That night, I tell ye, she looked *some!*
    She seemed to 've got a new soul,
For she felt sartin-sure he'd come,
    Down to her very shoe-sole.

She heered a foot, an' knowed it tu,
    A-raspin' on the scraper,—
All ways to once her feelins flew
    Like sparks in burnt-up paper.

He kin' o' l'itered on the mat,
    Some doubtfle o' the sekle,
His heart kep' goin' pity-pat,
    But hern went pity Zekle.

An' yit she gin her cheer a jerk
    Ez though she wished him furder,
An' on her apples kep' to work,
    Parin' away like murder.

'You want to see my Pa, I s'pose?'
    'Wal—no—I come dasignin''—
'To see my Ma? She's sprinklin' clo'es
    Agin to-morrer's i'nin'.'

To say why gals act so or so,
    Or don't, 'ould be presumin';
Mebbe to mean *yes* an' say *no*
    Comes nateral to women.

He stood a spell on one foot fust,
    Then stood a spell on t'other,
An' on which one he felt the wust
    He couldn't ha' told ye nuther.

Says he, 'I'd better call agin;'
    Says she, 'Think likely, Mister:'
Thet last word pricked him like a pin,
    An'—Wal, he up an' kissed her.

When Ma bimeby upon 'em slips,
    Huldy sot pale ez ashes,
All kin' o' smily roun' the lips
    An' teary roun' the lashes.

For she was jes' the quiet kind
    Whose naturs never vary,
Like streams that keep a summer mind
    Snow-hid in Jenooary.

The blood clost roun' her heart felt glued
  Too tight for all expressin',
Tell mother see how metters stood,
  An' gin 'em both her blessin'.

Then her red come back like the tide
  Down to the Bay o' Fundy,
An' all I know is they was cried
  In meetin' come nex' Sunday.   J. R. LOWELL.

612. GOD SENDS HIS TEACHERS UNTO EVERY AGE

GOD sends His teachers unto every age,
To every clime, and every race of men,
With revelations fitted to their growth
And shape of mind, nor gives the realm of Truth
Into the selfish rule of one sole race:
Therefore each form of worship that hath swayed
The life of man, and given it to grasp
The master-key of knowledge, reverence,
Infolds some germs of goodness and of right;
Else never had the eager soul, which loathes
The slothful down of pampered ignorance,
Found in it even a moment's fitful rest.

> J. R. LOWELL (*Rhoecus*).

613. HE SPOKE OF BURNS

HE spoke of Burns: men rude and rough
  Pressed round to hear the praise of one
Whose heart was made of manly, simple stuff,
  As homespun as their own.

And, when he read, they forward leaned,
  Drinking, with thirsty hearts and ears,
His brook-like songs whom glory never weaned
  From humble smiles and tears.

> J. R. LOWELL (*An Incident in a Railroad Car*).

614. TO W. L. GARRISON

IN a small chamber, friendless and unseen,
  Toiled o'er his types one poor, unlearned young man;
The place was dark, unfurnitured, and mean;
  Yet there the freedom of a race began.

.   .   .   .

O Truth! O Freedom! how are ye still born
  In the rude stable, in the manger nursed!
What humble hands unbar those gates of morn
  Through which the splendours of the New Day burst!

> J. R. LOWELL.

L 3

615. FROM 'THE SHEPHERD OF KING ADMETUS'

MEN granted that his speech was wise,
  But, when a glance they caught
Of his slim grace and woman's eyes,
  They laughed, and called him good-for-naught.

Yet after he was dead and gone,
  And e'en his memory dim,
Earth seemed more sweet to live upon,
  More full of love, because of him.

And day by day more holy grew
  Each spot where he had trod,
Till after-poets only knew
  Their first-born brother as a God.   J. R. LOWELL.

616. STANZAS ON FREEDOM

MEN! whose boast it is that ye
Come of fathers brave and free,
If there breathe on earth a slave,
Are ye truly free and brave?
If ye do not feel the chain,
When it works a brother's pain,
Are ye not base slaves indeed,
Slaves unworthy to be freed?

Women! who shall one day bear
Sons to breathe New England air,
If ye hear, without a blush,
Deeds to make the roused blood rush
Like red lava through your veins,
For your sisters now in chains,—
Answer! are ye fit to be
Mothers of the brave and free?

Is true Freedom but to break
Fetters for our own dear sake,
And, with leathern hearts, forget
That we owe mankind a debt?
No! true freedom is to share
All the chains our brothers wear,
And, with heart and hand, to be
Earnest to make others free!

They are slaves who fear to speak
For the fallen and the weak;
They are slaves who will not choose
Hatred, scoffing, and abuse,
Rather than in silence shrink
From the truth they needs must think;
They are slaves who dare not be
In the right with two or three.
                           J. R. LOWELL.

617. FROM 'THE PRESENT CRISIS'

ONCE to every man and nation comes the moment to decide,
In the strife of Truth with Falsehood, for the good or evil side;
Some great cause, God's new Messiah, offering each the bloom or blight,
Parts the goats upon the left hand, and the sheep upon the right,
And the choice goes by for ever 'twixt that darkness and that light.

. . . .

Careless seems the great Avenger; history's pages but record
One death-grapple in the darkness 'twixt old systems and the Word;
Truth for ever on the scaffold, Wrong for ever on the throne,—
Yet that scaffold sways the future, and, behind the dim unknown,
Standeth God within the shadow, keeping watch above His own.
                                        J. R. LOWELL.

618. SONG BY APELLES

Cupid and my Campaspe played
At cards for kisses, Cupid paid;
He stakes his quiver, bow, and arrows,
His mother's doves, and team of sparrows;
Loses them too; then, down he throws
The coral of his lip, the rose
Growing on 's cheek (but none knows how),
With these, the crystal of his brow,
And then the dimple of his chin:
All these did my Campaspe win.
At last he set her both his eyes;
She won, and Cupid blind did rise.
O Love! has she done this to thee?
What shall (alas!) become of me?

        J. Lyly (*Campaspe*).

619. APOLLO'S SONG

My Daphne's hair is twisted gold,
Bright stars apiece her eyes do hold,
My Daphne's brow enthrones the Graces,
My Daphne's beauty stains all faces,
On Daphne's cheek grow rose and cherry,
On Daphne's lip a sweeter berry,
Daphne's snowy hand but touched does melt,
And then no heavenlier warmth is felt,
My Daphne's voice tunes all the spheres,
My Daphne's music charms all ears.
Fond am I thus to sing her praise;
These glories now are turned to bays.

        J. Lyly (*Midas*).

620. SAPPHO'S SONG

O cruel Love! on thee I lay
My curse, which shall strike blind the day:
Never may sleep with velvet hand
Charm thine eyes with sacred wand;
Thy jailors shall be hopes and fears;
Thy prison-mates, groans, sighs, and tears;
Thy play to wear out weary times,
Fantastic passions, vows, and rhymes;
Thy bread be frowns, thy drink be gall,
Such as when you Phao call;
The bed thou liest on be despair;
Thy sleep, fond dreams; thy dreams, long care;
Hope (like thy fool) at thy bed's head,
Mock thee, till madness strike thee dead;
As Phao, thou dost me, with thy proud eyes;
In thee poor Sappho lives, for thee she dies.

        J. Lyly (*Sappho and Phao*).

621. PAN'S SONG

PAN's Syrinx was a girl indeed,
Though now she 's turned into a reed.
From that dear reed Pan's pipe does come,
A pipe that strikes Apollo dumb;
Nor flute, nor lute, nor gittern can
So chant it, as the pipe of Pan;
Cross-gartered swains, and dairy girls,
With faces smug and round as pearls,
When Pan's shrill pipe begins to play,
With dancing wear out night and day:
The bag-pipe's drone his hum lays by,
When Pan sounds up his minstrelsy.
His minstrelsy! O base! This quill
Which at my mouth with wind I fill,
Puts me in mind, though her I miss,
That still my Syrinx' lips I kiss.

J. LYLY (Midas).

622. TO APOLLO

SING to Apollo, god of day,
Whose golden beams with morning play,
And make her eyes so brightly shine,
Aurora's face is called divine.
Sing to Phoebus, and that throne
Of diamonds which he sits upon;
    Io, paeans let us sing
      To Physic's and to Poesy's King!

Crown all his altars with bright fire,
Laurels bind about his lyre,
A Daphnean coronet for his head,
The Muses dance about his bed;
When on his ravishing lute he plays,
Strew his temple round with bays.
    Io, paeans let us sing
      To the glittering Delian King!

J. LYLY (Midas).

623. TRICO'S SONG

WHAT bird so sings, yet so does wail?
Oh, 'tis the ravished Nightingale.
Jug, Jug, Jug, Jug, tereu, she cries,
And still her woes at midnight rise.
Brave prick-song! who is't now we hear?
None but the Lark so shrill and clear;
How at heaven's gates she claps her wings,
The morn not waking till she sings.

Hark, hark, with what a pretty throat
Poor Robin red-breast tunes his note;
Hark how the jolly cuckoos sing
Cuckoo, to welcome in the spring,
Cuckoo, to welcome in the spring.

J. LYLY (*Campaspe*).

624. THE OFFICER'S GRAVE

THERE is in the wide, lone sea,
A spot unmarked but holy;
For there the gallant and the free
In his ocean-bed lies lowly.

Down, down, within the deep
That oft to triumph bore him,
He sleeps a sound and pleasant sleep
With the salt waves washing
o'er him.

He sleeps serene and safe
From tempest or from billow,
Where the storms that high above
him chafe
Scarce rock his peaceful pillow.

The sea and him in death
They did not dare to sever:
It was his home while he had
breath:
'Tis now his rest for ever!

Sleep on, thou mighty dead!
A glorious tomb they've found
thee,
The broad blue sky above thee
spread,
The boundless waters round thee.

No vulgar foot treads here,
No hand profane shall move
thee,
But gallant fleets shall proudly
steer,
And warriors shout, above thee.

And when the last trump shall
sound,
And tombs are asunder riven,
Like the morning sun from the
wave thou'lt bound
To rise and shine in heaven.

H. F. LYTE.

625. TELL ME, MY HEART, IF THIS BE LOVE

WHEN Delia on the plain appears,
Awed by a thousand tender fears,
I would approach, but dare not move:
Tell me, my heart, if this be Love.

Whene'er she speaks, my ravished ear
No other voice but hers can hear,
No other wit but hers approve:
Tell me, my heart, if this be Love.

If she some other youth commend,
Though I was once his fondest friend,
His instant enemy I prove:
Tell me, my heart, if this be Love.

. . . . . .

When, fond of power, of beauty vain,
Her nets she spread for every swain,
I strove to hate, but vainly strove:
Tell me, my heart, if this be Love.

G. LYTTELTON, LORD LYTTELTON.

626. ABSENT YET PRESENT

As the flight of a river
  That flows to the sea,
My soul rushes ever
  In tumult to thee.

A twofold existence
  I am where thou art;
My heart in the distance
  Beats close to thy heart.

Look up, I am near thee,
  I gaze on thy face;
I see thee, I hear thee,
  I feel thine embrace.

As a magnet's control on
  The steel it draws to it,
Is the charm of thy soul on
  The thoughts that pursue it.

And absence but brightens
  The eyes that I miss,
And custom but heightens
  The spell of thy kiss.

It is not from duty,
  Though that may be owed,—
It is not from beauty,
  Though that be bestowed;

But all that I care for,
  And all that I know,
Is that, without wherefore,
  I worship thee so.

Through granite it breaketh
  A tree to the ray,
As a dreamer forsaketh
  The grief of the day,

My soul in its fever
  Escapes unto thee;
O dream to the griever,
  O light to the tree!

A twofold existence
  I am where thou art;
Hark, hear in the distance
  The beat of my heart!

                    EDWARD BULWER, LORD LYTTON.

627. THE ARMADA

ATTEND, all ye who list to hear our noble England's praise;
I tell of the thrice famous deeds she wrought in ancient days,
When that great fleet invincible against her bore in vain
The richest spoils of Mexico, the stoutest hearts of Spain.
It was about the lovely close of a warm summer day,
There came a gallant merchant-ship full sail to Plymouth Bay;
Her crew had seen Castile's black fleet beyond Aurigny's isle,
At earliest twilight, on the waves lie heaving many a mile.
At sunrise she escaped their van, by God's especial grace,
And the tall *Pinta*, till the noon, had held her close in chase.
Forthwith a guard at every gun was placed along the wall;
The beacon blazed upon the roof of Edgecumbe's lofty hall;
Many a light fishing-bark put out to pry along the coast,
And with loose rein and bloody spur rode inland many a post.
With his white hair, unbonneted, the stout old sheriff comes;
Behind him march the halberdiers; before him sound the drums;
His yeomen round the market cross make clear an ample space;
For there behoves him to set up the standard of Her Grace.
And haughtily the trumpets peal, and gaily dance the bells,
As slow upon the labouring wind the royal blazon swells.
Look how the Lion of the sea lifts up his ancient crown,
And underneath his deadly paw treads the gay lilies down.

So stalked he when he turned to flight, on that famed Picard field,
Bohemia's plume, and Genoa's bow, and Caesar's eagle shield.
So glared he when at Agincourt in wrath he turned to bay,
And crushed and torn beneath his claws the princely hunters lay.
Ho! strike the flagstaff deep, sir Knight: ho! scatter flowers, fair
    maids:
Ho! gunners, fire a loud salute: ho! gallants, draw your blades:
Thou sun, shine on her joyously; ye breezes, waft her wide;
Our glorious *semper eadem*, the banner of our pride.
The freshening breeze of eve unfurled that banner's massy fold;
The parting gleam of sunshine kissed that haughty scroll of gold:
Night sank upon the dusky beach, and on the purple sea,
Such night in England ne'er had been, nor e'er again shall be.
From Eddystone to Berwick bounds, from Lynn to Milford Bay,
That time of slumber was as bright and busy as the day;
For swift to east and swift to west the ghastly war-flame spread,
High on St. Michael's Mount it shone: it shone on Beachy Head.
Far on the deep the Spaniard saw, along each southern shire,
Cape beyond cape, in endless range, those twinkling points of fire.
The fisher left his skiff to rock on Tamar's glittering waves:
The rugged miners poured to war from Mendip's sunless caves:
O'er Longleat's towers, o'er Cranbourne's oaks, the fiery herald flew
And roused the shepherds of Stonehenge, the rangers of Beaulieu.
Right sharp and quick the bells all night rang out from Bristol
    town,
And ere the day three hundred horse had met on Clifton down;
The sentinel on Whitehall gate looked forth into the night,
And saw o'erhanging Richmond Hill that streak of blood-red light.
Then bugle's note and cannon's roar the death-like silence broke,
And with one start, and with one cry, the royal city woke.
At once on all her stately gates arose the answering fires;
At once the wild alarum clashed from all her reeling spires:
From all the batteries of the Tower pealed loud the voice of fear;
And all the thousand masts of Thames sent back a louder cheer:
And from the farthest wards was heard the rush of hurrying feet,
And the broad streams of pikes and flags rushed down each roaring
    street;
And broader still became the blaze, and louder still the din,
As fast from every village round the horse came spurring in:
And eastward straight from wild Blackheath the warlike errand went,
And roused in many an ancient hall the gallant squires of Kent.
Southward from Surrey's pleasant hills flew those bright couriers
    forth;
High on bleak Hampstead's swarthy moor they started for the north;
And on, and on, without a pause, untired they bounded still:
All night from tower to tower they sprang; they sprang from hill
    to hill:
Till the proud Peak unfurled the flag o'er Darwin's rocky dales
Till like volcanoes flared to heaven the stormy hills of Wales,

Till twelve fair counties saw the blaze on Malvern's lonely height,
Till streamed in crimson on the wind the Wrekin's crest of light,
Till broad and fierce the star came forth on Ely's stately fane,
And tower and hamlet rose in arms o'er all the boundless plain;
Till Belvoir's lordly terraces the sign to Lincoln sent,
And Lincoln sped the message on o'er the wide vale of Trent;
Till Skiddaw saw the fire that burned on Gaunt's embattled pile,
And the red glare on Skiddaw roused the burghers of Carlisle.

Thomas, Lord Macaulay.

628. FROM 'HORATIUS'

Lars Porsena of Clusium
  By the Nine Gods he swore
That the great house of Tarquin
  Should suffer wrong no more.
By the Nine Gods he swore it,
  And named a trysting day,
And bade his messengers ride
    forth,
East and west and south and
    north,
  To summon his array.

. . . . .

Fast by the royal standard,
  O'erlooking all the war,
Lars Porsena of Clusium
  Sat in his ivory car.
By the right wheel rode Mamilius,
  Prince of the Latian name;
And by the left false Sextus,
  That wrought the deed of shame.

But when the face of Sextus
  Was seen among the foes,
A yell that rent the firmament
  From all the town arose.
On the house-tops was no woman
  But spat towards him and
    hissed,
No child but screamed out curses,
  And shook its little fist.

But the Consul's brow was sad,
  And the Consul's speech was
    low,
And darkly looked he at the wall,
  And darkly at the foe.

'Their van will be upon us
  Before the bridge goes down;
And if they once may win the
    bridge
  What hope to save the town?'

Then out spake brave Horatius,
  The Captain of the Gate:
'To every man upon this earth
  Death cometh soon or late.
And how can man die better
  Than facing fearful odds,
For the ashes of his fathers,
  And the temples of his Gods,

'And for the tender mother
  Who dandled him to rest,
And for the wife who nurses
  His baby at her breast,
And for the holy maidens
  Who feed the eternal flame,
To save them from false Sextus
  That wrought the deed of
    shame?

'Hew down the bridge, Sir Con-
    sul,
  With all the speed ye may;
I, with two more to help me,
  Will hold the foe in play.
In yon strait path a thousand
  May well be stopped by three.
Now who will stand on either
    hand,
  And keep the bridge with
    me?'

Then out spake Spurius Lartius ;
  A Ramnian proud was he :
' Lo, I will stand at thy right hand,
  And keep the bridge with thee.'
And out spake strong Herminius ;
  Of Titian blood was he :
' I will abide on thy left side,
  And keep the bridge with thee.'

' Horatius,' quoth the Consul,
  ' As thou sayest, so let it be.'
And straight against that great
    array
  Forth went the dauntless Three.
For Romans in Rome's quarrel
  Spared neither land nor gold,
Nor son nor wife, nor limb nor life,
  In the brave days of old.

Then none was for a party ;
  Then all were for the state ;
Then the great man helped the
    poor,
  And the poor man loved the
    great ;
Then lands were fairly portioned ;
  Then spoils were fairly sold :
The Romans were like brothers
  In the brave days of old.

Now Roman is to Roman
  More hateful than a foe,
And the Tribunes beard the high,
  And the Fathers grind the low.
As we wax hot in faction,
  In battle we wax cold ;
Wherefore men fight not as they
    fought
  In the brave days of old.

  .   .   .   .   .   .

Was none who would be foremost
  To lead such dire attack :
But those behind cried ' Forward !'
  And those before cried ' Back ! '
And backward now and forward
  Wavers the deep array ;
And on the tossing sea of steel
To and fro the standards reel ;
And the victorious trumpet-peal
  Dies fitfully away.

Yet one man for one moment
  Stood out before the crowd;
Well known was he to all the
    Three,
  And they gave him greeting
    loud,
' Now welcome, welcome, Sextus !
  Now welcome to thy home !
Why dost thou stay and turn
    away ?
Here lies the road to Rome.'

Thrice looked he at the city ;
  Thrice looked he at the dead ;
And thrice came on in fury,
  And thrice turned back in
    dread :
And, white with fear and hatred,
  Scowled at the narrow way
Where, wallowing in a pool of
    blood,
  The bravest Tuscans lay.

But meanwhile axe and lever
  Have manfully been plied ;
And now the bridge hangs tottering
  Above the boiling tide.
' Come back, come back, Hora-
    tius ! '
  Loud cried the Fathers all.
' Back, Lartius ! back, Herminius !
  Back, ere the ruin fall ! '

Back darted Spurius Lartius ;
  Herminius darted back :
And, as they passed, beneath their
    feet
  They felt the timbers crack.
But when they turned their faces,
  And on the farther shore
Saw brave Horatius stand alone,
  They would have crossed once
    more.

But with a crash like thunder
  Fell every loosened beam,
And, like a dam, the mighty wreck
  Lay right athwart the stream ;
And a long shout of triumph
  Rose from the walls of Rome,
As to the highest turret-tops
  Was splashed the yellow foam.

And, like a horse unbroken
  When first he feels the rein,
The furious river struggled hard,
  And tossed his tawny mane,
And burst the curb, and bounded,
  Rejoicing to be free,
And whirling down, in fierce career,
Battlement, and plank, and pier,
  Rushed headlong to the sea.

Alone stood brave Horatius,
  But constant still in mind,
Thrice thirty thousand foes before,
  And the broad flood behind.
' Down with him ! ' cried false Sextus,
  With a smile on his pale face.
' Now yield thee,' cried Lars Porsena,
  ' Now yield thee to our grace.'

Round turned he, as not deigning
  Those craven ranks to see ;
Naught spake he to Lars Porsena,
  To Sextus naught spake he ;
But he saw on Palatinus
  The white porch of his home ;
And he spake to the noble river
  That rolls by the towers of Rome.

' O Tiber ! father Tiber !
  To whom the Romans pray,
A Roman's life, a Roman's arms,
  Take thou in charge this day ! '
So he spake, and speaking sheathed
  The good sword by his side.
And with his harness on his back,
  Plunged headlong in the tide.

No sound of joy or sorrow
  Was heard from either bank ;
But friends and foes in dumb surprise,
With parted lips and straining eyes,
  Stood gazing where he sank ;

And when above the surges
  They saw his crest appear,
All Rome sent forth a rapturous cry
And even the ranks of Tuscany
  Could scarce forbear to cheer.

. . . . . .

' Curse on him ! ' quoth false Sextus;
  ' Will not the villain drown ?
But for this stay, ere close of day
  We should have sacked the town.'
' Heaven help him,' quoth Lars Porsena,
  ' And bring him safe to shore ;
For such a gallant feat of arms
  Was never seen before.'

And now he feels the bottom ;
  Now on dry earth he stands ;
Now round him throng the Fathers
  To press his gory hands ;
And now, with shouts and clapping,
  And noise of weeping loud,
He enters through the River-Gate,
  Borne by the joyous crowd.

. . . . . .

When the oldest cask is opened,
  And the largest lamp is lit;
When the chestnuts glow in the embers,
  And the kid turns on the spit;
When young and old in circle
  Around the firebrands close;
When the girls are weaving baskets,
  And the lads are shaping bows;

When the goodman mends his armour,
  And trims his helmet's plume ;
When the goodwife's shuttle merrily
  Goes flashing through the loom ;
With weeping and with laughter
  Still is the story told,
How well Horatius kept the bridge
  In the brave days of old.
           LORD MACAULAY.

629. A JACOBITE'S EPITAPH

To my true king I offered, free from stain,
Courage and faith ; vain faith, and courage vain.
For him I threw lands, honours, wealth, away,
And one dear hope, that was more prized than they.
For him I languished in a foreign clime,
Grey-haired with sorrow in my manhood's prime ;
Heard on Lavernia Scargill's whispering trees,
And pined by Arno for my lovelier Tees ;
Beheld each night my home in fevered sleep,
Each morning started from the dream to weep ;
Till God, who saw me tried too sorely, gave
The resting-place I asked, an early grave.
O thou, whom chance leads to this nameless stone,
From that proud country which was once mine own,
By those white cliffs I never more must see,
By that dear language which I spake like thee,
Forget all feuds, and shed one English tear
O'er English dust. A broken heart lies here.

LORD MACAULAY.

630. BABY

WHERE did you come from, baby dear ?
Out of the everywhere into here.

Where did you get those eyes so blue ?
Out of the sky as I came through.

What makes the light in them sparkle and spin ?
Some of the starry spikes left in.

Where did you get that little tear ?
I found it waiting when I got here.

What makes your forehead so smooth and high ?
A soft hand stroked it as I went by.

What makes your cheek like a warm white rose ?
I saw something better than any one knows.

Whence that three-cornered smile of bliss ?
Three angels gave me at once a kiss.

Where did you get this pearly ear ?
God spoke, and it came out to hear.

Where did you get those arms and hands ?
Love made itself into bonds and bands.

Feet, whence did you come, you darling things ?
From the same box as the cherubs' wings.

How did they all just come to be you ?
God thought about me, and so I grew.

But how did you come to us, you dear ?
God thought about you, and so I am here.   G. MACDONALD.

631. LOVE NEW AND OLD

AND were they not the happy days
  When Love and I were young,
When earth was robed in heavenly light,
  And all creation sung ?
When gazing in my true love's face,
  Through greenwood alleys lone,
I guessed the secrets of her heart,
  By whispers of mine own.

And are they not the happy days
  When Love and I are old,
And silver evening has replaced
  A morn and noon of gold ?
Love stood alone mid youthful joy,
  But now by sorrow tried,
It sits and calmly looks to heaven
  With angels at its side.   C. MACKAY.

632. TUBAL CAIN

OLD Tubal Cain was a man of might
  In the days when Earth was young ;
By the fierce red light of his furnace bright
  The strokes of his hammer rung ;
And he lifted high his brawny hand
  On the iron glowing clear,
Till the sparks rushed out in scarlet showers,
  As he fashioned the sword and spear.
And he sang : ' Hurra for my handiwork !
  Hurra for the spear and sword !
Hurra for the hand that shall wield them well,
  For he shall be king and lord ! '

To Tubal Cain came many a one,
  As he wrought by his roaring fire,
And each one prayed for a strong steel blade
  As the crown of his desire :
And he made them weapons sharp and strong,
  Till they shouted loud for glee,
And gave him gifts of pearl and gold,
  And spoils of the forest free.
And they sang : ' Hurra for Tubal Cain,
  Who has given us strength anew !
Hurra for the smith, hurra for the fire,
  And hurra for the metal true ! '

But a sudden change came o'er his heart
  Ere the setting of the sun,
And Tubal Cain was filled with pain
  For the evil he had done ;

He saw that men, with rage and hate,
  Made war upon their kind,
That the land was red with the blood they shed,
  In their lust for carnage blind.
And he said : ' Alas ! that ever I made,
  Or that skill of mine should plan,
The spear and the sword for men whose joy
  Is to slay their fellow-man ! '

And for many a day old Tubal Cain
  Sat brooding o'er his woe ;
And his hand forbore to smite the ore,
  And his furnace smouldered low.
But he rose at last with a cheerful face,
  And a bright courageous eye,
And bared his strong right arm for work,
  While the quick flames mounted high.
And he sang : ' Hurra for my handiwork ! '
  And the red sparks lit the air ;
' Not alone for the blade was the bright steel made ; '
  And he fashioned the first ploughshare.

And men, taught wisdom from the past,
  In friendship joined their hands,
Hung the sword in the hall, the spear on the wall,
  And ploughed the willing lands ;
And sang : ' Hurra for Tubal Cain !
  Our stanch good friend is he ;
And for the ploughshare and the plough
  To him our praise shall be.
But while oppression lifts its head,
  Or a tyrant would be lord,
Though we may thank him for the plough,
  We'll not forget the sword ! '   C. MACKAY.

633. THE SHANDON BELLS

WITH deep affection,
And recollection,
I often think of
  Those Shandon bells,
Whose sounds so wild would,
In the days of childhood,
Fling around my cradle
  Their magic spells.
On this I ponder
Where'er I wander,
And thus grow fonder,
  Sweet Cork, of thee ;

With thy bells of Shandon,
That sound so grand on
The pleasant waters
  Of the River Lee.
I've heard bells chiming
Full many a clime in,
Tolling sublime in
  Cathedral shrine,
While at a glib rate
Brass tongues would vibrate—
But all the music
  Spoke naught like thine ;

For memory, dwelling
On each proud swelling
Of the belfry knelling
    Its bold notes free,
Made the bells of Shandon
Sound far more grand on
The pleasant waters
    Of the River Lee.

I've heard bells tolling
Old Adrian's Mole in,
Their thunder rolling
    From the Vatican,
And cymbals glorious
Swinging uproarious
In the glorious turrets
    Of Notre Dame ;
But thy sounds were sweeter
Than the dome of Peter
Flings o'er the Tiber,
    Pealing solemnly ;—

O, the bells of Shandon
Sound far more grand on
The pleasant waters
    Of the River Lee.

There's a bell in Moscow,
While in tower and kiosk O
In Saint Sophia
    The Turkman gets ;
And loud in air
Calls men to prayer
From the tapering summits
    Of tall minarets.
Such empty phantom
I freely grant them ;
But there's an anthem
    More dear to me,—
'Tis the bells of Shandon
That sound so grand on
The pleasant waters
    Of the River Lee.
       F. MAHONY (FATHER PROUT).

634.   THE BIRKS OF ENDERMAY

THE smiling morn, the breathing
    spring,
Invite the tuneful birds to sing ;
And, while they warble from each
    spray,
Love meets the universal lay.
Let us, Amanda, timely wise,
Like them, improve the hour that
    flies ;
And in soft raptures waste the day,
Among the shades of Endermay.

For soon the winter of the year,
And age, life's winter, will appear ;
At this thy living bloom must
    fade,
As that will strip the verdant
    shade.
Our taste of pleasure then is o'er,
The feathered songsters love no
    more ;
And when they droop and we decay,
Adieu the shades of Endermay !
       D. MALLET.

635.   DARK ROSALEEN

O MY Dark Rosaleen,
    Do not sigh, do not weep !
The priests are on the ocean green,
    They march along the deep.
There's wine from the royal Pope
    Upon the ocean green ;
And Spanish ale shall give you hope,
    My Dark Rosaleen !
    My own Rosaleen !
Shall glad your heart, shall give you hope,
Shall give you health, and help, and hope,
    My Dark Rosaleen !

Over hills, and through dales,
  Have I roamed for your sake ;
All yesterday I sailed with sails
  On river and on lake.
The Erne, at its highest flood,
  I dashed across unseen,
For there was lightning in my blood,
    My Dark Rosaleen !
    My own Rosaleen !
Oh, there was lightning in my blood,
Red lightning lightened through my blood,
    My Dark Rosaleen !

All day long, in unrest,
  To and fro, do I move.
The very soul within my breast
  Is wasted for you, love !
The heart in my bosom faints
  To think of you, my Queen,
My life of life, my saint of saints,
    My Dark Rosaleen !
    My own Rosaleen !
To hear your sweet and sad complaints,
My life, my love, my saint of saints,
    My Dark Rosaleen !

Woe and pain, pain and woe,
  Are my lot, night and noon,
To see your bright face clouded so,
  Like to the mournful moon.
But yet will I rear your throne
  Again in golden sheen ;
'Tis you shall reign, shall reign alone,
    My Dark Rosaleen !
    My own Rosaleen !
'Tis you shall have the golden throne,
'Tis you shall reign, and reign alone,
    My Dark Rosaleen !

Over dews, over sands,
  Will I fly, for your weal :
Your holy delicate white hands
  Shall girdle me with steel.
At home, in your emerald bowers,
  From morning's dawn till e'en,
You'll pray for me, my flower of flowers,
    My Dark Rosaleen !
    My fond Rosaleen !
You'll think of me through daylight hours,
My virgin flower, my flower of flowers,
    My Dark Rosaleen !

I could scale the blue air,
    I could plough the high hills,
Oh, I could kneel all night in prayer,
    To heal your many ills !
And one beamy smile from you
    Would float like light between
My toils and me, my own, my true,
        My Dark Rosaleen !
        My fond Rosaleen !
Would give me life and soul anew,
A second life, a soul anew,
        My Dark Rosaleen !

Oh, the Erne shall run red,
    With redundance of blood,
The earth shall rock beneath our tread,
    And flames wrap hill and wood,
And gun-peal and slogan-cry
    Wake many a glen serene,
Ere you shall fade, ere you shall die,
        My Dark Rosaleen !
        My own Rosaleen !
The Judgement Hour must first be nigh,
Ere you can fade, ere you can die,
        My Dark Rosaleen !   J. C. MANGAN.

636.   THE NAMELESS ONE

ROLL forth, my song, like the rushing river,
    That sweeps along to the mighty sea ;
God will inspire me while I deliver
    My soul of thee !

Tell thou the world, when my bones lie whitening
    Amid the last homes of youth and eld,
That once there was one whose veins ran lightning
    No eye beheld.

Tell how his boyhood was one drear night-hour,
    How shone for him, through his grief and gloom,
No star of all heaven sends to light our
    Path to the tomb.

Roll on, my song, and to after ages
    Tell how, disdaining all earth can give,
He would have taught men, from wisdom's pages,
    The way to live.

And tell how trampled, derided, hated,
    And worn by weakness, disease, and wrong,
He fled for shelter to God, who mated
    His soul with song—

With song which alway, sublime or vapid,
  Flowed like a rill in the morning-beam,
Perchance not deep, but intense and rapid—
    A mountain stream.

Tell how this Nameless, condemned for years long
  To herd with demons from hell beneath,
Saw things that made him, with groans and tears, long
    For even death.

Go on to tell how, with genius wasted,
  Betrayed in friendship, befooled in love,
With spirit shipwrecked, and young hopes blasted,
    He still, still strove ;

Till spent with toil, dreeing death for others,
  And some whose hands should have wrought for him
(If children live not for sires and mothers),
    His mind grew dim ;

And he fell far through that pit abysmal,
  The gulf and grave of Maginn and Burns,
And pawned his soul for the devil's dismal
    Stock of returns ;

But yet redeemed it in days of darkness,
  And shapes and signs of the final wrath,
When death, in hideous and ghastly starkness,
    Stood on his path.

And tell how now, amid wreck and sorrow,
  And want, and sickness, and houseless nights,
He bides in calmness the silent morrow,
    That no ray lights.

And lives he still, then ? Yes ! Old and hoary
  At thirty-nine, from despair and woe,
He lives, enduring what future story
    Will never know.

Him grant a grave to, ye pitying noble,
  Deep in your bosoms : there let him dwell !
He, too, had tears for all souls in trouble
    Here, and in hell.   J. C. MANGAN.

637. FAUSTUS' DYING SOLILOQUY

  Ah, Faustus,
Now hast thou but one bare hour to live,
And then thou must be damned perpetually !
Stand still, you ever-moving spheres of heaven,
That time may cease, and midnight never come ;
Fair Nature's eye, rise, rise again, and make
Perpetual day ; or let this hour be but
A year, a month, a week, a natural day,

That Faustus may repent and save his soul!
O lente, lente currite, noctis equi!
The stars move still, time runs, the clock will strike,
The devil will come, and Faustus must be damned.
O, I'll leap up to my God!—Who pulls me down?—
See, see, where Christ's blood streams in the firmament!
One drop would save my soul, half a drop: ah, my Christ!—
Ah, rend not my heart for naming of my Christ!
Yet will I call on Him: O, spare me, Lucifer!—
Where is it now? 'tis gone: and see, where God
Stretcheth out His arm, and bends His ireful brows!
Mountains and hills, come, come, and fall on me,
And hide me from the heavy wrath of God!
No, no!
Then will I headlong run into the earth:
Earth, gape! O, no, it will not harbour me
You stars that reigned at my nativity,
Whose influence hath allotted death and hell,
Now draw up Faustus, like a foggy mist,
Into the entrails of yon labouring clouds,
That, when you vomit forth into the air,
My limbs may issue from your smoky mouths,
So that my soul may but ascend to heaven!

C. MARLOWE (Faustus).

638.   THE PASSIONATE SHEPHERD TO HIS LOVE

COME live with me and be my love,
And we will all the pleasures prove
That hills and valleys, dale and field,
And all the craggy mountains yield.

There will we sit upon the rocks
And see the shepherds feed their flocks,
By shallow rivers, to whose falls
Melodious birds sing madrigals.

And I will make thee beds of roses
And a thousand fragrant posies,
A cap of flowers, and a kirtle
Embroidered all with leaves of myrtle.

A gown made of the finest wool,
Which from our pretty lambs we pull,
Fair linèd slippers for the cold,
With buckles of the purest gold.

A belt of straw and ivy buds
With coral clasps and amber studs:
And if these pleasures may thee move,
Come live with me and be my love.

The shepherd swains shall dance and sing
For thy delight each May-morning:
If these delights thy mind may move,
Then live with me and be my love.

C. MARLOWE.[1]

639. WHO EVER LOVED, THAT LOVED NOT AT
FIRST SIGHT?

IT lies not in our power to love or hate,
For will in us is overruled by fate.
When two are stripped, long ere the course begin,
We wish that one should lose, the other win;
And one especially do we affect
Of two gold ingots, like in each respect:
The reason no man knows; let it suffice
What we behold is censured by our eyes.
Where both deliberate, the love is slight:
Who ever loved, that loved not at first sight?

C. MARLOWE (*Hero and Leander*).

640. HELEN

WAS this the face that launched a thousand ships,
And burned the topless towers of Ilium?—
Sweet Helen, make me immortal with a kiss!—
Her lips suck forth my soul: see where it flees!—
Come, Helen, come, give me my soul again.
Here will I dwell, for heaven is in these lips,
And all is dross that is not Helena.
I will be Paris, and for love of thee,
Instead of Troy, shall Wittenberg be sacked,
And I will combat with weak Menelaus,
And wear thy colours on my plumèd crest;
Yes, I will wound Achilles in the heel,
And then return to Helen for a kiss.
Oh, thou art fairer than the evening air
Clad in the beauty of a thousand stars;
Brighter art thou than flaming Jupiter
When he appeared to hapless Semele;
More lovely than the monarch of the sky
In wanton Arethusa's azured arms;
And none but thou shalt be my paramour!

C. MARLOWE (*Faustus*).

[1] See Ralegh's reply, No. 771.

641. TO DETRACTION

FOUL canker of fair virtuous action,
Vile blaster of the freshest blooms on earth,
Envy's abhorrèd child, Detraction,
I here expose, to thy all-tainting breath,
    The issue of my brain: snarl, rail, bark, bite,
    Know that my spirit scorns Detraction's spite.

  . . . .

My spirit is not puffed up with fat fume
Of slimy ale, nor Bacchus' heating grape.
My mind disdains the dungy muddy scum
Of abject thoughts and Envy's raging hate.
    True judgement slight regards opinion;
    A sprightly wit disdains Detraction.   J. MARSTON.

642. TO EVERLASTING OBLIVION

THOU mighty gulf, insatiate cormorant!
Deride me not, though I seem petulant
    To fall into thy chops. Let others pray
    For ever their fair poems flourish may,
But as for me, hungry Oblivion
Devour me quick, accept my orison,
    My earnest prayers which do importune thee,
    With gloomy shade of thy still empery,
    To veil both me and my rude poesy.
Far worthier lines, in silence of thy state,
Do sleep securely, free from love or hate!
From which this living ne'er can be exempt,
But whilst it breathes will hate and fury tempt:
Then close his eyes with thy all-dimming hand,
Which not right glorious actions can withstand.
Peace, hateful tongues, I now in silence pace,
Unless some hound do wake me from my place,
    I with this sharp, yet well-meant poesy,
    Will sleep secure, right free from injury
    Of cankered hate, or rankest villany.   J. MARSTON.

643. THOUGHTS IN A GARDEN

How vainly men themselves amaze
To win the palm, the oak, or bays,
And their incessant labours see
Crowned from some single herb or tree,
Whose short and narrow-vergèd shade
Does prudently their toils upbraid;
While all the flowers and trees do close
To weave the garlands of repose!

Fair Quiet, have I found thee here,
And Innocence thy sister dear ?
Mistaken long, I sought you then
In busy companies of men :
Your sacred plants, if here below,
Only among the plants will grow :
Society is all but rude
To this delicious solitude.

No white nor red was ever seen
So amorous as this lovely green.
Fond lovers, cruel as their flame,
Cut in these trees their mistress' name ;
Little alas ! they know or heed
How far these beauties hers exceed !
Fair trees ! wheresoe'er your barks I wound,
No name shall but your own be found.

When we have run our passion's heat,
Love hither makes his best retreat :
The gods, that mortal beauty chase,
Still in a tree did end their race ;
Apollo hunted Daphne so
Only that she might laurel grow ;
And Pan did after Syrinx speed
Not as a nymph, but for a reed.

What wondrous life is this I lead !
Ripe apples drop about my head ;
The luscious clusters of the vine
Upon my mouth do crush their wine ;
The nectarine and curious peach
Into my hands themselves do reach ;
Stumbling on melons, as I pass,
Ensnared with flowers, I fall on grass.

Meanwhile the mind, from pleasure less,
Withdraws into its happiness ;
The mind, that ocean where each kind
Does straight its own resemblance find ;
Yet it creates, transcending these,
Far other worlds, and other seas ;
Annihilating all that 's made
To a green thought in a green shade.

Here at the fountain's sliding foot,
Or at some fruit-tree's mossy root,
Casting the body's vest aside,
My soul into the boughs does glide ;
There, like a bird, it sits and sings,
Then whets and combs its silver wings,
And, till prepared for longer flight,
Waves in its plumes the various light.

Such was that happy garden-state,
While man there walked without a mate;
After a place so pure and sweet,
What other help could yet be meet!
But 'twas beyond a mortal's share
To wander solitary there:
Two Paradises 'twere in one,
To live in Paradise alone.

How well the skilful gardener drew
Of flowers and herbs this dial new!
Where, from above, the milder sun
Does through a fragrant Zodiac run:
And, as it works, the industrious bee
Computes its time as well as we.
How could such sweet and wholesome hours
Be reckoned but with herbs and flowers?

A. MARVELL.

644. AN HORATIAN ODE

UPON CROMWELL'S RETURN FROM IRELAND

THE forward youth that would
  appear
Must now forsake his Muses dear,
  Nor in the shadows sing
  His numbers languishing.

'Tis time to leave the books in
  dust,
And oil the unused armour's rust,
  Removing from the wall,
  The corslet of the hall.

So restless Cromwell could not
  cease
In the inglorious arts of peace,
  But through adventurous war
  Urgèd his active star.

And like the three-forked light-
  ning, first
Breaking the clouds where it was
  nursed,
  Did thorough his own side,
  His fiery way divide.

(For 'tis all one to courage high,
The emulous, or enemy;
  And with such to enclose
  Is more than to oppose.)

Then burning through the air he
  went,
And palaces and temples rent;
  And Caesar's head at last
  Did through his laurels blast.

'Tis madness to resist or blame
The face of angry heaven's flame;
  And if we would speak true,
  Much to the man is due

Who, from his private gardens,
  where
He lived reservèd and austere
  (As if his highest plot
  To plant the bergamot),

Could by industrious valour climb
To ruin the great work of time,
  And cast the kingdoms old
  Into another mould.

Though Justice against Fate com-
  plain,
And plead the ancient rights in
  vain—
  But those do hold, or break
  As men are strong or weak—

Nature, that hateth emptiness,
Allows of penetration less,
　　And therefore must make room
　　Where greater spirits come.

What field of all the civil war
Where his were not the deepest
　　　　scar ?
　　And Hampton shows what part
　　He had of wiser art,

Where, twining subtle fears with
　　hope,
He wove a net of such a scope
　　That Charles himself might
　　　　chase
　　To Car'sbrook's narrow case ;

That thence the royal actor borne
The tragic scaffold might adorn :
　　While round the armèd bands
　　Did clap their bloody hands ;

He nothing common did or mean
Upon that memorable scene,
　　But with his keener eye
　　The axe's edge did try ;

Nor called the Gods, with vulgar
　　spite,
To vindicate his helpless right ;
　　But bowed his comely head
　　Down, as upon a bed.

This was that memorable hour
Which first assured the forcèd
　　power :
　　So when they did design
　　The Capitol's first line,

A bleeding head, where they
　　begun,
Did fright the architects to run
　　And yet in that the State
　　Foresaw its happy fate.

And now the Irish are ashamed
To see themselves in one year
　　tamed ;
　　So much one man can do,
　　That does both act and know.

They can affirm his praises best,
And have, though overcome, con-
　　fessed
　　How good he is, how just,
　　And fit for highest trust.

Nor yet grown stiffer with com-
　　mand,
But still in the Republic's hand,
　　How fit he is to sway,
　　That can so well obey.

He to the Commons' feet presents
A kingdom for his first year's
　　rents,
　　And (what he may !) forbears
　　His fame to make it theirs ;

And has his sword and spoils
　　ungirt,
To lay them at the public's skirt.
　　So when the falcon high
　　Falls heavy from the sky,

She, having killed, no more does
　　search,
But on the next green bough to
　　perch ;
　　Where, when he first does lure,
　　The falconer has her sure.

What may not then our isle
　　presume,
While Victory his crest does
　　plume ?
　　What may not others fear,
　　If thus he crowns each year ?

As Caesar, he ere long to Gaul,
To Italy, a Hannibal !
　　And to all states not free
　　Shall climacteric be.

The Pict no shelter now shall
　　find
Within his parti-coloured mind,
　　But (from his valour) sad
　　Shrink underneath the plaid.

Happy, if in the tufted brake
The English hunter him mistake ;
　　Nor lay his hounds in near
　　The Caledonian deer.

But thou, the war's and Fortune's son,
March indefatigably on,
    And for the last effect
    Still keep the sword erect.

Besides the force it has to fright
The spirits of the shady night,
    The same arts that did gain
    A power, must it maintain.

A. MARVELL.

645. THE NYMPH'S GRIEF FOR HER FAWN

THE wanton troopers, riding by,
Have shot my fawn, and it will die !
   .   .   .   .   .

I have a garden of my own,
But so with roses overgrown,
And lilies, that you would it guess
To be a little wilderness ;
And all the spring-time of the year
It only lovèd to be there.
Among the beds of lilies I
Have sought it oft, where it should
    lie ;
Yet could not, till itself would rise,
Find it, although before mine eyes ;

For in the flaxen lilies' shade,
It like a bank of lilies laid.
Upon the roses it would feed,
Until its lips e'en seemed to bleed ;
And then to me 'twould boldly
    trip,
And print those roses on my lip.
But all its chief delight was still
On roses thus itself to fill ;
And its pure virgin limbs to fold
In whitest sheets of lilies cold.
Had it lived long, it would have
    been
Lilies without, roses within.

A. MARVELL.

646. WHERE THE REMOTE BERMUDAS RIDE

WHERE the remote Bermudas ride
In the ocean's bosom unespied,
From a small boat that rowed along
The listening winds received this song.

What should we do but sing His praise
That led us through the watery maze
Unto an isle so long unknown,
And yet far kinder than our own ?
Where He the huge sea-monsters wracks,
That lift the deep upon their backs,
He lands us on a grassy stage,
Safe from the storms, and prelates' rage :
He gave us this eternal spring
Which here enamels everything,
And sends the fowls to us in care
On daily visits through the air.
He hangs in shades the orange bright
Like golden lamps in a green night,
And does in the pomegranates close
Jewels more rich than Ormus shows :
He makes the figs our mouths to meet,
And throws the melons at our feet ;
But apples plants of such a price,
No tree could ever bear them twice.

With cedars chosen by His hand
From Lebanon He stores the land;
And makes the hollow seas that roar
Proclaim the ambergris on shore.
He cast (of which we rather boast)
The Gospel's pearl upon our coast;
And in these rocks for us did frame
A temple where to sound His name.
O let our voice His praise exalt
Till it arrive at heaven's vault,
Which then perhaps rebounding may
Echo beyond the Mexique bay!
—Thus sung they in the English boat
A holy and a cheerful note:
And all the way, to guide their chime,
With falling oars they kept the time.   A. Marvell.

647. THE BLUSHING ROSE AND PURPLE FLOWER

The blushing rose and purple flower,
  Let grow too long, are soonest blasted!
Dainty fruits, though sweet, will sour,
  And rot in ripeness, left untasted!
    Yet here is one more sweet than these:
    The more you taste, the more she'll please.

Beauty, though enclosed with ice,
  Is a shadow chaste as rare;
Then, how much those sweets entice
  That have issue full as fair!
    Earth cannot yield from all her powers
    One equal, for Dame Venus' bowers!

P. Massinger.

648. TO DEATH

Why art thou slow, thou rest of trouble, Death,
  To stop a wretch's breath,
That calls on thee, and offers her sad heart
  A prey unto thy dart?
I am not young, nor fair; be therefore bold.
  Sorrow hath made me old.
Deformed, and wrinkled; all that I can crave
  Is quiet in my grave.
Such as live happy hold long life a jewel,
  But to me thou art cruel,
If thou end not my tedious misery,
  And I soon cease to be.
Strike, and strike home, then; pity unto me,
  In one short hour's delay is tyranny.

P. Massinger.

M

649. FROM 'LOGAN BRAES'

By Logan's streams that rin sae deep
Fu' aft wi' glee, I've herded sheep,
I've herded sheep, or gather'd slaes,
Wi' my dear lad, on Logan braes.
But wae's my heart! thae days are gane,
And fu' o' grief I herd alane,
While my dear lad maun face his faes,
Far, far frae me and Logan braes.

Nae mair at Logan kirk will he,
Atween the preachings, meet wi' me—
Meet wi' me, or when it's mirk,
Convoy me hame frae Logan kirk.
I weel may sing thae days are gane—
Frae kirk and fair I come alane,
While my dear lad maun face his faes,
Far, far frae me and Logan braes!   J. MAYNE.

650. THE MARINER'S WIFE

BUT are you sure the news is true ?
And are you sure he's well ?
Is this a time to think o' wark ?
Ye jades, fling by your wheel !
    There's nae luck about the
        house,
    There's nae luck at a' ;
    There's nae luck about the
        house
    When our goodman's awa' !

Is this a time to think of wark,
When Colin's at the door ?
Rax me my cloak ! I'll down the
        Quay
And see him come ashore !
    There's nae luck about the
        house, &c.

Rise up, and make a clean fireside !
Put on the muckle pat !
Gie little Kate her cotton gown,
And Jock his Sunday's coat.
    There's nae luck about the
        house, &c.

Make their shoon as black as slaes,
Their stockings white as snaw.
It's a' to pleasure our goodman,
He likes to see them braw !
    There's nae luck about the
        house, &c.

There are twa hens into the
        crib
Have fed this month and mair ;
Made haste, and thraw their necks
        about,
    That Colin well may fare.
    There's nae luck about the
        house, &c.

Bring down to me my bigonet,
My bishop-satin gown,
And then gae tell the bailie's
        wife
That Colin's come to town.
    There's nae luck about the
        house, &c.

My Turkey slippers I'll put on,
My stockings pearl-blue,
And a' to pleasure our goodman
For he's baith leal and true.
    There's nae luck about the
        house, &c.

Sae sweet his voice, sae smooth his
        tongue,
His breath's like cauler air,
His very tread has music in 't,
As he comes up the stair !
    There's nae luck about the
        house, &c.

And will I see his face again ?
And will I hear him speak ?
I'm downright dizzy with the joy ;
In troth, I'm like to greet !
    There 's nae luck about the house,
      There 's nae luck at a' ;
    There 's nae luck about the house
      When our goodman 's awa' !

W. J. MICKLE.

651. THE PALM AND THE PINE

BENEATH an Indian palm a girl
  Of other blood reposes,
Her cheek is clear and pale as
    pearl,
  Amid that wild of roses.

Beside a northern pine a boy
  Is leaning fancy-bound,
Nor listens where with noisy joy
  Awaits the impatient hound.

Cool grows the sick and feverish
    calm,—
  Relaxed the frosty twine,—
The pine-tree dreameth of the
    palm,
  The palm-tree of the pine.

As soon shall nature interlace
  Those dimly-visioned boughs,
As these young lovers face to face
  Renew their early vows !

R. M. MILNES, LORD HOUGHTON.

652. THE MEN OF OLD

I KNOW not that the men of
    old
  Were better than men now,
Of heart more kind, of hand more
    bold,
  Of more ingenuous brow :
I heed not those who pine for
    force
  A ghost of Time to raise,
As if they thus could check the
    course
  Of these appointed days.

Still is it true, and over-true,
  That I delight to close
This book of life self-wise and
    new,
  And let my thoughts repose
On all that humble happiness
  The world has since foregone—
The daylight of contentedness
  That on those faces shone !

With rights, though not too closely
    scanned,
  Enjoyed, as far as known—
With will, by no reverse un-
    manned—
  With pulse of even tone—
They from to-day and from
    to-night
  Expected nothing more
Than yesterday and yesternight
  Had proffered them before.

To them was life a simple art
  Of duties to be done,
A game where each man took his
    part,
  A race where all must run ;
A battle whose great scheme and
    scope
  They little cared to know,
Content, as men-at-arms, to cope
  Each with his fronting foe.

Man *now* his Virtue's diadem
  Puts on, and proudly wears—
Great thoughts, great feelings,
      came to them,
  Like instincts, unawares:
Blending their souls' sublimest
      needs
  With tasks of every day,
They went about their gravest
      deeds,
  As noble boys at play.

And what if Nature's fearful
      wound
  They did not probe and bare,
For that their spirits never
      swooned
  To watch the misery there—
For that their love but flowed
      more fast,
  Their charities more free,
Not conscious what mere drops
      they cast
  Into the evil sea.

A man's best things are nearest
      him,
  Lie close about his feet,
It is the distant and the dim
  That we are sick to greet:
For flowers that grow our hands
      beneath
  We struggle and aspire,—
Our hearts must die, except they
      breathe
  The air of fresh desire.

But, brothers, who up Reason's
      hill
  Advance with hopeful cheer—
Oh, loiter not, those heights are
      chill,
  As chill as they are clear;
And still restrain your haughty
      gaze,
  The loftier that ye go,
Remembering distance leaves a
      haze
  On all that lies below.

R. M. MILNES, LORD HOUGHTON.

653. SHADOWS

THEY seemed, to those who saw them meet,
  The casual friends of every day;
Her smile was undisturbed and sweet,
  His courtesy was free and gay.

But yet if one the other's name
  In some unguarded moment heard,
The heart you thought so calm and tame
  Would struggle like a captured bird:

And letters of mere formal phrase
  Were blistered with repeated tears,—
And this was not the work of days,
  But had gone on for years and years!

Alas, that love was not too strong
  For maiden shame and manly pride!
Alas, that they delayed so long
  The goal of mutual bliss beside!

Yet what no chance could then reveal,
  And neither would be first to own,
Let fate and courage now conceal,
  When truth could bring remorse alone.

R. M. MILNES, LORD HOUGHTON.

654. THE VENETIAN SERENADE

WHEN along the light ripple the far serenade
Has accosted the ear of each passionate maid,
She may open the window that looks on the stream,—
She may smile on her pillow and blend it in dream;
Half in words, half in music, it pierces the gloom,
' I am coming—Stalì—but you know not for whom!
   Stalì—not for whom ! '

Now the tones become clearer—you hear more and more
How the water divided returns on the oar,—
Does the prow of the gondola strike on the stair ?
Do the voices and instruments pause and prepare ?
Oh ! they faint on the ear as the lamp on the view,
' I am coming—Premì—but I stay not for you !
   Premì—not for you ! '

Then return to your couch, you who stifle a tear,
Then awake not, fair sleeper—believe he is here;
For the young and the loving no sorrow endures,
If to-day be another's, to-morrow is yours;—
May, the next time you listen, your fancy be true,
' I am coming—Sciàr—and for you and to you !
   Sciàr—and to you ! '
       R. M. MILNES, LORD HOUGHTON.

655. ON THE LATE MASSACRE IN PIEDMONT

AVENGE, O Lord, thy slaughtered saints, whose bones
Lie scattered on the Alpine mountains cold,
Even them who kept Thy truth so pure of old
When all our fathers worshipped stocks and stones,
Forget not : in Thy book record their groans
Who were Thy sheep, and in their ancient fold
Slain by the bloody Piedmontese that rolled
Mother with infant down the rocks. Their moans
The vales redoubled to the hills, and they
To Heaven. Their martyred blood and ashes sow
O'er all the Italian fields, where still doth sway
The triple tyrant : that from these may grow
A hundred-fold, who having learnt Thy way
Early may fly the Babylonian woe.
       J. MILTON.

656. TO THE LORD GENERAL CROMWELL

CROMWELL, our chief of men, who through a cloud
Not of war only, but detractions rude,
Guided by faith and matchless fortitude
To peace and truth thy glorious way hast ploughed,
And on the neck of crownèd Fortune proud
Hast reared God's trophies, and His work pursued,
While Darwen stream with blood of Scots imbrued
And Dunbar field resounds thy praises loud,
And Worcester's laureate wreath ; yet much remains
To conquer still ; peace hath her victories
No less renowned than war, new foes arise
Threatening to bind our souls with secular chains :
Help us to save free conscience from the paw
Of hireling wolves whose gospel is their maw. J. MILTON.

657. TO THE LADY MARGARET LEY

DAUGHTER to that good earl, once president
Of England's council, and her treasury,
Who lived in both, unstained with gold or fee,
And left them both, more in himself content,
Till the sad breaking of the Parliament
Broke him, as that dishonest victory
At Chaeronea, fatal to liberty,
Killed with report that old man eloquent,
Though later born, than to have known the days
Wherein your father flourished, yet by you,
Madam, methinks I see him living yet ;
So well your words his noble virtues praise,
That all both judge you to relate them true,
And to possess them, honoured Margaret.   J. MILTON.

658. HAIL, HOLY LIGHT

HAIL, holy Light ! offspring of heaven first-born !
Or of the Eternal Co-eternal beam,
May I express thee unblamed ? since God is light,
And never but in unapproachèd light
Dwelt from eternity, dwelt then in thee,
Bright effluence of bright essence increate.

.   .   .   .

With the year
Seasons return ; but not to me returns
Day, or the sweet approach of even or morn,
Or sight of vernal bloom, or summer's rose,
Or flocks, or herds, or human face divine ;
But cloud instead, and ever-during dark
Surrounds me, from the cheerful ways of men
Cut off, and for the book of knowledge fair

Presented with a universal blank
Of Nature's works, to me expunged and rased,
And wisdom at one entrance quite shut out.
So much the rather thou, celestial light,
Shine inward, and the mind through all her powers
Irradiate : there plant eyes, all mist from thence
Purge and disperse, that I may see and tell
Of things invisible to mortal sight.

J. MILTON (Paradise Lost, Bk. iii).

659. FROM ' L'ALLEGRO '

HASTE thee, Nymph, and bring with thee
Jest and youthful jollity,
Quips and cranks, and wanton wiles,
Nods, and becks, and wreathèd smiles,
Such as hang on Hebe's cheek,
And love to live in dimple sleek ;
Sport that wrinkled Care derides,
And Laughter holding both his sides.
Come, and trip it as you go
On the light fantastic toe,
And in thy right hand lead with thee,
The Mountain Nymph, sweet Liberty ;
And if I give thee honour due,
Mirth, admit me of thy crew,
To live with her, and live with thee,
In unreprovèd pleasures free ;

.   .   .   .   .   .

Then to the well-trod stage anon,
If Jonson's learnèd sock be on,
Or sweetest Shakespeare, Fancy's child,
Warble his native wood-notes wild.
    And ever against eating cares,
Lap me in soft Lydian airs,
Married to immortal verse
Such as the meeting soul may pierce
In notes, with many a winding bout
Of linkèd sweetness long drawn out,
With wanton heed and giddy cunning,
The melting voice through mazes running,
Untwisting all the chains that tie
The hidden soul of harmony.
That Orpheus' self may heave his head
From golden slumber on a bed
Of heaped Elysian flowers, and hear
Such strains as would have won the ear
Of Pluto, to have quite set free
His half-regained Eurydice.

J. MILTON.

660. PHILOSOPHY

How charming is divine Philosophy !
Not harsh, and crabbed, as dull fools suppose,
But musical as is Apollo's lute,
And a perpetual feast of nectared sweets,
Where no crude surfeit reigns.   J. MILTON (*Comus*).

661. ON BEING ARRIVED AT TWENTY-THREE YEARS OF AGE

How soon hath Time, the subtle thief of youth,
Stolen on his wing my three and twentieth year !
My hasting days fly on with full career,
But my late spring no bud or blossom showeth.
Perhaps my semblance might deceive the truth,
That I to manhood am arrived so near,
And inward ripeness doth much less appear,
That some more timely-happy spirits indueth.
Yet be it less or more, or soon or slow,
It shall be still in strictest measure even,
To that same lot, however mean, or high,
Toward which Time leads me, and the will of Heaven ;
All is, if I have grace to use it so,
As ever in my great Taskmaster's eye.   J. MILTON.

662. FROM 'THE HYMN ON THE NATIVITY'

It was the winter wild,
While the heaven-born child
   All meanly wrapt in the rude
      manger lies ;
Nature, in awe to him,
Had doffed her gaudy trim,
   With her great Master so to
      sympathize :
It was no season then for her
To ,wanton with the sun, her
   lusty paramour.

Only with speeches fair
She wooes the gentle air
   To hide her guilty front with
      innocent snow ;
And on her naked shame,
Pollute with sinful blame,
   The saintly veil of maiden
      white to throw ;
Confounded, that her Maker's eyes
Should look so near upon her
   foul deformities.

But he, her fears to cease,
Sent down the meek-eyed Peace ;
   She, crowned with olive green, came softly sliding
Down through the turning sphere,
His ready harbinger,
   With turtle wing the amorous clouds dividing ;
And, waving wide her myrtle wand,
She strikes a universal peace through sea and land.
                                        J. MILTON.

663. METHOUGHT I SAW MY LATE ESPOUSED SAINT

METHOUGHT I saw my late espousèd saint
Brought to me like Alcestis from the grave,
Whom Jove's great son to her glad husband gave,
Rescued from death by force though pale and faint.
Mine as whom washed from spot of child-bed taint,
Purification in the old law did save,
And such, as yet once more I trust to have
Full sight of her in heaven without restraint,
Came vested all in white, pure as her mind:
Her face was veiled, yet to my fancied sight,
Love, sweetness, goodness, in her person shined
So clear, as in no face with more delight.
But O, as to embrace me she inclined,
I waked, she fled, and day brought back my night.

J. MILTON.

664. NOW CAME STILL EVENING ON

Now came still evening on, and twilight grey
Had in her sober livery all things clad;
Silence accompanied, for beast and bird,
They to their grassy couch, these to their nests
Were slunk, all but the wakeful nightingale;
She all night long her amorous descant sung;
Silence was pleased: now glowed the firmament
With living sapphires: Hesperus that led
The starry host, rode brightest, till the moon
Rising in clouded majesty, at length,
Apparent queen, unveiled her peerless light,
And o'er the dark her silver mantle threw.

J. MILTON (*Paradise Lost*, Bk. iv).

665. THE NIGHTINGALE

O NIGHTINGALE, that on yon bloomy spray
Warbl'st at eve, when all the woods are still,
Thou with fresh hope the Lover's heart dost fill,
While the jolly hours lead on propitious May,
Thy liquid notes that close the eye of Day,
First heard before the shallow Cuckoo's bill
Portend success in love; O if Jove's will
Have linked that amorous power to thy soft lay,
Now timely sing, ere the rude Bird of Hate
Foretell my hopeless doom in some grove nigh:
As thou from year to year hast sung too late
For my relief; yet hadst no reason why,
Whether the Muse or Love call thee his mate,
Both them I serve, and of their train am I. J. MILTON.

666.　SATAN'S ADDRESS TO THE SUN

O THOU, that, with surpassing glory crowned,
Look'st from thy sole dominion like the god
Of this new world; at whose sight all the stars
Hide their diminished heads; to thee I call,
But with no friendly voice, and add thy name,
O sun! to tell thee how I hate thy beams,
That bring to my remembrance from what state
I fell, how glorious once above thy sphere,
Till pride and worse ambition threw me down
Warring in heaven against heaven's matchless king.
Ah, wherefore? He deserved no such return
From me, whom He created what I was
In that bright eminence, and with his good
Upbraided none; nor was his service hard.
. . . .
Me miserable! which way shall I fly
Infinite wrath and infinite despair?
Which way I fly is hell; myself am hell;
And, in the lowest deep, a lower deep
Still threatening to devour me opens wide,
To which the hell I suffer seems a heaven.

J. MILTON (Paradise Lost, Bk. iv).

667.　OF MAN'S FIRST DISOBEDIENCE

OF Man's first disobedience, and the fruit
Of that forbidden tree, whose mortal taste
Brought death into the world, and all our woe,
With loss of Eden, till one greater Man
Restore us, and regain the blissful seat,
Sing, heavenly Muse, that on the secret top
Of Oreb, or of Sinai, didst inspire
That shepherd, who first taught the chosen seed,
In the beginning how the heavens and earth
Rose out of chaos: or if Sion hill
Delight thee more, and Siloa's brook that flowed
Fast by the oracle of God; I thence
Invoke thy aid to my adventurous song,
That with no middle flight intends to soar
Above the Aonian mount, while it pursues
Things unattempted yet in prose or rhyme.
And chiefly thou, O Spirit, that dost prefer
Before all temples the upright heart and pure,
Instruct me, for Thou knowest; Thou from the first
Wast present, and with mighty wings outspread
Dove-like satst brooding on the vast Abyss
And mad'st it pregnant: what in me is dark
Illumine, what is low raise and support;

That to the height of this great argument
I may assert Eternal Providence,
And justify the ways of God to men.

> J. MILTON (*Paradise Lost*, Bk. i).

668. FAITHFUL AMONG THE FAITHLESS

THE seraph Abdiel, faithful found,
Among the faithless, faithful only he ;
Among innumerable false, unmoved,
Unshaken, unseduced, unterrified,
His loyalty he kept, his love, his zeal ;
Nor number, nor example with him wrought
To swerve from truth, or change his constant mind,
Though single.

> J. MILTON (*Paradise Lost*, Bk. v).

669. THESE ARE THY GLORIOUS WORKS

THESE are thy glorious works, Parent of good,
Almighty, Thine this universal frame,
Thus wondrous fair : Thyself how wondrous then !
Unspeakable, who sitt'st above these heavens
To us invisible, or dimly seen
In these thy lowest works ; yet these declare
Thy goodness beyond thought, and power divine.
Speak, ye who best can tell, ye sons of light,
Angels, for ye behold Him, and with songs
And choral symphonies, day without night,
Circle His throne rejoicing, ye, in heaven,
On earth join all ye creatures to extol
Him first, Him last, Him midst, and without end.

.   .   .   .

Join voices, all ye living souls, ye birds,
That, singing, up to heaven-gate ascend,
Bear on your wings and in your notes His praise.
Ye that in waters glide, and ye that walk
The earth, and stately tread, or lowly creep ;
Witness if I be silent, morn or even,
To hill, or valley, fountain, or fresh shade,
Made vocal by my song, and taught His praise.
Hail ! universal Lord ! be bounteous still
To give us only good ; and if the night
Have gathered aught of evil or concealed,
Disperse it, as now light dispels the dark !

> J. MILTON (*Paradise Lost*, Bk. v).

670. FROM 'COMUS'

To the Ocean now I fly,
And those happy climes that lie
Where day never shuts his eye,
Up in the broad fields of the sky ;
There I suck the liquid air
All amidst the Gardens fair
Of Hesperus, and his daughters three
That sing about the golden tree :
Along the crispèd shades and bowers
Revels the spruce and jocund Spring,
The Graces, and the rosy-bosomed Hours,
Thither all their bounties bring,
That there eternal Summer dwells,
And West winds, with musky wing
About the cedarn alleys fling
Nard, and Cassia's balmy smells.
Iris there, with humid bow,
Waters the odorous banks that blow
Flowers of more mingled hue
Than her purfled scarf can show,
And drenches with Elysian dew
(List, mortals, if your ears be true)
Beds of hyacinth, and roses
Where young Adonis oft reposes,
Waxing well of his deep wound
In slumber soft, and on the ground
Sadly sits the Assyrian Queen.

J. MILTON.

671. HE FOR GOD ONLY, SHE FOR GOD IN HIM

Two of far nobler shape, erect and tall,
Godlike erect, with native honour clad,
In naked majesty seemed lords of all,
And worthy seemed.

    .   .   .   .

Not equal, as their sex not equal seemed ;
For contemplation he and valour formed ;
For softness she and sweet attractive grace ;
He for God only, she for God in him.

J. MILTON (Paradise Lost, Bk. iv).

672. ON SHAKESPEARE, 1630

WHAT needs my Shakespeare for his honoured bones,
The labour of an age in pilèd stones,
Or that his hallowed relics should be hid
Under a star-ypointing pyramid ?
Dear son of memory, great heir of Fame,
What need'st thou such weak witness of thy name ?
Thou in our wonder and astonishment
Hast built thyself a livelong monument.
For whilst to the shame of slow-endeavouring art,
Thy easy numbers flow, and that each heart
Hath from the leaves of thy unvalued book,
Those Delphic lines with deep impression took,

Then thou our fancy of itself bereaving,
Dost make us marble with too much conceiving;
And so sepulchred in such pomp dost lie,
That kings for such a tomb would wish to die.

J. MILTON.

673. WOMAN'S HAPPIEST KNOWLEDGE

WHAT thou bidd'st

Unargued I obey: so God ordains;
God is thy law, thou mine: to know no more
Is woman's happiest knowledge, and her praise.
With thee conversing, I forget all time;
All seasons, and their change, all please alike.
Sweet is the breath of morn, her rising sweet,
With charm of earliest birds: pleasant the sun,
When first on this delightful land he spreads
His orient beams, on herb, tree, fruit, and flower,
Glistering with dew: fragrant the fertile earth
After soft showers; and sweet the coming on
Of grateful evening mild; then silent night,
With this her solemn bird, and this fair moon,
And these the gems of heaven, her starry train:
But neither breath of morn, when she ascends
With charm of earliest birds, nor rising sun
On this delightful land, nor herb, fruit, flower
Glistering with dew, nor fragrance after showers,
Nor grateful evening mild, nor silent night,
With this her solemn bird, nor walk by moon,
Or glittering star-light, without thee is sweet.

J. MILTON (Paradise Lost, Bk. iv).

674. ON HIS BLINDNESS

WHEN I consider how my light is spent,
Ere half my days, in this dark world and wide,
And that one talent which is death to hide,
Lodged with me useless, though my soul more bent
To serve therewith my Maker, and present
My true account, lest He returning chide,
Doth God exact day-labour, light denied?
I fondly ask; but Patience, to prevent
That murmur, soon replies, God doth not need
Either man's work or His own gifts: who best
Bear His mild yoke, they serve Him best; His state
Is kingly. Thousands at His bidding speed
And post o'er land and ocean without rest:
They also serve who only stand and wait.

J. MILTON.

675. LYCIDAS

Elegy on a Friend drowned in the Irish Channel

YET once more, O ye laurels, and once more
Ye myrtles brown, with ivy never sere,
I come to pluck your berries harsh and crude,
And with forced fingers rude
Shatter your leaves before the mellowing year.
Bitter constraint, and sad occasion dear
Compels me to disturb your season due :
For Lycidas is dead, dead ere his prime,
Young Lycidas, and hath not left his peer :
Who would not sing for Lycidas ? he knew
Himself to sing, and build the lofty rhyme.
He must not float upon his watery bier
Unwept, and welter to the parching wind,
Without the meed of some melodious tear.
  Begin then, Sisters of the sacred well
That from beneath the seat of Jove doth spring,
Begin, and somewhat loudly sweep the string.
Hence with denial vain and coy excuse,
So may some gentle Muse
With lucky words favour my destined urn ;
And as he passes turn,
And bid fair peace be to my sable shroud.
For we were nursed upon the selfsame hill,
Fed the same flock by fountain, shade, and rill.
  Together both, ere the high lawns appeared
Under the opening eye-lids of the morn,
We drove a-field, and both together heard
What time the gray-fly winds her sultry horn,
Battening our flocks with the fresh dews of night,
Oft till the star that rose, at evening, bright,
Towards heaven's descent had sloped his westering wheel.
Meanwhile the rural ditties were not mute,
Tempered to the oaten flute ;
Rough Satyrs danced, and Fauns with cloven heel,
From the glad sound would not be absent long,
And old Damoetas loved to hear our song.
  But, O the heavy change, now thou art gone,
Now thou art gone, and never must return !
Thee, Shepherd, thee the woods, and desert caves,
With wild thyme and the gadding vine o'ergrown,
And all their echoes mourn.
The willows and the hazel copses green
Shall now no more be seen
Fanning their joyous leaves to thy soft lays.
As killing as the canker to the rose,
Or taint-worm to the weanling herds that graze,

Or frost to flowers, that their gay wardrobe wear
When first the white-thorn blows;
Such, Lycidas, thy loss to shepherds' ear.
　Where were ye, Nymphs, when the remorseless deep
Closed o'er the head of your loved Lycidas?
For neither were ye playing on the steep
Where your old bards, the famous Druids, lie,
Nor on the shaggy top of Mona high,
Nor yet where Deva spreads her wizard stream:
Ay me, I fondly dream!
Had ye been there—for what could that have done?
What could the Muse herself that Orpheus bore,
The Muse herself, for her enchanting son,
Whom universal nature did lament,
When by the rout that made the hideous roar,
His gory visage down the stream was sent,
Down the swift Hebrus to the Lesbian shore?
　Alas! what boots it with uncessant care
To tend the homely slighted shepherd's trade
And strictly meditate the thankless Muse?
Were it not better done, as others use,
To sport with Amaryllis in the shade,
Or with the tangles of Neaera's hair?
Fame is the spur that the clear spirit doth raise
(That last infirmity of noble mind)
To scorn delights, and live laborious days:
But the fair guerdon when we hope to find,
And think to burst out into sudden blaze,
Comes the blind Fury with the abhorrèd shears
And slits the thin-spun life. But not the praise,
Phoebus replied, and touched my trembling ears;
Fame is no plant that grows on mortal soil,
Nor in the glistering foil
Set off to the world, nor in broad rumour lies:
But lives and spreads aloft by those pure eyes,
And perfect witness of all judging Jove;
As he pronounces lastly on each deed,
Of so much fame in heaven expect thy meed.
　O fountain Arethuse, and thou honoured flood
Smooth-sliding Mincius, crowned with vocal reeds,
That strain I heard was of a higher mood:
But now my oat proceeds,
And listens to the herald of the sea
That came in Neptune's plea,
He asked the waves, and asked the felon winds,
What hard mishap hath doomed this gentle swain?
And questioned every gust of rugged wings
That blows from off each beakèd promontory:
They knew not of his story;

And sage Hippotadès their answer brings,
That not a blast was from his dungeon strayed,
The air was calm, and on the level brine
Sleek Panopé with all her sisters played.
It was that fatal and perfidious bark
Built in the eclipse, and rigged with curses dark,
That sunk so low that sacred head of thine.
  Next Camus, reverend sire, went footing slow,
His mantle hairy, and his bonnet sedge,
Inwrought with figures dim, and on the edge
Like to that sanguine flower inscribed with woe :
Ah ! who hath reft (quoth he) my dearest pledge ?
Last came, and last did go
The pilot of the Galilean lake ;
Two massy keys he bore of metals twain
(The golden opes, the iron shuts amain) ;
He shook his mitred locks, and stern bespake,
How well could I have spared for thee, young swain,
Enow of such, as for their bellies' sake
Creep and intrude and climb into the fold !
Of other care they little reckoning make
Than how to scramble at the shearers' feast,
And shove away the worthy bidden guest.
Blind mouths ! that scarce themselves know how to hold
A sheep-hook, or have learned aught else the least
That to the faithful herdman's art belongs !
What recks it them ? What need they ? they are sped ;
And when they list, their lean and flashy songs
Grate on their scrannel pipes of wretched straw,
The hungry sheep look up, and are not fed,
But swoln with wind and the rank mist they draw,
Rot inwardly, and foul contagion spread :
Besides what the grim wolf with privy paw
Daily devours apace, and nothing said,
But that two-handed engine at the door
Stands ready to smite once, and smite no more.
  Return, Alpheus, the dread voice is past
That shrunk thy streams ; return, Sicilian Muse,
And call the vales, and bid them hither cast
Their bells and flowerets of a thousand hues.
Ye valleys low, where the mild whispers use,
Of shades and wanton winds, and gushing brooks,
On whose fresh lap the swart star sparely looks,
Throw hither all your quaint enamelled eyes
That on the green turf suck the honeyed showers,
And purple all the ground with vernal flowers.
Bring the rathe primrose that forsaken dies,
The tufted crow-toe, and pale jessamine,
The white pink, and the pansy freaked with jet,

The glowing violet,
The musk-rose, and the well-attired woodbine,
With cowslips wan that hang the pensive head,
And every flower that sad embroidery wears:
Bid Amaranthus all his beauty shed,
And daffodillies fill their cups with tears,
To strew tne laureat hearse where Lycid lies.
For so to interpose a little ease,
Let our frail thoughts dally with false surmise.
Ay me! whilst thee the shores and sounding seas
Wash far away, where'er thy bones are hurled,
Whether beyond the stormy Hebrides
Where thou perhaps under the whelming tide
Visit'st the bottom of the monstrous world;
Or whether thou, to our moist vows denied,
Sleep'st by the fable of Bellerus old,
Where the great Vision of the guarded mount
Looks towards Namancos and Bayona's hold;
Look homeward, Angel, now, and melt with ruth:
And, O ye dolphins, waft the hapless youth!

Weep no more, woful shepherds, weep no more,
For Lycidas, your sorrow, is not dead,
Sunk though he be beneath the watery floor;
So sinks the day-star in the ocean-bed,
And yet anon repairs his drooping head
And tricks his beams, and with new-spangled ore,
Flames in the forehead of the morning sky:
So Lycidas sunk low, but mounted high
Through the dear might of Him that walked the waves;
Where, other groves and other streams along,
With nectar pure his oozy locks he laves,
And hears the unexpressive nuptial song
In the blest kingdoms meek of joy and love.
There entertain him all the saints above
In solemn troops, and sweet societies,
That sing, and, singing, in their glory move,
And wipe the tears for ever from his eyes.
Now, Lycidas, the shepherds weep no more;
Henceforth thou art the Genius of the shore,
In thy large recompense, and shalt be good
To all that wander in that perilous flood.

Thus sang the uncouth swain to the oaks and rills,
While the still morn went out with sandals grey;
He touched the tender stops of various quills,
With eager thought warbling his Doric lay:
And now the sun had stretched out all the hills,
And now was dropt into the western bay:
At last he rose, and twitched his mantle blue:
To-morrow to fresh woods, and pastures new.   J. MILTON.

676. PRAYER

PRAYER is the soul's sincere desire,
  Uttered or unexpressed ;
The motion of a hidden fire,
  That trembles in the breast.

Prayer is the burden of a sigh ;
  The falling of a tear ;
The upward glancing of an eye,
  When none but God is near.

Prayer is the simplest form of speech
  That infant lips can try ;
Prayer, the sublimest strains that reach
  The Majesty on high.   J. MONTGOMERY.

677. THE FALLING LEAF

WERE I a trembling leaf
  On yonder stately tree,
After a season gay and brief,
  Condemned to fade and flee ;

I should be loath to fall
  Beside the common way,
Weltering in mire, and spurned by
    all,
  Till trodden down to clay.

Nor would I like to spread
  My thin and withered face
In hortus siccus, pale and dead,
  A mummy of my race.

No—on the wings of air
  Might I be left to fly,
I know not and I heed not where,
  A waif of earth and sky !
        J. MONTGOMERY.

678. BELIEVE ME, IF ALL THOSE ENDEARING YOUNG CHARMS

BELIEVE me, if all those endearing young charms,
  Which I gaze on so fondly to-day,
Were to change by to-morrow, and fleet in my arms,
  Like fairy-gifts fading away,
Thou wouldst still be adored, as this moment thou art,
  Let thy loveliness fade as it will,
And around the dear ruin each wish of my heart
  Would entwine itself verdantly still.

It is not while beauty and youth are thine own,
  And thy cheeks unprofaned by a tear,
That the fervour and faith of a soul can be known,
  To which time will but make thee more dear ;
No, the heart that has truly loved never forgets,
  But as truly loves on to the close,
As the sun-flower turns on her god, when he sets,
  The same look which she turned when he rose.
        T. MOORE.

679. A CANADIAN BOAT-SONG

FAINTLY as tolls the evening chime
Our voices keep tune and our oars keep time.
Soon as the woods on shore look dim,
We'll sing at St. Anne's our parting hymn.
Row, brothers, row, the stream runs fast,
The Rapids are near and the daylight's past!

Why should we yet our sail unfurl?
There is not a breath the blue wave to curl;
But, when the wind blows off the shore,
Oh! sweetly we'll rest our weary oar.
Blow, breezes, blow, the stream runs fast,
The Rapids are near and the daylight's past!

Utawa's tide! this trembling moon
Shall see us float over thy surges soon.
Saint of this green isle! hear our prayers,
Oh, grant us cool heavens and favouring airs.
Blow, breezes, blow, the stream runs fast,
The Rapids are near and the daylight's past!
                                                        T. MOORE.

680. OFT IN THE STILLY NIGHT

OFT, in the stilly night,
    Ere slumber's chain has bound me,
Fond Memory brings the light
    Of other days around me;
        The smiles, the tears,
        Of boyhood's years,
    The words of love then spoken;
        The eyes that shone,
        Now dimmed and gone,
    The cheerful hearts now broken!
Thus, in the stilly night,
    Ere Slumber's chain hath bound me,
Sad Memory brings the light
    Of other days around me.

When I remember all
    The friends, so linked together,
I've seen around me fall,
    Like leaves in wintry weather;
        I feel like one,
        Who treads alone
    Some banquet-hall deserted,
        Whose lights are fled,
        Whose garlands dead,
    And all but he departed!
Thus, in the stilly night,
    Ere Slumber's chain hath bound me,
Sad Memory brings the light
    Of other days around me.
                                                        T. MOORE.

681. OH! BREATHE NOT HIS NAME

OH! breathe not his name, let it sleep in the shade
Where cold and unhonoured his relics are laid:
Sad, silent, and dark, be the tears that we shed,
As the night-dew that falls on the grass o'er his head.

But the night-dew that falls, though in silence it weeps,
Shall brighten with verdure the grave where he sleeps;
And the tear that we shed, though in secret it rolls,
Shall long keep his memory green in our souls.   T. MOORE.

682. SHE IS FAR FROM THE LAND

SHE is far from the land where her young hero sleeps,
  And lovers are round her, sighing :
But coldly she turns from their gaze, and weeps,
  For her heart in his grave is lying.

She sings the wild songs of her dear native plains,
  Every note which he loved awaking ;—
Ah ! little they think, who delight in her strains,
  How the heart of the minstrel is breaking.

He had lived for his love, for his country he died,
  They were all that to life had entwined him ;
Nor soon shall the tears of his country be dried,
  Nor long will his love stay behind him.

Oh ! make her a grave where the sunbeams rest,
  When they promise a glorious morrow ;
They'll shine o'er her sleep, like a smile from the West,
  From her own loved island of sorrow.   T. MOORE.

683. THE HARP THAT ONCE THROUGH TARA'S HALLS

THE harp that once through Tara's halls
    The soul of music shed,
  Now hangs as mute on Tara's walls
    As if that soul were fled.
  So sleeps the pride of former days,
    So glory's thrill is o'er,
  And hearts, that once beat high for praise,
    Now feel that pulse no more.

  No more to chiefs and ladies bright
    The harp of Tara swells :
  The chord alone, that breaks at night,
    Its tale of ruin tells.
  Thus Freedom now so seldom wakes,
    The only throb she gives,
  Is when some heart indignant breaks,
    To show that still she lives.   T. MOORE.

684. THE MINSTREL-BOY

THE Minstrel-Boy to the war is gone,
    In the ranks of death you'll find him ;
  His father's sword he has girded on,
    And his wild harp slung behind him.
  'Land of song !' said the warrior-bard,
    'Though all the world betrays thee,
  One sword, at least, thy rights shall guard,
    One faithful harp shall praise thee !'

The Minstrel fell !—but the foeman's chain
  Could not bring his proud soul under ;
The harp he loved ne'er spoke again,
  For he tore his chords asunder ;
And said, ' No chains shall sully thee,
  Thou soul of love and bravery !
Thy songs were made for the brave and free,
  They shall never sound in slavery ! '   T. MOORE.

685. THE MEETING OF THE WATERS

THERE is not in the wide world a valley so sweet
As that vale in whose bosom the bright waters meet ;
Oh ! the last rays of feeling and life must depart,
Ere the bloom of that valley shall fade from my heart.

Yet it was not that nature had shed o'er the scene
Her purest of crystal and brightest of green ;
'Twas not her soft magic of streamlet or hill,
Oh ! no—it was something more exquisite still.

'Twas that friends, the beloved of my bosom, were near,
Who made every dear scene of enchantment more dear,
And who felt how the best charms of nature improve,
When we see them reflected from looks that we love.

Sweet vale of Avoca ! how calm could I rest
In thy bosom of shade, with the friends I love best,
Where the storms that we feel in this cold world should cease,
And our hearts, like thy waters, be mingled in peace.
                         T. MOORE.

686. THE LAST ROSE OF SUMMER

'TIS the last rose of summer
  Left blooming alone ;
All her lovely companions
  Are faded and gone ;
No flower of her kindred,
  No rosebud is nigh,
To reflect back her blushes,
  To give sigh for sigh.

I'll not leave thee, thou lone one !
  To pine on the stem ;
Since the lovely are sleeping,
  Go, sleep thou with them.

Thus kindly I scatter
  Thy leaves o'er the bed,
Where thy mates of the garden
  Lie scentless and dead.

So soon may I follow,
  When friendships decay,
And from Love's shining circle
  The gems drop away.
When true hearts lie withered
  And fond ones are flown,
Oh ! who would inhabit
  This bleak world alone ?
                T. MOORE.

687.　WHEN HE WHO ADORES THEE

When he who adores thee has left but the name
　Of his fault and his sorrows behind,
Oh ! say, wilt thou weep, when they darken the fame
　Of a life that for thee was resigned ?
Yes, weep, and however my foes may condemn,
　Thy tears shall efface their decree ;
For Heaven can witness, though guilty to them,
　I have been but too faithful to thee.

With thee were the dreams of my earliest love ;
　Every thought of my reason was thine ;
In my last humble prayer to the Spirit above
　Thy name shall be mingled with mine.
Oh ! blest are the lovers and friends who shall live
　The days of thy glory to see ;
But the next dearest blessing that Heaven can give
　Is the pride of thus dying for thee.　　　T. Moore.

688.　THE GILLIFLOWER OF GOLD

A golden gilliflower to-day
I wore upon my helm alway,
And won the prize of this tourney.
　　Hah ! hah ! la belle jaune giroflée.

However well Sir Giles might sit,
His sun was weak to wither it,
Lord Miles's blood was dew on it :
　　Hah ! hah ! la belle jaune giroflée.

Although my spear in splinters flew,
From John's steel-coat, my eye was true ;
I wheeled about, and cried for you,
　　Hah ! hah ! la belle jaune giroflée.

Yea, do not doubt my heart was good,
Though my spear flew like rotten wood,
To shout, although I scarcely stood,
　　Hah ! hah ! la belle jaune giroflée.

My hand was steady too, to take
My axe from round my neck, and break
John's steel-coat up for my love's sake.
　　Hah ! hah ! la belle jaune giroflée.

When I stood in my tent again,
Arming afresh, I felt a pain
Take hold of me, I was so fain,
　　Hah ! hah ! la belle jaune giroflée,

To hear : *Honneur aux fils des preux !*
Right in my ears again, and show
The gilliflower blossomed new.
  Hah ! hah ! la belle jaune giroflée.

The Sieur Guillaume against me came,
His tabard bore three points of flame
From a red heart : with little blame,
  Hah ! hah ! la belle jaune giroflée.

Our tough spears crackled up like straw,
He was the first to turn and draw
His sword, that had nor speck nor flaw ;
  Hah ! hah ! la belle jaune giroflée.

But I felt weaker than a maid,
And my brain, dizzied and afraid,
Within my helm a fierce tune played,
  Hah ! hah ! la belle jaune giroflée.

Until I thought of your dear head,
Bowed to the gilliflower bed,
The yellow flowers stained with red ;
  Hah ! hah ! la belle jaune giroflée.

Crash ! how the swords met : *giroflée !*
The fierce tune in my helm would play,
La belle ! la belle ! jaune giroflée !
  Hah ! hah ! la belle jaune giroflée.

Once more the great swords met again :
' *La belle ! la belle !* ' but who fell then ?
Le Sieur Guillaume, who struck down ten ;
  Hah ! hah ! la belle jaune giroflée.

And as with mazed and unarmed face,
Toward my own crown and the Queen's place,
They led me at a gentle pace,
  Hah ! hah ! la belle jaune. giroflée.

I almost saw your quiet head
Bowed o'er the gilliflower bed,
The yellow flowers stained with red.
  Hah ! hah ! la belle jaune giroflée.

         W. MORRIS.

689. PRAISE OF MY LADY

My lady seems of ivory
Forehead,   straight   nose,   and
    cheeks that be
Hollowed a little mournfully.
        Beata mea Domina !

Her forehead, overshadowed much
By bows of hair, has a wave such
As God was good to make for me.
        Beata mea Domina !

Not greatly long my lady's hair,
Nor yet with yellow colour fair,
But thick and crispèd wonderfully:
        Beata mea Domina !

Heavy to make the pale face sad,
And dark, but dead as though
    it had
Been forged by God most wonder-
    fully
        Beata mea Domina !

Of some strange metal, thread by
    thread,
To stand out from my lady's head,
Not moving much to tangle me.
        Beata mea Domina !

Beneath her brows the lids fall
    slow,
The lashes a clear shadow throw
Where I would wish my lips to be.
        Beata mea Domina !

Her great eyes, standing far apart,
Draw up some memory from her
    heart,
And gaze out very mournfully ;
        Beata mea Domina !

So beautiful and kind they are,
But most times looking out afar,
Waiting for something, not for me.
        Beata mea Domina !

I wonder if the lashes long
Are those that do her bright eyes
    wrong,
For always half tears seem to be
        Beata mea Domina !

Lurking below the underlid,
Darkening the place where they
    lie hid :
If they should rise and flow for
    me !
        Beata mea Domina !

Her full lips being made to kiss,
Curled up and pensive each one is ;
This makes me faint to stand and
    see.
        Beata mea Domina !

Her lips are not contented now,
Because the hours pass so slow
Towards a sweet time : (pray for
    me),
        Beata mea Domina !

Nay, hold thy peace ! for who
    can tell ?
But this at least I know full well,
Her lips are parted longingly,
        Beata mea Domina !

So passionate and swift to move,
To pluck at any flying love,
That I grow faint to stand and
    see.
        Beata mea Domina !

Yea ! there beneath them is her
    chin,
So fine and round, it were a sin
To feel no weaker when I see
        Beata mea Domina !

God's dealings ; for with so much
    care
And troublous, faint lines wrought
    in there,
He finishes her facè for me.
        Beata mea Domina !

Of her long neck what shall I
    say ?
What things about her body's
    sway,
Like a knight's pennon or slim
    tree
        Beata mea Domina !

Set gently waving in the wind ;
Or her long hands that I may
    find
On some day sweet to move o'er
    me ?
     Beata mea Domina !
God pity me though, if I missed
The telling, how along her wrist
The veins creep, dying languidly
     Beata mea Domina !

Inside her tender palm and thin.
Now give me pardon, dear,
    wherein
My voice is weak and vexes thee.
     Beata mea Domina !
All men that see her any time,
I charge you straightly in this
    rhyme,
What, and wherever you may be,
     Beata mea Domina !

To kneel before her ; as for me
I choke and grow quite faint to see
My lady moving graciously.
     Beata mea Domina !   W. MORRIS.

690. SUMMER DAWN

PRAY but one prayer for me 'twixt thy closed lips ;
    Think but one thought of me up in the stars.
The summer night waneth, the morning light slips
    Faint and grey 'twixt the leaves of the aspen, betwixt the
        cloud-bars,
That are patiently waiting there for the dawn :
    Patient and colourless, though Heaven's gold
Waits to float through them along with the sun.
Far out in the meadows, above the young corn,
    The heavy elms wait, and restless and cold
The uneasy wind rises ; the roses are dun ;
They pray the long gloom through for daylight new born,
Round the lone house in the midst of the corn.
    Speak but one word to me over the corn,
    Over the tender, bowed locks of the corn.   W. MORRIS.

691. SHAMEFUL DEATH

THERE were four of us about that
    bed ;
  The mass-priest knelt at the side,
I and his mother stood at the head,
  Over his feet lay the bride ;
We were quite sure that he was
    dead,
  Though his eyes were open wide.

He did not die in the night,
  He did not die in the day,
But in the morning twilight
  His spirit passed away,
When neither sun nor moon was
    bright,
  And the trees were merely grey.

He was not slain with the sword,
  Knight's axe, or the knightly
    spear,
Yet spoke he never a word
  After he came in here ;
I cut away the cord
  From the neck of my brother
    dear.

He did not strike one blow,
  For the recreants came behind,
In a place where the hornbeams
    grow,
  A path right hard to find,
For the hornbeam boughs swing so,
  That the twilight makes it blind.

They lighted a great torch then,
  When his arms were pinioned
    fast,
Sir John the knight of the Fen,
  Sir Guy of the Dolorous Blast,
With knights threescore and ten,
  Hung brave Lord Hugh at last.

I am threescore and ten,
  And my hair is all turned grey,
But I met Sir John of the Fen
  Long ago on a summer day,
And am glad to think of the
    moment when
  I took his life away.

I am threescore and ten,
  And my strength is mostly
    passed,
But long ago I and my men,
  When the sky was overcast,
And the smoke rolled over the
    reeds of the fen,
  Slew Guy of the Dolorous Blast.

And now, knights all of you,
  I pray you pray for Sir Hugh,
A good knight and a true,
  And for Alice, his wife, pray
    too.
                    W. MORRIS.

692. OLD LOVE

You must be very old, Sir Giles,
  I said; he said: Yea, very old!
Whereat the mournfullest of smiles
  Creased his dry skin with many a fold.

They hammered out my basnet point
  Into a round salade, he said,
The basnet being quite out of joint,
  Natheless the salade rasps my head.

He gazed at the great fire awhile:
  And you are getting old, Sir John;
(He said this with that cunning smile
  That was most sad) we both wear on;

Knights come to court and look at me,
  With eyebrows up; except my lord,
And my dear lady, none I see
  That know the ways of my old sword.

(My lady! at that word no pang
  Stopped all my blood.) But tell me, John,
Is it quite true that Pagans hang
  So thick about the east, that on

The eastern sea no Venice flag
  Can fly unpaid for? True, I said,
And in such way the miscreants drag
  Christ's cross upon the ground, I dread

That Constantine must fall this year.
  Within my heart: These things are small;
This is not small, that things outwear
  I thought were made for ever, yea, all,

All things go soon or late; I said.
  I saw the duke in court next day;
Just as before, his grand great head
  Above his gold robes dreaming lay,

Only his face was paler; there
  I saw his duchess sit by him;
And she, she was changed more; her hair
  Before my eyes that used to swim,

And make me dizzy with great bliss
  Once, when I used to watch her sit,
Her hair is bright still, yet it is
  As though some dust were thrown on it.

Her eyes are shallower, as though
  Some grey glass were behind; her brow
And cheeks the straining bones show through,
  Are not so good for kissing now.

Her lips are drier now she is
  A great duke's wife these many years,
They will not shudder with a kiss
  As once they did, being moist with tears.

Also her hands have lost that way
  Of clinging that they used to have;
They looked quite easy, as they lay
  Upon the silken cushions brave

With broidery of the apples green
  My Lord Duke bears upon his shield.
Her face, alas! that I have seen
  Look fresher than an April field,

This is all gone now; gone also
  Her tender walking; when she walks
She is most queenly I well know,
  And she is fair still. As the stalks

Of faded summer-lilies are,
  So is she grown now unto me
This spring-time, when the flowers star
  The meadows, birds sing wonderfully.

I warrant once she used to cling
  About his neck and kissed him so,
And then his coming step would ring
  Joy-bells for her; some time ago.

Ah! sometimes like an idle dream
  That hinders true life overmuch,
Sometimes like a lost heaven, these seem
  This love is not so hard to smutch.

W. MORRIS.

693. BEAUTY BATHING

BEAUTY sat bathing by a spring,
  Where fairest shades did hide her ;
The winds blew calm, the birds did sing,
  The cool streams ran beside her.
My wanton thoughts enticed mine eye
  To see what was forbidden :
But better memory said Fie ;
  So vain desire was chidden—
    Hey nonny nonny O !
    Hey nonny nonny !

Into a slumber then I fell,
  And fond imagination
Seemèd to see, but could not tell,
  Her feature or her fashion :
But even as babes in dreams do smile,
  And sometimes fall a-weeping,
So I awaked as wise that while
  As when I fell a-sleeping.   A. MUNDAY.

694. THE LAND O' THE LEAL

I'm wearin' awa', John,
Like snaw-wreaths in thaw, John !
I'm wearin' awa'
  To the land o' the leal !
There 's nae sorrow there, John ;
There 's neither cauld nor care,
  John ;
The day is aye fair
  In the land o' the leal.

Our bonnie bairn 's there, John,
She was baith gude and fair, John,
And, oh, we grudged her sair
  To the land o' the leal !
But sorrow 's sel' wears past,
  John !
And joy 's a-comin' fast, John !
The joy that 's aye to last
  In the land o' the leal.

Sae dear that joy was bought,
  John,
Sae free the battle fought, John,
That sinfu' man e'er brought
  To the land o' the leal.
Oh, dry your glist'ning e'e, John,
My saul langs to be free, John,
And angels beckon me
  To the land o' the leal.

Oh, haud ye leal and true, John !
Your day, it 's wearin' thro',
  John ;
And I'll welcome you
  To the land o' the leal.
Now fare ye weel, my ain John !
This warld 's cares are vain, John ;
We'll meet and we'll be fain
  In the land o' the leal !
    CAROLINA, LADY NAIRNE.

695. CALLER HERRIN'

Wha'll buy my caller herrin'?
They're bonnie fish and halesame
    farin';
  Wha'll buy my caller herrin',
  New drawn frae the Forth?

When ye were sleepin' on your
    pillows,
Dreamed ye aught o' our puir
    fellows,
Darkling as they faced the billows,
A' to fill the woven willows?
  Buy my caller herrin',
  New drawn frae the Forth!

Wha'll buy my caller herrin'?
They're no brought here without
    brave darin';
Buy my caller herrin',
Hauled thro' wind and rain.
  Wha'll buy my caller herrin',
  New drawn frae the Forth?

Wha'll buy my caller herrin'?
Oh, ye may ca' them vulgar farin';
Wives and mithers, maist de-
    spairin',
Ca' them lives o' men.
  Wha'll buy my caller herrin',—
  New drawn frae the Forth?

When the creel o' herrin' passes,
Ladies, clad in silks and laces,
Gather in their braw pelisses,
Cast their heads, and screw their
    faces.
  Wha'll buy my caller herrin',
  New drawn frae the Forth?

Caller herrin' 's no got lightly,
Ye can trip the spring fu' tightlie,
Spite o' tauntin', flauntin', flingin',
Gow has set you a' a-singing
  'Wha'll buy my caller herrin',
  New drawn frae the Forth?'

Neebour wives! now tent my tellin'
When the bonny fish ye're sellin',
At ae word be, in ye're dealin'!
Truth will stand, when a' thing's failin'!
  Wha'll buy my caller herrin',
  New drawn frae the Forth?

                        CAROLINA, LADY NAIRNE.

696. I NEVER LOVED AMBITIOUSLY TO CLIMB

I NEVER loved ambitiously to climb,
Or thrust my hand too far into the fire.
To be in heaven sure is a blessed thing;
But, Atlas-like, to prop heaven on one's back
Cannot but be more labour than delight.
Such is the state of men in honour placed:
They are gold vessels made for servile uses;
High trees that keep the weather from low houses,
But cannot shield the tempest from themselves.
I love to dwell betwixt the hills and dales,
Neither to be so great as to be envied,
Nor yet so poor the world should pity me.

                        T. NASH.

697. SPRING

Spring, the sweet Spring, is the year's pleasant king;
Then blooms each thing, then maids dance in a ring,
Cold doth not sting, the pretty birds do sing,
   Cuckoo, jug-jug, pu-we, to-witta-woo!

The palm and may make country houses gay,
Lambs frisk and play, the shepherds pipe all day,
And we hear aye birds tune this merry lay,
   Cuckoo, jug-jug, pu-we, to-witta-woo.

The fields breathe sweet, the daisies kiss our feet,
Young lovers meet, old wives a-sunning sit,
In every street these tunes our ears do greet,
   Cuckoo, jug-jug, pu-we, to-witta-woo!
      Spring! the sweet Spring!
         T. Nash (*Summer's Last Will and Testament*).

698. LEAD, KINDLY LIGHT

Lead, kindly Light, amid the encircling gloom,
      Lead Thou me on;
The night is dark, and I am far from home,
      Lead Thou me on.
Keep Thou my feet; I do not ask to see
The distant scene: one step enough for me.

I was not ever thus, nor prayed that Thou
      Shouldst lead me on;
I loved to choose and see my path, but now
      Lead Thou me on.
I loved the garish day, and, spite of fears,
Pride ruled my will: remember not past years.

So long Thy power hath blest me, sure it still
      Will lead me on,
O'er moor and fen, o'er crag and torrent, till
      The night is gone,
And with the morn those angel faces smile,
Which I have loved long since, and lost awhile.
                           J. H. Newman.

699. FLOWERS WITHOUT FRUIT

Prune thou thy words, the thoughts control
   That o'er thee swell and throng;
They will condense within thy soul,
   And change to purpose strong.

But he who lets his feelings run
   In soft luxurious flow,
Shrinks when hard service must be done,
   And faints at every woe.

> Faith's meanest deed more favour bears,
>   Where hearts and wills are weighed,
> Than brightest transports, choicest prayers,
>   Which bloom their hour and fade.
>
> J. H. Newman.

700. FROM 'THE DREAM OF GERONTIUS'

Take me away, and in the lowest deep
    There let me be,
And there in hope the lone night-watches keep,
    Told out for me.
There, motionless and happy in my pain,
    Lone, not forlorn,—
There will I sing my sad perpetual strain,
    Until the morn.
There will I sing, and soothe my stricken breast,
    Which ne'er can cease
To throb, and pine, and languish, till possest
    Of its Sole Peace.
There will I sing my absent Lord and Love :—
    Take me away,
That sooner I may rise, and go above,
And see Him in the truth of everlasting day.

J. H. Newman.

701. TO DARKNESS

Hail, thou most sacred, venerable thing !
    What muse is worthy thee to sing—
Thee, from whose pregnant, universal womb
All things, even Light, thy rival, first did come ?
What dares he not attempt that sings of thee,
    Thou first and greatest mystery ?
Who can the secrets of thy essence tell ?
Thou, like the light of God, art inaccessible.

Before great Love this monument did raise,
    This ample theatre of praise ;
Before the folding circles of the sky
Were tuned by Him who is all harmony ;
Before the morning stars their hymn began,
    Before the council held for man,
Before the birth of either time or place,
Thou reign'st unquestioned monarch in the empty space.

Thy native lot thou didst to Light resign,
    But still half of the globe is thine.
Here, with a quiet but yet awful hand,
Like the best emperors thou dost command.

To thee the stars above their brightness owe,
    And mortals their repose below ;
To thy protection fear and sorrow flee,
And those that weary are of Light find rest in thee.

Though light and glory be the Almighty's throne,
    Darkness is His pavilion ;
From that His radiant beauty, but from thee
He has His terror and His majesty :
Thus, when He first proclaimed His sacred law,
    And would His rebel subjects awe,
Like princes on some great solemnity,
He appeared in His robes of state, and clad Himself with thee.
                                                J. Norris.

702. LIKE ANGELS' VISITS

How fading are the joys we dote upon :
Like apparitions seen and gone.
But those which soonest take their flight
Are the most exquisite and strong,—
    Like angels' visits, short and bright ;
Mortality's too weak to bear them long.   J. Norris.

703. I DO NOT LOVE THEE

I DO not love thee !—no ! I do not love thee !
And yet when thou art absent I am sad ;
    And envy even the bright blue sky above thee,
Whose quiet stars may see thee and be glad.

I do not love thee !—yet, I know not why,
Whate'er thou dost seems still well done, to me :
    And often in my solitude I sigh
That those I do love are not more like thee !

I do not love thee !—yet, when thou art gone,
I hate the sound (though those who speak be dear)
    Which breaks the lingering echo of the tone
Thy voice of music leaves upon my ear.

I do not love thee !—yet thy speaking eyes,
With their deep, bright, and most expressive blue,
    Between me and the midnight heaven arise,
Oftener than any eyes I ever knew.

I know I do not love thee ! yet, alas !
Others will scarcely trust my candid heart ;
    And oft I catch them smiling as they pass,
Because they see me gazing where thou art.
                                    The Hon. Mrs. Norton.

704. I LATELY VOWED, BUT 'TWAS IN HASTE

I LATELY vowed, but 'twas in haste,
  That I no more would court
The joys which seem when they are past
  As dull as they are short.

I oft to hate my mistress swear,
  But soon my weakness find:
I make my oaths when she's severe,
  But break them when she's kind.   J. OLDMIXON.

705. BUSY, CURIOUS, THIRSTY FLY

BUSY, curious, thirsty fly,
Drink with me, and drink as I;
Freely welcome to my cup,
Couldst thou sip and sip it up.
Make the most of life you may,
Life is short and wears away.

Both alike are mine and thine
Hastening quick to their decline;
Thine's a summer, mine's no more,
Though repeated to threescore;
Threescore summers, when they're gone,
Will appear as short as one.
                          W. OLDYS.

706. WE ARE THE MUSIC-MAKERS

WE are the music-makers,
  And we are the dreamers of dreams,
Wandering by lone sea-breakers,
  And sitting by desolate streams;
World-losers and world-forsakers,
  On whom the pale moon gleams:
Yet we are the movers and shakers
  Of the world for ever, it seems.

With wonderful deathless ditties
We build up the world's great cities,
  And out of a fabulous story
  We fashion an empire's glory:
One man with a dream, at pleasure,
  Shall go forth and conquer a crown;
And three with a new song's measure
  Can trample a kingdom down.

      .   .   .   .   .   .

A breath of our inspiration
Is the life of each generation;
  A wondrous thing of our dreaming,
  Unearthly, impossible seeming—
The soldier, the king, and the peasant
  Are working together in one,
Till our dream shall become their present,
  And their work in the world be done.
                    A. W. E. O'SHAUGHNESSY.

N

707. THE ENCHANTMENT

I DID but look and love awhile—
    'Twas but for one half-hour;
Then to resist I had no will,
    And now I have no power.

To sigh, and wish, is all my ease,
    Sighs which do heat impart
Enough to melt the coldest ice,
    Yet cannot warm your heart.

Oh, would your pity give my heart
    One corner of your breast,
'Twould learn of yours the winning art,
    And quickly steal the rest.   T. OTWAY.

708. O WOMAN! LOVELY WOMAN

O WOMAN! lovely woman! Nature made thee
To temper man: we had been brutes without you;
Angels are painted fair, to look like you:
There's in you all that we believe of heaven,—
Amazing brightness, purity, and truth,
Eternal joy, and everlasting love.
    T. OTWAY (*Venice Preserved*).

709. WHAT MIGHTY ILLS HAVE NOT BEEN DONE BY WOMAN

WHAT mighty ills have not been done by woman!
Who was't betrayed the Capitol? A woman!
Who lost Mark Antony the world? A woman!
Who was the cause of a long ten years' war,
And laid old Troy in ashes? Woman,
Destructive, damnable, deceitful woman!
    T. OTWAY (*The Orphan*).

710. MAN'S PREROGATIVE

BOOKS are a part of man's prerogative,
    In formal ink they thoughts and voices hold,
That we to them our solitude may give,
    And make time present travel that of old.
Our life fame pieceth longer at the end,
And books it farther backward to extend.
    SIR T. OVERBURY (*The Wife*).

711. WHEN THY BEAUTY APPEARS

    WHEN thy beauty appears
    In its graces and airs
All bright as an angel new dropped from the sky,
At distance I gaze, and am awed by my fears,
    So strangely you dazzle my eye!

> But when without art,
>   Your kind thoughts you impart,
> When your love runs in blushes through every vein;
> When it darts from your eyes, when it pants in your heart,
>   Then I know you're a woman again.

> There's a passion and pride
>   In our sex (she replied),
> And thus, might I gratify both, I would do;
> Still an angel appear to each lover beside,
>   But still be a woman to you!   T. PARNELL.

712. WASTEFUL WOMAN

AH wasteful woman,—she that may
    On her sweet self set her own price,
Knowing he cannot choose but pay,—
    How has she cheapened Paradise!
How given for naught her priceless gift!
    How spoiled the bread and spilled the wine,
Which, spent with due respective thrift,
    Had made brutes men, and men divine!
            COVENTRY PATMORE (*The Angel in the House*, 1854).

713. THE TOYS

MY little Son, who looked from thoughtful eyes,
And moved and spoke in quiet grown-up wise,
Having my law the seventh time disobeyed,
I struck him, and dismissed
With hard words and unkissed,
—His Mother, who was patient, being dead.
Then, fearing lest his grief should hinder sleep,
I visited his bed,
But found him slumbering deep,
With darkened eyelids, and their lashes yet
From his late sobbing wet.
And I, with moan,
Kissing away his tears, left others of my own;
For, on a table drawn beside his head,
He had put, within his reach,
A box of counters and a red-veined stone,
A piece of glass abraded by the beach,
And six or seven shells,
A bottle with bluebells,
And two French copper coins, ranged there with careful art,
To comfort his sad heart.
So, when that night I prayed
To God, I wept, and said:
Ah, when at last we lie with trancèd breath,
Not vexing Thee in death,

And Thou rememberest of what toys
We made our joys,
How weakly understood
Thy great commanded good,
Then, fatherly not less
Than I whom Thou hast moulded from the clay,
Thou'lt leave Thy wrath, and say ;
' I will be sorry for their childishness.'

COVENTRY PATMORE.

714. THE SPOUSAL TIME OF MAY

'Twas when the spousal time of May
  Hangs all the hedge with bridal wreaths,
And air's so sweet the bosom gay
  Gives thanks for every breath it breathes,
When like to like is gladly moved,
  And each thing joins in Spring's refrain,
' Let those love now who never loved ;
  Let those who have loved love again ' ;
That I, in whom the sweet time wrought,
  Lay stretched within a lonely glade,
Abandoned to delicious thought
  Beneath the softly twinkling shade.
The leaves, all stirring, mimicked well
  A neighbouring rush of rivers cold,
And, as the sun or shadow fell,
  So these were green and those were gold ;
In dim recesses hyacinths drooped,
  And breadths of primrose lit the air,
Which, wandering through the woodland, stooped
  And gathered perfumes here and there ;
Upon the spray the squirrel swung,
  And careless songsters, six or seven,
Sang lofty songs the leaves among,
  Fit for their only listener, Heaven.

COVENTRY PATMORE (The Angel in the House).

715. THE MARRIED LOVER

Why, having won her, do I woo ?
  Because her spirit's vestal grace
Provokes me always to pursue,
  But, spirit-like, eludes embrace ;
Because her womanhood is such
  That, as on court-days subjects kiss
The Queen's hand, yet so near a touch
  Affirms no mean familiarness ;
Nay, rather marks more fair the height
  Which can with safety so neglect

To dread, as lower ladies might,
    That grace could meet with disrespect,
Thus she with happy favour feeds
    Allegiance from a love so high
That thence no false conceit proceeds
    Of difference bridged, or state put by;
Because, although in act and word
    As lowly as a wife can be,
Her manners, when they call me lord,
    Remind me 'tis by courtesy;
Not with her least consent of will,
    Which would my proud affection hurt,
But by the noble style that still
    Imputes an unattained desert;
Because her gay and lofty brows,
    When all is won which hope can ask,
Reflect a light of hopeless snows
    That bright in virgin ether bask;
Because, though free of the outer court
    I am, this Temple keeps its shrine
Sacred to Heaven; because, in short,
    She's not and never can be mine.
            COVENTRY PATMORE (*The Angel in the House*).

716. THE BEECH AND THE SAPLING OAK

FOR the tender beech and the sapling oak,
    That grow by the shadowy rill,
You may cut down both at a single stroke,
    You may cut down which you will.

But this you must know, that as long as they grow,
    Whatsoever change may be,
You can never teach either oak or beech
    To be aught but a greenwood tree.
            T. L. PEACOCK (*Maid Marian*).

717. THE GRAVE OF LOVE

I DUG, beneath the cypress shade,
    What well might seem an elfin's grave;
And every pledge in earth I laid,
    That erst thy false affection gave.

I pressed them down the sod beneath;
    I placed one mossy stone above;
And twined the rose's fading wreath
    Around the sepulchre of love.

Frail as thy love, the flowers were dead,
    Ere yet the evening sun was set:
But years shall see the cypress spread,
    Immutable as my regret.   T. L. PEACOCK.

718. LOVE AND AGE

I PLAYED with you 'mid cowslips blowing,
  When I was six and you were four;
When garlands weaving, flower-balls throwing,
  Were pleasures soon to please no more.
Through groves and meads, o'er grass and heather,
  With little playmates, to and fro,
We wandered hand in hand together;
  But that was sixty years ago.

You grew a lovely roseate maiden,
  And still our early love was strong;
Still with no care our days were laden,
  They glided joyously along;
And I did love you very dearly,
  How dearly words want power to show;
I thought your heart was touched as nearly;
  But that was fifty years ago.

Then other lovers came around you,
  Your beauty grew from year to year,
And many a splendid circle found you
  The centre of its glittering sphere.
I saw you then, first vows forsaking,
  On rank and wealth your hand bestow;
Oh, then I thought my heart was breaking,—
  But that was forty years ago.

And I lived on, to wed another:
  No cause she gave me to repine;
And when I heard you were a mother,
  I did not wish the children mine.
My own young flock, in fair progression,
  Made up a pleasant Christmas row:
My joy in them was past expression;—
  But that was thirty years ago.

You grew a matron plump and comely,
  You dwelt in fashion's brightest blaze;
My earthly lot was far more homely;
  But I too had my festal days.
No merrier eyes have ever glistened
  Around the hearth-stone's wintry glow,
Than when my youngest child was christened,—
  But that was twenty years ago.

Time passed. My eldest girl was married,
  And I am now a grandsire grey;
One pet of four years old I've carried
  Among the wild-flowered meads to play.

In our old fields of childish pleasure,
    Where now, as then, the cowslips blow,
She fills her basket's ample measure ;—
    And that is not ten years ago.

But though love's first impassioned blindness
    Has passed away in colder light,
I still have thought of you with kindness,
    And shall do, till our last good-night. .
The ever-rolling silent hours
    Will bring a time we shall not know,
When our young days of gathering flowers
    Will be an hundred years ago.
                T. L. PEACOCK (*Gryll Grange*).

719. IN HIS LAST BINN SIR PETER LIES

IN his last binn Sir Peter lies,
    Who knew not what it was to frown:
Death took him mellow, by surprise,
    And in his cellar stopped him down.
Through all our land we could not boast
    A knight more gay, more prompt than he,
To rise and fill a bumper toast,
    And pass it round with three times three.

None better knew the feast to sway,
    Or keep mirth's boat in better trim ;
For Nature had but little clay
    Like that of which she moulded him.
The meanest guest that graced his board
    Was there the freest of the free,
His bumper toast when Peter poured,
    And passed it round with three times three.

He kept at true good humour's mark
    The social flow of pleasure's tide:
He never made a brow look dark,
    Nor caused a tear, but when he died.
No sorrow round his tomb should dwell:
    More pleased his gay old ghost would be,
For funeral song, and passing bell,
    To hear no sound but three times three.
                T. L. PEACOCK (*Headlong Hall*).

720. IN THE DAYS OF OLD

IN the days of old,
Lovers felt true passion,
Deeming years of sorrow
By a smile repaid.

Now the charms of gold,
Spells of pride and fashion,
Bid them say good-morrow
To the best-loved maid.

Through the forests wild,
O'er the mountains lonely,
They were never weary
Honour to pursue:
If the damsel smiled
Once in seven years only,
All their wanderings dreary
Ample guerdon knew.

Now one day's caprice
Weighs down years of smiling,
Youthful hearts are rovers,
Love is bought and sold:
Fortune's gifts may cease,
Love is less beguiling;
Wiser were the lovers,
In the days of old.

T. L. PEACOCK (*Crotchet Castle*).

721. MARGARET LOVE PEACOCK

LONG night succeeds thy little day;
　O blighted blossom! can it be,
That this grey stone and grassy clay
　Have closed our anxious care of thee?

The half-formed speech of artless thought,
　That spoke a mind beyond thy years;
The song, the dance, by nature taught;
　The sunny smiles, the transient tears;

The symmetry of face and form,
　The eye with light and life replete;
The little heart so fondly warm;
　The voice so musically sweet—

These lost to hope, in memory yet
　Around the hearts that loved thee cling,
Shadowing, with long and vain regret,
　The too fair promise of thy spring.　T. L. PEACOCK.

722. LOVE AND OPPORTUNITY

OH! who art thou, so swiftly flying?
　My name is Love, the child replied;
Swifter I pass than south winds sighing,
　Or streams through summer vales that glide.
And who art thou, his flight pursuing?
　'Tis cold Neglect whom now you see:
The little god you there are viewing,
　Will die, if once he's touched by me.

Oh! who art thou so fast proceeding,
　Ne'er glancing back thine eyes of flame?
Marked but by few, through earth I'm speeding,
　And Opportunity's my name.
What form is that, which scowls beside thee?
　Repentance is the form you see;
Learn, then, the fate may yet betide thee:
　She seizes them who seize not me.

T. L. PEACOCK (*Headlong Hall*).

723. THE WAR SONG OF DINAS VAWR

THE mountain sheep are sweeter,
But the valley sheep are fatter;
We therefore deemed it meeter
To carry off the latter.
We made an expedition;
We met a host and quelled it;
We forced a strong position,
And killed the men who held
  it.

On Dyfed's richest valley,
Where herds of kine were browsing,
We made a mighty sally,
To furnish our carousing.
Fierce warriors rushed to meet us;
We met them, and o'erthrew them:
They struggled hard to beat us;
But we conquered them, and slew
  them.

As we drove our prize at leisure,
The king marched forth to catch
  us:
His rage surpassed all measure,
But his people could not match
  us.

He fled to his hall-pillars;
And, ere our force we led off,
Some sacked his house and cel-
  lars,
While others cut his head off.

We there, in strife bewildering,
Spilt blood enough to swim in:
We orphaned many children,
And widowed many women.
The eagles and the ravens
We glutted with our foemen;
The heroes and the cravens,
The spearmen and the bowmen.

We brought away from battle,
And much their land bemoaned
  them,
Two thousand head of cattle,
And the head of him who owned
  them:
Ednyfed, King of Dyfed,
His head was borne before us;
His wine and beasts supplied our
  feasts,
And his overthrow, our chorus.

T. L. PEACOCK (*The Misfortunes of Elphin*).

724. FOR ENGLAND WHEN WITH FAVOURING GALE

FOR England, when, with favouring gale
  Our gallant ship up channel steered,
And, scudding under easy sail,
  The high blue western land appeared;
To heave the lead the seaman sprung,
And to the pilot cheerly sung,
      'By the deep nine.'

And bearing up to gain the port,
  Some well-known object kept in view;
An abbey-tower, a harbour-fort,
  Or beacon, to the vessel true;
While oft the lead the seaman flung,
And to the pilot cheerly sung,
      'By the mark seven.'

N 3

And as the much-loved shore we near,
  With transport we behold the roof
Where dwelt a friend or partner dear,
  Of faith and love a matchless proof.
The lead once more the seaman flung,
And to the watchful pilot sung,
          'Quarter less five.'

Now to her berth the ship draws nigh:
  We shorten sail—she feels the tide—
'Stand clear the cable,' is the cry—
  The anchor's gone; we safely ride.
The watch is set, and through the night
We hear the seaman with delight
      Proclaim 'All's well.'   W. PEARCE.

725. OENONE'S SONG: CUPID'S CURSE

FAIR and fair and twice so fair,
  As fair as any may be,—
The fairest shepherd on our green,
  A love for any lady.

.   .   .   .

My love is fair, my love is gay,
As fresh as bin the flowers in May,
And of my love my roundelay,
My merry, merry roundelay,
  Concludes with Cupid's curse:
They that do change old love for new,
  Pray gods they change for worse.

My love can pipe, my love can sing,
My love can many a pretty thing,
And of his lovely praises ring
My merry, merry roundelays.
  Amen to Cupid's curse:
They that do change old love for new,
  Pray gods they change for worse.
      G. PEELE (*The Arraignment of Paris*).

726. HIS GOLDEN LOCKS TIME HATH TO SILVER TURNED

HIS golden locks time hath to silver turned;
  O time too swift, O swiftness never ceasing!
His youth 'gainst time and age hath ever spurned,
  But spurned in vain; youth waneth by increasing.
Beauty, strength, youth, are flowers but fading seen.
Duty, faith, love, are roots, and ever green.

His helmet now shall make a hive for bees,
  And lovers' sonnets turned to holy psalms;
A man at arms must now serve on his knees,
  And feed on prayers, which are Age his alms:
But though from court to cottage he depart,
His saint is sure of his unspotted heart.

And when he saddest sits in homely cell,
  He'll teach his swains this carol for a song:
'Blessed be the hearts that wish my Sovereign well,
  Cursed be the souls that think her any wrong.'
Goddess, allow this agèd man his right,
To be your beadsman now that was your knight.
                              G. PEELE (*Polyhymnia*).

727. TO CHARLOTTE PULTENEY

TIMELY blossom, infant fair,
Fondling of a happy pair,
Every morn and every night
Their solicitous delight,
Sleeping, waking, still at ease,
Pleasing, without skill to please;
Little gossip, blithe and hale,
Tattling many a broken tale,
Singing many a tuneless song,
Lavish of a heedless tongue;
Simple maiden, void of art,
Babbling out the very heart,
Yet abandoned to thy will,
Yet imagining no ill,
Yet too innocent to blush;
Like the linnet in the bush
To the mother-linnet's note
Moduling her slender throat;
Chirping forth thy petty joys,
Wanton in the change of toys,
Like the linnet green, in May
Flitting to each bloomy spray;
Wearied then and glad of rest,
Like the linnet in the nest:—
This thy present happy lot,
This, in time will be forgot:
Other pleasures, other cares,
Ever-busy Time prepares;
And thou shalt in thy daughter see,
This picture, once, resembled thee.   A. PHILIPS.

728. A COUNTRY LIFE

How sacred and how innocent
  A country-life appears,
How free from tumult, discontent,
  From flattery or fears!

This was the first and happiest life,
  When man enjoyed himself;
Till pride exchangèd peace for strife,
  And happiness for pelf.

'Twas here the Poets were inspired,
  Here taught the multitude;
The brave they here with honour fired,
  And civilized the rude.

That golden age did entertain
  No passion but of love;
The thoughts of ruling and of gain
  Did ne'er their fancies move!
.   .   .   .

They knew no law nor physic then,
  Nature was all their wit;
And if there yet remain to men
  Content, sure, this is it!   K. PHILIPS.

729. FROM 'LENORE'

Ah, broken is the golden bowl! the spirit flown forever!
Let the bell toll!—a saintly soul floats on the Stygian river!
And, Guy de Vere, hast *thou* no tear?—weep now or nevermore!
See! on yon drear and rigid bier low lies thy love, Lenore!
Come let the burial rite be read—the funeral song be sung!—
An anthem for the queenliest dead that ever died so young—
A dirge for her the doubly dead in that she died so young.

'Wretches! ye loved her for her wealth and hated her for her pride,
And when she fell in feeble health, ye blessed her—that she died!
How *shall* the ritual, then, be read?—the requiem how be sung
By you—by yours, the evil eye,—by yours, the slanderous tongue
That did to death the innocence that died, and died so young?'
Peccavimus ; but rave not thus! and let a Sabbath song
Go up to God so solemnly the dead may feel no wrong!

E. A. POE.

730. ANNABEL LEE

It was many and many a year ago,
    In a kingdom by the sea,
That a maiden there lived whom you may know
    By the name of Annabel Lee;
And this maiden she lived with no other thought
    Than to love and be loved by me.

I was a child and *she* was a child
    In this kingdom by the sea;
But we loved with a love that was more than love—
    I and my Annabel Lee;
With a love that the wingèd seraphs of heaven
    Coveted her and me.

And this was the reason that, long ago,
    In this kingdom by the sea,
A wind blew out of a cloud, chilling
    My beautiful Annabel Lee;
So that her high-born kinsman came
    And bore her away from me,
To shut her up in a sepulchre
    In this kingdom by the sea.

The angels, not half so happy in heaven,
    Went envying her and me—
Yes!—that was the reason (as all men know,
    In this kingdom by the sea)
That the wind came out of the cloud by night,
    Chilling and killing my Annabel Lee.

But our love it was stronger by far than the love
    Of those who were older than we—
    Of many far wiser than we—
And neither the angels in heaven above,
    Nor the demons down under the sea,
Can ever dissever my soul from the soul
    Of the beautiful Annabel Lee.

For the moon never beams without bringing me dreams
    Of the beautiful Annabel Lee ;
And the stars never rise but I feel the bright eyes
    Of the beautiful Annabel Lee ;
And so, all the night-tide, I lie down by the side
Of my darling—my darling—my life and my bride,
    In the sepulchre there by the sea,
    In her tomb by the sounding sea.   E. A. POE.

731. THE RAVEN

ONCE upon a midnight dreary, while I pondered, weak and weary,
Over many a quaint and curious volume of forgotten lore,
    While I nodded, nearly napping, suddenly there came a tapping,
    As of some one gently rapping, rapping at my chamber door.
' 'Tis some visitor,' I muttered, ' tapping at my chamber door—
        Only this, and nothing more.'

Ah, distinctly I remember it was in the bleak December,
And each separate dying ember wrought its ghost upon the floor.
    Eagerly I wished the morrow ;—vainly I had sought to borrow
    From my books surcease of sorrow—sorrow for the lost Lenore—
For the rare and radiant maiden whom the angels name Lenore—
        Nameless here for evermore.

And the silken sad uncertain rustling of each purple curtain
Thrilled me—filled me with fantastic terrors never felt before ;
    So that now, to still the beating of my heart, I stood repeating,
    ' 'Tis some visitor entreating entrance at my chamber door—
Some late visitor entreating entrance at my chamber door ;—
        This it is, and nothing more.'

Presently my soul grew stronger ; hesitating then no longer,
' Sir,' said I, ' or Madam, truly your forgiveness I implore ;
    But the fact is I was napping, and so gently you came rapping,
    And so faintly you came tapping, tapping at my chamber door,
That I scarce was sure I heard you '—here I opened wide the door ;——
        Darkness there, and nothing more.

Deep into that darkness peering, long I stood there wondering, fearing,
Doubting, dreaming dreams no mortals ever dared to dream before ;
    But the silence was unbroken, and the stillness gave no token,
    And the only word there spoken was the whispered word, ' Lenore !'
This I whispered, and an echo murmured back the word, ' Lenore ! '—
        Merely this, and nothing more.

Back into the chamber turning, all my soul within me burning,
Soon again I heard a tapping somewhat louder than before.
  'Surely,' said I, 'surely that is something at my window lattice :
  Let me see, then, what thereat is, and this mystery explore—
Let my heart be still a moment and this mystery explore ;—
        'Tis the wind and nothing more.'

Open here I flung the shutter, when, with many a flirt and flutter,
In there stepped a stately raven of the saintly days of yore ;
  Not the least obeisance made he ; not a minute stopped or stayed he ;
  But, with mien of lord or lady, perched above my chamber door—
Perched upon a bust of Pallas just above my chamber door—
        Perched, and sat, and nothing more.

Then this ebony bird beguiling my sad fancy into smiling,
By the grave and stern decorum of the countenance it wore,
  'Though thy crest be shorn and shaven, thou,' I said, 'art sure no
      craven,
Ghastly grim and ancient raven wandering from the Nightly shore—
Tell me what thy lordly name is on the Night's Plutonian shore !'
        Quoth the Raven, 'Nevermore.'

Much I marvelled this ungainly fowl to hear discourse so plainly,
Though its answer little meaning—little relevancy bore ;
  For we cannot help agreeing that no living human being
  Ever yet was blest with seeing bird above his chamber door—
Bird or beast upon the sculptured bust above his chamber door,
        With such name as 'Nevermore'.

But the raven, sitting lonely on the placid bust, spoke only
That one word, as if his soul in that one word he did outpour.
  Nothing further then he uttered ; not a feather then he fluttered—
  Till I scarcely more than muttered, 'Other friends have flown
      before—
On the morrow *he* will leave me, as my hopes have flown before.'
        Then the bird said, 'Nevermore.'

Startled at the stillness broken by reply so aptly spoken,
'Doubtless,' said I, 'what it utters is its only stock and store,
  Caught from some unhappy master whom unmerciful Disaster
  Followed fast and followed faster till his songs one burden bore—
Till the dirges of his Hope that melancholy burden bore
        Of "Never—nevermore".'

But the Raven still beguiling all my fancy into smiling,
Straight I wheeled a cushioned seat in front of bird, and bust, and
      door ;
  Then upon the velvet sinking, I betook myself to linking
  Fancy unto fancy, thinking what this ominous bird of yore—
What this grim, ungainly, ghastly, gaunt and ominous bird of yore
        Meant in croaking 'Nevermore'.

This I sat engaged in guessing, but no syllable expressing
To the fowl whose fiery eyes now burned into my bosom's core ;
  This and more I sat divining, with my head at ease reclining
  On the cushion's velvet lining that the lamplight gloated o'er,
But whose velvet violet lining with the lamplight gloating o'er,
     She shall press, ah, nevermore !

Then methought the air grew denser, perfumed from an unseen
    censer
Swung by Seraphim whose footfalls tinkled on the tufted floor.
  ' Wretch,' I cried, ' thy God hath lent thee—by these angels he hath
  sent thee
Respite—respite and nepenthe, from thy memories of Lenore !
Quaff, oh quaff this kind nepenthe and forget this lost Lenore ! '
     Quoth the Raven, ' Nevermore.'

' Prophet ! ' said I, ' thing of evil !—prophet still, if bird or devil !—
Whether Tempter sent, or whether tempest tossed thee here ashore,
  Desolate yet all undaunted, on this desert land enchanted—
  On this home by horror haunted—tell me truly, I implore—
Is there—*is* there balm in Gilead ?—tell me—tell me, I implore ! '
     Quoth the Raven, ' Nevermore.'

' Prophet ! ' said I, ' thing of evil—prophet still, if bird or devil !
By that Heaven that bends above us—by that God we both adore—
  Tell this soul with sorrow laden if, within the distant Aidenn,
  It shall clasp a sainted maiden whom the angels name Lenore—
Clasp a rare and radiant maiden whom the angels name Lenore.'
     Quoth the Raven, ' Nevermore.'

' Be that word our sign in parting, bird or fiend,' I shrieked, up-
    starting—
' Get thee back into the tempest and the Night's Plutonian shore !
  Leave no black plume as a token of that lie thy soul hath spoken !
  Leave my loneliness unbroken !—quit the bust above my door !
Take thy beak from out my heart, and take thy form from off my door ! '
     Quoth the Raven, ' Nevermore.'

And the Raven, never flitting, still is sitting, still is sitting
On the pallid bust of Pallas just above my chamber door ;
  And his eyes have all the seeming of a demon's that is dreaming,
  And the lamplight o'er him streaming throws his shadow on the floor ;
And my soul from out that shadow that lies floating on the floor
     Shall be lifted—nevermore !   E. A. POE.

732. FOR ANNIE

THANK Heaven ! the crisis—
  The danger is past,
And the lingering illness
  Is over at last—
And the fever called ' Living '
  Is conquered at last.

Sadly, I know
  I am shorn of my strength,
And no muscle I move
  As I lie at full length—
But no matter !—I feel
  I am better at length.

And I rest so composedly
  Now, in my bed,
That any beholder
  Might fancy me dead—
Might start at beholding me,
  Thinking me dead.

The moaning and groaning,
  The sighing and sobbing,
Are quieted now,
  With that horrible throbbing
At heart :—ah, that horrible,
  Horrible throbbing !

The sickness—the nausea—
  The pitiless pain—
Have ceased, with the fever
  That maddened my brain—
With the fever called ' Living '
  That burned in my brain.

And oh ! of all tortures
  That torture the worst
Has abated—the terrible
  Torture of thirst
For the naphthaline river
  Of Passion accurst :—
I have drunk of a water
  That quenches all thirst :—

Of a water that flows,
  With a lullaby sound,
From a spring but a very few
  Feet under ground—
From a cavern not very far
  Down under ground.

And ah ! let it never
  Be foolishly said
That my room it is gloomy
  And narrow my bed ;
For man never slept
  In a different bed—
And, *to sleep,* you must slumber
  In just such a bed.

My tantalized spirit
  Here blandly reposes,
Forgetting, or never
  Regretting its roses—
Its old agitations
  Of myrtles and roses ;

For now, while so quietly
  Lying, it fancies
A holier odour
  About it, of pansies—
A rosemary odour,
  Commingled with pansies—
With rue and the beautiful
  Puritan pansies.

And so it lies happily,
  Bathing in many
A dream of the truth
  And the beauty of Annie—
Drowned in a bath
  Of the tresses of Annie.

She tenderly kissed me,
  She fondly caressed,
And then I fell gently
  To sleep on her breast—
Deeply to sleep
  From the heaven of her breast.

When the light was extinguished,
  She covered me warm,
And she prayed to the angels
  To keep me from harm—
To the queen of the angels
  To shield me from harm.

And I lie so composedly,
  Now, in my bed
(Knowing her love),
  That you fancy me dead—
And I rest so contentedly,
  Now, in my bed
(With her love at my breast),
  That you fancy me dead—
That you shudder to look at me,
  Thinking me dead ;—

But my heart it is brighter
  Than all of the many
Stars in the sky,
  For it sparkles with Annie—
It glows with the light
  Of the love of my Annie—
With the thought of the light
  Of the eyes of my Annie.
               E. A. POE.

733. A LITTLE LEARNING IS A DANGEROUS THING

A LITTLE learning is a dangerous thing;
Drink deep, or taste not the Pierian spring:
These shallow draughts intoxicate the brain,
And drinking largely sobers us again.
Fired at first sight with what the Muse imparts,
In fearless youth we tempt the heights of arts,
While from the bounded level of our mind,
Short views we take, nor see the lengths behind;
But more advanced, behold with strange surprise,
New distant scenes of endless science rise!
So pleased at first the towering Alps we try,
Mount o'er the vales, and seem to tread the sky,
The eternal snows appear already past,
And the first clouds and mountains seem the last:
But those attained, we tremble to survey
The growing labours of the lengthened way,
The increasing prospect tires our wandering eyes,
Hills peep o'er hills, and Alps on Alps arise!
                              A. POPE (*Essay on Criticism*).

734. THE MAN OF ROSS

ALL our praises why should Lords engross?
Rise, honest Muse! and sing the man of Ross.

.   .   .   .

Behold the market-place with poor o'erspread!
The Man of Ross divides the weekly bread;
He feeds yon almshouse, neat, but void of state,
Where Age and Want sit smiling at the gate;
Him portioned maids, apprenticed orphans blessed,
The young who labour, and the old who rest.
Is any sick? the Man of Ross relieves,
Prescribes, attends, the medicine makes, and gives.
Is there a variance? enter but his door,
Balked are the courts, and contest is no more.
Despairing quacks with curses fled the place,
And vile attorneys, now a useless race.
    Thrice happy man! enabled to pursue
What all so wish, but want the power to do!
O say! what sums that generous hand supply?
What mines, to swell that boundless charity?
    Of debts and taxes, wife and children clear,
This man possessed—five hundred pounds a year.
Blush, grandeur, blush! proud Courts, withdraw your blaze!
Ye little stars! hide your diminished rays.
                              A. POPE (*Moral Essays*).

735. THE ART OF WRITING

But most by numbers judge a poet's song,
And smooth or rough, with them, is right or wrong:
In the bright Muse though thousand charms conspire,
Her voice is all these tuneful fools admire;
Who haunt Parnassus but to please their ear,
Not mend their minds; as some to church repair,
Not for the doctrine, but the music there.
These equal syllables alone require,
Though oft the ear the open vowels tire;
While expletives their feeble aid do join;
And ten low words oft creep in one dull line:
While they ring round the same unvaried chimes
With sure returns of still expected rhymes;
Where'er you find ' the cooling western breeze ',
In the next line, it ' whispers through the trees ':
If crystal streams ' with pleasing murmurs creep ',
The reader's threatened, not in vain, with ' sleep ':
Then, at the last and only couplet fraught
With some unmeaning thing they call a thought,
A needless Alexandrine ends the song
That, like a wounded snake, drags its slow length along.

. . . .

True ease in writing comes from art, not chance,
As those move easiest who have learned to dance.

A. Pope (Essay on Criticism).

736. THE UNIVERSAL PRAYER

Father of all! in every age,
  In every clime adored,
By saint, by savage, and by sage,
  Jehovah, Jove, or Lord!

Thou great First Cause, least
    understood!
  Who all my sense confined
To know but this, that Thou art
    good,
  And that myself am blind;

Yet gave me in this dark estate,
  To see the good from ill:
And binding nature fast in fate,
  Left free the human will.

. . . . . .

To Thee, whose temple is all space,
  Whose altar, earth, sea, skies,
One chorus let all being raise;
  All nature's incense rise!

A. Pope.

737. ODE ON SOLITUDE

Happy the man, whose wish and care
A few paternal acres bound,
Content to breathe his native air,
  In his own ground.

Whose herds with milk, whose fields with bread,
Whose flocks supply him with attire,
Whose trees in summer yield him shade,
    In winter fire.

Blessed, who can unconcern'dly find
Hours, days, and years slide soft away,
In health of body, peace of mind,
    Quiet by day,

Sound sleep by night; study and ease,
Together mixed; sweet recreation;
And Innocence, which most does please
    With meditation.

Thus let me live, unseen, unknown,
Thus unlamented let me die,
Steal from the world, and not a stone
    Tell where I lie.   A. POPE.

738. ON MRS. CORBET

Who died of a cancer in her breast.

HERE rests a woman, good without pretence,
Blessed with plain reason, and with sober sense:
No conquests she, but o'er herself, desired,
No arts essayed, but not to be admired.
Passion and pride were to her soul unknown,
Convinced that virtue only is our own.
So unaffected, so composed a mind;
So firm, so soft; so strong, yet so refined;
Heaven, as its purest gold, by tortures tried;
The saint sustained it, but the woman died. A. POPE.

739. ON A CERTAIN LADY AT COURT

[HENRIETTA HOWARD, COUNTESS OF SUFFOLK]

I KNOW the thing that's most uncommon
    (Envy, be silent, and attend);
I know a reasonable woman,
    Handsome and witty, yet a friend.

Not warped by passion, awed by rumour,
    Not grave through pride, or gay through folly;
An equal mixture of good humour,
    And sensible soft melancholy.

'Has she no faults then,' Envy says, 'Sir?'
    Yes, she has one, I must aver;
When all the world conspires to praise her,
    The woman's deaf, and does not hear!   A. POPE.

740. FROM THE 'ESSAY ON MAN'

Know then thyself, presume not God to scan;
The proper study of mankind is Man.

Vice is a monster of so frightful mien,
As, to be hated, needs but to be seen.

For modes of faith let graceless zealots fight;
His can't be wrong whose life is in the right;
In faith and hope the world will disagree,
But all mankind's concern is charity.

Honour and shame from no condition rise;
Act well your part, there all the honour lies.

What can ennoble sots, or slaves, or cowards?
Alas! not all the blood of all the Howards.

A wit's a feather, and a chief a rod;
An honest man's the noblest work of God.

If parts allure thee, think how Bacon shined,
The wisest, brightest, meanest of mankind:
Or ravished with the whistling of a name,
See Cromwell, damned to everlasting fame.

Know then this truth (enough for Man to know),
Virtue alone is happiness below.   A. Pope.

741. LO, THE POOR INDIAN

Lo, the poor Indian! whose untutored mind
Sees God in clouds, or hears him in the wind;
His soul, proud science never taught to stray
Far as the solar walk, or milky way;
Yet simple nature to his hope has given,
Behind the cloud-topped hill, a humbler heaven;
Some safer world in depth of woods embraced,
Some happier island in the watery waste,
Where slaves once more their native land behold,
No fiends torment, no Christians thirst for gold.
To Be, contents his natural desire,
He asks no angel's wing, no seraph's fire;
But thinks, admitted to that equal sky,
His faithful dog shall bear him company.
                              A. Pope (*Essay on Man*).

742. INTENDED FOR SIR ISAAC NEWTON IN WESTMINSTER ABBEY

Nature and Nature's Laws lay hid in Night:
God said, *Let Newton be!* and all was Light.
                                        A. Pope.

743. EPITAPH ON GAY IN WESTMINSTER ABBEY

Of manners gentle, of affections mild ;
In wit, a man ; simplicity, a child :
With native humour tempering virtuous rage,
Formed to delight at once and lash the age :
Above temptation, in a low estate,
And uncorrupted, even among the great :
A safe companion, and an easy friend,
Unblamed through life, lamented in thy end.
These are thy honours ! not that here thy bust
Is mixed with heroes, or with kings thy dust ;
But that the worthy and the good shall say,
Striking their pensive bosoms—' *Here* lies Gay.'

A. POPE.

744. ADDISON (1732-4)

Statesman, yet friend to Truth ! of soul sincere,
In action faithful, and in honour clear ;
Who broke no promise, served no private end,
Who gained no title, and who lost no friend ;
Ennobled by himself, by all approved,
And praised, unenvied, by the Muse he loved.

A. POPE (*Moral Essays*).

745. FROM THE PROLOGUE TO ' CATO '

To wake the soul by tender strokes of art,
To raise the genius, and to mend the heart ;
To make mankind in conscious virtue bold,
Live o'er each scene, and be what they behold :
For this the Tragic Muse first trod the stage,
Commanding tears to stream through every age ;
Tyrants no more their savage nature kept,
And foes to virtue wondered how they wept.
Our author shuns by vulgar springs to move
The hero's glory, or the virgin's love ;
In pitying love, we but our weakness show,
And wild ambition well deserves its woe.
Here tears shall flow from a more generous cause,
Such tears as patriots shed for dying laws :
He bids your breast with ancient ardour rise,
And calls forth Roman drops from British eyes.
Virtue confessed in human shape he draws,
What Plato thought, and godlike Cato was :
No common object to your sight displays,
But what with pleasure Heaven itself surveys,

A brave man struggling in the storms of fate,
And greatly falling, with a falling State.

. . . .

Your scene precariously subsists too long
On French translation, and Italian song.
Dare to have sense yourselves; assert the stage,
Be justly warmed with your own native rage:
Such plays alone should win a British ear,
As Cato's self had not disdained to hear.   A. POPE.

746. VITAL SPARK OF HEAVENLY FLAME

VITAL spark of heavenly flame!
Quit, oh quit this mortal frame;
Trembling, hoping, lingering, flying,
Oh the pain, the bliss of dying!
Cease, fond Nature, cease thy strife,
And let me languish into life.

Hark! they whisper; Angels say,
'Sister Spirit, come away!'
What is this absorbs me quite?
Steals my senses, shuts my sight,
Drowns my spirits, draws my breath?
Tell me, my Soul, can this be death?

The world recedes; it disappears!
Heaven opens on my eyes! my ears
    With sounds seraphic ring:
Lend, lend your wings! I mount! I fly!
O Grave! where is thy victory?
    O Death! where is thy sting?   A. POPE.

747. ADDISON (1735)

WERE there one whose fires
True genius kindles, and fair fame inspires;
Blest with each talent and each art to please,
And born to write, converse, and live with ease:
Should such a man, too fond to rule alone,
Bear, like the Turk, no brother near the throne,
View him with scornful, yet with jealous eyes,
And hate for arts that caused himself to rise;
Damn with faint praise, assent with civil leer,
And, without sneering, teach the rest to sneer;
Willing to wound, and yet afraid to strike,
Just hint a fault, and hesitate dislike;
Alike, reserved to blame, or to commend,
A timorous foe, and a suspicious friend;

Dreading even fools, by flatterers besieged,
And so obliging that he ne'er obliged ;
Like Cato, give his little Senate laws,
And sit attentive to his own applause ;
While wits and Templars every sentence raise,
And wonder with a foolish face of praise—
Who but must laugh, if such a man there be ?
Who would not weep, if Atticus were he !

A. POPE (Epistle to Dr. Arbuthnot).

748. FROM ' THE OLD MAN'S WISH '

WITH a pudding on Sunday, and stout humming liquor,
And remnants of Latin to puzzle the vicar ;
With a hidden reserve of Burgundy wine
To drink the King's health as oft as I dine :
  May I govern my passions with an absolute sway,
  And grow wiser and better as my strength wears away,
  Without gout or stone, by a gentle decay.

With Plutarch and Horace and one or two more
Of the best wits that lived in the ages before ;
With a dish of roast mutton, not venison nor teal,
And clean, though coarse, linen at every meal :
  May I govern my passions with an absolute sway,
  And grow wiser and better as my strength wears away,
  Without gout or stone, by a gentle decay.   W. POPE.

749. DEATH

'TWAS man himself
Brought Death into the world ; and man himself
Gave keenness to his darts, quickened his pace,
And multiplied destruction on mankind.

.   .   .   .

One murder made a villain,
Millions a hero. Princes were privileged
To kill, and numbers sanctified the crime. B. PORTEUS.

750. THE VICAR

HIS talk was like a spring, which runs
  With rapid change from rocks to roses :
It slipped from politics to puns,
  It passed from Mahomet to Moses ;
Beginning with the laws which keep
  The planets in their radiant courses,
And ending with some precept deep
  For dressing eels, or shoeing horses.

.   .   .   .   .   .

His sermon never said or showed
　　That Earth is foul, that Heaven is gracious,
Without refreshment on the road
　　From Jerome or from Athanasius:
And sure a righteous zeal inspired
　　The hand and head that penned and planned them,
For all who understood admired,
　　And some who did not understand them.
　　　　　　　　W. M. Praed (*Every-day Characters*).

751. STANZAS TO THE SPEAKER ASLEEP

Sleep, Mr. Speaker; it's surely fair
If you don't in your bed, that you should in your chair.
Longer and longer still they grow,
Tory and Radical, Aye and No;
Talking by night, and talking by day;—
Sleep, Mr. Speaker; sleep, sleep while you may!

Sleep, Mr. Speaker; slumber lies
Light and brief on a Speaker's eyes;
Fielden or Finn, in a minute or two,
Some disorderly thing will do;
Riot will chase repose away;—
Sleep, Mr. Speaker; sleep, sleep while you may:

Sleep, Mr. Speaker; Cobbett will soon
Move to abolish the sun and moon;
Hume, no doubt, will be taking the sense
Of the House on a saving of thirteen pence;
Grattan will growl, or Baldwin bray;—
Sleep, Mr. Speaker; sleep, sleep while you may!

Sleep, Mr. Speaker; dream of the time
When loyalty was not quite a crime;
When Grant was a pupil in Canning's school,
When Palmerston fancied Wood a fool;
Lord, how principles pass away!
Sleep, Mr. Speaker; sleep, sleep while you may!

Sleep, Mr. Speaker; sweet to men
Is the sleep that cometh but now and then;
Sweet to the sorrowful, sweet to the ill,
Sweet to the children that work in a mill,
You have more need of sleep than they;—
Sleep, Mr. Speaker; sleep, sleep while you may!
　　　　　　　　　　　　　W. M. Praed.

752. SCHOOL AND SCHOOLFELLOWS

' Floreat Etona '

TWELVE years ago I made a mock
  Of filthy trades and traffics :
I wondered what they meant by stock ;
  I wrote delightful sapphics ;
I knew the streets of Rome and Troy ;
  I supped with Fates and Furies,—
Twelve years ago I was a boy,
  A happy boy, at Drury's.

Twelve years ago !—how many a thought
  Of faded pains and pleasures
Those whispered syllables have brought
  From Memory's hoarded treasures !
The fields, the farms, the bats, the books,
  The glories and disgraces,
The voices of dear friends, the looks
  Of all familiar faces !

Kind *Mater* smiles again to me,
  As bright as when we parted ;
I seem again the frank, the free,
  Stout-limbed and simple-hearted !
Pursuing every idle dream,
  And shunning every warning ;
With no hard work but Bovney stream,
  No chill except Long Morning :

Now stopping Harry Vernon's ball
  That rattled like a rocket ;
Now hearing Wentworth's ' Fourteen all ! '
  And striking for the pocket ;
Now feasting on a cheese and flitch,—
  Now drinking from the pewter ;
Now leaping over Chalvey ditch,
  Now laughing at my tutor.

Where are my friends ? I am alone ;
  No playmate shares my beaker :
Some lie beneath the churchyard stone,
  And some—before the Speaker ;
And some compose a tragedy,
  And some compose a rondeau ;
And some draw sword for liberty,
  And some draw pleas for John Doe.

Tom Mill was used to blacken eyes
  Without the fear of sessions ;
Charles Medlar loathed false quantities
  As much as false professions ;

Now Mill keeps order in the land,
  A magistrate pedantic ;
And Medlar's feet repose unscanned
  Beneath the wide Atlantic.

Wild Nick, whose oaths made such a din,
  Does Dr. Martext's duty ;
And Mullion, with that monstrous chin,
  Is married to a Beauty ;
And Darrell studies, week by week,
  His Mant, and not his Manton ;
And Ball, who was but poor at Greek,
  Is very rich at Canton.

And I am eight-and-twenty now ;—
  The world's cold chains have bound me ;
And darker shades are on my brow,
  And sadder scenes around me :
In Parliament I fill my seat,
  With many other noodles ;
And lay my head in Jermyn Street,
  And sip my hock at Boodle's.

But often when the cares of life
  Have sent my temples aching,
When visions haunt me of a wife,
  When duns await my waking,
When Lady Jane is in a pet,
  Or Hoby in a hurry,
When Captain Hazard wins a bet,
  Or Beaulieu spoils a curry,—

For hours and hours I think and talk
  Of each remembered hobby ;
I long to lounge in Poets' Walk,
  To shiver in the Lobby ;
I wish that I could run away
  From House and Court and Levée,
Where bearded men appear to-day
  Just Eton boys grown heavy,—

That I could bask in childhood's sun,
  And dance o'er childhood's roses,
And find huge wealth in one pound one,
  Vast wit in broken noses,
And play Sir Giles at Datchet Lane,
  And call the milkmaids Houris,—
That I could be a boy again,—
  A happy boy,—at Drury's.   W. M. PRAED.

753. A LETTER OF ADVICE

(From Miss Medora Trevilian, at Padua, to Miss Araminta Vavasour, in London.)

You tell me you're promised a lover,
  My own Araminta, next week ;
Why cannot my fancy discover
  The hue of his coat and his cheek ?
Alas ! if he look like another,
  A vicar, a banker, a beau,
Be deaf to your father and mother,
  My own Araminta, say ' No ! '

Miss Lane, at her Temple of Fashion,
  Taught us both how to sing and to speak,
And we loved one another with passion,
  Before we had been there a week :
You gave me a ring for a token ;
  I wear it wherever I go ;
I gave you a chain—is it broken ?
  My own Araminta, say ' No ! '

O think of our favourite cottage,
  And think of our dear Lalla Rookh !
How we shared with the milkmaids their pottage,
  And drank of the stream from the brook ;
How fondly our loving lips faltered,
  ' What further can grandeur bestow ? '
My heart is the same ;—is yours altered ?
  My own Araminta, say ' No ! '

Remember the thrilling romances
  We read on the bank in the glen ;
Remember the suitors our fancies
  Would picture for both of us then.
They wore the red cross on their shoulder,
  They had vanquished and pardoned their foe—
Sweet friend, are you wiser or colder ?
  My own Araminta, say ' No ! '

You know when Lord Rigmarole's carriage
  Drove off with your cousin Justine,
You wept, dearest girl, at the marriage,
  And whispered, ' How base she has been ! '
You said you were sure it would kill you
  If ever your husband looked so ;
And you will not apostatize,—will you ?
  My own Araminta, say ' No ! '

When I heard I was going abroad, love,
 I thought I was going to die;
We walked arm-in-arm to the road, love,
 We looked arm-in-arm to the sky;
And I said, 'When a foreign postilion
 Has hurried me off to the Po,
Forget not Medora Trevilian:
 My own Araminta, say "No!"'

We parted! but sympathy's fetters
 Reach far over valley and hill;
I muse o'er your exquisite letters,
 And feel that your heart is mine still;
And he who would share it with me, love,—
 The richest of treasures below,—
If he's not what Orlando should be, love,
 My own Araminta, say 'No!'

If he wears a top-boot in his wooing,
 If he comes to you riding a cob,
If he talks of his baking or brewing,
 If he puts up his feet on the hob,
If he ever drinks port after dinner,
 If his brow or his breeding is low,
If he calls himself 'Thompson' or 'Skinner',—
 My own Araminta, say 'No!'

If he studies the news in the papers
 While you are preparing the tea,
If he talks of the damps or the vapours,
 While moonlight lies soft on the sea,
If he's sleepy while you are capricious,
 If he has not a musical 'Oh!'
If he does not call *Werther* delicious,—
 My own Araminta, say 'No!'

If he ever sets foot in the City
 Among the stockbrokers and Jews,
If he has not a heart full of pity,
 If he don't stand six feet in his shoes,
If his lips are not redder than roses,
 If his hands are not whiter than snow,
If he has not the model of noses,—
 My own Araminta, say 'No!'

If he speaks of a tax or a duty,
 If he does not look grand on his knees,
If he's blind to a landscape of beauty,
 Hills, valleys, rocks, waters, and trees,

If he dotes not on desolate towers,
  If he likes not to hear the blast blow,
If he knows not the language of flowers,—
  My own Araminta, say ' No ! '

He must walk—like a god of old story
  Come down from the home of his rest;
He must smile—like the sun in his glory
  On the bud, he loves ever the best;
And oh ! from its ivory portal
  Like music his soft speech must flow !
If he speak, smile, or walk like a mortal,
  My own Araminta, say ' No ! '

Don't listen to tales of his bounty,
  Don't hear what they say of his birth,
Don't look at his seat in the county,
  Don't calculate what he is worth;
But give him a theme to write verse on,
  And see if he turns out his toe;
If he's only an excellent person,—
  My own Araminta, say ' No ! '   W. M. PRAED.

754. EPITAPH

NOBLES and heralds, by your leave,
  Here lies what once was Matthew Prior,
The son of Adam and of Eve;
  Can Bourbon or Nassau claim higher ?   M. PRIOR.

755. THE DYING ADRIAN TO HIS SOUL

POOR, little, pretty, fluttering thing,
  Must we no longer live together ?
And dost thou prune thy trembling wing,
  To take thy flight thou knowst not whither ?
Thy humorous vein, thy pleasing folly,
  Lies all neglected, all forgot:
And pensive, wavering, melancholy,
  Thou dread'st and hop'st thou know'st not what.
                                          M. PRIOR.

756. THE MERCHANT, TO SECURE HIS TREASURE

  THE merchant, to secure his treasure,
    Conveys it in a borrowed name:
  Euphelia serves to grace my measure,
    But Chloe is my real flame.

My softest verse, my darling lyre,
    Upon Euphelia's toilet lay—
When Chloe noted her desire
    That I should sing, that I should play.

My lyre I tune, my voice I raise,
    But with my numbers mix my sighs;
And whilst I sing Euphelia's praise,
    I fix my soul on Chloe's eyes.

Fair Chloe blushed: Euphelia frowned:
    I sung, and gazed; I played, and trembled:
And Venus to the Loves around
    Remarked how ill we all dissembled.   M. PRIOR.

757. EPIGRAM

To John I owed great obligation;
    But John unhappily thought fit
To publish it to all the nation,
    Sure John and I are more than quit.   M. PRIOR.

758. THE LADY WHO OFFERS HER LOOKING-GLASS TO VENUS

VENUS, take my votive glass;
Since I am not what I was,
What from this day I shall be,
Venus, let me never see.   M. PRIOR.

759. NATURE AND ART

WHAT I speak, my fair Chloe, and what I write, shows
    The difference there is betwixt nature and art:
I court others in verse—but I love thee in prose;
    And they have my whimsies—but thou hast my heart.

The God of us verse-men, you know, child, the Sun,
    How after his journeys he sets up his rest:
If at morning o'er Earth 'tis his fancy to run;
    At night he declines on his Thetis's breast.

So when I am wearied with wandering all day,
    To thee, my delight, in the evening I come:
No matter what beauties I saw in my way,
    They were but my visits, but thou art my home.

Then finish, dear Chloe, this pastoral war;
    And let us like Horace and Lydia agree;
For thou art a girl as much brighter than her,
    As he was a poet sublimer than me.   M. PRIOR.

760. WHAT SEEMS SO DARK TO THY DIM SIGHT

WHAT seems so dark to thy dim sight
May be a shadow, seen aright,
Making some brightness doubly bright.

. . . . . .

The cry wrung from thy spirit's pain
May echo on some far-off plain,
And guide a wanderer home again.

Fail—yet rejoice ; because no less
The failure that makes thy distress
May teach another full success.

. . . . . .

And trust,—as if already plain,
How just thy share of loss and pain
Is for another fuller gain.

A. A. PROCTER (*Light and Shade*).

761. COME, ALL YE FEATHERY PEOPLE

COME, all ye feathery people of mid air,
Who sleep 'midst rocks, or on the mountain summits
Lie down with the wild winds ; and ye who build
Your homes amidst green leaves by grottos cool ;
And ye who on the flat sands hoard your eggs
For suns to ripen, come ! O phoenix rare !
If death hath spared thee, or philosophic search
Permit thee still to own thy haunted nest,
Perfect Arabian ;—lonely nightingale !
Dark creature, who art silent all day long,
But when pale eve unseals thy clear throat, loosest
Thy twilight music on the dreamy boughs
Until they waken ; and thou, cuckoo bird,
Who art the ghost of sound, having no shape
Material, but dost wander far and near,
Like untouched Echo whom the woods deny
Sight of her love,—come all to my slow charm !
Come, thou sky-climbing bird, wakener of morn,
Who springest like a thought unto the sun,
And from his golden floods dost gather wealth
(Epithalamium and Pindaric song),
And with it enrich our ears ; come all to me,
Beneath the chamber where my lady lies,
And, in your several musics, whisper—Love !

B. W. PROCTER.

762. KING DEATH

KING DEATH was a rare old fellow,
    He sat where no sun could shine,
And he lifted his hand so yellow,
    And poured out his coal-black wine.
        Hurrah, for the coal-black wine !

There came to him many a maiden
    Whose eyes had forgot to shine,
And widows with grief o'erladen,
    For a draught of his coal-black wine.
        Hurrah, for the coal-black wine !

The scholar left all his learning,
    The poet his fancied woes,
And the beauty her bloom returning
    Like life to the fading rose.
        Hurrah, for the coal-black wine !

All came to the rare old fellow,
    Who laughed till his eyes dropped brine,
And he gave them his hand so yellow,
    And pledged them in Death's black wine.
        Hurrah, for the coal-black wine !

                                B. W. PROCTER.

763. ADDRESS TO THE OCEAN

O THOU vast Ocean ! ever-sounding sea !
Thou symbol of a drear immensity !
Thou thing that windest round the solid world
Like a huge animal, which, downward hurled
From the black clouds, lies weltering and alone,
Lashing and writhing till its strength be gone.
Thy voice is like the thunder, and thy sleep
Is as a giant's slumber, loud and deep.
Thou speakest in the east and in the west
At once, and on thy heavily-laden breast
Fleets come and go, and shapes that have no life
Or motion, yet are moved and meet in strife.
The earth hath naught of this : no chance or change
Ruffles its surface, and no spirits dare
Give answer to the tempest-wakened air ;
But o'er its wastes the weakly tenants range
At will, and wound its bosom as they go :
Ever the same, it hath no ebb, no flow ;
But in their stated rounds the seasons come,
And pass like visions to their wonted home ;
And come again, and vanish ; the young Spring
Looks ever bright with leaves and blossoming ;

And Winter always winds his sullen horn,
When the wild Autumn, with a look forlorn,
Dies in his stormy manhood; and the skies
Weep, and flowers sicken, when the summer flies.

Oh! wonderful thou art, great element:
And fearful in thy spleeny humours bent,
And lovely in repose; thy summer form
Is beautiful, and when thy silver waves
Make music in earth's dark and winding caves,
I love to wander on thy pebbled beach,
Marking the sunlight at the evening hour,
And hearken to the thoughts thy waters teach—
Eternity—Eternity—and Power.   B. W. PROCTER.

764. ON THE DOWAGER LADY E. H——D

VAIN are the charms of white and red,
  Which divide the blooming fair;
Give me the nymph whose snow is spread
  Not o'er her breast, but hair.

Of smoother cheeks, the winning grace,
  As open forces I defy;
But in the wrinkles of her face
  Cupids, as in ambush, lie.

If naked eyes set hearts on blaze,
  And amorous warmth inspire;
Through glass who darts her pointed rays,
  Lights up a fiercer fire!
        W. PULTENEY, EARL OF BATH.

765. LORD, WHEN WE LEAVE THE WORLD

LORD, when we leave the world and come to Thee,
  How dull, how slug are we!

If Pleasure beckon with her balmy hand,
  Her beck's a strong command:
If Honour calls us with her courtly breath,
  An hour's delay is death:
If Profit's golden-fingered charm inveigles,
  We clip more swift than eagles:
Let Auster weep, or blustering Boreas roar,
  Till eyes or lungs be sore:
Let Neptune swell, until his dropsy sides
  Burst into broken tides:

How fast and fearless do our footsteps flee!
The lightfoot roebuck's not so swift as we.
        F. QUARLES.

o

766. ON THE LIFE AND DEATH OF MAN

The world's a theatre. The earth, a stage
Placed in the midst: where both prince and page,
Both rich and poor, fool, wise man, base and high,
All act their parts in life's short tragedy.
    Our life's a tragedy. Those secret rooms,
Wherein we 'tire us, are our mothers' wombs.
The music ushering in the play is mirth
To see a man-child brought upon the earth.
That fainting gasp of breath which first we vent,
Is a dumb show; presents the argument.
Our new-born cries, that new-born griefs bewray,
Are the sad prologue of the ensuing play.
False hopes, true fears, vain joys, and fierce distracts,
Are like the music that divides the Acts.
Time holds the glass, and when the hour's outrun,
Death strikes the epilogue, and the play is done.
F. Quarles.

767. SWEET PHOSPHOR

Will 't ne'er be morning ? Will that promised light
  Ne'er break, and clear those clouds of night ?
    Sweet Phosphor, bring the day,
      Whose conquering ray
May chase these fogs: sweet Phosphor, bring the day.

.   .   .   .

Let those have night that slily love to immure
  Their cloistered crimes, and sin secure ;
Let those have night that blush to let men know
  The baseness they ne'er blush to do ;
Let those have night that love to take a nap,
  And loll in Ignorance's lap :
Let those whose eyes, like owls, abhor the light,
  Let those have night, that love the night :
    Sweet Phosphor, bring the day :
      How sad delay
Afflicts dull hopes ! sweet Phosphor, bring the day.
F. Quarles.

768. HOW SHOULD I YOUR TRUE LOVE KNOW

As you came from the holy land
  Of Walsingham,
Met you not with my true love,
  By the way, as you came ?

How shall I know your true love,
  That have met many one,
As I went to the holy land,
  That have come, that have gone?

She is neither white, nor brown ;
  But as the heavens fair !
There is none hath a form so divine,
  In the earth, or the air !

Such a one did I meet, good sir,
  Such an angelic face,
Who like a queen, like a nymph,
    did appear
  By her gait, by her grace.

She hath left me here all alone,
  All alone, as unknown ;
Who sometimes did me lead with
    herself,
  And me loved as her own.

What's the cause that she leaves
    you alone,
  And a new way doth take ;
Who loved you once as her own,
  And her joy did you make ?

I have loved her all my youth,
  But now old, as you see,
Love likes not the falling fruit
  From the withered tree.

Know that Love is a careless
    child,
  And forgets promise past ;
He is blind ; he is deaf when he
    list,
  And in faith never fast !

His desire is a dureless content,
  And a trustless joy.
He is won, with a world of despair ;
  And is lost, with a toy.

Of womenkind such indeed is the
    love,—
  Or the word love abused ;
Under which many childish desires
  And conceits are excused.

But true love is a durable fire,
  In the mind ever burning,
Never sick, never old, never dead,
  From itself never turning. Sir W. Ralegh.

769. THE CONCLUSION

Even such is Time, which takes in trust
  Our youth, our joys, our all we have,
And pays us but with earth and dust ;
  Who, in the dark and silent grave,
When we have wandered all our ways,
Shuts up the story of our days ;
But from this earth, this grave, this dust,
My God shall raise me up, I trust. Sir W. Ralegh.

770. HIS PILGRIMAGE

Give me my scallop-shell of quiet,
  My staff of faith to walk upon,
My scrip of joy, immortal diet,
  My bottle of salvation,
My gown of glory, hope's true
    gage :
And thus I'll take my pilgrimage.
Blood must be my body's balmer ;
  No other balm will there be
    given ;
Whilst my soul, like quiet palmer,
  Travelleth towards the land of
    heaven ;

Over the silver mountains,
Where spring the nectar fountains:
    There will I kiss
    The bowl of bliss ;
And drink mine everlasting fill
Upon every milken hill.
My soul will be a-dry before ;
But, after, it will thirst no more.

Of death and judgement, heaven
    and hell
Who oft doth think, must needs
    die well. Sir W. Ralegh.

771. THE NYMPH'S REPLY TO THE PASSIONATE SHEPHERD

If all the world and love were young,
And truth in every shepherd's tongue,
These pretty pleasures might me move
To live with thee and be thy love.

But Time drives flocks from field to fold,
When rivers rage and rocks grow cold;
And Philomel becometh dumb;
The rest complains of cares to come.

The flowers do fade; and wanton fields
To wayward winter reckoning yields:
A honey tongue, a heart of gall,
Is fancy's spring, but sorrow's fall.

Thy gowns, thy shoes, thy beds of roses,
Thy cap, thy kirtle, and thy posies
Soon break, soon wither, soon forgotten,
In folly ripe, in reason rotten.

Thy belt of straw and ivy-buds,
Thy coral clasps and amber studs,
All these in me no means can move
To come to thee and be thy love.

But could youth last, and love still breed,
Had joys no date, nor age no need,
Then these delights my mind might move
To live with thee and be thy love.

SIR W. RALEGH.[1]

772. LIFE'S TRAGI-COMEDY

What is our life? A play of passion:
Our mirth? The music of division.
Our mothers' wombs the tiring-houses be,
Where we are dressed for this short comedy.
Heaven the judicious sharp spectator is,
That sits and marks still who do act amiss.
Our graves that hide us from the searching sun,
Are like drawn curtains when the play is done.
Thus march we, playing, to our latest rest;
Only we die in earnest; that's no jest.

SIR W. RALEGH.

[1] See Marlowe's poem, No. 638.

773. AN THOU WERE MY AIN THING

An thou were my ain thing,
I would love thee, I would love thee ;
An thou were my ain thing
  How dearly I would love thee.

Like bees that suck the morning dew,
Frae flowers of sweetest scent and hue,
Sae wad I dwell upon thy mow
  And gar the gods envy me.

Sae lang 's I had the use of light
I'd on thy beauties feast my sight,
Syne in saft whispers through the night
  I'd tell how much I loved thee.

. . . .

I'd grasp thee to this breast of mine,
Whilst thou like ivy or the vine
Around my stronger limbs should twine,
  Formed handy to defend thee.   A. Ramsay.

774. THE POET

From witty men and mad
All poetry conception had.

No sires but these will poetry admit :
Madness or wit.

This definition poetry doth fit :
It is witty madness, or mad wit.

Only these two poetic heat admits :
A witty man, or one that 's out of 's wits.
                                    T. Randolph.

775. I HAVE A MISTRESS, FOR PERFECTIONS RARE

I have a mistress, for perfections rare
In every eye, but in my thought most fair.
Like tapers on the altar shine her eyes ;
Her breath is the perfume of sacrifice ;
And wheresoe'er my fancy would begin,
Still her perfection lets religion in.
We sit and talk, and kiss away the hours
As chastely as the morning dews kiss flowers :
I touch her, like my beads, with devout care,
And come unto my courtship as my prayer.
                                    T. Randolph.

776. WE BE THREE POOR MARINERS

We be three poor mariners,
  Newly come from the seas ;
We spend our lives in jeopardy,
  While others live at ease.
Shall we go dance the round,
    around ?
Shall we go dance the round ?
And he that is a bully-boy
  Come, pledge me on this ground !

We care not for those martial men
  That do our states disdain ;
But we care for those merchant men
  That do our states maintain :
To them we dance this round,
    around,
  To them we dance this round ;
And he that is a bully-boy
  Come, pledge me on this ground !
                    T. RAVENSCROFT.

777. AN ITALIAN SONG

Dear is my little native vale,
  The ring-dove builds and murmurs there ;
Close by my cot she tells her tale
  To every passing villager.
The squirrel leaps from tree to tree,
And shells his nuts at liberty.

In orange groves and myrtle-bowers,
  That breathe a gale of fragrance round,
I charm the fairy-footed hours
  With my loved lute's romantic sound ;
Or crowns of living laurel weave
For those that win the race at eve.

The shepherd's horn at break of day,
  The ballet danced in twilight glade,
The canzonet and roundelay
  Sung in the silent greenwood shade ;
These simple joys, that never fail,
Shall bind me to my native vale.   S. ROGERS.

778. MELANCHOLY

Go—you may call it madness, folly ;
  You shall not chase my gloom away.
There's such a charm in melancholy,
  I would not, if I could, be gay.

Oh, if you knew the pensive pleasure
  That fills my bosom when I sigh,
You would not rob me of a treasure
  Monarchs are too poor to buy !   S. ROGERS.

779. MINE BE A COT BESIDE THE HILL

MINE be a cot beside the hill ;
   A bee-hive's hum shall soothe my ear ;
A willowy brook, that turns a mill,
   With many a fall shall linger near.

The swallow, oft, beneath my thatch,
   Shall twitter from her clay-built nest ;
Oft shall the pilgrim lift the latch,
   And share my meal, a welcome guest.

Around my ivied porch shall spring
   Each fragrant flower that drinks the dew ;
And Lucy, at her wheel, shall sing
   In russet-gown and apron blue.

The village-church, among the trees,
   Where first our marriage-vows were given,
With merry peals shall swell the breeze,
   And point with taper spire to Heaven.   S. ROGERS.

780. NATURE'S GIFT

NATURE denied him much,
But gave him at his birth what most he values :
A passionate love for music, sculpture, painting,
For poetry, the language of the gods,
For all things here, or grand or beautiful,
A setting sun, a lake among the mountains,
The light of an ingenuous countenance,
And, what transcends them all, a noble action.
                S. ROGERS (*Italy*).

781. VENICE

THERE is a glorious City in the sea.
The sea is in the broad, the narrow streets,
Ebbing and flowing ; and the salt sea-weed
Clings to the marble of her palaces.
No track of men, no footsteps to and fro,
Lead to her gates. The path lies o'er the sea,
Invisible ; and from the land we went,
As to a floating city—steering in,
And gliding up her streets as in a dream,
So smoothly, silently—by many a dome
Mosque-like, and many a stately portico,
The statues ranged along an azure sky ;
By many a pile in more than eastern pride,
Of old the residence of merchant-kings ;
The fronts of some, though Time had shattered them,
Still glowing with the richest hues of art,
As though the wealth within them had run o'er.
                S. ROGERS (*Italy*).

782.　THE ROBIN'S GRAVE

TREAD lightly here, for here, 'tis said,
When piping winds are hushed around,
A small note wakes from underground,
Where now his tiny bones are laid.
No more in lone and leafless groves,
With ruffled wing and faded breast,
His friendless, homeless spirit roves;
—Gone to the world where birds are blessed!
Where never cat glides o'er the green,
Or schoolboy's giant form is seen;
But Love, and Joy, and smiling Spring
Inspire their little souls to sing.　　　　S. ROGERS.

783.　UP-HILL

DOES the road wind up-hill all the way?
　Yes, to the very end.
Will the day's journey take the whole long day?
　From morn to night, my friend.

But is there for the night a resting-place?
　A roof for when the slow dark hours begin.
May not the darkness hide it from my face?
　You cannot miss that inn.

Shall I meet other wayfarers at night?
　Those who have gone before.
Then must I knock, or call when just in sight?
　They will not keep you standing at that door.

Shall I find comfort, travel-sore and weak?
　Of labour you shall find the sum.
Will there be beds for me and all who seek?
　Yea, beds for all who come.　　　C. G. ROSSETTI.

784.　A BIRTHDAY

MY heart is like a singing bird
　Whose nest is in a watered shoot;
My heart is like an apple-tree
　Whose boughs are bent with thickset fruit;
My heart is like a rainbow shell
　That paddles in a halcyon sea;
My heart is gladder than all these,
　Because my love is come to me.

Raise me a dais of silk and down ;
  Hang it with vair and purple dyes ;
Carve it in doves, and pomegranates,
  And peacocks with a hundred eyes ;
Work it in gold and silver grapes,
  In leaves, and silver fleurs-de-lys ;
Because the birthday of my life
  Is come, my love is come to me.

C. G. ROSSETTI.

785. REST

O EARTH, lie heavily upon her eyes ;
Seal her sweet eyes weary of watching, Earth ;
Lie close around her ; leave no room for mirth
With its harsh laughter, nor for sound of sighs.
She hath no questions, she hath no replies,
Hushed in and curtained with a blessèd dearth
Of all that irked her from the hour of birth ;
With stillness that is almost Paradise.
Darkness more clear than noonday holdeth her,
Silence more musical than any song ;
Even her very heart has ceased to stir :
Until the morning of Eternity
Her rest shall not begin nor end,. but be ;
And when she wakes she will not think it long.

C. G. ROSSETTI.

786. ROSES FOR THE FLUSH OF YOUTH

OH roses for the flush of youth,
  And laurel for the perfect
    prime ;
But pluck an ivy branch for me
  Grown old before my time.

Oh violets for the grave of youth,
  And bay for those dead in their
    prime ;
Give me the withered leaves I chose
  Before in the old time.

C. G. ROSSETTI.

787. WHEN I AM DEAD, MY DEAREST

WHEN I am dead, my dearest,
  Sing no sad songs for me ;
Plant thou no roses at my head,
  Nor shady cypress tree :
Be the green grass above me
  With showers and dewdrops
    wet :
And if thou wilt, remember,
  And if thou wilt, forget.

I shall not see the shadows,
  I shall not feel the rain ;
I shall not hear the nightingale
  Sing on, as if in pain :
And dreaming through the twilight
  That doth not rise nor set,
Haply I may remember,
  And haply may forget.

C. G. ROSSETTI.

788. THE BLESSED DAMOZEL

THE blessèd Damozel leaned out
  From the gold bar of Heaven ;
Her eyes knew more of rest and
    shade
Than waters stilled at even ;
She had three lilies in her hand,
  And the stars in her hair were
    seven.

Her robe, ungirt from clasp to hem,
  No wrought flowers did adorn,
But a white rose of Mary's gift,
  For service meetly worn ;
And her hair lying down her back
  Was yellow like ripe corn.

Her seemed she scarce had been
    a day
  One of God's choristers ;
The wonder was not yet quite gone
  From that still look of hers ;
Albeit, to them she left, her day
  Had counted as ten years.

(To *one*, it is ten years of years.
  . . . Yet now, and in this place,
Surely she leaned o'er me—her
    hair
  Fell all about my face . . .
Nothing : the Autumn fall of
    leaves.
  The whole year sets apace.)

It was the rampart of God's house
  That she was standing on ;
By God built over the sheer depth
  The which is Space begun ;
So high, that looking downward
    thence
  She scarce could see the sun.

It lies in Heaven, across the flood
  Of ether, as a bridge.
Beneath, the tides of day and
    night
  With flame and blackness ridge
The void, as low as where this
    earth
  Spins like a fretful midge.

She scarcely heard her sweet new
    friends :
  Playing at holy games,
Softly they spake among them-
    selves
  Their virginal chaste names ;
And the souls, mounting up to
    God,
  Went by her like thin flames.

And still she bowed above the vast
  Waste sea of worlds that swarm;
Until her bosom must have made
  The bar she leaned on warm,
And the lilies lay as if asleep
  Along her bended arm.

From the fixed place of Heaven,
    she saw
  Time like a pulse shake fierce
Through all the worlds. Her gaze
    still strove
  Within the gulf to pierce
Its path ; and now she spoke, as
    when
  The stars sung in their spheres.

The sun was gone now. The
    curled moon
  Was like a little feather
Fluttering far down the gulf.
    And now
  She spoke through the still
    weather.
Her voice was like the voice the
    stars
  Had when they sung together.

' I wish that he were come to
    me,
  For he will come,' she said.
' Have I not prayed in Heaven ?
    —on earth,
  Lord, Lord, has he not prayed ?
Are not two prayers a perfect
    strength ?
  And shall I feel afraid ?

' When round his head the aureole
  clings,
And he is clothed in white,
I'll take his hand and go with him
  To the deep wells of light,
And we will step down as to a
    stream
And bathe there in God's sight.
' We two will stand beside that
    shrine,
  Occult, withheld, untrod,
Whose lamps are stirred continually
  With prayers sent up to God;
And see our old prayers, granted,
    melt
  Each like a little cloud.
' We two will lie i' the shadow of
  That living mystic tree,
Within whose secret growth the
    Dove
  Is sometimes felt to be,
While every leaf that His plumes
    touch
  Saith His Name audibly.
' And I myself will teach to him,
  I myself, lying so,
The songs I sing here; which his
    voice
  Shall pause in, hushed and slow,
And find some knowledge at each
    pause,
  Or some new thing to know.'
(Ah sweet! Just now, in that
    bird's song,
  Strove not her accents there
Fain to be hearkened? When
    those bells
  Possessed the midday air,
Was she not stepping to my side
  Down all the trembling stair?)
' We two,' she said, ' will seek the
    groves
  Where the Lady Mary is,
With her five handmaidens, whose
    names
  Are five sweet symphonies,
Cecily, Gertrude, Magdalen,
  Margaret, and Rosalys.

' Circlewise sit they, with bound
    locks
  And foreheads garlanded;
Into the fine cloth white like
    flame
  Weaving the golden thread,
To fashion the birth-robes for
    them
  Who are just born, being dead.
' He shall fear, haply, and be
    dumb;
  Then I will lay my cheek
To his, and tell about our love,
  Not once abashed or weak:
And the dear Mother will approve
  My pride, and let me speak.
' Herself shall bring us, hand in
    hand
  To Him round whom all souls
Kneel, the unnumbered ransomed
    heads
  Bowed with their aureoles:
And angels meeting us shall sing
  To their citherns and citoles.
' There will I ask of Christ the
    Lord
  Thus much for him and me:—
Only to live as once on earth
  At peace—only to be
As then awhile, for ever now
  Together, I and he.'
She gazed, and listened, and then
    said,
  Less sad of speech than mild,
' All this is when he comes.' She
    ceased.
The light thrilled past her, filled
With angels in strong level lapse.
  Her eyes prayed, and she smiled.
(I saw her smile.) But soon their
    flight
  Was vague in distant spheres;
And then she laid her arms along
  The golden barriers,
And laid her face between her
    hands,
  And wept. (I heard her tears.)
                    D. G. ROSSETTI.

789. FROM 'OUR BLESSED LADY'S LULLABY'

UPON my lap my Sovereign sits,
　And sucks upon my breast;
Meanwhile his love sustains my life,
　And gives my body rest.
　　Sing lullaby, my little boy!
　　Sing lullaby, my life's joy!

When thou hast taken thy repast,
　Repose, my babe, on me!
So may thy mother and thy nurse
　Thy cradle also be.
　　Sing lullaby, my little boy!
　　Sing lullaby, my life's joy!

. . . .

My babe, my bliss, my child, my choice,
　My fruit, my flower, and bud;
My Jesus, and my only joy,
　The sum of all my good!
　　Sing lullaby, my little boy!
　　Sing lullaby, my life's joy!

R. ROWLANDS.

790. SIDNEY

A SWEET attractive kind of grace,
　A full assurance given by looks,
Continual comfort in a face,
　The lineaments of Gospel books!
　　I trow that countenance cannot lie
　　Whose thoughts are legible in the eye.

Was ever eye did see that face,
　Was ever ear did hear that tongue,
Was ever mind did mind his grace
　That ever thought the travel long?
　　But eyes and ears, and every thought
　　Were with his sweet perfections caught

. . . .

Did never love so sweetly breathe
　In any mortal breast before,
Did never Muse inspire beneath
　A poet's brain with finer store;
　　He wrote of love with high conceit,
　　And beauty reared above her height.

M. ROYDON (*Friend's Passion for his Astrophill*).

791. ALAS, FOR MAN!

Alas, for man! who hath no sense
Of gratefulness nor confidence,
  But still rejects and raves;
That all God's love can hardly
    win
One soul from taking pride in
    sin,
  And pleasures over graves.

But teach me, God, a milder
    thought,
Lest I, of all Thy blood hath bought,
  Least honourable be;
And this that moves me to con-
    demn,
Be rather want of love for them,
  Than jealousy for Thee.

J. Ruskin (*Mont Blanc Revisited*).

792. DORINDA

Dorinda's sparkling wit and eyes
  United, cast too fierce a light,
Which blazes high, but quickly dies;
  Pains not the heart, but hurts the sight.

Love is a calmer, gentler joy;
  Smooth are his looks, and soft his pace;
Her Cupid is a blackguard boy,
  That runs his link full in your face.

C. Sackville, Earl of Dorset.

793. MAY THE AMBITIOUS EVER FIND

May the ambitious ever find
  Success in crowds and noise,
While gentle love does fill my mind
  With silent real joys.

May knaves and fools grow rich and great,
  And the world think them wise,
While I lie dying at her feet,
  And all that world despise!

Let conquering kings new triumphs raise,
  And melt in court delights;
Her eyes can give much brighter days,
  Her arms much softer nights.

C. Sackville, Earl of Dorset.

794. THE ADVICE

Phyllis, for shame, let us improve
  A thousand several ways,
These few short minutes stolen by
    love
  From many tedious days.

Whilst you want courage to
    despise
  The censure of the grave,
For all the tyrants in your eyes,
  Your heart is but a slave.

My love is full of noble pride,
  And never will submit
To let that fop, Discretion, ride
  In triumph over wit.

False friends I have, as well as you,
  That daily counsel me
Vain frivolous trifles to pursue,
  And leave off loving thee.

When I the least belief bestow
  On what such fools advise,
May I be dull enough to grow
  Most miserably wise.

C. SACKVILLE, EARL OF DORSET.

795. A BALLAD WHEN AT SEA

To you, fair ladies, now at land,
  We men at sea indite;
But, first, would have you understand
  How hard it is to write.
The Muses now, and Neptune too,
We must implore, to write to you,
    With a fa, la, la, la, la !

But though the Muses should be kind,
  And fill our empty brain:
Yet if rough Neptune cause the wind
  To rouse the azure main,
Our paper, pens, and ink, and we
Roll up and down our ships at sea,
    With a fa, la, la, la, la !

Then if we write not by each post,
  Think not that we're unkind !
Nor yet conclude that we are lost
  By Dutch, by French, or wind.
Our griefs will find a speedier way:
The tide shall bring them twice a day,
    With a fa, la, la, la, la !

The King, with wonder and surprise,
  Will think the sea's grown bold,
For that the tide does higher rise
  Than e'er it did of old.
But let him know that 'tis our tears
Send floods of grief to Whitehall Stairs,
    With a fa, la, la, la, la !

Should Count Toulouse but come to know
  Our sad and dismal story,
The French would scorn so weak a foe,
  Where they can get no glory,
For what resistance can they find
From men, who've left their hearts behind,
    With a fa, la, la, la, la !

To pass our tedious time away
  We throw the merry Main,
Or else at serious Ombre play.
  But why should we in vain
Each other's ruin thus pursue ?
We were undone when we left you,
    With a fa, la, la, la, la !

When any mournful tune you hear,
  That dies in every note,
As if it sighed for each man's care,
  For being so remote,
Then think how often love we've made
To you, while all those tunes were played
    With a fa, la, la, la, la !

Let wind and weather do their worst,
  Be you to us but kind,
Let Frenchmen vapour, Dutchmen curse,
  No sorrows we shall find.
'Tis then no matter how things go,
Nor who's our friend, nor who's our foe,
    With a fa, la, la, la, la !

Thus, having told you all our loves,
  And likewise all our fears,
In hopes this declaration moves
  Some pity to our tears,
Let's hear of no inconstancy ;
We have too much of that at sea,
    With a fa, la, la, la, la !
          C. SACKVILLE, EARL OF DORSET.

796. MISERY

His face was lean, and some-deal pined away,
And eke his hands consumèd to the bone,
But what his body was I cannot say,
For on his carcass raiment had he none
Save clouts and patches, piecèd one by one ;
With staff in hand, and scrip on shoulders cast,
His chief defence against the winter's blast.

His food, for most, was wild fruits of the tree,
Unless sometime some crumbs fell to his share,
Which in his wallet long, God wot, kept he
As on the which full daintily would he fare ;
His drink, the running stream, his cup, the bare
Of his palm closed ; his bed, the hard cold ground ;
To this poor life was Misery ybound.
T. SACKVILLE, EARL OF DORSET (*The Mirrour for Magistrates*).

797. ODE ON HEARING THE DRUM

I HATE that drum's discordant sound,
Parading round, and round, and round :
To thoughtless youth it pleasure yields,
And lures from cities and from fields,
To sell their liberty for charms
Of tawdry lace and glittering arms,
And when Ambition's voice commands,
To march, and fight, and fall in foreign lands.

I hate that drum's discordant sound,
Parading round, and round, and round :
To me it talks of ravaged plains,
And burning towns, and ruined swains,
And mangled limbs, and dying groans,
And widows' tears and orphans' moans ;
And all that misery's hand bestows
To fill the catalogue of human woes.   J. SCOTT.

798. A WEARY LOT IS THINE

' A WEARY lot is thine, fair maid,
    A weary lot is thine !
To pull the thorn thy brow to
    braid,
And press the rue for wine !
A lightsome eye, a soldier's mien,
    A feather of the blue,
A doublet of the Lincoln green,—
No more of me you knew,
          My Love !
No more of me you knew.

' This morn is merry June, I trow,
    The rose is budding fain ;
But she shall bloom in winter
    snow,
    Ere we two meet again.'
He turned his charger as he spake,
    Upon the river shore,
He gave his bridle-reins a shake,
    Said, ' Adieu for evermore,
          My Love !
And àdieu for evermore.'
          SIR W. SCOTT (*Rokeby*).

799. COUNTY GUY

AH ! County Guy, the hour is nigh,
    The sun has left the lea,
The orange-flower perfumes the
    bower,
    The breeze is on the sea.
The lark, his lay who trilled all day,
    Sits hushed his partner nigh ;
Breeze, bird, and flower confess
    the hour,
But where is County Guy ?

The village maid steals through
    the shade
    Her shepherd's suit to hear ;
To Beauty shy, by lattice high,
    Sings high-born Cavalier.
The star of Love, all stars above,
    Now reigns o'er earth and sky,
And high and low the influence
    know,
    But where is County Guy ?
          SIR W. SCOTT (*Quentin Durward*).

800. AVE MARIA

AVE MARIA ! maiden mild !
 Listen to a maiden's prayer !
Thou canst hear though from the
 wild,
 Thou canst save amid despair.
Safe may we sleep beneath thy
 care,
 Though banished, outcast, and
 reviled ;
Maiden ! hear a maiden's prayer—
 Mother, hear a suppliant child !
 Ave Maria !

Ave Maria ! undefiled !
 The flinty couch we now must
 share,
Shall seem with down of eider piled,
 If thy protection hover there.
The murky cavern's heavy air
 Shall breathe of balm if thou
 hast smiled ;
Then, Maiden ! hear a maiden's
 prayer ;
 Mother, list a suppliant child !
 Ave Maria !

Ave Maria ! stainless styled !
 Foul demons of the earth and air
From this their wonted haunt exiled,
 Shall flee before thy presence fair.
We bow us to our lot of care,
 Beneath thy guidance reconciled ;
Hear for a maid a maiden's prayer,
 And for a father hear a child !
 Ave Maria !
 SIR W. SCOTT (*The Lady of the Lake*).

801. BREATHES THERE THE MAN WITH SOUL SO DEAD

BREATHES there the man, with soul so dead,
Who never to himself hath said,
 This is my own, my native land !
Whose heart hath ne'er within him burned,
As home his footsteps he hath turned,
 From wandering on a foreign strand !
If such there breathe, go, mark him well ;
For him no Minstrel raptures swell ;
High though his titles, proud his name,
Boundless his wealth as wish can claim ;
Despite those titles, power, and pelf,
The wretch, concentred all in self,
Living, shall forfeit fair renown,
And, doubly dying, shall go down
To the vile dust, from whence he sprung,
Unwept, unhonoured, and unsung.
 O Caledonia ! stern and wild,
Meet nurse for a poetic child !
Land of brown heath and shaggy wood,
Land of the mountain and the flood,

Land of my sires ! what mortal hand
Can e'er untie the filial band,
That knits me to thy rugged strand !
Still as I view each well-known scene,
Think what is now, and what hath been,
Seems as, to me, of all bereft,
Sole friends thy woods and streams were left ;
And thus I love them better still,
Even in extremity of ill.

Sir W. Scott (*The Lay of the Last Minstrel*).

802. CORONACH

He is gone on the mountain,
He is lost to the forest,
Like a summer-dried fountain,
When our need was the sorest.
The font, reappearing,
From the rain-drops shall borrow,
But to us comes no cheering,
To Duncan no morrow !

The hand of the reaper
Takes the ears that are hoary,
But the voice of the weeper
Wails manhood in glory.

The autumn winds rushing
Waft the leaves that are searest,
But our flower was in flushing
When blighting was nearest.

Fleet foot on the correi,
Sage counsel in cumber,
Red hand in the foray,
How sound is thy slumber !
Like the dew on the mountain,
Like the foam on the river,
Like the bubble on the fountain,
Thou art gone and for ever !

Sir W. Scott (*The Lady of the Lake*).

803. IF THOU WOULD'ST VIEW FAIR MELROSE ARIGHT

If thou would'st view fair Melrose aright,
Go visit it by the pale moonlight ;
For the gay beams of lightsome day
Gild, but to flout, the ruins grey.
When the broken arches are black in night,
And each shafted oriel glimmers white ;
When the cold light's uncertain shower
Streams on the ruined central tower ;
When buttress and buttress, alternately,
Seem framed of ebon and ivory ;
When silver edges the imagery,
And the scrolls that teach thee to live and die ;
When distant Tweed is heard to rave,
And the owlet to hoot o'er the dead man's grave,
Then go—but go alone the while—
Then view St. David's ruined pile ;
And home returning, soothly swear,
Was never scene so sad and fair !

Sir W. Scott (*The Lay of the Last Minstrel*).

804. LOVE

In peace, Love tunes the shepherd's reed ;
In war, he mounts the warrior's steed ;
In halls, in gay attire is seen ;
In hamlets, dances on the green.
Love rules the court, the camp, the grove,
And men below, and saints above ;
For love is heaven, and heaven is love.
Sir W. Scott (The Lay of the Last Minstrel).

805. LOOK NOT THOU ON BEAUTY'S CHARMING

Look not thou on beauty's charming,
Sit thou still when kings are arming,
Taste not when the wine-cup glistens,
Speak not when the people listens,
Stop thine ear against the singer,
From the red gold keep thy finger ;
Vacant heart and hand and eye,
Easy live and quiet die.
Sir W. Scott (The Bride of Lammermoor).

806. THE OUTLAW

O Brignal banks are wild and fair,
  And Greta woods are green,
And you may gather garlands there
  Would grace a summer queen.
And as I rode by Dalton-hall
  Beneath the turrets high,
A maiden on the castle-wall
  Was singing merrily,—
' O, Brignal Banks are fresh and fair,
  And Greta woods are green ;
I'd rather rove with Edmund there,
  Than reign our English queen.'

' If, maiden, thou wouldst wend with me,
  To leave both tower and town,
Thou first must guess what life lead we,
  That dwell by dale and down.
And if thou canst that riddle read,
  As read full well you may,
Then to the greenwood shalt thou speed,
  As blithe as Queen of May.'
Yet sung she, ' Brignal banks are fair,
  And Greta woods are green ;
I'd rather rove with Edmund there,
  Than reign our English queen.

I read you, by your bugle-horn,
    And by your palfrey good,
I read you for a ranger sworn
    To keep the king's greenwood.'
' A ranger, lady, winds his horn,
    And 'tis at peep of light ;
His blast is heard at merry morn,
    And mine at dead of night.'
Yet sung she, ' Brignal banks are fair,
    And Greta woods are gay ;
I would I were with Edmund there,
    To reign his Queen of May !

With burnished brand and musketoon,
    So gallantly you come,
I read you for a bold dragoon
    That lists the tuck of drum.'
' I list no more the tuck of drum,
    No more the trumpet hear ;
But when the beetle sounds his hum,
    My comrades take the spear.
And O ! though Brignal banks be fair,
    And Greta woods be gay,
Yet mickle must the maiden dare
    Would reign my Queen of May !

Maiden ! a nameless life I lead,
    A nameless death I'll die ;
The fiend, whose lantern lights the mead,
    Were better mate than I !
And when I'm with my comrades met
    Beneath the greenwood bough,
What once we were we all forget,
    Nor think what we are now.
Yet Brignal banks are fresh and fair,
    And Greta woods are green,
And you may gather garlands there
    Would grace a summer queen.'

                                    SIR W. SCOTT (*Rokeby*).

807. OH, HUSH THEE, MY BABIE

OH, hush thee, my babie, thy sire was a knight,
Thy mother a lady, both lovely and bright ;
The woods and the glens, from the towers which we see,
They all are belonging, dear babie, to thee.
        O ho ro, i ri ri, cadul gu lo,
        O ho ro, i ri ri, &c.

Oh, fear not the bugle, though loudly it blows,
It calls but the warders that guard thy repose ;
Their bows would be bended, their blades would be red,
Ere the step of a foeman drew near to thy bed.
    O ho ro, i ri ri, &c.

Oh, hush thee, my babie, the time soon will come
When thy sleep shall be broken by trumpet and drum ;
Then hush thee, my darling, take rest while you may,
For strife comes with manhood, and waking with day.
    O ho ro, i ri ri, &c.   SIR W. SCOTT.

808.   O WOMAN ! IN OUR HOURS OF EASE

O WOMAN ! in our hours of ease,
Uncertain, coy, and hard to please,
And variable as the shade
By the light quivering aspen made ;
When pain and anguish wring the brow,
A ministering angel thou !
                        SIR W. SCOTT (*Marmion*).

809.   PROUD MAISIE

PROUD Maisie is in the wood,
    Walking so early ;
Sweet Robin sits on the bush,
    Singing so rarely.

' Tell me, thou bonny bird,
    When shall I marry me ? '
' When six braw gentlemen
    Kirkward shall carry ye.'

' Who makes the bridal bed,
    Birdie, say truly ? '
' The grey-headed sexton
    That delves the grave duly.'

' The glow-worm o'er grave and stone
    Shall light thee steady.
The owl from the steeple sing
    " Welcome, proud lady ".'

                SIR W. SCOTT (*The Heart of Midlothian*).

810.   SOLDIER, REST ! THY WARFARE O'ER

SOLDIER, rest ! thy warfare o'er,
    Sleep the sleep that knows not breaking ;
Dream of battled fields no more,
    Days of danger, nights of waking.
In our isle's enchanted hall
    Hands unseen thy couch are strewing,
Fairy strains of music fall,
    Every sense in slumber dewing.
Soldier, rest ! thy warfare o'er,
Dream of fighting fields no more :
Sleep the sleep that knows not breaking,
Morn of toil, nor night of waking.

No rude sound shall reach thine ear,
　Armour's clang, or war-steed champing,
Trump nor pibroch summon here
　Mustering clan, or squadron tramping.
Yet the lark's shrill fife may come
　At the daybreak from the fallow,
And the bittern sound his drum,
　Booming from the sedgy shallow.
Ruder sounds shall none be near,
Guards nor warders challenge here,
Here 's no war-steed's neigh and champing,
Shouting clans or squadrons stamping.

Huntsman, rest ! the chase is done ;
　While our slumbrous spells assail ye,
Dream not, with the rising sun,
　Bugles here shall sound reveillé.
Sleep ! the deer is in his den ;
　Sleep ! thy hounds are by thee lying ;
Sleep ! nor dream in yonder glen,
　How thy gallant steed lay dying.
Huntsman, rest ! thy chase is done,
Think not of the rising sun,
For at dawning to assail ye
Here no bugles sound reveillé.

　　　　　　　Sir W. Scott (*The Lady of the Lake*).

811. SOUND, SOUND THE CLARION

Sound, sound the clarion, fill the fife !
　To all the sensual world proclaim,
One crowded hour of glorious life
　Is worth an age without a name.

　　　　　　　Sir W. Scott (*Old Mortality*).

812.　THE WAY WAS LONG, THE WIND WAS COLD

The way was long, the wind was cold,
The Minstrel was infirm and old ;
His withered cheek, and tresses grey,
Seemed to have known a better day ;
The harp, his sole remaining joy,
Was carried by an orphan boy.
The last of all the Bards was he,
Who sung of Border chivalry ;
For, welladay ! their date was fled,
His tuneful brethren all were dead ;
And he, neglected and oppressed,
Wished to be with them, and at rest.
No more, on prancing palfrey borne,
He carolled, light as lark at morn ;

No longer courted and caressed,
High placed in hall, a welcome guest,
He poured to lord and lady gay
The unpremeditated lay:
Old times were changed, old manners gone;
A stranger filled the Stuarts' throne;
The bigots of the iron time
Had called his harmless art a crime.
A wandering Harper, scorned and poor,
He begged his bread from door to door,
And tuned, to please a peasant's ear,
The harp a king had loved to hear.

SIR W. SCOTT (*The Lay of the Last Minstrel*).

813. REBECCA'S HYMN

WHEN Israel, of the Lord beloved,
  Out from the land of bondage came,
Her fathers' God before her moved,
  An awful guide in smoke and flame.
By day, along the astonished lands
  The cloudy pillar glided slow;
By night, Arabia's crimsoned sands
  Returned the fiery column's glow.

There rose the choral hymn of praise,
  And trump and timbrel answered keen,
And Zion's daughters poured their lays
  With priest's and warrior's voice between.
No portents now our foes amaze,
  Forsaken Israel wanders lone:
Our fathers would not know Thy ways,
  And Thou hast left them to their own.

But present still, though now unseen!
  When brightly shines the prosperous day,
Be thoughts of Thee a cloudy screen
  To temper the deceitful ray.
And oh, when stoops on Judah's path
  In shade and storm the frequent night,
Be Thou, long-suffering, slow to wrath,
  A burning and a shining light!

Our harps we left by Babel's streams,
  The tyrant's jest, the Gentile's scorn;
No censer round our altar beams,
  And mute are timbrel, harp, and horn.
But Thou hast said, The blood of goat,
  The flesh of rams I will not prize;
A contrite heart, a humble thought,
  Are Mine accepted sacrifice.

SIR W. SCOTT (*Ivanhoe*).

814. JOCK OF HAZELDEAN

' WHY weep ye by the tide, ladie ?
  Why weep ye by the tide ?
I'll wed ye to my youngest son,
  And ye sall be his bride ;
And ye sall be his bride, ladie,
  Sae comely to be seen '—
But aye she loot the tears down fa'
  For Jock of Hazeldean.[1]

' Now let this wilfu' grief be done,
  And dry that cheek so pale ;
Young Frank is chief of Errington,
  And lord of Langley-dale ;
His step is first in peaceful ha',
  His sword in battle keen '—
But aye she loot the tears down fa'
  For Jock of Hazeldean.

' A chain of gold ye sall not lack,
  Nor braid to bind your hair ;
Nor mettled hound, nor managed hawk,
  Nor palfrey fresh and fair ;
And you, the foremost o' them a',
  Shall ride our forest queen '—
But aye she loot the tears down fa'
  For Jock of Hazeldean.

The kirk was decked at morning-tide,
  The tapers glimmered fair ;
The priest and bridegroom wait the bride,
  And dame and knight are there.
They sought her baith by bower and ha' ;
  The ladie was not seen !
She 's o'er the Border, and awa'
  Wi' Jock of Hazeldean.   SIR W. SCOTT.

815. CHILD AND MAIDEN

AH, Chloris ! that I now could sit
  As unconcerned as when
Your infant beauty could beget
  No pleasure, nor no pain !

When I the dawn used to admire,
  And praised the coming day,
I little thought the growing fire
  Must take my rest away.

Your charms in harmless childhood lay,
  Like metals in the mine ;
Age from no face took more away
  Than youth concealed in thine.

But as your charms insensibly
  To their perfection prest,
Fond love as unperceived did fly,
  And in my bosom rest.

---

[1] The first stanza is ancient.

My passion with your beauty grew;
  And Cupid at my heart
Still, as his mother favoured you,
  Threw a new flaming dart:

Each gloried in their wanton part;
  To make a lover, he
Employed the utmost of his art—
  To make a beauty, she.
Sir C. Sedley.

816. LOVE STILL HAS SOMETHING OF THE SEA

Love still has something of the sea
  From whence his mother rose;
No time his slaves from doubt
    can free,
  Nor give their thoughts repose.

They are becalmed in clearest
    days,
  And in rough weather tossed;
They wither under cold delays,
  Or are in tempests lost.

    One while they seem to touch the port:
      Then straight into the main,
    Some angry wind in cruel sport,
      Their vessel drives again.
Sir C. Sedley.

817. PHYLLIS

Phyllis is my only joy,
  Faithless as the winds or seas,
Sometimes cunning, sometimes
    coy,
  Yet she never fails to please:
    If with a frown
    I am cast down,
    Phyllis, smiling
    And beguiling,
Makes me happier than before.

Though alas! too late I find
  Nothing can her fancy fix;
Yet the moment she is kind
  I forgive her all her tricks,
    Which though I see,
    I can't get free:
    She deceiving,
    I believing,
What need lovers wish for more?
Sir C. Sedley.

818. ARIEL'S SONG

Come unto these yellow sands,
  And then take hands:
Curtsied when you have, and kissed,—
  The wild waves whist,—
Foot it featly here and there;
  And, sweet sprites, the burden bear.
    Hark, hark!
    The watch-dogs bark:
    Hark, hark! I hear
The strain of strutting Chanticleer.
W. Shakespeare (The Tempest, Act I, Sc. ii).

819.　FULL FATHOM FIVE THY FATHER LIES

FULL fathom five thy father lies;
　　Of his bones are coral made:
Those are pearls that were his eyes:
　　Nothing of him that doth fade,
But doth suffer a sea-change
Into something rich and strange.
Sea-nymphs hourly ring his knell:
Hark! now I hear them,—ding-dong, bell.

　　　　　W. SHAKESPEARE (*The Tempest*, Act I, Sc. ii).

820.　WE ARE SUCH STUFF AS DREAMS ARE MADE ON

OUR revels now are ended. These our actors,
As I foretold you, were all spirits and
Are melted into air, into thin air:
And, like the baseless fabric of this vision,
The cloud-capped towers, the gorgeous palaces,
The solemn temples, the great globe itself,
Yea, all which it inherit, shall dissolve
And, like this insubstantial pageant faded,
Leave not a rack behind. We are such stuff
As dreams are made on, and our little life
Is rounded with a sleep.

　　　　　W. SHAKESPEARE (*The Tempest*, Act IV, Sc. i).

821.　WHERE THE BEE SUCKS

WHERE the bee sucks, there suck I:
In a cowslip's bell I lie;
There I couch when owls do cry.
On the bat's back I do fly
After summer merrily:
Merrily, merrily shall I live now
Under the blossom that hangs on the bough.

　　　　　W. SHAKESPEARE (*The Tempest*, Act V, Sc. i).

822.　WHO IS SILVIA

WHO is Silvia? what is she?
　　That all our swains commend her?
Holy, fair, and wise is she;
　　The heaven such grace did lend her,
That she might admirèd be.

Is she kind as she is fair?
　　For beauty lives with kindness:
Love doth to her eyes repair,
　　To help him of his blindness;
And, being helped, inhabits there.

Then to Silvia let us sing,
    That Silvia is excelling ;
She excels each mortal thing
    Upon the dull earth dwelling ;
    To her let us garlands bring.
W. SHAKESPEARE (*The Two Gentlemen of Verona*, Act IV, Sc. ii).

823. AYE, BUT TO DIE

AYE, but to die, and go we know not where ;
To lie in cold obstruction and to rot ;
This sensible warm motion to become
A kneaded clod ; and the delighted spirit
To bathe in fiery floods, or to reside
In thrilling region of thick-ribbèd ice ;
To be imprisoned in the viewless winds,
And blown with restless violence round about
The pendant world ; or to be worse than worst
Of those that lawless and incertain thoughts
Imagine howling : 'tis too horrible !
The weariest and most loathèd worldly life
That age, ache, penury and imprisonment
Can lay on nature is a paradise
To what we fear of death.
        W. SHAKESPEARE (*Measure for Measure*, Act III, Sc. i).

824. MAN

MAN, proud man,
Dressed in a little brief authority,
Most ignorant of what he's most assured,
His glassy essence, like an angry ape,
Plays such fantastic tricks before high heaven
As make the angels weep ; who, with our spleens,
Would all themselves laugh mortal.
        W. SHAKESPEARE (*Measure for Measure*, Act II, Sc. ii).

825. SIGH NO MORE, LADIES

SIGH no more, ladies, sigh no more,
    Men were deceivers ever ;
One foot in sea, and one on shore ;
    To one thing constant never.
        Then sigh not so,
        But let them go,
And be you blithe and bonny,
Converting all your sounds of woe
Into Hey nonny, nonny.

Sing no more ditties. Sing no mo
    Of dumps so dull and heavy ;
The fraud of men was ever so,
    Since summer first was leavy.
        Then sigh not so,
        But let them go,
And be you blithe and bonny,
Converting all your sounds of woe
Into Hey nonny, nonny.
        W. SHAKESPEARE (*Much Ado about Nothing*, Act II, Sc. iii).

826. ON A DAY

On a day, alack the day !
Love, whose month is ever May,
Spied a blossom passing fair
Playing in the wanton air ;
Through the velvet leaves the
     wind,
All unseen, 'gan passage find ;
That the lover, sick to death,
Wished himself the heaven's
     breath.
Air, quoth he, thy cheeks may blow;
Air, would I might triumph so !

But alack ! my hand is sworn
Ne'er to pluck thee from thy
     thorn :
Vow, alack ! for youth unmeet,
Youth so apt to pluck a sweet.
Do not call it sin in me,
That I am forsworn for thee ;
Thou for whom e'en Jove would
     swear
Juno but an Ethiop were ;
And deny himself for Jove,
Turning mortal for thy love.

W. SHAKESPEARE (*Love's Labour's Lost*, Act IV, Sc. iii).

827. SPRING

When daisies pied and violets blue
     And lady-smocks all silver-white
And cuckoo-buds of yellow hue
     Do paint the meadows with delight,
The cuckoo then, on every tree,
Mocks married men ; for thus sings he,
                Cuckoo ;
Cuckoo, cuckoo : O, word of fear,
Unpleasing to a married ear !

When shepherds pipe on oaten straws,
     And merry larks are ploughmen's clocks,
When turtles tread, and rooks, and daws,
     And maidens bleach their summer smocks,
The cuckoo then, on every tree,
Mocks married men ; for thus sings he,
                Cuckoo ;
Cuckoo, cuckoo ; O, word of fear,
Unpleasing to a married ear !

W. SHAKESPEARE (*Love's Labour's Lost*, Act v, Sc. ii).

828. WINTER

When icicles hang by the wall,
     And Dick the shepherd blows his nail,
And Tom bears logs into the hall,
     And milk comes frozen home in pail,
When blood is nipped, and ways be foul,
Then nightly sings the staring owl,
                Tu-who ;
Tu-whit, tu-who—a merry note,
While greasy Joan doth keel the pot.

When all around the wind doth blow,
  And coughing drowns the parson's saw,
And birds sit brooding in the snow,
  And Marian's nose looks red and raw,
When roasted crabs hiss in the bowl,
Then nightly sings the staring owl,
         Tu-who ;
Tu-whit, tu-who—a merry note,
While greasy Joan doth keel the pot.
W. SHAKESPEARE (*Love's Labour's Lost*, Act v, Sc. ii).

829.   I NEVER MAY BELIEVE

    I NEVER may believe
These antique fables, nor these fairy toys.
Lovers and madmen have such seething brains,
Such shaping fantasies, that apprehend
More than cool reason ever comprehends.
The lunatic, the lover, and the poet,
Are of imagination all compact :
One sees more devils than vast hell can hold,
That is, the madman ; the lover, all as frantic,
Sees Helen's beauty in a brow of Egypt :
The poet's eye, in a fine frenzy rolling,
Doth glance from heaven to earth, from earth to heaven ;
And, as imagination bodies forth
The forms of things unknown, the poet's pen
Turns them to shapes, and gives to airy nothing
A local habitation and a name.
Such tricks hath strong imagination,
That, if it would but apprehend some joy,
It comprehends some bringer of that joy ;
Or in the night, imagining some fear,
How easy is a bush supposed a bear !
W. SHAKESPEARE (*A Midsummer-Night's Dream*, Act v, Sc. i).

830.   THE FAIRIES' SONG

YOU spotted snakes with double tongue,
  Thorny hedge-hogs, be not seen ;
Newts, and blind-worms, do no wrong ;
  Come not near our fairy queen.
    Philomel, with melody,
    Sing in our sweet lullaby ;
Lulla, lulla, lullaby ; lulla, lulla, lullaby :
    Never harm,
    Nor spell, nor charm,
  Come our lovely lady nigh ;
  So, good night, with lullaby.

Weaving spiders come not here;
　Hence, you long-legged spinners, hence!
Beetles black, approach not near;
　Worm nor snail, do no offence.
　　Philomel, with melody,
　　Sing in our sweet lullaby;
Lulla, lulla, lullaby; lulla, lulla, lullaby:
　　Never harm,
　　Nor spell, nor charm,
　　Come our lovely lady nigh;
　　So, good night, with lullaby.
Fairy.　Hence, away! now all is well.
One aloof stand sentinel.

W. SHAKESPEARE (*A Midsummer-Night's Dream*, Act II, Sc. ii).

831. HOW SWEET THE MOONLIGHT SLEEPS

How sweet the moonlight sleeps upon this bank!
Here will we sit, and let the sounds of music
Creep in our ears: soft stillness and the night
Become the touches of sweet harmony.
Sit, Jessica: look, how the floor of heaven
Is thick inlaid with patines of bright gold:
There's not the smallest orb which thou behold'st
But in his motion like an angel sings,
Still quiring to the young-eyed cherubins;
Such harmony is in immortal souls;
But, whilst this muddy vesture of decay
Doth grossly close it in, we cannot hear it.
　　．　　．　　．　　．　　．　　．
The man that hath no music in himself,
Nor is not moved with concord of sweet sounds,
Is fit for treasons, stratagems, and spoils,
The motions of his spirit are dull as night,
And his affections dark as Erebus:
Let no such man be trusted.

W. SHAKESPEARE (*The Merchant of Venice*, Act V, Sc. i).

832. TELL ME WHERE IS FANCY BRED

TELL me where is fancy bred,
　Or in the heart or in the head?
　How begot, how nourishèd?
　　　Reply, reply.
It is engendered in the eyes,
　With gazing fed; and fancy dies
　In the cradle where it lies.
　　Let us all ring fancy's knell:
　　I'll begin it,—Ding, dong, bell.
　　　Ding, dong, bell.

W. SHAKESPEARE (*The Merchant of Venice*, Act III, Sc. ii).

833. THE QUALITY OF MERCY

THE quality of mercy is not strained,
It droppeth as the gentle rain from heaven
Upon the place beneath : it is twice blessed ;
It blesseth him that gives and him that takes :
'Tis mightiest in the mightiest ; it becomes
The thronèd monarch better than his crown ;
His sceptre shows the force of temporal power,
The attribute to awe and majesty,
Wherein doth sit the dread and fear of kings ;
But mercy is above this sceptred sway,
It is enthronèd in the hearts of kings,
It is an attribute to God himself,
And earthly power doth then show likest God's
When mercy seasons justice. Therefore, Jew,
Though justice be thy plea, consider this,
That in the course of justice none of us
Should see salvation : we do pray for mercy,
And that same prayer doth teach us all to render
The deeds of mercy.

W. SHAKESPEARE (*The Merchant of Venice*, Act IV, Sc. i).

834. ALL THE WORLD'S A STAGE

ALL the world's a stage,
And all the men and women merely players :
They have their exits and their entrances ;
And one man in his time plays many parts,
His acts being seven ages. At first the infant,
Mewling and puking in the nurse's arms.
And then the whining schoolboy, with his satchel,
And shining morning face, creeping like snail
Unwillingly to school. And then the lover,
Sighing like furnace, with a woeful ballad
Made to his mistress' eyebrow. Then a soldier,
Full of strange oaths, and bearded like the pard,
Jealous in honour, sudden and quick in quarrel,
Seeking the bubble reputation
Even in the cannon's mouth. And then the justice,
In fair round belly with good capon lined,
With eyes severe, and beard of formal cut,
Full of wise saws and modern instances ;
And so he plays his part. The sixth age shifts
Into the lean and slippered pantaloon,
With spectacles on nose and pouch on side,
His youthful hose well saved, a world too wide
For his shrunk shank ; and his big manly voice,

Turning again toward childish treble, pipes
And whistles in his sound. Last scene of all,
That ends this strange eventful history,
Is second childishness and mere oblivion,
Sans teeth, sans eyes, sans taste, sans everything.
>   W. SHAKESPEARE (*As You Like It*, Act II, Sc. vii).

835. BLOW, BLOW, THOU WINTER WIND

BLOW, blow, thou winter wind,
Thou art not so unkind
>   As man's ingratitude ;
Thy tooth is not so keen,
Because thou art not seen,
>   Although thy breath be rude.
Heigh-ho ! sing, heigh-ho ! unto the green holly :
Most friendship is feigning, most loving mere folly.
>   Then heigh-ho ! the holly !
>   This life is most jolly.

Freeze, freeze, thou bitter sky,
Thou dost not bite so nigh
>   As benefits forgot :
Though thou the waters warp,
Thy sting is not so sharp
>   As friend remembered not.
Heigh-ho ! sing, heigh-ho ! unto the green holly :
Most friendship is feigning, most loving mere folly.
>   Then heigh-ho ! the holly !
>   This life is most jolly.
>   W. SHAKESPEARE (*As You Like It*, Act II, Sc. vii).

836. IT WAS A LOVER AND HIS LASS

IT was a lover and his lass,
>   With a hey, and a ho, and a hey nonino,
That o'er the green corn-field did pass,
>   In the spring time, the only pretty ring time,
When birds do sing, hey ding a ding, ding ;
Sweet lovers love the spring.

Between the acres of the rye,
>   With a hey, and a ho, and a hey nonino,
These pretty country folks would lie,
>   In the spring time, &c.

This carol they began that hour,
>   With a hey, and a ho, and a hey nonino,
How that a life was but a flower
>   In the spring time, &c.

And therefore take the present time,
  With a hey, and a ho, and a hey nonino ;
For love is crowned with the prime
  In the spring time, the only pretty ring time,
When birds do sing, hey ding a ding, ding ;
Sweet lovers love the spring.
    W. SHAKESPEARE (*As You Like It*, Act v, Sc. iii).

837. UNDER THE GREENWOOD TREE

UNDER the greenwood tree
Who loves to lie with me,
And turn his merry note
Unto the sweet bird's throat,
Come hither, come hither, come
    hither :
  Here shall he see
  No enemy
But winter and rough weather.

Who doth ambition shun,
And loves to live i' the sun,
Seeking the food he eats,
And pleased with what he gets,
Come hither, come hither, come
    hither :
  Here shall he see
  No enemy
But winter and rough weather.
    W. SHAKESPEARE (*As You Like It*, Act II, Sc. v).

838. WHY SHOULD THIS A DESERT BE

WHY should this a desert be ?
  For it is unpeopled ? No ;
Tongues I'll hang on every tree,
  That shall civil sayings show.
Some, how brief the life of man
  Runs his erring pilgrimage,
That the stretching of a span
  Buckles in his sum of age ;
Some, of violated vows
  'Twixt the souls of friend and
    friend :
But upon the fairest boughs,
  Or at every sentence' end,

Will I Rosalinda write ;
  Teaching all that read to
    know
The quintessence of every sprite
  Heaven would in little show.
Therefore Heaven Nature charged
  That one body should be filled
With all graces wide enlarged :
  Nature presently distilled
Helen's cheek, but not her heart,
  Cleopatra's majesty,
Atalanta's better part,
  Sad Lucretia's modesty.
    W. SHAKESPEARE (*As You Like It*, Act III, Sc. ii).

839. COME AWAY, DEATH

COME away, come away, death,
  And in sad cypress let me be
    laid ;
Fly away, fly away, breath ;
  I am slain by a fair cruel maid.
My shroud of white, stuck all with
    yew,
  O ! prepare it.
My part of death, no one so true
  Did share it.

Not a flower, not a flower sweet,
  On my black coffin let there be
    strown ;
Not a friend, not a friend greet
  My poor corse, where my bones
    shall be thrown.
A thousand thousand sighs to save,
  Lay me, O ! where
Sad true lover never find my grave,
  To weep there.
    W. SHAKESPEARE (*Twelfth Night*, Act II, Sc. iv).

P

840. IF MUSIC BE THE FOOD OF LOVE

IF music be the food of love, play on ;
Give me excess of it, that, surfeiting,
The appetite may sicken, and so die.
That strain again ! it had a dying fall :
O ! it came o'er my ear like the sweet sound
That breathes upon a bank of violets,
Stealing and giving odour.   Enough ! no more :
'Tis not so sweet now as it was before.
O spirit of love ! how quick and fresh art thou,
That, notwithstanding thy capacity
Receiveth as the sea, nought enters there,
Of what validity and pitch soe'er,
But falls into abatement and low price,
Even in a minute : so full of shapes is fancy,
That it alone is high fantastical.

                    W. SHAKESPEARE (*Twelfth Night*, Act I, Sc. i).

841. O MISTRESS MINE, WHERE ARE YOU ROAMING

O MISTRESS mine, where are you roaming ?
O ! stay and hear ! your true-love's coming,
       That can sing both high and low ;
Trip no further, pretty sweeting ;
Journeys end in lovers meeting,
       Every wise man's son doth know.

What is love ? 'tis not hereafter ;
Present mirth hath present laughter ;
       What's to come is still unsure :
In delay there lies no plenty ;
Then come kiss me, Sweet-and-twenty,
       Youth's a stuff will not endure.

             W. SHAKESPEARE (*Twelfth Night*, Act II, Sc. iii).

842. SHE NEVER TOLD HER LOVE

             SHE never told her love,
But let concealment, like a worm i' the bud,
Feed on her damask cheek : she pined in thought,
And with a green and yellow melancholy,
She sat like Patience on a monument,
Smiling at grief.

             W. SHAKESPEARE (*Twelfth Night*, Act II, Sc. iv).

843. COME BUY

LAWN as white as driven snow ;
Cypress black as e'er was crow ;
Gloves as sweet as damask roses ;
Masks for faces and for noses ;
Bugle-bracelet, necklace-amber,
Perfume for a lady's chamber ;
Golden quoifs and stomachers,
For my lads to give their dears ;
Pins and poking-sticks of steel ;
What maids lack from head to heel :
Come buy of me, come ; come buy, come buy ;
Buy, lads, or else your lasses cry :
   Come buy.

    W. SHAKESPEARE (*The Winter's Tale*, Act IV, Sc. iii).

844. O PROSERPINA

O PROSERPINA !
For the flowers now that frighted thou let'st fall
From Dis's wagon ! daffodils
That come before the swallow dares, and take
The winds of March with beauty ; violets dim,
But sweeter than the lids of Juno's eyes
Or Cytherea's breath ; pale primroses,
That die unmarried, ere they can behold
Bright Phoebus in his strength, a malady
Most incident to maids ; bold oxlips and
The crown imperial ; lilies of all kinds,
The flower-de-luce being one.

    W. SHAKESPEARE (*The Winter's Tale*, Act IV, Sc. iii).

845. WHEN DAFFODILS BEGIN TO PEER

WHEN daffodils begin to peer,
   With heigh ! the doxy, over the dale,
Why, then comes in the sweet o' the year ;
   For the red blood reigns in the winter's pale.

The white sheet bleaching on the hedge,
   With heigh ! the sweet birds, O, how they sing !
Doth set my pugging tooth on edge ;
   For a quart of ale is a dish for a king.

The lark, that tirra-lirra chants,
   With, heigh ! with, heigh ! the thrush and the jay,
Are summer songs for me and my aunts,
   While we lie tumbling in the hay.

    W. SHAKESPEARE (*The Winter's Tale*, Act IV, Sc. ii).

846. IF ENGLAND TO ITSELF DO REST BUT TRUE

THIS England never did, nor never shall,
Lie at the proud foot of a conqueror,
But when it first did help to wound itself.
Now these her princes are come home again,
Come the three corners of the world in arms,
And we shall shock them. Naught shall make us rue,
If England to itself do rest but true.

> W. SHAKESPEARE (*King John*, Act v, Sc. vii).

847. TO GILD REFINÈD GOLD

To gild refinèd gold, to paint the lily,
To throw a perfume on the violet,
To smooth the ice, or add another hue
Unto the rainbow, or with taper-light
To seek the beauteous eye of heaven to garnish,
Is wasteful and ridiculous excess.

> W. SHAKESPEARE (*King John*, Act IV, Sc. ii).

848. CHRIST'S SOLDIER

MANY a time hath banished Norfolk fought
For Jesu Christ in glorious Christian field,
Streaming the ensign of the Christian cross
Against black pagans, Turks, and Saracens ;
And toiled with works of war, retired himself
To Italy ; and there at Venice gave
His body to that pleasant country's earth,
And his pure soul unto his captain Christ,
Under whose colours he had fought so long.

> W. SHAKESPEARE (*King Richard II*, Act IV, Sc. i).

849. O ! WHO CAN HOLD A FIRE IN HIS HAND

O ! WHO can hold a fire in his hand
By thinking on the frosty Caucasus ?
Or cloy the hungry edge of appetite
By bare imagination of a feast ?
Or wallow naked in December snow
By thinking on fantastic summer's heat ?
O, no ! the apprehension of the good
Gives but the greater feeling to the worse :
Fell sorrow's tooth doth never rankle more
Than when it bites, but lanceth not the sore.

> W. SHAKESPEARE (*King Richard II*, Act I, Sc. iii).

850. SAD STORIES OF THE DEATH OF KINGS

OF comfort no man speak :
Let 's talk of graves, of worms, and epitaphs ;
Make dust our paper, and with rainy eyes
Write sorrow on the bosom of the earth ;
Let 's choose executors and talk of wills :
And yet not so—for what can we bequeath
Save our deposèd bodies to the ground ?
Our lands, our lives, and all are Bolingbroke's,
And nothing can we call our own but death,
And that small model of the barren earth
Which serves as paste and cover to our bones.
For God's sake, let us sit upon the ground
And tell sad stories of the death of kings :
How some have been deposed, some slain in war,
Some haunted by the ghosts they have deposed,
Some poisoned by their wives, some sleeping killed ;
All murdered : for within the hollow crown
That rounds the mortal temples of a king
Keeps Death his court, and there the antic sits,
Scoffing his state and grinning at his pomp ;
Allowing him a breath, a little scene,
To monarchize, be feared, and kill with looks,
Infusing him with self and vain conceit
As if this flesh which walls about our life
Were brass impregnable ; and humoured thus
Comes at the last, and with a little pin
Bores through his castle wall, and farewell king !

W. SHAKESPEARE (*King Richard II*, Act III, Sc. ii).

851. THIS THRONE OF KINGS, THIS SCEPTERED ISLE

THIS royal throne of kings, this sceptered isle,
This earth of majesty, this seat of Mars,
This other Eden, demi-paradise,
This fortress built by Nature for herself
Against infection and the hand of war,
This happy breed of men, this little world,
This precious stone set in the silver sea,
Which serves it in the office of a wall,
Or as a moat defensive to a house,
Against the envy of less happier lands,
This blessèd plot, this earth, this realm, this England.

W. SHAKESPEARE (*King Richard II*, Act II, Sc. i).

852.　SLEEP

How many thousand of my poorest subjects
Are at this hour asleep ! O sleep ! O gentle sleep !
Nature's soft nurse, how have I frighted thee,
That thou no more wilt weigh my eyelids down
And steep my senses in forgetfulness ?
Why rather, sleep, liest thou in smoky cribs,
Upon uneasy pallets stretching thee,
And hushed with buzzing night-flies to thy slumber,
Than in the perfumed chambers of the great,
Under the canopies of costly state,
And lulled with sound of sweetest melody ?
O thou dull god ! why liest thou with the vile
In loathsome beds, and leav'st the kingly couch
A watch-case or a common 'larum bell ?
Wilt thou upon the high and giddy mast
Seal up the ship-boy's eyes, and rock his brains
In cradle of the rude imperious surge,
And in the visitation of the winds,
Who take the ruffian billows by the top,
Curling their monstrous heads, and hanging them
With deafening clamour in the slippery clouds,
That with the hurly death itself awakes ?
Canst thou, O partial sleep ! give thy repose
To the wet sea-boy in an hour so rude,
And in the calmest and most stillest night,
With all appliances and means to boot,
Deny it to a king ? Then, happy low, lie down !
Uneasy lies the head that wears a crown.

  W. SHAKESPEARE (*King Henry IV*, Pt. II, Act III, Sc. i).

853.　FROM HENRY'S ADDRESS TO HIS ARMY

I AM not covetous for gold,
Nor care I who doth feed upon my cost ;
It yearns me not if men my garments wear ;
Such outward things dwell not in my desires :
But if it be a sin to covet honour,
I am the most offending soul alive.
 . . . . . .
We few, we happy few, we band of brothers ;
For he to-day that sheds his blood with me
Shall be my brother ; be he ne'er so vile
This day shall gentle his condition :
And gentlemen in England, now a-bed
Shall think themselves accursed they were not here,
And hold their manhoods cheap whiles any speaks
That fought with us upon Saint Crispin's day.

  W. SHAKESPEARE (*King Henry V*, Act IV, Sc. iii).

854. SO WORK THE HONEY-BEES

So work the honey-bees,
Creatures that by a rule in nature teach
The act of order to a peopled kingdom.
They have a king and officers of sorts ;
Where some, like magistrates, correct at home,
Others, like merchants, venture trade abroad,
Others, like soldiers, armèd in their stings,
Make boot upon the summer's velvet buds ;
Which pillage they with merry march bring home
To the tent-royal of their emperor :
Who, busied in his majesty, surveys
The singing masons building roofs of gold,
The civil citizens kneading up the honey,
The poor mechanic porters crowding in
Their heavy burdens at his narrow gate,
The sad-eyed justice, with his surly hum,
Delivering o'er to executors pale
The lazy yawning drone.
              W. SHAKESPEARE (*King Henry V*, Act I, Sc. ii).

855. METHOUGHT WHAT PAIN IT WAS TO DROWN

METHOUGHT what pain it was to drown:
What dreadful noise of water in mine ears !
What sights of ugly death within mine eyes !
Methought I saw a thousand fearful wracks ;
A thousand men that fishes gnawed upon ;
Wedges of gold, great anchors, heaps of pearl,
Inestimable stones, unvalued jewels,
All scattered in the bottom of the sea.
Some lay in dead men's skulls ; and in those holes
Where eyes did once inhabit, there were crept,
As 'twere in scorn of eyes, reflecting gems,
That wooed the slimy bottom of the deep,
And mocked the dead bones that lay scattered by.
              W. SHAKESPEARE (*King Richard III*, Act I, Sc. iv).

856. NOW IS THE WINTER OF OUR DISCONTENT

Now is the winter of our discontent
Made glorious summer by this sun of York ;
And all the clouds that loured upon our house
In the deep bosom of the ocean buried.
Now are our brows bound with victorious wreaths ;
Our bruisèd arms hung up for monuments ;
Our stern alarums changed to merry meetings ;
Our dreadful marches to delightful measures.

Grim-visaged war hath smoothed his wrinkled front ;
And now,—instead of mounting barbèd steeds,
To fright the souls of fearful adversaries,—
He capers nimbly in a lady's chamber
To the lascivious pleasing of a lute.
> W. SHAKESPEARE (*King Richard III*, Act I, Sc. i).

857.   FAREWELL TO ALL MY GREATNESS

FAREWELL ! a long farewell, to all my greatness !
This is the state of man : to-day he puts forth
The tender leaves of hopes ; to-morrow blossoms,
And bears his blushing honours thick upon him ;
The third day comes a frost, a killing frost ;
And, when he thinks, good easy man, full surely
His greatness is a-ripening, nips his root,
And then he falls, as I do. I have ventured,
Like little wanton boys that swim on bladders,
This many summers in a sea of glory,
But far beyond my depth : my high-blown pride
At length broke under me, and now has left me,
Weary and old with service, to the mercy
Of a rude stream, that must for ever hide me.
Vain pomp and glory of this world, I hate ye :
I feel my heart new opened. O ! how wretched
Is that poor man that hangs on princes' favours.
There is, betwixt that smile we would aspire to,
That sweet aspect of princes, and their ruin,
More pangs and fears than wars or women have ;
And when he falls, he falls like Lucifer,
Never to hope again.
> W. SHAKESPEARE (*King Henry VIII*, Act III, Sc. ii).

858.   ORPHEUS WITH HIS LUTE

ORPHEUS with his lute made trees,
And the mountain tops that freeze,
  Bow themselves, when he did sing :
To his music plants and flowers
Ever sprung ; as sun and showers
  There had made a lasting spring.

Everything that heard him play,
Even the billows of the sea,
  Hung their heads, and then lay by.
In sweet music is such art,
Killing care and grief of heart
  Fall asleep, or hearing, die.
> W. SHAKESPEARE (*King Henry VIII*, Act III, Sc. i).

859. HE JESTS AT SCARS, THAT NEVER FELT A WOUND

HE jests at scars, that never felt a wound.
But, soft ! what light through yonder window breaks ?
It is the east, and Juliet is the sun !
Arise, fair sun, and kill the envious moon,
Who is already sick and pale with grief,
That thou her maid art far more fair than she :
Be not her maid, since she is envious ;
Her vestal livery is but sick and green,
And none but fools do wear it ; cast it off.
It is my lady ; O ! it is my love :
O ! that she knew she were.
She speaks, yet she says nothing : what of that ?
Her eye discourses ; I will answer it.
I am too bold, 'tis not to me she speaks :
Two of the fairest stars in all the heaven,
Having some business, do entreat her eyes
To twinkle in their spheres till they return.
What if her eyes were there, they in her head ?
The brightness of her cheek would shame those stars
As daylight doth a lamp ; her eyes in heaven
Would through the airy region stream so bright
That birds would sing and think it were not night.
See ! how she leans her cheek upon her hand :
O ! that I were a glove upon that hand,
That I might touch that cheek.
      W. SHAKESPEARE (*Romeo and Juliet,* Act II, Sc. ii).

860. QUEEN MAB

SHE is the fairies' midwife, and she comes
In shape no bigger than an agate-stone
On the fore-finger of an alderman,
Drawn with a team of little atomies
Athwart men's noses as they lie asleep :
Her wagon-spokes made of long spinners' legs ;
The cover, of the wings of grasshoppers ;
The traces, of the smallest spider's web ;
The collars, of the moonshine's watery beams ;
Her whip, of cricket's bone ; the lash, of film ;
Her waggoner, a small grey-coated gnat
Not half so big as a round little worm
Pricked from the lazy finger of a maid ;
Her chariot is an empty hazel-nut,
Made by the joiner squirrel or old grub,
Time out o' mind the fairies' coach-makers.

And in this state she gallops night by night
Through lovers' brains, and then they dream of love ;
O'er courtiers' knees, that dream on curtsies straight ;
O'er lawyers' fingers, who straight dream on fees ;
O'er ladies' lips, who straight on kisses dream ;
Which oft the angry Mab with blisters plagues,
Because their breaths with sweetmeats tainted are.
Sometimes she gallops o'er a courtier's nose,
And then dreams he of smelling out a suit ;
And sometimes comes she with a tithe-pig's tail,
Tickling a parson's nose as a' lies asleep,
Then dreams he of another benefice ;
Sometime she driveth o'er a soldier's neck,
And then dreams he of cutting foreign throats,
Of breaches, ambuscadoes, Spanish blades,
Of healths five fathom deep ; and then anon
Drums in his ear, at which he starts and wakes ;
And, being thus frighted, swears a prayer or two,
And sleeps again.
                 W. SHAKESPEARE (*Romeo and Juliet*, Act i, Sc. iv).

861. MARK ANTONY'S ORATION

FRIENDS, Romans, countrymen, lend me your ears ;
I come to bury Caesar, not to praise him.
The evil that men do lives after them,
The good is oft interrèd with their bones ;
So let it be with Caesar. The noble Brutus
Hath told you Caesar was ambitious ;
If it were so, it was a grievous fault,
And grievously hath Caesar answered it.
Here, under leave of Brutus and the rest,—
For Brutus is an honourable man ;
So are they all, all honourable men,—
Come I to speak in Caesar's funeral.
He was my friend, faithful and just to me :
But Brutus says he was ambitious ;
And Brutus is an honourable man.
He hath brought many captives home to Rome,
Whose ransoms did the general coffers fill :
Did this in Caesar seem ambitious ?
When that the poor have cried, Caesar hath wept ;
Ambition should be made of sterner stuff :
Yet Brutus says he was ambitious ;
And Brutus is an honourable man.
You all did see that on the Lupercal
I thrice presented him a kingly crown,
Which he did thrice refuse : was this ambition ?

Yet Brutus says he was ambitious ;
And, sure, he is an honourable man.
I speak not to disprove what Brutus spoke,
But here I am to speak what I do know.
You all did love him once, not without cause :
What cause withholds you then to mourn for him ?
O judgement ! thou art fled to brutish beasts,
And men have lost their reason. Bear with me ;
My heart is in the coffin there with Caesar,
And I must pause till it come back to me.

W. SHAKESPEARE (Julius Caesar, Act III, Sc. ii).

862. THERE IS A TIDE IN THE AFFAIRS OF MEN

THERE is a tide in the affairs of men,
Which, taken at the flood, leads on to fortune ;
Omitted, all the voyage of their life
Is bound in shallows and in miseries.
On such a full sea are we now afloat ;
And we must take the current when it serves,
Or lose our ventures.

W. SHAKESPEARE (Julius Caesar, Act IV, Sc. iii).

863. BRUTUS

THIS was the noblest Roman of them all ;
All the conspirators save only he
Did that they did in envy of great Caesar ;
He only, in a general honest thought
And common good to all, made one of them.
His life was gentle, and the elements
So mixed in him that Nature might stand up
And say to all the world, ' This was a man ! '

W. SHAKESPEARE (Julius Caesar, Act V, Sc. v).

864. A MIND DISEASED

CANST thou not minister to a mind diseased,
Pluck from the memory a rooted sorrow,
Raze out the written troubles of the brain,
And with some sweet oblivious antidote
Cleanse the stuffed bosom of that perilous stuff
Which weighs upon the heart ?

W. SHAKESPEARE (Macbeth, Act V, Sc. iii).

865. IF IT WERE DONE WHEN 'TIS DONE

If it were done when 'tis done, then 'twere well
It were done quickly ; if the assassination
Could trammel up the consequence, and catch
With his surcease success ; that but this blow
Might be the be-all and the end-all here,
But here, upon this bank and shoal of time,
We'd jump the life to come. But in these cases
We still have judgement here ; that we but teach
Bloody instructions, which, being taught, return
To plague the inventor ; this even-handed justice
Commends the ingredients of our poisoned chalice
To our own lips. He's here in double trust :
First, as I am his kinsman and his subject,
Strong both against the deed ; then, as his host,
Who should against his murderer shut the door,
Not bear the knife myself. Besides, this Duncan
Hath borne his faculties so meek, hath been
So clear in his great office, that his virtues
Will plead like angels trumpet-tongued against
The deep damnation of his taking-off ;
And pity, like a naked new-born babe,
Striding the blast, or heaven's cherubin, horsed
Upon the sightless couriers of the air,
Shall blow the horrid deed in every eye,
That tears shall drown the wind. I have no spur
To prick the sides of my intent, but only
Vaulting ambition, which o'er-leaps itself
And falls on the other.

W. SHAKESPEARE (*Macbeth*, Act i, Sc. vii).

866. IS THIS A DAGGER WHICH I SEE BEFORE ME

Is this a dagger which I see before me,
The handle toward my hand ? Come, let me clutch thee :
I have thee not, and yet I see thee still.
Art thou not, fatal vision, sensible
To feeling as to sight ? or art thou but
A dagger of the mind, a false creation,
Proceeding from the heat-oppressèd brain ?
I see thee yet, in form as palpable
As this which now I draw.
Thou marshall'st me the way that I was going ;
And such an instrument I was to use.
Mine eyes are made the fools o' the other senses,
Or else worth all the rest : I see thee still ;
And on thy blade and dudgeon gouts of blood,
Which was not so before. There's no such thing :

It is the bloody business which informs
Thus to mine eyes. Now o'er the one half-world
Nature seems dead, and wicked dreams abuse
The curtained sleep ; witchcraft celebrates
Pale Hecate's offerings ; and withered murder,
Alarumed by his sentinel, the wolf,
Whose howl's his watch, thus with his stealthy pace,
With Tarquin's ravishing strides, toward his design
Moves like a ghost. Thou sure and firm-set earth,
Hear not my steps, which way they walk, for fear
Thy very stones prate of my whereabout,
And take the present horror from the time,
Which now suits with it. Whiles I threat he lives :
Words to the heat of deeds too cold breath gives.
I go, and it is done ; the bell invites me.
Hear it not, Duncan ; for it is a knell
That summons thee to heaven or to hell.

W. SHAKESPEARE (*Macbeth*, Act II, Sc. i).

867. TO-MORROW

TO-MORROW, and to-morrow, and to-morrow,
Creeps in this petty pace from day to day,
To the last syllable of recorded time ;
And all our yesterdays have lighted fools
The way to dusty death. Out, out, brief candle !
Life's but a walking shadow, a poor player
That struts and frets his hour upon the stage,
And then is heard no more ; it is a tale
Told by an idiot, full of sound and fury,
Signifying nothing.

W. SHAKESPEARE (*Macbeth*, Act V, Sc. v).

868. O! THAT THIS TOO TOO SOLID FLESH WOULD MELT

O ! THAT this too too solid flesh would melt,
Thaw and resolve itself into a dew ;
Or that the Everlasting had not fixed
His canon 'gainst self-slaughter ! O God ! O God !
How weary, stale, flat, and unprofitable
Seem to me all the uses of this world.

        · · · · · · ·

        Frailty, thy name is woman !
A little month ; or ere those shoes were old
With which she followed my poor father's body,
Like Niobe, all tears.

W. SHAKESPEARE (*Hamlet*, Act I, Sc. ii).

869. THE CHARIEST MAID IS PRODIGAL ENOUGH

Laertes.   The chariest maid is prodigal enough
If she unmask her beauty to the moon ;
Virtue herself 'scapes not calumnious strokes ;
The canker galls the infants of the spring
Too oft before their buttons be disclosed,
And in the morn and liquid dew of youth
Contagious blastments are most imminent.
Be wary then ;   best safety lies in fear :
Youth to itself rebels, though none else near.
  Ophelia.   I shall the effect of this good lesson keep,
As watchman to my heart.   But, good my brother,
Do not, as some ungracious pastors do,
Show me the steep and thorny way to heaven,
Whiles, like a puffed and reckless libertine,
Himself the primrose path of dalliance treads,
And recks not his own rede.

W. SHAKESPEARE (*Hamlet*, Act I, Sc. iii).

870.   TO THINE OWN SELF BE TRUE

THERE, my blessing with thee !
And these few precepts in thy memory
Look thou character.   Give thy thoughts no tongue,
Nor any unproportioned thought his act.
Be thou familiar, but by no means vulgar ;
The friends thou hast, and their adoption tried,
Grapple them to thy soul with hoops of steel ;
But do not dull thy palm with entertainment
Of each new-hatched, unfledged comrade.   Beware
Of entrance to a quarrel, but, being in,
Bear 't that the opposèd may beware of thee.
Give every man thine ear, but few thy voice ;
Take each man's censure, but reserve thy judgement.
Costly thy habit as thy purse can buy,
But not expressed in fancy ; rich, not gaudy ;
For the apparel oft proclaims the man,
And they in France of the best rank and station
Are most select and generous, chief in that.
Neither a borrower, nor a lender be ;
For loan oft loses both itself and friend,
And borrowing dulls the edge of husbandry.
This above all : to thine own self be true,
And it must follow, as the night the day,
Thou canst not then be false to any man.

W. SHAKESPEARE (*Hamlet*, Act I, Sc. iii).

871. TO BE, OR NOT TO BE

To be, or not to be: that is the question:
Whether 'tis nobler in the mind to suffer
The slings and arrows of outrageous fortune,
Or to take arms against a sea of troubles,
And by opposing end them? To die: to sleep;
No more; and, by a sleep to say we end
The heart-ache and the thousand natural shocks
That flesh is heir to, 'tis a consummation
Devoutly to be wished. To die, to sleep;
To sleep: perchance to dream: aye, there's the rub;
For in that sleep of death what dreams may come
When we have shuffled off this mortal coil,
Must give us pause. There's the respect
That makes calamity of so long life;
For who would bear the whips and scorns of time,
The oppressor's wrong, the proud man's contumely,
The pangs of disprized love, the law's delay,
The insolence of office, and the spurns
That patient merit of the unworthy takes,
When he himself might his quietus make
With a bare bodkin? who would fardels bear,
To grunt and sweat under a weary life,
But that the dread of something after death,
The undiscovered country from whose bourn
No traveller returns, puzzles the will,
And makes us rather bear those ills we have
Than fly to others that we know not of?
Thus conscience does make cowards of us all;
And thus the native hue of resolution
Is sicklied o'er with the pale cast of thought,
And enterprises of great pith and moment
With this regard their currents turn awry,
And lose the name of action.

                    W. SHAKESPEARE (*Hamlet*, Act III, Sc. i).

872. ON DOVER CLIFF

                              How fearful
And dizzy 'tis to cast one's eyes so low!
The crows and choughs that wing the midway air
Show scarce so gross as beetles; half way down
Hangs one that gathers samphire, dreadful trade!
Methinks he seems no bigger than his head.
The fishermen that walk upon the beach
Appear like mice, and yond tall anchoring bark
Diminished to her cock, her cock a buoy
Almost too small for sight. The murmuring surge,

That on the unnumbered idle pebbles chafes,
Cannot be heard so high. I'll look no more,
Lest my brain turn, and the deficient sight
Topple down headlong.

> W. SHAKESPEARE (*King Lear*, Act IV, Sc. vi).

873. FAREWELL THE TRANQUIL MIND

FAREWELL the tranquil mind ; farewell content !
Farewell the plumèd troop and the big wars
That make ambition virtue ! O, farewell !
Farewell the neighing steed, and the shrill trump,
The spirit-stirring drum, the ear-piercing fife,
The royal banner, and all quality,
Pride, pomp, and circumstance of glorious war !
And, O you mortal engines, whose rude throats
The immortal Jove's dread clamours counterfeit,
Farewell ! Othello's occupation 's gone !

> W. SHAKESPEARE (*Othello*, Act III, Sc. iii).

874. GOOD NAME

GOOD name in man and woman, dear my lord,
Is the immediate jewel of their souls :
Who steals my purse steals trash ; 'tis something, nothing ;
'Twas mine, 'tis his, and has been slave to thousands ;
But he that filches from me my good name
Robs me of that which not enriches him,
And makes me poor indeed.

> W. SHAKESPEARE (*Othello*, Act III, Sc. iii).

875. I HAVE DONE THE STATE SOME SERVICE

I HAVE done the state some service, and they know 't ;
No more of that. I pray you, in your letters,
When you shall these unlucky deeds relate,
Speak of me as I am ; nothing extenuate,
Nor set down aught in malice ; then, must you speak
Of one that loved not wisely but too well ;
Of one not easily jealous, but, being wrought,
Perplexed in the extreme ; of one whose hand,
Like the base Indian, threw a pearl away
Richer than all his tribe ; of one whose subdued eyes
Albeit unusèd to the melting mood,
Drop tears as fast as the Arabian trees
Their medicinable gum.

> W. SHAKESPEARE (*Othello*, Act V, Sc. ii).

876. OTHELLO'S WOOING

I WILL a round unvarnished tale deliver
Of my whole course of love. . . . .
Her father loved me ; oft invited me ;
Still questioned me the story of my life
From year to year, the battles, sieges, fortunes
That I have passed.
I ran it through, even from my boyish days,
To the very moment that he bade me tell it ;
Wherein I spake of most disastrous chances,
Of moving accidents by flood and field,
Of hair-breadth 'scapes i' the imminent deadly breach,
Of being taken by the insolent foe,
And sold to slavery, of my redemption thence
And portance in my travel's history :
Wherein of antres vast, and deserts idle,
Rough quarries, rocks and hills whose heads touch heaven,
It was my hint to speak, such was the process ;
And of the Cannibals that each other eat,
The Anthropophagi, and men whose heads
Do grow beneath their shoulders. This to hear
Would Desdemona seriously incline : . . . .
          . . . . My story being done,
She gave me for my pains a world of sighs :
She swore, in faith, 'twas strange, 'twas passing strange ;
'Twas pitiful, 'twas wondrous pitiful :
She wished she had not heard it, yet she wished
That heaven had made her such a man : she thanked me ;
And bade me, if I had a friend that loved her,
I should but teach him how to tell my story,
And that would woo her. Upon this hint, I spake :
She loved me for the dangers I had passed ;
And I loved her, that she did pity them.

W. SHAKESPEARE (Othello, Act I, Sc. iii).

877. SHE THAT WAS EVER FAIR

SHE that was ever fair and never proud,
Had tongue at will and yet was never loud,
Never lacked gold and yet went never gay,
Fled from her wish and yet said ' Now I may ',
She that being angered, her revenge being nigh,
Bade her wrong stay and her displeasure fly,
She that in wisdom never was so frail
To change the cod's head for the salmon's tail,
She that could think and ne'er disclose her mind,
See suitors following and not look behind,
She was a wight, if ever such wight were,—
To suckle fools and chronicle small beer.

W. SHAKESPEARE (Othello, Act II, Sc. i).

878.   A DIRGE

FEAR no more the heat o' the sun,
  Nor the furious winter's rages ;
Thou thy worldly task hast done,
  Home art gone, and ta'en thy wages ;
Golden lads and girls all must,
As chimney-sweepers, come to dust.

Fear no more the frown o' the great,
  Thou art past the tyrant's stroke ;
Care no more to clothe and eat ;
  To thee the reed is as the oak :
The sceptre, learning, physic, must
All follow this, and come to dust.

Fear no more the lightning-flash
  Nor the all-dreaded thunder-stone ;
Fear not slander, censure rash ;
  Thou hast finished joy and moan :
All lovers young, all lovers must
Consign to thee, and come to dust.

             W. SHAKESPEARE (*Cymbeline*, Act IV, Sc. ii).

879.   HARK ! HARK ! THE LARK

HARK ! hark ! the lark at heaven's gate sings,
  And Phoebus 'gins arise,
His steeds to water at those springs
  On chaliced flowers that lies ;
And winking Mary-buds begin
  To ope their golden eyes :
With everything that pretty is,
  My lady sweet, arise :
    Arise, arise !
             W. SHAKESPEARE (*Cymbeline*, Act II, Sc. iii).

880.   CRABBÈD AGE AND YOUTH

CRABBÈD Age and Youth cannot live together :
  Youth is full of pleasure, age is full of care ;
Youth like summer morn, age like winter weather,
  Youth like summer brave, age like winter bare :
Youth is full of sport, age's breath is short ;
  Youth is nimble, age is lame :
Youth is hot and bold, age is weak and cold,
  Youth is wild, and age is tame.
Age, I do abhor thee, youth, I do adore thee ;
  O ! my love, my love is young :
Age, I do defy thee : O ! sweet shepherd, hie thee,
  For methinks thou stay'st too long.
             W. SHAKESPEARE (*The Passionate Pilgrim*)

881. FAREWELL! THOU ART TOO DEAR FOR MY POSSESSING

FAREWELL! thou art too dear for my possessing,
And like enough thou know'st thy estimate:
The charter of thy worth gives thee releasing;
My bonds in thee are all determinate.
For how do I hold thee but by thy granting?
And for that riches where is my deserving?
The cause of this fair gift in me is wanting,
And so my patent back again is swerving.
Thyself thou gav'st, thy own worth then not knowing,
Or me, to whom thou gav'st it, else mistaking;
So thy great gift, upon misprision growing,
Comes home again, on better judgement making.
    Thus have I had thee, as a dream doth flatter,
    In sleep a king, but, waking, no such matter.
                W. SHAKESPEARE (Sonnet LXXXVII).

882. FULL MANY A GLORIOUS MORNING HAVE I SEEN

FULL many a glorious morning have I seen
Flatter the mountain-tops with sovereign eye,
Kissing with golden face the meadows green,
Gilding pale streams with heavenly alchemy;
Anon permit the basest clouds to ride
With ugly rack on his celestial face,
And from the forlorn world his visage hide,
Stealing unseen to west with this disgrace:
Even so my sun one early morn did shine,
With all-triumphant splendour on my brow;
But, out! alack! he was but one hour mine,
The region cloud hath masked him from me now.
    Yet him for this my love no whit disdaineth;
    Suns of the world may stain when heaven's sun staineth.
                W. SHAKESPEARE (Sonnet XXXIII).

883. LET ME NOT TO THE MARRIAGE OF TRUE MINDS

LET me not to the marriage of true minds
Admit impediments. Love is not love
Which alters when it alteration finds,
Or bends with the remover to remove:
O no! it is an ever-fixèd mark
That looks on tempests and is never shaken;
It is the star to every wandering bark,
Whose worth's unknown, although his height be taken.
Love's not Time's fool, though rosy lips and cheeks
Within his bending sickle's compass come;
Love alters not with his brief hours and weeks,
But bears it out even to the edge of doom.
    If this be error, and upon me proved,
    I never writ, nor no man ever loved.
                W. SHAKESPEARE (Sonnet CXVI).

884. SHALL I COMPARE THEE TO A SUMMER'S DAY

SHALL I compare thee to a summer's day ?
Thou art more lovely and more temperate :
Rough winds do shake the darling buds of May,
And summer's lease hath all too short a date :
Sometime too hot the eye of heaven shines,
And often is his gold complexion dimmed :
And every fair from fair sometime declines,
By chance, or nature's changing course, untrimmed.
But thy eternal summer shall not fade,
Nor lose possession of that fair thou ow'st,
Nor shall death brag thou wander'st in his shade,
When in eternal lines to time thou grow'st ;
  So long as men can breathe, or eyes can see,
  So long lives this, and this gives life to thee.

W. SHAKESPEARE (Sonnet XVIII).

885. TO ME, FAIR FRIEND, YOU NEVER CAN BE OLD

To me, fair friend, you never can be old,
For as you were when first your eye I eyed,
Such seems your beauty still. Three winters cold
Have from the forests shook three summers' pride,
Three beauteous springs to yellow autumn turned
In process of the seasons have I seen,
Three April perfumes in three hot Junes burned,
Since first I saw you fresh, which yet are green.
Ah ! yet doth beauty, like a dial-hand,
Steal from his figure, and no pace perceived ;
So your sweet hue, which methinks still doth stand,
Hath motion, and mine eye may be deceived :
  For fear of which, hear this, thou age unbred :
  Ere you were born was beauty's summer dead.

W. SHAKESPEARE (Sonnet CIV).

886. WHEN IN THE CHRONICLE OF WASTED TIME

WHEN in the chronicle of wasted time
I see descriptions of the fairest wights,
And beauty making beautiful old rhyme
In praise of ladies dead and lovely knights,
Then, in the blazon of sweet beauty's best,
Of hand, of foot, of lip, of eye, of brow,
I see their antique pen would have expressed
Even such a beauty as you master now.
So all their praises are but prophecies
Of this our time, all you prefiguring ;
And, for they looked but with divining eyes,
They had not skill enough your worth to sing :
  For we, which now behold these present days,
  Have eyes to wonder, but lack tongues to praise.

W. SHAKESPEARE (Sonnet CVI).

887. WHEN TO THE SESSIONS OF SWEET SILENT THOUGHT

When to the sessions of sweet silent thought
I summon up remembrance of things past,
I sigh the lack of many a thing I sought,
And with old woes new wail my dear times' waste:
Then can I drown an eye, unused to flow,
For precious friends hid in death's dateless night,
And weep afresh love's long since cancelled woe,
And moan the expense of many a vanished sight:
Then can I grieve at grievances foregone,
And heavily from woe to woe tell o'er
The sad account of fore-bemoanèd moan,
Which I new pay as if not paid before.
But if the while I think on thee, dear friend,
All losses are restored and sorrows end.

W. Shakespeare (Sonnet xxx).

888. GOOD-NIGHT

Good-night? ah! no; the hour is ill
  Which severs those it should unite;
Let us remain together still,
  Then it will be *good* night.

How can I call the lone night good,
  Though thy sweet wishes wing its flight?
Be it not said, thought, understood,
  Then it will be—*good* night.

To hearts which near each other move
  From evening close to morning light,
The night *is* good; because, my love,
  They never *say* good-night. P. B. Shelley.

889. TO A SKYLARK

Hail to thee, blithe Spirit!
  Bird thou never wert,
That from heaven, or near it,
  Pourest thy full heart
In profuse strains of unpremeditated art.

Higher still and higher
  From the earth thou springest
Like a cloud of fire;
  The blue deep thou wingest,
And singing still dost soar, and soaring ever singest.

In the golden lightning
  Of the sunken sun,
O'er which clouds are brightening,
  Thou dost float and run ;
Like an unbodied joy whose race is just begun.

The pale purple even
  Melts around thy flight ;
Like a star of Heaven
  In the broad daylight
Thou art unseen, but yet I hear thy shrill delight,

Keen as are the arrows
  Of that silver sphere,
Whose intense lamp narrows
  In the white dawn clear
Until we hardly see—we feel that it is there.

All the earth and air
  With thy voice is loud,
As, when night is bare,
  From one lonely cloud
The moon rains out her beams, and heaven is overflowed.

What thou art we know not ;
  What is most like thee ?
From rainbow clouds there flow not
  Drops so bright to see
As from thy presence showers a rain of melody.

Like a Poet hidden
  In the light of thought
Singing hymns unbidden,
  Till the world is wrought
To sympathy with hopes and fears it heeded not :

Like a high-born maiden
  In a palace-tower,
Soothing her love-laden
  Soul in secret hour
With music sweet as love, which overflows her bower :

Like a glow-worm golden
  In a dell of dew,
Scattering unbeholden
  Its aerial hue
Among the flowers and grass, which screen it from the view !

Like a rose embowered
  In its own green leaves,
By warm winds deflowered,
  Till the scent it gives
Makes faint with too much sweet those heavy-wingèd thieves :

Sound of vernal showers
    On the twinkling grass,
Rain-awakened flowers,
    All that ever was
Joyous, and clear, and fresh, thy music doth surpass:

Teach us, Sprite or Bird,
    What sweet thoughts are thine:
I have never heard
    Praise of love or wine
That panted forth a flood of rapture so divine.

Chorus Hymeneal,
    Or triumphal chant,
Matched with thine would be all
    But an empty vaunt,
A thing wherein we feel there is some hidden want.

What objects are the fountains
    Of thy happy strain?
What fields, or waves, or mountains?
    What shapes of sky or plain?
What love of thine own kind? what ignorance of pain?

With thy clear keen joyance
    Languor cannot be:
Shadow of annoyance
    Never came near thee:
Thou lovest—but ne'er knew love's sad satiety.

Waking or asleep,
    Thou of death must deem
Things more true and deep
    Than we mortals dream,
Or how could thy notes flow in such a crystal stream?

We look before and after,
    And pine for what is not:
Our sincerest laughter
    With some pain is fraught;
Our sweetest songs are those that tell of saddest thought.

Yet if we could scorn
    Hate, and pride, and fear;
If we were things born
    Not to shed a tear,
I know not how thy joy we ever should come near.

Better than all measures
    Of delightful sound,
Better than all treasures
    That in books are found,
Thy skill to poet were, thou scorner of the ground!

Teach me half the gladness
   That thy brain must know,
Such harmonious madness
   From my lips would flow
The world should listen then—as I am listening now !

P. B. SHELLEY.

890.   HE HAS OUTSOARED THE SHADOW OF OUR NIGHT

He has outsoared the shadow of our night ;
Envy and calumny and hate and pain,
And that unrest which men miscall delight,
Can touch him not and torture not again ;
From the contagion of the world's slow stain
He is secure, and now can never mourn
A heart grown cold, a head grown grey in vain.

P. B. SHELLEY (Adonais).

891.   ON KEATS

WHO DESIRED THAT ON HIS TOMB SHOULD BE INSCRIBED ——

' HERE lieth One whose name was writ on water.'
   But, ere the breath that could erase it blew,
Death, in remorse for that fell slaughter,
   Death, the immortalizing winter, flew
Athwart the stream,—and time's printless torrent grew
A scroll of crystal, blazoning the name
   Of Adonais !

P. B. SHELLEY.

892.   HOW WONDERFUL IS DEATH

How wonderful is Death,
   Death and his brother Sleep !
One, pale as yonder waning moon,
   With lips of lurid blue ;
   The other, rosy as the morn
When throned on ocean's wave
   It blushes o'er the world :
Yet both so passing wonderful !

   Hath then the gloomy Power
Whose reign is in the tainted sepulchres
   Seized on her sinless soul ?
   Must then that peerless form
Which love and admiration cannot view
Without a beating heart, those azure veins
Which steal like streams along a field of snow,
   That lovely outline, which is fair
         As breathing marble, perish ?

Must putrefaction's breath
Leave nothing of this heavenly sight
But loathsomeness and ruin ?
Spare nothing but a gloomy theme,
On which the lightest heart might moralize ?
Or is it only a sweet slumber
Stealing o'er sensation,
Which the breath of roseate morning
Chaseth into darkness ?
Will Ianthe wake again,
And give that faithful bosom joy
Whose sleepless spirit waits to catch
Light, life and rapture from her smile ?

P. B. SHELLEY (*Queen Mab*).

893. LINES TO AN INDIAN AIR

I ARISE from dreams of thee
In the first sweet sleep of night,
When the winds are breathing low,
And the stars are shining bright :
I arise from dreams of thee,
And a spirit in my feet
Has led me—who knows how ?
To thy chamber-window, Sweet !

The wandering airs they faint
On the dark, the silent stream—
The Champak odours fail
Like sweet thoughts in a dream ;
The nightingale's complaint,
It dies upon her heart ;—
As I must on thine,
Oh, belovèd as thou art !

Oh lift me from the grass !
I die ! I faint ! I fail !
Let thy love in kisses rain
On my lips and eyelids pale.
My cheek is cold and white, alas !
My heart beats loud and fast ;—
Oh ! press it to thine own again,
Where it will break at last.   P. B. SHELLEY.

894. FROM 'THE CLOUD'

I BRING fresh showers for the thirsting flowers,
    From the seas and the streams ;
I bear light shade for the leaves when laid
    In their noonday dreams.
From my wings are shaken the dews that waken
    The sweet buds every one,
When rocked to rest on their mother's breast,
    As she dances about the sun.
I wield the flail of the lashing hail,
    And whiten the green plains under ;
And then again I dissolve it in rain,
    And laugh as I pass in thunder.

I sift the snow on the mountains below,
    And their great pines groan aghast;
And all the night 'tis my pillow white,
    While I sleep in the arms of the blast.
Sublime on the towers of my skiey bowers,
    Lightning my pilot sits;
In a cavern under is fettered the thunder,
    It struggles and howls at fits.   P. B. SHELLEY.

895. TO ——

I FEAR thy kisses, gentle maiden,
    Thou needest not fear mine;
My spirit is too deeply laden
    Ever to burthen thine.

I fear thy mien, thy tones, thy motion,
    Thou needest not fear mine;
Innocent is the heart's devotion
    With which I worship thine.   P. B. SHELLEY.

896. TO ——

MUSIC, when soft voices die,
Vibrates in the memory——
Odours, when sweet violets sicken,
Live within the sense they quicken.

Rose leaves, when the rose is dead,
Are heaped for the belovèd's bed;
And so thy thoughts, when thou art gone,
Love itself shall slumber on.   P. B. SHELLEY.

897. ODE TO THE WEST WIND

I

O WILD West Wind, thou breath of Autumn's being,
Thou, from whose unseen presence the leaves dead
Are driven, like ghosts from an enchanter fleeing,

Yellow, and black, and pale, and hectic red,
Pestilence-stricken multitudes: O thou,
Who chariotest to their dark wintry bed

The wingèd seeds, where they lie cold and low,
Each like a corpse within its grave, until
Thine azure sister of the Spring shall blow

Her clarion o'er the dreaming earth, and fill
(Driving sweet buds like flocks to feed in air)
With living hues and odours plain and hill:

Wild Spirit, which art moving everywhere;
Destroyer and preserver; hear, oh, hear!

II

Thou on whose stream, 'mid the steep sky's commotion,
Loose clouds like earth's decaying leaves are shed,
Shook from the tangled boughs of Heaven and Ocean,

Angels of rain and lightning: there are spread
On the blue surface of thine aery surge,
Like the bright hair uplifted from the head

Of some fierce Maenad, even from the dim verge
Of the horizon to the zenith's height,
The locks of the approaching storm. Thou dirge

Of the dying year, to which this closing night
Will be the dome of a vast sepulchre,
Vaulted with all thy congregated might

Of vapours, from whose solid atmosphere
Black rain, and fire, and hail will burst: oh, hear!

III

Thou who didst waken from his summer dreams,
The blue Mediterranean, where he lay,
Lulled by the coil of his crystàlline streams,

Beside a pumice isle in Baiae's bay,
And saw in sleep old palaces and towers
Quivering within the wave's intenser day,

All overgrown with azure moss and flowers
So sweet, the sense faints picturing them! Thou
For whose path the Atlantic's level powers

Cleave themselves into chasms, while far below
The sea-blooms and the oozy woods which wear
The sapless foliage of the ocean, know

Thy voice, and suddenly grow grey with fear
And tremble and despoil themselves: oh, hear!

IV

If I were a dead leaf thou mightest bear;
If I were a swift cloud to fly with thee;
A wave to pant beneath thy power, and share

The impulse of thy strength, only less free
Than thou, O uncontrollable! If even
I were as in my boyhood, and could be

The comrade of thy wanderings over heaven,
As then, when to outstrip thy skiey speed
Scarce seemed a vision; I would ne'er have striven

As thus with thee in prayer in my sore need.
Oh, lift me as a wave, a leaf, a cloud!
I fall upon the thorns of life! I bleed!

A heavy weight of hours has chained and bowed
One too like thee: tameless, and swift, and proud.

v

Make me thy lyre, even as the forest is :
What if my leaves are falling like its own !
The tumult of thy mighty harmonies

Will take from both a deep, autumnal tone,
Sweet though in sadness. Be thou, Spirit fierce,
My spirit ! Be thou me, impetuous one !

Drive my dead thoughts over the universe
Like withered leaves to quicken a new birth !
And, by the incantation of this verse,

Scatter, as from an unextinguished hearth
Ashes and sparks, my words among mankind !
Be through my lips to unawakened earth

The trumpet of a prophecy ! O Wind,
If Winter comes, can Spring be far behind ? P. B. SHELLEY.

898. A LAMENT

O WORLD ! O life ! O time !
On whose last steps I climb,
   Trembling at that where I had stood before ;
When will return the glory of your prime ?
      No more—Oh, never more !

Out of the day and night
A joy has taken flight ;
   Fresh spring, and summer, and winter hoar,
Move my faint heart with grief, but with delight
      No more—Oh, never more !   P. B. SHELLEY.

899. ON A POET'S LIPS I SLEPT

On a poet's lips I slept
Dreaming like a love-adept
In the sound his breathing kept ;
Nor seeks nor finds he mortal blisses,
But feeds on the aerial kisses
Of shapes that haunt thought's wildernesses.
He will watch from dawn to gloom
The lake-reflected sun illume
The yellow bees in the ivy-bloom,
Nor heed, nor see, what things they be ;
But from these create he can
Forms more real than living man,
Nurslings of immortality !
One of these awakened me,
And I sped to succour thee.
         P. B. SHELLEY (*Prometheus Unbound*).

900. ONE WORD IS TOO OFTEN PROFANED

ONE word is too often profaned
  For me to profane it,
One feeling too falsely disdained
  For thee to disdain it ;
One hope is too like despair
  For prudence to smother,
And pity from thee more dear
  Than that from another.

I can give not what men call love,
  But wilt thou accept not
The worship the heart lifts above
  And the Heavens reject not,—
The desire of the moth for the star,
  Of the night for the morrow,
The devotion to something afar
  From the sphere of our sorrow ?

P. B. SHELLEY.

901. TO THE NIGHT

SWIFTLY walk o'er the western wave,
    Spirit of Night !
Out of the misty eastern cave,
Where, all the long and lone daylight,
Thou wovest dreams of joy and fear,
Which make thee terrible and dear,—
    Swift be thy flight !

Wrap thy form in a mantle grey,
    Star-inwrought !
Blind with thine hair the eyes of Day ;
Kiss her until she be wearied out,
Then wander o'er city, and sea, and land,
Touching all with thine opiate wand—
    Come, long-sought !

When I arose and saw the dawn,
    I sighed for thee ;
When light rode high, and the dew was gone,
And noon lay heavy on flower and tree,
And the weary Day turned to his rest
Lingering like an unloved guest,
    I sighed for thee.

Thy brother Death came, and cried
    Wouldst thou me ?
Thy sweet child Sleep, the filmy-eyed,
Murmured like a noontide bee,
Shall I nestle near thy side ?
Wouldst thou me ?—And I replied
    No, not thee !

Death will come when thou art dead,
    Soon, too soon—
Sleep will come when thou art fled ;
Of neither would I ask the boon
I ask of thee, belovèd Night—
Swift be thine approaching flight,
    Come soon, soon !
P. B. SHELLEY.

902. LOVE'S PHILOSOPHY

THE fountains mingle with the river
  And the rivers with the Ocean,
The winds of heaven mix for ever
  With a sweet emotion ;
Nothing in the world is single ;
  All things by a law divine
In one spirit meet and mingle.
  Why not I with thine ?—

See the mountains kiss high heaven
  And the waves clasp one another ;
No sister-flower would be forgiven
  If it disdained its brother ;
And the sunlight clasps the earth,
  And the moonbeams kiss the sea :
What is all this sweet work worth,
  If thou kiss not me ?   P. B. SHELLEY.

903. OCEAN'S NURSLING

UNDERNEATH Day's azure eyes
Ocean's nursling, Venice lies,
A peopled labyrinth of walls,
Amphitrite's destined halls,
Which her hoary sire now paves
With his blue and beaming waves.
Lo ! the sun upsprings behind,
Broad, red, radiant, half-reclined
On the level quivering line
Of the waters crystalline ;
And before that chasm of light,
As within a furnace bright,
Column, tower, and dome, and
    spire,
Shine like obelisks of fire,

Pointing with inconstant motion
From the altar of dark ocean
To the sapphire-tinted skies ;
As the flames of sacrifice
From the marble shrines did rise,
As to pierce the dome of gold
Where Apollo spoke of old.

Sun-girt City ! thou hast been
Ocean's child, and then his queen ;
Now is come a darker day,
And thou soon must be his prey,
If the power that raised thee
    here
Hallow so thy watery bier.

P. B. SHELLEY (*Lines written among the Euganean Hills*).

904. TIME

UNFATHOMABLE Sea ! whose waves are years,
  Ocean of Time, whose waters of deep woe
Are brackish with the salt of human tears !
  Thou shoreless flood, which in thy ebb and flow
Claspest the limits of mortality,
And sick of prey, yet howling on for more,
Vomitest thy wrecks on its inhospitable shore ;
Treacherous in calm, and terrible in storm,
  Who shall put forth on thee,
    Unfathomable Sea ?   P. B. SHELLEY.

905. WHEN THE LAMP IS SHATTERED

When the lamp is shattered
The light in the dust lies dead—
When the cloud is scattered,
The rainbow's glory is shed.
When the lute is broken,
Sweet tones are remembered not ;
When the lips have spoken,
Loved accents are soon forgot.

As music and splendour
Survive not the lamp and the lute,
The heart's echoes render
No song when the spirit is mute :—
No song but sad dirges,
Like the wind through a ruined cell,
Or the mournful surges
That ring the dead seaman's knell.

When hearts have once mingled,
Love first leaves the well-built nest ;
The weak one is singled
To endure what it once possessed.
O Love ! who bewailest
The frailty of all things here,
Why choose you the frailest
For your cradle, your home, and your bier ?

Its passions will rock thee
As the storms rock the ravens on high ;
Bright reason will mock thee,
Like the sun from a wintry sky.
From thy nest every rafter
Will rot, and thine eagle home
Leave thee naked to laughter,
When leaves fall and cold winds come.   P. B. Shelley.

906. WRITTEN AT AN INN AT HENLEY

To thee, fair freedom ! I retire
   From flattery, cards, and dice, and din ;
Nor art thou found in mansions higher
   Than the low cot, or humble inn.

'Tis here with boundless power I reign ;
   And every health which I begin,
Converts dull port to bright champagne ;
   Such freedom crowns it, at an inn.

I fly from pomp, I fly from plate !
   I fly from falsehood's specious grin ;
Freedom I love, and form I hate,
   And choose my lodgings at an inn.

Here, waiter ! take my sordid ore,
   Which lackeys else might hope to win ;
It buys, what courts have not in store ;
   It buys me freedom at an inn.

Whoe'er has travelled life's dull round,
   Where'er his stages may have been,
May sigh to think he still has found
   The warmest welcome at an inn.   W. Shenstone.

907. HAD I A HEART FOR FALSEHOOD FRAMED

HAD I a heart for falsehood framed,
    I ne'er could injure you ;
For though your tongue no promise claimed,
    Your charms would make me true.
To you no soul shall bear deceit,
    No stranger offer wrong ;
But friends in all the aged you'll meet,
    And lovers in the young.

But when they learn that you have blest
    Another with your heart,
They'll bid aspiring passion rest,
    And act a brother's part :
Then, lady, dread not here deceit
    Nor fear to suffer wrong ;
For friends in all the aged you'll meet,
    And brothers in the young.

R. B. SHERIDAN (*The Duenna*).

908. I NE'ER COULD ANY LUSTRE SEE

I NE'ER could any lustre see
In eyes that would not look on me ;
I ne'er saw nectar on a lip,
But where my own did hope to sip.
Has the maid who seeks my heart
Cheeks of rose, untouched by art ?
I will own the colour true
When yielding blushes aid their hue.

Is her hand so soft and pure ?
I must press it, to be sure ;
Nor can I be certain then,
Till it, grateful, press again.
Must I, with attentive eye,
Watch her heaving bosom sigh ?
I will do so, when I see
That heaving bosom sigh for me.

R. B. SHERIDAN (*The Duenna*).

909. THE SUN OF OUR TABLE

THIS bottle's the sun of our table,
    His beams are rosy wine ;
We, planets, that are not able
    Without his help to shine.
Let mirth and glee abound !
        You'll soon grow bright
        With borrowed light,
And shine as he goes round !

R. B. SHERIDAN (*The Duenna*).

910. THE GLORIES OF OUR BLOOD AND STATE

THE glories of our blood and state
    Are shadows, not substantial things ;
There is no armour against fate ;
    Death lays his icy hand on kings :
        Sceptre and Crown
        Must tumble down,
And in the dust be equal made
With the poor crookèd scythe and spade.

Some men with swords may reap the field,
    And plant fresh laurels where they kill :
But their strong nerves at last must yield ;
    They tame but one another still :
        Early or late
        They stoop to fate,
And must give up their murmuring breath,
When they, pale captives, creep to death.

The garlands wither on your brow,
    Then boast no more your mighty deeds ;
Upon Death's purple altar now
    See, where the victor-victim bleeds :
        Your heads must come
        To the cold tomb ;
Only the actions of the just
Smell sweet, and blossom in their dust.   J. SHIRLEY.

911. VICTORIOUS MEN OF EARTH

VICTORIOUS men of earth, no more
    Proclaim how wide your empires are ;
Though you bind in every shore,
    And your triumphs reach as far
        As night or day,
    Yet you, proud monarchs, must obey
And mingle with forgotten ashes, when
Death calls ye to the crowd of common men.

Devouring Famine, Plague, and War,
    Each able to undo mankind,
Death's servile emissaries are ;
    Nor to these alone confined,
        He hath at will
    More quaint and subtle ways to kill ;
A smile or kiss, as he will use the art,
Shall have the cunning skill to break a heart.
                       J. SHIRLEY.

912.   PIPING PEACE

You virgins that did late despair
  To keep your wealth from cruel
    men,
Tie up in silk your careless hair :
  Soft peace is come again.

Now lovers' eyes may gently
    shoot
  A flame that would not kill :
The drum was angry, but the
    lute
  Shall whisper what you will.

Sing ' Io, Io ! ' for his sake
  Who hath restored your droop-
    ing heads ;
With choice of sweetest flowers
    make
  A garden where he treads ;

Whilst we whole groves of laurel
    bring,
  A petty triumph to his brow,
Who is the master of our spring
  And all the bloom we owe.
                          J. SHIRLEY.

913.   SLEEP

COME, Sleep ! O Sleep, the certain knot of peace,
The baiting-place of wit, the balm of woe,
The poor man's wealth, the prisoner's release,
The indifferent judge between the high and low ;
With shield of proof shield me from out the press
Of those fierce darts Despair at me doth throw :
O make in me those civil wars to cease ;
I will good tribute pay, if thou do so.
Take thou of me smooth pillows, sweetest bed,
A chamber deaf to noise and blind to light,
A rosy garland and a weary head :
And if these things, as being thine in right,
  Move not thy heavy grace, thou shalt in me,
  Livelier than elsewhere, Stella's image see.
                          SIR P. SIDNEY.

914.   WOOING STUFF

FAINT Amorist ! what, dost thou think
To taste Love's honey, and not drink
One dram of gall ? or to devour
A world of sweet, and taste no sour ?
Dost thou ever think to enter
The Elysian fields, that dar'st not venture
In Charon's barge ? A lover's mind
Must use to sail with every wind.
He that loves, and fears to try,
Learns his mistress to deny.
  Doth she chide thee ? 'Tis to show it,
That thy coldness makes her do it.
  Is she silent ? Is she mute ?
Silence fully grants thy suit.

Doth she pout and leave the room ?
Then she goes, to bid thee come.
  Is she sick ? Why then, be sure
She invites thee to the cure.
  Doth she cross thy suit with ' No ' ?
Tush ! She loves to hear thee woo.
  Doth she call the faith of man
In question ? Nay, she loves thee then.
And if e'er she makes a blot,
She's lost if that thou hitt'st her not.
  He that after ten denials
Dares attempt no further trials,
Hath no warrant to acquire
The dainties of his chaste desire.   SIR P. SIDNEY.

915. LEAVE ME, O LOVE

LEAVE me, O Love ! which reachest but to dust,
And thou, my mind, aspire to higher things ;
Grow rich in that which never taketh rust.
Whatever fades, but fading pleasure brings.
Draw in thy beams, and humble all thy might
To that sweet yoke, where lasting freedoms be,
Which breaks the clouds, and opens forth the light,
That doth both shine and give us sight to see.
Oh, take fast hold ! Let that Light be thy guide
In this small course, which birth draws out to death,
And think how evil becometh him to slide
Who seeketh heaven, and comes of heavenly breath.
  Then, farewell, world ! Thy uttermost I see.
  Eternal Love, maintain thy life in me.   SIR P. SIDNEY.

916. LOOK IN THY HEART AND WRITE

LOVING in truth, and fain in verse my love to show,
That she, dear she, might take some pleasure of my pain—
Pleasure might cause her read, reading might make her know,
Knowledge might pity win, and pity grace obtain—
I sought fit words to paint the blackest face of woe,
Studying inventions fine, her wits to entertain ;
Oft turning others' leaves, to see if thence would flow
Some fresh and fruitful showers upon my sunburned brain.
But words came halting forth, wanting Invention's stay ;
Invention, Nature's child, fled step-dame Study's blows ;
And others' feet still seemed but strangers in my way.
Thus, great with child to speak, and helpless in my throes,
  Biting my truant pen, beating myself for spite,
  ' Fool,' said my Muse to me, ' look in thy heart and write ! '
                                        SIR P. SIDNEY.

917.　A SUGARED KISS

My Star, because a sugared kiss
In sport I sucked while she asleep did lie,
Doth lour, nay chide, nay threat for only this !
Sweet, it was saucy Love, not humble I.
But no 'scuse serves ; she makes her wrath appear
In Beauty's throne : see now, who dares come near
Those scarlet judges, threatening bloody pain.
O heavenly fool, thy most kiss-worthy face
Anger invests with such a lovely grace,
That Anger's self I needs must kiss again.

　　　　　　　　　　SIR P. SIDNEY (*Astrophel and Stella*).

918.　MY TRUE-LOVE HATH MY HEART

My true-love hath my heart, and I have his,
By just exchange one for the other given :
I hold his dear, and mine he cannot miss,
There never was a better bargain driven :
His heart in me keeps me and him in one,
My heart in him his thoughts and senses guides :
He loves my heart, for once it was his own,
I cherish his because in me it bides :
His heart his wound receivèd from my sight.
My heart was wounded with his wounded heart,
For as from me on him his heart did light,
So still me thought in me his heart did smart,
　　Both equal hurt in this change sought our bliss :
　　My true-love hath my heart, and I have his.

　　　　　　　　　　SIR P. SIDNEY.

919.　NO MORE, MY DEAR

No more, my dear, no more these counsels try !
O give my passions leave to run their race !
Let Fortune lay on me her worst disgrace,
Let folk o'ercharged with brain, against me cry,
Let clouds bedim my face, break in mine eye,
Let me no steps but of lost labour trace,
Let all the earth in scorn recount my case,
But do not will me from my love to fly.
I do not envy Aristotle's wit,
Nor do aspire to Caesar's bleeding fame,
Nor aught do care, though some above me sit,
Nor hope nor wish another course to frame,
　　But that which once may win thy cruel heart.
　　Thou art my wit and thou my virtue art.

　　　　　　　　　　SIR P. SIDNEY.

920. TO THE MOON

With how sad steps, O Moon, thou climb'st the skies !
How silently, and with how wan a face !
What, may it be, that e'en in heavenly place
That busy archer his sharp arrows tries ?
Sure, if that long-with-love-acquainted eyes
Can judge of love, thou feel'st a lover's case ;
I read it in thy looks ; thy languished grace,
To me, that feel the like, thy state descries.
Then, even of fellowship, O Moon, tell me,
Is constant love deemed there but want of wit ?
Are beauties there as proud as here they be ?
Do they above love to be loved, and yet
    Those lovers scorn whom that love doth possess ?
    Do they call virtue, there, ungratefulness ? Sir P. Sidney.

921. TO MARGARET

Merry Margaret,
As midsummer flower,
Gentle as falcon,
Or hawk of the tower ;
With solace and gladness,
Much mirth and no madness,
All good and no badness ;
So joyously,
So maidenly,
So womanly
Her demeaning
In every thing,
Far, far passing
That I can indite,
Or suffice to write
Of Merry Margaret
As midsummer flower,
Gentle as falcon,
Or hawk of the tower.
As patient and as still
And as full of good will
As fair Isaphill,
Coliander,
Sweet pomander,
Good Cassander ;
Steadfast of thought,
Well made, well wrought,
Far may be sought,
Ere that ye can find
So courteous, so kind,
As merry Margaret,
This midsummer flower,
Gentle as falcon,
Or hawk of the tower.

    J. Skelton (*To Mistress Margaret Hussey*)

922. TULLOCHGORUM

Oh, Tullochgorum's my delight,
It gars us a' in ane unite,
And ony sumph that keeps up spite,
    In conscience I abhor him.
For blythe and cheery we's be a',
Blythe and cheery, blythe and cheery,
Blythe and cheery we's be a',
    And mak' a happy quorum.
For blythe and cheery we's be a',
As lang as we hae breath to draw,
And dance, till we be like to fa',
    The reel of Tullochgorum.   J. Skinner.

923. FROM ' A SONG TO DAVID '

HE sang of God—the mighty source
Of all things—the stupendous force
    On which all strength depends ;
From whose right arm, beneath whose eyes.
All period, power, and enterprise
    Commences, reigns, and ends.

Tell them, I AM, Jehovah said
To Moses ; while earth heard in dread,
    And, smitten to the heart,
At once above, beneath, around,
All Nature, without voice or sound,
    Replied, O LORD, THOU ART.

.   .   .   .   .   .

Glorious the sun in mid career ;
Glorious the assembled fires appear ;
    Glorious the comet's train :
Glorious the trumpet and alarm ;
Glorious the Almighty's stretched-out arm ;
    Glorious the enraptured main :

Glorious the northern lights a-stream ;
Glorious the song, when God's the theme ;
    Glorious the thunder's roar :
Glorious Hosanna from the den ;
Glorious the catholic Amen ;
    Glorious the martyr's gore :

Glorious—more glorious, is the crown
Of Him that brought salvation down,
    By meekness called thy Son :
Thou that stupendous truth believed ;—
And now the matchless deed's achieved,
    Determined, dared, and done.   C. SMART.

924. BARBARA

ON the Sabbath-day,
Through the churchyard old and grey,
Over the crisp and yellow leaves, I held my rustling way ;
And amid the words of mercy, falling on my soul like balms ;
'Mid the gorgeous storms of music—in the mellow organ-calms,
'Mid the upward streaming prayers, and the rich and solemn psalms,
    I stood careless, Barbara.

My heart was otherwhere
While the organ shook the air,
And the priest, with outspread hands, blessed the people with a prayer ;

But, when rising to go homeward, with a mild and saint-like shine
Gleamed a face of airy beauty with its heavenly eyes on mine—
Gleamed and vanished in a moment—O that face was surely thine
    Out of heaven, Barbara !

O pallid, pallid face !
O earnest eyes of grace !
When last I saw thee, dearest, it was in another place.
You came running forth to meet me with my love-gift on your wrist :
The flutter of a long white dress, then all was lost in mist—
A purple stain of agony was on the mouth I kissed,
    That wild morning, Barbara !

I searched in my despair,
Sunny noon and midnight air ;
I could not drive away the thought that you were lingering there.
O many and many a winter night I sat when you were gone,
My worn face buried in my hands, beside the fire alone.
Within the dripping churchyard, the rain plashing on your stone,
    You were sleeping, Barbara.

'Mong angels, do you think
Of the precious golden link
I clasped around your happy arm while sitting by yon brink ?
Or when that night of gliding dance, of laughter and guitars,
Was emptied of its music, and we watched, through latticed bars,
The silent midnight heaven creeping o'er us with its stars,
    Till the day broke, Barbara ?

In the years I've changed ;
Wild and far my heart hath ranged,
And many sins and errors now have been on me avenged :
But to you I have been faithful, whatsoever good I lacked :
I loved you, and above my life still hangs that love intact—
Your love the trembling rainbow, I the reckless cataract.
    Still I love you, Barbara !

Yet, love, I am unblest ;
With many doubts oppressed,
I wander like a desert wind, without a place of rest.
Could I but win you for an hour from off that starry shore,
The hunger of my soul were stilled, for Death hath told you more
Than the melancholy world doth know ; things deeper than all lore
    Will you teach me, Barbara ?

In vain, in vain, in vain,
You will never come again.
There droops upon the dreary hills a mournful fringe of rain ;
The gloaming closes slowly round, loud winds are in the tree,
Round selfish shores for ever moans the hurt and wounded sea,
There is no rest upon the earth, peace is with Death and thee,
    Barbara !   A. SMITH (*Horton*).

925. THE SPRING CHANSON

Sing to the spring ; but through the spring I look
And see, when fields are bare, the woodlands pale,
And hear a sad unmated redbreast wail
In beechen russets by a leaden brook.
For I am tortured by a boding eye,
That, gazing on the morning's glorious grain,
Beholds late shreds of fiery sunset stain
The marble pallor of a western sky.
Sweet is thy song, oh merle ! and sweetly sung
Thy forefathers in our forefathers' ears ;
And this—far more than all—the song endears,
In that it knits the old world with the young.
Men live and die, the song remains, and when
I list the passion of thy vernal breath,
Methinks thou singest best to love and death,
To happy lovers and to dying men.   A. Smith.

926. FROM 'AN ADDRESS TO THE MUMMY IN BELZONI'S EXHIBITION'

And thou hast walked about (how strange a story !)
    In Thebes' streets three thousand years ago,
When the Memnonium was in all its glory,
    And time had not begun to overthrow
Those temples, palaces, and piles stupendous,
Of which the very ruins are tremendous !

Speak ! for thou long enough hast acted dummy ;
    Thou hast a tongue, come, let us hear its tune ;
Thou'rt standing on thy legs above ground, mummy !
    Revisiting the glimpses of the moon,
Not like thin ghosts or disembodied creatures,
But with thy bones and flesh, and limbs and features.

Tell us—for doubtless thou canst recollect—
    To whom we should assign the Sphinx's fame ?
Was Cheops or Cephrenes architect
    Of either Pyramid that bears his name ?
Is Pompey's Pillar really a misnomer ?
Had Thebes a hundred gates, as sung by Homer ?

Perhaps thou wert a mason, and forbidden
    By oath to tell the secrets of thy trade—
Then say, what secret melody was hidden
    In Memnon's statue, which at sunrise played ?
Perhaps thou wert a priest—if so, my struggles
Are vain, for priestcraft never owns its juggles.

Perchance that very hand, now pinioned flat,
 Has hob-a-nobbed with Pharaoh, glass to glass;
Or dropped a halfpenny in Homer's hat,
 Or doffed thine own to let Queen Dido pass,
Or held, by Solomon's own invitation,
A torch at the great Temple's dedication.   H. SMITH.

927. MOURN, HAPLESS CALEDONIA, MOURN
[1746.]

MOURN, hapless Caledonia, mourn
Thy banished peace, thy laurels torn!
Thy sons, for valour long renowned,
Lie slaughtered on their native ground;
Thy hospitable roofs no more
Invite the stranger to the door;
In smoky ruins sunk they lie,
The monuments of cruelty.

The wretched owner sees afar
His all become the prey of war;
Bethinks him of his babes and wife,
Then smites his breast, and curses life.
Thy swains are famished on the rocks,
Where once they fed their wanton flocks:
Thy ravished virgins shriek in vain;
Thy infants perish on the plain.

What boots it, then, in every clime,
Through the wide-spreading waste of time,
Thy martial glory, crowned with praise,
Still shone with undiminished blaze?
Thy towering spirit now is broke,
Thy neck is bended to the yoke.
What foreign arms could never quell,
By civil rage and rancour fell.   T. G. SMOLLETT.

928. ODE TO LEVEN WATER

ON Leven's banks, while free to rove,
And tune the rural pipe to love,
I envied not the happiest swain
That ever trod the Arcadian plain.
 Pure stream, in whose transparent wave
My youthful limbs I wont to lave;
No torrents stain thy limpid source,
No rocks impede thy dimpling course,
That sweetly warbles o'er its bed,
With white round polished pebbles spread;
While, lightly poised, the scaly brood
In myriads cleave thy crystal flood;

The springing trout in speckled pride,
The salmon, monarch of the tide;
The ruthless pike, intent on war,
The silver eel, and mottled par.
Devolving from thy parent lake,
A charming maze thy waters make,
By bowers of birch and groves of pine,
And edges flowered with eglantine.
   Still on thy banks so gaily green
May numerous herds and flocks be seen:
And lasses chanting o'er the pail,
And shepherds piping in the dale;
And ancient faith that knows no guile,
And industry embrowned with toil;
And hearts resolved and hands prepared
The blessings they enjoy to guard!   T. G. SMOLLETT.

929. WHEN SAPPHO TUNED THE RAPTURED STRAIN

WHEN Sappho tuned the raptured strain
The listening wretch forgot his pain;
With art divine the lyre she strung,
Like thee she played, like thee she sung.

For while she struck the quivering wire,
The eager breast was all on fire;
And when she joined the vocal lay,
The captive soul was charmed away.

But had she added still to these
Thy softer, chaster power to please,
Thy beauteous air of sprightly youth,
Thy native smiles of artless truth:

She ne'er had pined beneath disdain,
She ne'er had played and sung in vain,
Despair had ne'er her soul possessed
To dash on rocks the tender breast.   T. G. SMOLLETT.

930. HOW BEAUTIFUL IS NIGHT

How beautiful is night!
A dewy freshness fills the silent air;
No mist obscures, nor cloud, nor speck, nor stain,
Breaks the serene of heaven;
In full-orbed glory yonder moon divine
Rolls through the dark blue depths.
Beneath her steady ray
The desert-circle spreads,
Like the round ocean, girdled with the sky.
How beautiful is night!   R. SOUTHEY (*Thalaba*).

931. THE BATTLE OF BLENHEIM

It was a summer evening,
  Old Kaspar's work was done,
And he before his cottage door
  Was sitting in the sun,
And by him sported on the green
His little grandchild Wilhelmine.

She saw her brother Peterkin
  Roll something large and round,
Which he beside the rivulet
  In playing there had found ;
He came to ask what he had found,
That was so large, and smooth,
    and round.

Old Kaspar took it from the boy,
  Who stood expectant by ;
And then the old man shook his
    head,
  And with a natural sigh,
' 'Tis some poor fellow's skull,'
    said he,
' Who fell in the great victory.

' I find them in the garden,
  For there's many here about ;
And often when I go to plough,
  The ploughshare turns them out !
For many thousand men,' said he,
' Were slain in that great victory.'

' Now tell us what 'twas all about,'
  Young Peterkin, he cries ;
And little Wilhelmine looks up
  With wonder-waiting eyes ;
' Now tell us all about the war,
And what they fought each other
    for.'

' It was the English,' Kaspar cried,
  ' Who put the French to rout ;
But what they fought each other
    for
  I could not well make out ;
But everybody said,' quoth he,
' That 'twas a famous victory.

' My father lived at Blenheim
    then,
  Yon little stream hard by ;
They burnt his dwelling to the
    ground,
  And he was forced to fly :
So with his wife and child he
    fled,
Nor had he where to rest his head.

' With fire and sword the country
    round
  Was wasted far and wide,
And many a childing mother then,
  And new-born baby died ;
But things like that, you know,
    must be
At every famous victory.

' They say it was a shocking
    sight
  After the field was won ;
For many thousand bodies here
  Lay rotting in the sun ;
But things like that, you know,
    must be
After a famous victory.

' Great praise the Duke of Marlbro'
    won,
  And our good Prince Eugene.'
' Why, 'twas a very wicked
    thing ! '
  Said little Wilhelmine.
' Nay . . . nay . . . my little girl,'
    quoth he,
' It was a famous victory.

' And everybody praised the Duke
  Who this great fight did win.'
' But what good came of it at
    last ? '
  Quoth little Peterkin.
' Why, that I cannot tell,' said
    he,
' But 'twas a famous victory.'

R. SOUTHEY.

932. MY DAYS AMONG THE DEAD ARE PASSED

My days among the Dead are passed ;
   Around me I behold,
Where'er these casual eyes are cast,
   The mighty minds of old ;
My never-failing friends are they,
With whom I converse day by day.

With them I take delight in weal,
   And seek relief in woe ;
And while I understand and feel
   How much to them I owe,
My cheeks have often been bedewed
With tears of thoughtful gratitude.

My thoughts are with the Dead ; with them
   I live in long-past years,
Their virtues love, their faults condemn,
   Partake their hopes and fears,
And from their lessons seek and find
Instruction with an humble mind.

My hopes are with the Dead ; anon
   My place with them will be,
And I with them shall travel on
   Through all Futurity ;
Yet leaving here a name, I trust,
That will not perish in the dust.   R. SOUTHEY.

933. THE IMMORTALITY OF LOVE

They sin who tell us Love can die.
With life all other passions fly,
All others are but vanity.
In Heaven Ambition cannot dwell,
Nor Avarice in the vaults of Hell ;
Earthly these passions of the Earth,
They perish where they have their birth ;
But Love is undestructible.
Its holy flame for ever burneth,
From Heaven it came, to Heaven returneth ;
Too oft on Earth a troubled guest,
At times deceived, at times oppressed,
It here is tried and purified,
Then hath in heaven its perfect rest ;
It soweth here with toil and care,
But the harvest time of Love is there.

Oh! when a mother meets on high
The Babe she lost in infancy,
Hath she not then, for pains and fears,
The day of woe, the watchful night,
For all her sorrow, all her tears,
An over-payment of delight?
                    R. SOUTHEY (*The Curse of Kehama*).

934. UPON THE IMAGE OF DEATH

BEFORE my face the picture hangs,
    That daily should put me in mind
Of those cold names and bitter pangs
    That shortly I am like to find;
But yet, alas! full little I
Do think hereon, that I must die.

.   .   .   .   .   .

My ancestors are turned to clay
    And many of my mates are gone;
My youngers daily drop away,
    And can I think to 'scape alone?
No, no; I know that I must die,
And yet my life amend not I.   R. SOUTHWELL.

935. NEW PRINCE, NEW POMP

BEHOLD a silly tender Babe,
    In freezing winter night,
In homely manger trembling lies;
    Alas, a piteous sight!

The inns are full. No man will yield
    This little Pilgrim bed;
But forced He is, with silly beasts,
    In crib to shroud his head.

Despise him not for lying there:
    First what He is inquire.
An orient pearl is often found
    In depth of dirty mire.

Weigh not his crib, his wooden dish,
    Nor beasts that by him feed;
Weigh not his mother's poor attire,
    Nor Joseph's simple weed.

This stable is a Prince's court;
    The crib, his chair of state;
The beasts are parcel of his pomp;
    The wooden dish his plate.

The persons in that poor attire
    His royal liveries wear.
The Prince himself is come from heaven;
    This pomp is prizèd there.

With joy approach, O Christian wight!
    Do homage to thy King;
And highly praise his humble pomp
    Which He from heaven doth bring.
                    R. SOUTHWELL.

936. LOSS IN DELAYS

SHUN delays, they breed remorse,
    Take thy time while time doth serve thee,
Creeping snails have weakest force,
    Fly their fault lest thou repent thee,
Good is best when soonest wrought,
Lingering labours come to nought.

   .   .   .   .   .   .

Time wears all his locks before,
    Take thou hold upon his forehead;
When he flies he turns no more
    And behind his scalp is naked.
Works adjourned have many stays;
Long demurs breed new delays.   R. SOUTHWELL.

937. TIMES GO BY TURNS

THE loppèd tree in time may grow again,
Most naked plants renew both fruit and flower;
The sorriest wight may find release of pain,
The driest soil suck in some moistening shower;
Times go by turns, and chances change by course,
From foul to fair, from better hap to worse.

The sea of Fortune doth not ever flow,
She draws her favours to the lowest ebb;
Her tides have equal times to come and go,
Her loom doth weave the fine and coarsest web;
No joy so great but runneth to an end,
No hap so hard but may in fine amend.

Not always fall of leaf, nor ever spring,
No endless night, yet not eternal day;
The saddest birds a season find to sing,
The roughest storm a calm may soon allay:
Thus, with succeeding turns, God tempereth all,
That man may hope to rise, yet fear to fall.

A chance may win that by mischance was lost;
That net that holds no great, takes little fish;
In some things all, in all things none are crossed;
Few all they need, but none have all they wish.
Unmingled joys here to no man befall;
Who least, hath some; who most, hath never all.
            R. SOUTHWELL.

938. TO ——

Too late I stayed—forgive the crime ;
   Unheeded flew the hours ;
How noiseless falls the foot of Time,
   That only treads on flowers !

What eye with clear account remarks
   The ebbing of the glass,
When all its sands are diamond sparks,
   That dazzle as they pass !

Oh, who to sober measurement
   Time's happy swiftness brings,
When birds of Paradise have lent
   Their plumage for his wings !   W. R. SPENCER.

939. THE REDCROSS KNIGHT

A GENTLE knight was pricking on the plain,
Yclad in mighty arms and silver shield,
Wherein old dints of deep wounds did remain,
The cruel marks of many a bloody field ;
Yet arms till that time did he never wield.
His angry steed did chide his foaming bit,
As much disdaining to the curb to yield :
Full jolly knight he seemed and fair did sit,
As one for knightly jousts and fierce encounters fit.

And on his breast a bloody cross he bore,
The dear remembrance of his dying Lord,
For whose sweet sake that glorious badge he wore,
And dead, as living, ever Him adored :
Upon his shield the like was also scored,
For sovereign hope, which in his help he had.
Right faithful true he was in deed and word ;
But of his cheer did seem too solemn sad :
Yet nothing did he dread, but ever was ydrad.
          E. SPÉNSER (*The Faerie Queene*).

940. FROM 'PROTHALAMION'

CALM was the day, and through the trembling air
Sweet-breathing Zephyrus did softly play,
A gentle spirit that lightly did delay
Hot Titan's beams, which then did glister fair ;
When I (whom sullen care,
Through discontent of my long fruitless stay
In Prince's court, and expectation vain
Of idle hopes, which still do fly away,

Like empty shadows, did afflict my brain)
Walked forth to ease my pain
Along the shore of silver streaming Thames ;
Whose rutty bank, the which his river hems,
Was painted all with variable flowers,
And all the meads adorned with dainty gems
Fit to deck maidens' bowers
And crown their paramours
Against the bridal day, which is not long :
   Sweet Thames ! run softly, till I end my song.

There, in a meadow, by the river's side,
A flock of nymphs I chancèd to espy,
All lovely daughters of the flood thereby,
With goodly greenish locks, all loose untied,
As each had been a bride ;
And each one had a little wicker basket,
Made of fine twigs, entrailèd curiously,
In which they gathered flowers to fill their flasket,
And with fine fingers cropped full feateously
The tender stalks on high.
Of every sort, which in that meadow grew,
They gathered some ; the violet, pallid blue,
The little daisy that at evening closes,
The virgin lily, and the primrose true,
With store of vermeil roses,
To deck their bridegrooms' posies
Against the bridal day, which was not long :
   Sweet Thames ! run softly, till I end my song.

With that I saw two swans of goodly hue
Come softly swimming down along the lea ;
Two fairer birds I yet did never see ;
The snow, which doth the top of Pindus strew,
Did never whiter show ;
Nor Jove himself, when he a swan would be,
For love of Leda, whiter did appear ;
Yet Leda was (they say) as white as he,
Yet not so white as these, nor nothing near ;
So purely white they were,
That even the gentle stream, the which them bare,
Seemed foul to them, and bade his billows spare
To wet their silken feathers, lest they might
Soil their fair plumes with water not so fair,
And mar their beauties bright,
That shone as heaven's light,
Against their bridal day, which was not long :
   Sweet Thames ! run softly till I end my song.

E. SPENSER.

941. WHAT HELL IT IS

FULL little knowest thou that hast not tried,
What hell it is in suing long to bide;
To lose good days that might be better spent;
To waste long nights in pensive discontent,
To speed to-day, to be put back to-morrow;
To feed on hope, to pine with fear and sorrow;
To have thy princess' grace, yet want her peers';
To have thy asking, yet wait many years;
To pet thy soul with crosses and with cares;
To eat thy heart through comfortless despairs;
To fawn, to crouch, to wait, to ride, to run,
To spend, to give, to wait, to be undone.

E. SPENSER (*Mother Hubbard's Tale*).

942. MOST GLORIOUS LORD OF LIFE

MOST glorious Lord of life! that, on this day,
Didst make Thy triumph over death and sin;
And, having harrowed hell, didst bring away
Captivity thence captive, us to win:
This joyous day, dear Lord, with joy begin;
And grant that we, for whom Thou didest die,
Being with Thy dear blood clean washed from sin,
May live for ever in felicity!
And that Thy love we weighing worthily,
May likewise love Thee for the same again;
And for Thy sake that all like dear didst buy,
With love may one another entertain:
  So let us love, dear Love, like as we ought;
  Love is the lesson which the Lord us taught.

E. SPENSER.

943. ONE DAY I WROTE HER NAME

ONE day I wrote her name upon the strand,
But came the waves and washèd it away:
Again I wrote it with a second hand,
But came the tide and made my pains his prey.
'Vain man,' said she, 'that dost in vain essay
A mortal thing so to immortalize;
For I myself shall like to this decay,
And eke my name be wipèd out likewise.'
'Not so,' quoth I; 'let baser things devise
To die in dust, but you shall live by fame;
My verse your virtues rare shall eternize,
And in the heavens write your glorious name:
  Where, whenas Death shall all the world subdue,
  Our love shall live, and later life renew. E. SPENSER.

944. THE SEASONS

SPRING

So forth issued the Seasons of the year ;
First, lusty Spring, all dight in leaves of flowers
That freshly budded and new blooms did bear,
In which a thousand birds had built their bowers
That sweetly sung to call forth paramours ;
And in his hand a javelin he did bear,
And on his head (as fit for warlike stoures)
A gilt engraven morion he did wear ;
That as some did him love, so others did him fear.

SUMMER

Then came the jolly Summer, being dight
In a thin silken cassock coloured green,
That was unlinèd all, to be more light :
And on his head a garland well beseen
He wore, from which, as he had chafèd been,
The sweat did drop ; and in his hand he bore
A bow and shafts, as he in forest green
Had hunted late the leopard or the boar,
And now would bathe his limbs with labour heated sore.

AUTUMN

Then came the Autumn all in yellow clad,
As though he joyèd in his plenteous store,
Laden with fruits that made him laugh, full glad
That he had banished hunger, which to-fore
Had by the belly oft him pinchèd sore :
Upon his head a wreath, that was enrolled
With ears of corn of every sort, he bore ;
And in his hand a sickle he did hold,
To reap the ripened fruits the which the earth had yold.

WINTER

Lastly came Winter, clothèd all in freize,
Chattering his teeth for cold that did him chill ;
Whilst on his hoary beard his breath did freeze,
And the dull drops that from his purpled bill
As from a limbeck did adown distil :
In his right hand a tippèd staff he held,
With which his feeble steps he stayèd still ;
For he was faint with cold, and weak with eld ;
That scarce his loosèd limbs he able was to weld.

E. SPENSER (*The Faerie Queene*).

945. SWEET AND SOUR

SWEET is the rose, but grows upon a brier;
Sweet is the juniper, but sharp his bough;
Sweet is the eglantine, but pricketh near;
Sweet is the fir-bloom, but his branches rough;
Sweet is the cypress, but his rind is tough;
Sweet is the nut, but bitter is his pill;
Sweet is the broom-flower, but yet sour enough;
And sweet is moly, but his root is ill:
So every sweet with sour is tempered still.
That maketh it be coveted the more;
For easy things, that may be got at will,
Most sorts of men do set but little store.
  Why then should I account of little pain,
    That endless pleasure shall unto me gain? E. SPENSER.

946. FROM THE 'EPITHALAMIUM'

WAKE now, my love, awake; for it is time;
The rosy morn long since left Tithon's bed,
All ready to her silver coach to climb;
And Phoebus 'gins to show his glorious head.
Hark! how the cheerful birds do chant their lays,
And carol of love's praise.
The merry lark his matins sings aloft;
The thrush replies; the mavis descant plays;
The ousel shrills; the ruddock warbles soft;
So goodly all agree, with sweet consent,
To this day's merriment.
Ah! my dear love, why do ye sleep thus long?
When meeter were that ye should now awake,
To await the coming of your joyous make,
And hearken to the birds' love-learnèd song,
The dewy leaves among!
For they of joy and pleasance to you sing,
That all the woods them answer, and their echo ring.

  .   .   .   .

Tell me, ye merchants' daughters, did ye see
So fair a creature in your town before;
So sweet, so lovely, and so mild as she,
Adorned with beauty's grace and virtue's store?

  .   .   .   .

Why stand ye still, ye virgins, in amaze,
Upon her so to gaze,
While ye forget your former lay to sing,
To which the woods did answer, and your echo ring?

But if ye saw that which no eyes can see,
The inward beauty of her lively sprite,
Garnished with heavenly gifts of high degree,
Much more then would ye wonder at that sight,

. . . .

Had ye once seen these her celestial treasures,
And unrevealèd pleasures,
Then would ye wonder, and her praises sing,
That all the woods should answer, and your echo ring.

Open the temple-gates unto my love,
Open them wide that she may enter in,
And all the posts adorn as doth behove,
And all the pillars deck with garlands trim,
For to receive this saint with honour due,
That cometh in to you.
With trembling steps and humble reverence,
She cometh in before the Almighty's view:
Of her ye virgins learn obedience,
When so ye come into these holy places,
To humble your proud faces:
Bring her up to the high altar, that she may
The sacred ceremonies there partake,
The which do endless matrimony make;
And let the roaring organs loudly play
The praises of the Lord, in lively notes,
The while, with hollow throats,
The choristers the joyous anthem sing,
That all the woods may answer, and their echo ring.

Behold, while she before the altar stands,
Hearing the holy priest that to her speaks,
And blesseth her with his two happy hands,
How the red roses flush up in her cheeks,
And the pure snow, with goodly vermeil stain,
Like crimson dyed in grain:
That even the angels, which continually
About the sacred altar do remain,
Forget their service and about her fly,
Oft peeping in her face, that seems more fair
The more they on it stare.
But her sad eyes, still fastened on the ground,
Are governèd with goodly modesty,
That suffers not one look to glance awry,
Which may let in a little thought unsound,
Why blush ye, love, to give to me your hand,
The pledge of all our band!
Sing, ye sweet angels, alleluia sing,
That all the woods may answer, and your echo ring.

Now all is done : bring home the bride again ;
Bring home the triumph of our victory :
Bring home with you the glory of her gain,
With joyance bring her, and with jollity.
Never had man more joyful day than this,
Whom Heaven would heap with bliss.
Make feast, therefore, now all this livelong day :
This day for ever to me holy is.
Pour out the wine without restraint or stay,
Pour not by cups, but by the bellyful,
Pour out to all that wull,
And sprinkle all the posts and walls with wine,
That they may sweat, and drunken be withal.
Crown ye god Bacchus with a coronal,
And Hymen also crown with wreaths of vine,
And let the Graces dance unto the rest,
For they can do it best :
The while the maidens do their carol sing
To which the woods shall answer, and their echo ring.

E. Spenser.

947. A DEPOSITION FROM BEAUTY

Though when I loved thee thou wert fair,
    Thou art no longer so ;
These glories all the pride they wear
    Unto opinion owe.
Beauties, like stars, in borrowed lustre shine ;
And 'twas my love that gave thee thine.

The flames that dwelt within thine eye
    Do now with mine expire ;
Thy brightest graces fade and die
    At once with my desire.
Love's fires thus mutual influence return ;
Thine cease to shine, when mine to burn.

Then, proud Celinda, hope no more
    To be implored or wooed,
Since by thy scorn thou dost restore
    The wealth my love bestowed ;
And thy despised disdain too late shall find
That none are fair but who are kind.   T. Stanley.

948. ENVOY

Go, little book, and wish to all
Flowers in the garden, meat in the hall,
A bin of wine, a spice of wit,
A house with lawns enclosing it,
A living river by the door,
A nightingale in the sycamore !   R. L. Stevenson.

949. REQUIEM

UNDER the wide and starry sky,
Dig the grave and let me lie.
Glad did I live and gladly die,
    And I laid me down with a will.

This be the verse you grave for me:
Here he lies where he longed to be;
Home is the sailor, home from sea,
    And the hunter home from the hill.
                            R. L. STEVENSON.

950. THE SPANISH ARMADA

FROM merciless invaders,
    From wicked men's device,
O God, arise and help us,
    To quell our enemies.

Sink deep their potent navies,
    Their strength and courage
        break,
O God! arise and arm us,
    For Jesus Christ, His sake.

Though cruel Spain and Parma
    With heathen legions come,
O God! arise and arm us,
    We'll die for our home!

We will not change our credo
    For Pope, nor book, nor bell;
And if the Devil come himself,
    We'll hound him back to hell.
                            J. STILL.

951. ALE

I CANNOT eat but little meat,
    My stomach is not good;
But sure, I think that I can
        drink
    With him that wears a hood.
Though I go bare, take ye no
        care,
    I am nothing a-cold;
I stuff my skin so full within
    Of jolly good ale and old.
Back and side go bare, go bare,
    Both foot and hand go cold;
But, belly, God send thee good ale
        enough,
    Whether it be new or old.

I love no roast but a nut-brown
        toast,
    And a crab laid in the fire;
A little bread shall do me stead;
    Much bread I not desire.
No frost, nor snow, no wind, I trow,
    Can hurt me if I would;
I am so wrapped, and throughly
        lapped
    Of jolly good ale and old.
Back and side go bare, go bare, &c.

And Tyb my wife, that as her life
    Loveth well good ale to seek,
Full oft drinks she, till ye may see
    The tears run down her cheek;
Then doth she troll to me the bowl,
    Even as a malt-worm should;
And saith, 'Sweetheart, I took
        my part
    Of this jolly good ale and old!'
Back and side go bare, go bare, &c.

Now let them drink till they nod
        and wink,
    Even as good fellows should do;
They shall not miss to have the bliss
    Good ale doth bring men to;
And all poor souls that have
        scoured bowls
    Or have them lustily trolled,
God save the lives of them and
        their wives,
    Whether they be young or old,
Back and side go bare, go bare,
    Both foot and hand go cold;
But, belly, God send thee good ale
        enough,
    Whether it be new or old.
                            J. STILL.

952. HAST THOU SEEN THE DOWN IN THE AIR

HAST thou seen the down in the air,
When wanton blasts have tossed it ?
Or the ship on the sea,
When ruder winds have crossed it ?

Hast thou marked the crocodile's weeping,
Or the fox's sleeping ?
Or hast thou viewed the peacock in his pride,
Or the dove by his bride ? . . .
O so fickle, O so vain, O so false, so false is she !

SIR J. SUCKLING.

953. I PRITHEE SEND ME BACK MY HEART

I PRITHEE send me back my heart,
Since I cannot have thine ;
For if from yours you will not part,
Why, then, shouldst thou have
mine ?

Yet now I think on't, let it lie,
To find it were in vain ;
For thou hast a thief in either eye
Would steal it back again.

Why should two hearts in one
breast lie,
And yet not lodge together ?
O Love ! where is thy sympathy,
If thus our breasts thou sever ?

But love is such a mystery,
I cannot find it out ;
For when I think I'm best resolved,
I then am in most doubt.

Then farewell care, and farewell woe ;
I will no longer pine ;
For I'll believe I have her heart,
As much as she hath mine.   SIR J. SUCKLING.

954. FROM 'A BALLAD UPON A WEDDING'

I TELL thee, Dick, where I have been,
Where I the rarest things have seen,
Oh, things beyond compare !
Such sights again cannot be found
In any place on English ground,
Be it at wake or fair.

At Charing Cross, hard by the way
Where we (thou know'st) do sell our hay,
There is a house with stairs ;
And there did I see coming down
Such folk as are not in our town,
Forty at least, in pairs.

Amongst the rest, one pestilent fine
(His beard no bigger, though, than thine !)
Walked on before the rest.
Our landlord looks like nothing to him ;
The king (God bless him !), 'twould undo him,
Should he go still so dressed. . . .

But wot you what ? The youth was going
To make an end of all his wooing ;
    The Parson for him stayed.
Yet, by his leave, for all his haste,
He did not so much wish all passed,
    Perchance, as did the maid.

The maid (and thereby hangs a tale)
For such a maid no Whitsun ale
    Could ever yet produce ;
No grape that 's kindly ripe could be
So round, so plump, so soft, as she ;
    Nor half so full of juice !

Her finger was so small, the ring
Would not stay on ; which they did bring.
    It was too wide a peck !
And to say truth, for out it must,
It looked like the great collar (just)
    About our young colt's neck.

Her feet, beneath her petticoat,
Like little mice stole in and out,
    As if they feared the light :
But oh ! she dances such a way,
No sun, upon an Easter Day,
    Is half so fine a sight ! . . .

Her cheeks so rare a white was on ;
No daisy makes comparison,
    Who sees them is undone.
For streaks of red were mingled there,
Such as are on a Katherine pear
    (The side that 's next the sun).

Her lips were red, and one was thin
Compared to that was next her chin
    (Some bee had stung it newly).
But, Dick, her eyes so guard her face,
I durst no more upon them gaze,
    Than on the sun in July.

Her mouth so small, when she does speak
Thou'dst swear her teeth her words did break,
    That they might passage get :
But she so handled still the matter,
They came as good as ours or better,
    And are not spent a whit ! . . .

Passion o' me ! how I run on ;
There 's that that would be thought upon,
    I trow, besides the bride :

The business of the Kitchen's great,
For it is fit that men should eat ;
   Nor was it there denied.

Just in the nick, the cook knocked thrice,
And all the waiters, in a trice,
   His summons did obey.
Each serving-man, with dish in hand,
Marched boldly up like our trained band,
   Presented, and away !

When all the meat was on the table
What man of knife or teeth was able
   To stay to be entreated ?
And this the very reason was,
Before the Parson could say grace
   The company was seated.

The business of the kitchen's great,
For it is fit that men should eat ;
   Nor was it there denied.
(Passion o' me, how I run on !
There's that, that would be thought upon,
   I trow, beside the bride).

Now hats fly off ; and youths carouse :
Healths first go round, and then the house.
   The bride's came thick and thick.
And when 'twas named another's health,
Perhaps he made it hers by stealth.
   (And who could help it, Dick ?)

O' th' sudden, up they rise and dance :
Then sit again and sigh and glance,
   Then dance again and kiss.
Thus several ways the time did pass ;
Whilst every woman wished her place,
   And every man wished his !

Sir J. Suckling.

955. OUT UPON IT, I HAVE LOVED

Out upon it, I have loved
   Three whole days together !
And am like to love three more,
   If it prove fair weather.

Time shall moult away his wings
   Ere he shall discover
In the whole wide world again
   Such a constant lover.

But the spite on't is, no praise
   Is due at all to me :
Love with me had made no stays,
   Had it any been but she.

Had it any been but she,
   And that very face,
There had been at least ere this
   A dozen dozen in her place.

Sir J. Suckling.

956. WHY SO PALE AND WAN, FOND LOVER

WHY so pale and wan, fond lover ?
    Prithee, why so pale ?
Will, when looking well can't move her,
    Looking ill prevail ?
    Prithee, why so pale ?

Why so dull and mute, young sinner ?
    Prithee, why so mute ?
Will, when speaking well can't win her,
    Saying nothing do't ?
    Prithee, why so mute ?

Quit, quit, for shame ! this will not move,
    This cannot take her ;
If of herself she will not love,
    Nothing can make her :
    The Devil take her !   SIR J. SUCKLING.

957. FROM 'A RHAPSODY ON POETRY'

HOBBES clearly proves that every creature
Lives in a state of war by nature.
The greater for the smallest watch,
But meddle seldom with their match.
A whale of moderate size will draw
A shoal of herrings down his maw ;
A fox with geese his belly crams ;
A wolf destroys a thousand lambs.
But search among the rhyming race,
The brave are worried by the base.
If on Parnassus' top you sit,
You rarely bite, are always bit.

   .   .   .   .   .   .

The vermin only tease and pinch
Their foes superior by an inch.
So, naturalists observe, a flea
Hath smaller fleas that on him prey ;
And these have smaller still to bite 'em,
And so proceed *ad infinitum.*
Thus every poet in his kind
Is bit by him that comes behind :
Who, though too little to be seen,
Can tease, and gall, and give the spleen.
                        J. SWIFT.

958. FROM 'ON THE DEATH OF DR. SWIFT'

PERHAPS I may allow the Dean
Had too much satire in his vein;
And seemed determined not to starve it,
Because no age could more deserve it.
Yet malice never was his aim;
He lashed the vice, but spared the name;
No individual could resent,
Where thousands equally were meant;
His satire points at no defect,
But what all mortals may correct;
For he abhorred that senseless tribe
Who call it humour when they gibe:
He spared a hump, or crooked nose,
Whose owners set not up for beaux.
True genuine dullness moved his pity,
Unless it offered to be witty.
Those who their ignorance confessed,
He ne'er offended with a jest;
But laughed to hear an idiot quote
A verse from Horace learned by rote.   J. SWIFT.

959. CEASE NOT TO LEARN

CEASE not to learn until thou cease to live:
Think that day lost, wherein thou draw'st no letter,
Nor gain'st no lesson, that new grace may give,
To make thyself learneder, wiser, better.

. . . . . .

Who readeth much, and never meditates,
Is like the greedy eater of much food,
Who so surcloys his stomach with his cates,
That commonly they do him little good.   J. SYLVESTER.

960. THE GLORIOUS STARS OF HEAVEN

I'LL ne'er believe that the Arch-Architect
With all these fires the heavenly arches decked
Only for show, and with their glistening shields
To amaze poor shepherds watching in the fields:
I'll ne'er believe that the least flower that pranks
Our garden borders, or the common banks,
And the least stone that in her warming lap
Our kind nurse Earth doth covetously wrap
Hath some peculiar virtue of its own,
And that the glorious stars of Heaven have none,
But shine in vain, and have no charge precise,
But to be walking in Heaven's galleries,
And through the palace up and down to clamber
As golden gulls about a presence-chamber.
                J. SYLVESTER (*Translation of Du Bartas*).

961. WERE I AS BASE AS IS THE LOWLY PLAIN

Were I as base as is the lowly plain,
And you, my love, as high as heaven above,
Yet should the thoughts of me, your humble swain,
Ascend to heaven, in honour of my love;
Were I as high as heaven above the plain,
And you, my love, as humble and as low
As are the deepest bottoms of the main,
Wheresoe'er you were, with you my love should go;
Were you the earth, dear love, and I the skies,
My love should shine on you like to the sun,
And look upon you with ten thousand eyes
Till heaven waxed blind, and till the world were done.
  Wheresoe'er I am, below, or else above you,
  Wheresoe'er you are, my heart shall truly love you.
                                        J. Sylvester.

962. ELENA'S SONG

Quoth tongue of neither maid nor wife
  To heart of neither wife nor maid,
Lead we not here a jolly life
  Betwixt the shine and shade?

Quoth heart of neither maid nor wife
  To tongue of neither wife nor maid,
Thou wag'st but I am worn with strife,
  And feel like flowers that fade.
                Sir H. Taylor (*Philip van Artevelde*).

963. IN THE VALLEY OF CAUTERETS

All along the valley, stream that flashest white,
Deepening thy voice with the deepening of the night,
All along the valley, where thy waters flow,
I walked with one I loved two and thirty years ago.
All along the valley while I walked to-day,
The two and thirty years were a mist that rolls away;
For all along the valley, down thy rocky bed,
Thy living voice to me was as the voice of the dead,
And all along the valley, by rock and cave and tree,
The voice of the dead was a living voice to me.
                          Alfred, Lord Tennyson.

964. AS THROUGH THE LAND AT EVE WE WENT

As through the land at eve we went,
    And plucked the ripened ears,
We fell out, my wife and I,
O we fell out I know not why,
    And kissed again with tears.
And blessings on the falling out
    That all the more endears,
When we fall out with those we love
    And kiss again with tears !
For when we came where lies the child
    We lost in other years,
There above the little grave,
O there above the little grave,
    We kissed again with tears.

LORD TENNYSON (*The Princess*).

965. BREAK, BREAK, BREAK

BREAK, break, break,
    On thy cold grey stones, O Sea !
And I would that my tongue could utter
    The thoughts that arise in me.

O well for the fisherman's boy,
    That he shouts with his sister at play !
O well for the sailor lad,
    That he sings in his boat on the bay !

And the stately ships go on
    To their haven under the hill ;
But O for the touch of a vanished hand,
    And the sound of a voice that is still !

Break, break, break,
    At the foot of thy crags, O Sea !
But the tender grace of a day that is dead
    Will never come back to me.

LORD TENNYSON.

966. COME DOWN, O MAID

COME down, O maid, from yonder mountain height:
What pleasure lives in height (the shepherd sang),
In height and cold, the splendour of the hills ?
But cease to move so near the heavens, and cease
To glide a sunbeam by the blasted pine,
To sit a star upon the sparkling spire ;

And come, for Love is of the valley, come,
For Love is of the valley, come thou down
And find him ; by the happy threshold, he,
Or hand in hand with Plenty in the maize,
Or red with spirted purple of the vats,
Or foxlike in the vine ; nor cares to walk
With Death and Morning on the silver horns,
Nor wilt thou snare him in the white ravine,
Nor find him dropped upon the firths of ice,
That huddling slant in furrow-cloven falls
To roll the torrent out of dusky doors :
But follow ; let the torrent dance thee down
To find him in the valley ; let the wild
Lean-headed Eagles yelp alone, and leave
The monstrous ledges there to slope, and spill
Their thousand wreaths of dangling water-smoke,
That like a broken purpose waste in air :
So waste not thou ; but come ; for all the vales
Await thee ; azure pillars of the hearth
Arise to thee ; the children call, and I
Thy shepherd pipe, and sweet is every sound,
Sweeter thy voice, but every sound is sweet ;
Myriads of rivulets hurrying through the lawn,
The moan of doves in immemorial elms,
And murmuring of innumerable bees.

                              LORD TENNYSON (*The Princess*).

967.   THE LOTOS-EATERS

' COURAGE ! ' he said, and pointed toward the land,
' This mounting wave will roll us shoreward soon.'
In the afternoon they came unto a land,
In which it seemèd always afternoon.
All round the coast the languid air did swoon,
Breathing like one that hath a weary dream.
Full-faced above the valley stood the moon ;
And like a downward smoke, the slender stream
Along the cliff to fall and pause and fall did seem.

A land of streams ! some, like a downward smoke,
Slow-dropping veils of thinnest lawn, did go ;
And some through wavering lights and shadows broke,
Rolling a slumbrous sheet of foam below.
They saw the gleaming river seaward flow
From the inner land : far off, three mountain-tops,
Three silent pinnacles of aged snow,
Stood sunset-flushed : and, dewed with showery drops,
Up-clomb the shadowy pine above the woven copse.

The charmèd sunset lingered low adown
In the red West : through mountain clefts the dale
Was seen far inland, and the yellow down
Bordered with palm, and many a winding vale
And meadow, set with slender galingale ;
A land where all things always seemed the same !
And round about the keel with faces pale,
Dark faces pale against that rosy flame,
The mild-eyed melancholy Lotos-eaters came.

Branches they bore of that enchanted stem,
Laden with flower and fruit, whereof they gave
To each, but whoso did receive of them,
And taste, to him the gushing of the wave
Far far away did seem to mourn and rave
On alien shores ; and if his fellow spake
His voice was thin, as voices from the grave ;
And deep-asleep he seemed, yet all awake,
And music in his ears his beating heart did make.

They sat them down upon the yellow sand,
Between the sun and moon upon the shore ;
And sweet it was to dream of Fatherland,
Of child, and wife, and slave ; but evermore
Most weary seemed the sea, weary the oar,
Weary the wandering fields of barren foam.
Then some one said, ' We will return no more ';
And all at once they sang, ' Our island home
Is far beyond the wave ; we will no longer roam.'

CHORIC SONG

Hateful is the dark-blue sky,
Vaulted o'er the dark-blue sea.
Death is the end of life ; ah, why
Should life all labour be ?
Let us alone. Time driveth onward fast,
And in a little while our lips are dumb.
Let us alone. What is it that will last ?
All things are taken from us, and become
Portions and parcels of the dreadful Past.
Let us alone. What pleasure can we have
To war with evil ? Is there any peace
In ever climbing up the climbing wave ?
All things have rest, and ripen towards the grave
In silence ; ripen, fall, and cease.
Give us long rest or death, dark death, or dreamful ease.

Dear is the memory of our wedded lives,
And dear the last embraces of our wives
And their warm tears : but all hath suffered change :
For surely now our household hearths are cold :
Our sons inherit us : our looks are strange :
And we should come like ghosts to trouble joy.
Or else the island princes over-bold
Have eat our substance, and the minstrel sings
Before them of the ten-years' war in Troy,
And our great deeds, as half-forgotten things.

. . . .

The Lotos blooms below the barren peak :
The Lotos blows by every winding creek :
All day the wind breathes low with mellower tone :
Through every hollow cave and alley lone
Round and round the spicy downs the yellow Lotos-dust is blown.
We have had enough of action and of motion we,
Rolled to starboard, rolled to larboard, when the surge was seething
    free,
Where the wallowing monster spouted his foam-fountains in the sea.
Let us swear an oath, and keep it with an equal mind,
In the hollow Lotos-land to live and lie reclined
On the hills like Gods together, careless of mankind.
For they lie beside their nectar, and the bolts are hurled
Far below them in the valleys, and the clouds are lightly curled
Round their golden houses, girdled with the gleaming world :
Where they smile in secret, looking over wasted lands,
Blight and famine, plague and earthquake, roaring deeps and fiery
    sands,
Clanging fights, and flaming towns, and sinking ships, and praying
    hands.
But they smile, they find a music centred in a doleful song
Steaming up, a lamentation and an ancient tale of wrong,
Like a tale of little meaning though the words are strong ;
Chanted from an ill-used race of men that cleave the soil,
Sow the seed, and reap the harvest with enduring toil,
Storing yearly little dues of wheat, and wine, and oil ;
Till they perish and they suffer—some, 'tis whispered,—down in hell
Suffer endless anguish, others in Elysian valleys dwell,
Resting weary limbs at last on beds of asphodel.
Surely, surely, slumber is more sweet than toil, the shore
Than labour in the deep mid-ocean, wind and wave and oar ;
Oh rest ye, brother mariners, we will not wander more.

                                        LORD TENNYSON.

968. ST. AGNES' EVE

DEEP on the convent-roof the snows
  Are sparkling to the moon:
My breath to heaven like vapour goes:
  May my soul follow soon!
The shadows of the convent-towers
  Slant down the snowy sward,
Still creeping with the creeping hours
  That lead me to my Lord:
Make Thou my spirit pure and clear
  As are the frosty skies,
Or this first snowdrop of the year
  That in my bosom lies.

As these white robes are soiled and dark,
  To yonder shining ground;
As this pale taper's earthly spark,
  To yonder argent round;
So shows my soul before the Lamb,
  My spirit before Thee;
So in mine earthly house I am,
  To that I hope to be.
Break up the heavens, O Lord! and far,
  Through all yon starlight keen,
Draw me, Thy bride, a glittering star,
  In raiment white and clean.

He lifts me to the golden doors;
  The flashes come and go;
All heaven bursts her starry floors,
  And strows her lights below,
And deepens on and up! the gates
  Roll back, and far within
For me the Heavenly Bridegroom waits,
  To make me pure of sin.
The sabbaths of Eternity,
  One sabbath deep and wide—
A light upon the shining sea—
  The Bridegroom with His bride!   LORD TENNYSON.

969. TO QUEEN VICTORIA

HER court was pure; her life serene;
  God gave her peace; her land reposed;
  A thousand claims to reverence closed
In her as Mother, Wife, and Queen;

And statesmen at her council met
  Who knew the seasons when to take
  Occasion by the hand, and make
The bounds of freedom wider yet

R

By shaping some august decree,
  Which kept her throne unshaken still,
  Broad-based upon her people's will,
And compassed by the inviolate sea.

LORD TENNYSON.

970.   HOME THEY BROUGHT HER WARRIOR DEAD

HOME they brought her warrior dead:
  She nor swooned, nor uttered cry:
All her maidens, watching, said,
  'She must weep or she will die.'

Then they praised him, soft and low,
  Called him worthy to be loved,
Truest friend and noblest foe;
  Yet she neither spoke nor moved.

Stole a maiden from her place,
  Lightly to the warrior stepped,
Took the face-cloth from the face;
  Yet she neither moved nor wept.

Rose a nurse of ninety years,
  Set his child upon her knee—
Like summer tempest came her tears—
  'Sweet my child, I live for thee.'

LORD TENNYSON (The Princess).

971.   IF LOVE BE LOVE

'IN Love, if Love be Love, if Love be ours,
Faith and unfaith can ne'er be equal powers:
Unfaith in aught is want of faith in all.

'It is the little rift within the lute,
That by and by will make the music mute,
And ever widening slowly silence all.

'The little rift within the lover's lute
Or little pitted speck in garnered fruit,
That rotting inward slowly moulders all.

'It is not worth the keeping: let it go:
But shall it? answer, darling, answer, no.
And trust me not at all or all in all.'
LORD TENNYSON (Idylls of the King: Merlin and Vivien).

972.   FROM 'LOCKSLEY HALL'

IN the Spring a fuller crimson comes upon the robin's breast;
In the Spring the wanton lapwing gets himself another crest;

In the Spring a livelier iris changes on the burnished dove;
In the Spring a young man's fancy lightly turns to thoughts of love.

    .   .   .   .

As the husband is, the wife is: thou art mated with a clown,
And the grossness of his nature will have weight to drag thee down.

He will hold thee, when his passion shall have spent its novel force,
Something better than his dog, a little dearer than his horse.

    .   .   .   .

Men, my brothers, men the workers, ever reaping something new:
That which they have done but earnest of the things that they shall do:

For I dipped into the future, far as human eye could see,
Saw the Vision of the world, and all the wonder that would be;

Saw the heavens fill with commerce, argosies of magic sails,
Pilots of the purple twilight, dropping down with costly bales;

Heard the heavens fill with shouting, and there rained a ghastly dew
From the nations' airy navies grappling in the central blue;

Far along the world-wide whisper of the south-wind rushing warm,
With the standards of the peoples plunging through the thunder-storm;

Till the war-drum throbbed no longer, and the battle-flags were furled
In the Parliament of man, the Federation of the world.

    .   .   .   .

Yet I doubt not through the ages one increasing purpose runs,
And the thoughts of men are widened with the process of the suns.

    .   .   .   .

Not in vain the distance beacons. Forward, forward let us range,
Let the great world spin for ever down the ringing grooves of change.

Through the shadow of the globe we sweep into the younger day:
Better fifty years of Europe than a cycle of Cathay.

LORD TENNYSON.

973. THE MILLER'S DAUGHTER

IT is the miller's daughter,
  And she is grown so dear, so dear,
That I would be the jewel
  That trembles at her ear:
For hid in ringlets day and night,
I'd touch her neck so warm and
  white.

And I would be the necklace,
  And all day long to fall and rise
Upon her balmy bosom,
  With her laughter or her sighs,
And I would lie so light, so light,
I scarce should be unclasped at night.

And I would be the girdle
  About her dainty dainty waist
And her heart would beat against
  me,
  In sorrow and in rest:
And I should know if it beat right,
I'd clasp it round so close and tight.

LORD TENNYSON.

974. ULYSSES

It little profits that an idle king,
By this still hearth, among these barren crags,
Matched with an agèd wife, I mete and dole
Unequal laws unto a savage race
That hoard, and sleep, and feed, and know not me.
I cannot rest from travel : I will drink
Life to the lees : all times I have enjoyed
Greatly, have suffered greatly, both with those
That loved me, and alone ; on shore and when
Through scudding drifts the rainy Hyades
Vexed the dim sea : I am become a name ;
For always roaming with a hungry heart
Much have I seen and known ; cities of men,
And manners, climates, councils, governments,
Myself not least, but honoured of them all ;
And drunk delight of battle with my peers,
Far on the ringing plains of windy Troy.
I am a part of all that I have met ;
Yet all experience is an arch wherethrough
Gleams that untravelled world, whose margin fades
For ever and for ever when I move.
How dull it is to pause, to make an end,
To rest unburnished, not to shine in use !
As though to breathe were life. Life piled on life
Were all too little, and of one to me
Little remains : but every hour is saved
From that eternal silence, something more,
A bringer of new things ; and vile it were
For some three suns to store and hoard myself,
And this grey spirit yearning in desire
To follow knowledge, like a sinking star,
Beyond the utmost bound of human thought.
     This is my son, mine own Telemachus,
To whom I leave the sceptre and the isle—
Well-loved of me, discerning to fulfil
This labour, by slow prudence to make mild
A rugged people, and through soft degrees
Subdue them to the useful and the good.
Most blameless is he, centred in the sphere
Of common duties, decent not to fail
In offices of tenderness, and pay
Meet adoration to my household gods,
When I am gone. He works his work, I mine.
     There lies the port : the vessel puffs her sail :
There gloom the dark broad seas. My mariners,
Souls that have toiled, and wrought, and thought with me—
That ever with a frolic welcome took
The thunder and the sunshine, and opposed

Free hearts, free foreheads—you and I are old;
Old age hath yet his honour and his toil;
Death closes all: but something ere the end,
Some work of noble note, may yet be done,
Not unbecoming men that strove with Gods.
The lights begin to twinkle from the rocks:
The long day wanes: the slow moon climbs: the deep
Moans round with many voices. Come, my friends,
'Tis not too late to seek a newer world.
Push off, and sitting well in order smite
The sounding furrows; for my purpose holds
To sail beyond the sunset, and the baths
Of all the western stars, until I die.
It may be that the gulfs will wash us down:
It may be we shall touch the Happy Isles,
And see the great Achilles, whom we knew.
Though much is taken, much abides; and though
We are not now that strength which in old days
Moved earth and heaven; that which we are, we are;
One equal temper of heroic hearts,
Made weak by time and fate, but strong in will
To strive, to seek, to find, and not to yield.

LORD TENNYSON.

975. FROM 'SIR GALAHAD'

MY good blade carves the casques of men,
   My tough lance thrusteth sure,
My strength is as the strength of ten,
   Because my heart is pure.
The shattering trumpet shrilleth high,
   The hard brands shiver on the steel,
The splintered spear-shafts crack and fly,
   The horse and rider reel:
They reel, they roll in clanging lists,
   And when the tide of combat stands,
Perfume and flowers fall in showers,
   That lightly rain from ladies' hands.

How sweet are looks that ladies bend
   On whom their favours fall!
For them I battle till the end,
   To save from shame and thrall:
But all my heart is drawn above,
   My knees are bowed in crypt and shrine:
I never felt the kiss of love,
   Nor maiden's hand in mine.
More bounteous aspects on me beam,
   Me mightier transports move and thrill;
So keep I fair through faith and prayer
   A virgin heart in work and will.   LORD TENNYSON.

976. NOW SLEEPS THE CRIMSON PETAL

Now sleeps the crimson petal, now the white ;
Nor waves the cypress in the palace walk ;
Nor winks the gold fin in the porphyry font :
The fire-fly wakens : waken thou with me.

Now droops the milkwhite peacock like a ghost,
And like a ghost she glimmers on to me.

Now lies the Earth all Danaë to the stars,
And all thy heart lies open unto me.

Now slides the silent meteor on, and leaves
A shining furrow, as thy thoughts in me.

Now folds the lily all her sweetness up,
And slips into the bosom of the lake :
So fold thyself, my dearest, thou, and slip
Into my bosom and be lost in me.

                    LORD TENNYSON (*The Princess*).

977. O SWALLOW, SWALLOW, FLYING, FLYING SOUTH

O SWALLOW, Swallow, flying, flying South,
Fly to her, and fall upon her gilded eaves,
And tell her, tell her, what I tell to thee.

O tell her, Swallow, thou that knowest each,
That bright and fierce and fickle is the South,
And dark and true and tender is the North.

O Swallow, Swallow, if I could follow, and light
Upon her lattice, I would pipe and trill,
And cheep and twitter twenty million loves.

O were I thou that she might take me in,
And lay me on her bosom, and her heart
Would rock the snowy cradle till I died.

Why lingereth she to clothe her heart with love,
Delaying as the tender ash delays
To clothe herself, when all the woods are green ?

O tell her, Swallow, that thy brood is flown :
Say to her, I do but wanton in the South,
But in the North long since my nest is made.

O tell her, brief is life but love is long,
And brief the sun of summer in the North,
And brief the moon of beauty in the South.

O Swallow, flying from the golden woods,
Fly to her, and pipe and woo her, and make her mine,
And tell her, tell her, that I follow thee.

                    LORD TENNYSON (*The Princess*).

978. O THAT 'TWERE POSSIBLE

O THAT 'twere possible
After long grief and pain
To find the arms of my true love
Round me once again!

  .   .   .   .   .

A shadow flits before me,

Not thou, but like to thee;
Ah Christ, that it were possible
For one short hour to see
The souls we loved, that they
      might tell us
What and where they be.

          LORD TENNYSON (*Maud*).

979. THE LADY OF SHALOTT

PART I

ON either side the river lie
Long fields of barley and of rye,
That clothe the wold and meet the sky;
And through the field the road runs by
      To many-towered Camelot;
And up and down the people go,
Gazing where the lilies blow
Round an island there below,
      The island of Shalott.

Willows whiten, aspens quiver,
Little breezes dusk and shiver
Through the wave that runs for ever
By the island in the river
      Flowing down to Camelot.
Four grey walls, and four grey towers,
Overlook a space of flowers,
And the silent isle embowers
      The Lady of Shalott.

By the margin, willow-veiled,
Slide the heavy barges trailed
By slow horses; and unhailed
The shallop flitteth silken-sailed
      Skimming down to Camelot:
But who hath seen her wave her hand?
Or at the casement seen her stand?
Or is she known in all the land,
      The Lady of Shalott?

Only reapers reaping early
In among the bearded barley,
Hear a song that echoes cheerly
From the river winding clearly,
      Down to towered Camelot:
And by the moon the reaper weary,
Piling sheaves in uplands airy,
Listening, whispers ' 'Tis the fairy
      Lady of Shalott.'

PART II

There she weaves by night and day
A magic web with colours gay.
She has heard a whisper say,
A curse is on her if she stay
  To look down to Camelot.
She knows not what the curse may be,
And so she weaveth steadily,
And little other care hath she,
  The Lady of Shalott.

And moving through a mirror clear
That hangs before her all the year,
Shadows of the world appear.
There she sees the highway near
  Winding down to Camelot:
There the river eddy whirls,
And there the surly village-churls,
And the red cloaks of market girls,
  Pass onward from Shalott.

Sometimes a troop of damsels glad,
An abbot on an ambling pad,
Sometimes a curly shepherd-lad,
Or long-haired page in crimson clad,
  Goes by to towered Camelot;
And sometimes through the mirror blue
The knights come riding two and two:
She hath no loyal knight and true,
  The Lady of Shalott.

But in her web she still delights
To weave the mirror's magic sights,
For often through the silent nights
A funeral, with plumes and lights,
  And music, went to Camelot.
Or when the moon was overhead,
Came two young lovers lately wed;
' I am half sick of shadows,' said
  The Lady of Shalott.

PART III

A bow-shot from her bower-eaves,
He rode between the barley-sheaves,
The sun came dazzling through the leaves,
And flamed upon the brazen greaves
  Of bold Sir Lancelot.
A red-cross knight for ever kneeled
To a lady in his shield,
That sparkled on the yellow field,
  Beside remote Shalott.

The gemmy bridle glittered free,
Like to some branch of stars we see
Hung in the golden Galaxy.
The bridle-bells rang merrily
        As he rode down to Camelot:
And from his blazoned baldric slung
A mighty silver bugle hung,
And as he rode his armour rung,
        Beside remote Shalott.

All in the blue unclouded weather
Thick-jewelled shone the saddle-leather,
The helmet and the helmet-feather
Burned like one burning flame together,
        As he rode down to Camelot.
As often through the purple night,
Below the starry clusters bright,
Some bearded meteor, trailing light,
        Moves over still Shalott.

His broad clear brow in sunlight glowed;
On burnished hooves his war-horse trode;
From underneath his helmet flowed
His coal-black curls as on he rode,
        As he rode down to Camelot.
From the bank and from the river
He flashed into the crystal mirror,
'Tirra lirra,' by the river
        Sang Sir Lancelot.

She left the web, she left the loom,
She made three paces through the room,
She saw the water-lily bloom,
She saw the helmet and the plume,
        She looked down to Camelot.
Out flew the web and floated wide;
The mirror cracked from side to side;
'The curse is come upon me,' cried
        The Lady of Shalott.

Part IV

In the stormy east-wind straining
The pale yellow woods were waning,
The broad stream in his banks complaining,
Heavily the low sky raining
        Over towered Camelot;
Down she came and found a boat
Beneath a willow left afloat,
And round about the prow she wrote
        The Lady of Shalott.

And down the river's dim expanse—
Like some bold seër in a trance,
Seeing all his own mischance—
With a glassy countenance
          Did she look to Camelot.
And at the closing of the day
She loosed the chain and down she lay;
The broad stream bore her far away,
          The Lady of Shalott.

Lying, robed in snowy white—
That loosely flew to left and right—
The leaves upon her falling light—
Through the noises of the night
          She floated down to Camelot:
And as the boat-head wound along
The willowy hills and fields among,
They heard her singing her last song,
          The Lady of Shalott.

Heard a carol, mournful, holy,
Chanted loudly, chanted lowly,
Till her blood was frozen slowly,
And her eyes were darkened wholly,
          Turned to towered Camelot;
For ere she reached upon the tide
The first house by the water-side,
Singing in her song she died,
          The Lady of Shalott.

Under tower and balcony,
By garden-wall and gallery,
A gleaming shape she floated by,
Dead-pale between the houses high,
          Silent into Camelot.
Out upon the wharfs they came,
Knight and burgher, lord and dame,
And round the prow they read her name,
          The Lady of Shalott.

Who is this? and what is here?
And in the lighted palace near
Died the sound of royal cheer;
And they crossed themselves for fear,
          All the knights at Camelot:
But Lancelot mused a little space;
He said, ' She has a lovely face;
God in His mercy lend her grace,
          The Lady of Shalott.'   LORD TENNYSON.

980. THE FLOWER

Once in a golden hour
  I cast to earth a seed.
Up there came a flower,
  The people said, a weed.

To and fro they went
  Through my garden-bower,
And muttering discontent
  Cursed me and my flower.

Then it grew so tall
  It wore a crown of light,
But thieves from o'er the wall
  Stole the seed by night.

Sowed it far and wide
  By every town and tower,
Till all the people cried,
  'Splendid is the flower.'

Read my little fable:
  He that runs may read.
Most can raise the flower now,
  For all have got the seed.

            LORD TENNYSON.

981. FROM 'IN MEMORIAM'

Strong Son of God, immortal Love,
  Whom we, that have not seen thy face
  By faith, and faith alone, embrace,
Believing where we cannot prove;

    .   .   .   .   .   .

Thou seemest human and divine,
  The highest, holiest manhood, thou:
  Our wills are ours, we know not how;
Our wills are ours, to make them thine.

Our little systems have their day;
  They have their day and cease to be:
  They are but broken lights of thee,
And thou, O Lord, art more than they.

    .   .   .   .   .   .

Let knowledge grow from more to more,
  But more of reverence in us dwell;
  That mind and soul, according well,
May make one music as before,
But vaster. . . .

            v

I sometimes hold it half a sin
  To put in words the grief I feel;
  For words, like Nature, half reveal
And half conceal the Soul within.

But, for the unquiet heart and brain,
   A use in measured language lies;
   The sad mechanic exercise,
Like dull narcotics, numbing pain.

LIII

How many a father have I seen,
   A sober man, among his boys,
   Whose youth was full of foolish noise,
Who wears his manhood hale and green:

And dare we to this fancy give,
   That had the wild oat not been sown,
   The soil, left barren, scarce had grown
The grain by which a man may live?

Or, if we held the doctrine sound
   For life outliving heats of youth,
   Yet who would preach it as a truth
To those that eddy round and round?

Hold thou the good: define it well:
   For fear divine Philosophy
   Should push beyond her mark, and be
Procuress to the Lords of Hell.

LIV

Oh yet we trust that somehow good
   Will be the final goal of ill,
   To pangs of nature, sins of will,
Defects of doubt, and taints of blood;

That nothing walks with aimless feet;
   That not one life shall be destroyed,
   Or cast as rubbish to the void,
When God hath made the pile complete;

That not a worm is cloven in vain;
   That not a moth with vain desire
   Is shrivelled in a fruitless fire,
Or but subserves another's gain.

Behold, we know not anything;
   I can but trust that good shall fall
   At last—far off—at last, to all,
And every winter change to spring.

So runs my dream: but what am I?
   An infant crying in the night:
   An infant crying for the light:
And with no language but a cry.

LV

I falter where I firmly trod,
   And falling with my weight of cares
   Upon the great world's altar-stairs
That slope through darkness up to God,

I stretch lame hands of faith, and grope,
   And gather dust and chaff, and call
   To what I feel is Lord of all,
And faintly trust the larger hope.

CVI

Ring out, wild bells, to the wild sky,
   The flying cloud, the frosty light:
   The year is dying in the night;
Ring out, wild bells, and let him die.

Ring out the old, ring in the new,
   Ring, happy bells, across the snow:
   The year is going, let him go;
Ring out the false, ring in the true.

Ring out the grief that saps the mind,
   For those that here we see no more;
   Ring out the feud of rich and poor,
Ring in redress to all mankind.

Ring out a slowly dying cause,
   And ancient forms of party strife;
   Ring in the nobler modes of life,
With sweeter manners, purer laws.

Ring out the want, the care, the sin,
   The faithless coldness of the times;
   Ring out, ring out my mournful rhymes,
But ring the fuller minstrel in.

Ring out false pride in place and blood,
   The civic slander and the spite;
   Ring in the love of truth and right,
Ring in the common love of good.

Ring out old shapes of foul disease;
   Ring out the narrowing lust of gold;
   Ring out the thousand wars of old,
Ring in the thousand years of peace.

Ring in the valiant man and free,
   The larger heart, the kindlier hand;
   Ring out the darkness of the land,
Ring in the Christ that is to be.

LORD TENNYSON.

982.　SWEET AND LOW

SWEET and low, sweet and low,
　Wind of the western sea,
Low, low, breathe and blow,
　Wind of the western sea !
Over the rolling waters go,
Come from the dying moon, and
　　blow,
　Blow him again to me ;
While my little one, while my
　pretty one, sleeps.

Sleep and rest, sleep and rest,
　Father will come to thee soon ;
Rest, rest, on mother's breast,
　Father will come to thee soon ;
Father will come to his babe in
　　the nest,
Silver sails all out of the west
　Under the silver moon :
Sleep, my little one, sleep, my
　pretty one, sleep.

LORD TENNYSON (*The Princess*).

983.　TEARS, IDLE TEARS

TEARS, idle tears, I know not what they mean,
Tears from the depth of some divine despair
Rise in the heart, and gather to the eyes,
In looking on the happy Autumn-fields,
And thinking of the days that are no more.

Fresh as the first beam glittering on a sail,
That brings our friends up from the underworld,
Sad as the last which reddens over one
That sinks with all we love below the verge ;
So sad, so fresh, the days that are no more.

Ah, sad and strange as in dark summer dawns
The earliest pipe of half-awakened birds
To dying ears, when unto dying eyes
The casement slowly grows a glimmering square ;
So sad, so strange, the days that are no more.

Dear as remembered kisses after death,
And sweet as those by hopeless fancy feigned
On lips that are for others ; deep as love,
Deep as first love, and wild with all regret ;
O Death in Life, the days that are no more.

LORD TENNYSON (*The Princess*).

984.　THE OLD ORDER CHANGETH

THE old order changeth, yielding place to new,
And God fulfils Himself in many ways,
Lest one good custom should corrupt the world.
Comfort thyself : what comfort is in me ?
I have lived my life, and that which I have done
May He within Himself make pure ! but thou,
If thou shouldst never see my face again,
Pray for my soul.　More things are wrought by prayer

Than this world dreams of. Wherefore, let thy voice
Rise like a fountain for me night and day.
For what are men better than sheep or goats
That nourish a blind life within the brain,
If, knowing God, they lift not hands of prayer
Both for themselves and those who call them friend ?
For so the whole round earth is every way
Bound by gold chains about the feet of God.
But now farewell. I am going a long way
With these thou seëst—if indeed I go
(For all my mind is clouded with a doubt)—
To the island-valley of Avilion ;
Where falls not hail, or rain, or any snow,
Nor ever wind blows loudly : but it lies
Deep-meadowed, happy, fair with orchard-lawns
And bowery hollows crowned with summer sea,
Where I will heal me of my grievous wound.

LORD TENNYSON (Morte d'Arthur).

985.   THE SPLENDOUR FALLS ON CASTLE WALLS

THE splendour falls on castle walls
    And snowy summits old in story :
The long light shakes across the lakes,
    And the wild cataract leaps in glory.
Blow, bugle, blow, set the wild echoes flying,
Blow, bugle ; answer, echoes, dying, dying, dying.

O hark, O hear ! how thin and clear,
    And thinner, clearer, farther going !
O sweet and far from cliff and scar
    The horns of Elfland faintly blowing !
Blow, let us hear the purple glens replying :
Blow, bugle ; answer, echoes, dying, dying, dying.

O love, they die in yon rich sky,
    They faint on hill or field or river :
Our echoes roll from soul to soul,
    And grow for ever and for ever.
Blow, bugle, blow, set the wild echoes flying,
And answer, echoes, answer, dying, dying, dying.

LORD TENNYSON (The Princess).

986.   WOMAN AND MAN

THE woman's cause is man's : they rise or sink
Together, dwarfed or godlike, bond or free.

  .   .   .   .

For woman is not undeveloped man
But diverse : could we make her as the man,

Sweet Love were slain : his dearest bond is this,
Not like to like, but like in difference.
Yet in the long years liker must they grow ;
The man be more of woman, she of man ;
He gain in sweetness and in moral height,
Nor lose the wrestling thews that throw the world ;
She mental breadth, nor fail in childward care,
Nor lose the childlike in the larger mind ;
Till at the last she set herself to man,
Like perfect music unto noble words.

LORD TENNYSON (The Princess).

987.   THERE LIES A VALE IN IDA

THERE lies a vale in Ida, lovelier
Than all the valleys of Ionian hills.
The swimming vapour slopes athwart the glen,
Puts forth an arm, and creeps from pine to pine,
And loiters, slowly drawn.   On either hand
The lawns and meadow-ledges midway down
Hang rich in flowers, and far below them roars
The long brook falling through the cloven ravine
In cataract after cataract to the sea.
Behind the valley topmost Gargarus
Stands up and takes the morning : but in front
The gorges, opening wide apart, reveal
Troas and Ilion's columned citadel,
The crown of Troas.

             Hither came at noon
Mournful Oenone, wandering forlorn
Of Paris, once her playmate on the hills.
Her cheek had lost the rose, and round her neck
Floated her hair or seemed to float in rest.
She, leaning on a fragment twined with vine,
Sang to the stillness, till the mountain-shade
Sloped downward to her seat from the upper cliff.

   ' O mother Ida, many-fountained Ida,
Dear mother Ida, hearken ere I die.
For now the noonday quiet holds the hill :
The grasshopper is silent in the grass :
The lizard, with his shadow on the stone,
Rests like a shadow, and the cicala sleeps.
The purple flowers droop : the golden bee
Is lily-cradled : I alone awake.
My eyes are full of tears, my heart of love,
My heart is breaking, and my eyes are dim,
And I am all aweary of my life.'

LORD TENNYSON (Oenone).

988. ALBERT THE GOOD

WE know him now : all narrow jealousies
Are silent ; and we see him as he moved,
How modest, kindly, all-accomplished, wise,
With what sublime repression of himself,
And in what limits, and how tenderly ;
Not swaying to this faction or to that ;
Not making his high place the lawless perch
Of winged ambitions, nor a vantage-ground
For pleasure ; but through all this tract of years
Wearing the white flower of a blameless life,
Before a thousand peering littlenesses,
In that fierce light which beats upon a throne,
And blackens every blot.

> LORD TENNYSON (Dedication to the *Idylls of the King*).

989. WHAT DOES LITTLE BIRDIE SAY

WHAT does little birdie say
In her nest at peep of day ?
Let me fly, says little birdie,
Mother, let me fly away.
Birdie, rest a little longer,
Till the little wings are stronger.
So she rests a little longer,
Then she flies away.

What does little baby say,
In her bed at peep of day ?
Baby says, like little birdie,
Let me rise and fly away.
Baby, sleep a little longer,
Till the little limbs are stronger.
If she sleeps a little longer,
Baby too shall fly away.

> LORD TENNYSON (*Sea-Dreams*).

990. AT THE CHURCH GATE

ALTHOUGH I enter not,
Yet round about the spot
    Oft-times I hover ;
And near the sacred gate,
With longing eyes I wait,
    Expectant of her.

The Minster bell tolls out
Above the city's rout
    And noise and humming :
They've hushed   the   Minster
        bell :
The organ 'gins to swell :
    She's coming, she's coming !

My lady comes at last,
Timid, and stepping fast,
    And hastening hither,
With modest eyes downcast :
She comes — she's here — she's
        past—
    May Heaven go with her !

Kneel, undisturbed, fair Saint !
Pour out your praise or plaint
    Meekly and duly ;
I will not enter there,
To sully your pure prayer
    With thoughts unruly.

But suffer me to pace
Round the forbidden place,
    Lingering a minute,
Like outcast spirits who wait
And see through heaven's gate
    Angels within it.   W. M. THACKERAY.

991. AD MINISTRAM

DEAR Lucy, you know what my wish is,—
    I hate all your Frenchified fuss :
Your silly entrées and made dishes
    Were never intended for us.
No footman in lace and in ruffles
    Need dangle behind my arm-chair ;
And never mind seeking for truffles,
    Although they be ever so rare.

But a plain leg of mutton, my Lucy,
    I prithee get ready at three :
Have it smoking, and tender and juicy,
    And what better meat can there be ?
And when it has feasted the master,
    'Twill amply suffice for the maid ;
Meanwhile I will smoke my canaster,
    And tipple my ale in the shade.
                              W. M. THACKERAY.

992. THE AGE OF WISDOM

Ho, pretty page, with the dimpled chin,
    That never has known the barber's shear,
All your wish is woman to win,
This is the way that boys begin,—
    Wait till you come to Forty Year.

Curly gold locks cover foolish brains,
    Billing and cooing is all your cheer ;
Sighing and singing of midnight strains,
Under Bonnybell's window panes,—
    Wait till you come to Forty Year.

Forty times over let Michaelmas pass,
    Grizzling hair the brain doth clear—
Then you know a boy is an ass,
Then you know the worth of a lass,
    Once you have come to Forty Year.

Pledge me round, I bid ye declare,
    All good fellows whose beards are grey,
Did not the fairest of the fair
Common grow and wearisome ere
    Ever a month was passed away ?

The reddest lips that ever have kissed,
    The brightest eyes that ever have shone,
May pray and whisper, and we not list,
Or look away, and never be missed,
    Ere yet ever a month is gone.

Gillian's dead, God rest her bier,
  How I loved her twenty years syne !
Marian's married, but I sit here
Alone and merry at Forty Year,
  Dipping my nose in the Gascon wine.
                    W. M. THACKERAY.

993. 'THE NOBLE ART OF MURDERING'

LAST year, my love, it was my hap
  Behind a grenadier to be,
And, but he wore a hairy cap,
  No taller man, methinks, than me.

Prince Albert and the Queen, God wot
  (Be blessings on the glorious pair !),
Before us passed. I saw them not—
  I only saw a cap of hair.

Your orthodox historian puts
  In foremost rank the soldier thus,
The red-coat bully in his boots,
  That hides the march of men from us.

He puts him there in foremost rank,
  You wonder at his cap of hair :
You hear his sabre's cursèd clank,
  His spurs are jingling everywhere.

Go to ! I hate him and his trade :
  Who bade us so to cringe and bend,
And all God's peaceful people made
  To such as him subservient ?

Tell me what find we to admire
  In epaulets and scarlet coats,
In men, because they load and fire,
  And know the art of cutting throats ?
      W. M. THACKERAY (*The Chronicle of the Drum*).

994. VANITAS VANITATUM

O VANITY of Vanities !
  How wayward the decrees of Fate are ;
How very weak the very wise,
  How very small the very great are !

  .   .   .   .

Though thrice a thousand years are past
  Since David's son, the sad and splendid,
The weary King Ecclesiast,
  Upon his awful tablets penned it,—

Methinks the text is never stale,
  And life is every day renewing
Fresh comments on the old, old tale
  Of Folly, Fortune, Glory, Ruin.

Hark to the Preacher, preaching still!
  He lifts his voice and cries his sermon,
Here at St. Peter's of Cornhill,
  As yonder on the Mount of Hermon:

For you and me to heart to take
  (O dear beloved brother readers)
To-day, as when the good King spake
  Beneath the solemn Syrian cedars.
                              W. M. THACKERAY.

995. THE END OF THE PLAY

THE play is done; the curtain drops,
Slow falling, to the prompter's bell:
A moment yet the actor stops,
And looks around, to say farewell.
It is an irksome word and task;
And, when he's laughed and said his say,
He shows, as he removes the mask,
A face that's anything but gay.

One word, ere yet the evening ends,
Let's close it with a parting rhyme,
And pledge a hand to all young friends,
As fits the merry Christmas-time.
On life's wide scene you, too, have parts,
That Fate ere long shall bid you play;
Good night! with honest gentle hearts
A kindly greeting go alway!

    .   .   .   .

Come wealth or want, come good or ill.
Let young and old accept their part,
And bow before the Awful Will,
And bear it with an honest heart,
Who misses, or who wins the prize.
Go, lose or conquer as you can;
But if you fail, or if you rise,
Be each, pray God, a gentleman.

A gentleman, or old or young!
(Bear kindly with my humble lays);
The sacred chorus first was sung
Upon the first of Christmas Days:

The shepherds heard it overhead—
The joyful angels raised it then:
Glory to Heaven on high, it said,
And peace on earth to gentle men.

My song, save this, is little worth;
I lay the weary pen aside,
And wish you health, and love, and mirth,
As fits the solemn Christmas-tide.
As fits the holy Christmas birth,
Be this, good friends, our carol still—
Be peace on earth, be peace on earth,
To men of gentle will.   W. M. THACKERAY.

996. THE KING OF BRENTFORD

THERE was a King in Brentford,—of whom no legends tell,
But who, without his glory,—could eat and sleep right well.
His Polly's cotton nightcap,—it was his crown of state,
He slept of evenings early,—and rose of mornings late.

All in a fine mud palace,—each day he took four meals,
And for a guard of honour,—a dog ran at his heels.
Sometimes to view his kingdoms,—rode forth this monarch good.
And then a prancing jackass—he royally bestrode.

There were no costly habits—with which this King was cursed,
Except (and where's the harm on't?)—a somewhat lively thirst;
But people must pay taxes,—and Kings must have their sport;
So out of every gallon—his Grace he took a quart.

He pleased the ladies round him,—with manners soft and bland;
With reason good, they named him,—the father of his land.
Each year his mighty armies—marched forth in gallant show;
Their enemies were targets,—their bullets they were tow.

He vexed no quiet neighbour,—no useless conquest made,
But by the laws of pleasure,—his peaceful realm he swayed.
And in the years he reignèd,—through all this country wide,
There was no cause for weeping,—save when the good man died.

The faithful men of Brentford,—do still their King deplore,
His portrait yet is swinging,—beside an alehouse door.
And topers, tender-hearted,—regard his honest phiz,
And envy times departed,—that knew a reign like his.
                                        W. M. THACKERAY.

997. BOUILLABAISSE

THIS Bouillabaisse a noble dish is—
  A sort of soup or broth, or brew,
Or hotchpotch of all sorts of fishes,
  That Greenwich never could outdo ;
Green herbs, red peppers, mussels, saffern,
  Soles, onions, garlic, roach, and dace ;
All these you eat at Terré's tavern,
  In that one dish of Bouillabaisse.

Indeed, a rich and savoury stew 'tis ;
  And true philosophers, methinks,
Who love all sorts of natural beauties,
  Should love good victuals and good drinks.
And Cordelier and Benedictine
  Might gladly, sure, his lot embrace,
Nor find a fast-day too afflicting
  Which served him up a Bouillabaisse.
    W. M. THACKERAY (*The Ballad of Bouillabaisse*).

998. THE SORROWS OF WERTHER

WERTHER had a love for Charlotte
  Such as words could never utter ;
Would you know how first he met her ?
  She was cutting bread-and-butter.

Charlotte was a married lady,
  And a moral man was Werther,
And, for all the wealth of Indies,
  Would do nothing for to hurt her.

So he sighed and pined and ogled,
  And his passion boiled and bubbled,
Till he blew his silly brains out,
  And no more was by it troubled.

Charlotte, having seen his body
  Borne before her on a shutter,
Like a well-conducted person,
  Went on cutting bread-and-butter.
              W. M. THACKERAY.

999. A PLEASING LAND OF DROWSYHED

A PLEASING land of drowsyhed it was :
Of dreams that wave before the half-shut eye ;
And of gay castles in the clouds that pass,
For ever flushing round a summer sky :
There eke the soft delights that witchingly
Instil a wanton sweetness through the breast,
And the calm pleasures always hovered nigh ;
But whate'er smacked of noyance, or unrest,
Was far far off expelled from this delicious nest.
        J. THOMSON (*The Castle of Indolence*):

1000. THE SNOW-STORM

THE keener tempests come : and, fuming dun
From all the livid east or piercing north,
Thick clouds ascend, in whose capacious womb
A vapoury deluge lies, to snow congealed.
Heavy they roll their fleecy world along,
And the sky saddens with the gathered storm.
Through the hushed air the whitening shower descends,
At first thin-wavering ; till at last the flakes
Fall broad and wide and fast, dimming the day
With a continual flow. The cherished fields
Put on their winter-robe of purest white.
'Tis brightness all ; save where the new snow melts
Along the mazy current. Low the woods
Bow their hoar head ; and, ere the languid sun
Faint from the west emits his evening ray,
Earth's universal face, deep-hid and chill,
Is one wild dazzling waste, that buries wide
The works of man. Drooping, the labourer-ox
Stands covered o'er with snow, and then demands
The fruit of all his toil. The fowls of heaven,
Tamed by the cruel season, crowd around
The winnowing store, and claim the little boon
Which Providence assigns them. One alone,
The redbreast, sacred to the household gods,
Wisely regardful of the embroiling sky,
In joyless fields and thorny thickets leaves
His shivering mates, and pays to trusted man
His annual visit. Half afraid, he first
Against the window beats ; then brisk alights
On the warm hearth ; then, hopping o'er the floor,
Eyes all the smiling family askance,
And pecks, and starts, and wonders where he is—
Till, more familiar grown, the table-crumbs
Attract his slender feet.   J. THOMSON (*The Seasons*).

1001. RULE BRITANNIA

WHEN Britain first, at Heaven's command,
  Arose from out the azure main,
This was the charter of the land,
  And guardian angels sung this strain—
    ' Rule, Britannia, rule the waves ;
    Britons never will be slaves.'

The nations, not so blest as thee,
  Must in their turns to tyrants fall ;
Whilst thou shalt flourish great and free,
  The dread and envy of them all.

Still more majestic shalt thou rise,
　　More dreadful from each foreign stroke ;
As the loud blast that tears the skies
　　Serves but to root thy native oak.

Thee haughty tyrants ne'er shall tame ;
　　All their attempts to bend thee down
Will but arouse thy generous flame,
　　But work their woe and thy renown.

To thee belongs the rural reign ;
　　Thy cities shall with commerce shine ;
All thine shall be the subject main,
　　And every shore it circles thine.

The Muses, still with freedom found,
　　Shall to thy happy coast repair :
Blest isle ! with matchless beauty crowned,
　　And manly hearts to guard the fair.
　　　　' Rule, Britannia, rule the waves ;
　　　　Britons never will be slaves.'　　J. THOMSON.

1002. AS WE RUSH IN THE TRAIN

As we rush, as we rush in the Train,
　　The trees and the houses go wheeling back,
But the starry heavens above the plain
　　Come flying on our track.

Oh the beautiful stars in the sky,
　　The silver doves of the forest of Night,
Over the dull earth swarm and fly,
　　Companions of our flight.

We will rush ever on without fear ;
　　Let the goal be far, the flight be fleet !
For we carry the Heavens with us, dear,
　　While the earth slips from our feet !　　J. THOMSON.

1003. FROM ' ON NEWS '

WHAT sacred instinct did inspire
My soul in childhood with a hope so strong ?
　　What secret force moved my desire
To expect my joys beyond the seas, so young ?
　　　　Felicity I knew
　　　　　　Was out of view,
　　　　And being here alone,
　　I saw that happiness was gone
　　　　From me ! For this
　　　　I thirsted absent bliss,
And thought that sure beyond the seas,
　　Or else in something near at hand
I knew not yet (since naught did please
　　I knew) my bliss did stand.

But little did the infant dream
That all the treasures of the world were by:
　And that himself was so the cream
And crown of all which round about did lie.
　　　Yet thus it was: The gem,
　　　　The diadem,
　　　The ring enclosing all
　That stood upon this earthly ball;
　　　The Heavenly Eye
　　Much wider than the sky,
Wherein they all included were;
　The glorious Soul, that was the King
Made to possess them, did appear
　　A small and little thing!　　　T. TRAHERNE.

1004. FROM 'THE KINGDOM OF GOD'

I SAY to thee, do thou repeat
To the first man thou mayest meet
In lane, highway, or open street—

That he and we and all men move
Under a canopy of love,
As broad as the blue sky above;

That doubt and trouble, fear and pain
And anguish, all are shadows vain,
That death itself shall not remain;

That weary deserts we may tread,
A dreary labyrinth may thread,
Through dark ways underground be led;

Yet, if we will one Guide obey,
The dreariest path, the darkest way
Shall issue out in heavenly day;

And we, on divers shores now cast,
Shall meet, our perilous voyage past,
All in our Father's house at last.　　R. C. TRENCH.

1005. SOME MURMUR, WHEN THEIR SKY IS CLEAR

SOME murmur, when their sky is clear
　And wholly bright to view,
If one small speck of dark appear
　In their great heaven of blue.
And some with thankful love are filled
　If but one streak of light,
One ray of God's good mercy gild
　The darkness of their night.

In palaces are hearts that ask,
    In discontent and pride,
Why life is such a dreary task,
    And all good things denied.
And hearts in poorest huts admire
    How love has in their aid
(Love that not ever seems to tire)
    Such rich provision made.   R. C. TRENCH.

1006. THE LATTICE AT SUNRISE

As on my bed at dawn I mused and prayed,
I saw my lattice prankt upon the wall,
The flaunting leaves and flitting birds withal—
A sunny phantom interlaced with shade ;
' Thanks be to heaven,' in happy mood I said,
' What sweeter aid my matins could befall
Than this fair glory from the East hath made ?
What holy sleights hath God, the Lord of all,
To bid us feel and see ! we are not free
To say we see not, for the glory comes
Nightly and daily, like the flowing sea ;
His lustre pierceth through the midnight glooms ;
And, at prime hour, behold ! He follows me
With golden shadows to my secret rooms ! '
                              C. TENNYSON TURNER.

1007. THE BUOY-BELL

How like the leper, with his own sad cry
Enforcing his own solitude, it tolls !
That lonely bell set in the rushing shoals,
To warn us from the place of jeopardy !
O friend of man ! sore-vexed by ocean's power,
The changing tides wash o'er thee day by day ;
Thy trembling mouth is filled with bitter spray,
Yet still thou ringest on from hour to hour ;
High is thy mission, though thy lot is wild—
To be in danger's realm a guardian sound ;
In seamen's dreams a pleasant part to bear,
And earn their blessing as the year goes round ;
And strike the key-note of each grateful prayer,
Breathed in their distant homes by wife or child !
                              C. TENNYSON TURNER.

1008. THE OCEAN

THE ocean at the bidding of the moon
For ever changes with his restless tide ;
Flung shoreward now, to be regathered soon
With kingly pauses of reluctant pride

And semblance of return :—Anon from home
He issues forth anew, high ridged and free—
The gentlest murmur of his seething foam
Like armies whispering where great echoes be !
O leave me here upon this beach to rove,
Mute listener to that sound so grand and lone—
A glorious sound, deep drawn and strongly thrown,
And reaching those on mountain heights above,
To British ears (as who shall scorn to own ?)
A tutelar fond voice, a saviour-tone of Love !

C. TENNYSON TURNER.

1009. TO HIS BOOKS

By sucking you the wise, like bees, do grow
Healing and rich, though this they do most slow,
Because most choicely ; for as great a store
Have we of books as bees of herbs, or more ;
And the great task to try, then know, the good,
To discern weeds, and judge of wholesome food,
Is a rare scant performance. For man dies
Oft ere 'tis done, while the bee feeds and flies.
But you were all choice flowers ; all set and dressed
By old sage florists, who well knew the best.

H. VAUGHAN.

1010. NIGHT

DEAR Night ! this world's defeat ;
The stop to busy fools ; care's check and curb ;
The day of spirits ; my soul's calm retreat
　　　Which none disturb !
　　Christ's progress, and His prayer-time ;
　　The hours to which high Heaven doth chime.

　　God's silent, searching flight ;
When my Lord's head is filled with dew, and all
His locks are wet with the clear drops of night ;
　　　His still, soft call ;
　　His knocking time ; the soul's dumb watch,
　　When spirits their fair kindred catch.

．　　．　　．　　．　　．

　　There is in God—some say—
A deep, but dazzling darkness ; as men here
Say it is late and dusky, because they
　　　See not all clear.
　　O for that Night ! where I in Him
　　Might live invisible and dim !　　H. VAUGHAN.

1011. THE RETREAT

Happy those early days, when I
Shined in my Angel-infancy.
Before I understood this place
Appointed for my second race,
Or taught my soul to fancy aught
But a white, celestial thought;
When yet I had not walked above
A mile or two from my first Love,
And looking back, at that short space
Could see a glimpse of His bright face;
When on some gilded cloud or flower
My gazing soul would dwell an hour,
And in those weaker glories spy
Some shadows of eternity;
Before I taught my tongue to wound
My conscience with a sinful sound,
Or had the black art to dispense
A several sin to every sense,
But felt through all this fleshly dress
Bright shoots of everlastingness.

O how I long to travel back,
And tread again that ancient track!
That I might once more reach that plain,
Where first I left my glorious train;
From whence the enlightened spirit sees
That shady city of palm trees!
But ah! my soul with too much stay
Is drunk, and staggers in the way!
Some men a forward motion love,
But I by backward steps would move;
And when this dust falls to the urn,
In that state I came, return.　　　H. Vaughan.

1012. CHILDHOOD

I cannot reach it; and my striving eye
Dazzles at it, as at eternity.
Were now that chronicle alive,
Those white designs which children drive,
And the thoughts of each harmless hour,
With their content, too, in my power,
Quickly would I make my path even,
And by mere playing go to heaven.　　　H. Vaughan.

1013. I WALKED THE OTHER DAY, TO SPEND MY HOUR

I WALKED the other day—to spend my hour—
    Into a field,
Where I sometimes had seen the soil to yield
    A gallant flower,
But Winter now had ruffled all the bower,
    And curious store
I knew there heretofore.

.   .   .   .

Then taking up what I could nearest spy,
    I digged about
That place where I had seen him to grow out;
    And by and by
I saw the warm recluse alone to lie,
    Where fresh and green
He lived of us unseen.   H. VAUGHAN.

1014. A SONG TO AMORET

If I were dead, and, in my place,
  Some fresher youth designed
To warm thee, with new fires; and grace
  Those arms I left behind:

Were he as faithful as the Sun,
  That's wedded to the Sphere;
His blood as chaste and temperate run,
  As April's mildest tear;

Or were he rich; and, with his heap
And spacious share of earth,
Could make divine affection cheap,
And court his golden birth;

For all these arts, I'd not believe
  (No! though he should be thine!),
The mighty Amorist could give
  So rich a heart as mine!

Fortune and beauty thou might'st find,
  And greater men than I;
But my true resolvèd mind
  They never shall come nigh.

For I not for an hour did love,
  Or for a day desire,
But with my soul had from above
  This endless holy fire.
                 H. VAUGHAN.

1015. PEACE

My soul, there is a country
  Far beyond the stars,
Where stands a wingèd sentry,
  All skilful in the wars.

There, above noise and danger,
  Sweet Peace sits, crowned with smiles,
And One, born in a manger,
  Commands the beauteous files.

He is thy gracious friend,
  And (O my soul, awake!)
Did in pure love descend
  To die here, for thy sake.

If thou canst get but thither;
  There grows the flower of Peace,
The Rose that cannot wither,
  Thy fortress, and thy ease.

Leave then thy foolish ranges;
  For none can thee secure,
But One who never changes,
  Thy God, thy life, thy cure.   H. VAUGHAN.

1016. DULL, WRETCHED WORMS

NINE months Thy hands are fashioning us,
    And many years—alas !
Ere we can lisp, or aught discuss
    Concerning Thee, must pass :
Yet have I known Thy slightest things,
    A feather, or a shell,
A stick, or rod, which some chance brings,
    The best of us excel.
Dull, wretched worms ! that would not keep
    Within our first fair bed,
But out of Paradise must creep
    For every foot to **tread**.   H. VAUGHAN.

1017. TIMBER

SURE thou didst flourish once ! and many springs,
    Many bright mornings, much dew, many showers,
Passed o'er thy head ; many light hearts and wings,
    Which now are dead, lodged in thy living bowers.

And still a new succession sings and flies ;
    Fresh groves grow up, and their green branches shoot
Towards the old and still enduring skies,
    While the low violet thrives at their root.   H. VAUGHAN.

1018. BEYOND THE VEIL

THEY are all gone into the world of light,
    And I alone sit lingering here ;
Their very memory is fair and bright,
        And my sad thoughts doth clear.

It glows and glitters in my cloudy breast,
    Like stars upon some gloomy grove,
Or those faint beams in which this hill is dressed,
        After the sun's remove.

I see them walking in an air of glory,
    Whose light doth trample on my days ;
My days, which are at best but dull and hoary,
        Mere glimmerings and decays.

O holy Hope, and high Humility,
    High as the heavens above !
These are your walks, and you have showed them me,
        To kindle my cold love.

Dear, beauteous Death, the jewel of the just,
    Shining nowhere but in the dark,
What mysteries do lie beyond thy dust,
        Could Man outlook that mark !

He that hath found some fledged bird's nest, may know
  At first sight, if the bird be flown ;
But what fair well or grove he sings in now,
      That is to him unknown.

And yet, as angels in some brighter dreams
  Call to the soul when man doth sleep,
So some strange thoughts transcend our wonted themes,
      And into glory peep.

If a star were confined into a tomb,
  Her captive flames must needs burn there ;
But when the hand that locked her up, gives room,
      She'll shine through all the sphere.

O Father of Eternal Life, and all
  Created glories under Thee !
Resume Thy spirit from this world of thrall
      Into true liberty.

Either disperse these mists, which blot and fill
  My perspective still, as they pass ;
Or else remove me hence unto that hill
      Where I shall need no glass.   H. VAUGHAN.

1019. MAN

WEIGHING the steadfastness and state
Of some mean things which here below reside,
Where birds, like watchful clocks, the noiseless date
  And intercourse of times divide,
Where bees at night get home and hive, and flowers,
    Early as well as late,
Rise with the sun, and set in the same bowers ;

I would, said I, my God would give
The staidness of these things to man ! for these
To His divine appointments ever cleave,
  And no new business breaks their peace ;
The birds nor sow nor reap, yet sup and dine,
    The flowers without clothes live,
Yet Solomon was never dressed so fine.

Man hath still either toys, or care ;
He hath no root, nor to one place is tied,
But ever restless and irregular
  About this earth doth run and ride ;
He knows he hath a home, but scarce knows where ;
    He says it is so far,
That he hath quite forgot how to go there.

He knocks at all doors, strays and roams;
Nay, hath not so much wit as some stones have,
Which in the darkest nights point to their homes
    By some hid sense their Maker gave;
Man is the shuttle, to whose winding quest
    And passage through these looms
God ordered motion, but ordained no rest.

                                    H. VAUGHAN.

1020. ON A CONTENTED MIND

WHEN all is done and said,
    In the end thus shall you find,
He most of all doth bathe in bliss
    That hath a quiet mind:
And, clear from worldly cares,
    To deem can be content
The sweetest time in all his life
    In thinking to be spent.

The body subject is
    To fickle Fortune's power,
And to a million of mishaps
    Is casual every hour:
And Death in time doth change
    It to a clod of clay;
When as the mind, which is divine
    Runs never to decay.

Companion none is like
    Unto the mind alone;
For many have been harmed by speech,
    Through thinking, few or none.
Fear oftentimes retaineth words,
    But makes not thought to cease;
And he speaks best that hath the skill
    When for, to hold his peace.

Our wealth leaves us at death;
    Our kinsmen at the grave;
But virtues of the mind unto
    The heavens with us we have.
Wherefore, for virtue's sake
    I can be well content,
The sweetest time of all my life
    To deem in thinking spent.

                        THOMAS, LORD VAUX.

1021. THE ROCK OF CASHEL

ROYAL and saintly Cashel! I would gaze
Upon the wreck of thy departed powers
Not in the dewy light of matin hours,
Nor the meridian pomp of summer's blaze,
But at the close of dim autumnal days,
When the sun's parting glance, through slanting showers,
Sheds o'er thy rock-throned battlements and towers
Such awful gleams as brighten o'er Decay's
Prophetic cheek. At such a time, methinks,
There breathes from thy lone courts and voiceless aisles
A melancholy moral, such as sinks
On the lone traveller's heart, amid the piles
Of vast Persepolis on her mountain stand,
Or Thebes half buried in the desert sand.

                        SIR AUBREY DE VERE.

1022. THE RIGHT USE OF PRAYER

THEREFORE when thou wouldst pray, or dost thine alms,
Blow not a trump before thee : hypocrites
Do thus, vaingloriously ; the common streets
Boast of their largess, echoing their psalms.
On such the laud of men, like unctuous balms,
Falls with sweet savour. Impious counterfeits !
Prating of heaven, for earth their bosom beats !
Grasping at weeds, they lose immortal palms !
God needs not iteration nor vain cries :
That man communion with his God might share
Below, Christ gave the ordinance of prayer :
Vague ambages, and witless ecstasies,
Avail not : ere a voice to prayer be given
The heart should rise on wings of love to heaven.

SIR AUBREY DE VERE.

1023. SORROW

COUNT each affliction, whether light or grave,
God's messenger sent down to thee ; do thou
With courtesy receive him ; rise and bow ;
And, ere his shadow pass thy threshold, crave
Permission first his heavenly feet to lave ;
Then lay before him all thou hast ; allow
No cloud of passion to usurp thy brow,
Or mar thy hospitality ; no wave
Of mortal tumult to obliterate
The soul's marmoreal calmness : Grief should be
Like joy, majestic, equable, sedate ;
Confirming, cleansing, raising, making free ;
Strong to consume small troubles ; to commend
Great thoughts, grave thoughts, thoughts lasting to the end.

AUBREY DE VERE (THE YOUNGER).

1024. SONG

SING the old song, amid the sounds dispersing
  That burden treasured in your hearts too long ;
    Sing it, with voice low-breathed, but never name her :
She will not hear you, in her turrets nursing
  High thoughts, too high to mate with mortal song—
    Bend o'er her, gentle Heaven, but do not claim her !

In twilight caves, and secret lonelinesses,
  She shades the bloom of her unearthly days ;
    And the soft winds alone have power to woo her :
Far off we catch the dark gleam of her tresses ;
  And wild birds haunt the wood-walks where she strays,
    Intelligible music warbling to her.

S

That Spirit charged to follow and defend her,—
 He also, doubtless, suffers this love-pain ;
  And she, perhaps, is sad, hearing his sighing :
And yet that face is not so sad as tender ;
 Like some sweet singer's, when her sweetest strain
  From the heaved heart is gradually dying !
        AUBREY DE VERE (THE YOUNGER).

1025.   IF WOMEN COULD BE FAIR AND YET NOT FOND

IF women could be fair and yet not fond,
 Or that their love were firm, not fickle still,
I would not marvel that they make men bond
 By service long to purchase their goodwill ;
But when I see how frail those creatures are,
I laugh that men forget themselves so far.

To mark the choice they make, and how they change,
 How oft from Phoebus they do flee to Pan ;
Unsettled still, like haggards wild they range,
 These gentle birds that fly from man to man ;
Who would not scorn and shake them from the fist,
And let them fly, fair fools, which way they list ?

Yet for our sport we fawn and flatter both,
 To pass the time when nothing else can please,
And train them to our lure with subtle oath,
 Till, weary of our wiles, ourselves we ease ;
And then we say when we their fancy try, ·
To play with fools, Oh what a fool was I.
       E. VERE, EARL OF OXFORD.

1026.   AN EPITAPH UPON THOMAS, LORD FAIRFAX

   UNDER this stone does lie
   One born for victory.

Fairfax, the valiant ! and the only he
Who e'er, for that alone, a conqueror would be.
 Both sexes' virtues were in him combined :
 He had the fierceness of the manliest mind,
 And all the meekness too of womankind.
He never knew what envy was, or hate.
 His soul was filled with worth and honesty,
 And with another thing, quite out of date,
   Called modesty.

When all the nation he had won,
And with expense of blood had bought
  Store great enough, he thought,
  Of fame and of renown :
  He then his arms laid down
    With full as little pride,
As if he had been of his enemy's side ;
Or one of them could do, that were undone.
  He neither wealth nor places sought ;
  For others, not himself, he fought.
    He was content to know
    (For he had found it so)
That, when he pleased, to conquer he was able ;
And leave the spoil and plunder to the rabble.
    He might have been a king,
    But yet he understood
  How much it is a meaner thing
To be unjustly great than honourably good.
        G. VILLIERS, DUKE OF BUCKINGHAM.

1027. THE TRUE MARTYR

THE Martyr worthiest of the bleeding name
Is he whose life a bloodless part fulfils ;
Whom racks nor tortures tear, nor poniard kills,
Nor heat of bigots' sacrificial flame :
But whose great soul can to herself proclaim
The fullness of the everlasting ills
With which all pained Creation writhes and thrills,
And yet pursue unblenched her solemn aim ;
Who works, all-knowing work's futility ;
Creates, all-conscious of ubiquitous death ;
And hopes, believes, adores, while Destiny
Points from life's steep to all her graves beneath ;
  Whose Thought 'mid scorching woes is found apart—
  Perfect amid the flames, like Cranmer's heart !
        T. WADE.

1028. TO A LADY SINGING

CHLORIS, yourself you so excel,
  When you vouchsafe to breathe my thought,
That like a spirit, with this spell
  Of my own teaching I am caught.

That eagle's fate and mine is one,
  Which, on the shaft that made him die,
Espied a feather of his own,
  Wherewith he wont to soar so high.

Had Echo, with so sweet a grace,
  Narcissus' loud complaints returned ;
Not for reflection of his face,
  But of his voice, the boy had mourned.
                              E. WALLER.

1029. GO, LOVELY ROSE

Go, lovely rose !
Tell her, that wastes her time and
    me,
  That now she knows,
When I resemble her to thee,
How sweet and fair she seems to be.

Tell her that's young
And shuns to have her graces spied,
  That hadst thou sprung
In deserts, where no men abide,
Thou must have uncommended
    died.

Small is the worth
Of beauty from the light retired :
  Bid her come forth,
Suffer herself to be desired ;
And not blush so to be admired.

Then die ! that she
The common fate of all things rare
  May read in thee :
How small a part of time they
    share
That are so wondrous sweet and
    fair !
                              E. WALLER.

1030. THE ENGLISH AND THE SEA

OTHERS may use the ocean as their road,
Only the English make it their abode,
Whose ready sails with every wind can fly,
And make a covenant with the inconstant sky ;
Our oaks secure as if they there took root,
We tread on billows with a steady foot.
                    E. WALLER (*A War with Spain*).

1031. ON A GIRDLE

THAT which her slender waist confined
Shall now my joyful temples bind :
No monarch but would give his crown
His arms might do what this has done.

It was my heaven's extremest sphere,
The pale which held that lovely dear :
My joy, my grief, my hope, my love
Did all within this circle move.

A narrow compass ! and yet there
Dwelt all that's good, and all that's fair :
Give me but what this riband bound,
Take all the rest the sun goes round.   E. WALLER.

1032. OLD AGE

THE seas are quiet when the winds give o'er ;
So calm are we when passions are no more ;
For then we know how vain it was to boast
Of fleeting things so certain to be lost.
Clouds of affection from our younger eyes
Conceal that emptiness which age descries.

The soul's dark cottage, battered and decayed,
Lets in new light through chinks that time hath made :
Stronger by weakness, wiser men become
As they draw near to their eternal home :
Leaving the Old, both worlds at once they view
That stand upon the threshold of the New.

E. WALLER.

1033. TO MR. HENRY LAWES

WHO HAD NEWLY SET A SONG OF MINE IN THE YEAR 1635

VERSES make heroic virtue live ;
But you can life to verses give.
As when in open air we blow,
The breath, though strained, sounds flat and low ;
But if a trumpet takes the blast,
It lifts it high and makes it last ;
So in your airs our numbers dressed
Make a shrill sally from the breast
Of nymphs, who, singing what we penned,
Our passions to themselves commend ;
While love, victorious with thy art,
Governs at once their voice and heart.   E. WALLER.

1034. TO THE YOUNGER LADY LUCY SYDNEY

WHY came I so untimely forth
Into a world which, wanting thee,
Could entertain us with no worth,
Or shadow of felicity ?
That time should me so far remove
From that which I was born to love.

Yet, fairest Blossom ! do not slight
That eye which you may know so soon ;
The rosy morn resigns her light
And milder splendours to the noon :
If such thy dawning beauty's power
Who shall abide its noon-tide hour ?

Hope waits upon the flowery prime ;
And summer though it be less gay,
Yet is not looked on as a time
Of declination or decay ;
For with a full hand she doth bring
All that was promised by the spring.   E. WALLER.

1035. RIVALS IN LOVE

OF all the torments, all the cares,
  With which our lives are cursed;
Of all the plagues a lover bears,
  Sure, rivals are the worst !
By partners in each other kind,
  Afflictions easier grow ;
In love alone we hate to find
  Companions of our woe.

Sylvia, for all the pangs you see
  Are labouring in my breast,
I beg not you would favour me,
  Would you but slight the rest.
How great soe'er your rigours are
  With them alone I'll cope :—
I can endure my own despair,
  But not another's hope.
                W. WALSH.

1036. TO HIS MISTRESS

AGAINST MARRIAGE

YES, all the world must sure agree,
He who 's secured of having thee,
    Will be entirely blest :
But 'twere in me too great a wrong,
To make one who has been so long
    My queen, my slave at last.

Nor ought those things to be confined,
That were for public good designed :
    Could we, in foolish pride,
Make the sun always with us stay,
'Twould burn our corn and grass away,
    To starve the world beside.

Let not the thoughts of parting fright,
Two souls, which passion does unite ;
    For while our love does last,
Neither will strive to go away ;
And why the devil should we stay,
    When once that love is past ?   W. WALSH.

1037. THE SOLDIER WORN WITH WARS

THE soldier, worn with wars, delights in peace ;
  The pilgrim, in his ease, when toils are past ;
The ship, to gain the port, when storms do cease ;
  And I rejoice, from love discharged at last !
    Whom while I served, peace, rest, and land I lost,
    With grievesome wars, with toils, with storms betost.

Sweet liberty now gives me leave to sing.
  What world it was, where love the rule did bear !
How foolish chance, by lots, ruled every thing !
  How error was mainsail ! each wave a tear !
    The master, Love himself ! Deep sighs the wind !
    Cares rowed with vows the ship *Unmerry Mind*.

False hope as helm oft turned the boat about.
Inconstant faith stood up for middle mast.
Despair the cable, twisted all with doubt,
  Held griping grief, the pikèd anchor, fast ;
    Beauty was all the rocks. But I, at last,
    Am now twice free ; and all my love is past !
                             T. WATSON.

1038. FROM 'A CRADLE HYMN'

HUSH ! my dear, lie still and slumber,
  Holy angels guard thy bed !
Heavenly blessings without number
  Gently falling on thy head.

Sleep, my babe ; thy food and raiment,
  House and home thy friends provide ;
All without thy care or payment,
  All thy wants are well supplied.

How much better thou'rt attended
  Than the Son of God could be,
When from heaven He descended,
  And became a child like thee !

    .   .   .   .

Lo, He slumbers in His manger,
  Where the hornèd oxen fed ;
Peace, my darling, here's no danger,
  Here's no ox anear thy bed !

'Twas to save thee, child, from dying,
  Save my dear from burning flame,
Bitter groans and endless crying,
  That thy blest Redeemer came.

Mayst thou live to know and fear Him,
  Trust and love Him all thy days ;
Then go dwell for ever near Him,
  See His face, and sing His praise !   I. WATTS.

1039. THE HARDY SOLDIER

To the Right Hon. John, Lord Cutts,
at the siege of Namur

' Oh, why is man so thoughtless grown ?
    Why guilty souls in haste to die ?
Venturing the leap to the worlds unknown,
    Heedless, to arms and blood they fly.

' Are lives but worth a soldier's pay ?
    Why will ye join such wide extremes,
And stake immortal souls, in play
    At desperate chance, and bloody games ?

' Valour 's a nobler turn of thought,
    Whose pardoned guilt forbids her fears ;
Calmly she meets the deadly shot,
    Secure of life beyond the stars :

' But Frenzy dares eternal Fate ;
    And, spurred with Honour's airy dreams,
Flies to attack the infernal gate
    And force a passage to the flames.'

Thus, hovering o'er Namuria's plains,
    Sang heavenly Love, in Gabriel's form.
Young Thraso left the moving strains,
    And vowed to pray before the storm.

Anon, the thundering trumpet calls.
    ' Vows are but wind ! ' the hero cries,
Then swears by Heaven, and scales the walls,
    Drops in the ditch, despairs, and dies.   I. Watts.

1040. TRUE GREATNESS

Were I so tall to reach the pole
Or grasp the ocean with my span,
I must be measured by my soul :
The mind 's the standard of the man.   I. Watts.

1041. THE DAY OF JUDGEMENT

When the fierce north wind with his airy forces
Rears up the Baltic to a foaming fury ;
And the red lightning with a storm of hail comes
                    Rushing amain down,

How the poor sailors stand amazed and tremble !
Whilst the hoarse thunder, like a bloody trumpet,
Roars a loud onset to the gaping waters
                    Quick to devour them.

Such shall the noise be, and the wild disorder
(If things eternal may be like these earthly),
Such the dire terror when the great Archangel
    Shakes the creation ;

Tears the strong pillars of the vault of heaven,
Breaks up old marble, the repose of princes ;
See the graves open, and the bones arising,
    Flames all around them.

Hark, the shrill outcries of the guilty wretches !
Lively bright horror, and amazing anguish,
Stare through their eye-lids, while the living worm lies
    Gnawing within them.

Thoughts, like old vultures, prey upon their heart-strings,
And the smart twinges, when the eye beholds the
Lofty Judge frowning, and a flood of vengeance
    Rolling before him.

Hopeless immortals ! how they scream and shiver,
While devils push them to the pit wide-yawning
Hideous and gloomy to receive them headlong
    Down to the centre.

Stop here, my fancy (all away, ye horrid
Doleful ideas !) : come, arise to Jesus,
How he sits God-like, and the saints around him
    Throned, yet adoring !

Oh, may I sit there when he comes triumphant,
Dooming the nations ! then ascend to glory,
While our hosannas all along the passage
    Shout the Redeemer.   I. WATTS.

1042. ALL THE FLOWERS OF THE SPRING

ALL the flowers of the spring
Meet to perfume our burying ;
These have but their growing
    prime,
And man does flourish but his
    time.
Survey our progress from our birth:
We are set, we grow, we turn to
    earth.
Courts adieu, and all delights,
All bewitching appetites !

Sweetest breath and clearest eye
Like perfumes go out and die ;
And consequently this is done
As shadows wait upon the
    sun.
Vain the ambition of kings
Who seek by trophies and dead
    things
To leave a living name behind,
And weave but nets to catch the
    wind.

J. WEBSTER (*The Devil's Law Case*).

1043. CALL FOR THE ROBIN-REDBREAST

CALL for the robin-redbreast and the wren,
Since o'er shady groves they hover
And with leaves and flowers do cover
The friendless bodies of unburied men.
Call unto his funeral dole
The ant, the field-mouse, and the mole
To rear him hillocks that shall keep him warm
And (when gay tombs are robbed) sustain no harm ;
But keep the wolf far thence, that 's foe to men,
For with his nails he'll dig them up again.

J. WEBSTER (*The White Devil*).

1044. DIRGE

HARK ! now everything is still ;
This screech-owl, and the whistler shrill,
Call upon our dame aloud,
And bid her quickly don her shroud.
Much you had of land and rent ;
Your length in clay 's now competent.
A long war disturbed your mind ;
Here your perfect peace is signed.
Of what is 't fools make such vain keeping ?
Sin, their conception : their birth, weeping :
Their life, a general mist of error ;
Their death, a hideous storm of terror.
Strew your hair with powders sweet,
Don clean linen, bathe your feet :
And—the foul fiend more to check—
A crucifix let bless your neck.
'Tis now full tide 'tween night and day :
End your groan and come away.

J. WEBSTER (*The Duchess of Malfi*).

1045. O LET US HOWL SOME HEAVY NOTE

O, LET us howl some heavy note,
  Some deadly doggèd howl,
Sounding, as from the threatening throat
  Of beasts and fatal fowl !
As ravens, screech-owls, bulls, and bears,
  We'll bell and bawl our parts,
Till irksome noise have cloyed your ears,
  And corrosived your hearts.
At last, whenas our quire wants breath,
  Our bodies being blessed,
We'll sing, like swans, will wèlcome death,
  And die in love and rest.

J. WEBSTER (*The Duchess of Malfi*).

1046. LOVE IS A LAW

Love is a law, a discord of such force,
That 'twixt our sense and reason makes divorce ;
Love 's a desire, that to obtain betime,
We lose an age of years plucked from our prime ;
Love is a thing to which we soon consent,
As soon refuse, but sooner far repent.

Then what must women be that are the cause
That love hath life ?   that lovers feel such laws ?
They're like the winds upon Lepanthae's shore
That still are changing : O, then love no more !
A woman's love is like that Syrian flower,
That buds, and spreads, and withers in an hour.
  J. Webster and W. Rowley (*The Thracian Wonder*).

1047. WOMAN'S POWER

I am a woman, and am proud of it.
We are content that man shall take the lead,
Knowing he ever will look back on us
With doting eye, not caring how he steps.
Walking thus blindly, we may guide him so
That he shall turn which way shall please us best :
So we can beckon him where'er we will,
And lead him ever round about his grave,
And in whene'er we list.—
All matters that are greater than ourselves
Do trace their secret graces to our hands.
For glory captains struggle in the fight,
And play against the bulwark of the foe
The o'erbrowing engines in the stubborn siege ;
But love doth brace the garland on his head,
Making proud victory sweeter than it is.
What warlike prince did doff his laurel yet
But he did cast it in some fair maid's lap,
Saying, ' My greatness I commit to thee,
Mistress of it, and me, and my proud heart ' ?

. . . .

Nay, even high offices, renown and praise,
Greatness of name, honour of men's regard,
Power and state and sumptuous array,
Do pay a tribute to the lips of love,
Fetching their freshness and their darling grace
From woman's approbation,—waiting still
Close to her elbow till she please to smile
Upon the cause whereof the man is proud,
And say that it is well.

. . . .

Our will is the strong rudder to our bark ;
Our wit, the sails ; beauty, the swelling tide ;
Caprice, the tackle, serving to all winds,—
Though light as nothing, yet it tells like truth ;
And constancy, the anchor that's upheaved,
For ever falling and yet never struck.

C. J. WELLS (*Joseph and his Brethren*).

1048. RACHEL

THE dim blue-lacèd veins on either brow,
Neath the transparent skin meandering,
That with the silvery-leavèd lily vied ;
Her full dark eye, whose brightness glistened through
The sable lashes soft as camel-hair ;
Her slanting head curved like the maiden moon
And hung with hair luxuriant as a vine
And blacker than a storm ; her rounded ear
Turned like a shell upon some golden shore ;
Her whispering foot that carried all her weight,
Nor left its little pressure on the sand ;
Her lips as drowsy poppies, soft and red,
Gathering a dew from her escaping breath ;
Her voice melodious, mellow, deep, and clear,
Lingering like sweet music in the ear ;
Her neck o'ersoftened like to unsunned curd ;
Her tapering fingers rounded to a point ;
The silken softness of her veinèd hand ;
Her dimpled knuckles answering to her chin ;
And teeth like honeycombs o' the wilderness.

C. J. WELLS (*Joseph and his Brethren*).

1049. WHAT MAN HAD NOT RATHER BE POOR

WHAT man in his wits had not rather be poor,
    Than for lucre his freedom to give,
Ever busy the means of his life to secure,
    And so ever neglecting to live ?

Environed from morning to night in a crowd,
    Not a moment unbent, or alone ;
Constrained to be abject, though never so proud,
    And at every one's call but his own.

Still repining, and longing for quiet, each hour,
    Yet studiously flying it still ;
With the means of enjoying his wish, in his power ;
    But accursed with his wanting the will.

For a year must be past, or a day must be come,
  Before he has leisure to rest;
He must add to his store this or that pretty sum,
  And then he will have time to be blessed.

But his gains more bewitching the more they increase,
  Only swell the desire of his eye:
Such a wretch, let mine enemy live if he please,
  Let not even mine enemy die.   S. WESLEY.

1050. IN YOUTH IS PLEASURE

IN an arbour green asleep I lay,
The birds sang sweet in the middle of the day,
I dreamèd fast of mirth and play:
    In youth is pleasure, in youth is pleasure.

Methought I walked still to and fro,
And from her company I could not go—
But when I waked it was not so:
    In youth is pleasure, in youth is pleasure.

Therefore my heart is surely pyght
Of her alone to have a sight
Which is my joy and heart's delight:
    In youth is pleasure, in youth is pleasure.
                    R. WEVER (*Lusty Juventus*).

1051. TO AN EARLY PRIMROSE

MILD offspring of a dark and sullen sire!
Whose modest form, so delicately fine,
    Was nursed in whirling storms,
    And cradled in the winds.

Thee, when young Spring first questioned Winter's way,
And dared the sturdy blusterer to the fight,
    Thee on this bank he threw
    To mark his victory.

In this low vale, the promise of the year,
Serene, thou openest to the nipping gale,
    Unnoticed and alone,
    Thy tender elegance.

So virtue blooms, brought forth amid the storms
Of chill adversity; in some lone walk
    Of life she rears her head,
    Obscure and unobserved;

While every bleaching breeze that on her blows,
Chastens her spotless purity of breast,
    And hardens her to bear
    Serene the ills of life.   H. KIRKE WHITE.

1052. TO NIGHT

MYSTERIOUS Night ! when our first parent knew
Thee from report divine, and heard thy name,
Did he not tremble for this lovely frame,
This glorious canopy of light and blue ?
Yet 'neath a curtain of translucent dew,
Bathed in the rays of the great setting flame,
Hesperus with the host of heaven came,
And lo ! Creation widened in man's view.

Who could have thought such darkness lay concealed
Within thy beams, O sun ! or who could find,
Whilst fly and leaf and insect stood revealed,
That to such countless orbs thou mad'st us blind !
Why do we then shun death with anxious strife ?
If Light can thus deceive, wherefore not Life ?

J. BLANCO WHITE.

1053. JE NE SAIS QUOI

YES, I'm in love, I feel it now,
  And Celia has undone me !
And yet I'll swear I can't tell how
  The pleasing plague stole on me.

'Tis not her face that love creates,
  For there no graces revel ;
'Tis not her shape, for there the Fates
  Have rather been uncivil.

'Tis not her air, for, sure, in that
  There's nothing more than common ;
And all her sense is only chat,
  Like any other woman.

Her voice, her touch, might give the alarm,
  'Twas both, perhaps, or neither !
In short, 'twas that provoking charm
  Of Celia all together.

W. WHITEHEAD.

1054. A SIGHT IN CAMP

A SIGHT in camp in the daybreak grey and dim,
As from my tent I emerge so early, sleepless,
As slow I walk in the cool fresh air, the path near by the hospital tent,
Three forms I see on stretchers lying, brought out there, untended lying,
Over each the blanket spread, ample brownish woollen blanket,
Grey and heavy blanket, folding, covering all.
Curious, I halt, and silent stand ;
Then with light fingers I from the face of the nearest, the first, just lift the blanket :

Who are you, elderly man so gaunt and grim, with well-greyed hair,
    and flesh all sunken about the eyes ?
Who are you, my dear comrade ?
Then to the second I step—And who are you, my child and darling ?
Who are you, sweet boy, with cheeks yet blooming ?
Then to the third—a face nor child, nor old, very calm, as of beautiful
    yellow-white ivory ;
Young man, I think I know you—I think this face of yours is the
    face of the Christ himself ;
Dead and divine, and brother of us all, and here again he lies.

WALT WHITMAN (Drum-Taps).

1055. BEAT ! BEAT ! DRUMS !

I

BEAT ! beat ! drums !—Blow ! bugles ! blow !
Through the windows—through doors—burst like a force of ruthless
    men,
Into the solemn church, and scatter the congregation ;
Into the school where the scholar is studying ;
Leave not the bridegroom quiet—no happiness must he have now
    with his bride ;
Nor the peaceful farmer any peace, ploughing his field or gathering
    his grain ;
So fierce you whirr and pound, you drums—so shrill you bugles blow.

II

Beat ! beat ! drums !—Blow ! bugles ! blow !
Over the traffic of cities—over the rumble of wheels in the streets :
Are beds prepared for sleepers at night in the houses ? No sleepers
    must sleep in those beds ;
No bargainers' bargains by day—no brokers or speculators—Would
    they continue ?
Would the talkers be talking ? would the singer attempt to sing ?
Would the lawyer rise in the court to state his case before the judge ?
Then rattle quicker, heavier drums—you bugles wilder blow.

III

Beat ! beat ! drums !—Blow ! bugles ! blow !
Make no parley—stop for no expostulation ;
Mind not the timid—mind not the weeper or prayer ;
Mind not the old man beseeching the young man ;
Let not the child's voice be heard, nor the mother's entreaties ;
Make even the trestles to shake the dead, where they lie awaiting the
    hearses,
So strong you thump, O terrible drums—so loud you bugles blow.

WALT WHITMAN (Drum-Taps).

1056. DID YOU ASK DULCET RHYMES FROM ME

Dᴵᴰ you ask dulcet rhymes from me ?
Did you find what I sang erewhile so hard to follow, to understand ?
Why I was not singing erewhile for you to follow, to understand—nor
    am I now ;
—What to such as you, anyhow, such a poet as I ?—therefore leave
    my works,
And go lull yourself with what you can understand ;
For I lull nobody,—and you will never understand me.

WALT WHITMAN (*Drum-Taps*).

1057. ANIMALS

I ᴛʜɪɴᴋ I could turn and live with animals, they are so placid and
    self-contained ;
I stand and look at them long and long.
They do not sweat and whine about their condition ;
They do not lie awake in the dark and weep for their sins ;
They do not make me sick discussing their duty to God ;
Not one is dissatisfied—not one is demented with the mania of owning
    things ;
Not one kneels to another, nor to his kind that lived thousands of
    years ago ;
Not one is respectable or industrious over the whole earth.

WALT WHITMAN (*Song of Myself*).

1058. O CAPTAIN ! MY CAPTAIN !

O Cᴀᴘᴛᴀɪɴ ! my Captain ! our fearful trip is done,
The ship has weathered every rack, the prize we sought is won,
The port is near, the bells I hear, the people all exulting,
While follow eyes the steady keel, the vessel grim and daring ;
            But O heart ! heart ! heart !
                O the bleeding drops of red,
                    Where on the deck my Captain lies,
                        Fallen cold and dead.

O Captain ! my Captain ! rise up and hear the bells ;
Rise up—for you the flag is flung—for you the bugle trills,
For you bouquets and ribboned wreaths—for you the shores a-crowding,
For you they call, the swaying mass, their eager faces turning ;
            Here Captain ! dear father !
                This arm beneath your head !
                    It is some dream that on the deck
                        You've fallen cold and dead.

My Captain does not answer, his lips are pale and still,
My father does not feel my arm, he has no pulse nor will,
The ship is anchored safe and sound, its voyage closed and done,
From fearful trip the victor ship comes in with object won ;
  Exult, O shores, and ring, O bells !
  But I, with mournful tread,
   Walk the deck my Captain lies,
   Fallen cold and dead.
    WALT WHITMAN (*Memories of President Lincoln*).

1059. SPIRIT WHOSE WORK IS DONE

SPIRIT whose work is done ! spirit of dreadful hours !
Ere, departing, fade from my eyes your forests of bayonets ;
Spirit of gloomiest fears and doubts, (yet onward ever unfaltering
 pressing ;)
Spirit of many a solemn day, and many a savage scene ! Electric
 spirit !
That with muttering voice, through the war now closed, like a tireless
 phantom flitted,
Rousing the land with breath of flame, while you beat and beat the
 drum ;
—Now, as the sound of the drum, hollow and harsh to the last, rever-
 berates round me ;
As your ranks, your immortal ranks, return, return from the battles ;
While the muskets of the young men yet lean over their shoulders ;
While I look on the bayonets bristling over their shoulders ;
While those slanted bayonets, whole forests of them, appearing in the
 distance, approach and pass on, returning homeward,
Moving with steady motion, swaying to and fro, to the right and left,
Evenly, lightly rising and falling, as the steps keep time ;
—Spirit of hours I knew, all hectic red one day, but pale as death
 next day ;
Touch my mouth ere you depart—press my lips close !
Leave me your pulses of rage ! bequeath them to me ! fill me with
 currents convulsive !
Let them scorch and blister out of my chants, when you are gone ;
Let them identify you to the future, in these songs.
    WALT WHITMAN (*Drum-Taps*).

1060. WHEN LILACS LAST IN THE DOORYARD BLOOMED

WHEN lilacs last in the dooryard bloomed,
And the great star early drooped in the western sky in the night,
I mourned, and yet shall mourn with ever-returning spring.

O ever-returning spring, trinity sure to me you bring,
Lilac blooming perennial and drooping star in the west,
And thought of him I love.

O powerful western fallen star !
O shades of night—O moody, tearful night !
O great star disappeared—O the black murk that hides the star !
O cruel hands that hold me powerless—O helpless soul of me !
O harsh surrounding cloud that will not free my soul.

In the dooryard fronting an old farm-house near the white-washed palings,
Stands the lilac-bush tall-growing with heart-shaped leaves of rich green.
With many a pointed blossom rising delicate, with the perfume strong I love
With every leaf a miracle—and from this bush in the dooryard,
With its delicate-coloured blossoms and heart-shaped leaves of rich green,
A sprig with its flower I break.

. . . .

Over the breast of the spring, the land, amid cities,
Amid lanes and through old woods, where lately the violets peeped from the ground, spotting the grey debris,
Amid the grass in the fields each side of the lanes, passing the endless grass,
Passing the yellow-speared wheat, every grain from its shroud in the dark-brown fields uprising,
Passing the apple-tree blows of white and pink in the orchards,
Carrying a corpse to where it shall rest in the grave,
Night and day journeys a coffin.

Coffin that passes through lanes and streets,
Through day and night with the great cloud darkening the land,
With the pomp of the inlooped flags, with the cities draped in black,
With the show of the States themselves as of crape-veiled women standing,
With processions long and winding and the flambeaus of the night,
With the countless torches lit, with the silent sea of faces and the unbared heads,
With the waiting depôt, the arriving coffin and the sombre faces,
With dirges through the night, with the thousand voices rising strong and solemn,
With all the mournful voices of the dirges poured around the coffin,

The dim-lit churches and the shuddering organs—where amid these you journey,
With the tolling tolling bells' perpetual clang,
Here, coffin that slowly passes,
I give you my sprig of lilac.

(Nor for you, for one alone,
Blossoms and branches green to coffins all I bring,
For fresh as the morning, thus would I chant a song for you, O sane
    and sacred death. . . .)

Come, lovely and soothing Death ;
Undulate round the world ; serenely arriving, arriving,
In the day, in the night, to all, to each ;
Sooner, or later, delicate Death.

Praised be the fathomless Universe
For life and joy, and for objects and knowledge curious ;
And for love, sweet love. But praise ! O praise and praise,
For the sure-enwinding arms of cool-enfolding Death.

Dark Mother, always gliding near, with soft feet,
Have none chanted for thee a chant of fullest welcome ?
Then I chant it for thee ; I glorify thee above all.
I bring thee a song that when thou must indeed come, come un-
    falteringly.

Approach, encompassing Death—strong deliveress,
When it is so, when thou hast taken them, I joyously sing the dead,
Lost in the loving floating ocean of thee,
Laved in the flood of thy bliss, O Death.

From me to thee glad serenades,
Dances for thee I propose, saluting thee, adornments and feastings
    for thee,
And the sights of the open landscape and the high-spread sky are
    fitting,
And life and the fields, and the huge and thoughtful night.

The night in silence under many a star,
The ocean shore and the husky whispering wave whose voice I know,
And the soul turning to thee, O vast and well-veiled Death,
And the body gratefully nestling close to thee.

Over the tree-tops I float thee a song,
Over the rising and sinking waves, over the myriad fields and the
    prairies wide,
Over the dense-packed cities all and the teeming wharves and ways,
I float this carol with joy, with joy to thee, O Death.

        WALT WHITMAN (*Memories of President Lincoln*).

1061. FROM 'THE MEETING'

I ASK no organ's soulless breath
To drone the themes of life and
death,
No altar candle-lit by day,
No ornate wordsman's rhetoric-
play,
No cool philosophy to teach
Its bland audacities of speech
To double-tasked idolaters
Themselves their gods and wor-
shippers,
No pulpit hammered by the fist
Of loud-asserting dogmatist,
Who borrows for the Hand of
love
The smoking thunderbolts of
Jove.

I know how well the fathers
taught,
What work the ancient schoolmen
wrought ;
I reverence old-time faith and men,
But God is near us now as then ;
His force of love is still unspent,
His hate of sin as imminent ;
And still the measure of our needs
Outgrows the cramping bounds of
creeds ;
The manna gathered yesterday
Already savours of decay ;
Doubts to the world's child-heart
unknown
Question us now from star and
stone.

J. G. WHITTIER.

1062. VESTA

O CHRIST of God ! whose life and
death
Our own have reconciled,
Most quietly, most tenderly
Take home Thy star-named
child !

Thy grace is in her patient eyes,
Thy words are on her tongue ;
The very silence round her seems
As if the angels sung.

Her smile is as a listening child's
Who hears its mother call ;
The lilies of Thy perfect peace
About her pillow fall.

She leans from out our clinging
arms
To rest herself in Thine ;
Alone to Thee, dear Lord, can
we
Our well-beloved resign !

Oh, less for her than for ourselves
We bow our heads and pray ;
Her setting star, like Bethlehem's,
To Thee shall point the way.

J. G. WHITTIER.

1063. FROM 'CHILD-SONGS'

STILL linger in our noon of time
And on our Saxon tongue
The echoes of the home-born hymns
The Aryan mothers sung.

And childhood had its litanies
In every age and clime ;
The earliest cradles of the race
Were rocked to poet's rhyme.

Nor sky, nor wave, nor tree, nor
  flower,
  Nor green earth's virgin sod,
So moved the singer's heart of old
  As these small ones of God.

The mystery of unfolding life
  Was more than dawning morn,
Than opening flower or crescent
  moon
  The human soul new-born !

And still to childhood's sweet
  appeal
  The heart of genius turns,
And more than all the sages teach
  From lisping voices learns,—

The voices loved of him who sang,
  Where Tweed and Teviot glide,
That sound to-day on all the
  winds
  That blow from Rydal-side,—

Heard in the Teuton's household songs,
  And folk-lore of the Finn,
Where'er to holy Christmas hearths
  The Christ-child enters in !   J. G. WHITTIER.

1064. COME, CHLOE, AND GIVE ME SWEET KISSES

COME, Chloe, and give me sweet kisses,
  For sweeter sure never girl gave ;
But why, in the midst of my blisses,
  Do you ask me how many I'd have ?
I'm not to be stinted in pleasure,
  Then, prithee, my charmer, be kind,
For whilst I love thee above measure,
  To numbers I'll ne'er be confined.
Count the bees that on Hybla are playing,
  Count the flowers that enamel its fields,
Count the flocks that on Tempe are straying,
  Or the grain that rich Sicily yields,
Go number the stars in the heaven,
  Count how many sands on the shore,
When so many kisses you've given,
  I still shall be craving for more.
To a heart full of love, let me hold thee,
  To a heart that, dear Chloe, is thine ;
In my arms I'll for ever enfold thee,
  And twist round thy limbs like a vine.
What joy can be greater than this is ?
  My life on thy lips shall be spent !
But the wretch that can number his kisses,
  With few will be ever content.

SIR C. HANBURY WILLIAMS.

1065. BROADWAY

THE shadows lay along Broadway,
  'Twas near the twilight tide,
And slowly there a lady fair
  Was walking in her pride.
Alone walked she, but viewlessly
  Walked spirits at her side.

Peace charmed the street beneath her feet,
  And Honour charmed the air,
And all astir looked kind on her,
  And called her good as fair;
For all God ever gave to her
  She kept with chary care.

She kept with care her beauties rare
  From lovers warm and true,
For her heart was cold to all but gold,
  And the rich came not to woo:
But honoured well are charms to sell,
  If priests the selling do.

Now walking there was one more fair
  A slight girl, lily-pale;
And she had unseen company
  To make the spirit quail:
'Twixt Want and Scorn she walked forlorn,
  And nothing could avail.

No mercy now can clear her brow
  For this world's peace to pray;
For, as love's wild prayer dissolved in air,
  Her woman's heart gave way!—
But the sin forgiven by Christ in Heaven,
  By man is cursed alway.   N. P. WILLIS.

1066. EPITAPH ON CHARLES II

HERE lies our Sovereign Lord the King,
  Whose word no man relies on,
Who never said a foolish thing,
  Nor ever did a wise one.
    J. WILMOT, EARL OF ROCHESTER.

1067. CONSTANCY

I CANNOT change, as others do,
  Though you unjustly scorn;
Since that poor swain that sighs for you,
  For you alone was born.
No, Phillis, no! your heart to move,
  A surer way I'll try,
And to revenge my slighted love,
Will still love on, will still love on, and die!

When killed with grief Amyntas lies,
    And you to mind shall call
The sighs that now unpitied rise,
    The tears that vainly fall:
That welcome hour, that ends this smart,
    Will then begin your pain,
For such a faithful, tender heart
Can never break, can never break, in vain.

J. WILMOT, EARL OF ROCHESTER.

1068. MY LIGHT THOU ART

My light thou art, without thy glorious sight
My eyes are darkened with eternal night;
My Love, thou art my way, my life, my light.

Thou art my way, I wander if thou fly;
Thou art my light, if hid, how blind am I!
Thou art my life, if thou withdraw'st I die.

Thou art my life; if thou but turn away,
My life's a thousand deaths. Thou art my way;
Without thee, Love, I travel not, but stray.

J. WILMOT, EARL OF ROCHESTER.

1069. UPON HIS DRINKING IN A BOWL.

Vulcan, contrive me such a cup
    As Nestor used of old;
Show all thy skill to trim it up,
    Damask it round with gold.

Make it so large that, filled with sack
    Up to the swelling brim,
Vast toasts on the delicious lake
    Like ships at sea may swim.

Engrave not battle on his cheek:
    With war I've nought to do.
I'm none of those that took Maestrich,
    Nor Yarmouth leaguer knew.

Let it no name of planets tell,
    Fixed stars or constellations,
For I am no Sir Sidrophel,
    Nor none of his relations.

But carve thereon a spreading vine,
    Then add two lovely boys;
Their limbs in amorous folds entwine,
    The type of future joys.

Cupid and Bacchus my saints are;
    May drink and love still reign!
With wine I wash away my cares
    And then to love again.

J. WILMOT, EARL OF ROCHESTER.

1070. A SLEEPING CHILD

FAIR was that face as break of dawn,
When o'er its beauty sleep was drawn
Like a thin veil which half concealed
The light of soul and half revealed.
While thy hushed heart with visions wrought
Each trembling eyelash moved with thought,
And things we dream, but ne'er can speak,
Like clouds come floating o'er thy cheek—
Such summer clouds as travel light
When the soul's heaven lies calm and bright ;—
Till thou awak'st,—then to thine eye
Thy whole heart leapt in ecstacy !
And lovely is that heart of thine,
Or sure those eyes could never shine
With such a wild, yet bashful glee,
Gay, half-o'ercome timidity.

J. WILSON ('CHRISTOPHER NORTH').

1071. AMARYLLIS I DID WOO

AMARYLLIS I did woo ;
And I courted Phillis too ;
Daphne for her love I chose ;
Chloris, for that damask rose
In her cheek I held as dear ;
Yea, a thousand liked, well near ;
And, in love with all together,
Fearèd the enjoying either,
'Cause to be of one possessed,
Barred the hope of all the rest.

G. WITHER (The Mistress of Philarete).

1072. BEHOLD THE SUN THAT SEEMED BUT NOW

BEHOLD the sun, that seemed but now
　Enthronèd overhead,
Beginning to decline below
　The globe whereon we tread ;
And he, whom yet we look upon
　With comfort and delight,
Will quite depart from hence anon,
　And leave us to the night.

Thus time, unheeded, steals away
　The life which nature gave ;
Thus are our bodies every day
　Declining to the grave ;
Thus from us all our pleasures fly
　Whereon we set our heart ;
And when the night of death draws
　nigh
Thus will they all depart.

Lord! though the sun forsake our sight,
   And mortal hopes are vain,
Let still thine everlasting light
   Within our souls remain;
And in the nights of our distress
   Vouchsafe those rays divine,
Which from the Sun of Righteousness
   For ever brightly shine!   G. WITHER.

1073. I LOVED A LASS, A FAIR ONE

I LOVED a lass, a fair one,
   As fair as e'er was seen;
She was indeed a rare one,
   Another Sheba Queen!
But, fool as then I was,
   I thought she loved me too:
But now, alas! she's left me,
   Falero, lero, loo.

Her hair like gold did glister,
   Each eye was like a star,
She did surpass her sister,
   Which passed all others far;
She would me honey call,
   She'd,—oh she'd kiss me too:
But now, alas! she's left me,
   Falero, lero, loo.

   .   .   .   .

Many a merry meeting
   My love and I have had;
She was my only sweeting,
   She made my heart full glad;
The tears stood in her eyes
   Like to the morning dew:
But now, alas! she's left me,
   Falero, lero, loo.

  .   .   .   .   .

Her cheeks were like the cherry,
   Her skin as white as snow;
When she was blithe and merry,
   She angel-like did show;
Her waist exceeding small,
   The fives did fit her shoe:
But now, alas! she's left me,
   Falero, lero, loo.

In summer time or winter
   She had her heart's desire;
I still did scorn to stint her
   From sugar, sack, or fire;
The world went round about,
   No cares we ever knew:
But now, alas! she's left me,
   Falero, lero, loo.

As we walked home together
   At midnight through the town,
To keep away the weather
   O'er her I'd cast my gown.
No cold my love should feel,
   Whate'er the heavens could do;
But now, alas! she's left me,
   Falero, lero, loo.

Like doves we should be billing,
   And clip and kiss so fast;
Yet she would be unwilling
   That I should kiss the last.
They're Judas-kisses now,
   Since that they proved untrue;
For now, alas! she's left me,
   Falero, lero, loo.

To maidens' vows and swearing
   Henceforth no credit give
You may give them the hearing
   But never them believe;
They are as false as fair,
   Unconstant, frail, untrue:
For mine, alas! hath left me,
   Falero, lero, loo.
            G. WITHER.

1074. THE FLOWER OF FLOWERS

LET who list, for me, advance
The admirèd flowers of France,
Let who will praise and behold
The reservèd marigold ;
Let the sweet-breathed violet now
Unto whom she pleaseth bow ;
And the fairest lily spread
Where she will her golden head ;
I have such a flower to wear
That for those I do not care.
. . . .

Let all times, both present, past,
And the age that shall be last,
Vaunt the beauties they bring
    forth.
I have found in one such worth,
That content I neither care
What the best before me were ;
Nor desire to live and see
Who shall fair hereafter be ;
For I know the hand of Nature
Will not make a fairer creature.

G. WITHER (*The Mistress of Philarete*).

1075. SHALL I, WASTING IN DESPAIR

SHALL I, wasting in despair,
Die because a woman 's fair ?
Or make pale my cheeks with care
'Cause another's rosy are ?
Be she fairer than the day,
Or the flowery meads in May,
  If she be not so to me
  What care I how fair she be ?

Should my heart be grieved or
    pined
'Cause I see a woman kind ?
Or a well-disposèd nature
Joinèd with a lovely feature ?
Be she meeker, kinder than
Turtle-dove, or pelican,
  If she be not so to me,
  What care I how kind she
    be ?

Shall a woman's virtues move
Me to perish for her love ?
Or her well-deserving, known,
Make me quite forget my own ?
Be she with that goodness blest
Which may gain her name of best,
  If she be not such to me
  What care I how good she be ?

'Cause her fortune seems too high,
Shall I play the fool, and die ?
Those that bear a noble mind,
Where they want of riches find,
Think what with them they would
    do
That without them dare to woo ;
  And unless that mind I see,
  What care I though great she
    be ?

Great, or good, or kind, or fair,
I will ne'er the more despair :
If she love me, this believe
I will die ere she shall grieve :
If she slight me when I woo,
I can scorn and let her go ;
  For if she be not for me,
  What care I for whom she be ?   G. WITHER.

1076. SWEET BABY, SLEEP

Sweet baby, sleep! what ails my dear,
  What ails my darling thus to cry?
Be still, my child, and lend thine ear
  To hear me sing thy lullaby:
My pretty lamb, forbear to weep;
Be still, my dear; sweet baby, sleep.

.   .   .   .

The King of kings, when He was born,
  Had not so much for outward ease:
By Him such dressings were not worn,
  Nor such like swaddling-clothes as these.
Sweet baby, then forbear to weep;
Be still, my babe; sweet baby, sleep.

Within a manger lodged thy Lord,
  Where oxen lay, and asses fed:
Warm rooms we do to thee afford,
  An easy cradle or a bed.
Sweet baby, then forbear to weep;
Be still, my babe; sweet baby, sleep.   G. Wither.

1077. WHAT PEARLS, WHAT RUBIES

What pearls, what rubies can
Seem so lovely fair to man,
As her lips whom he doth love,
When in sweet discourse they move,
Or her lovelier teeth, the while
She doth bless him with a smile?
  Stars indeed fair creatures be;
Yet amongst us where is he
Joys not more the while he lies
Sunning in his mistress' eyes,
Than in all the glimmering light
Of a starry winter's night?

.   .   .   .   .   .

Look on moon, on stars, on sun,
All God's creatures overrun,
See if all of them presents
To your mind such sweet con-
    tents;
Or, if you from them can take
Aught that may a beauty make,
Shall one half so pleasing prove,
As is hers whom you do love.

.   .   .   .   .   .

  Note the beauty of an eye—
And if aught you praise it by
Leave such passion in your mind,
Let my reason's eye be blind.
Mark if ever red or white
Anywhere gave such delight
As when they have taken place
In a worthy woman's face.

G. Wither (*The Mistress of Philarete*).

1078. TO A KISS

SOFT child of love, thou balmy bliss,
Inform me, O delicious kiss,
Why thou so suddenly art gone,
Lost in the moment thou art won ?

Yet go ! For wherefore should I sigh ?
On Delia's lips, with raptured eye,
On Delia's blushing lips I see
A thousand full as sweet as thee.   J. WOLCOT.

1079. TO A FISH OF THE BROOKE

WHY flyest thou away with fear ?
Trust me there 's naught of danger near,
    I have no wicked hooke
All covered with a snaring bait,
Alas, to tempt thee to thy fate,
    And dragge thee from the brooke.

O harmless tenant of the flood,
I do not wish to spill thy blood,
    For Nature unto thee
Perchance hath given a tender wife,
And children dear, to charm thy life,
    As she hath done for me.

Enjoy thy stream, O harmless fish ;
And when an angler for his dish,
    Through gluttony's vile sin,
Attempts, a wretch, to pull thee *out*,
God give thee strength, O gentle trout,
    To pull the raskall *in* !   J. WOLCOT.

1080. TO MARY

IF I had thought thou couldst have died,
    I might not weep for thee ;
But I forgot, when by thy side
    That thou couldst mortal be :
It never through my mind had past
    The time would e'er be o'er,
And I on thee should look my last,
    And thou shouldst smile no more !

And still upon that face I look,
    And think 'twill smile again ;
And still the thought I will not brook,
    That I must look in vain.
But when I speak—thou dost not say
    What thou ne'er left'st unsaid ;
And now I feel, as well I may,
    Sweet Mary, thou art dead !

If thou wouldst stay, e'en as thou art,
  All cold and all serene—
I still might press thy silent heart,
  And where thy smiles have been.
While e'en thy chill, bleak corpse I have,
  Thou seemest still mine own ;
But there—I lay thee in thy grave,
  And I am now alone !

I do not think, where'er thou art,
  Thou hast forgotten me ;
And I, perhaps, may soothe this heart
  In thinking too of thee :
Yet there was round thee such a dawn
  Of light ne'er seen before,
As fancy never could have drawn,
  And never can restore !

                                              C. WOLFE.

1081. THE BURIAL OF SIR JOHN MOORE AT CORUNNA

NOT a drum was heard, not a funeral note,
  As his corpse to the rampart we hurried ;
Not a soldier discharged his farewell shot
  O'er the grave where our hero we buried.

We buried him darkly at dead of night,
  The sods with our bayonets turning ;
By the struggling moonbeam's misty light
  And the lantern dimly burning.

No useless coffin enclosed his breast,
  Not in sheet nor in shroud we wound him ;
But he lay like a warrior taking his rest
  With his martial cloak around him.

Few and short were the prayers we said,
  And we spoke not a word of sorrow ;
But we steadfastly gazed on the face that was dead,
  And we bitterly thought of the morrow.

We thought, as we hollowed his narrow bed
  And smoothed down his lonely pillow,
That the foe and the stranger would tread o'er his head,
  And we far away on the billow !

Lightly they'll talk of the spirit that 's gone
  And o'er his cold ashes upbraid him,—
But little he'll reck, if they let him sleep on
  In the grave where a Briton has laid him.

But half of our heavy task was done
  When the clock struck the hour for retiring :
And we heard the distant and random gun
  That the foe was sullenly firing.

Slowly and sadly we laid him down,
  From the field of his fame fresh and gory;
We carved not a line, and we raised not a stone,
  But we left him alone with his glory.   C. WOLFE.

1082. DAWN

O LILY with the heavenly sun
  Shining upon thy breast!
My scattered passions toward thee
    run,
And poise to awful rest.

The darkness of our universe
  Smothered my soul in night;
Thy glory shone; whereat the
    curse
Passed molten into light.

Raised over envy; freed from pain;
  Beyond the storms of chance
Blessed king of my own world I reign,
  Controlling circumstance.
            T. WOOLNER (*My Beautiful Lady*).

1083. THE REVERIE OF POOR SUSAN

AT the corner of Wood Street, when daylight appears,
Hangs a Thrush that sings loud, it has sung for three years:
Poor Susan has passed by the spot, and has heard
In the silence of morning the song of the Bird.

'Tis a note of enchantment; what ails her? She sees
A mountain ascending, a vision of trees;
Bright volumes of vapour through Lothbury glide,
And a river flows on through the vale of Cheapside.

Green pastures she views in the midst of the dale
Down which she so often has tripped with her pail;
And a single small cottage, a nest like a dove's,
The one only dwelling on earth that she loves.

She looks, and her heart is in heaven: but they fade,
The mist and the river, the hill and the shade:
The stream will not flow, and the hill will not rise,
And the colours have all passed away from her eyes!
            W. WORDSWORTH.

1084. THE SOLITARY REAPER

BEHOLD her, single in the field,
Yon solitary Highland Lass!
Reaping and singing by herself;
Stop here, or gently pass!
Alone she cuts and binds the
    grain,
And sings a melancholy strain;
O listen! for the Vale profound
Is overflowing with the sound.

No Nightingale did ever chaunt
More welcome notes to weary bands
Of travellers in some shady haunt,
Among Arabian sands:
A voice so thrilling ne'er was heard
In Spring-time from the Cuckoo-
    bird,
Breaking the silence of the seas
Among the farthest Hebrides.

Will no one tell me what she
    sings ?—
Perhaps the plaintive numbers flow
For old, unhappy, far-off things,
And battles long ago :
Or is it some more humble lay,
Familiar matter of to-day ?
Some natural sorrow, loss, or pain,
That has been, and may be again ?

Whate'er the theme, the Maiden
    sang
As if her song could have no ending ;
I saw her singing at her work,
And o'er the sickle bending ;—
I listened, motionless and still ;
And, as I mounted up the hill,
The music in my heart I bore,
Long after it was heard no more.

W. WORDSWORTH.

1085. FROM ' A POET'S EPITAPH '

BUT who is He, with modest looks,
And clad in homely russet brown ?
He murmurs near the running brooks
A music sweeter than their own.

He is retired as noontide dew,
Or fountain in a noon-day grove ;
And you must love him, ere to you
He will seem worthy of your love.

The outward shows of sky and earth,
Of hill and valley, he has viewed ;
And impulses of deeper birth
Have come to him in solitude.

In common things that round us lie
Some random truths he can impart,—
The harvest of a quiet eye
That broods and sleeps on his own heart.

But he is weak ; both Man and Boy,
Hath been an idler in the land ;
Contented if he might enjoy
The things which others understand.

W. WORDSWORTH.

1086. TO A YOUNG LADY

WHO HAD BEEN REPROACHED FOR TAKING LONG WALKS IN THE COUNTRY

DEAR Child of Nature, let them rail !
—There is a nest in a green dale,
A harbour and a hold ;
Where thou, a Wife and Friend, shalt see
Thy own heart-stirring days, and be
A light to young and old.

There, healthy as a shepherd boy,
And treading among flowers of joy
Which at no season fade,
Thou, while thy babes around thee cling,
Shalt show us how divine a thing
A Woman may be made.

Thy thoughts and feelings shall not die,
Nor leave thee, when grey hairs are nigh,
A melancholy slave ;
But an old age serene and bright,
And lovely as a Lapland night,
Shall lead thee to thy grave.   W. WORDSWORTH.

1087. BOOKS

DREAMS, books, are each a world ; and books, we know,
Are a substantial world, both pure and good :
Round these, with tendrils strong as flesh and blood,
Our pastime and our happiness will grow.
There find I personal themes, a plenteous store,
Matter wherein right voluble I am,
To which I listen with a ready ear ;
Two shall be named, pre-eminently dear,—
The gentle Lady married to the Moor ;
And heavenly Una with her milk-white Lamb.

W. WORDSWORTH (*Personal Talk*).

1088. COMPOSED UPON WESTMINSTER BRIDGE

Sept. 3, 1802

EARTH has not anything to show more fair :
Dull would he be of soul who could pass by
A sight so touching in its majesty :
This City now doth, like a garment, wear
The beauty of the morning : silent, bare,
Ships, towers, domes, theatres, and temples lie
Open unto the fields, and to the sky,
All bright and glittering in the smokeless air.
Never did sun more beautifully steep
In his first splendour, valley, rock, or hill ;
Ne'er saw I, never felt, a calm so deep !
The river glideth at his own sweet will :
Dear God ! the very houses seem asleep ;
And all that mighty heart is lying still !

W. WORDSWORTH.

1089. I TRAVELLED AMONG UNKNOWN MEN

I TRAVELLED among unknown men,
In lands beyond the sea ;
Nor, England ! did I know till then
What love I bore to thee.

'Tis past, that melancholy dream !
Nor will I quit thy shore
A second time ; for still I seem
To love thee more and more.

Among thy mountains did I feel
The joy of my desire ;
And she I cherished turned her wheel
Beside an English fire.

Thy mornings showed, thy nights concealed,
The bowers where Lucy played :
And thine too is the last green field
That Lucy's eyes surveyed.

W. WORDSWORTH.

1090. I WANDERED LONELY AS A CLOUD

I WANDERED lonely as a cloud
That floats on high o'er vales and hills,
When all at once I saw a crowd,
A host, of golden daffodils ;
Beside the lake, beneath the trees,
Fluttering and dancing in the breeze.

Continuous as the stars that shine
And twinkle on the milky way,
They stretched in never-ending line
Along the margin of a bay :
Ten thousand saw I at a glance
Tossing their heads in sprightly dance.

The waves beside them danced ; but they
Out-did the sparkling waves in glee :
A poet could not but be gay
In such a jocund company :
I gazed—and gazed—but little thought
What wealth the show to me had brought :

For oft, when on my couch I lie
In vacant or in pensive mood,
They flash upon that inward eye
Which is the bliss of solitude ;
And then my heart with pleasure fills,
And dances with the daffodils.

W. WORDSWORTH.

1091. COMPOSED UPON THE BEACH NEAR CALAIS, 1802

IT is a beauteous evening, calm and free,
The holy time is quiet as a Nun
Breathless with adoration ; the broad sun
Is sinking down in its tranquillity ;
The gentleness of heaven broods o'er the Sea :
Listen ! the mighty Being is awake,
And doth with his eternal motion make
A sound like thunder—everlastingly.
Dear Child ! dear Girl ! that walkest with me here,
If thou appear untouched by solemn thought,
Thy nature is not therefore less divine :
Thou liest in Abraham's bosom all the year ;
And worshipp'st at the Temple's inner shrine,
God being with thee when we know it not.

W. WORDSWORTH.

1092. WE MUST BE FREE OR DIE

IT is not to be thought of that the flood
Of British freedom, which, to the open sea
Of the world's praise, from dark antiquity
Hath flowed, ' with pomp of waters, unwithstood ',
Roused though it be full often to a mood
Which spurns the check of salutary bands,
That this most famous Stream in bogs and sands
Should perish ; and to evil and to good
Be lost for ever. In our halls is hung
Armoury of the invincible knights of old :
We must be free or die, who speak the tongue
That Shakespeare spoke ; the faith and morals hold
Which Milton held.—In everything we are sprung
Of Earth's first blood, have titles manifold.

W. WORDSWORTH.

1093. LONDON, 1802

MILTON ! thou shouldst be living at this hour :
England hath need of thee : she is a fen
Of stagnant waters : altar, sword, and pen,
Fireside, the heroic wealth of hall and bower,
Have forfeited their ancient English dower
Of inward happiness. We are selfish men ;
Oh ! raise us up, return to us again ;
And give us manners, virtue, freedom, power.
Thy soul was like a Star, and dwelt apart ;
Thou hadst a voice whose sound was like the sea :
Pure as the naked heavens, majestic, free,
So didst thou travel on life's common way,
In cheerful godliness ; and yet thy heart
The lowliest duties on herself did lay.

W. WORDSWORTH.

1094. MY HEART LEAPS UP WHEN I BEHOLD

MY heart leaps up when I behold
  A rainbow in the sky :
So was it when my life began ;
So is it now I am a man ;
So be it when I shall grow old,
  Or let me die !
The Child is father of the Man ;
And I could wish my days to be
Bound each to each by natural piety.

W. WORDSWORTH.

1095. NUNS FRET NOT AT THEIR CONVENT'S NARROW ROOM

Nuns fret not at their convent's narrow room;
And hermits are contented with their cells;
And students with their pensive citadels;
Maids at the wheel, the weaver at his loom,
Sit blithe and happy; bees that soar for bloom,
High as the highest Peak of Furness-fells,
Will murmur by the hour in foxglove bells:
In truth the prison, unto which we doom
Ourselves, no prison is: and hence for me,
In sundry moods, 'twas pastime to be bound
Within the Sonnet's scanty plot of ground;
Pleased if some Souls (for such there needs must be)
Who have felt the weight of too much liberty,
Should find brief solace there, as I have found.

W. WORDSWORTH.

1096. WRITTEN IN LONDON, 1802

O FRIEND! I know not which way I must look
For comfort, being, as I am, oppressed,
To think that now our life is only dressed
For show; mean handy-work of craftsman, cook,
Or groom!—We must run glittering like a brook
In the open sunshine, or we are unblessed:
The wealthiest man among us is the best:
No grandeur now in nature or in book
Delights us. Rapine, avarice, expense,
This is idolatry; and these we adore:
Plain living and high thinking are no more:
The homely beauty of the good old cause
Is gone; our peace, our fearful innocence,
And pure religion breathing household laws.

W. WORDSWORTH.

1097. ON THE EXTINCTION OF THE VENETIAN REPUBLIC

ONCE did She hold the gorgeous east in fee;
And was the safeguard of the west: the worth
Of Venice did not fall below her birth,
Venice, the eldest Child of Liberty.
She was a maiden City, bright and free;
No guile seduced, no force could violate;
And, when she took unto herself a Mate,
She must espouse the everlasting Sea.
And what if she had seen those glories fade,
Those titles vanish, and that strength decay;
Yet shall some tribute of regret be paid
When her long life hath reached its final day:
Men are we, and must grieve when even the Shade
Of that which once was great is passed away.

W. WORDSWORTH.

1098. SCORN NOT THE SONNET

Scorn not the Sonnet; Critic, you have frowned,
Mindless of its just honours; with this key
Shakespeare unlocked his heart; the melody
Of this small lute gave ease to Petrarch's wound;
A thousand times this pipe did Tasso sound;
With it Camöens soothed an exile's grief;
The Sonnet glittered a gay myrtle leaf
Amid the cypress with which Dante crowned
His visionary brow: a glow-worm lamp,
It cheered mild Spenser, called from Faery-land
To struggle through dark ways; and when a damp
Fell round the path of Milton, in his hand
The Thing became a trumpet; whence he blew
Soul-animating strains—alas, too few !

W. WORDSWORTH.

1099. SHE DWELT AMONG THE UNTRODDEN WAYS

She dwelt among the untrodden ways
  Beside the springs of Dove,
A Maid whom there were none to praise
  And very few to love:

A violet by a mossy stone
  Half-hidden from the eye !
—Fair as a star, when only one
  Is shining in the sky.

She lived unknown, and few could know
  When Lucy ceased to be;
But she is in her grave, and, oh,
  The difference to me !

W. WORDSWORTH.

1100. SHE WAS A PHANTOM OF DELIGHT

She was a Phantom of delight
When first she gleamed upon my
    sight;
A lovely Apparition, sent
To be a moment's ornament;
Her eyes as stars of Twilight fair;
Like Twilight's, too, her dusky hair;
But all things else about her
    drawn
From May-time and the cheerful
    Dawn;
A dancing Shape, an Image gay,
To haunt, to startle, and way-lay.

I saw her upon nearer view,
A Spirit, yet a Woman too !
Her household motions light and
    free,
And steps of virgin-liberty;
A countenance in which did meet
Sweet records, promises as sweet;
A Creature not too bright or good
For human nature's daily food;
For transient sorrows, simple
    wiles,
Praise, blame, love, kisses, tears,
    and smiles.

And now I see with eye serene
The very pulse of the machine ;
A Being breathing thoughtful breath,
A Traveller between life and death ;
The reason firm, the temperate will,
Endurance, foresight, strength, and skill ;
A perfect Woman, nobly planned,
To warn, to comfort, and command ;
And yet a Spirit still, and bright
With something of angelic light.

W. WORDSWORTH.

1101. TO A CHILD
WRITTEN IN HER ALBUM

SMALL service is true service while it lasts :
Of humblest Friends, bright Creature ! scorn not one :
The Daisy, by the shadow that it casts
Protects the lingering dew-drop from the sun.

W. WORDSWORTH.

1102. THE STILL SAD MUSIC OF HUMANITY

THE sounding cataract
Haunted me like a passion : the tall rock,
The mountain, and the deep and gloomy wood,
Their colours and their forms, were then to me
An appetite ; a feeling and a love,
That had no need of a remoter charm,
By thought supplied, or any interest
Unborrowed from the eye.—That time is past,
And all its aching joys are now no more,
And all its dizzy raptures. Not for this
Faint I, nor mourn nor murmur ; other gifts
Have followed ; for such loss, I would believe,
Abundant recompense. For I have learned
To look on nature, not as in the hour
Of thoughtless youth ; but hearing oftentimes
The still, sad music of humanity,
Nor harsh nor grating, though of ample power
To chasten and subdue. . . .
                    Therefore am I still
A lover of the meadows and the woods,
And mountains ; and of all that we behold
From this green earth ; of all the mighty world
Of eye, and ear,—both what they half create,
And what perceive ; well pleased to recognize
In nature and the language of the sense
The anchor of my purest thoughts, the nurse,
The guide, the guardian of my heart, and soul
Of all my moral being.

W. WORDSWORTH (Tintern Abbey).

1103. THE WORLD IS TOO MUCH WITH US

THE world is too much with us ; late and soon,
Getting and spending, we lay waste our powers :
Little we see in Nature that is ours ;
We have given our hearts away, a sordid boon !
This Sea that bares her bosom to the moon ;
The winds that will be howling at all hours,
And are up-gathered now like sleeping flowers ;
For this, for everything, we are out of tune ;
It moves us not.—Great God ! I'd rather be
A Pagan suckled in a creed outworn ;
So might I, standing on this pleasant lea,
Have glimpses that would make me less forlorn ;
Have sight of Proteus rising from the sea ;
Or hear old Triton blow his wreathèd horn.

W. WORDSWORTH.

1104. ODE ON INTIMATIONS OF IMMORTALITY FROM RECOLLECTIONS OF EARLY CHILDHOOD

THERE was a time when meadow, grove, and stream,
The earth, and every common sight,
          To me did seem
        Apparelled in celestial light,
The glory and the freshness of a dream.
It is not now as it hath been of yore ;—
          Turn wheresoe'er I may,
            By night or day,
The things which I have seen I now can see no more.

        The Rainbow comes and goes,
          And lovely is the Rose,
          The Moon doth with delight
Look round her when the heavens are bare
          Waters on a starry night
          Are beautiful and fair ;
        The sunshine is a glorious birth ;
        But yet I know, where'er I go,
That there hath passed away a glory from the earth.

Now, while the birds thus sing a joyous song,
          And while the young lambs bound
          As to the tabor's sound,
To me alone there came a thought of grief :
A timely utterance gave that thought relief,
          And I again am strong :
The cataracts blow their trumpets from the steep ;
No more shall grief of mine the season wrong ;
I hear the echoes through the mountains throng,
The winds come to me from the fields of sleep,

And all the earth is gay ;
Land and sea
Give themselves up to jollity,
And with the heart of May
Doth every Beast keep holiday ;—
Thou Child of Joy
Shout round me, let me hear thy shouts, thou happy
Shepherd-boy !

Ye blessèd Creatures, I have heard the call
Ye to each other make ; I see
The heavens laugh with you in your jubilee ;
My heart is at your festival,
My head hath its coronal,
The fullness of your bliss, I feel—I feel it all.
Oh evil day ! if I were sullen
While Earth herself is adorning
This sweet May-morning,
And the children are culling
On every side,
In a thousand valleys far and wide,
Fresh flowers ; while the sun shines warm,
And the Babe leaps up on his Mother's arm :—
I hear, I hear, with joy I hear !
—But there 's a Tree, of many, one,
A single Field which I have looked upon,
Both of them speak of something that is gone :
The Pansy at my feet
Doth the same tale repeat :
Whither is fled the visionary gleam ?
Where is it now, the glory and the dream ?

Our birth is but a sleep and a forgetting :
The Soul that rises with us, our life's Star,
Hath had elsewhere its setting,
And cometh from afar :
Not in entire forgetfulness,
And not in utter nakedness,
But trailing clouds of glory do we come
From God, who is our home :
Heaven lies about us in our infancy !
Shades of the prison-house begin to close
Upon the growing Boy,
But he beholds the light, and whence it flows,
He sees it in his joy ;
The Youth, who daily farther from the east
Must travel, still is Nature's Priest,
And by the vision splendid
Is on his way attended ;
At length the Man perceives it die away,
And fade into the light of common day.

Earth fills her lap with pleasures of her own ;
Yearnings she hath in her own natural kind,
And, even with something of a Mother's mind,
   And no unworthy aim,
 The homely Nurse doth all she can
To make her Foster-child, her inmate Man,
   Forget the glories he hath known,
And that imperial palace whence he came.

Behold the Child among his new-born blisses,
A six years' darling of a pigmy size !
See, where 'mid work of his own hand he lies,
Fretted by sallies of his mother's kisses,
With light upon him from his father's eyes !
See, at his feet, some little plan or chart,
Some fragment from his dream of human life,
Shaped by himself with newly-learnèd art ;
  A wedding or a festival,
  A mourning or a funeral ;
   And this hath now his heart,
  And unto this he frames his song :
   Then will he fit his tongue
To dialogues of business, love, or strife ;
   But it will not be long
   Ere this be thrown aside,
  And with new joy and pride
The little actor cons another part ;
Filling from time to time his ' humorous stage '
With all the Persons, down to palsied Age,
That Life brings with her in her equipage ;
   As if his whole vocation
   Were endless imitation.

Thou, whose exterior semblance doth belie
   Thy Soul's immensity ;
Thou best Philosopher, who yet dost keep
Thy heritage, thou Eye among the blind,
That, deaf and silent, read'st the eternal deep,
Haunted for ever by the eternal mind,—
   Mighty Prophet ! Seer blest !
   On whom those truths do rest
Which we are toiling all our lives to find,
In darkness lost, the darkness of the grave ;
Thou, over whom thy Immortality
Broods like the Day, a Master o'er a Slave,
A Presence which is not to be put by ;
Thou little Child, yet glorious in the might
Of heaven-born freedom on thy being's height,
Why with such earnest pains dost thou provoke
The years to bring the inevitable yoke,

Thus blindly with thy blessedness at strife ?
Full soon thy Soul shall have her earthly freight,
And custom lie upon thee with a weight,
Heavy as frost, and deep almost as life !

    O joy ! that in our embers
    Is something that doth live,
    That Nature yet remembers
    What was so fugitive !
The thought of our past years in me doth breed
Perpetual benediction : not indeed
For that which is most worthy to be blessed,
Delight and liberty, the simple creed
Of Childhood, whether busy or at rest,
With new-fledged hope still fluttering in his breast :—
    Not for these I raise
    The song of thanks and praise ;
  But for those obstinate questionings
    Of sense and outward things,
    Fallings from us, vanishings,
    Blank misgivings of a Creature
Moving about in worlds not realized,
High instincts before which our mortal Nature
Did tremble like a guilty Thing surprised :
    But for those first affections,
    Those shadowy recollections,
      Which, be they what they may,
Are yet the fountain-light of all our day,
Are yet a master-light of all our seeing ;
    Uphold us, cherish, and have power to make
Our noisy years seem moments in the being
Of the eternal Silence : truths that awake,
      To perish never :
Which neither listlessness, nor mad endeavour,
    Nor Man nor Boy,
Nor all that is at enmity with joy,
Can utterly abolish or destroy !
  Hence, in a season of calm weather
    Though inland far we be,
Our Souls have sight of that immortal sea
    Which brought us hither,
    Can in a moment travel thither,
And see the Children sport upon the shore,
And hear the mighty waters rolling evermore.

Then, sing, ye Birds, sing, sing a joyous song !
    And let the young Lambs bound
    As to the tabor's sound !
We in thought will join your throng,

Ye that pipe and ye that play
Ye that through your hearts to-day
Feel the gladness of the May!
What though the radiance which was once so bright
Be now for ever taken from my sight,
Though nothing can bring back the hour
Of splendour in the grass, of glory in the flower;
We will grieve not, rather find
Strength in what remains behind;
In the primal sympathy
Which having been must ever be;
In the soothing thoughts that spring
Out of human suffering;
In the faith that looks through death,
In years that bring the philosophic mind.

And O, ye Fountains, Meadows, Hills, and Groves,
Forebode not any severing of our loves!
Yet in my heart of hearts I feel your might;
I only have relinquished one delight
To live beneath your more habitual sway.
I love the Brooks which down their channels fret,
Even more than when I tripped lightly as they;
The innocent brightness of a new-born Day
Is lovely yet;
The Clouds that gather round the setting sun
Do take a sober colouring from an eye
That hath kept watch o'er man's mortality;
Another race hath been, and other palms are won.
Thanks to the human heart by which we live,
Thanks to its tenderness, its joys, and fears,
To me the meanest flower that blows can give
Thoughts that do often lie too deep for tears.

W. WORDSWORTH.

1105. THREE YEARS SHE GREW

THREE years she grew in sun and shower,
Then Nature said, ' A lovelier flower
On earth was never sown;
This Child I to myself will take;
She shall be mine, and I will make
A Lady of my own.

' Myself will to my darling be
Both law and impulse: and with me
The Girl, in rock and plain,
In earth and heaven, in glade and bower,
Shall feel an overseeing power
To kindle or restrain.

' She shall be sportive as the fawn
That wild with glee across the lawn
Or up the mountain springs ;
And hers shall be the breathing balm,
And hers the silence and the calm
Of mute insensate things.

' The floating clouds their state shall lend
To her ; for her the willow bend ;
Nor shall she fail to see
Even in the motions of the Storm
Grace that shall mould the Maiden's form
By silent sympathy.

' The stars of midnight shall be dear
To her ; and she shall lean her ear
In many a secret place
Where rivulets dance their wayward round,
And beauty born of murmuring sound
Shall pass into her face.

' And vital feelings of delight
Shall rear her form to stately height,
Her virgin bosom swell ;
Such thoughts to Lucy I will give
While she and I together live
Here in this happy dell.'

Thus Nature spake—The work was done—
How soon my Lucy's race was run !
She died, and left to me
This heath, this calm, and quiet scene ;
The memory of what has been,
And never more will be.   W. WORDSWORTH.

1106. UP ! UP ! MY FRIEND

UP ! up ! my Friend, and quit your
    books ;
Or surely you'll grow double :
Up ! up ! my Friend, and clear
    your looks,
Why all this toil and trouble ?

The sun, above the mountain's
    head,
A freshening lustre mellow
Through all the long green fields
    has spread,
His first sweet evening yellow.

Books ! 'tis a dull and endless
    strife :
Come, hear the woodland linnet,
How sweet his music ! on my
    life,
There 's more of wisdom in it.

And hark ! how blithe the throstle
    sings !
He, too, is no mean preacher :
Come forth into the light of things,
Let Nature be your teacher.

.   .   .   .   .   .

One impulse from a vernal wood
May teach you more of man,
Of moral evil and of good,
Than all the sages can.
W. WORDSWORTH (*The Tables Turned*).

1107. FROM 'THE AFFLICTION OF MARGARET'

WHERE art thou, my beloved Son,
Where art thou, worse to me than
dead ?
Oh find me, prosperous or un-
done !
Or, if the grave be now thy bed,
Why am I ignorant of the same
That I may rest, and neither blame
Nor sorrow may attend thy name ?

.　　.　　.　　.　　.

My Son, if thou be humbled, poor,
Hopeless of honour and of gain,
Oh ! do not dread thy mother's
door ;
Think not of me with grief and
pain :
I now can see with better eyes ;
And worldly grandeur I despise,
And fortune with her gifts and lies.

.　　.　　.　　.　　.　　.

Perhaps some dungeon hears thee
groan,
Maimed, mangled by inhuman
men ;
Or thou upon a desert thrown
Inheritest the lion's den ;
Or hast been summoned to the
deep,
Thou, thou and all thy mates, to
keep
An incommunicable sleep.

I look for ghosts ; but none will
force
Their way to me : 'tis falsely said
That there was ever intercourse
Between the living and the dead ;
For, surely, then I should have
sight
Of him I wait for day and night,
With love and longings infinite.
W. WORDSWORTH.

1108. UPON THE DEATH OF SIR ALBERTUS MORTON'S WIFE

HE first deceased ; she for a little tried
To live without him, liked it not, and died.
SIR H. WOTTON.

1109. CHARACTER OF A HAPPY LIFE

How happy is he born and taught,
That serveth not another's will ;
Whose armour is his honest thought,
And simple truth his utmost skill ;

Whose passions not his masters are ;
Whose soul is still prepared for death,
Untied unto the world by care
Of public fame or private breath ;

Who envies none that chance doth raise,
Nor vice ; hath never understood
How deepest wounds are given by praise ;
Nor rules of state, but rules of good :

Who hath his life from rumours freed ;
Whose conscience is his strong retreat ;
Whose state can neither flatterers feed,
Nor ruin make accusers great ;

Who God doth late and early pray,
More of His grace than gifts to lend,
And entertains the harmless day
With a well-chosen book or friend ;

—This man is freed from servile bands
Of hope to rise or fear to fall ;
Lord of himself, though not of lands ;
And having nothing, yet hath all.

Sir H. Wotton.

1110. ON THE SPRING

This Day Dame Nature seemed in love :
The lusty sap began to move ;
Fresh juice did stir the embracing vines,
And birds had drawn their valentines,
The jealous trout, that low did lie,
Rose at a well-dissembled fly ;
There stood my friend with patient skill,
Attending of his trembling quill.
Already were the eaves possessed
With the swift pilgrims' daubèd nest :
The groves already did rejoice,
In Philomel's triumphing voice :
The showers were short, the weather mild,
The morning fresh, the evening smiled.
Joan takes her neat rubbed pail, and now
She trips to milk the sand-red cow ;
Where, for some sturdy football swain,
Joan strokes a syllabub or twain ;
The fields and gardens were beset
With tulip, crocus, violet,
And now, though late, the modest rose
Did more than half a blush disclose.
Thus all looked gay, and full of cheer
To welcome the new-liveried year.

Sir H. Wotton.

1111.   ON HIS MISTRESS, THE QUEEN
OF BOHEMIA

You meaner beauties of the night,
   That poorly satisfy our eyes
More by your number than your light,
   You common people of the skies ;
What are you, when the Moon shall rise ?

You curious chanters of the wood
   That warble forth Dame Nature's lays,
Thinking your passions understood
   By your weak accents ; what's your praise
When Philomel her voice shall raise ?

You violets that first appear,
   By your pure purple mantles known
Like the proud virgins of the year,
   As if the spring were all your own,
What are you, when the Rose is blown ?

So, when my Mistress shall be seen
   In form and beauty of her mind,
By virtue first, then choice, a Queen,
   Tell me, if she were not designed
Th' eclipse and glory of her kind ?

                         SIR H. WOTTON.

1112.   AND WILT THOU LEAVE ME THUS

AND wilt thou leave me thus ?
Say nay, say nay, for shame !
To save thee from the blame
Of all my grief and grame.
And wilt thou leave me thus ?
Say nay, say nay !

And wilt thou leave me thus,
That hath loved thee so long
In wealth and woe among ?
And is thy heart so strong
As for to leave me thus ?
Say nay, say nay !

And wilt thou leave me thus,
That hath given thee my heart
Never for to depart,
Neither for pain nor smart :
And wilt thou leave me thus ?
Say nay, say nay !

And wilt thou leave me thus,
And have no more pity
Of him that loveth thee ?
Alas, thy cruelty !
And wilt thou leave me thus ?
Say nay, say nay !

                         SIR T. WYATT.

1113. BLAME NOT MY LUTE

BLAME not my Lute! for he must sound
   Of this or that as liketh me;
For lack of wit the Lute is bound
   To give such tunes as pleaseth me;
Though my songs be somewhat strange,
And speak such words as touch thy change,
        Blame not my Lute!

My Lute, alas! doth not offend,
   Though that perforce he must agree
To sound such tunes as I intend
   To sing to them that heareth me;
Then though my songs be somewhat plain,
And toucheth some that use to feign,
        Blame not my Lute!

My Lute and strings may not deny,
   But as I strike they must obey;
Break not them then so wrongfully,
   But wreak thyself some other way;
And though the songs which I indite
Do quit thy change with rightful spite,
        Blame not my Lute!

.   .   .   .   .   .

Blame but thyself that hast misdone,
   And well deservèd to have blame;
Change thou thy way, so evil begone,
   And then my Lute shall sound that same;
But if till then my fingers play,
By thy desert their wonted way,
        Blame not my Lute!   SIR T. WYATT.

1114. FORGET NOT YET

FORGET not yet the tried intent
Of such a truth as I have meant;
My great travail so gladly spent
      Forget not yet!

Forget not yet when first began
The weary life ye know, since whan
The suit, the service none tell can;
      Forget not yet!

Forget not yet the great assays,
The cruel wrong, the scornful ways,
The painful patience in delays,
      Forget not yet!

Forget not! oh! forget not this,
How long ago hath been, and is
The mind that never meant amiss—
      Forget not yet!

Forget not then thine own approved,
The which so long hath thee so loved,
Whose steadfast faith yet never moved—
      Forget not this!
            SIR T. WYATT.

1115. THEY FLEE FROM ME THAT SOMETIME DID ME SEEK

THEY flee from me that sometime did me seek,
  With naked foot stalking within my chamber:
Once have I seen them gentle, tame, and meek,
  That now are wild, and do not once remember
That sometime they have put themselves in danger
To take bread at my hand; and now they range,
  Busily seeking in continual change.

Thankèd be fortune, it hath been otherwise
  Twenty times better; but once especial—
In thin array—after a pleasant guise,
  When her loose gown did from her shoulders fall,
And she me caught in her arms long and small,
And therewithal so sweetly did me kiss,
  And softly said, ' Dear heart, how like you this ? '

It was no dream; for I lay broad awaking:
  But all is turned now, through my gentleness,
Into a bitter fashion of forsaking;
  And I have leave to go of her goodness;
And she also to use new-fangleness.
But since that I unkindly so am servèd,
  ' How like you this ? '—what hath she now deservèd ?
                         SIR T. WYATT.

1116. THE FAIR THIEF

BEFORE the urchin well could go,
She stole the whiteness of the snow;
And more, that whiteness to adorn,
She stole the blushes of the morn;
Stole all the sweetness ether sheds
On primrose buds and violet beds.

Still to reveal her artful wiles
She stole the Graces' silken smiles;
She stole Aurora's balmy breath;
And pilfered orient pearl for teeth;
The cherry, dipped in morning dew,
Gave moisture to her lips, and hue.

These were her infant spoils, a store;
And she, in time, still pilfered more !
At twelve, she stole from Cyprus' queen
Her air and love-commanding mien;
Stole Juno's dignity; and stole
From Pallas sense to charm the soul.

Apollo's wit was next her prey;
Her next, the beam that lights the day;
She sang;—amazed, the Sirens heard;
And to assert their voice appeared.
She played;—the Muses from their hill,
Wondered who thus had stole their skill.

Great Jove approved her crimes and art;
And, t'other day, she stole my heart!
If lovers, Cupid, are thy care,
Exert thy vengeance on this Fair:
To trial bring her stolen charms,
And let her prison be my arms!

C. WYNDHAM, EARL OF EGREMONT.

1117. THE WHEEDLER

IN vain, dear Chloe, you suggest
That I, inconstant, have possessed
   Or loved a fairer she;
Would you with ease at once be cure
Of all the ills you've long endured,
   Consult your glass and me!

If then you think that I can find
A nymph more fair, or one more kind,
   You've reason for your fears;
But if impartial you will prove
To your own beauty and my love,
   How needless are your tears!

If, in my way, I should by chance
Receive, or give, a wanton glance,
   I like but while I view;
How slight the glance, how faint the kiss,
Compared to that substantial bliss
   Which I receive from you!

With wanton flight the curious bee
From flower to flower still wanders free;
   And where each blossom blows,
Extracts the juice of all he meets,
But for his quintessence of sweets,
   He ravishes the rose.

So, my fond fancy to employ
On each variety of joy
   From nymph to nymph I roam;
Perhaps see fifty in a day!
Those are but visits which I pay—
   For Chloe is my home!   SIR W. YONGE.

1118. PROCRASTINATION

Be wise to-day: 'tis madness to defer;
Next day the fatal precedent will plead;
Thus on, till wisdom is pushed out of life.
Procrastination is the thief of time.

. . . .

All promise is poor dilatory man,
And that through every stage: when young, indeed,
In full content we, sometimes, nobly rest,
Unanxious for ourselves; and only wish,
As duteous sons, our fathers were more wise.
At thirty man suspects himself a fool;
Knows it at forty, and reforms his plan;
At fifty chides his infamous delay,
Pushes his prudent purpose to resolve;
In all the magnanimity of thought
Resolves; and re-resolves; then, dies the same.

E. Young (*Night Thoughts*).

1119. NIGHT

O majestic Night!
Nature's great ancestor! Day's elder born!
And fated to survive the transient sun!
By mortals and immortals seen with awe!
A starry crown thy raven brow adorns,
An azure zone thy waist; clouds, in heaven's loom
Wrought through varieties of shape and shade,
In ample folds of drapery divine,
Thy flowing mantle form, and, heaven throughout,
Voluminously pour thy pompous train:
Thy gloomy grandeurs—Nature's most august,
In spirit aspect!—claim a grateful verse;
And like a sable curtain starred with gold,
Drawn o'er my labours past, shall clothe the scene.

E. Young (*Night Thoughts*).

1120. SLEEP

Tired Nature's sweet restorer, balmy Sleep!
He, like the world, his ready visit pays
Where fortune smiles; the wretched he forsakes,
Swift on his downy pinions flies from woe,
And lights on lids unsullied by a tear!

E. Young (*Night Thoughts*).

1121. AUTHORS AND CRITICS

With fame in just proportion envy grows ;
The man that makes a character makes foes ;
Slight peevish insects round a genius rise,
As a bright day awakes the world of flies ;
With hearty malice, but with feeble wing,
To show they live, they flutter and they sting :
But as by depredations wasps proclaim
The fairest fruit, so these the fairest fame.

E. YOUNG (*Epistle to Pope*).

1122. THE BIRKENHEAD

AMID the loud ebriety of war,
With shouts of ' la République ' and ' la Gloire ',
The *Vengeur's* crew, 'twas said, with flying flag
And broadside blazing level with the wave
Went down erect, defiant, to their grave
Beneath the sea. 'Twas but a Frenchman's brag,
Yet Europe rang with it for many a year.
Now we recount no fable : England, hear !
And when they tell thee ' England is a fen
Corrupt, a kingdom tottering to decay,
Her nerveless burghers lying an easy prey
For the first comer,' tell how the other day
A crew of half a thousand Englishmen
Went down into the deep in Simon's Bay !

Not with the cheer of battle in the throat,
Or cannon-glare or din to stir their blood,
But, roused from dreams of home to find their boat
Fast sinking, mustered on the deck they stood,
Biding God's pleasure and their chief's command.
Calm was the sea, but not less calm that band
Close ranged upon the poop, with bated breath,
But flinching not though eye to eye with death.
Heroes ! Who were these heroes ? Veterans steeled
To face the King of Terrors mid the scaith
Of many a hurricane and trenchèd field ?
Far other : weavers from the stocking-frame ;
Boys from the plough ; cornets with beardless chin,
But steeped in honour and in discipline.

Weep, Britain, for the Cape whose ill-starred name,
Long since divorced from Hope suggests but shame,
Disaster, and thy captains held at bay
By naked hordes ; but, as thou weepest, thank
Heaven for those undegenerate sons who sank
Aboard the *Birkenhead* in Simon's Bay !   SIR H. YULE.

1123. THE TWA CORBIES

As I was walking all alane
I heard twa corbies making a mane ;
The tane unto the t'other say,
' Where sall we gang and dine to-day ? '

—In behint yon auld fail dyke,
I wot there lies a new-slain Knight ;
And naebody kens that he lies there,
But his hawk, his hound, and lady fair.

' His hound is to the hunting gane,
His hawk to fetch the wild-fowl hame,
His lady 's ta'en another mate,
So we may mak our dinner sweet.

' Ye'll sit on his white hause-bane,
And I'll pick out his bonny blue een :
Wi' ae lock o' his gowden hair
We'll theek our nest when it grows bare.

' Mony a ane for him makes mane,
But nane sall ken where he is gane ;
O'er his white banes, when they are bare,
The wind sall blaw for evermair.'
(SCOTT's *Minstrelsy of the Scottish Border.*)

1124. FROM 'LADY ANNE BOTHWELL'S LAMENT'

BALOW, my babe ! lie still and sleep,
It grieves me sair to see thee weep :
If thoust be silent, Ise be glad,
Thy maining maks my heart full sad.
Balow, my boy ! thy mother's joy !
Thy father breeds me great annoy.
    Balow, my babe ! lie still and sleep,
    It grieves me sair to see thee weep.

When he began to court my luve,
And with his sugared words to move,
His feignings false and flattering cheer
To me that time did not appear :
But now I see, most cruel he
Cares neither for my babe nor me.
    Balow, my babe, &c.

Lie still, my darling! sleep awhile,
And when thou wakest, sweetly smile;
But smile not as thy father did,
To cozen maids; nay, God forbid!
But yet I fear thou wilt gae near
Thy father's heart and face to bear.
    Balow, my babe, &c.

I canna choose but ever will
Be luving to thy father still:
Where'er he gae, where'er he ride,
My luve with him doth still abide:
In weel or wae, where'er he gae,
Mine heart can ne'er depart him frae.
    Balow, my babe! lie still and sleep,
    It grieves me sair to see thee weep.
                            (PERCY'S *Reliques*.)

1125. THE QUEEN OF FAIRIES

COME follow, follow me,
You, fairy elves that be,
Which circle on the green;
Come follow me, your queen.
Hand in hand, let's dance a round,
For this place is fairy ground.

When mortals are at rest,
And snorting in their nest;
Unheard and unespied,
  Through key-holes we do glide;
Over tables, stools, and shelves,
We trip it with our fairy elves.

And, if the house be foul,
Or platter, dish, or bowl,
Up stairs we nimbly creep,
And find the sluts asleep:
There we pinch their arms and thighs—
None escapes; nor none espies.

But if the house be swept,
And from uncleanness kept,
We praise the household maid,
And surely she is paid:
For we do use before we go,
To drop a tester in her shoe.

Upon a mushroom's head,
Our table we do spread;
A grain of rye, or wheat,
Is manchet, which we eat;
Pearly drops of dew we drink
In acorn cups filled to the brink.

The brains of nightingales,
With unctuous dew of snails,
Between two nutshells stewed,
Is meat that's easily chewed;
And the beards of little mice
Do make a feast of wondrous price.

The grasshopper and the fly,
Serve for our minstrelsy;
Grace said, we dance a while,
And so the time beguile:
And when the moon doth hide her head,
The glow-worm lights us home to bed.

On tops of dewy grass,
So nimbly do we pass,
The young and tender stalk
Ne'er bends when we do walk;
Yet in the morning may be seen
Where we, the night before, have been.

(1658)

1126.　WILLIE DROWNED IN YARROW

Down in yon garden sweet and
　　gay
　Where bonnie grows the lily,
I heard a fair maid sighing say,
　' My wish be wi' sweet Willie !

' Willie 's rare, and Willie 's fair,
　And Willie 's wondrous bonny ;
And Willie hecht to marry me
　Gin e'er he married ony.

' O gentle wind, that bloweth south
　From where my Love repaireth,
Convey a kiss frae his dear
　　mouth
　And tell me how he fareth ! ·

' O tell sweet Willie to come
　　down
　And hear the mavis singing,
And see the birds on ilka bush
　And leaves around them hing-
　　ing.

' The lav'rock there, wi' her white
　　breast
　And gentle throat sae narrow !
There 's sport eneuch for gentle-
　　men
　On Leader haughs and Yarrow.

' O Leader haughs are wide and
　　braid,
　And Yarrow haughs are bonny ;
There Willie hecht to marry me
　If e'er he married ony.

' But Willie 's gone, whom I
　　thought on,
　And does not hear me weeping ;
Draws many a tear frae 's true
　　love's e'e,
　When other maids are sleeping.

'Yestreen I made my bed fu' braid,
　The night I'll mak' it narrow
For a' the live-lang winter night
　I lie twined o' my marrow.

' O came ye by yon water-side ?
　Pou'd you the rose or lily ?
Or came you by yon meadow green,
　Or saw you my sweet Willie ? '

She sought him up, she sought him
　　down,
　She sought him braid and nar-
　　row ;
Syne, in the cleaving of a crag,
　She found him drowned in Yar-
　　row.

(*c.* 17th cent. *Palgrave's version.*)

1127.　TO TIME

Eternal Time, that wastest without waste,
　That art and art not ! diest, and livest still ;
Most slow of all ; and yet of greatest haste ;
　Both ill and good ; and neither good nor ill :
　　How can I justly praise thee, or dispraise ?
　Dark are thy nights, but bright and clear thy days.

Both free and scarce, thou giv'st and tak'st again ;
　Thy womb that all doth breed, is tomb to all ;
What so by thee hath life, by thee is slain ;
　From thee do all things rise, by thee they fall !
　　Constant, inconstant, moving, standing still ;
　Was, Is, Shall Bee, do thee both breed and kill !

I lose thee, while I seek to find thee out ;
  The farther off, the more I follow thee ;
The faster hold, the greater cause of doubt !
    Was, *Is*, I know ; but *Shall* I cannot see.
      All things by thee are measured ; thou, by none :
      All are in thee ! Thou, in thyself alone !

                       (A. W., 1602.)

1128. GOD BE IN MY HEAD

God be in my head,
And in my understanding ;

God be in mine eyes,
And in my looking ;

God be in my mouth,
And in my speaking ;

God be in my heart,
And in my thinking ;

God be at mine end,
And at my departing.

              (*Sarum Primer*, 1558.)

1129. I SAW MY LADY WEEP

I saw my lady weep,
And sorrow proud to be advancèd so
In those fair eyes, where all perfections keep.
  Her face was full of woe,
But such a woe, believe me, as wins more hearts
Than mirth can do with her enticing parts.

  Sorrow was there made fair,
And passion wise ! Tears, a delightful thing,
Silence, beyond all speech a wisdom rare !
  She made her sighs to sing ;
And all things with so sweet a sadness move,
As made my heart at once both grieve and love.

  Oh fairer than aught else
The world can show ! Leave off in time to grieve.
Enough, enough ! your joyful look excels,
  Tears kill the heart, believe.
Oh, strive not to be excellent in woe,
Which only breeds your beauty's overthrow.   (1600)

1130. HELEN OF KIRCONNELL

I WISH I were where Helen lies ;
Night and day on me she cries ;
O that I were where Helen lies
    On fair Kirconnell lea !

Curst be the heart that thought the thought,
And curst the hand that fired the shot,
When in my arms burd Helen dropt,
    And died to succour me !

O think na ye my heart was sair
When my Love dropt down and spak nae mair !
There did she swoon wi' meikle care
    On fair Kirconnell lea.

As I went down the water-side,
None but my foe to be my guide,
None but my foe to be my guide,
    On fair Kirconnell lea ;

I lighted down my sword to draw,
I hackèd him in pieces sma',
I hackèd him in pieces sma',
    For her sake that died for me.

O Helen fair, beyond compare !
I'll make a garland of thy hair
Shall bind my heart for evermair
    Until the day I die.

O that I were where Helen lies !
Night and day on me she cries ;
Out of my bed she bids me rise,
    Says, ' Haste and come to me ! '

O Helen fair ! O Helen chaste !
If I were with thee, I were blest,
Where thou lies low and takes thy rest
    On fair Kirconnell lea.

I wish my grave were growing green,
A winding-sheet drawn ower my een,
And I in Helen's arms lying,
    On fair Kirconnell lea.

I wish I were where Helen lies ;
Night and day on me she cries ;
And I am weary of the skies,
    For her sake that died for me.

           (SCOTT's *Minstrelsy of the Scottish Border*.)

1131. THE HEAVENLY JERUSALEM

Jerusalem, my happy home,
　When shall I come to thee ?
When shall my sorrows have an
　end ?
　Thy joys when shall I see ?

O happy harbour of the saints !
　O sweet and pleasant soil !
In thee no sorrow may be found,
　No grief, no care, no toil.

In thee no sickness may be seen,
　No hurt, no ache, no sore ;
There is no death, nor ugly devil,
　There is life for evermore.

No dampish mist is seen in thee
　No cold, nor darksome night ;
There every soul shines as the
　sun,
　There God Himself gives light.

There lust and lucre cannot dwell,
　There envy bears no sway ;
There is no hunger, heat, nor cold,
　But pleasure every way.

Jerusalem ! Jerusalem !
　God grant I once may see
Thy endless joys, and of the same
　Partaker ay to be !

Thy walls are made of precious
　stones ;
　Thy bulwarks diamonds square ;
Thy gates are of right orient
　pearl,
　Exceeding rich and rare.

Thy turrets and thy pinnacles
　With carbuncles do shine ;
Thy very streets are paved with
　gold,
　Surpassing clear and fine.

Thy houses are of ivory ;
　Thy windows crystal clear ;
Thy tiles are made of beaten gold ;
　O God that I were there !
　.　　.　　.　　.　　.　　.

We that are here in banishment
　Continually do mourn ;
We sigh and sob, we weep and
　wail ;
　Perpetually we groan.

Our sweet is mixed with bitter gall ;
　Our pleasure is but pain ;
Our joys scarce last the looking on;
　Our sorrows still remain.

But there they live in such delight,
　Such pleasure and such play,
As that to them a thousand years
　Doth seem as yesterday.

Thy vineyards and thy orchards are
　Most beautiful and fair ;
Full furnishèd with trees and fruits
　Most wonderful and rare.

Thy gardens and thy gallant walks
　Continually are green ;
There grow such sweet and pleas-
　ant flowers
　As nowhere else are seen.

There 's nectar and ambrosia
　made ;
　There 's musk and civet sweet ;
There many a fair and dainty drug
　Are trodden under feet.
　.　　.　　.　　.　　.

There David stands, with harp in
　hand
　As master of the quire ;
Ten thousand times that man were
　blest
　That might this music hear !

Our Lady sings *Magnificat*
　With tune surpassing sweet,
And all the virgins bear their parts,
　Sitting about her feet.

Te Deum doth St. Ambrose sing ;
　St. Austin doth the like ;
Old Simeon and Zacharie
　Have not their songs to seek.

There Magdalene hath left her moan,
    And cheerfully doth sing
With blessed saints, whose harmony
    In every street doth ring.

Jerusalem, my happy home,
    Would God I were in thee !
Would God my woes were at an end,
    Thy joys that I might see !
                    (F. B. P. 16th cent.)

1132. THE CANADIAN BOAT SONG

LISTEN to me, as when ye heard our father
    Sing long ago the song of other shores—
Listen to me, and then in chorus gather
    All your deep voices as ye pull your oars :
        Fair these broad meads—these hoary woods are grand ;
        But we are exiles from our fathers' land.

From the lone shieling of the misty island
    Mountains divide us, and the waste of seas—
Yet still the blood is strong, the heart is Highland,
    And we in dreams behold the Hebrides :
        Fair these broad meads, &c.

We ne'er shall tread the fancy-haunted valley,
    Where 'tween the dark hills creeps the small clear stream,
In arms around the patriarch banner rally,
    Nor see the moon on royal tombstones gleam :
        Fair these broad meads, &c.

When the bold kindred, in the time long-vanished,
    Conquered the soil and fortified the keep,—
No seer foretold the children would be banished,
    That a degenerate Lord might boast his sheep :
        Fair these broad meads, &c.

Come foreign rage—let Discord burst in slaughter !
    O then for clansmen true, and stern claymore—
The hearts that would have given their blood like water,
    Beat heavily beyond the Atlantic roar :
        Fair these broad meads—these hoary woods are grand ;
        But we are exiles from our fathers' land.
                    (18—, ? J. WILSON.)

1133. LOVE IN THY YOUTH, FAIR MAID

LOVE in thy youth, fair maid, be wise,
    Old Time will make thee colder,
And though each morning new arise,
    Yet we each day grow older.

Thou as heaven art fair and young,
　Thine eyes like twin stars shining ;
But ere another day be sprung,
　All these will be declining ;

Then winter comes with all his fears,
　And all thy sweets shall borrow ;
Too late then wilt thou shower thy tears,
　And I, too late, shall sorrow.　　　　　(1632)

1134.　FROM 'LOVE ME LITTLE, LOVE ME LONG'

Love me little, love me long,
Is the burden of my song :
Love that is too hot and strong
　Burneth soon to waste.
Still I would not have thee cold,
Not too backward nor too bold ;
Love that lasteth till 'tis old
　Fadeth not in haste.
Love me little, love me long
Is the burden of my song.

　　　　　　　　　　　　　　　(1569–70)

1135.　LOVE NOT ME FOR COMELY GRACE

Love not me for comely grace,
For my pleasing eye or face ;
Nor for any outward part,
No, nor for my constant heart :
　For those may fail or turn to ill,
　　So thou and I shall sever.
Keep therefore a true woman's eye,
And love me still, but know not why ;
　So hast thou the same reason still
　　To doat upon me ever.　　　　　(1609)

1136.　MY LOVE IN HER ATTIRE DOTH SHOW HER WIT.

My Love in her attire doth show her wit,
It doth so well become her ;
For every season she hath dressings fit,
For winter, spring, and summer.
No beauty she doth miss
When all her robes are on ;
But Beauty's self she is
When all her robes are gone.　　　　　(1602)

1137. O WALY WALY UP THE BANK

O waly waly up the bank,
  And waly waly down the brae,
And waly waly yon burn-side
  Where I and my Love wer wont to gae !
I leant my back unto an aik,
  I thought it was a trusty tree ;
But first it bow'd, and syne it brak,
  Sae my true Love did lichtly me.

O waly waly, but love be bonny
  A little time while it is new ;
But when it's auld, it waxeth cauld
  And fades awa' like morning dew.
O wherfore shuld I busk my head ?
  Or wherfore shuld I kame my hair ?
For my true Love has me forsook,
  And says he'll never loe me mair.

Now Arthur-seat sall be my bed ;
  The sheets shall ne'er be fyl'd by me :
Saint Anton's well sall be my drink,
  Since my true Love has forsaken me.
Marti'mas wind, when wilt thou blaw
  And shake the green leaves aff the tree ?
O gentle Death, whan wilt thou come ?
  For of my life I am wearie.

'Tis not the frost, that freezes fell,
  Nor blawing snaw's inclemencie ;
'Tis not sic cauld that makes me cry.
  But my Love's heart grawn cauld to me.
When we came in by Glasgow town
  We were a comely sight to see ;
My Love was cled in black velvet,
  And I mysell in cramasie.

But had I wist, before I kist,
  That love had been sae ill to win ;
I had lockt my heart in a case of gowd
  And pinn'd it with a siller pin.
And, O ! if my young babe were born.
  And set upon the nurse's knee,
And I mysell were dead and gane,
  For a maid again I'se never be.

(Percy's *Reliques*.)

1138. ROSES, THEIR SHARP SPINES BEING GONE

ROSES, their sharp spines being
    gone,
Not royal in their smells alone,
    But in their hue;
Maiden-pinks, of odour faint,
Daisies smell-less, yet most quaint,
    And sweet thyme true;

Primrose, first-born child of Ver,
Merry spring-time's harbinger,
    With her bells dim;
Oxlips, in their cradles grow-
    ing,
Marigolds, on death-beds blow-
    ing,
    Lark-heels trim;

All, dear Nature's children sweet,
Lie 'fore bride and bridegroom's
    feet,
    Blessing their sense.
Not an angel of the air,
Bird melodious or bird fair,
    Be absent hence!

The crow, the slanderous cuckoo,
    nor
The boding raven, nor chough hoar,
    Nor chattering pie,
May on our bride-house perch or
    sing,
Or with them any discord bring,
    But from it fly.

(1634, *Two Noble Kinsmen*, ? J. FLETCHER.)

1139. SINCE FIRST I SAW YOUR FACE

SINCE first I saw your face I resolved to honour and renown ye;
If now I be disdainèd I wish my heart had never known ye.
What? I that loved and you that liked, shall we begin to wrangle?
No, no, no, my heart is fast, and cannot disentangle.

If I admire or praise you too much, that fault you may forgive me;
Or if my hands had strayed but a touch, then justly might you leave me.
I asked you leave, you bade me love; is't now a time to chide me?
No, no, no, I'll love you still what fortune e'er betide me.

The Sun, whose beams most glorious are, rejecteth no beholder,
And your sweet beauty past compare made my poor eyes the bolder:
Where beauty moves and wit delights and signs of kindness bind me
There, O there! where'er I go I'll leave my heart behind me!

(1607)

1140. DRAKE

SIR Drake, whom well the world's end knew,
    Which thou didst compass round,
And whom both poles of heaven once saw,
    Which north and south do bound,

The stars above would make thee known,
    If men here silent were;
The sun himself cannot forget
    His fellow-traveller.

1141. SISTER, AWAKE

SISTER, awake! close not your eyes!
  The day her light discloses,
And the bright morning doth arise
  Out of her bed of roses.

See the clear sun, the world's bright eye,
  In at our window peeping:
Lo, how he blusheth to espy
  Us idle wenches sleeping!

Therefore awake! make haste, I say,
  And let us, without staying,
All in our gowns of green so gay
  Into the park a-maying. (1604)

1142. SUMMER IS COMING

SUMMER is a-coming in!
  Loud sing cuckoo:
Groweth seed and bloweth mead,
  And springeth the wood now.
    Sing cuckoo, cuckoo.

Ewe bleateth after lamb,
  Loweth after calf the cow;
Bullock starteth, buck verteth;
  Merry sing, cuckoo,
    Cuckoo, cuckoo.

Well singest thou cuckoo;
  Nor cease thou never now,
    Sing cuckoo now,
      Sing cuckoo. (c. 1250)

1143. SWEET SUFFOLK OWL

SWEET Suffolk owl, so trimly dight
With feathers, like a lady bright;
Thou sing'st alone, sitting by night,
  ' Te whit! Te whoo!'

Thy note that forth so freely rolls
With shrill command the mouse controls;
And sings a dirge for dying souls.
  ' Te whit! Te whoo!' (1619)

1144. A PROPHET THAT CASSANDRA-LIKE

THE sea hath many thousand
    sands,
The sun hath motes as many;
The sky is full of stars, and Love
As full of woes as any:
Believe me, that do know the elf,
And make no trial by thyself.

It is in truth a pretty toy
For babes to play withal;
But O, the honies of our youth
Are oft our age's gall:
Self-proof in time will make thee
    know
He was a prophet told thee so:

A prophet that, Cassandra-like,
Tells truth without belief;
For headstrong youth will run his race,
Although his goal be grief:
Love's martyr, when his heat is past,
Proves Care's confessor at the last.

(1610)

1145. CHERRY-RIPE

THERE is a garden in her face
  Where roses and white lilies blow;
A heavenly paradise is that place,
  Wherein all pleasant fruits do grow;
There cherries grow that none may buy,
Till cherry-ripe themselves do cry.

Those cherries fairly do enclose
  Of orient pearl a double row,
Which when her lovely laughter shows,
  They look like rose-buds filled with snow:
Yet them no peer nor prince may buy,
Till cherry-ripe themselves do cry.

Her eyes like angels watch them still;
  Her brows like bended bows do stand,
Threat'ning with piercing frowns to kill
  All that approach with eye or hand
These sacred cherries to come nigh—
Till Cherry-ripe themselves do cry!

(1616, ? T. CAMPION)

1146. THE THREE RAVENS

THERE were three ravens sat on a tree,
    Down a down!
They were as black as they might be,
    With a down!
The one of them said to his mate,
'Where shall we our breakfast take?'
'Down in yonder green field,
There lies a knight slain, under his shield.
His hounds they lie down at his feet,
So well they can their master keep!
His hawks, they fly so eagerly,
There's no small fowl dare him come nigh!'
Down there comes a fallow doe,
As great with young as she might go.
She lifted up his bloody head,
And kissed his wounds that were so red.

She got him up upon her back,
And carried him to earthen lake.
She buried him before the prime ;
She was dead herself ere evensong time.

God send every gentleman,
        Down a down !
Such hawks, such hounds, and such a leman
        With a down !

(1611)

1147. WEEP YOU NO MORE, SAD FOUNTAINS

WEEP you no more, sad fountains ;
    What need you flow so fast ?
Look how the snowy mountains
    Heaven's sun doth gently waste.
But my sun's heavenly eyes
    View not your weeping,
    That now lies sleeping
Softly, now softly lies
        Sleeping.

Sleep is a reconciling,
    A rest that peace begets ;
Doth not the sun rise smiling
    When fair at eve he sets ?
Rest you, then, rest, sad eyes,
    Melt not in weeping
    While she lies sleeping
Softly, now softly lies
        Sleeping.   (1603)

1148. WHEN MOLLY SMILES

WHEN Molly smiles beneath her cow,
I feel my heart—I can't tell how ;
When Molly is on Sunday dressed,
On Sundays I can take no rest.

What can I do ? on worky days
I leave my work on her to gaze.
What shall I say ? At sermons, I
Forget the text when Molly's by.

Good master curate, teach me how
To mind your preaching and my plough :
And if for this you'll raise a spell,
A good fat goose shall thank you well.   (1732)

1149. THE FAITHLESS LOVER

WHILE that the sun with his beams hot
    Scorchèd the fruits in vale and mountain,
Philon, the shepherd, late forgot,
    Sitting beside a crystal fountain
        In the shadow of a green oak tree,
        Upon his pipe this song played he :
Adieu, Love, adieu, Love, untrue Love !
Untrue Love, untrue Love, adieu Love !
Your mind is light, soon lost for new love.

So long as I was in your sight
  I was your heart, your soul, your treasure ;
And evermore you sobbed and sighed,
    Burning in flames beyond all measure :
      —Three days endured your love to me,
      And it was lost in other three !
Adieu, Love, &c.

Another shepherd you did see
  To whom your heart was soon enchainèd ;
Full soon your love was leapt from me,
    Full soon my place he had obtainèd.
      Soon came a third your love to win,
      And we were out and he was in.
Adieu, Love, &c.

Sure you have me passing glad
  That you your mind so soon removèd
Before that I the leisure had
    To choose you for my best belovèd :
      For all my love was passed and done
      Two days before it was begun.
Adieu, Love, adieu, Love, untrue Love !
Untrue Love, untrue Love, adieu Love !
Your mind is light, soon lost for new love.   (1589)

1150. THE BONNY EARL OF MURRAY

YE Highlands, and ye Lawlands,
  Oh, where have you been ?
They have slain the Earl of
    Murray,
  And they laid him on the green.

Now wae to thee, Huntley,
  And wherefore did you sae ?
I bade you bring him wi' you,
  But forbad you him to slay.

He was a braw gallant,
  And he rid at the ring ;
And the bonny Earl of Murray,
  Oh, he might have been a King !

He was a braw gallant,
  And he play'd at the ba' ;
And the bonny Earl of Murray
  Was the flower amang them a'.

He was a braw gallant,
  And he play'd at the glove ;
And the bonny Earl of Murray
  Oh, he was the Queen's Love !

Oh ! lang will his lady
  Look o'er the Castle Down,
Ere she see the Earl of Murray
  Come sounding through the
    town !
    (HERD'S *Scots Songs :* 1769)

U

INDEX TO FIRST LINES

SUBJECT INDEX

[In this Index, which does not pretend to be exhaustive, the poems have been classified under main headings. The references are to the numbers of the poems, not to the pages.]

OXFORD : HORACE HART
PRINTER TO THE UNIVERSITY